Published in 2024 by Connor Court Publishing Pty Ltd.

Connor Court Publishing Pty Ltd.

PO Box 7257

Redland Bay QLD 4165

sales@connorcourt.com

www.connorcourt.com

ISBN: 9781923224278

Cover Design by Ian James

Front cover illustration: Maestro Cillario rehearsing the Overture to *La Forza del destino*, Sydney Domain, 9 January 1998. *The Daily Telegraph*, 10 January 1998. Photo by Jeff Darmanin/Newspix. Licensed as front cover illustration by Newspix.

Printed in Australia.

1: Maestro Cillario, early 1960s.

Bruce Duffie:

'When you're conducting then, you're conscious of the audience behind you?'

Cillario:

'Of course. Every artist is in touch with his public.'

(1982 interview)

CONTENTS

FOREWORD

I worked alongside Carlo Felice Cillario for over twenty years. He was a man and a conductor I could admire and respect, and we became great friends. He was extremely kind and helpful to me.

He was personally responsible for the development of the opera in Australia. His love of opera and theatre strongly showed in his performances. He loved the orchestra and understood its supreme importance and he loved singers, or at least many of them. He did not suffer fools gladly, but he knew how to bring the best out of those he worked with.

The period of Puccini and late Verdi belonged to him, and he truly loved these works and it showed. His *Otello* and *Falstaff*, along with *La Bohème*, *Madama Butterfly* and especially *Fanciulla del West* are among my memorable theatrical experiences.

I asked him to conduct *Otello* with Joan and it was obvious that they adored each other and made magic together.

He was a man of great energy – he would swim and walk miles before morning rehearsals well into his eighties. His death at over ninety was a great loss to opera and especially to opera in Australia. He is greatly missed for the care and love he showed in guiding so many young musicians.

Richard Bonynge AC CBE

2: Carlo Felice Cillario, violinist, c1939.

ACKNOWLEDGEMENTS

Following the death of Carlo Felice Cillario in 2007, I formed the idea of producing a publication that would outline his Australian career in the context of his wider international achievements. It was not until 2016 that I contacted his grandson, Alessandro Cillario, and outlined my plan to him. Alessandro was immediately encouraging of the project, and while he also plans to produce a book about his grandfather's career in other parts of the world, he has been constantly supportive of my work. As Alessandro described to me, his grandfather would disappear to Australia once or twice each year, while the family speculated about what called him to an opera company on the other side of the world. I hope that this book goes some way to providing an explanation.

I am grateful to the Cillario family, in particular Carlo's grandsons, Alessandro Cillario, and Dario Bernardini, for their understanding, hospitality and support of my research. They provided invaluable assistance in making primary source material from the archives of their grandfather available, and helped me to unravel details of the Cillario family history at moments when I found myself becoming lost in a maze of detail.

In Australia I am foremost indebted to Moffatt Oxenbould AM, who has been unfailingly supportive and generous with his time since I first contacted him, following my visit to Cillario's country house, outside Bologna, when it was opened for my inspection for the first time since his death. Moffatt's enthusiasm for a comprehensive book that revealed Cillario's legacy in Australia encouraged me to produce (as the full scope of the available research material became apparent) a sizeable, detailed book, as befitted the subject. Moffatt made himself available to be interviewed, and to answer any questions I had as they arose. When it came to working with primary material that is at times contradictory, he was forthcoming with suggestions, documentation, and other crucial material as well as sharing with me his unerring eye for fine detail. As the book was nearing completion, Moffatt agreed to proof-read the entire manuscript, affording me the peace of mind that the information within is as accurate as it can possibly be. I am grateful to Moffatt for writing an Afterword, and to Richard Bonynge AC CBE, for contributing a Foreword, in personal appreciation of their colleague.

My thanks are also due to Sharolyn Kimmorley AM, who suggested (in 1996) that I would find it a unique and enriching experience to play for Cillario's rehearsals. She was absolutely correct, and what I gleaned from the experience of working on nearly a dozen productions with him has formed the seeds of this book. Sharolyn was variously Cillario's musical assistant and prompter, particularly during his later years, and in our conversations since his death she has been constantly supportive of this book, as the idea developed into reality.

My former colleague, Brian Castles-Onion has provided advice, primary material, and recordings to assist in my research. I am delighted that Brian agreed to provide a discography of Cillario's recorded legacy, as well as a personal memoir of their association, both of which can be found in the Appendix. I am grateful to Dr David Kim-Boyle, of the Sydney Conservatorium, the University of Sydney, for the restoration of the 78RPM recording files of Cillario playing the violin.

The scope of this project was considerably expanded when material was located and made available to me from the archives of Opera Australia, in particular their press files from 1969-c1990 and their artist files, which cover a similar period. For their assistance and efforts in locating material that was thought lost, I would like to thank Peter Alexander and Jennifer Fung, from the Opera Australia Music Library for allowing me unrestricted access to the materials they hold. I would also like to thank Joanne Goodman, Artistic Senior Manager of Opera Australia, for dealing with the legalities of copyright and permissions regarding the material that the company holds.

In addition, I would like to thank Jacqui Smith, Peter Quantrill, Peter Robinson, Tom Woods, Simon Towle, Simon Lobelson, Anne Spira, Patrick Togher, Alistair McKeen, Stephenie Calahan, Caroline

Alcorso, Adrian Keating, Raymond Holden, Vincent Plush, Phillip Sametz, Anke Höppner-Ryan, Alan Hicks, Kathryn Roberts Parker, the staff of the National Library of Australia, and Tom Volf, of the Maria Callas Foundation (Fonds de Dotation Maria Callas).

The production of this work was made possible, in part, through Special Studies Program leave awarded in 2023 by the Sydney Conservatorium of Music, University of Sydney. This work is an output of Australian Research Council (ARC) Discovery Early Career Researcher Award (DECRA) DE230100469.

Associate Professor Stephen Mould
The Sydney Conservatorium of Music,
The University of Sydney 2024.

CILLARIO IN ENGLISH

Cillario was a true polyglot, whose sentences would typically include words borrowed from several other languages. He spoke Italian, Spanish, Romanian and English, and likely some Russian, French and German. When he arrived in Australia in 1968, he had previously worked in the UK and North America and spoke functional English, though in his first year he used an interpreter for some interviews. During his decades of visiting Australia, his English evolved, although he was always keen to point out that he spoke a 'poor' ('poooor') English. His meaning and intention were rarely in doubt, he expressed himself very clearly about matters that interested him.

Both his spoken and his written English were inimitable – they were part of his personal hallmark. His speech was often reproduced exactly by reviewers, his personal charm and style was somehow embedded in his use of syntax and choice of words. Cillario wrote and, at times, typed. A study of the resulting documents often raises the suspicion that some of his mis-spellings were, in fact deliberate. Resulting ironies and slights that emerge in his communications could, at times be read as being intentional – this would be fully in keeping with his personality which exuded a dry and, at times, strangely ironic sense of humour.

A document written to the Australian Opera and Ballet Orchestra, and reproduced in Appendix 9 illustrates the ambiguity. He writes (types) that the orchestra is 'playing better than never [ever]', and asks the players to consider 'which is more closed [close] to *bel canto*.'

One will never know, but like many of those who interviewed him, I have gone to lengths to retain, wherever possible his own conception of English, both in quoting his spoken words, and also in transcribing his writings. In the transcription of documents, typed or written, I have allowed spelling and grammatical mistakes to stand, wherever possible, noting them with [sic]. When I felt an explanation was needed, I have clarified with a footnote. In the translation and editing of selections from his memoirs (see Appendix 7), I have taken all care to present Cillario's 'voice' (which I still recall vividly) as authentically as possible.

ILLUSTRATIONS

Front cover: Maestro Cillario rehearsing the Overture to *La Forza del destino*, Sydney Domain, 9 January 1998. *The Daily Telegraph*, 10 January 1998. Photo by Jeff Darmanin/Newspix.

Back cover: Carlo Felice Cillario 1980s. Photo by Marie Thérèse Driscoll. Oxenbould/Ewer Collection, National Library of Australia.

1: Maestro Cillario, early 1960s. Opera Australia Library archives.

2: Carlo Felice Cillario, violinist, c1939. Cillario family archive, Bologna.

3: Carlo Felice Cillario conducting the Bucharest Philharmonic Orchestra in the Atheneum, Bucharest, 1940s. Cillario family archive, Bologna.

4: Stars of the ETOC, 1968. *The Australian*, 19 February 1968.

5: Carlo Felice Cillario, 'The baton breaker.' "I did not lose my baton … I broke it.' Shortly before leaving last night for San Francisco, New York and Naples, Mr Cillario was explaining an incident.' *The Sydney Morning Herald,* June 27, 1968. Nine media.

6: Carlo Felice Cillario reunited with his pet goldfish, Adeline. *The Australian*, 4 January 1969.

7: Cillario and Renzo Frusca rehearsing *La forza del destino. The Bulletin*, Vol. 92; No.4708. 13 June 1970. Are Media Ltd.

8: Carlo Felice Cillario applauding the *Otello* cast, Capitol Theatre, Sydney. *The Bulletin,* Vol.92; No.4717.15 August 1970. Are Media Ltd.

9: Cillario inspecting the unfinished Sydney Opera House, July 1970. *The Herald* (Saturday), 25 July 1970. Photo by Rick Stevens/Nine media.

10: 'Three views of an $85m. compromise'. *The Herald* (Saturday), 25 July 1970. Photo by Rick Stevens/Nine media.

11: Cillario rehearsing the Elizabethan Sydney Orchestra for *Aida*, 1975. *The Sunday Telegraph*, 1 February 1981. Photo by Neil Duncan/ Newspix.

12: Cillario Felice Cillario. *The Sydney Morning Herald*, October 5 1977. Nine media.

13: Carlo Felice Cillario at the Sydney Opera House for the *'Cav & Pag'* season, 13 September 1978. Nine media.

14: Conductor Carlo Felice Cillario, with the Australian Opera, Dress

Rehearsal for *Madama Butterfly*, June 12, 1978. Photo by Martin James Brannan/Sydney Morning Herald.

15: Conductor Carlo Felice Cillario, with the Australian Opera, Dress Rehearsal for *Madama Butterfly*, June 12, 1978. Photo by Martin James Brannan/Sydney Morning Herald.

16: One of Cillario's infamous 'doodles' – corrections for Italian pronunciation. Collection of the author.

17: Moffatt Oxenbould and Carlo Felice Cillario c2000. Opera Australia Library archives.

18: Snapshot of Maestro Cillario in 18th-century costume and wig, operating the wind-machine backstage at the Court Theatre of Drottningholm Sweden, 1980s. Oxenbould/Ewer Collection, National Library of Australia.

19: Music Consultant and Principal Guest Conductor, Carlo Felice Cillario, 29 September 1987. Nine Media.

20: Cillario studying a score, 1989. Photo by Andrew Tait.

21: Cillario rehearsing *Otello*, Melbourne, 1989. Photo by Andrew Tait.

22: Reproduced with permission.

23: Reproduced with permission.

24: Maestro Cillario conducting the Sydney Symphony Orchestra in the Sydney Town Hall, *The Australian,* 23 April 1992. Photo by Patrick Hamilton/Newspix.

25: Maestro Cillario conducting the Sydney Symphony Orchestra, Sydney Town Hall. April 22, 1992. Photo by Colin Townsend/The Sydney Morning Herald.

26: The presentation of the Australian Opera Trophy, Sydney Opera House, 1994, following a performance of *La traviata*. Photo by Branco Gaica/National Library of Australia.

27: Maestro Cillario rehearsing *La bohème*, Redfern, NSW, 1999. Photo by Stephen Mould.

28: 'Carlo keeps secret score,' *Sunday Herald*, Sunday, 6 April 1997. Photo by David Geraghty/Newspix.

29: 'Dial M for Maestro,' *The Daily Telegraph*, 17 January 1997. Photo by Bob Barker/Newspix.

30: Rehearsing *La bohème* with Moffatt Oxenbould, 1999. Photo by Stephen Mould.

31: Maestro Carlo Felice Cillario conductor for Saturday Night's Opera in the Domain. Photo by Steven Siewert/The Sydney Morning Herald.

32: The programme cover of 'Maestro Cillario Exposed'. Cillario's added text is a parody of a text from Mozart's *La clemenza di Tito*. Collection of the author.

33: Cillario, note to Robert Allman (performing Marcello), *La bohème*, 1981. Courtesy of Sharolyn Kimmorley.

34: A caricature of Maestro Cillario launching into a performance of *La traviata*, by Caroline Johns, tuba player of the Australian Opera and Ballet Orchestra. A copy was presented to the conductor at the gala celebration. Reproduced with permission.

35: Memorial card produced by the Cillario family to mark the funeral of Carlo Felice Cillario (1915–2007). Cillario Family Archive, Bologna.

36: Faces of Cillario – Bucharest, 1944; Sydney, 1970; Sydney 1992. Cillario family archive/ Are Media Ltd./Newspix.

37: The Odesa Opera House, 1941.

38: Nikolai N. Chernyatinsky. Photo by V. M. Gridin.

39: Maestro Gino Marinuzzi in discussion with Carlo Felice Cillario c1945. Cillario family archive, Bologna.

40: Broadsheet published by the Italian branch of HMV to publicise the release of Cillario's recordings c1937. Cillario family archive, Bologna.

41: A postcard from the composer Manuel de Falla, thanking Cillario for his recordings of Szymanowski and Bach, late 1930s. Cillario family archive, Bologna.

42: 'King had a right royal time,' Tito Gobbi in the Moomba Parade, crowned 'King of Moomba.' *The Sun News Pictorial, Melbourne*, 11 March 1969. Photo by Staff Photographer/Newspix.

43: Carlo Felice Cillario, rehearsing in the Opera Theatre orchestra pit c1999. Photo by Jennifer Soo/Nine media.

44: 'Tuxedo or Apron, he's a Maestro', *The Age*, 5 June 1979/Nine media.

45-6: Maria Callas, letter to Carlo Felice Cillario, 6 December 1963. Reproduced with permission.

All reasonable efforts have been made to locate the copyright owners of the images reproduced in this book. The author invites any relevant copyright owners to make contact at: stephen.mould@sydney.edu.au

LIST OF REVIEWERS

Nadine Amadio (1929–2009) was a member of the distinguished Amadio family and a devotee of several branches of the Australian arts. She worked as an author, journalist, critic and film scriptwriter. She regularly contributed music and arts reviews for *The Sydney Morning Herald*.

Fred Blanks (1925–2011) was a scientist and widely-respected Sydney-based critic, 'whose reviews of concerts and operas were eloquent, illuminating and sometimes trenchant.' (*The Sydney Morning Herald*, 18 March 2011). He was born in Germany, from where his family fled to London in 1937, arriving in Australia in 1938. He reviewed for the *Australian Jewish News* (from 1952) and *The Sydney Morning Herald* (1963-98).

'B. Canto' or 'Bel Canto' - David Brown, a Sydney-based arts and music critic, who reviewed principally for the *Australian Jewish News*. He was also an artist biographer for the Australian Opera and the founding conductor and Chairperson of the Sydney Jewish Choral Society.

Peter Burch a Melbourne-based critic who for 32 years was the Victorian concerts manager for Musica Viva. He also worked as a lecturer at RMIT, teaching arts administration to postgraduate students. He reviewed chiefly for *The Australian* in Melbourne.

John Cargher (1919–2008) was a British-born Australian journalist, author, broadcaster and critic of opera and ballet. His long running broadcast 'Singers of Renown' played a significant role in the development of taste making among Australian opera goers, a radio programme that he presented until a week before he death. He juggled many occupations, and was a colourful, flamboyant character, with strong opinions which informed his reviews.

John ('Jack') Carmody (b. 1940) a lecturer in physiology and pharmacology on the Faculty of Medicine at the University of NSW, in Sydney: for over 25 years he was also a music critic and book reviewer for publications in Australia and overseas, as well as being a radio broadcaster. His reviews of opera performances are among the more colourful of the period.

Clive O'Connell Melbourne-based O'Connell was music critic for *The Australian* (1974–77) and chief music critic for *The Age* in Melbourne (1978-2019). He occasionally reviewed for David Gyger's *Opera Australia*.

Romola Constantino (1930–1988) was an Australian pianist, accompanist, and teacher, who also worked as a music, film, and theatre critic. She was a senior lecturer at Sydney University and a regular music critic with *The Sydney Morning Herald*.

Roger Covell (1931–2019) was a musicologist and Professor Emeritus in the School of Arts and Media at the University of New South Wales, Sydney. He was also a critic, author and conductor. His reviews were published chiefly by *The Sydney Morning Herald*, for whom he was the principal music critic from 1960 until the late 1990s.

Alison Gyger (b.1933) although not a reviewer, Alison Gyger is of significance as an Associate editor of *Opera-Opera* (see David Gyger). She also conducted extensive research into Australia's early operatic history, producing three books which are among the leading research in the field.

David Gyger (1931–2019) was a 'respected arts journalist, opera critic and music lover' (*The Sydney Morning Herald, obituary*). He is particularly remembered for his monthly newspaper *Opera-Opera* (1978–2007) which passed through several name changes: *Opera Australia* (1978–93), *Opera Australasia* (1994–January 1997), and *Opera-Opera* (Feb. 1997–2007). The final name change was the result of the renaming of the national company.

Ken Healey (b. 1936) has been a reviewer, chiefly for the Fairfax Press, in both Canberra and Sydney. He later became a regular reviewer for David Gyger's *Opera-Opera* newspaper, and for over 20 years taught playwriting at NIDA as Literary Manager.

Kenneth Hince (1926–2018) was a Melbourne-based critic and antiquarian bookseller. He became a reviewer for *The Australian* in 1964. Later, he also reviewed for *the Age*.

Brian Hoad (1938–2006) was a British-born journalist, who came to Australia as a 'Ten-pound Pom'. He was a reviewer for *The Bulletin*.

W. L. Hoffmann ('Bill') (1920–2011) was one of the founding members of the Canberra Critics Circle. He reviewed for *The Canberra Times*, with whom he had a long association, and was long regarded as Australia's senior music critic. He travelled around Australia (particularly to Sydney and Melbourne) writing reviews of concerts and operas which appeared in *The Canberra Times*.

David Malouf (b. 1934) is an Australian poet, novelist and playwright. He has also written the libretti for three operas, most notably *Voss*, by Richard Meale. He has regularly reviewed opera performances, interviewed artists – including Cillario – and written extended pieces about the art form, notably of the 1995 *Nabucco* production. The recipient of many awards, he served for many years on the board of Opera Australia.

Maria Prerauer (1922–2006) studied to be a singer, and left Australia during the 1950s to pursue a career in Europe. Following her return, she became a leading arts critic in Sydney, becoming critic and arts editor for *The Australian*, where her strong opinions caused her to be nicknamed 'Maria Piranha' in some circles.

3: Carlo Felice Cillario conducting the Bucharest Philharmonic
Orchestra in the Atheneum, Bucharest, 1940s.

PREFACE – THE LOST MAESTRO

This study explores a rich and decisive period in Australian operatic history, during which the national company defined its raison d'être and moved into its principal performance home – the Sydney Opera House. The development of the company can be charted through a series of name changes – the Elizabethan Trust Opera Company (ETOC, 1957–69), the Australian Opera (AO, 1970–96), and Opera Australia (OA, 1996–present).

A constant musical force through those decisive periods was the Argentinian-born, Italian conductor, Carlo Felice Cillario (1915–2007). Cillario enjoyed a 35–year career in Australia (1968–2003), chronicled here and examined with a view to defining a sense of his legacy. This book gathers surviving documentary records of Cillario's Australian career, including material that may serve to illuminate the character and sensibilities of this extraordinary musician.

Cillario first visited Australia in 1968. He was 53 years old but exuded a youthful vigour that he retained throughout much of his tenure with the company. He was enjoying an international career crowned by the run of *Tosca* in January 1964, starring Maria Callas and Tito Gobbi, which marked his debut at the Royal Opera House in London. Montserrat Caballé, Renata Scotto, Renata Tebaldi and Luciano Pavarotti numbered among the many singers who performed with him regularly.

The highlight of Cillario's first season in Australia took place at the Adelaide Festival, where he conducted *Tosca* with the London-based Australian soprano, Marie Collier, Tito Gobbi and the Australian tenor, Donald Smith. These Adelaide performances subsequently acquired an almost legendary significance in Australian operatic history. In his memoirs, Tito Gobbi recalled his first Antipodean visit with pleasure: 'When I had a chance to drive out into the country I was overwhelmed by the beauty of the scenery and the invigorating quality of the atmosphere. It made me feel younger, full of life and immensely refreshed.'[1]

---

[1] Tito Gobbi, *My Life* (Great Britain, Macdonald and Jane's Publishers, 1979), 226.

Two years younger than Gobbi, Cillario had a similar reaction to Australia, which may have also reminded him of his childhood in Argentina. He was charmed by what he found – the people, the landscape and the cultural scene – and gladly entertained the prospect of further visits. While Europe and the Americas offered more glamorous and lucrative engagements, involving much less 'spade work', Cillario seemed to thrive on hard work, rather than coasting on long-established, routine working traditions. Moffatt Oxenbould wrote that 'from the day of his first rehearsal in Australia in 1968, Maestro Cillario has had a clearly defined focus in his work – to seriously make music with the best possible available artistic resources.'[2] While the Adelaide *Tosca* performances formed the highlight of his first season, Australia also offered enticing opportunities for Cillario to conduct works by Wagner and Mozart, repertoire that European and American houses tended to give to his colleagues.

Following their successes in 1968, both Cillario and Gobbi returned the following year, but the singer's second Australian season was less well-received. Nevertheless, both were engaged to return again in 1970, with Gobbi planned to direct *Otello* and sing the role of Iago, but this did not eventuate due to financial issues that could not be satisfactorily resolved between Gobbi's manager, the Sydney management and the Australian Tax Office.[3] Like many conductors before and after him, Cillario entertained hopes of a trans-continental career, which led him to accept the post of Music Director of the Australian Opera in 1970. This quickly became unsustainable, as the Australian Opera and his international career

---

[2] Moffatt Oxenbould *Carlo Felice Cillario and Opera Australia*, programme essay for 'A Gala Celebration for Carlo Felice Cillario,' Opera Australia programme, 23 March 2003. Oxenbould joined the Elizabethan Trust Opera Company in 1963. He held several key positions with the evolving organisation, eventually becoming Artistic Director in 1984. He worked closely with Cillario for virtually his entire tenure with the company.

[3] Alison Gyger [in: *Australia's Operatic Phoenix, From World War II to War and Peace* (Sydney, Pellinor Pty Ltd, 2005)] states that 'unknown to Gobbi, his agent demanded an outrageous fee, beyond the company's budget,' while *The Sydney Morning Herald* reported ('Singer in Tax Dispute,' 21 January 1970) that Gobbi owed the Australian Tax Office more than $10,000.

each made demands that were impossible to meet. It was planned that he would continue in Australia as a guest conductor, but a series of competing demands in early 1971 led to him resigning from his Australian commitments, a decision he felt himself to have been forced into.[4] Cillario did not return until 1975, when he was greeted by a completed Sydney Opera House, a building about whose final design phase he had expressed strong opinions.

Until 2003, the conductor would visit Australia each year, leading dynamic performances of the Italian repertoire, as well as satisfying his wider musical interests and allegiances, particularly his passion for the works of Wagner. He played a crucial role in developing the opera orchestra in Sydney (today the Australian Opera and Ballet Orchestra) into a cohesive, flexible, and stylish entity, which boasted a sound that breathed his inimitable hallmark. Over this period, managements shifted, music directors came and went, crises arose, and funding models were thrown out. Through all of this, Cillario was a constant force, continuing his annual visits, undertaking an intensive schedule, working with leading directors on important new stagings, and reviving existing productions with an array of casts.

Over time, Sydney, became a second home to Cillario. It was hardly a matter of professional necessity for him to conduct in Australia, in fact the months that he spent here, far from the 'main circuit' probably caused him to be overlooked for prestigious international engagements. Nevertheless, Cillario was drawn back to Australia time and time again, over the course of three decades. It was here that he created an operatic legacy of substance: achieved by a steady commitment over time and the exercise of patience and persistence.

While in Australia, Cillario lived simply, and devoted himself to his art, his profession and his colleagues. In overseas circles, surprise was often expressed that the conductor had chosen to eschew the limelight and the jet-set lifestyle of an international

---

[4] The company artist files from this period are preserved by Opera Australia ('Carlo Felice Cillario – Artist Files, Opera Australia Library archives') and contain extensive documentary material relating to the years 1968–1988.

maestro, effectively depriving himself of a wider career. From today's perspective, it becomes clear that in the antipodes, Cillario found the conditions that he needed to create his life's work, and that it was here, far from the established opera houses of the world, that he created his musical home.

OVERTURE
An International Maestro

Carlo Felice Cillario's arrival in Australia brought to these shores an international opera maestro whose career was in full flight. During the 1960s, he had made important debuts at Glyndebourne Festival Opera, Chicago Lyric Opera, the Royal Opera in London and the Metropolitan Opera in New York, leading performances with many of the star singers of the day.

His career was managed by the leading impresario, Sandor Gorlinsky, a polyglot born in Kyiv and raised in Berlin. In 1940 he fled to the UK, where he took advantage of a post-war boom in opera. He promoted regional tours and arranged his own seasons of Italian operas in London, which remained his base.[5] Gorlinsky represented many of the outstanding singers of the day, including Callas, Gobbi, del Monaco, Tebaldi, Scotto, Caballé and di Stefano. The astute agent quickly discovered that his leading artists were delighted to perform with the support of Cillario in the pit. When he secured engagements for them, the conductor was frequently included in the deal.

The celebrated run in London of *Tosca* in January 1964 was brokered by Gorlinsky who employed all his diplomatic skills to ease Callas out of the semi-retirement that she appeared to be slipping into. Callas and Cillario had never worked together previously,[6] but a letter from the diva to the maestro attests to her respect for him.[7] A young Australian stage manager was working at Covent Garden

---

[5] Information relating to Gorlinsky in this paragraph is derived from: http://Archiveshuib.jisc.ac.uk, accessed 12 February 2023.

[6] Their previous contact seems to have been of a business, rather a musical nature – see Appendix 7, for Cillario's recollections that seem almost fanciful in their detail.

[7] The letter is preserved in the Cillario family archive, Bologna. It is reproduced in Appendix 10.

at the time: Stephen Hall[8] became acquainted with Tito Gobbi, who expressed a desire to sing in Australia. Following his return to Australia, Hall took up a position with the Elizabethan Trust Opera Company,[9] which had determined to make an ambitious statement of intent with its 1968 season. A run of *Tosca* performances at the Adelaide Festival,[10] would feature a world-class cast, and Hall was instrumental in engaging Gobbi to perform the role of Scarpia. According to Hall, the baritone was the company's 'first real major international star' engaged partly in a move to 'bring out people by whom Australian artists could measure themselves.'[11]

Gobbi and Cillario were regular musical collaborators as well as friends, and the baritone's suggestion for Cillario to conduct was greeted with enthusiasm by Hall. The conductor found the offer interesting, but he was not short of offers to conduct *Tosca* around the world. What clinched the deal was the offer to conduct two further operas, Mozart's *The Magic Flute* and Wagner's *Tannhäuser*. In conversations and interviews, Cillario often spoke of Mozart as the greatest composer,[12] but his forays into this repertoire were few and far between. When he did conduct Mozart in Australia, it was usually sung in English translation, a convention at the time, which aroused in him strong, if conflicting opinions.[13] Wagner was also a

---

[8] Stephen Hall was associated with the ETOC from the early 1960s, occupying several administrative roles with the company. He eventually became Artistic Director of the Australian Opera, and following a successful production of *Aida*, produced in 1975 for the company, he became the founding director of the Sydney Festival, a position that he held for 18 years. He died in 2014.

[9] Henceforth ETOC.

[10] Which had been founded in 1960.

[11] Alison Gyger (2005), 221.

[12] See Cillario's memoir about Josef Krips, p. 93.

[13] Carlo Felice Cillario and Bruce Duffie, *Conductor Carlo Felice Cillario: A conversation with Bruce Duffie* (A conversation recorded in Chicago, 8 November 1982), and portions broadcast on WNIB in 1986, 1990, 1995 and 2000. The conversation was transcribed in 2015 and is available at: http://www.bruceduffie.com/cillario.html, accessed 2 January 2023. Moffatt Oxenbould has written that 'Probably he regrets that he did not conduct Mozart operas as often as he would have liked in Australia.' Moffatt Oxenbould, *Carlo Felice Cillario and Opera Australia*, essay in 'A Gala Celebration for Carlo Felice Cillario' commemorative programme. Opera Australia, Concert Hall, Sydney Opera House, 23 March 2003.

lifelong interest,[14] and Cillario would conduct most of the Bayreuth canon in Australia.[15] When accepting the antipodean engagement, the conductor could hardly have anticipated how it would eventually influence his subsequent life and career.

By 1968, Cillario had established impeccable operatic credentials internationally, and was enjoying a thriving conducting career. He had made a career-change during the Second World War, when a broken wrist during a soccer game stalled his career as a violinist. By the end of the war his career was primarily focused upon conducting which he pursued in Romania, Odesa, and then in Italy. In 1948 he relocated to Argentina, where he felt that he would have more possibilities than in post-war Europe. The development of his career can be traced through his 1952 conducting debut and subsequent engagements at the Teatro Colón, but during the latter part of the 1950s he gradually made a return to Europe. He was invited to the Gran Teatro Liceu di Barcelona in 1956, which was followed by performances of *Aida* and *La Gioconda* in Buenos Aires (1960) and *La bohème* and *Tosca* in Mexico.

Cillario's 1961 debut with the Lyric Opera of Chicago led to him returning as an annual guest for several years and his Glyndebourne debut the same year also initiated a relationship that continued until 1967.[16] At Glyndebourne, Cillario established a rapport with Franco

---

14 There are important connections between Wagner and the city of Bologna, of which Cillario was extremely proud. In particular, the first Italian staging of *Lohengrin* was given in Bologna (1 November 1871) following which the composer was made an honorary citizen of the city (1 August 1872). At that time, he expressed a wish to visit Bologna, which finally occurred on 4 December 1876, when he attended a performance of *Rienzi* at the Teatro Comunale. luigiverdi.it/engl/musica_a_bologna-ingl.html, accessed 28 October 2023.

15 Cillario was engaged to conduct the entire *Ring* cycle for the Australian Opera during the 1980s. The project floundered amid successive artistic and music directors, criticism of the production concept, issues with the artistic and theatrical demands made by the tetralogy, and the limitations of the Opera Theatre pit. The project was jettisoned following the *Das Rheingold* season (*Die Walküre* was staged first).

16 Vittorio Gui was the Music Director of the Glyndebourne Festival Opera at this time and was a mentor to the younger conductor. Gui's correspondence with Cillario, rich in musical insights and advice, is held in the Cillario family archive, Bologna (see Bibliography).

Zeffirelli, conducting his production of *L'elisir d'amore* with Mirella Freni and Luigi Alva in the leading roles.[17]

Cillario and Zeffirelli renewed their artistic partnership with the 1964 Callas *Tosca* at Covent Garden. On opening night, a 40-minute ovation followed the fall of the curtain, with 27 stage calls, along with 20 minutes of applause at the end of each of the two earlier acts. Also in 1964, Cillario made his début at the Teatro San Carlo in Naples, with Donizetti's *Roberto Devereux*,[18] which signalled the conductor's growing interest in the revival of the neglected *bel canto* operas of the 19th century. In 1966, Cillario appeared at Carnegie Hall, New York, with Montserrat Caballé in a concert performance of the same Donizetti rarity.[19]

In addition to these achievements, by the time he appeared in Australia, the conductor had already appeared at theatres in Madrid, Venice (La Fenice), Rome, and the Paris Opéra, conducting the leading singers of the day, including, over the coming decade, Renata Tebaldi, Mirella Freni, Luigi Alva, Franco Corelli and Luciano Pavarotti. His star was clearly in the ascendant, and on arriving in Australia, there was no doubt that audiences were witnessing the work of an international conductor of the highest pedigree and reputation.

As will be described later in this book, Cillario's formative musical years and subsequent career convey a sense of adventure and restlessness which came to underpin his life. One senses in the unfolding of his career, a longing to transcend frontiers and conquer the unknown. The career that Cillario enjoyed in Australia contains elements of these characteristics, which became an integral part of his makeup, harking back perhaps to his origins as the child of émigrés, born in 1915 in a small town in Argentina – a birth of which there is no surviving official record.

---

[17] On this occasion, Cillario led from the keyboard, playing the recitatives.
[18] With Leyla Gencer.
[19] Cillario is credited with having steered Caballé towards the *bel canto* repertoire. The legacy is available on several recordings, notably *Rossini Rarities* (1968) and *Donizetti Rarities* (1970) for RCA. See also: Helena Matheopolous, *Diva* (London: Gollancz, 1991), 68.

Opera in Australia 1954–68

The post-war era in Australia was characterised by growth and optimism in most areas of society, symbolised by the Melbourne Olympic Games (1956), which brought the country to international attention. This period also heralded a period of optimism within the arts, with the establishment of The Australian Elizabethan Theatre Trust (1954), in the wake of the coronation of Queen Elizabeth II. It was hoped that her reign would foster a new 'Elizabethan' age in the cultural life of the country. The Australian Opera Company was established in the Olympic year (1956) and commemorated the Mozart bicentenary by presenting four of the composers' operas in all capital cities, travelling more than 10,000 kilometres, and giving 169 performances.[20] From these beginnings, the Australian Opera Company became the Elizabethan Trust Opera Company in 1957. At the beginning of that year, the Danish architect, Jørn Utzon, won a competition for his design for the Sydney Opera House.[21]

During the nineteenth century, Australia had enjoyed a livelier operatic culture than might be assumed from the convict origins of the British colony,[22] financed by gold rushes and property booms. This European art form was adapted from established models, and reinvented the Old World within new, often trail-blazing contexts. Early operatic activities were touring enterprises, with local companies, such as that of William Lyster vying with imported Italian opera troupes for the market.[23] These peripatetic conditions persisted into the 1950s and were noted by Eugene Goossens when he arrived in Sydney to take up the positions of Chief Conductor of the Sydney Symphony Orchestra (SSO) and Director of the New South Wales Conservatorium of Music between 1946 and 1956.

Goossens found an embryonic operatic culture, in comparison

---

[20] https://en.wikipedia.org/wiki/Opera_Australia#Australian_Opera_Company, 1956%E2%80%9357, accessed 25 April 2023.

[21] A. Gyger (2005), 117.

[22] See: Alison Gyger, *Civilising the Colonies, Pioneering Opera in Australia* (Sydney, Pellinor Pty Ltd, 1999).

[23] See: Harold Love, *The Golden Age of Australian Opera, W.S. Lyster and his Companies 1861–1880* (Sydney, Currency Press Pty Ltd, 1981).

with the established professionalism of his orchestra and its administration. He developed opera seasons at the Conservatorium, presenting ambitious programmes that included the works of Wagner, Mozart, Mussorgsky, Debussy, and his own *Judith*, for which he engaged a young Joan Sutherland to sing the title role. Rather than casting vocal students, Goossens usually sourced local, experienced singers, and supplemented the student orchestra with players from the pool of SSO members. During his tenure, Goossens formed a vision of an opera house for Sydney, identifying the Harbour site at Bennelong Point for its construction, where it stands today. Goossens was one of the few figures at the time who possessed the vision, political connections, and status to push such an ambitious idea forward. Despite the conductor resigning his positions and quitting Australia in 1956, the opera house project was officially established in 1957, when the design competition for the building was announced. Construction of the Sydney Opera House commenced on 2 March 1959.

The ETOC was an enterprising company which, over the decade following its establishment, emerged as a strong local entity. During the late 1950s and early 1960s, London was the preferred travel destination for young Australian singers, directors, conductors, and administrators who were looking to gain experience and a foothold in the profession. Many found work at The Royal Opera, Covent Garden or Sadler's Wells. Future leaders of the opera industry in Australia – such as Stephen Hall and Moffatt Oxenbould – developed their careers in London, acquiring skills that would be put to good use in the development of the new, antipodean enterprise. The stellar rise of Joan Sutherland cemented the idea of Australia as an aspiring operatic nation. Her return home in 1965 for a 14-week tour, presented by J.C. Williamson Ltd. and organized by Sir Frank Tait,[24] further influenced the emerging operatic culture. On the tour, several singers from the UK – either British nationals or long-term

[24] Tait hailed from a family of entrepreneurs and managers who were major players in Australian theatres. He became the managing director of J. C. Williamson's, who owned and managed theatres throughout Australia, dominating the industry.

expatriate Australians[25] – were inspired by the sense of purpose and positive spirit of the local company and decided to make their home in Australia, joining the developing operatic industry.[26]

The career of an opera singer was becoming something to aspire to,[27] assisted by a solid stable of conductors and music staff. These included the Viennese Georg Tintner, Walter Stiasny, and William Reid, a British 'ex-pat' who could conduct most of the repertoire on short notice and little rehearsal. In 1967 Robert Feist – an American conductor with international experience – had been engaged as a guest conductor. The leaders of the ETOC had reason to feel optimistic about both available resources and the fulfilment of artistic ambitions. However, they were in search of overseas expertise to provide suitable musical leadership for their company.

As the Sydney Opera House gradually took shape on the waterfront at Bennelong Point, it became clear that the city would acquire a unique edifice, which promised to become an operatic centre of world-class excellence. Thus, a parallel flurry of artistic and administrative activity took place alongside the physical construction of Utzon's design, to expand the opera company and make it worthy of the new building. The company required a diverse ensemble of singers, a comprehensive repertoire of productions, a strong core of administrators, conductors and directors, music staff, a chorus, and an orchestra. Such a company self-evidently required a strong artistic leader – in those days, the model generally accepted worldwide was that of a music director[28] – a post that awaited the right candidate.

---

[25] For example, Morag Beaton (Scottish) and Elizabeth Fretwell (Australian).

[26] Opinion is divided about the impact of the 'Williamson–Sutherland Opera Company' tour. Neil Warren-Smith, representing the singer's perspective, noted that the tour posed a threat to the Trust Company, which 'went back into the woodwork'. See: Neil Warren-Smith and Frank Salter, *25 Years of Australian Opera* (Melbourne, Oxford University Press, 1983), 142–3.

[27] However, it remained a precarious means of earning a living: the bass-baritone Neil Warren-Smith, for example, combined the earlier part of his singing career with that of his learned trade as a butcher. Ibid, 140.

[28] The term 'music director' is usual today, whereas during this period 'musical director' was often used to denote the same function.

ACT 1 (1968–1971)
Scene 1 – 1968

Elizabethan Trust Season

It is often assumed that the Adelaide Festival performances of *Tosca* marked the Australian debut of Maestro Cillario, but his first Australian performances occurred earlier in the season, in Canberra. In 1968, the ETOC opened their season in the Australian capital, then toured to Adelaide for the festival, thence to Melbourne and Brisbane, before concluding in Sydney.[29] Cillario was to conduct in all five cites. He opened the season in February with Wagner's *Tannhäuser,* which featured a mainly local cast of soloists,[30] and a chorus of just 24 singers. In Canberra, he also conducted Mozart's *The Magic Flute* (sung in English). He was the sole conductor for this first leg of the season, and received particularly positive reviews, as *The Canberra Times*, reviewing *Tannhäuser* reported:

> Fortunately, in this production the conductor, Carlo Felice Cillario, does not allow the musical interest to lag; in particular his forward-moving tempi maintain the impulse of the drama so that the lack of sustained musical inspiration is never obvious and the periodic stretches of operatic padding never tedious ... under his baton the moments of high intensity, such as the end of the Venusberg scene, the

---

[29] The first opera conducted by Cillario in Australia has been a source of confusion, with Australian Opera programmes on occasion citing *The Magic Flute*, or *La fanciulla del West* in their artist profiles. *Tannhäuser* is correctly listed as his debut in: *The Canberra Times*, 3 November 1967 and Moffatt Oxenbould's *Timing is Everything* (2005), 153.

[30] Cast: Donald Shanks (Hermann, Landgraf of Thuringia), Kenneth Neate (Tannhäuser), Marcella Reale, Rosemary Gordon, Mary Hayman (Elisabeth), Morag Beaton (Venus), Ronald Maconaghie, Raymond Myers, Alexander Major (Wolfram), Robin Gordon (Walther), Luciano Borghi and Joseph Grunfelder (Biterolf), John Germain (Heinrich), John Pringle (Reinmar), Janice Taylor (Shepherd).

entry of the guests in Act 2, and the final apotheosis were quite electrifying.[31]

The same reviewer was equally enthusiastic about Cillario's Mozart performances, finding that 'there was stylish and generally well-toned support from the Trust Orchestra under the visiting Italian conductor … Cillario … he was again able to maintain its [the music's] flow, so that there was a sense of unity of purpose to the whole of the first act.'[32] In Sydney and Melbourne, there was some critical division about the merits of the *Tannhäuser* production by Stephan Beinl.[33] One reviewer found Wagner to be at fault,[34] while another suggested that the composer had not always been well served by the conductor,[35] though it was acknowledged that Cillario and the orchestra achieved 'dramatic impact in the overture' and allied passages, while both critics felt that the 'long drawn-out passages', particularly in Act 3 caused boredom.

The preparations for *The Magic Flute* had not been without tensions. At the first rehearsal in Sydney, Cillario shouted at Stephen Hall (within earshot of the players): 'You promised me an orchestra!' Hall calmly replied: 'With your coaching, Carlo, they are soon bound to become very good.'[36] According to Hall, he received a 'sneering smile' in response, but Cillario 'then began to work in earnest and carefully explained to every section what he wanted them to do.'[37] The eventual result was positively received. John Cargher quipped that the '"Magic Flute" may get most of its magic from the brilliant conducting of Carlo Felice Cillario'[38] and went on to praise the local cast.[39] The conductor himself was not happy that the opera was sung

---

[31] W.L. Hoffmann, *The Canberra Times*, 26 February 1968.

[32] Hoffmann, *The Canberra Times*, 28 February 1968.

[33] Stephan Beinl (1903–1970) was a Viennese-born opera producer who enjoyed a significant career in Austria and Switzerland before arriving in Australia in 1962. He worked as a producer with the Elizabethan Theatre Trust.

[34] Fred R. Blanks, *The Australian Jewish Times* (Sydney), 4 July 1968.

[35] 'H.L.' *The Australian Jewish News* (Melbourne), 19 April 1968.

[36] Hall, Cillario Obituary, 20 December 2007.

[37] Ibid.

[38] John Cargher, *The Bulletin*, 20 April 1968.

[39] Casts: Robert Gard (Tamino), Betty Westwater, Maureen Howard, Diane Holmes (1st, 2nd, 3rd Lady), Ronald Maconaghie (Papageno), Helen Kerby

in English rather than the original German. In Canberra the vocal strength of the ensemble was acknowledged by critics, along with the 'stylish and generally well-toned support from the Trust Orchestra'.[40] With hindsight it was felt that the season 'was well conducted by Cillario, though the orchestra was not yet in command of Mozart'.[41]

In spite of the fact that Cillario was working with an orchestra formed only the previous year, his vigour and his artistic integrity resulted in a musical and dramatic fusion of a standard well above the norm at the time with the company. In Wagner's complex divided and exposed string passages, he began to create the lustrous sheen of string sound that became a hallmark of the company orchestra; the fruit of his work could still be discerned in the orchestra for some years after his retirement. One might wonder what was going through his mind as he conducted *Tannhäuser* in Canberra, with a reduced orchestra and a chorus barely half the size of an accepted norm for this repertoire. It is evident that from his first appearances in Australia, Cillario brought a fresh energy and a set of particular skills which breathed new life into the nation's operatic culture. He coaxed, he inspired, he challenged, and occasionally he shouted, but all the while he worked to raise the standard of music-making to a level that would eventually bear comparison with other operatic centres of the world.

At the conclusion of the Canberra season, en route to Adelaide, Cillario made a short stop in Melbourne, where he conducted in the annual Moomba Festival. On 4 March, the ETOC presented a Gala Concert at the Myer Music Bowl, conducted jointly by the 'famous Italian maestro' Cillario; the 'American conductor' Robert Feist; and 'the Company's new resident conductor, Mr William Reid (formerly of Sadler's Wells)'. This was Cillario's first experience of Melbourne, a city where he would regularly perform for the next 30 years. It

(Queen of Night), John Pringle (Speaker), Neil Warren-Smith (Sarastro), Rosemary Gordon and Janice Taylor (Pamina), Robin Gordon (Monostatos), Joan Shute, Mary Hayman, Beryl Biggs (1st, 2nd, 3rd Genii), Joseph Powell, Kevin Mills (Two Priests), Janice Taylor and Janice Hill (Papagena), Neville Grave, John Pooley (Two Men in Armour).
[40] Hoffmann, *The Canberra Times*, 28 February 1968.
[41] A. Gyger (2005), 218.

was also the first time he shared the podium with two conductors already known to Australian audiences: Feist, who was subsequently overlooked in favour of Cillario; and Reid who became a long-standing colleague of Cillario, often taking over performance runs from the Italian maestro.

After the Met our opera is just great, say the stars

THE CONDUCTORS Robert Feist (left) and Carlo Cillario (right) and between them the singers Kenneth Neate, Raymond Myers and Marcella Reale.

4: The stars of the ETOC season, 1968 compare the company favourably with the Metropolitan Opera, New York.

Adelaide Festival

Established in 1960, the Adelaide Festival of the Arts was loosely modelled on the Edinburgh International Festival, with the aim of overcoming 'the tyranny of distance in bringing to South Australia the culture which arts lovers in other countries experience.'[42] As well as engaging artists from Europe and the US, the festival brought together national forces for special events such as the 1968 performances of Mahler's Eighth Symphony, which combined the Sydney and Adelaide ABC orchestras. The participation of the ETOC in 1968 was described as a 'change of emphasis', to bring the company 'deservedly to the fore … and its new orchestra [that] La Scala's [sic] Carlo Cillario and America's Robert Feist will conduct.'[43]

---

[42] http://www.yooyahcloud.com/ADELAIDE_FESTIVAL_OF_ARTS/CH6bM/
Adelaide_Festival_of_Arts_History.pdf, accessed 24 February 2023.

[43] [No author named], *Walkabout*, Vol 34, No. 1, 1 January 1968.

Having been formed only one year previously, the Trust Orchestra inevitably drew comparison with Australia's better-established orchestral resources, funded by the ABC which had previously played for the opera seasons.[44] According to the bass-baritone Neil Warren-Smith, a company member of the ETOC since its inception, 'Cillario was one of the first conductors to work with our new ... *personal* orchestra.' Warren-Smith sometimes 'had the feeling that the ABC orchestras were getting in our way. With this lot, I never did.' He admired the 'speed with which they established their own identity'.[45] A clear concern of the Trust management during this time was to raise and maintain orchestral standards through the hiring of quality operatic specialists. Several conductors already resident in Australia could be relied upon to produce solid performances. But they were not 'star' conductors; Cillario's visit was perhaps the first experience of an opera conductor of such flair and dynamism on these shores.

The contrasting styles and artistic backgrounds of the two conductors were inevitably played out in the press. Robert Feist had made his Australian debut the previous year, conducting *Tosca* and other repertoire to good reviews. He was billed as an 'international conductor', and his seriousness of purpose and interpretative abilities with the larger Verdi and Puccini repertoire were admired. He would have been a long-term solid musical asset for the company, but Cillario was generally favoured for the greater discipline and refinement he brought to the orchestral sound, and for his keener sense of dramatic pacing. Where Feist led respectful performances, Cillario produced authentically Italian *melodramma*.

The ETOC began its Adelaide season with well-received performances of *Tannhäuser*,[46] which transferred from Canberra. Cillario's 'control of the stage' was noted, as well as the 'cleanly

---

[44] The Australian Broadcasting Commission, which, at that time administrated the state orchestras.

[45] Warren-Smith and Salter (1983), 140.

[46] For cast see FN 30.

polished sound' that he drew from his 'small orchestra'.[47] An incident occurred during the opening night which has passed into Australian operatic lore. John Cargher recalled it many years later: 'He [Cillario] conducted with such verve and energy that he knocked his score to the ground and nearly lost his trousers, when his braces gave way.'[48] Cillario was of short stature, and in trying to communicate with his players, he fell from the podium, which collapsed underneath him. He landed amid the flute section, at which point his braces gave way and the performance came to a halt. The cast remained onstage while a member of the music staff (William Reid) attempted to return the maestro's clothes to a decent state. In some accounts, Reid held the maestro's trousers up for the remainder of the act. Cillario appeared unfazed by the incident (which could have had more serious consequences) and continued conducting 'with zest'.[49]

This sartorial mishap was not an isolated incident in Cillario's Australian career. Other conductors might have found such incidents mortifying, but Cillario always resumed unabashed. As recalled by Stephen Hall: 'Cillario merely got the giggles and continued to joke about it years later.'[50] For Cillario, a performance was '*un spettacolo*', reflecting life in all its richness and never without an element of risk.

Tosca was to be the highlight of the festival. It was advertised that the best Australian singers[51] would appear alongside "internationally

---

[47] Comments taken from Kenneth Hince's reviews in: *The Australian*, 11 March 1968, and 16 March 1968.

[48] John Cargher, *Opera and ballet in Australia* (Cassell Australia, 1977), 130.

[49] Information in this paragraph is derived from Cargher (Ibid), and *The Daily Telegraph*, 22 March 1968 ('The show must go on'). Stephen Hall, in his obituary of Cillario (*The Australian*, 20 December 2007), recalls the incident slightly differently. Cillario himself recalled it in an interview for *The Australian*, 6 February 1970. Oxenbould gives another version in his 2005 book (157–8). William Reid who was present, seated next to the conductor as prompter, has written a somewhat confused account in 'The Day Cillario Lost His Trousers' (Image, April 1987, 71–2).

[50] Hall, Cillario Obituary (Ibid).

[51] Adelaide Cast: Marie Collier (Tosca), Donald Smith (Cavaradossi), Tito Gobbi (Scarpia), Luciano Borghi (Angelotti), Ronald Maconaghie (Sacristan), John Heffernan (Spoletta), John Pringle (Sciarrone), Janice Taylor (Shepherd).

Australian" Marie Collier,[52] 'who holds La Scala, Covent Garden and New York's "Met" in eager tribute, and Italy's celebrated Tito Gobbi.'[53] The epithet 'internationally Australian' is quaint and reflects the times. Ballarat-born Marie Collier was already well on her way to a major career, having understudied Callas as Tosca at Covent Garden in 1964 and substituted for her in 1965. Adelaide audiences had heard her at the 1964 festival in the Australian premiere of William Walton's *Troilus and Cressida*.[54] Cavaradossi was sung by Donald Smith, who had sung with success at Sadler's Wells in London, but as the operatic culture became more established, he settled back in Australia, a place more suited to his temperament. Tito Gobbi was a force familiar to all opera *cognoscenti*, at least through recordings, and was widely recognised as one of the world's leading interpreters of Scarpia.[55]

The opera was to be televised – the first time an opera performance had been made available across Australia on a commercial station (Channel 9), and while the film does not survive, a sound recording does.[56] According to Warren-Smith, 'Gobbi's performance was every bit as superb as had been heralded. So was Marie Collier's. But even more exciting – and certainly more lasting – than the visit of Tito Gobbi, was the arrival of Carlo Felice Cillario.'[57]

The response to this cast of principal singers was electric: in an article titled 'A "Tosca" of Toscas' W.L. Hoffmann wrote: 'In the history of opera in Australia certain moments, certain performances stand out above all others. No one who was present at this performance of 'Tosca' could doubt that this was one of those rare and memorable

---

52 She was also hailed as 'World-famous Ballarat-born Soprano,' *The Australian Jewish News* (Melbourne), 16 February 1968.

53 Alongside these high-level stars of opera, the same publication notes that Marlene Dietrich will also appear at the Festival 'and collect the highest fee ever paid to an Adelaide Festival star.' ['Publisher's column' – no author identified], *Walkabout* Vol. 34, No. 1, 1 January 1968.

54 The production was by Robin Lovejoy, with designs by Frank Hinder.

55 His reputation as a 'malignant and chilling Scarpia' was upheld in Adelaide. [No author named], *Walkabout*, Vol. 34, No. 10, 1 October 1968.

56 https://youtu.be/lZN8zW3yXNQ, accessed 15 January 2023.

57 Warren-Smith and Salter (1983), 139–40.

moments.' While lavishing praise upon the three principals, he also noted that 'the Trust orchestra under the skilful direction of Italian conductor Cillario [gave a] glowing and balanced realisation of the score.'[58]

The scrutinising of the work of the newly founded Trust Orchestra led to Cillario and Feist being, in effect, in competition. Cillario's conducting was enthusiastically received, while Feist's work, while worthy and professional, was left in the shade. Critical opinion remained divided. However, reviewers at this time were not immune to using their influence in order to side with particular artists, especially when foreign guest artists came into play with locals. One such reviewer (who for a time acted as a singer's agent, creating an awkward conflict) was John Cargher, a flamboyant opera commentator and raconteur, who was openly critical of Cillario. His review of the opening night of *Tosca* praised the equality of the three principals, finding that 'Gobbi at 53 [sic] sang and acted like a 20-year-old', and that Donald Smith possessed a 'voice to compete' with the Italian. Cargher then noted that Collier had 'an unaccountable and unnecessary case of first-night nerves' and that vocally she declined in the third act, 'before then, she had poured forth the most glorious sound an audience can expect of a singer.' Cargher then made a cryptic mention of some backstage disagreement between Cillario and Smith, evidently not discernible from the performance but conveyed anecdotally to the reviewer. When it came to assessing the musical direction, Cargher wrote:

> Regrettably I must note that conductor Carlo Felice Cillario did not add to the enjoyment of the evening. I am reluctant to believe that this 'Tosca' is a yardstick of his qualities in the Italian repertoire. Ragged playing may be due to lack of

---

[58] Hoffmann, *The Canberra Times*, 16 March 1968. The continuation of the review is worth quoting: 'And this was purely because of the magnificent musical–dramatic projection of the three principals, Marie Collier, Tito Gobbi and Donald Smith. … The settings, the production, the chorus and orchestra were all practically identical with what we had in Canberra last year. However, it must be added that the Trust Orchestra, under the skilful direction of the Italian conductor Cillario … gave a far more glowing and balanced realisation of the score.'

rehearsal; the ignoring of Puccini's precise intentions, such as the hasty dismissal of the great funeral march in the last act, would seem to be out of character with what we have heard of Signor Cillario's admirable qualities.[59]

Cargher was one of the more colourful and outspoken of the reviewers of the period, and in his ongoing assessments of Cillario's work, a note of personal disapproval regularly creeps in. Every point scored by Cillario was typically followed by a qualifying note of disdain. The fact was that there had been a clash between Cillario and Smith (not for the last time in their working collaborations), and Cargher had publicly taken the side of the tenor. In engaging a volatile Italian conductor, the company had chosen a provocative musical force who needed to 'stir the pot' – not only in performance, but frequently in rehearsal. He would create a voluble atmosphere around which he could improvise, creating something visceral and unpredictable, ensuring that each performance would be a unique event. Nearly a decade later, in 1977, Cillario explained in an interview 'in opera you have surprises during the performances … I like that sort of thing'.[60] And, it must be said that if Cillario found himself without surprises in his performances, he instinctively turned towards creating an environment where they would occur. This volatility was a characteristic of both his own personality, and the repertoire with which he was particularly associated.

Cargher's criticisms of these performances come across as heavy-handed, and perhaps personally motivated. All the same, another leading reviewer of the period, Kenneth Hince, also indicated that Cillario was pushing his histrionic approach to the limit. Hince found the conducting of *Tosca* to be 'neither precise enough in detail, nor sympathetic in tone', and criticised the 'hard, driving tempos and the lack of any give or take within the pulse of the music' which was in stark contrast to his reception of the earlier performances of *Tannhäuser*. Hince also made a veiled reference to dissension

---

[59] Quotes in this paragraph from Cargher, 'Triumph, tragedy', *The Bulletin*, 30 March 1968.

[60] Stephen Downes, 'Cillario: noble maestro of the opera world', *The Age*, 18 April 1977.

among the cast, concluding that 'this surely is an opera which has to be played most flexibly … Cillario apparently sees it otherwise: but I think he will have to persuade some of his singers that he is right before there is a perfect liaison between voice and orchestra.'[61]

There was no doubt that the Adelaide *Tosca* season was highly charged, an operatic experience on a level not often encountered in Australia at that time. Things seemed to settle down in the pit once the company reached Melbourne, where Felix Werder wrote:

> Conductor Carlo Felice Cillario put on a magnificent performance to translate the score and its dramatic implications into a living reality. He showed a vigorous sense of style, fine orchestral control and an inner conception of the fitness of things which inspired his charges.[62]

Hince also revised his views in Melbourne, finding that Cillario's 'severity, which was marked in Adelaide, relaxed … the music is living and breathing far more easily than it was.'[63] He also alluded to tensions remaining between the conductor and Donald Smith.

The 1967 visit of conductor Robert Feist had been successful, and it is likely that he was being considered for some future role with the developing company. He had been entrusted with some of the major warhorses of the Italian repertoire, including *Don Carlo* and *La fanciulla del West*. Feist's career in America and Italy via New Zealand,[64] gave him 'international' status in the eyes of the company, but it was not of the pedigree of Cillario, a fact which became obvious during the 1968 season. A week before his negative review of Cillario's *Tosca*, John Cargher posted a review ('Half-baked "Don Carlo[s]"'), comparing Feist's conducting of *Don Carlo* and Cillario's reading of *Tannhäuser*.[65] With Feist, Cargher found that 'while his efforts down there were far from bad, he failed to

---

[61] Hince, 'Night of the long tiaras, the festival's operatic night of nights,' *The Australian*, 16 March 1968.

[62] Felix Werder, *The Age*, Melbourne, 6 April 1968.

[63] Hince, 'A foothold on the ramparts,' *The Australian*, 9 April 1968.

[64] https://www.emmickfunerals.com/obituary/Robert-Feist, accessed 9 January 2023.

[65] Cargher, 'Half-baked Don Carlo[s],' *The Bulletin*, 23 March 1968.

produce the drive and urgency which are needed to bring a Verdi opera to life', whereas:

> under Carlo Felice Cillario the orchestral playing and the extremely difficult ensembles on stage come to life brilliantly. One can no longer plead inexperience for the Trust's orchestra; after this we know that it is a major musical unit which is just as good as the man at the helm.[66]

While Cillario's performances aroused conflicting reactions and some division in the press, it is clear that the management of the ETOC and its resident musicians saw in him a potential asset for the future of the company.

Melbourne and Sydney Seasons

The ETOC performed in Melbourne from 4 April to 11 May in the Princess Theatre. The Tosca of Marie Collier was celebrated as something of a homecoming for the soprano with her Ballarat origins. Donald Smith also reprised his Cavaradossi, but Gobbi had only been contracted for Adelaide, and Australian-born, overseas–based Raymond Myers undertook the role of Scarpia, which was judged to be musically impressive but dramatically 'tentative'.[67] The rehearsal period in Melbourne was tense – Myers was inexperienced and not yet reliable in his role. The dress rehearsal descended into something of a farce, and at the end of the second act, as Scarpia expires, Collier delivered Tosca's line 'È morto! Or gli perdono!'[68] – only to be met by Cillario's cry of 'Io! No!'[69] Such spontaneous eruptions from the pit became something of a Cillario speciality over the years, and were not always confined to the rehearsals.[70]

Following *Tosca*, the cast for *The Magic Flute* featured many Australian singers who would go on to work with Cillario regularly in subsequent years, including Neil Warren-Smith, Robert Gard,

---

[66] Ibid.

[67] A. Gyger (2005), 223.

[68] 'He's dead! Now I forgive him!'

[69] 'Not I!'

[70] This incident is recounted in Oxenbould (2005), 158–9.

Ronald Maconaghie and John Pringle.[71] Cillario conducted only the
initial Melbourne performances, then relinquished the podium to
Feist and Reid. The revival of the twelve-year-old production, which
had been created by Stefan Haag was criticised in some circles, and
it was felt that the orchestra was still some way from establishing a
'Mozart style'.

The Melbourne *Tannhäuser* largely replicated the cast from
Adelaide.[72] It comprised local artists, with some overseas-based
Australians who had built wider careers and were now returning
– singers such as Kenneth Neate, Morag Beaton (a Scottish singer
who came to Australia for the 1965 Sutherland–Williamson season
and eventually settled here), and Raymond Myers. The season was
deemed to be a success and it was clear that Cillario committed as
much passion and industry to working with local casts as he did
with visiting stars.

After further performances in Brisbane, the company completed
the 1968 season in Sydney, where a partially completed Sydney
Opera House stood on the harbour foreshore. The building had been
a hot topic when Cillario and Collier were interviewed in Adelaide
and questioned about operatic life in Australia. By 1968, the Sydney
Opera House (originally scheduled for completion in 1963)[73] was
being openly spoken of as a 'let-down of the company's hopes'. Collier
was critical of the new plans for a smaller auditorium to stage opera
and ballet. Calling it a 'tragedy', she said that the space would not
supply the dimensions necessary for grand opera. Cillario likewise
cast doubt on whether 'a full-scale orchestra can be accommodated
in the smaller hall of the opera house', with a maximum pit size of
51 players, as opposed to 75 at Covent Garden.[74]

At the time of the Sydney season, the technical director of the
Lincoln Centre in New York visited Sydney to advise on the viability
of the plan to create an opera theatre from what had originally been

---

[71] For cast see FN 39.
[72] See FN 30.
[73] Roger Covell, *Australia's Music, Themes of a new Society* (Sun Books, Melbourne, 1967), 257.
[74] Pamela Ruskin, *Walkabout*, Vol. 34, No. 1, 1 January 1968.

planned as the Drama Theatre. Hans Sondheimer found fault only with the curved pit wall. Otherwise, he judged that '80% of the operas could be played there' … it 'will do for a long time' and that it is 'a place for young singers.' Some condescension could be detected in his closing remark: 'If you really succeed here, I am sure someone, someday, will build you a house for grand opera.' Sondheimer optimistically estimated that the pit would seat 74 players.[75] Cillario's reservations were ignored at the time, and the limitations of the Opera Theatre and its pit were to have consequences for his musical aspirations with the company over subsequent years.

In Sydney, Cillario continued to enjoy success, though there were some slippery moments backstage. The season was due to open on 11 June with *Tosca,* starring a new Italian soprano in the title role, Antonietta Stella.[76] Three hours before the premiere Donald Smith withdrew due to illness, and one hour prior to curtain up Stella also fell ill. The opening was postponed until 15 June,[77] with Nicola Filacuridi replacing Smith,[78] and Stella recovered from her indisposition. She enjoyed a triumphant success as Tosca: 'all a prima donna should be: beautiful sounding, good-looking … gracious, elegant … a modern diva. … She wears fine gowns with style.'[79] Her flamboyant demeanour and wardrobe led to Stella being a very popular and much interviewed figure in the press. Roger Covell gave

---

[75] All quotes in this paragraph, from A. Gyger (2005), 225–6.

[76] Alison Gyger (2005) states (205) that she sang only in Canberra and Brisbane, but then (223) talks of her having to cancel the opening night in Sydney, which was postponed until 15 June, when a recovered Stella sang. Stella had enjoyed a major career, singing around the world, including in Vienna, London and the Metropolitan Opera, New York.

[77] Sydney Casts: Antonietta Stella and Maureen Howard (Tosca), Donald Smith and Reginald Byers (Cavaradossi), Raymond Myers (Scarpia), Luciano Borghi and Joseph Grunfelder (Angelotti), Ronald Maconaghie (Sacristan), John Heffernan (Spoletta), John Pringle (Sciarrone), Paul Rutenis (Gaoler).

[78] An artist who had sung with Stella in Europe and had taken up residence in Sydney where he became a real estate agent and was, from time-to-time called upon when the company had an emergency, as on this occasion (A. Gyger (2005), 223–4).

[79] Foley, *Daily Telegraph* 17 June 1968. Information in this paragraph also derived from A. Gyger (2005), 223–24.

the production a favourable review and noted that Cillario seemed 'more at ease with his forces than at earlier openings of the season,' shaping the 'flexible contours of Puccini's style with a keen regard for the unity of stage and pit.'[80]

The musical qualities of *Tannhäuser* were well received in Sydney: as Elisabeth, Marcella Reale was praised for her 'rich voice, … elegant phrasing and convincing characterisation'. Morag Beaton had success as Venus, 'singing with sensuous allure and thrilling abandon,' and Raymond Myers was deemed a 'restrained and stylish Wolfram.'[81]

Touring to five major cities, the 1968 season was a notable success, commercially as well as artistically, largely due to the efforts of John Young[82] and Stefan Haag[83], as well as the entrepreneur Harry Miller[84] who had the responsibility to 'sell' the season. His idea to offer tickets on a subscription basis revolutionised the local market for live cultural events, making opera a fashionable and sought-after commodity. The operas sold out in most cities, and in Sydney, 3000 ticket requests had to be turned down. The Adelaide *Tosca* was considered to have been the highlight of the festival. It displayed the potential of a strong local company, with an international presence, against whom local talent was tested and not found wanting.

In Sydney, Robert Feist shared the conducting of *Tosca* and *Tannhäuser* with Cillario. The critics had by now become less positive about the American. It was noted in his reading of *La forza*

[80] Covell, *The Sydney Morning Herald*, 18 June 1968.
[81] Hoffmann, *The Canberra Times*, 26 February 1968.
[82] New-Zealand born John Young had a career as a singer in musicals and opera prior to joining the ETOC, where he eventually became the company Administrator.
[83] Stefan Haag (1925–1986) was a Viennese-born stage director, designer, and arts administrator. As a member of the Vienna Boys Choir, he was stranded in Australia during World War II. He was Executive Director (1962–1968) and Artistic Advisor (1968–1969) of the Elizabethan Theatre Company. https://adb.anu.edu.au/biography/haag-stefan-hermann-12577, accessed 8 November 2023.
[84] Harry M. Miller (1934–2018) was a New Zealand-born promoter, publicist, and media agent. For a time, he worked on the staff of the ETOC and was influential in developing the system of season subscriptions.

del destino that 'there were some uneasy aspects to Robert Feist's characteristically thorough and intense direction.'[85] Regarding his direction of *La fanciulla del West*, 'Feist's conducting reflected his love and knowledge of the score, but there were suggestions that the orchestra was not quite up to its intricacies.'[86]

Cillario emerged victoriously from his first antipodean season. He also clearly enjoyed his time in Australia. As Moffatt Oxenbould justly observed, he 'was enchanted to find a vitality and lack of pretension in the Elizabethan Trust Opera Company. He loved the sense of ensemble among the artists and revelled in being able to participate in the artistic growth of individual singers and instrumentalists.'[87] He enjoyed the atmosphere of this new world, unfettered by European mores and traditions. Cillario was essentially an 'Italian maestro', with all that the term implies, but an iconoclastic, wild frontier spirit also coursed through his veins. While he knew all the traditions and conventions of the repertoire, he was always questioning received wisdom, searching for new ways of understanding the printed score, inventing and finding new freedoms between the notes. This was a process that constantly preoccupied him, and it became the means for him to shun the routine of the repertory opera conductor. Even in his final years, he would approach a classic opera such as *La traviata* as if for the first time, sometimes to the frustration of seasoned, *routinièr* singers. His expertise and knowledge were, unusually, accompanied by a child-like sense of wonder upon opening a score, even one that he had conducted many times before.

The arrival of Cillario in 1968 had a major impact on the development of opera in Australia. His sense of style, his dynamic energy and zeal for excellence were eagerly received in a land of operatic opportunity, whose openness and unpretentiousness were embraced by the conductor in turn. During the Sydney season, John Cargher remarked on the lack of operatic traditions in Australia,

---

[85] A. Gyger (2005), 221; quoting Covell, *The Sydney Morning Herald*, 18 June 1968.

[86] Ibid, 224.

[87] Oxenbould, *Carlo Felice Cillario and Opera Australia*, 2003.

which 'until recently has relied on scratch companies of overseas artists for limited tours.' While lamenting the 'total absence of artistic direction' in the operatic sphere (which may be taken to mean musical direction), he saw in Cillario the hope of a long-awaited remedy.[88]

Future Plans

Behind the scenes of the ETOC, the management had come to the same conclusion as Cargher. They recognised in Cillario a future musical leader, who could strengthen and lead the company into their future home. Cillario had made a huge impact with the company and displayed great enthusiasm for his work with the ETOC, and a sense of personal investment in the company and its future. During this first visit, the company moved quickly to secure the conductor, with negotiations taking place against other structural changes within the organisation, and it seems that neither side had considered all the implications of the commitment.

In Australia, opera had long been understood as a primarily Italian art form, a notion cemented by the visits of a number of Italian touring companies during the nineteenth and early twentieth centuries. Cillario's performances radiated the high energy of Italian *melodramma*. Under his baton, there was a sense that audiences were imbibing their opera from the source. He could speak about his experiences – conducting Callas, recording with Caballé – and inspire the whole company. He also demonstrated a combative element in his character which boded well. Here would be a figure willing to go and fight for the cause of opera in Australia, which at the time meant the Sydney Opera House and all that it represented.

Cillario was, however, in the midst of a busy and lucrative international career, and the ETOC was seeking a time commitment which would significantly diminish his availability on the international circuit. An undated telegram from 1968 confirms that an initial offer for the position of Musical Director for 1969 was

[88] Material in this paragraph is derived from Cargher, 'Hope is with the singers,' *The Bulletin*, 22 June 1968.

made.[89] Why that title was subsequently wound back to 'Principal Conductor' is not certain, but records of the negotiations suggest that the impending incorporation of the ETOC was a factor hindering it from making long-term appointments.

There were two people who particularly influenced Cillario's future Australian career at this pivotal time. Stephen Hall, who had been largely responsible for Cillario's 1968 visit played a central role in the events between 1968 and 1975, when Cillario returned as guest conductor. Hall saw the world of opera in global terms. He went to great lengths to secure Cillario's commitment to working with the ETOC, seeing him as a potential conduit through which the company would make connections with the wider world and secure an international reputation.

At the time of incorporation, a compatriot of Cillario's, Claudio Alcorso[90] became Chairman of the Board of the Australian Opera. He and Cillario enjoyed close professional and personal associations. Alcorso had made his home in Australia, where he became a successful businessman as well as a cultured patron of the arts. He recognised the potential benefits for the Australian Opera to have Cillario at its helm. The correspondence between the two men reveals deep cultural affinities as well as a shared vision for an operatic culture in Australia, but it also discloses a good deal of shrewd diplomacy on Alcorso's part. Cillario liked to profess that

---

[89] John Young to Carlo Felice Cillario, at Teatro San Carlo, Naples, Undated (1968) telegram. 'Carlo Felice Cillario – Artist Files 'Misc.', Opera Australia Library archives'.

[90] Claudio Alcorso was born in 1913, educated in Rome, and emigrated as a business migrant to Australia with his family in 1939 following the Fascist government's persecution of Jews. Later interned as an enemy alien, he settled in Tasmania in 1948. In addition to his subsequent involvement in the textile and wine industries, and his participation in conservation movements in Tasmania, he was the Chairman of the Board of the ETOC and then the Australian Opera. He and Cillario corresponded regularly when the conductor was overseas. Part of this correspondence is preserved at the Tasmanian Archives and Heritage Office [NS3001/1/14]. I am grateful to Moffatt Oxenbould and Stephenie Cahalan for drawing my attention to these documents. See also Stephenie Cahalan, *Colour and Movement – the life of Claudio Alcorso* (Hobart, Tasmania, Forty South Publishing Pty. Ltd., 2019) 72.

he was not interested in money, politics, or anything other than his art. Meanwhile, Sandor Gorlinsky operated behind the scenes as his agent, ensuring that the conductor's career remained grounded in business, rather than altruism. Alcorso worked hard to organise a structure for Cillario's involvement with the company that would serve the needs of both parties. He even expressed a hope that Cillario might leave the 'old world' and bring his family to Australia, but Cillario never seriously entertained the idea.

Following Hall's departure as artistic director in 1977 a third person, Moffatt Oxenbould, whose history with the ETOC dated back to 1963, became the guiding figure behind Cillario's work with the company, and by 1986 they had become a symbiotic team of 'artistic director' and 'principal guest conductor'. Through Oxenbould's diplomatic and administrative talents, Australia gained Cillario on his own terms, as guest conductor and artistic advisor, unfettered by the title of music director, and thus freed from the restrictions and responsibilities that went with it.

The appointment of a music director was a momentous undertaking for the ETOC, an essential step in the legitimisation of the company in the eyes of the world opera stage. The appointee would be responsible for the development and expansion of the company in the lead-up to the completion of the Opera House. They would also lead the first staged opera performances in the new building and assume overall artistic responsibility for the programming of the inaugural season. Cillario was not the first conductor to have been considered for this role. The British conductor, Edward Downes,[91] had been first approached in 1963, and was offered the job,[92] but plans fell through. Many Australian singers who travelled to the UK to further their operatic careers knew Downes through his work at The Royal Opera in London, where he had begun as a *répétiteur* and risen to become a staff conductor of long standing. Several of those singers wrote to the ETOC, paying tribute to Downes as

---

[91] Edward Downes (1924–2009) British conductor, particularly of opera. He had a long association with The Royal Opera House from 1952 and was also a long-time conductor with the BBC Philharmonic. He was particularly noted as a Verdi and Russian-opera specialist.

[92] Oxenbould (2005), 127.

both a conductor and an individual.[93] Their testimony paints him as both a 'company man' and a redoubtable creative force, capable of delivering excellent performances over a wide repertoire. The Royal Opera was celebrated at the time for its musical standards, instilled by the stringent leadership of Georg Solti as its Music Director. At this stage of his career, Downes was seeking his own domain. He was also a good friend of George Lascelles, the Earl of Harewood, who had wielded considerable power in London operatic life ever since his founding of *Opera* magazine in 1950. In 1970, Lord Harewood was appointed as the 'overseas member' of the new Australian Opera Board; probably, at least in part, in order to maintain a dialogue with Downes.

It is impossible to assess here how much Jørn Utzon's winning design for the Opera House affected the development of the ETOC and its choice of inaugural Music Director. No one could be sure how the Opera House would look, sound or function when completed, though the developing concrete shells suggested a monumental scale of music making. 'Grand Opera' was a resonant term which had shifted in meaning through the course of the nineteenth century. It still had currency in Australia during the 1960s and 70s, as a gold standard signifying the largest and weightiest works in the repertoire: those of Wagner, Verdi, Puccini and Richard Strauss.

During the building phase of the Opera House, it was not clear until a fairly late stage that the Opera Theatre of the new edifice would be unable to adequately host this repertoire. The company's attempts to secure the services of high-profile international conductors have often since foundered due both to the limitations of the pit and the acoustic of the Opera Theatre. For all the exciting potential of Utzon's design, what eventuated was a poorly resourced theatre which failed to satisfy its brief. Whoever was appointed as Music Director would face the challenge of overcoming these contradictions and limitations while building cohesive seasons of opera.

---

[93] Tasmanian Archives and Heritage Office, Item NS3001/1/14. 'Correspondence Claudio Alcorso and Carlo Cillario, a conductor and at one time Musical Director of the Australian Opera.'

In this unofficial contest between Downes and Cillario that was to emerge, Claudio Alcorso emerges as a skilled strategist in keeping two strong candidates in the field. Following the tour of 1968, Cillario became the preferred candidate, with an agreement in place for him to return as Principal Conductor the following year.

5: 'The Baton Breaker', Carlo Felice Cillario, 1968.

Alcorso and Hall set the company on a course that would see him named as Music Director in 1970 and conduct the first season in the Opera House in 1973. For the moment, Cillario was open to offers, doubtless flattered by the attention. However, the path to naming him as Music Director in 1970 was not a smooth one.

Scene 2 – 1969

Return as Principal Conductor

In January 1969, Cillario's new position was announced, and John Cargher wrote:

> Carlo Felice Cillario's re-engagement as principal conductor must meet with universal approval. Conductors are a commodity which this country cannot produce unassisted, and the likelihood of the availability of a Mackerras being remote, the Trust cannot do better than to rely on the Cillarios of this world.[94]

The transitory title of 'Principal Conductor' evoked a set of expectations which were untested. In this role, Cillario likely acted in the knowledge that he was soon to become the Music Director, and assumed responsibilities that aligned with his own understanding of what that role would entail. This lack of clarity was to have repercussions.

Upon his return to Australia, Cillario prepared and conducted three operas in the 1969 season: *Falstaff*, *Madama Butterfly*, and *Un ballo in maschera*.[95] *Falstaff* was keenly anticipated due to the return of Tito Gobbi in the title role for the Melbourne performances.[96] Gobbi's portrayal was well received by the public, and most critics praised him for his 'experienced mastery of the role and powerful singing.'[97] Cargher's review of the Melbourne *Falstaff* was generally positive, though a predictable note of disdain crept in:

> Falstaff will never be a box-office opera, no matter how

---

[94] Cargher, *The Bulletin,* 11 Jan 1969.

[95] The season was completed by Wolf-Ferrari's *School for Fathers*, and Mussorgsky's *Boris Godunov.*

[96] Melbourne Cast: Tito Gobbi (Falstaff), John Pringle and Alan Light (Ford), Robert Gard and Reginald Byers (Fenton), Ian Campbell (Dr Caius), Adelio Zagonara (Bardolfo), Donald Shanks (Pistola), Elizabeth Fretwell (Alice Ford), Janice Taylor and Glenys Fowles (Nannetta), Justine Rettick (Mistress Quickly), Diane Holmes (Meg Page).

[97] A. Gyger (2005), 232.

much the more serious critics may hail it as a masterpiece. Its appearance in a Trust opera season can be justified by the availability of Gobbi and a substantially fine supporting cast. Carlo Felice Cillario, as usual, works miracles with the orchestra, who make one wonder whether they deliberately sabotage other conductors or whether Cillario is some kind of minor Toscanini.[98]

Cargher qualified his position with a longer and more critical piece published the following week. It was not a matter of under-rehearsal, he judged, rather that the 'failure … lay in the awe with which the large cast treated its celebrated guest'.[99] Within the company, there were rumblings that something was amiss. Moffatt Oxenbould felt that Gobbi's second visit to Australia was 'as disastrous as the first was marvellous.'[100] He had made a highly positive impression during the production of *Tosca* the previous year, when he was helpful and supportive of younger local singers who were performing minor roles. In particular John Pringle, who played Sciarrone, was grateful for the advice and support he received from Gobbi at the start of his career.[101]

Such mutual warmth had cooled by the time of the *Falstaff* staging. Between differing accounts there emerges a sense of resentment within the company towards an artist, who, no matter how famous, had arrived at the last minute and failed to blend into a production which had already been solidly rehearsed. Perhaps Gobbi was simply less at home in an ensemble work such as *Falstaff*. Nevertheless, Cillario's command of the score won praise, with W.L. Hoffmann noting that he 'elicited some fine playing from the orchestra and shaped the whole performance with a sure hand so that, although it moved like quicksilver, the details of Verdi's delicate and lovely score were always apparent.'[102]

The 'insider' reservations about Gobbi's Falstaff were in stark

---

[98] Cargher, *The Bulletin*, 1 March 1968.

[99] Cargher, *The Bulletin*, 8 March 1968.

[100] A. Gyger (2005), 232.

[101] Ibid., 233.

[102] Hoffmann, *The Canberra Times*, 10 February 1969.

contrast to the ecstatic reception accorded to him at the 1969 Moomba Festival where Cillario also appeared, conducting the final act of Verdi's *Un ballo in maschera* as part of a presentation of highlights from the season.[103] Gobbi was named the 'King of Moomba' and basked in both public acclaim and attention from the press (as well as some threats from members of the public, hostile that a person associated with the arts, and foreign to boot, was appointed to this role), which was on a scale rarely granted to an opera singer, even a star import.[104]

Madama Butterfly was a new production, directed by Yoshie Fujiwara, with sets and costumes created by Toshi Tosa, whose work was already known to Sydney audiences. Fujiwara was a veteran of opera, having enjoyed a singing career in Europe and run his own opera company in Japan, for which he had previously directed five productions of *Butterfly*. The Administrator of the ETOC, John Young, had decided to engage a Japanese production team in order to create a staging that was 'authentically Japanese … not the often-seen mishmash of *Mikado* and Kabuki imitations that sometimes pass as Western interpretations of this Japanese theme.'[105]

Fujiwara was critical of the opera's plot, and arrived with limited English, at which point it became clear that he was uncertain about his exact role in the production.[106] However he found the music 'unfailingly convincing', and it was doubtless a shared admiration for Puccini's score that brought him and Cillario together in creating a production that was generally praised. Tosa's designs created widespread interest, with images being published in popular magazines such as the *Australian Women's Weekly*, where it was reported that 'for the first time Australian audiences are seeing an authentic "Madame Butterfly" [sic] produced and designed by the Japanese … presented in true Japanese setting, mood and costume …

---

[103] [No author identified], *Listener In-TV*, 2–8 March 1968.

[104] The Opera Australia press files contain over 30 such articles, considerably more reportage than any opera production would receive. See also Appendix 7, pp. 435-43.

[105] ETOC 1969 season booklet, quoted in: A. Gyger (2005), 228.

[106] See also: Oxenbould (2005), 170–8.

completely authentic.'[107] The cast was led by Maureen Howard as Cio-Cio-San, with Sharpless sung by Robert Allman, who had returned to Australia after several years as a freelance singer in Europe.[108]

As Principal Conductor, Cillario began to assume new powers related to casting, while conflicts brewed between him and some of the singers. When he arrived for his first rehearsal, he had already made known his reservations about Maureen Howard, who had been cast as the alternate Butterfly. He walked into the rehearsal room and greeted all the singers except Howard, who he ignored. During the final rehearsals, Cillario announced that neither Donald Smith (Pinkerton), Adelio Zagonara (Goro) nor Justine Rettick (Suzuki) would sing the opening night in Canberra.[109] This was a decisive turn of events in the company's history, when for the first time a conductor intervened in casting decisions, which would formerly have been under the control of the company management. It seems that Cillario had assumed that the term 'principal conductor' had a similar purview as 'music director' carries in the European operatic milieu.

In the event, the musical direction of these performances was uniformly praised, with W.L. Hoffmann writing that the premiere in Canberra

> stands high among the company's distinguished presenta-
> tions of the past – it is beautifully mounted, brilliantly pro-
> duced and magnificently sung. Again, Carlo Felice Cillario
> displayed his ability to penetrate to the heart of the music
> … musically and visually a memorable Butterfly indeed.[110]

In Melbourne, Cargher declared that

> Cillario in Puccini's *Madama Butterfly* is comparable to
> anything which can be heard on disc, i.e., it can hold its own

---

[107] [No author named], *The Australian Women's Weekly*, 9 April 1969, 8.

[108] Cast: Maureen Howard (Cio-Cio-San), Jean Valerio and Justine Rettick (Suzuki), Dawn Walsh (Kate Pinkerton), Donald Smith and David Parker (B.F. Pinkerton), Ronald Maconaghie and Robert Allman (Sharpless), Graeme Ewer and Adelio Zagonara (Goro), John Germain (Yamadori), Lucio Borghi (Bonze), William Coombes (Imperial Commissioner), John Brady (Official Registrar).

[109] This is discussed in greater detail in: Oxenbould (2005), 172–6.

[110] Hoffmann, *The Canberra Times*, 12 February 1969.

against the best in the world. It is a mystery how he achieves such effects with the limited resources at his disposal, but he does so, and we should be humbly grateful.[111]

These sentiments were echoed by Felix Werder:

Carlo Felice Cillario demonstrated his outstanding ability of total involvement. He believes in what he is doing and so sweeps you along with his conviction. Obvious phrases are made sublime by subtle articulation. Details of counterpoint and dynamics are so finely etched that an ordinary score is transformed into symphonic proportion[s]. Without doubt the orchestra was the hero of the night and they richly deserved their particular ovation.[112]

In Adelaide the production was equally successful, and Cillario 'after an appearance of haste in the first act, achieved splendid results from the Elizabethan Trust Orchestra.'[113]

Directed by Tom Brown, a new staging of *Un ballo in maschera* was given in Melbourne and Sydney to great acclaim, becoming the 'hit' of the season. It was designed by Desmond Digby and created to fit the stage of the SOH Opera Theatre, four years ahead of its opening. The casting was based solidly around local artists and included Glenys Fowles (as Oscar), who had just returned from New York, having won the Metropolitan Opera Auditions.[114] Cargher paid Cillario another back-handed compliment for his conducting of *Ballo*: 'Carlo Felice Cillario's conducting was again so monotonously good that it is almost a pleasure to report that he was let down on two occasions, first by a singer, and then his strings.'[115]

As Cillario began to exert his influence as Principal Conductor,

---

[111] Cargher, *The Bulletin*, 8 March 1969.

[112] Werder, *The Age* (Melbourne), 24 February 1969.

[113] Harold Tidemann, *The Adelaide Advertiser*, 9 April 1969.

[114] Cast: Donald Smith (Gustavus III), Elizabeth Fretwell and Rosemary Gordon and Mary Hayman (Amelia), Robert Allman (Anckarstroem), Neil Warren-Smith and Peter North (Count Ribbing), Donald Shanks and John Pooley (Count Horn), John Germain and William Coombes (Cristian), Glenys Fowles (Oscar), Morag Beaton (Mlle Arvidson), Kevin Mills (Arnfelt), Ian Campbell (Servant).

[115] Cargher, *The Bulletin*, 22 March 1969.

the press became eager to learn more about the company's new appointment, leading to a curious article about his pet goldfish, named Adeline (Ill. 6) with whom he was reunited when he returned to Australia at the start of 1969.[116] The press had produced good copy from some of Cillario's colourful behaviour during the 1968 season, such as an incident where his baton seemed to disappear during a performance, the details of which were denied by the conductor (Ill. 5): 'I did not lose my baton … I broke it specially.'[117] The incident had occurred during a performance of *Tosca* when a clattering noise emerged from the pit, followed by a view of Cillario conducting with 'about three inches of baton in his right hand'. Cillario's response records his unique and yet expressive command of English:

> This job, this marvellous job of a conductor, is very difficult in many cases … the conductor is the centre. To perform together with the orchestra is a kind of love. When a people is loving I think it is important to look at the eyes of the partner, and so it is with the conductor.[118]

He explained that there had been personnel changes in the orchestra due to rostering. Some of the fresh players were inexperienced and had not attended sufficient rehearsals.

> During the first act we had new singers. … All the singers needed that I follow them, and just at this moment one section of the orchestra was not looking at me in the eyes. For to save a difficult situation, I was obliged to call their attention with the baton and with a little too much temperament.[119]

Cillario said that the breakage had cost him 70 cents. The reviewer asked why he had continued to use the broken baton throughout the second act when he had a spare that he used for the third. He replied '… that's very observing of you to notice … it was

---

[116] [No author named], *The Sydney Morning Herald*, 4 January 1969.

[117] 'DATA', *The Sydney Morning Herald*, 27 June 1968.

[118] Ibid.

[119] Ibid.

just a little joke to remind this section that had not been looking at me in the eyes… '.[120]

Praise for the musical direction was a thread that ran through the reception of the season, credited by Roger Covell to Cillario, 'ably seconded by William Reid.'[121] John Small noted that 'two features of *Falstaff* and *Butterfly* deserve special attention: the orchestra was uniformly excellent, and Carlo Cillario's conducting was a model of accuracy and clarity.'[122] It was also noted within the company that Cillario was ready to roll up his sleeves and improve standards by

6: Carlo Felice Cillario reunited with his pet goldfish, Adeline, 1969.

hard work and persistence. He may have been critical about individual orchestral players or singers, but he was (once his initial irritation had passed) equally prepared to find solutions and offer help and advice. Moffatt Oxenbould has recalled that Cillario:

> loved the sense of ensemble amongst the artists and revelled in being able to participate in the artistic growth of individual singers and instrumentalists. Most mornings on tour … he could be found in the theatre pit or in a dressing room, playing chamber music with members of the orchestra or sitting in on a coaching session with a principal singer or chorister, making suggestions about technique, repertoire and career path. If he recognised potential, he became passionately interested in its development and sought to provide assistance, either personally or by contact with other conductors, coaches or singers.[123]

[120] Ibid.
[121] Covell, *The Sydney Morning Herald*, 23 May 1969.
[122] John Small, *The Bulletin*, 8 March 1969.
[123] Oxenbould, *Carlo Felice Cillario and Opera Australia*, 2003.

Behind the Scenes

Correspondence between Cillario and Claudio Alcorso confirms
that even while he was Principal Conductor, it was mutually
recognised that the scope of his appointment included work as
'artistic advisor'.[124] As part of this role, during the 1969 season,
Cillario wrote a report for Alcorso about the state of the company,
making recommendations for artistic improvements. According
to Cillario, the orchestral musicians have 'exceptional goodwill
and discipline and also good qualities for operatic style but some
have scant technical preparation, and their contribution is not
sufficient.'[125] He notes that the development of 'technical integrity'
could be achieved by forming chamber music groups from within
the orchestra – string quartets, double quintets with winds and so
on.[126] He asks for more strings and notes the inadequate pit size.
He states that 'the Union will not oppose us if we need to import
musicians from overseas', and mentions interest from players in UK,
Italy and France to relocate to Australia to take up such positions. He
sees this as an imperative, due to the 'birth of the second orchestra'
– the opera orchestra that was being formed in Melbourne. Much
of Cillario's correspondence with the company during 1969–70 was
concerned with reports and recommendations about players that he
auditioned during his conducting engagements in Europe and the
Americas.

Cillario remarks on the improvement in the chorus brought
about by Geoffrey Arnold, the new chorus master, and he
acknowledges William Reid's work with the principals. He makes
recommendations for additions to the music staff, including
a 'substitute Maestro of Italian origin so that he may teach the
tradition and correct pronunciation as approximately 60% of the
repertoire is sung in Italian ... The same man could be employed as

---

[124] Cillario to Alcorso, 4 December 1970. 'Carlo Felice Cillario – Artist Files '1',
Opera Australia Library archives.'
[125] Cillario to Alcorso (in Italian), translation by Alcorso, forwarded to Stephen
Hall and John Young, inter-office memo, 2 May 1969. 'Carlo Felice Cillario –
Artist Files '1', Opera Australia Library archives.'
[126] Ibid, all quotes in this paragraph are from the 2 May 1969 document.

prompter. This is a function which it is urgent to reinstate.' Cillario always required a prompter ('suggeritore') for his performances, which was a long-held tradition in Italy. He says that not to have this position is a 'senseless dream' and that 'all the major theatres in the world use a prompter.'[127] He also recommended the engagement of Jani Strasser,[128] the Head of Music Staff at Glyndebourne to provide further expertise on the music staff.

Cillario also proposed a bold commissioning policy, inviting composers to write short works of 20–30 minutes' duration for semi-staged production. His list of suggested composers was wide in scope, including Benjamin Britten, Nino Rota, Samuel Barber, and Alberto Ginastera. He also reported on a meeting that he had with Dr Catherine Ellis of the Elder Conservatorium of Music Adelaide, about First Nations communities, and the possibility of developing them as future opera singers. He writes that 'it may be worthwhile to consider after further enquiries the possibility of sending a music teacher to aboriginal missions to discover potential talent on the spot.'[129] The culture of the First Nations held an abiding interest for Cillario, and he would later make several visits to remote settlements in order to learn more about their music and their customs.

Such reports to the management became a regular part of his work with the company. On occasion, Cillario's enthusiasm for singers he had discovered overseas would result in spontaneous invitations, and the management in Sydney would have to wind back undertakings that had been made in the heat of the moment. Cillario undertook a sizeable and detailed correspondence, acting as a talent scout in several areas for the company and positioning himself as its musical leader. On occasion, however, misunderstandings caused tempers to fray, and Cillario would fire off a torpedo, such as this communication to Stephen Hall:

> You know that I consider my duty just to indicate to you the really good elements and now you doubt about my seriousness and my experience, sending me advices like to

---

[127] Ibid.
[128] See p. 42.
[129] See pp. 107-8.

a 'scugnizzo Napolitano'[130] or a 'carpet seller'! Sincerely I hope you will save in the future your strongness for more justified occasions ...[131]

The source of this hubris becomes clear in the context of other correspondence during the same period, which was dominated by discussions over the unfilled post of Music Director. There was no doubt within the ETOC that Cillario was the man for the job, but several outstanding issues required resolution. The most pressing among them concerned the level of commitment which would be required of him: the length of time he would spend in Australia each year, and how many performances he would lead. In 1968, Cillario had conducted in five of the country's capital cities. During 1969, his national touring was considerably reduced, and in 1970 he conducted only in Sydney. An internal company memo states that Cillario conducted 51 performances during 1968, 32 in 1969 (due to reduced availability) but that if he were to conduct all performances of three operas over six months in 1970, he could achieve a total of 90 performances.'[132] In reality, that figure was a gross over-estimate.

Cillario evidently coveted the position of Music Director of an opera house, a position he had never held. Yet the negotiations were marked by mutual misunderstandings and fundamental differences. In July, Cillario wrote to Hall: 'In my last letters I declared that I can be Musical Director in 1970 if the Trust can transform in reality a few basic[s] projects we fixed a few months ago.'[133] These included the hiring of the stage director Renzo Frusca, the vocal coach Jani Strasser, and the expansion of the orchestra.

When the appointment was finally ratified, it was for one year only, and acrimony ensued. On 6 August Cillario, writing also on behalf of Gorlinsky, objected to Stephen Hall: 'In our opinion just a

---

[130] A Neapolitan street-urchin.
[131] Cillario (in Bologna) to Stephen Hall, 13 August 1969. 'Carlo Felice Cillario – Artist Files '1', Opera Australia Library archives.'
[132] John Young to Donald McDonald, 14 May 1969. 'Carlo Felice Cillario – Artist Files '1', Opera Australia Library archives.'
[133] Cillario (in Bologna) to Stephen Hall, 17 July 1969. 'CFC – Artist Files '1', Opera Australia Library archives.'

season as MD is nothing.'[134] Hall replied on 11 August: 'You must not be upset by this. You know very well that Claude [Claudio] and I want you to be Musical Director for many years but at this stage it is political [sic] that we announce only the plans for 1970.'[135] The reason given was that the company was to be incorporated in that year, at which point the new Board would become authorised to make long-term appointments. While this was true, the management was also trying to manage the timing so that the newly named company, and its inaugural music director could be announced simultaneously.

Cillario and Gorlinsky were unmoved by such arguments. Nevertheless, Cillario was publicly confirmed as Music Director at the start of September 1969. A few days later, Gorlinsky wrote to Stephen Hall, saying that his artist was unhappy about the announcement and under other circumstances, he would resile from the commitment 'because he does not like to play politics and is only concerned with making music.' Gorlinsky complained that the position was announced without Cillario's consent and that when he heard of it, he [Cillario] 'assumed that it was for at least three years … You will agree that it is unheard of to appoint a Musical Director for only a single season … one appoints a Musical Director to have a long-term policy.' [136]

At this point, Alcorso sprang into action. By 16 September he had circulated a memorandum to the Australian Opera Executive Committee. Alcorso stated that Cillario had written to him, complaining that a one-year appointment is 'meaningless.' Expanding on Gorlinsky's comments, the Chairman continued:

> It is impossible for a Musical Director to bring his work to fruition in one year and … if he is going to be Musical Director … for a longer period, he must know it in advance

---

[134] Cillario (in Riccione) to Stephen Hall, 6 August 1969. 'CFC – Artist Files '1', Opera Australia Library archives.'

[135] Hall to Cillario, 11 August 1969. 'CFC – Artist Files '1', Opera Australia Library archives.'

[136] Gorlinsky to Stephen Hall, 9 September 1969. 'Carlo Felice Cillario – Artist Files '1', Opera Australia Library archives.'

or he may enter into commitments in other parts of the world which are booked sometimes two or three years in advance.[137]

Alcorso had consulted with his executives, who agreed that Cillario was 'a person who combines high artistic standards with qualities of leadership and human understanding. These qualities are not often found in the same person ... His knowledge of the language and Australian attitudes is good and has been tested over the two last seasons.' Alcorso proposed that the appointment of a Musical Director 'should extend over a period of time from a minimum of three to a maximum of five years.' He concluded by requesting that the Committee approve the appointment 'for a period of time which will include the first complete season at the Sydney Opera House.'[138]

On 24 October, Cillario wrote to Hall, confirming that he had received a revised offer of a three-year contract. However, he wanted the contract extended by a further year, up to the opening of the Sydney Opera House, which he intended to conduct. During 1970, he told Hall he planned to 'develop my activity as M.D.', proposing paradoxically that he conduct fewer performances, and accordingly spend less time in Australia. It then emerged that he had been offered a contract in Mexico City and fulfilling it would require his schedule to be revised, because he needed the money for his 'familiona'.[139]

While the company had been naïve to imagine that a musical director active on the world stage would be happy to settle for a contract of a single year, there is something wilful in Cillario's subsequent reactions, which convey a sense of his conflicting feelings over the appointment, even while negotiating for it to be extended. The pride of winning and fulfilling a prestigious directorship clashed with the freedom (and remuneration) he enjoyed as a freelance

[137] Claudio Alcorso to the Australian Opera Executive Committee, 16 September 1969. 'Carlo Felice Cillario – Artist Files '1', Opera Australia Library archives.'

[138] Ibid.

[139] Quotes in this paragraph from Cillario (in Bologna) to Hall, 24 October 1969. 'CFC – Artist Files '1', OA Library archives.'

conductor. His actions indicate that he was not prepared to 'settle down' as a music director who would assume far-reaching artistic and administrative responsibilities.

A draft contract was eventually drawn up for 'four consecutive annual seasons of Grand Opera, the first commencing in 1970 and the last in 1973.' Cillario was engaged to conduct the opening night and first season in the Sydney Opera House. He was required to conduct 'at least three operas per annum' and to spend 20 weeks of the year in Australia, whether in one long or two shorter stays. The fee structure included a sum covering all his work in Australia (including performances) along with another component, as a 'reimbursement of expenses incurred outside of Australia while engaged in work on behalf of The Australian Opera.'[140] There is no evidence that this contract was ever signed.

When Cillario departed Australia following the season in April 1969, he shared with the press a typical barbed compliment, saying that he admired Australian singers, many of whom had gone to all parts of the world for opportunities. 'I speak a bad English, but I feel you people do also … it makes a better sound for opera.'[141] Cillario was to be the Music Director from 1970, but the contracting process had been a long and bumpy negotiation. On the one hand he wanted a longer contract that would see him open the inaugural opera season in the new Sydney Opera House, on the other hand, he expected a level of flexibility which called into question his commitment to the company. Something would have to give.

---

[140] Contract draft between Cillario and the Australian Opera, undated, (1969). 'CFC – Artist Files '1', OA Library archives.'

[141] [No author named], *The Sydney Morning Herald*, 23 April 1969.

Scene 3 – 1970

Music Director, the Australian Opera

Cillario returned to Sydney in mid-May 1970, having just conducted *Falstaff* in Paris, with Tito Gobbi in the title role. As Music Director of the renamed and newly incorporated Australian Opera, he announced plans to expand the repertoire, and in particular to introduce one 'new' work each year. The forthcoming season would feature *The Rake's Progress* of Stravinsky, which Cillario did not conduct, and which received poor reviews. The call went up for more new operas by Australian composers.[142]

Cillario had been impressed by the organisation of the music staff when he conducted in Glyndebourne in 1961. The company was renowned for its high level of musical and ensemble preparation, and Cillario wished to emulate those practices in Australia. To that end he engaged the legendary vocal coach Jani Strasser for his first season as Music Director, thereby raising the musical standards and instilling disciplined ensemble. In flight from the Nazis, the Hungarian-born Strasser had left Austria in 1934 and settled in the UK. He had been the vocal coach of Audrey Mildmay, the wife of John Christie, who both founded the Glyndebourne Festival Opera. [143] Strasser brought knowledge and expertise to the company in Australia, accompanied by an inimitable continental charm, and Cillario could rely on him for meticulous preparation of the repertoire.

Considerable optimism surrounded Cillario's return to Sydney in 1970. The Opera House had reached its final phase of construction and the halls had been switched around.[144] The company's orchestra had already been enlarged, in the expectation that the pit would be commensurately expanded from its original design in order to mount the largest operas of the repertoire. However, it was still far

---

[142] See A. Gyger (2005), 245.

[143] See Oxenbould (2005), 187.

[144] Harewood interviewed by Tony Frewin in the 1970 Australian Opera season booklet.

from clear how the original pit, designed for 28 players, could be enlarged to achieve this capacity.[145] When questioned about the size of the pit and the 'rather small flying space', Lord Harewood replied that the theatre 'should be able to accommodate operas like those of Mozart as well as the biggest of Verdi.'[146]

Cillario conducted three operas in the 1970 season at Her Majesty's Theatre in Sydney, all of them belonging to his core repertoire: new productions of *La bohème*, *La forza del destino*, and *Otello*. *La bohème* featured a youthful local cast,[147] under the direction of Renzo Frusca, with designs by Tom Lingwood. It was remembered with affection by Stephen Hall,[148] and was a 'hit' with audiences. The cast of younger singers projected 'a more with-it image',[149] in a strategy that the company also employed in two later productions of the opera.[150] This *Bohème* remained in the repertory until 1986. According to Fred Blanks, 'here was a beautifully designed and above all conducted performance of a work that has never been surpassed for sheer irresistible delight', and he praised the entire cast.[151] John Cargher was equally enthusiastic:

> In the midst of such visual splendours there rests a musical performance dominated by Carlo Felice Cillario's conducting of the difficult score. The singers are notably good dramatically, blending so well into the whole that their contribution almost becomes submerged. This is music drama at its best, as Puccini intended it to be ... Glenys Fowles takes another giant step up the ladder of success as

---

[145] Information in this paragraph derived from A. Gyger (2005), 240-1.

[146] See FN 144.

[147] Cast: Anson Austin and John Serge (Rodolfo), Glenys Fowles (Mimì), Ronald Maconaghie (Marcello), Maureen Howard and Beryl Furlan (Musetta), Donald Shanks (Colline), Robert Eddie (Schaunard), Robert Simmons and John Germain (Benoit), Luciano Borghi (Alcindoro), Ian Campbell (Parpignol), John Durham (Customs Sergeant), Paul Rutenis (Customs Officer).

[148] Hall, Cillario Obituary, 20 December 2007.

[149] David Gyger, *The Australian*, 20 June 1970.

[150] The 1996 production by Baz Luhrmann, and the 1999 production by Moffatt Oxenbould.

[151] Blanks, *Australian Jewish Times* (Sydney), 2 July 1970.

Mimì, and Donald Shanks is the most impressive Colline I have seen or heard.[152]

Roger Covell echoed Cargher's verdict: 'Cillario's direction in the pit gave the fullest value to those fleet, scherzo-like passages in the music ... that helped *La bohème* to retain its character as the freshest of Puccini's major works.' Covell also noted that some of Cillario's fast tempi were extreme, challenging the players to their limit, but 'the overall effect was ardent and committed' with the music direction creating 'tenderness and delicacy in the instrumental work for the famous slow, soft-centred arias and ensembles.'[153]

Otello was the next to open, in a new production by Bernd Benthaak.[154] Again, the cast was a local one,[155] except for Rome-based Umberto Borsò, an Italian tenor who had first sung in Australia in the 1955 J.C. Williamson Italian Opera Season. Iago was sung by John Shaw, who had been based overseas since 1964, and eventually re-joined the company's ensemble in 1973. Cargher was not uncritical of Cillario's work in the pit: 'For all the superb sound he squeezed out of his orchestra, [he] still suffered from the occasional unreasonable desire to catch the last train home at any cost; you simply can't hurry a carefully thought-out monologue like "Dio, mi potevi scagliar".'[156] His assessment of the singing, however, evoked comparisons with leading artists of the day:

> Anybody can engage del Monaco, Gobbi and Tebaldi if they have the money. To produce this kind of vocal splendour without them is quite a different proposition. The Australian Opera has done nothing better for admirers of good singing since its creation 16 years ago.

---

[152] Cargher, *The Bulletin*, 4 July 1970.
[153] Covell, *The Sydney Morning Herald*, 22 June 1970.
[154] Bernd Benthaak (1943–2009) was a German-born opera director, who began his career at the Hamburg State Opera during the 1960s. He worked as a resident director with the newly incorporated Australia Opera during the 1970-80s.
[155] Cast: Umberto Borsò (Otello), John Shaw (Iago), Reginald Byers (Cassio), Ian Campbell (Roderigo), Donald Shanks (Lodovico), Luigi Borghi (Montano), Robert Eddie (Herald), Rosemary Gordon (Desdemona), Dawn Walsh (Emilia).
[156] Cargher, *The Bulletin*, 18 July 1970.

While finding the conductor's pace at times hectic, he admired the orchestra which had:

> come in for a share of opprobrium this season and much of it is undeserved. Not so long ago the sound from pit orchestras in Australia was a combination of the strident, the inept and the uncertain, but this criticism is no longer valid. Both the ensemble and string tone in the last act of *Otello* were absolutely first class and even the notorious bass passage was negotiated with reasonable accuracy.[157]

7: Cillario and Renzo Frusca rehearsing *La forza del destino*, 1970.

La forza del destino was also directed by Renzo Frusca, with Tom Lingwood as designer. Here too, the casting was strong,[158] with Donald Smith (Alvaro), Robert Allman (Don Carlos), and the Italian 'star' import Franca Como as Leonora. Cargher noted, unkindly that 'what she loses in appearance, she makes up for in her singing'.[159] Cillario's incisive and impassioned conducting was admired: 'The

---

[157] Ibid.

[158] Cast: Franca Como (Leonora), Morag Beaton (Preziosilla), Donald Smith (Don Alvaro), Robert Allman (Don Carlos), Neil Warren-Smith (Padre Guardiano), Luciano Borghi (Marchese di Calatrava), Ronald Maconaghie and Robert Simmons (Fra Melitone), Isabel Veale (Curra), Joseph Grunfelder (The Mayor), Ian Campbell (Trabuco), John Germain (A Surgeon).

[159] Cargher, *The Bulletin*, 11 July 1970.

orchestra under the mastery of Cillario is at its best'.[160] As the
season progressed, performances varied in quality, Cargher noting
on 11 July that 'the admirable Cillario had a decided off-night, but
Verdi, as usual, overcame all opposition, even lack of coordination
between stage and pit, and some incredible misjudgements in
tempo: 'Solenne in quest'ora' is too well-known to pass at double
the normal speed.'[161] Fred Blanks put forward a more positive
view: 'The work itself has times of ennui, but its sections of high
drama are stirring and its music – excellently conducted by Carlo
Felice Cillario – has many high points of beauty and force.'[162] In
some circles, the opera was regarded as 'dull', while production of
it contained 'excellent singing', with the addition of Cillario's 'firm,
imaginative and powerful control over the orchestra.'[163]

The 1970 season had opened on 13 June, and all was progressing
well, until the evening of 30 July, when Her Majesty's Theatre burned
down following a performance of *Otello*. The aftermath of the fire
was a testament to the determination and resilience of the company.
All concerned were committed to continue the season in whatever
form possible. Although the loss of some productions affected the
touring arrangements for that year (and beyond), it was determined
that concert performances would be given in the 'dilapidated
and disused' Capitol Theatre, whose décor was described as 'pure
MGM Roman-Gothic Revival.'[164] It was even suggested that the
results in the new venue were 'musically stronger than the staged
performances.' The Capitol Theatre was found to have 'splendid
acoustics' and 'patrons were experiencing the musical calibre of the
company for the first time.'

Presenting the operas in concert also shifted the dynamic

---

[160] [No author named], 'Sydney Life and Times,' *The Australian Jewish Times*
      (Sydney), 9 July 1970.
[161] Cargher had made similar comments about Cillario conducting twice as fast
      as usual in *Tosca* in Adelaide in 1968. See: Cargher, 'Triumph, tragedy,' *The
      Bulletin*, 30 March 1968.
[162] Blanks, *The Australian Jewish Times* (Sydney), 16 July 1970.
[163] 'R.J.R.', 'Verdi opera was dull', *The Catholic Weekly*, July 1970.
[164] Kenneth Robins, *The Bulletin*, 15 August 1970.

between performers and audience.[165] Kenneth Robins wrote that 'it was inevitable that there would be a change of emphasis, and the emergence of the conductor as the star turn was the main one.' Robins noted that Cillario and Reid were 'both "opera" conductors, conscious of the tremendous range of emotional dynamics required and with a superhuman alertness.' He further observed that Cillario in particular possesses 'an incandescent theatricalism when on the podium which strikes sparks from the orchestra and singers.'[166]

Despite serious disruption to the company's performance schedule and uncertainty surrounding the forthcoming touring plans, Cillario ensured the success of this, his first and only season as Music Director. In the aftermath of the fire, the Australian Opera management

8: Cillario applauding the *Otello* cast, Capitol Theatre, Sydney, August 1970.

remained on course in their goal of occupying their long-awaited home, the Sydney Opera House, now scheduled to open in March 1973. Cillario found himself in the Capitol Theatre, where the acoustic and atmosphere impressed him so much that he proposed that the company should programme concert performances of Ponchielli's *La Gioconda* there in 1971.[167] Nevertheless, as the year

---

[165] A. Gyger (2005), 242.

[166] Robins, 15 August 1970.

[167] Cillario (from San Francisco) to Alcorso, 18 October 1970. Tasmanian Archives and Heritage Office, Hobart. Item NS3001/1/14: 'Correspondence Claudio Alcorso and Carlo Cillario, a conductor and at one time Musical Director of The Australian Opera.'

wore on, Cillario's doubts about the responsibilities he had accepted increased, and the question remains: why had he accepted the position of Music Director?

Discontent

By 1970, the operatic world was Cillario's oyster. He was 55 years old, in excellent health and at the peak of his musical powers. His engagements were managed by an astute and powerful agent. He was being offered work in Europe and America, where he enjoyed working with the best singers in leading opera houses. A number of emerging stars of the operatic world chose to work with him, in particular Montserrat Caballé, whose rise to stardom also benefitted the conductor.

High-profile engagements and profitable recording contracts were in the pipeline. Operatically speaking, Australia was off the international radar, and the local company was still to prove itself in their future home. Why would he choose to spend large parts of the year in Australia, effectively cutting himself off from major opportunities, at a time when international travel between Australia and Europe had only just become usual?

This question was posed to Cillario in an interview early in 1970.[168] Highlights and low points of his career were recalled: losing his trousers during a performance in 1968,[169] recent engagements with Caballé, and a return to the Paris Opéra for *Falstaff* with Gobbi. Recalling his conducting debut in Odesa during the Second World War, as bombs fell around the opera house, Cillario remarked: 'It is impossible to have opera without problems. When people say to me "Maestro, we have no problems," then that is a problem.'[170] Following Cillario's account of his recent and forthcoming engagements, the interviewer thought it 'odd' that he would spend so much time in Australia. Cillario took umbrage: he was 'wildly enthusiastic' about the local scene, he insisted, and he had shared the news of

[168] [No author named], 'Despite losing his pants, he thinks our opera's great,' *The Australian*, 3 February 1970.

[169] See pp.14 and FN 49.

[170] See FN 168.

the company's successes with colleagues in Italy and Paris, where he believes the methods developed in Australia should be adopted. 'From the first time I came here I have been convinced that the future is very, very bright, … it is for this reason I am now tied to the Australian Opera.'[171]

Privately, however, Cillario had come to the realisation that these ties were unsustainable. Having previously pushed for a four-year contract, he dragged his feet over committing to sign. A company memo from April 1970 indicates that a final contract was still being drafted, late in the season. [172] A further re-draft was dated 26 June. On 5 August, Alcorso took steps to secure Cillario's commitment before his departure on 20 August. Alcorso produced a contract engaging him 'for a period of 3 to 5 years.' Some provisions were added: an assurance that 'the Australian Opera is your first concern, and that it has first call on your time for a total of six months each year (probably to be divided into two periods) … we believe that it is to the mutual benefit of the Musical Director and The Australian Opera for the Musical Director to spend six months of the year outside of Australia.' [173] Cillario was given a deadline of 9 August.

Once again, the contract went unsigned.[174] Cillario informed Alcorso of his withdrawal as Music Director, and the Chairman secured the conductor's agreement to continue as Music Director until the end of 1971, cutting short his period of contract by two years (or three years, depending on which contract is considered). In the aftermath of the fire at the end of July, this was indeed a significant blow to the company, which was attempting to plan a revised schedule of activity both for the remainder of 1970, and for the following year, while publicly making a show of artistic solidarity with a Musical Director firmly in place. By October, Cillario's correspondence betrays a waning enthusiasm for planning

---

[171] Ibid.

[172] Bruce Lane to Donald McDonald, inter-office memo, 20 April 1970. 'Carlo Felice Cillario – Artist Files '1', Opera Australia Library archives.'

[173] Alcorso to Cillario, 5 August 1970. 'Carlo Felice Cillario – Artist Files '1', Opera Australia Library archives.'

[174] Draft copy (undated) in 'CFC – Artist Files '1', Opera Australia Library archives.'

his work in Australia for the forthcoming season. He did not wish to conduct any revivals, he was critical of casting proposals for the works he had agreed to conduct, and the revised season dates for 1971 (in response to the fire) were not possible for him, as he was locked into concerts in Bologna.[175]

Such date clashes and irreconcilable positions led to an unresolvable crisis early in 1971. Cillario seems to have felt that he was now in a position to be more selective about the periods that he elected to spend in Australia, and the productions he wished to conduct. He assumed he would have an ongoing association with the Australian Opera, and it took him time to grasp that his decision not to continue as Musical Director had far-reaching consequences for both parties.

Alcorso and his colleagues on the Australian Opera Board turned to their alternative candidate for musical director, Edward Downes. Georg Solti was coming to the end of his decade-long tenure as Music Director of the Royal Opera, and Downes entertained fair hopes of being appointed Solti's successor; the Australian Opera would have been far from his mind. It was then announced that Colin Davis would succeed Solti at Covent Garden. While Davis' appointment came as a blow to Downes, it left him free to further consider the position of music director in Sydney, influenced by his friend Lord Harewood. Downes accepted an offer and was quickly engaged by the company as Music Director Designate, effective as of the conclusion of Cillario's tenure in 1972.

In their efforts to be ready to occupy the Opera House, the company members of the Australian Opera held out hopes for an accessible leader: ideally a full-time resident of Australia, not a globetrotter who flew in and out. However unrealistic this may have been, it was a tacit expectation, and one that has been at the root of executive turbulence not only in the Australian Opera but in other antipodean performing-arts organisations in subsequent decades. According to his correspondence with Alcorso, Cillario felt under

---

[175] Cillario (in Bologna) to Hall, 29 October 1970. 'CFC – Artist Files '1', Opera Australia Library archives.'

unsustainable pressure in the post, his responsibilities began to overwhelm him, and his health suffered.[176] He felt as though he had been 'talked into' the post of Musical Director from the outset. While he wished to retain a relationship with the company, he could only do so as 'guest conductor and musical advisor'.[177] Alcorso accepted the situation, in the knowledge that Edward Downes was available and willing to take up the musical leadership on a more committed basis.

Snippets of this backstage turmoil gradually reached the press. In July 1970, Kenneth Hince had written an article about Cillario's appointment as Music Director. In it he summed up his experiences of Cillario as a conductor, and the qualities that he brought to the developing artform in Australia.

> In each of the operas he has conducted for us, the orchestra has been strongly impressive. Cillario seems to feel, rightly, that the ensemble of the whole opera has to rest on the strongest foundations he can supply for it. He finds these, or makes them, in the precision and discipline of the playing in the pit. By the time this year's operas were over the orchestra was working pretty nearly as well as you could expect from a group of this size in any standard repertory company.[178]

Hince notes that Cillario's appointment as Music Director was a first for the company, observing that 'as an idea, it is excellent', while noting that 'nothing much has been said about the terms of the appointment' and suggesting that:

> As music[al] director, he ought to have a decisive say in pretty well all aspects of the season – repertory, casting, production, staging, decor. Obviously, this will bring problems with it – some old, and some new. The company's administration must be flexible and magnanimous in its

---

[176] Cillario to Alcorso, 4 December 1970, and Cillario to Hall, 21 January 1971. 'Carlo Felice Cillario – Artist Files '1', Opera Australia Library archives.'

[177] Cillario to Hall, 21 January 1971. 'CFC – Artist Files '1', Opera Australia Library archives.'

[178] Hince, 'Cillario's challenge', *The Australian*, 26 July 1970.

handling of the new position. Cillario himself will have to be as strong in the conference room as he is at the conductor's desk.[179]

Cillario had arrived at the helm of a vibrant, expanding organisation which was hungry for his expertise and leadership, one which had only in the recent past achieved full-time employment for its solo singers, orchestra and chorus. In juggling what was potentially a full-time position with the demands of a busy international career, Cillario was working against the tide of the company. As the management worked to expand the Sydney orchestra as Cillario had advocated, he became less and less available to work with it and create the ensemble he had envisaged. Resentment began to grow about his absences. During 1970, there were already doubts raised about whether the company was 'getting enough' of Cillario to adequately meet the expectations of a Music Director. In August, John Moses published a review of the Sydney seasons, which had been led by

> resident conductor Reid, and a visiting Musical Director of some accomplishment, Carlo Felice Cillario. Here again is a problem. Cillario's accomplishment is not to be doubted and his services are greatly in demand overseas. But this is the trouble. He arrived here, I'm told by the opera people, about the middle of May, to begin preparing as musical director a season which opened in the middle of June. He is to leave Australia at the end of this month [August], leaving the company without its musical director for the rest of the Australian tour. In any other terms except those which are apparently acceptable here, this is musically and operatically unthinkable. The musical director, one would think, is the man who is continually shaping performances, checking on standards, weeding out the incompetents and either making them play the notes or sacking them. A company simply cannot have a musical director who is here only four months of the year, or it can, and get the results it deserves.[180]

---

[179] Ibid.
[180] John Moses, *The Bulletin*, 8 August 1970.

Moses made a proposal:

> Have a full-time musical director so that fundamental training can go along with preparation for specific operas; alternatively, make peace with the ABC and borrow some experienced players from its orchestras to stiffen the sinews in the weak spots. I feel that the appointment of an artistic director is crucial. The Australian Opera has a distinguished board of directors, to which, presumably, the whole organisation is responsible. But a board which includes a textile man, an academic, a sharebroker, a Minister of the Crown, the editor of a trendy woman's magazine and a nuclear physicist is hardly likely to be in a position rigidly to enforce the standards that are necessary. A really strong man wouldn't be easy to find. And he would have to be paid a lot of money if he were to be any good. But on the other hand, the Australian Opera got $871,000 in taxpayer's money to mount this season and it earned another three-quarter million at the box-office. There should be something out of all that to spare for the right man. And he'd earn it with only two years to go to the Big Night.[181]

The issues around Cillario's appointment and subsequent resignation have become tropes of the company's history. They embody a dilemma (partly of distance and access) regarding the company's musical leadership that have never been resolved. Any serious overseas contender for the role of Music Director would be effectively committing professional suicide by relocating to Australia and devoting themselves full-time to the national company. Symphonic institutions in Australia have similarly lured conductors with offers of three-year contracts, vague promises into the future, and the possibility for concurrent positions, in educational institutions, for example. History shows that international conductors have not lasted long in such precarious circumstances, and a number have been left high and dry.

Late in 1970, once Cillario had returned to Europe, the senior management of the Australian Opera was overhauled. Stephen Hall

---

[181] Ibid.

was promoted from Administrator to Artistic Director, Donald McDonald became General Manager and Moffatt Oxenbould became the Coordinator of Planning. The company continued to prepare the 1971 season, which was significantly revised due to the knock-on effects of the fire the previous July.[182] Having initially raised a clash of dates with engagements in Bologna, Cillario undertook to withdraw from these to be available in Australia. However, he was unhappy about both the casting and the rehearsal dates for the new production of *The Marriage of Figaro*. He wrote to Hall with the suggestion that he be replaced by Kurt Herbert Adler (from San Francisco, where Cillario was conducting at the time). An offer to Adler from Hall, suggested Cillario, could be reciprocated by Hall being invited to direct an opera in San Francisco.

Hall did not take the bait. He reminded Cillario of his agreed commitments and remarked that he was 'the best person to conduct *Figaro* and ... the only person who has the skill and personality to attract the young players who will improve our Sydney orchestra.'[183] Concurrently, Alcorso was overseeing a recruitment process for the orchestra in response to Cillario's recommendations. In early November, Hall wrote again to Cillario, promising 'important new ingredients for the rebirth of the Sydney orchestra, but we need you here to mould them and prepare them....'[184]

In November, Cillario assured Lord Harewood of his commitment to the Australian Opera for the 1971 season. He noted that he had been released from the agreement to conduct in Bologna (by the Lord Mayor, no less), and went on to say that he had turned down an offer to conduct *Norma* in London with Caballé. He mentioned that Hall would shortly visit Harewood in London, and regarding the outstanding issue of the post of music director, Cillario requested: 'Please do not take any decision before to let me know it. As you know,

---

[182] Hall to Cillario, 12 October 1970, states that the fire had cost the company an estimated $90,000. 'Carlo Felice Cillario – Artist Files '1', Opera Australia Library archives.'

[183] Hall to Cillario, 26 October 1970. 'CFC – Artist Files '1', Opera Australia Library archives.'

[184] Hall to Cillario, 6 November 1970. 'CFC – Artist Files '1', Opera Australia Library archives.'

I consider my collaboration with A.O. my principal and interesting job. And I wish to be sure that my collaboration will be extended also during the following years.'[185] Cillario was probably aware that his unreliable availability posed problems for the company's short- and long-term plans. He would also have known that a replacement music director was being sought, and that Harewood was involved with the appointment process.

On 27 November Alcorso wrote to Cillario, setting out their difference of opinion over the issue of a Musical Director. In his letter, Alcorso reminds Cillario that an MD is needed who could spend 'a minimum of six months in Australia (eight if necessary).' The offer had been made, and Cillario refused it.

> You told me you had spoken to your wife ... you mentioned how old your parents were, and you said that 'if you had not got stuck in the quicksands of South America ... and if you had been 15 years younger.' You were in difficulty, a little confused, touched (as was I too) and completely honest. It was after that interview that we decided to look for another Musical Director.[186]

Alcorso refers to Cillario's comment that there was no need for a Musical Director, and that if they found someone good 'they will be very busy elsewhere'. This is countered by Alcorso, who also rejects Cillario's view that "if such a person were mediocre, it would be better to commit mass suicide." He replies: 'I can assure you that we will not appoint a mediocre person! You know that I will do my utmost to ensure that this Company ... will be among the best and most "creative" in the world.' Alcorso mentions Edward Downes and Charles Mackerras as the shortlisted candidates for the role Cillario had refused:[187]

As if to continue our fateful Sunday morning interview, I

---

[185] Cillario (in Bologna) to Lord Harewood (London), 14 November 1970. 'CFC – Artist Files '1', Opera Australia Library archives.'

[186] Alcorso to Cillario (in Italian), 27 November 1970. 'CFC – Artist Files '1', Opera Australia Library archives.' English translation by Simon Towle.

[187] Ibid. Alcorso wrote that Cillario 'must have had some presentiment about all this when you wrote to Harewood on November 14th!'

believe, my dearest Carlo, that you would like to resolve your inner conflict between 'Australia and the rest' with a compromise (the English say: "You want to have your cake and eat it!"). I fully understand and sympathise with you, but I cannot detract from my primary and utter loyalty that stems from the responsibilities I undertook with the A. O. And you know that everyone wanted you here both as musical director and as a person.

As I already wrote to you, and you still quote this phrase: I would like the 'bonds that tie us not to be rescinded', but Carlo … how can you write 'keep me tied in any way!' when it was you who rejected those bonds?! And please forgive me for reminding you that the decision to have a minimum period … for the MD to be in Australia was, and must remain ours! … Now I do not know if we will conclude the arrangement with Downes or … – if you are right – with nobody. But I promise you that I will do all I can to ensure that there will be a close relationship between the Music Director and yourself in the hope that you remain as Principal Conductor and continue to come every year.[188]

Cillario replied on 4 December, referring to the 'decisive interview' in August when he had renounced his role, despite offers to delay his decision, and 'reconsider'. He speaks of having lost his 'usual joy in working … loss of sleep' and 'heavy burden of more general responsibilities'. He says that in June 1969, Alcorso had 'encouraged me to accept the position/role without hesitation' and that Cillario 'accepted, even if with modest enthusiasm.' He notes that at that time 'any mention of taking on more responsibility and even extending the duration of this type of work, felt like an attack on my health and artistic capacity,' hence, his refusal and 'advising not to insist doubling up my responsibilities (conductor and MD).'[189]

Cillario refers further to the 'decisive meeting' and recalled Alcorso asking if he intended breaking off ties with Australia, to

---

[188] See FN 186.

[189] All quotes in this paragraph are from: Cillario to Alcorso (In Italian), 4 December 1970. 'Carlo Felice Cillario – Artist Files '1', Opera Australia Library archives.' English translation by Simon Towle.

which he had replied that 'if at some time in the future I have to give up coming here … I will be extremely sad.' He quotes Alcorso's response: 'I would like the bonds that tie us not to be rescinded,' which he took to mean: 'It is understood that the four months of my stay per year, as well as my interest during the rest of the year, should continue not only for 1971 but also for future years.' Cillario indicates that he had also agreed (with Stephen Hall) to conduct at the 1972 Adelaide Festival (February/March) and in Melbourne (April/May), as well as engagements for 'the first part of '73 for the preparation and entrance into the Opera House.'[190]

Instead, he now finds to his dismay that 'everything has been reduced to your promise to "do what you can" to ensure that there will be a close relationship between the future MD and myself.' Cillario refers to the imminent announcement of Downes as his successor and cites 'the esteem and support of Lord Harewood' as well as other correspondence on this matter between Cillario and Alcorso, which Cillario admits may have been written in a 'slightly mischievous tone'. He compliments Alcorso on the choice of Downes: 'If you have Downes on board then you have done a good job.'[191] He asks for the opportunity to:

> turn to full account the work I have started in developing young artists and to give me time to untie my bonds – if necessary – in a gradual way, including spiritually from you. At the moment I am speaking to everybody with such enthusiasm for Australia and the AO, that if I were not to return to you for at least a couple of seasons, then everyone would think that you gave me the boot. That would cause a lot of harm to my cursed career and my personality in general.[192]

Cillario had evidently not counted upon Alcorso's resolve, in the face of his resignation to guide the company in a new direction. In December 1970, Downes flew to Australia, with the apparent purpose of discussing a new production of *Der Rosenkavalier* projected for

---

[190] Ibid.
[191] Ibid.
[192] Ibid.

1972. The timing was right to secure him as the Music Director, who would conduct the first operatic performances in the soon-to-be-completed Sydney Opera House. It was widely recognised that Cillario was unwilling to devote the time he needed to be in Australia.[193] Stephen Hall reflected: 'The appointment of Downes was crucial to the company's success. Carlo didn't want to do all the day-to-day stuff. He could also be a capricious individual when he chose. ... He changed his mind about the music director's job, still had his eyes set on bigger things.'[194]

9: Cillario inspecting the unfinished Sydney Opera House, July 1970. 'Asked his opinion of the orchestra pit, Cillario turned, eyes black, mouth drawn, a Latin face silently eloquent.'

---

[193] Cargher, *The Bulletin*, 27 February 1971.
[194] A. Gyger (2005), 253.

Intermezzo – 1971

Departure

By late February 1971, Edward Downes had been announced as Music Director Designate of the Australian Opera, effective from 1972; he would be named Music Director when the company moved into the Opera House.[195] Cillario would meanwhile fulfil his contract until the end of the 1971 season. He congratulated Stephen Hall over the appointment of Downes: 'I am very happy for you and the Company for Ted Downes' decision to accept. He is a very fine musician and responsible person and ... his English is better than my ...!'[196]

Cillario sent similar compliments about his successor to several members of the company, including Alcorso and Lord Harewood. On 21 January Cillario wrote to Hall from Bari, where he was conducting at the opera house. He wishes to amend a draft press release, which stated that he would continue as Music Director until the end of 1971. He asks:

> only to omit the phrase 'Maestro Cillario will remain as the Company's Music Director for the '71 season.' You know well that I never had the ambition to have that appointment. I accepted it just because Claudio and you asked me that, for helping the Trust in a delicate situation. But you know that I consider wrong to have double responsibilities (Principal Conductor and Music Director) on the same person. Amount of responsibilities who forced me to eat tablets to sleep.[197]

Regarding 1971, Cillario wrote: 'Be sure that I will be your most devote[d] and loyal collaborator.'[198] He was due to conduct a new

[195] Covell, 'Hope fulfilled,' *The Sydney Morning Herald*, 3 March 1971.
[196] Cillario to Hall, 31 January 1971. 'Carlo Felice Cillario – Artist Files '1', Opera Australia Library archives.'
[197] Cillario to Hall, 21 January 1971. 'CFC – Artist Files '1', Opera Australia Library archives.'
[198] Ibid.

production of *Nabucco* in the Sydney season that would open in May, and *Otello* in Canberra. This would be followed by a new production of *The Marriage of Figaro*. Despite agreements about dates, Cillario seems to have regarded his relinquishing of the Music Director post as also a loosening of prior commitments.

On 26 January, Hall responded in writing to a phone call he had received from Cillario, who asked to shorten his already renegotiated dates by a further 10 days. Hall sets out the compromised position in which such a request would leave the company. Cillario had already been advertised as the conductor of the Canberra *Otello*, and his absence from the Melbourne season made his presence in Sydney and Canberra all the more critical. It would also compromise the orchestral schedule (which had been organised around Cillario's availability) and those of the other conductors. In consultation with Alcorso, Hall informed Cillario that the company was unable to agree to his request. 'You realise that under normal circumstances we would do anything to try and fit in your other engagements with our schedule. I hope you will understand ... that we did not make the decision lightly.'[199] Hall found the letter urgent to the extent that he summarised the information in a cable sent on the same day.[200]

Having been delayed in the mail, an earlier letter from Cillario now arrived late,[201] and explained in more detail the significance of the engagement. Cillario had received a prestigious offer to conduct *Norma* in a concert performance in London (under the auspices of the London Opera Society) with Caballé, Cossotto, Marti and Vinco. This was tied to the possibility of a recording for Deutsche Gramophon in August and further performances in 1973 at the Metropolitan Opera. Hall replied to Cillario by cable: 'Did not realise recording and Met involved *STOP* Will discuss matter

---

[199] Information in this paragraph derived from: Hall to Cillario, 26 January 1971. 'CFC – Artist Files '1', Opera Australia Library archives.'

[200] Hall to Cillario, cable, 26 January 1971. 'CFC – Artist Files '1', Opera Australia Library archives.'

[201] Cillario to Hall, 13 January 1971. 'Carlo Felice Cillario – Artist Files '1', Opera Australia Library archives.'

again with Claudio in effort to find solution.'[202] The resulting clashes were revised by Hall and referred to Alcorso, who was not happy about being forced to reschedule, and told Hall that he bore the responsibility if *Figaro* and *Nabucco* were not as good as had been hoped.[203] Cillario was released for ten days to undertake the London *Norma*.

Following this disruption, and prior to his arrival in Australia, Cillario received a further invitation, to conduct Donizetti's *Maria Stuarda* at the Teatro alla Scala in Milan, starring Caballé. This would be a La Scala debut for both soprano and conductor. With his music director role in Australia coming to its conclusion, Cillario felt within his rights to ask to be released from the first rehearsals of *Nabucco*; the kind of 'late arrival' which today is not unusual practice among conductors. Cillario was aware that William Reid was well used to deputising for him while he was away, and they had a clear musical understanding.

In Europe, there is a general convention whereby an artist who receives an offer which is more prestigious than an existing contract is usually granted a release, so Cillario's request was not without precedent in his own cultural milieu. In the early 1970s, however, the convention in Australia was for the conductor to be present from the first rehearsal of an opera, as part of their responsibilities as the 'principal conductor'. While Downes did not take up his role as Music Director Designate until 1972, both he and Lord Harewood were consulted about the matter which was referred to Downes for a determination.[204] With the arrival of a new musical leader from another musical culture, the parameters of Downes' role also remained to be tested. He told the company to refuse the request, and Cillario was obliged to choose between Sydney and Milan.

Alcorso acted immediately. Cillario was effectively in breach of contract, and the following telegram was sent via Gorlinsky:

---

[202] Hall to Cillario, undated cable, c29 January 1971. 'CFC – Artist Files '1', Opera Australia Library archives.'

[203] Hall to Cillario, 8 February 1971. 'CFC – Artist Files '1', Opera Australia Library archives.'

[204] See also: Oxenbould (2005), 202-3.

Unless Cillario arrives March 28 for preparation and rehearsals until April 18 and returns April 28 for rehearsals and performances as agreed, we must regretfully consider Cillario has broken his contract which will therefore be entirely cancelled *STOP* confirmation of Cillario having received this commitment must be received by 6pm Saturday in Melbourne. Alcorso Chairman Australian Opera.[205]

Cillario replied: 'Surprised you easily renounce for a few rehearsals the collaboration of a *scaligero*[206] conductor letter follows love Carlo.'[207]

Alcorso cabled Gorlinsky about the announcement of Cillario's resignation:

Cillario cable means he renounces contract *STOP* we accept contract has been cancelled and both parties released from all obligations past present and future *STOP* we must make public announcement without delay and will publish on Wednesday 24 March following statement *QUOTE* Maestro Cillario has been given the opportunity to conduct at La Scala opera house and his acceptance of that offer will preclude his carrying out his entire obligations to the Australian Opera for the Sydney season. It has therefore been agreed that his contract with the Australian Opera should be cancelled. This decision has been made with reluctance and regret *UNQUOTE* will consider amendments if requested by Cillario and if received in time. ALCORSO.[208]

At the bottom of this cable is a handwritten draft message, which was possibly also sent by cable at the time to Cillario: 'Official cable to Gorlinsky does not change my feelings of friendship towards you

[205] Alcorso to Cillario C/- Gorlinsky, London, cable, 19 March 1971 'Carlo Felice Cillario – Artist Files '1', Opera Australia Library archives.'

[206] An artist associated with Teatro alla Scala, Milan.

[207] Cillario to Alcorso, cable, 20 March 1971. 'CFC – Artist Files '1', Opera Australia Library archives.'

[208] Alcorso to Gorlinsky, undated sheet, typed, c22 March 1971. 'CFC – Artist Files '1', Opera Australia Library archives.'

or those of many other Australian friends affectionately, Claudio.'[209] There followed a telegram, from Cillario to 'Alcorso Theatre Trust': 'Forced to accept your decision but beg to inform the public that in reality, I asked only to renounce first rehearsals, best wishes, CILLARIO'.[210]

It may have just been a matter of reinforcing company policy, but it cannot be denied that for several years following these events, Cillario was 'frozen out' of the Australian Opera. In the commemorative booklet and LP recording issued to celebrate the company in its new home,[211] Cillario, the founding Music Director of the company, received no mention. Downes and Cillario hailed from quite different musical cultures, and they made a study in contrasts. It is also significant to note that when Cillario conducted Callas in *Tosca* at the Royal Opera in 1964, Edward Downes had been at work in the prompt box.

The reactions to Cillario's departure in the Australian press were of disappointment, and some anger at the perception that they were being abandoned by this inspiring figure:

> The influence that a first-rate and widely experienced musical director can bring to a company has been shown by the continuously improving standard of performances since Carlo Felice Cillario has held that position with the Australian Opera. Now he apparently finds that his international commitments make it impossible for him to spend sufficient time each year in Australia and he is relinquishing the position at the end of the present season.[212]
>
> Cillario 'walked out, ostensibly so that he could conduct

---

[209] Ibid, handwritten note. 'CFC – Artist Files '1', Opera Australia Library archives.'

[210] Cillario to Alcorso, cable, 22 March 1971. 'CFC – Artist Files '1', Opera Australia Library archives.'

[211] Presentation box, to mark the Australian Opera's first season in the Sydney Opera House. Folder containing a broadsheet, costume designs and a commemorative LP ('Great Australian Singers') titled 'The Australian Opera 1973. General Editor – Leo Schofield; Printed by John Sands Pty. Ltd. Sydney, Australia.

[212] Hoffmann, *The Canberra Times,* 25 February 1971.

the debut of his friend, the soprano Montserrat Caballé at La Scala, Milan. A rather public row blew up between the administration and the company's leading tenor, Donald Smith.[213]

Italian maestro Carlo Felice Cillario who was to be guest conductor with the Australian Opera's Sydney season beginning on May 15 at the Elizabethan Theatre, Newtown, will not be available. His contract has been cancelled because he has had an offer to conduct at La Scala, Milan. The company's resident conductor, William Reid, guest conductor, Walter Stiasny, associate conductor, Vanco Cavdarski and another member of the staff, Geoffrey Arnold, will conduct the season.[214]

This volatile gentleman certainly knew how to produce superb sound from the Trust orchestras. He deserves credit for improving conducting and playing standards. Until the arrival of Edward Downes ... we will have to be satisfied with others whose work is better on the whole than that which we used to get from visiting conductors.[215]

The company moved on. Musical responsibility for the *Nabucco* staging was taken over by Reid. Cillario's appearance at La Scala was reported by Roger Covell, who cited several reviews that had praised the conductor's 'understanding of style, professional control and musicianly collaboration with the singers.' Covell expressed the view that the 'severance of his regular connection' or 'any permanent breach' would be unfortunate, and noted that it would be 'very pleasant and musically beneficial if he could be invited back periodically as a guest conductor of works with which he has shown himself to be particularly in sympathy.'[216] Cillario, Covell noted, was fond of both Australia, and of the Australian Opera, and the article may have been carefully 'placed' in order to keep the door open to an important figure. In due course Covell's stated wishes would eventuate.

[213] Cargher, *The Bulletin*, 11 March 1972.
[214] [No author named], 'Opera Change,' *The Canberra Times*, 29 March 1971.
[215] Cargher, *The Bulletin*, 10 April 1971.
[216] Covell, 'Cillario success,' *The Sydney Morning Herald*, 19 May 1971.

Writing to Cillario in May, Stephen Hall congratulated him on his La Scala debut. He enclosed Covell's article and added: 'You will see from this that there is great sympathy for you in the press and I can only add that the sentiments expressed by Roger Covell are similar to my own.'[217] Cillario replied with gratitude: 'I plunged my memory into a charming past.'[218] The Australian Opera had done all it could to accommodate Cillario. While recovering from the major setback of the 1970 fire, the company was struggling to prepare and present an artistically rewarding season. It is not clear the extent to which Cillario realised that his demands, exacerbated by his recent resignation as music director, pushed the company's leadership beyond their limits.

Cillario wrote to Hall two days after the final cables. He felt that the course of events had run out of control, saying that 'Destiny was the protagonist.' He also accused Hall of having chosen 'the intransigent way. And in this case the intransigence makes difficult the incomprehension, even if it is right.' Nevertheless, Cillario sent his hope 'that artistically it may be the best for the Trust and that you have not taken such a decision only to give me a lesson.'[219] Cillario was by now aware that Downes and Lord Harewood had been consulted over the question of his release for La Scala.

Just over a month later, directly after his triumphant *Norma* with Caballé at the Royal Festival Hall, Cillario wrote to Donald McDonald:[220] 'I know that the officer who receive[s] the order to kill a prisoner is not responsible of his act. But I can imagine how sad you were, sending me the official cables signed from Claudio! I was very sad receiving them ...'[221]

By late May, Cillario was at home in Bologna, where he replied to another letter from Hall:

---

[217] Hall to Cillario, 25 May 1971. 'Carlo Felice Cillario – Artist Files '1', Opera Australia Library archives.'

[218] Cillario to Hall, 31 May 1971. 'CFC – Artist Files '1', Opera Australia Library archives.'

[219] Cillario (at Waldorf Hotel, London) to Hall, 21 March 1971. 'Carlo Felice Cillario – Artist Files '1', Opera Australia Library archives.'

[220] At that time, McDonald was the General Manager of the Australian Opera.

[221] Cillario (in London) to Donald McDonald, 27 April 1971. 'CFC – Artist Files '1', Opera Australia Library archives.'

Frankly I am not convinced that the decision was take[n] "with regret and reluctance". If the Trust t[h]ought that my job would have benefited the Company, I think some other[s] solutions were possible. Any case now it is too late, and I repeat[e] you that I hope it was the best solution for the Australian Opera.[222]

Communication continued sporadically. By the end of the year, Hall wrote 'Carissimo Carlo, I was so happy to hear from you and to find that you realise we still think of you and want you.'[223] Time would show that Hall's words were not empty.

Cillario was deeply hurt by the course of events. His responses swerved between anger and an abiding belief that he had proposed solutions which would not compromise the artistic quality of the season in Australia. A sense of loss can also be discerned at having been abruptly removed (or finally resigned) from a great enterprise and estranged from colleagues with whom he felt himself to be in artistic accord and sympathy. On the side of Hall and Alcorso there is a sense of both artistic and personal loss, tempered by the professional imperative to move forward.

Both Alcorso and Hall remained in contact with Cillario. He wrote to them from one or another city where he had been engaged, mentioning singers and orchestral players whom he had encountered and who would be happy to come and work in Australia. The new artistic leadership, however, had its own networks. Cillario continued to correspond with Hall over potential dates to conduct at the Opera House in 1973 between October and December. He referred back to the proposal of Hall producing an opera in San Francisco, and both Hall and Alcorso wrote of tentative possibilities for Cillario to return as a guest. Hall raised a plan to stage Puccini's *Il trittico*, and the idea that Cillario would conduct it.[224] In the event, the production went ahead with three

[222] Cillario to Hall, 30 May 1971. 'CFC – Artist Files '1', Opera Australia Library archives.'
[223] Hall to Cillario, 24 November 1971. 'CFC – Artist Files '1', Opera Australia Library archives.'
[224] For example: Cillario to Hall, 30 November 1971; Hall to Cillario, 17 January 1972; Hall to Cillario, 1972 (no date). 'Carlo Felice Cillario – Artist Files '3', Opera Australia Library Archives.'

conductors, one for each work, with Downes joined by two of his assistants on the music staff. Both Hall and Alcorso expressed a genuine desire to see Cillario return, and to conduct in the Sydney Opera House. Doubtless there was also a need for a certain time to elapse, and for some wounds to heal.

In 1972, Cillario made his debut at the Metropolitan Opera in New York, conducting Bellini's *La sonnambula*, with Renata Scotto in the title role. He also conducted a run of *La traviata* at the Royal Opera, in which Caballé made her house debut. In 1973, he returned to the Met for Caballé's debut in *Norma*. It was not until the 1975 season, Downes' last as Music Director, that Cillario returned to Australia.

10: 'Three views of an $85m. compromise' – Bernd Benthaak, Tom Lingwood and Carlo Felice Cillario on the steps of the incomplete Sydney Opera House. July 1970.

ACT 2 (1975–1993)

Scene 1

1975 – *Ritorna Vincitor*

Cillario's return to the Australian Opera should be placed in the context of the tortuous debate over the eventual design of the Sydney Opera House. He had first-hand experience of opera houses all over the world – from smaller, provincial theatres to the largest houses. While he loved to conduct Mozart and Rossini – and had particularly enjoyed working at Glyndebourne (a 'Mozart house') during the 1960s – his aspirations for opera in Australia revolved around the creation of a suitably sizeable theatre that could do justice to the 'grand' operas of Verdi, Puccini, Wagner, and Richard Strauss.[225] Cillario had been critical of the projected pit size in the Opera Theatre since his first visit in 1968, and also of the overall size and resources of the stage, including a lack of wing space for ease of scene changes and to facilitate multiple productions in a repertoire season.

The dual-purpose symphony and opera hall that had originally been planned had become the Concert Hall, the new home of the Sydney Symphony Orchestra and the projected Drama Theatre was reconceived as the Opera Theatre. The size of and acoustic of the opera pit has remained a point of contention – one that outlasted Cillario's tenure with the company.[226] During his tenure as Music Director, Edward Downes along with the Earl of Harewood tended to gloss over the problem, making unfortunate comparisons between the Sydney Opera Theatre and Glyndebourne, even going as far as suggesting that a Mozart-size theatre was 'good enough' or a 'good start'. Such comments hardly addressed the issue of a monumentally expensive building, ostensibly designed for the production of opera, in which the largest and greatest works of the repertoire could not

---

[225] Renamed the Joan Sutherland Theatre in 2012.

[226] Even after a major renovation, it remains a point of contention today (2024).

be performed, without significant diminution of their scale. The issue became acute when comparisons were raised with leading international opera houses across the world. As a regular conductor in such houses, Cillario was ideally placed to voice an authoritative opinion. He did not hesitate to do so, often in abrasive terms, but he also recognised that other major theatres in the world were also (as he said) 'imperfect'. Perhaps in the knowledge that the problems were beyond any easy resolution, he generally focused upon making the best of the circumstances.

It was probably Stephen Hall who played the decisive role in Cillario's return to Sydney. An offer was made to conduct Verdi's *Aida*, Cillario accepted, and arrived late in 1974 to commence rehearsals. Hall had an eye for spectacle, and he wished to see the opera company performing in the new Concert Hall. Accordingly, he devised a simple but monumental production in collaboration with the stage designer Tom Lingwood. The company's General Manager, John Winther[227] was also a leading force in driving the project. All the elements of a traditional *Aida* were represented: even elephants,[228] in slightly ridiculous likenesses.

The logistics of mounting an opera in the Concert Hall were considerable. Nothing could be removed from or screwed down in the venue. Backstage areas could barely accommodate the requirements of offstage brass ensembles and choruses. The 230 people who appeared on stage had to be accommodated in both the Concert Hall and the Opera Theatre dressing rooms, and meticulous signage directed artists between the venues. In retrospect, designer Tom Lingwood found that there were fewer logistical issues with using the Concert Hall than in mounting smaller productions in the Opera Theatre. He viewed *Aida* as the beginning of 'an era of unlimited possibilities' for the Australian Opera in the Opera

---

[227] John Winther (1933–2012) was General Manager of the company between 1971 and 1977. He had previously been the opera director at the Royal Danish Theatre, and in addition to working as an arts administrator, was a noted pianist.

[228] There was a regulation banning of animals in the Sydney Opera House. (Romola Constantino, '*Aida* a traffic problem,' *The Sydney Morning Herald*, 27 January 1975.)

House. In her review of *Aida*, Romola Constantino declared that the company should 'run up a flag' on the Opera House, for having 'taken over' the Concert Hall 'from which they were ousted when the home of Sydney Opera was shifted from the main auditorium to the cramped hall known as the Opera Theatre.' She predicted that 'this is a company ready to take up any challenge.'[229] Soon afterwards, Hall was invited to become founder-director of the Sydney Festival at least partly due to the success of this *Aida*.

On his return to Sydney, Cillario for the first time entered the completed Sydney Opera House, about which he had expressed so many reservations. A good deal was at stake, as he would have been aware, on the success of a production designed to reinvent opera within its walls (or sails) on a monumental scale. The orchestra was 'about 80 people'[230] placed in the open, visible to the public. Listed as a 'Guest Conductor', Cillario had at his disposal a first-class cast of singers,[231] many of whom were familiar to him from previous visits with the company. Marilyn Richardson created the role of Aida, in her debut with the company, the role was also sung by Elizabeth Fretwell. As Radamès, Donald Smith alternated with Reginald Byers, and Lauris Elms alternated with Elizabeth Connell as Amneris. They were joined by Donald Shanks (Ramfis), John Shaw alternating with Raymond Myers as Amonasro, and Alan Light (The King). Richardson and Connell would go on to have distinguished careers with the company.

Aida opened on 30 January 1975 and won immediate success for the company, further reinforced by a national broadcast during the run. Cillario made a triumphant return, reaping the advantage of the excellent acoustic in the Concert Hall with space for a larger, more visible orchestra. The conductor did not change out of his white tuxedo for the opening-night reception, at which Margaret

---

[229] Ibid.

[230] Ibid.

[231] Cast: Marilyn Richardson and Elizabeth Fretwell (Aida), Elizabeth Connell and Lauris Elms (Amneris), Donald Smith and Reginald Byers (Radamès), John Shaw and Raymond Myers (Amonasro), Donald Shanks (Ramfis), Alan Light (The King), Gregory Martin (Messenger), Noela Strange-Mure (High Priestess).

Whitlam (wife of the Prime Minister, Gough Whitlam) handed Cillario her empty glass, mistaking him for a waiter.[232]

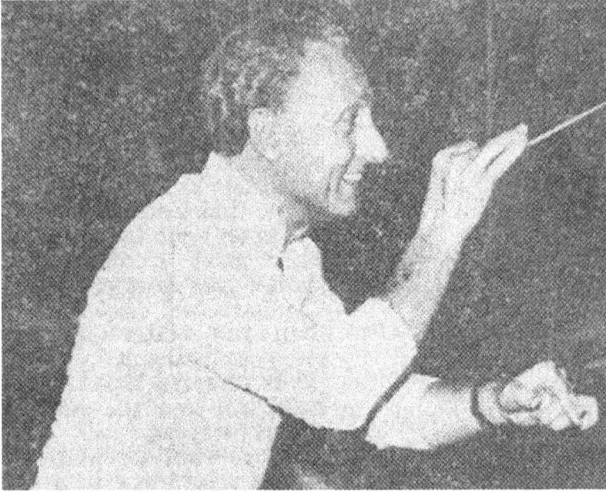

11: Cillario rehearsing the Elizabethan Sydney Orchestra for *Aida*, 1975.

Aida was revived in 1976 and 1977, further attesting both to its practical nature and its commercial appeal. In the following years, Cillario conducted other works such as *Otello* and *Tristan und Isolde* in the Concert Hall, and reviews of these performances noted the improved sound of the orchestra under his direction, free from the constraints of the opera pit.

Cillario stayed on in Sydney to lead stagings of Verdi's *Rigoletto* and Donizetti's *L'elisir d'amore* (sung in English), making a total of three productions, as many as for his final season as Music Director in 1970. He had made his name in the UK with *L'elisir* at Glyndebourne in 1961, where he became acquainted with the conductor John Pritchard, who made his Australian Opera debut in 1974. Following Cillario's return later that year, a singer with the company drew an illuminating comparison: Cillario 'throws himself into an opera and is awaaaay' whereas John Pritchard 'is completely, sublimely relaxed. With no exertion whatsoever, he stands there

---

[232] Ava Hubble, *The Strange Case of Eugene Goossens and other tales from the Sydney Opera House* (Sydney, Collins Publishers Australia, 1988), 34.

and out pours great orchestral playing.'[233] Illustration 34 personifies Cillario's 'awaaaay', as experienced by a member of the Australian Opera and Ballet Orchestra.

L'elisir d'amore was given in a new production by Stefan Haag, who had played a decisive role with the company in its formative years. His work met with lukewarm appreciation, unlike 'the orchestra under the excellent direction of Carlo Felice Cillario' who 'found the right mood'.[234] Roger Covell wrote that Cillario 'conducted with complete authority and untiring energy, taking firm hold of the musical reading of the piece.'[235] The cast featured Eilene Hannan (Adina), Henri Wilden (Nemorino), Ronald Maconaghie (Belcore), and Donald Shanks (Dulcamara). *Rigoletto* was the revival of a production by John Copley, and Cillario shared the conducting with William Reid, taking over the second run.[236]

Cillario's return to Australia in 1975 began a new phase of his relationship with the Australian Opera: his 'golden years' with the company. He found his place as a regular guest conductor, established his repertoire and 'after his welcome return as a guest artist, he was part of every successive year of the company's performances until 2003.'[237]

1976 – A New Music Director

Cillario's return for the 1976 season coincided with the appointment of a new music director, Richard Bonynge, the third incumbent of that position in seven years. Bonynge continued in the post for just shy of a decade: something of a feat, considering the upheavals which the company continued to experience following the long-

---

[233] Warren-Smith and Salter (1983), 146.

[234] 'E.S.' *The Australian Jewish Times* (Sydney), 4 September 1975.

[235] Covell, *The Sydney Morning Herald*, 23 August 1975.

[236] Casts: Donald Smith (Duke of Mantua), Raymond Myers and John Shaw (Rigoletto), Glenys Fowles and June Bronhill (Gilda), Neil Warren-Smith and Donald Shanks (Sparafucile), Jacqueline Kensett-Smith (Maddalena), Robin Lawler (Giovanna), Grant Dixon (Monterone), John Germain (Marullo), William Bamford (Borsa), Joseph Grunfelder (Count Ceprano), Rosemary Gunn (Countess Ceprano), John Durham (Usher), Janice Hill (Page).

[237] Oxenbould, Cillario obituary, 20 December 2007.

delayed opening of the Opera House. He stepped down 1984, when he was named 'Conductor Emeritus and Principal Guest Conductor', and continued to work with the company until the early 2000s, his achievements in this later period included returning Bellini's works to the company's repertoire and mentoring their casts in the *bel canto* tradition.

Unlike Cillario before him, Bonynge succeeded in balancing the demands of the post with those of his own career. He was a peripatetic music director, in a position to dictate his availability around his international schedule and leave the day-to-day running of the company to others. He had negotiated a favourable contract in this regard, and one which took account of Joan Sutherland's relationship with the company; he conducted all his wife's performances, with one notable exception, discussed below. This period was the height of 'Sutherland mania', when the soprano was in demand all over the world, and her ongoing availability to the Australian Opera became a linchpin in the company's financial modelling.

Bonynge focused on the *bel canto* operas, neglected repertoire from the 18th and 19th centuries, and the Italian and French lyric repertoire. This emphasis would not normally be considered prudent as a commercial strategy, nor did it always succeed as such, but if Sutherland appeared in a production, a healthy box-office return was almost guaranteed. The couple attracted artists such as Luciano Pavarotti and Marilyn Horne to sing in Australia, and successfully revived repertoire that had rarely been heard in Sydney. Exactly what Sutherland sang, was less important to the public than the fact that she was singing.

This risky artistic strategy depended on the availability of first-rate conductors who would take on the standard repertoire usually regarded as the natural property of any music director. The core of the company's repertoire centred on Verdi and Puccini, which Bonynge left alone aside from early Verdi. In his stead, Cillario conducted most of the Puccini productions, and a good deal of Verdi. On average, he conducted as many productions per season as Bonynge, including major works such as *Der fliegende Holländer*,

Parsifal, The Cunning Little Vixen and *La fanciulla del West*, which were not among Bonynge's conducting interests.

The 1976 Sydney season began with a revival of *Aida*, a sold-out run of performances, with some significant cast changes.[238] The Swedish soprano Helena Döse alternated with Elizabeth Fretwell as Aida, and Heather Begg alternated with Margreta Elkins as Amneris. Roger Covell was critical of several of the casting choices but praised Raymond Myers (Amonasro) for his 'vocal clarity, power, … and energy.' The other protagonist singled out for praise was Cillario, 'whose masterly conducting of Verdi's score deserves to be treasured in any operagoer's memory.'[239] Cargher referred to 'just sitting back and enjoying a brilliant score unleashed from the orchestra by Carlo Felice Cillario with often stunning immediacy, an involving, enveloping and often totally overwhelming experience for the audience and also at times for some of the singers, too.'[240] In the Concert Hall, Cargher declared that the company had found a suitable performance venue, and hinted at the possibility of some of the larger works of Wagner and Richard Strauss appearing there in the future.

The company management was focused upon improving their performance conditions in the Opera House, and the use of the Concert Hall for hybrid (semi-staged) productions was felt to be a good, if occasional alternative. However, a setback to their plans was announced in June 1976, after a structural survey had found that increasing the pit size in the Opera Theatre could have grave implications. Frank Barnes, the General Manager of the Opera House, stated that performing opera or ballet in the Concert Hall was relatively easy, as an orchestral pit could be created in front of the stage, by taking out the first rows of seats. He continued:

---

[238] Cast: Helena Döse and Elizabeth Fretwell (Aida), Heather Begg and Margreta Elkins (Amneris), Donald Smith and Reginald Byers (Radamès), John Shaw and Raymond Myers (Amonasro), Donald Shanks and Grant Dixon (Ramfis), Alan Light (The King), Gregory J. Martin (Messenger), Beryl Furlan (High Priestess). Both Begg and Elkins were making their Australian Opera debuts.

[239] Covell, *The Sydney Morning Herald*, 19 January 1976.

[240] Cargher, *The Bulletin*, 1 May 1976.

As far as the Opera Theatre is concerned, on the face of it, that looks easy. Remove some seats, dig down to pit level and then extend the pit back into the stalls area to the point where you can accommodate 120 to 140 musicians. But below the [Opera Theatre] floor level ... tight under the first row of seats there are stressing cables which help to hold the roof up. In other words, you could not effect the changes to the pit by digging down into the stalls area without risking a structural calamity of stupendous proportions.[241]

The Melbourne season which followed included *Tosca*,[242] in a staging directed by David Neal. Donald Smith returned as Cavaradossi, John Shaw as Scarpia; Floria Tosca was sung by Orianna Santunione, who had been billed as 'one of Italy's most sensational operatic talents.' Cargher's review was peppered with backhanded provocation:

It was a very professional, well and truly 'verismo' belting of the score, led by Carlo Felice Cillario with immense gusto. There is just one question: is it the function of the Australian Opera to spend some thousands of dollars of public money to imitate professional Italian standards? Surely not.[243]

Verdi's *Simon Boccanegra*, a relative rarity in Australia, also transferred from Sydney. Melbourne critics found fault with Tito Capobianco's staging and questioned the decision to mount the opera at all. The cast included Joan Carden as Amelia, Donald Shanks & Neil Warren-Smith alternating as Fiesco, and Robert Allman and John Shaw alternating as the Doge.[244] Cillario's music-making was

---

[241] [No author named], 'Size limit on opera orchestra,' *The Sun Herald*, 6 June 1976.

[242] Cast: Orianna Santunione (Tosca), Donald Smith (Cavaradossi), John Shaw (Scarpia), Alan Light (Angelotti), William Bamford (Spoletta), John Germain (Sacristan), Robert Eddie (Sciarrone), Donald Solomon (Gaoler).

[243] References in this paragraph are derived from: Cargher, *The Bulletin*, 1 May 1976.

[244] Cast: Joan Carden (Amelia), Reginald Byers and Robin Donald (Adorno), Robert Allman and John Shaw (Boccanegra), Donald Shanks and Neil Warren-Smith (Fiesco), Gregory Yurisich (Paolo), Josef Grunfelder (Pietro), David Rampy (Captain), Janice Hill (Lady in Waiting).

praised as 'a wonder of shaped, unobtrusive splendour. … The most memorable of those passages … were in the first scene in which Boccanegra recognises Amelia as his granddaughter and tries to talk her into marrying against her will, and also the quartet with chorus at the end of the second scene, where overlapping and alternating melodies were brought to a shimmering, polychromatic climax by Cillario and his singers.'[245] Cillario well knew how to realise the unique *tinta* of this elusive work, and by all accounts, he succeeded admirably.

The same Melbourne autumn season included Janáček's *The Cunning Little Vixen* in a Jonathan Miller production which had been originally staged at Glyndebourne, in an English translation by Norman Tucker.   John Winther was eager to bring this work and production to the company's repertoire, but the Melbourne season, conducted by Georg Tintner initially attracted criticism, with Cargher lamenting the absence of a set defining a forest: 'not a leaf, not a tree in this forest'.[246]

Vixen fared better in the Sydney winter season under Cillario's baton.[247] Nadine Amadio praised the opera company for mounting this 'unknown but meaningful work', which boasted 'elemental vitality' eschewing 'operatic devices and operatic over-sentimentality' in favour of 'the potency of melody and the dynamic rhythmic content'. Among the cast,[248] Eilene Hannan (The Vixen), Robert

---

[245] Leonard Glickfield, *The Australian Jewish News* (Melbourne), 19 March 1976. '"Boccanegra" of Lusagne Verdi'.

[246] Cargher, *The Bulletin*, 3 April 1976.

[247] With the later performances conducted by Georg Tintner.

[248] Cast: John Pringle (The Forester), Elizabeth Fretwell (The Forester's Wife), Kieran Casey (Pepík), Paul Clark and Nicholas Martin (Frantík), Donald Shanks (The Parson), Robert Gard (The Schoolmaster), David Rampy and Robin Donald (Pásek, the Innkeeper), Etela Piha (The Innkeeper's Wife), Gregory Yurisich and Robert Eddie (Harašta), Eilene Hannan and Cynthia Johnston (The Vixen), Robert Gard (The Dog), William Bamford (The Cock), Dawn Walsh (The Hen), Donald Shanks (The Badger), Anson Austin and Ron Stevens (The Fox), Elizabeth Fretwell (The Owl), Christopher Casey and John Boyle (The Cricket), Michael Terry and Hugh Sullivan (The Grasshopper), Laurie Bennett (The Gnat), Phillip Buchanan and Stephen Molony (The Frog), Mark Furneaux (The Dragonfly), Hellen Sky (The Doe), Keith Macdonald (The Stag), Keith Macdonald (The Stag), Linda Tenen-

Allman (The Forester), and Ronald Dowd (The Schoolmaster) were particularly singled out for praise. In a well-informed review, Amadio felt that the opera had 'special meaning in the Australia of today.' She praised both Miller's production and the orchestral contribution led by Cillario, in a 'fine performance that pulsed with the life-forces of nature and was often stirring.'[249] Irwin Imhof found that 'the orchestra under Cillario played splendidly and managed to imbue the score with life.'[250]

In fact, with this *Cunning Little Vixen*, Cillario was approaching Janáček afresh. British conductors were more accepted in Australia as 'all-rounders', but the combination of Cillario's nationality,[251] and the clear authority of his work in his native repertoire, tended to reinforce stereotypes of him as an 'Italian maestro' who would be less at home in repertoire from beyond his native borders. In the same way, he was considered an operatic conductor first and foremost, despite his extensive concert work with orchestras across Europe and South America. Cillario himself was reticent about his rich, polyglot past, his vast knowledge of musical byways and his intellectual hunger for new repertoire. He was not given to excessive name-dropping or self-publicity. Aspects of his professional background therefore remained almost unknown and unacknowledged in Australia. Cillario immersed himself fully into Janáček's sound world; *Vixen* requires a conductor with a profound knowledge of the orchestra, particularly the strings, to shape Janacek's at times unidiomatic instrumental writing and hold its many textural strands in balance. Cillario unquestionably succeeded in doing so.

The third production conducted by Cillario in the winter season was *The Abduction from the Seraglio*, again sung in English with dialogue by the theatre director George Ogilvie, in another rare but welcome Mozartian foray for the conductor. Cillario's opinions about

baum (The Cat). Bears, Fox Cubs, Hedgehogs, Squirrels, Flies, Birds – National Boys' Choir; Chorus Master – Kevin Casey.

[249] Nadine Amadio, *The Financial Review*, 27 August 1976.

[250] Irwin Imhof, *The Australian Jewish News* (Sydney), 27 August 1976.

[251] It was often forgotten that he was Argentinian-born and is still considered an Argentinian conductor in South America.

opera in translation were inconstant: he remarked to Bruce Duffie that 'In Sydney, all the critics prefer in the local language … English. I fight against it, but they asked for English to be used in comedy like *Don Pasquale*, *L'elisir d'amore*, and also Mozart, unfortunately. I was forced to conduct *The Magic Flute* in English. It's terrible!'[252] On at least one occasion he turned down a production of *The Magic Flute* with the company, because it was to be performed in English. However, he later conducted a staging in English (by Ogilvie) of Verdi's *Falstaff*, which seems an unlikely match.

Roger Covell lavished praise on much of the singing in *Seraglio*, with the performances of Joan Carden (Konstanze), June Bronhill (Blonde), and Donald Shanks (Osmin) particularly singled out.[253] He also felt that this was a 'stately' *Seraglio*, speaking in terms both of the production and the musical values. He mused that Cillario, who as he noted 'can set a tempo as brisk as anyone when he wishes' may have been influenced by Ogilvie's staging to develop a complementary approach, which lent the performances a 'spacious, ample style.'[254] Nadine Amadio felt that youthfulness was the hallmark of the production, realised in both the conducting and stage direction, and she praised Cillario for 'working magic with the Elizabethan Sydney Orchestra', and 'allowing Mozart his earnest youth.'[255] Both conductor and director were 'deeply aware of the style and the feelings of the young Mozart.' Another critic noted that the orchestra 'was at its best under the direction of Carlo Felice Cillario', and both the production and cast were warmly praised.[256] Cillario's final assignment in the Sydney winter season was *Rigoletto*, a revival from the previous year, with an almost identical cast.[257]

[252] Cillario and Duffie, *Interview*, 1982.
[253] Cast: Joan Carden (Konstanze), June Bronhill (Blonde), Anson Austin and Henri Wilden (Belmonte), Graeme Ewer and Gordon Wilcock (Pedrillo), Donald Shanks (Osmin), Pieter van der Stolk (Pasha Selim).
[254] Covell, *The Sydney Morning Herald*, 24 June 1976.
[255] Amadio, *The Financial Review*, 25 June 1976.
[256] 'E.S.,' *The Australian Jewish Times* (Sydney), 8 July 1976.
[257] Cast: [Changes from previous season are underlined.] Reginald Byers (Duke of Mantua), Raymond Myers and John Shaw (Rigoletto), Glenys Fowles and June Bronhill (Gilda), Donald Shanks (Sparafucile), Lesley Stender (Maddalena), Rosemary Gunn (Giovanna), Grant Dixon (Monterone),

1977 – A Watershed Year

If 1976 had been a busy year in Australia for Cillario, the following year was even more so, when he conducted nine runs of seven productions. *Aida* was revived for the third year in a row, with its title role triple cast across ten performances: Orianna Santunione opened the run, followed by Marilyn Richardson, and then Dolores Cambridge. Roger Covell summed up Santunione's Aida as 'a prolonged blare of powerful or strenuous singing, largely devoid of dramatic meaning.' Her voice was 'of a considerable size and flooding presence … without demonstrating any significant ability to shape her phrasing with a pressure of meaning and feeling.' Marilyn Richardson's 'decidedly smaller' voice, on the other hand was employed with purpose and 'she found meaning in every phrase and clinched that meaning with gestures and movement that were as apt as they were simple and contained.' Perhaps Richardson benefited from the presence of Ronald Dowd as her Radamès (Reginald Byers had sung with Santunione).[258] At the cast change, Margreta Elkins was found to be an improvement over Lauris Elms and Robert Allman was preferred over John Shaw.[259] Cillario continued to have success throughout the production, one of the most popular mounted by the company at that time.

Madama Butterfly was given in Canberra, Sydney and Melbourne, in a new production directed by John Copley. Cillario conducted three of the director's productions during 1977 two of them new, and they bore further witness to an enduring, artistically symbiotic relationship between the visual language that Copley

---

Robert Eddie (Marullo), Lamberto Furlan (Borsa), Joseph Grunfelder (Count Ceprano), Etela Piha (Countess Ceprano), John Durham (Usher), Janice Hill (Page).

[258] Cast: Orianna Santunione and Marilyn Richardson and Dolores Cambridge (Aida), Lauris Elms and Margreta Elkins and Heather Begg (Amneris), Reginald Byers and Ronald Dowd (Radamès), John Shaw and Robert Allman and Raymond Myers (Amonasro), Alan Light (The King), Kevin Mills (Messenger), Isobel Buchanan and Beryl Furlan and Judith Saliba (High Priestess).

[259] Information in this paragraph derived from: Roger Covell, 'Blare into opera,' *The Sydney Morning Herald*, 17 January 1977.

created onstage, and the culture of sound that Cillario conjured up in the orchestra pit. *Butterfly* premiered in Sydney, with the rising star Leona Mitchell, who was making her debut with the Australian Opera.[260] She was 'well supported by the orchestra and, above all by Carlo Felice Cillario.'[261] The company had not appeared in Canberra during 1976, so to make amends, an international guest was engaged to sing the role of Cio-Cio-San – Mietta Sighele, who was praised for her 'fine tonal quality, evenly spread throughout the range, and with sufficient power to ride over the sometimes too-exuberant orchestral climaxes, her singing was a constant delight' … the orchestra 'playing under Carlo Felice Cillario provided a warm and glowing, if at times a somewhat enthusiastic account of Puccini's score.'[262]

Santunione reprised *Tosca* in Sydney, alongside Reginald Byers (Cavaradossi) and John Shaw (Scarpia), and an emerging star, Gregory Yurisich as Angelotti.[263] Both these productions were extensively reviewed by Roger Covell, in an article titled 'Tosca, Butterfly a Cillario Triumph':

> The primary allotment of credit for the success of both eve-
> nings must go to [neither Orianna Santunione nor Leona
> Mitchell], but to the conducting of Carlo Felice Cillario. His
> direction established in vivid, unforced fashion the abrupt
> drive of many passages in *Tosca* and those characteristic
> moments when the music of this score gathers itself for a

[260] Cast: Leona Mitchell [and Mietta Sighele, Canberra and Melbourne] (Cio-Cio-San), Lesley Stender and Jennifer Bermingham (Suzuki), Lamberto Furlan and Robin Donald (B.F. Pinkerton), Ronald Maconaghie and John Pringle (Sharpless), Gordon Wilcock [and Kevin Mills, Canberra and Melbourne](Goro), Gregory Yurisich and Pieter van der Stolk (Yamadori), Joseph Grunfelder [and Grant Dixon, Canberra and Melbourne] (Bonze), Rosemary Gunn [and Helga Willis-Golding, Canberra] (Kate Pinkerton), Robert Eddie (Imperial Commissioner), Trevor Brown (Registrar), Beaumont Cox [Sydney] (Trouble).

[261] 'E.S.', *The Australian Jewish Times* (Sydney), 10 February 1977.

[262] Hoffmann, *The Canberra Times*, 5 March 1977.

[263] Cast: Orianna Santunione (Tosca), Reginald Byers (Cavaradossi), John Shaw (Scarpia), Gregory Yurisich (Angelotti), Graeme Ewer (Spoletta), Alan Light (Sacristan), Robert Eddie (Sciarrone), Donald Solomon (Gaoler).

crucial accent with the focused ease of a cat about to spring. *Madama Butterfly*, even more fluid in tempo and volatile in contrast, came together under his leadership with unerring emotional logic and sense of pace. Conducting as good as this is not common (least of all in Puccini performances in Australia) as to be taken for granted. It provides the context in which every instrumentalist and singer can do his or her best. With rare exceptions orchestra and cast responded to their opportunity. The results gave us cause to cherish Mr Cillario more than ever.[264]

Also in Sydney, Cillario conducted a stellar cast[265] in Copley's new staging of Verdi's *Macbeth,* taking over the end of the run which had opened with Sir John Pritchard in the pit. Covell found John Shaw 'vocally strong' in the title role, but the proceedings were dominated by Elizabeth Connell as Lady Macbeth: an already 'splendid portrayal' on opening night 'had grown into one of the most decisive and commanding vocal-dramatic performances seen and heard by operagoers in this country.' Covell compared the two conductors, finding Pritchard's first-night direction 'slack', whereas when Cillario took the reins, his conducting 'was notably more effective in its grip on the performance' communicating 'the fire and force of a more enlivening and committed musical personality.'[266]

This was already a heavy load, but Cillario's year also included three major German operas. Beethoven's *Fidelio* was performed in the Melbourne autumn season, with a Copley staging from 1970 revived by Elke Neidhardt, in which an excellent local cast[267] supported the Danish soprano Lone Koppel Winther as

[264] Covell, *The Sydney Morning Herald*, 31 January 1977.
[265] Cast: Elizabeth Connell (Lady Macbeth), John Shaw (Macbeth), Clifford Grant (Banquo), Reginald Byers and Lamberto Furlan (Macduff), Mary Jane Corderoy and Dolores Cambridge (Lady in Waiting), Paul Ferris and Anson Austin (Malcolm), Pieter van der Stolk (Dottore), Geoffrey Harris (Servant to Macbeth), Guido Martin, Kathleen Moore, Judith Saliba (Apparitions).
[266] Covell, *The Sydney Morning Herald*, 3 September 1977.
[267] Cast: Graeme Ewer and Anson Austin (Jaquino); Beryl Furlan and Cynthia Johnston (Marzelline); Neil Warren-Smith and Donald Shanks (Rocco); Lone Koppel Winther and Nance Grant (Leonore); John Shaw (Pizarro); Ronald Dowd (Florestan); Robert Allman and Grant Dixon (Don Fernando).

Leonore. She had moved to Australia and joined the company of the Australian Opera with her husband, John Winther, who was General Manager.

More controversial was the poor standard of the orchestral playing in this Melbourne season. *Fidelio* was singled out, particularly the horn obbligati in the treacherous first act 'Abscheulicher', but critics found fault elsewhere, too. However, they took care to exempt Cillario from blame, instead attributing the malaise to systemic problems that lay beyond the responsibility of a guest conductor.[268] While praising the 'spacious... sensitive... and precise' conducting of Cillario, John Sinclair observed that an orchestra's quality is determined by its administration, which no guest conductor can influence.[269] Felix Werder amplified such feelings:

> Conductor Carlo Felice Cillario laboured away at his Herculean task, but with each wrong intonation, with each faulty entry that he slaughtered, 10 rose up in its place. It was all a case of an orchestra that does not play together does not stay together, particularly when we had a pair of horns, ill winds that nobody blew good. Still, Cillario's fine musicianship and his vast experience as a man of the theatre, [were evident] in the way ... he nursed the singers through the accompaniments and in the way he indicated climaxes did, in the end produce more plus than minus.[270]

The crisis of faith in the orchestral management was such that Cillario was moved to reply to *The Age*:

> Sir,
>
> Melbourne critics have accused the Trust orchestra of poor form. They are right. Fidelio *is* symphonic theatre; Beethoven's music is so clear and truthful that it does not permit weakness or imperfections. I have often declared my keen interest in contributing to the building up of the

---

[268] By this time the Elizabethan Trust orchestra had split into separate Melbourne and Sydney entities, and Cillario was effectively a 'guest conductor' in Melbourne.

[269] John Sinclair, 'The decline of Fidelio,' *The Herald*, 25 April 1977.

[270] Werder, *The Age*, 25 April 1977.

Melbourne Elizabethan orchestra … [in which] we note, unfortunately, a deterioration. … I will try to enumerate the reasons for this alarming regress.

In 1976 the Trust was forced to take the disastrous step of sacking 12 players from each of the orchestras. The Melbourne horn section, for instance was reduced from five to four players, who now have to support the heavy load of all rehearsals and performances without any rest. This overwork reflects on the standard of performances. No other orchestra in the world is in such an incredible position.

Because of the small size of pits in Australia it is necessary to perform the great operas of Beethoven, Verdi and Wagner with half the normal number of strings. Therefore, all the players must be both outstanding and experienced. There are many superb young players in Australia, but not many of them are attracted to joining the Trust orchestras. Those that do frequently only make themselves available for one season. With players always changing, there is little possibility of establishing a rapport or developing the ensemble.

A resident conductor is vital in establishing the physiognomy of an orchestra. But here we have the singular situation of a resident conductor who is never asked to conduct his own orchestra.

The opening night of Fidelio was badly affected by the illness of a key player, and because of the petrol strike, a replacement could not be flown in from Sydney.

… It is about time that Australia, mother of so many great artists and a country with a public so evidently interested in artistic progress, took more seriously its responsibility for supporting adequately its opera orchestras, given that they are not only instruments of entertainment, but also of art and culture. CFC.[271]

By 1977, the Australian Opera was spreading its wings, both in terms of artistic ambitions and number of performances given;

---

[271] C.F. Cillario, 'Orchestra set an impossible task,' *The Age*, 30 April 1977.

the season was one of Cillario's busiest in Australia. Had he been the company's music director, some responsibility for orchestral deficiencies would likely have fallen on him, but as a guest conductor he was able to side-step any direct fallout and write with impunity about the issues that occurred behind the scenes. Musicians are usually wise to keep their counsel in the face of published criticism, but Cillario felt no such compunction. On the eve of conducting *Madama Butterfly* in Sydney, he had shared frank opinions with the journalist Maria Prerauer.

Prerauer began by asking Cillario: 'What is an international conductor like you doing in a place like this?' He replied that he loved Sydney, and loved the orchestra: 'so enthusiastic... I teach them tricks, yes, but *they* teach me also.' He noted the danger of becoming a specialised 'Herr Doktor' in a post in Europe, whereas Australia offered him the opportunity to maintain a broad repertoire, conducting Wagner, Mozart and Janáček, which he found 'more interesting'. The conversation turned to casting. 'Does he have a hand in casting his own operas here?' Cillario paused and covered his face. 'Er, sometimes, perhaps ...?' Prerauer asked him: 'Meaning not very often? He smiles and spreads his arms in a gesture that speaks louder than the words he does not say.'[272]

Cillario was more forthcoming on the lack of vocal talent. The Australian Opera was 'fast becoming a company without voices. Without *real*, large operatic voices. Where are the tenors?' ... All this miscasting! ... The Australian public accepts the wrong voices. They do not understand. In Italy you could not get away with it. The public would scream. They would riot.' Damning with faint praise, he observed: 'Here you have a company of good actors ... But where do we get the tenors? They do not grow on gumtrees.' And in a salvo at the administration, he remarked that he heard many fine tenors in Europe. 'I ask Australian Opera. Please, can I engage? But they do not trust. John Winther was just before in Europe: has no time.'

Even more rashly, Cillario moved on to the critics. He was particularly incensed when one of them accused him of not following the tempo of a certain singer. '"A critic not to know that

---

[272] Maria Prerauer, 'Hooked, Happy, High,' *The Australian*, 28 January 1977.

in opera the SINGER MUST FOLLOW THE CONDUCTOR!" he exclaims.' With the rant receding, Cillario turns the conversation towards soccer. "'Soccer was good for me, you see?" [273] he grins. "A violinist cannot play forever. And as a violinist I am now getting old. But as a conductor I am still a little baby.'" [274] There were no apparent repercussions from such candid reflections.

Earlier in the year Cillario had conducted *Parsifal* in concert: a momentous event for several reasons. The performance in Sydney was billed as the 'First Australian Concert Performance', on the basis of evidence that *Parsifal* may have been staged in the city around 1900. That particular date seems unlikely, given that the opera was not performed outside Bayreuth until New Year's Eve 1903.[275] *Parsifal* had been the last of Wagner's works to find a place in opera houses, not because of the scale and resources required, but because the composer had stipulated a ban on performances elsewhere as a means of securing a legacy for his wife Cosima and their children.

Parsifal in 1977 also marked the first occasion on which the Australian Opera presented a late work of Wagner's in its new home. The project brought together several institutions: the Australian Opera, the ABC, the Sydney Symphony Orchestra, Sydney Philharmonia Choirs and the Sydney Grammar School Choir (led by Peter Seymour). The cast, too, was local, [276] except for the American bass Reid Bunger as Klingsor. [277] This collaboration between the

---

[273] He was referring to breaking his wrist during a soccer game in c1942, after which he turned to conducting.

[274] See FN 272.

[275] The first 'performance' of *Parsifal* in Australia was probably the radio broadcast of 1936, with the work given in three parts, on 7, 9 and 10 April. See A. Gyger, 'Opera in the Antipodes' (1990), 331.

[276] Cast: John Shaw (Amfortas), Alan Light (Titurel), Donald Shanks (Gurnemanz), Ronald Dowd (Parsifal), Reid Bunger (Klingsor), Lone Koppel Winther (Kundry), Sandra Hahn (Alto Solo). Geoffrey Harris, John Germain (Two Grail Knights), Judith Saliba, Kathleen Moore, Henri Wilden, Jonathan Hughes (Four Squires), Rhonda Bruce, Dolores Cambridge, Jennifer Lindfield, Kathleen Moore, Judith Saliba, Amanda Thane (Six Flower Maidens).

[277] A regular guest with the Vienna State Opera.

opera company and the ABC was influential in establishing a 'house style' of collaboration for larger-scale works.

It did not go unnoticed among the critical fraternity that, four years after the opening of the Sydney Opera House, Wagner was finally being presented not in the Opera Theatre but the Concert Hall. David Ahern anticipated the event as a 'half-hearted though well-intentioned substitute' given Wagner's ambition to create a synthesis between music, drama and décor.[278] Under the headline 'The good points of a bad idea', Roger Covell shared his scepticism in advance of *Parsifal* in concert form, but conceded that it could be a stepping-stone towards full-scale Australian Opera-ABC collaboration in late Wagner (which finally took place with *Tristan und Isolde* 13 years later).[279]

Maria Prerauer represented the reservations of several other critics who were concerned that the 'length of *Parsifal*, without the benefit of a staged production to scaffold it, may result in boredom among audiences ... akin to witnessing a live recording that could not be switched off'.[280] Audiences as well as critics were wary of the scale of Wagner's works, not least due to lack of familiarity. The use of the Concert Hall inevitably drew attention back to the much-publicised flaws of the Opera Theatre. The building of the Opera House had attracted relentless publicity, good and bad, with updates regularly posted on the front pages of national newspapers. Now that it was complete and the issues with the finished structure had been quantified, each new venture within the building became a subject of public controversy. The period leading up to the *Parsifal* performance was an example of this.

It was Cillario, more than any other individual, who turned scepticism to success. Presented with an opportunity that no European house had afforded him, he ignored the squabbles, wrote no further letters of protest, and immersed himself in the profound beauty of Wagner's last music-drama. '*Parsifal* is a mysterious work. The music is a dangerous drug, a heavenly narcotic. One needs a great

[278] David Ahern, *The Sunday Telegraph*, 10 April 1977.
[279] Covell, *The Sydney Morning Herald*, 4 April 1977.
[280] Prerauer, *The Australian*, 4 July 1977.

deal of preparation for *Parsifal*,' he said.[281] The performances were a great success, mainly due to the absolute musical commitment and expertise of the conductor. David Ahern was mollified by the result: 'From a musical point of view, this surrogate' flowed with supreme ease of direction, shape and architecture under the guiding hand of conductor Carlo Felice Cillario. It was a wise choice that the joint produc[ers] (ABC and Australian Opera) made when they engaged Cillario, for he is eminently able to provide a complete overview of the work.'[282] Among the cast, Ahern singled out the 'veteran singer Ronald Dowd' for particular praise in the title role.

Roger Covell was generally positive about the vocal performances, without singling out anyone in particular. His praise was reserved for the conductor:

> The first was the playing of the Sydney Symphony Orches-tra under the direction of Carlo Felice Cillario. No one would have [previously] assumed that Mr Cillario was a Wagnerian Conductor; but, as with everything he does, he brought skill, insight, enthusiasm and sympathy to bear on the score, with memorable results.' 'This was not among the slowest of Parsifals (I make no complaint about that) but neither was it rushed or unidiomatic. ...
>
> The music maintained propulsion without sacrificing its innate tendency towards contemplation and rumination. The moulding of the brass and woodwind ensemble, the phrasing and terracing of string dynamics were both firm and sensitive. The climaxes had power without blare. Only at the very beginning of the performance did Cillario seem inclined to flatten out dynamic contrasts.[283]

Fred Blanks echoed these sentiments when he wrote that the per-formance 'was as grand as could be imagined ... Cillario conduct-ing with tremendous verve, intensity and authority', and the Sydney Symphony Orchestra 'thoroughly rehearsed'. Reid Bunger 'showed

---

[281] Amadio, '*Parsifal*: at last we can see Wagner's dynamic "farewell"', *The Finan-cial Review*, 25 February 1977.

[282] Ahern, *The Sunday Telegraph*, 10 April 1977.

[283] Covell, *The Sydney Morning Herald*, 4 April 1977.

off a big voice full of dramatically apt malice', Donald Shanks, as Gurnemanz was 'sonorous', Ronald Dowd's Parsifal 'sometimes slightly underweight' and Lone Koppel Winther created 'a sultry, emotionally plausible Kundry.'[284] Imhof lavished praise on

> the magnificent playing of the orchestra and the dynamic and impressive conducting of Cillario. He seemed to be completely at home with Wagner's difficult score and while his tempi were on the fast side, it helped to increase the tension of the drama.[285]

Maria Prerauer, who had been so concerned about the length of the work, ate her words:

> What took place was a minor miracle. And there can be no doubt at all that the chief perpetrator was … Cillario. Through his masterly and passionate involvement, it was suddenly all there. His baton somehow seemed to paint with brilliance and splendour even the visual colour and spectacle of this grandiose medieval mystery play…. The Sydney Symphony Orchestra responded superbly, providing a vast canvas of sizzling instrumental sound. So overwhelming was the illusion that you could actually see the ritual, the ceremonial processions, the Round Table, the knights and the Holy Grail they guarded, as well as the magician Klingsor's evil garden stocked with seductive flower-maidens. Apparently, this was only our second *Parsifal* since the turn of the century or so. Will it take as long again before we get it on stage at last?[286]

Prerauer's plea seemed finally set for fulfilment in the Sydney summer season of 1993, when a stage production of *Parsifal* was planned under Cillario's baton. Budgetary issues caused the project to be abandoned and replaced by a revival of *Tristan und Isolde*.[287] The 1977 *Parsifal* had consolidated Cillario's credentials

---

[284] Blanks, *The Australian Jewish Times* (Sydney), 14 April 1977.

[285] Imhof, *The Australian Jewish Times* (Sydney), 22 April 1977.

[286] Prerauer, *The Australian*, 4 July 1977.

[287] For more detail, see: Oxenbould (2005), 570–71. As of 2023, Opera Australia has not yet presented a staging of *Parsifal*, with its most recent performance (again in concert) taking place in 2017.

as a 'Wagner conductor' in Australia, an epithet not easily earned. It was recognised that with the Sydney Symphony Orchestra, and a favourable acoustic, the conductor could produce results of the highest artistic quality. It also revealed that he possessed a profound inner grasp of Wagner's compositional processes. The energy he unleashed in the pit when conducting Italian melodramas, at times bordering on the manic, could be harnessed, and refined, to realise a complex and subtle architectural structure that conveyed a sense of truth and rightness in one of the most complex and elusive works of the operatic canon.

To complete his Germanic assignments in 1977, Cillario conducted a new production of *Der fliegende Holländer*, directed by Peter Peterson and designed by Søren Frandsen in the Sydney winter season. The company's only previous forays into Wagner were *Holländer* from a decade earlier, *Tannhäuser* in 1968, and a *Lohengrin* production in 1958. The 'new' *Holländer* was, in fact, a reworking by Peterson of a Bayreuth production created by Wieland Wagner, which had been adapted by the Royal Danish Opera, before being brought to Australia by John Winther. The production met with a mixed reception and was reported as 'far from an unqualified success'[288] as boos mingled with applause on the opening night. The two casts were excellent, with the qualities of the alternating Sentas (Lone Koppel Winther and Nance Grant) and Holländers (Robert Allman and Raymond Myers) being enthusiastically compared and discussed. The singing was uniformly well received.[289] There was no doubt as to the quality of the music direction:

> With Carlo Felice at the helm, the performance is tremendously exciting. The orchestra shudders and rages as tempests break out in the woodwinds and strings, and all hell is set loose. Yet the sound remains wonderfully clear, the speeds are perfectly balanced and the rhythms clean-cut.[290]

---

[288] Hoffmann, *The Canberra Times*, 15 September 1977.

[289] Cast: Neil Warren-Smith and Donald Shanks (Daland), Lone Koppel Winther and Nance Grant (Senta), Ronald Dowd and Robin Donald (Erik), Rosina Raisbeck and Lesley Stender (Mary), Anson Austin and Geoffrey Harris (Steuermann), Robert Allman and Raymond Myers (Holländer).

[290] Prerauer, 'Bon voyage, Dutchman,' *The Australian*, 3 September 1976.

In another review, Prerauer notes that 'the real hero remains the conductor Carlo Felice Cillario, whose brilliant direction results in a musical voyage that is never less than exciting, sometimes spine-chillingly terrifying and always in the finest *echt* Wagnerian mode.'[291] Brian Hoad found the production to be 'both exceptionally gloomy and exceptionally enlightening'. He noted the significance of a Bayreuth staging being seen in Australia, lending a sense of Wagnerian authenticity to the experience.[292] Roger Covell remarked that because

> the action ... has been stripped to tableaux, the attention focused on the orchestra is ... greater than usual. Under Carlo Felice Cillario's well-judged and impassioned direction, it survives this scrutiny more creditably than I had dared to hope and the conductor's masterful instinct fuels the whole performance.[293]

This was not Cillario's first foray into the world of the *Holländer*. He had conducted an Italian staging ('*Il Vascello fantasma*') a few years earlier in Bergamo. His formidable energy and mastery of the score drove the musical force of this production and the quality of the orchestral sound he created was recognised by all. *Holländer* is the work of a composer who was yet to master the orchestra in the sense that he reveals his art in the later music dramas, and it requires a deft hand and mind to recreate the sound world of the first work of the Bayreuth canon.

The 1977 season was a landmark year for Cillario in Australia. He undertook an enormous workload, created two new productions, and revealed new facets of his musical personality to audiences. He conducted three seminal works of the German canon, each posing their own interpretative challenges, all of which he solved admirably. Cillario was recognised as a force within the company, not just in his own 'signature' repertoire (which had long been undisputed) but as a searching interpreter of German repertoire and Wagner

[291] Prerauer, 'Double Dutchman,' *The Australian*, 12 September 1971.
[292] Brian Hoad, A Dutchman with its colour flying,' *The Bulletin* 10 September 1977.
[293] Covell, *The Sydney Morning Herald*, 2 September 1977.

in particular. Writing of the success of the 1977 summer season, David Malouf declared that 'a good deal of that is due to Carlo Felice Cillario's vigorous and uncompromising direction from the pit.'[294] Later in the year, Nadine Amadio reported that Cillario 'has been an important part of the recent rapid growth of the Australian Opera and he has conducted 14 major productions over the last eight years.'[295]

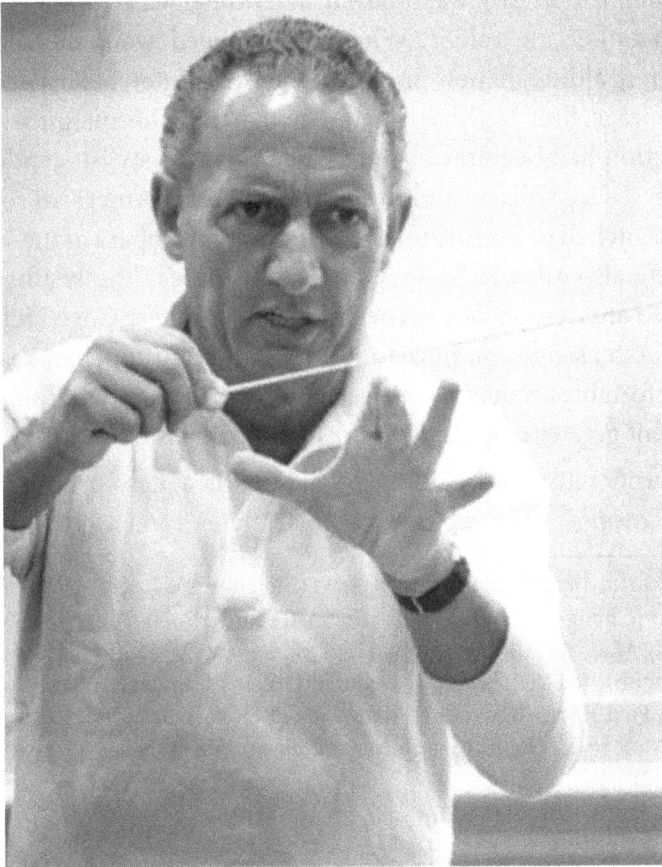

12: Cillario at work, 1977.

In 1978, Cillario conducted five productions, three of which were revivals from the previous season. The *Holländer* was given in Melbourne, with one significant change of cast – Donald Smith as

---

[294] David Malouf, *The National Times*, 21–26 February 1977.
[295] Amadio, *The Financial Review*, 26 August 1977.

Erik, 'at his Verdian best ... strong, positive singing.'[296] For *Macbeth* in Melbourne, Elizabeth Fretwell undertook took the role of Lady Macbeth,[297] in a performance of 'dramatic conviction' which Cillario 'conducted impeccably, with nicely-judged tempos and scrupulous care for the balance of voices and orchestra.'[298] It was noted that this was the first performance of *Macbeth* in Melbourne since 1964, and the best production of the current season.'[299]

Madama Butterfly was revived in Sydney, with Leona Mitchell reprising the title role.[300] What had changed were the sets and costumes; although new in 1977, they had later been destroyed in a storage fire. Nadine Amadio noted that the integrity of the production had been preserved by 'the superbly stylish conducting of Carlo Felice Cillario and the casting of young American soprano Leona Mitchell in the title role.'[301] As the opening opera of the season, *Butterfly* also allowed Sydney audiences to hear the results of an enlarged and remodelled orchestra pit which Roger Covell reported sent 'a better string and horn tone into the auditorium, to reveal with uncomfortable accuracy some eccentricities in woodwind solos and to permit greater emphasis for brass and percussion.'[302]

Cillario returned again to Mozart with a new production of *Don Giovanni*, directed by George Ogilvie[303] and cast with local

---

[296] Glickfield, *The Australian Jewish News* (Melbourne), 7 April 1978.

[297] Cast: [Changes from previous season are underlined.] Elizabeth Fretwell (Lady Macbeth), Robert Allman and John Shaw (Macbeth), Clifford Grant (Banquo), Reginald Byers (Macduff), Dolores Cambridge (Lady in Waiting), Paul Ferris (Malcolm), Pieter van der Stolk (Dottore), Luciano Borghi (Servant to Macbeth), Guido Martin, Dawn Walsh, Helga Willis-Golding (Apparitions).

[298] Sinclair, *The Herald* (Melbourne), 12 April 1978.

[299] Ibid.

[300] Cast. Leona Mitchell (Cio-Cio-San), Jennifer Bermingham (Suzuki), Lamberto Furlan (B.F. Pinkerton), Robert Allman (Sharpless), Gordon Wilcock (Goro), Gregory Yurisich (Yamadori), Joseph Grunfelder (Bonze), Rosemary Gunn (Kate Pinkerton), Robert Eddie (Imperial Commissioner), Trevor Brown (Registrar).

[301] Amadio, *The Financial Review*, 16 June 1978.

[302] Covell, *The Sydney Morning Herald*, 16 June 1978.

[303] With whom he had previously collaborated on a production of *The Abduction from the Seraglio*.

Mozartian singers.[304] This production also toured to Newcastle, the only occasion on which Cillario conducted in that city.

Opportunities to conduct Mozart were always special occasions for Cillario. He recalled an encounter with the conductor Josef Krips, a renowned Mozartian:

> One morning I poked my nose into the theatre while he [Krips] was rehearsing Masetto's "Batti batti" with the orchestra alone; and I was surprised that such a grumpy-looking man could obtain such a seductive result from the crawling cellos and tender violas. The accompaniment alone created Zerlina's magic without the need for voice and words.
>
> When we met following the rehearsal, I told him this and he, finally fixing his eyes at my face, asked me: "Do you love Mozart?" I answered something I had thought in some moments of the highest Mozartian ecstasy: "Maestro Krips: one of the main reasons why I will be sorry to die – if it is true that one must – is the lack of certainty that Mozart's music exists in the afterlife."
>
> He collected himself for a moment and said: "I thought this too. I am older than you. If I die first, I'll let you know." He smiled and the ice was broken.[305]

Cillario's repertoire in 1977 also included a double bill that he conducted around the world with great success, and yet which elicited from him the most contradictory expressions of love and hate: *Cav & Pag*. The original production was created by Stephen Hall and designed by Desmond Digby, and the cast[306] was not short

---

[304] Cast: John Pringle (Don Giovanni), Clifford Grant (The Commendatore), Nance Grant (Donna Anna), Henri Wilder (Don Ottavio), Margreta Elkins (Donna Elvira), Neil Warren-Smith (Leporello), Gregory Yurisich (Masetto), Jennifer Bermingham (Zerlina).

[305] From an unpublished memoir.

[306] Cast: *Cavalleria Rusticana*: Elizabeth Fretwell (Santuzza), Kathleen Moore (Lola), Rosina Raisbeck (Mamma Lucia), Robin Donald and Reginald Byers (Turiddu), Neville Wilkie (Alfio). *I pagliacci*: Etela Piha (Nedda), Donald Smith (Canio), John Shaw (Tonio), Paul Ferris (Beppe), Gregory Yurisich (Silvio), Anthony Clark and Guido Martin (2 Villagers).

of large personalities. In *Cavalleria,* revived by Bernd Benthaak, Elizabeth Fretwell was praised for her portrayal of Santuzza, and the much-loved Rosina Raisbeck was acknowledged in reviews for her cameo performance of Mamma Lucia.

However, the tenor Robin Donald was forced to withdraw due to illness at the last minute, and Reginald Byers stepped in to sing Turiddu. According to Nadine Amadio, the 'not particularly inspired' *Cavalleria* production was 'saved only by the warm and illuminating conducting of Cillario and the playing of the Elizabethan Sydney Orchestra.'[307] The set toppled over at one point, and Byers suffered memory lapses which marred the opening night. John Carmody was more enthusiastic about the production: 'Ably encouraged by Carlo Cillario, the orchestra put plenty of the right spirit into their playing and ... Cillario's professionalism held everything together admirably through all of the anxiety of the last pages of *Cavalleria,* when Byers' memory began to rebel.' [308] Revived by Elke Neidhardt, *Pagliacci* received stronger praise for a 'very different standard of performance' and both Donald Smith and John Shaw were well reviewed. Nadine Amadio remarked that Cillario was the unifying force behind the evening.[309]

Cillario seems to have relished these moments of unpredictable, unplanned drama. He was certainly adept at recognising them in the nick of time and turning them around in the spirit of 'the show must go on'. *Cav & Pag* was regarded as core repertoire for the conductor; ironically so, given his strong and contradictory feelings towards the double bill.

---

[307] Amadio, 'Bravos for a conductor', *The Financial Review*, 29 September 1978.
[308] Carmody, *The National Times*, week ending 7 October 1978.
[309] See FN 307.

Ballabile

13. Carlo Felice Cillario at the Sydney Opera House for the *Cav & Pag* season, 1978.

Cav & Pag – 'Che cosa brutta'

Cillario entertained strong, if conflicted feelings about *verismo* in general, and the perennially popular pairing of Mascagni and Leoncavallo in particular. 'If I was Minister for Culture in Italy, I would do something like Hitler. I would put '*Cav*' and '*Pag*' in the street and burn the scores.' He admitted to 'a love-hate relationship with the double bill: he loves to say [that] he hates to conduct it.'[310]

Conduct it he did, however, at the frequent invitation of theatres across the world. He explained his feelings at greater length to Bruce Duffie in 1982.

---

[310] Michael Shmith, 'Some even hate the cause of their fame,' *The Age* (Melbourne), 9 May 1988.

Many times I discussed this with my father. He loved everything in music. ... But he loved especially Wagner, and
also Verdi and Puccini. We had terrible fights because I said
verismo style opera is dead. Mascagni's music was smelling
too much of onion and Leoncavallo was mediocre. He said
that I must be mediocre because they are two great composers. They are successful. ... so then I was forced to accept *Cav & Pag* because Madrid offered me a lot of opera[s]
with just two performances of each [*Cav & Pag*] ... [if I did
not accept all] they would call another conductor. ... So, I
sent a cable to my father, "At last I will conduct *Cavalleria*,"
and the answer of my father ... was "Poor Mascagni!"[311]

Later in the same interview, he warmed to the double bill:

I was talking against *Pagliacci*, and often I have been trying
to discover which was worse – *Cavalleria* or *Pagliacci*?
Working with them both, honestly, I think *Cavalleria*
is superior, yes. But when I was conducting *Pagliacci*
with a great cast of singers at the Met – [Richard Tucker,
Cornell MacNeil, Teresa Stratas, Zeffirelli production] ...
I discovered that *Pagliacci* can be better than *Cavalleria*![312]

Listening to a Karajan recording of *Cavalleria* again took him
unawares:

I try to listen to Karajan because he is a real genius. [With]
Cavalleria, he surprised me, because I didn't believe that he
was interested in that work. I thought he was much better
if he was conducting more works like *Parsifal*. ... But he
conducted the best *Cavalleria* that was ever performed. He
transformed *Cavalleria* in[to] a masterpiece of Romantic
music that even Mascagni couldn't believe could be so
good![313]

Cillario admitted that when performing these works himself 'you
know that when we are involved, then I like them, because they are
masterpieces in their way.... During the performance I am very

---

[311] Cillario and Duffie, *Interview*, 1982.

[312] Ibid.

[313] Ibid.

excited. I must be, otherwise … it's better not to conduct it.'[314] The intensity of his performances radiated a conviction in the heat of the moment which tended to cool off in the cold light of day.

Matters were not helped by the fact that for the runs of *Cav & Pag* there were serious casting issues, which Cillario had flagged to the management. He summed up his feelings about the season:

> I am forced to confirm the opinion that I already had before the premiere … the reality is even worse than my expectation. In my opinion we haven't the right cast for this opera. After such a disastrous experience, I suggest that this opera should not be performed until a suitable cast is found.[315]

He held to his position, saying that he would not conduct *Cav & Pag* unless there were suitable singers. During this period in the '70's, he would forthrightly refuse to conduct productions unless he was in agreement with the casting. He also wanted the operas to be double cast as a surety. In 1979, he wrote further to Peter Hemmings stating that during *Cavalleria* performances, he felt 'like a torero fighting against 5 BULLS!'[316]

Later in life Cillario held firm to his stated antipathy. A 1987 interview opens with the bold declaration: 'I'd like to burn the scores of all those *verismo* operas!' This comment was made to the accompaniment of the conductor thumping a score of Puccini's 'cloying' *Suor Angelica* and continued: 'I hate these operas … ears bitten off in the street! I like my real life and my opera to be kept separate.' *Cav & Pag* and the Puccini canon were consigned to an inferior category of 'entertainment', which he admitted also applied to some works of Donizetti. [317]

Cillario consistently held up Mozart as an ideal, an antipode to *verismo*: 'I hate, really, *verismo*, especially starting with *Pagliacci*

---

[314] Ibid.

[315] Cillario to Hemmings, 6 October 1978. Carlo Felice Cillario – Artist Files '1', Opera Australia Library archives.

[316] Cillario to Hemmings, 1978 (no date). Carlo Felice Cillario – Artist Files '1', Opera Australia Library archives.

[317] Carmody, *The Sydney Morning Herald*, 6 October 1987.

and *Cavalleria Rusticana*. I don't say Puccini because Puccini was an opera composer. But I am a Mozart lover, so I cannot accept people on stage biting ears and making funny things that destroy the music.'[318] Even *Tosca*, drew a stinging remark: 'I hate it – yes you can say that. It is the opera that gave me fortune. I have conducted the *Tosca* of the century, at Covent Garden with Callas, and recently with [Montserrat] Caballé and [Luciano] Pavarotti at the Met. Now everyone calls me for *Tosca*. I say I prefer to go to Australia, where they give me other things – Mozart, Wagner....'[319]

Much of this posturing was aimed to provide the press with entertaining copy and was an expression of the conductor's ironic and often bizarre sense of humour. He rarely spoke about personal affairs or matters beyond his musical and professional work. He cultivated the image of the 'maestro', as practiced by Italian conductors of an older generation and exemplified by Arturo Toscanini.

By contrast, the star singers that visited Australia were generally open to sharing aspects of their lives with the press. Tito Gobbi spoke of his grandchildren, and his pride on being crowned 'King of Moomba'. Cillario used quips and distractions to turn the course of an interview when the line of questioning came too close to home. At work he revealed to his colleagues a restlessly enquiring mind, and broad musical culture. He disliked being typecast and he had a horror of routine: he never took 'anything for granted and never presumed to have a fixed view of any score, no matter how familiar.'[320]

The author recalls assisting Cillario during a run of *La traviata* in 2001, one of the conductor's last productions. The cast of singers was well known to him, and it could have been a relaxed season. But Cillario was not inclined to take things easy. He constantly interrogated the score, looking for new ways of shaping phrases, new places to breathe, new colours, to the frequent bewilderment of several cast members. He was concerned to avoid allowing this

[318] Ibid.

[319] Shmith, *The Age* (Melbourne), 9 May 1988.

[320] Oxenbould, *Carlo Felice Cillario and Opera Australia*, 2003.

canonic work, with which he undoubtedly had a great affinity, to become stale, and he maintained this stance until his final performance.

One might see Cillario's musical career as falling into two parts, divided at some point in 1942, when he broke his wrist playing football in Odesa. Hitherto, he had built a career as a violinist, with the rewards of competition prizes, concert engagements across Italy and farther afield, and a recording contract with HMV. He was also composing and was, in all respects, a very serious-minded concert artist. Later in life, however, he maintained that 'opera was his first love',[321] and recalled playing from a piano score of *Die Walküre* as a child.[322]

Cillario struggled with the paradox of opera encompassing both serious music-drama and entertainment. On some level, he felt that his career as an opera conductor was at odds with his idealised concept of music as 'high art', with its epitome in the works of Mozart. He masked this in public by playing the clown when questioned on such matters.[323] The Australian poet and novelist David Malouf once succeeded in glimpsing behind the mask, when he persuaded Cillario to consider the nature of opera. The final paragraphs of his interview, 'Cillario the Aristocrat', are worth quoting in full:

> Opera tries to please many tastes, but it is also an art and demands the highest possible standards of us. This is something I feel very strongly about. There is a word you use in English that I hate very much when it is translated into Italian: entertainment (*divertimento, passatempo*). It makes me sick to hear some great work like Parsifal or The Magic Flute called an entertainment. If people go to an exhibition of Van Gough or to see a Giotto or a Fra Angelico in a church they don't talk about entertainment.

---

[321] For example: Malouf, *The National Times*, 12–17 July 1976.

[322] See memoir 'Art in the Heart' (Appendix 7).

[323] In Australia, at this time, journalists from diverse areas (particularly sport) could be sent to interview arts figures. Often the reviews were unsatisfactory, and Cillario would have been one of the more challenging interviewees for the uninitiated. In situations where he felt ill at ease, he would typically employ humour to enliven the exchanges.

I like to think of what Bach used to write at the end of his compositions – and Handel and Haydn too: 'For the Glory of God and the Elevation of the Human Spirit.'

Well, I won't speak about God for the moment, but the second part of that phrase must be the goal of every artist, composer or interpreter, but also the goal of the public as well. Of course, the public is composed of people who have been working all day and they may be tired and not in an ideal mood for listening to a masterpiece. But really, they must be if they are to enjoy the sort of art that requires something of them as well.[324]

Cillario was a deeply serious musician, with a strong feeling of responsibility to his muse, be it comic or serious. His notion of art and its place in society was deeply Central European in its outlook and aligns with the German concept of *Bildung*. Aside from his inconstant thoughts on their musical qualities, he held a lasting distaste for the brutality and violence ('ears bitten off in the street') which are central to both *Cav & Pag* and equally much of the *verismo* canon, such as Puccini's *Tosca* and *Il tabarro*. He even insisted on the distribution of a leaflet, addressed to the audience of *Cav & Pag* when he conducted it in Melbourne, which stated his pacifist position on these works.

As a pragmatic man of the theatre, however, Cillario well understood the place of such works within the repertoire. Despite his reservations, he was highly regarded as a pre-eminent interpreter of *verismo* opera, and of Puccini in particular.

---

[324] Malouf, 'Cillario the Aristocrat,' *The National Times*, 12–17 July 1976.

Scene 2

The double bill of *Cav & Pag* was repeated in Melbourne the following year, with almost the same cast, but now with Elke Neidhardt as stage director for both works. In Melbourne and Brisbane, Cillario also conducted *La bohème* in a production both designed and staged by Tom Lingwood. The cast was led by Joan

14: Carlo Felice Cillario, dress rehearsal for *Madama Butterfly*, June 1978.

Carden as Mimì[325] and Lamberto Furlan as Rodolfo, who got off to a bad start, with an announcement before Act 3 on the first night requesting indulgence for an indisposition. John Pringle and the other bohemians attracted praise, and the orchestra played well, but was found overwhelming due to the Palais Theatre's unsuitability for opera.[326] Peter Burch commented, 'Carlo Felice Cillario conducted the Elizabethan Melbourne Orchestra with his customary intelligence and sensitivity, not rushing the singers, but allowing the music to expand.'[327]

The *Butterfly*[328] of the previous year was also revived in Melbourne, with Ron Stevens replacing Lamberto Furlan as Pinkerton, and Joan Carden as Cio-Cio-San, in which she enjoyed a great success. Robert Allman (Sharpless) and Jennifer Bermingham (Suzuki) won praise; only Stevens failed to receive positive reviews. A restaging of the ending by an assistant producer was felt to have weakened the original production. Critics were unanimous in their appreciation of the musical leadership, with Cillario described as 'exemplary',[329] and 'exceptional'.[330]

The 1977 *Fidelio* production was due to be revived in the Sydney summer season, until the sets went up in flames in a storeroom fire during 1978, a disaster from which an opportunity arose to present the work in the Concert Hall, following the successful precedents of *Aida* and *Parsifal* in the same venue. Cillario spoke

---

[325] Cast: Lamberto Furlan (Rodolfo), Joan Carden and Beryl Furlan (Mimì), John Pringle (Marcello), Etela Piha (Musetta), Clifford Grant and Grant Dixon (Colline), Gregory Yurisich (Schaunard), John Germain (Benoit), Alan Light (Alcindoro), Grahame Macfarlane (Parpignol), Gregory Martin (Customs Sergeant), Donald Solomon (Customs Officer).

[326] Hince, *The Australian*, 14 March 1979.

[327] Peter Burch, *The Australian* (Melbourne), 15 March 1979.

[328] Cast: Joan Carden and Elizabeth Tippett (Cio-Cio-San), Jennifer Bermingham (Suzuki), Ron Stevens (B.F. Pinkerton), Robert Allman and Ronald Maconaghie (Sharpless), Gordon Wilcock (Goro), Pieter van der Stolk (Yamadori), Joseph Grunfelder (Bonze), Rosemary Gunn (Kate Pinkerton), Robert Eddie (Commissario Imperiale), Kevin Mills (Uffiziale del Registro).

[329] Sinclair, *The Herald* (Melbourne), 23 April 1979.

[330] Cargher, *The National Times*, 23 April 1979.

with Romola Constantino, expressing his enthusiasm for the project which will

> enable him to give the importance he believes is owing to the musical side of Beethoven's opera. He says that *Fidelio* is not a grand opera which needs the Concert Hall for size, but, he feels, it needs it for sound, more than any other opera. He considers that the combination of *Fidelio* and the Concert Hall will give him his most valuable challenge since he began conducting in Australia 10 years ago – the big 1977 *Parsifal* concert performance notwithstanding.[331]

In Cillario's own words: '*Fidelio* is a perfect opera, although many hold that Beethoven was not an operatic composer.' He noted that 'it is sometimes unjustly called a conductor's opera ... that fault may lie with a tradition started by Mahler, who added *Leonora* Overture No 3.' Cillario did not follow suit: 'he believes that Beethoven's final decisions make a perfectly proportioned opera.' Performing the overture, he said, 'causes the audience to clap madly, but it destroys the balance, stealing the thunder from the last scene.' In the Concert Hall, the orchestra would be placed in the full view of the audience:

> For Cillario, this is an opportunity, with the hall's favour-able acoustics, to give greater measure to the sound quali-ties he considers are the vital link with the philosophical and moral spirit of the opera, so important to Beethoven. ... Beethoven's sound, he thinks is the most mysterious of any composers ... and the unspoken profundities of his instrumental music were expressed most explicitly in his much-laboured opera.[332]

He continued:

> I am looking at times, for a certain harshness and percus-siveness – even in the vocal and chorus parts. This is not easy-flowing Mozart, or Italian *bel canto*. It has a character of its own.... The sound of a composer, the sound of an

---

[331] Constantino, 'Cillario against the wind,' *The Sydney Morning Herald*, 13 January 1979.

[332] Ibid.

epoch – it's like a taste, you cannot define it precisely, but you know it.[333]

A semi-staging was created by the original producer, Bernd Benthaak, amounting to 'almost an acted oratorio on a few flights of stairs.'[334] There were two notable cast changes from 1977 – Marilyn Richardson stepped into the role of Leonore, and Donald Smith the role of Florestan.[335] One critic described their performances together as 'memorable'.[336] Others were less convinced. Romola Constantino praised Smith for his 'ample ringing sound' while noting that his German was 'incomprehensible.'[337] John Carmody concurred with that assessment and found further fault with Richardson as Leonore and John Shaw as Don Pizarro, granting Donald Shanks the distinction of having given the finest performance as Rocco. Carmody found the ensembles frequently inaudible and wrote that *Fidelio* is a *Singspiel* 'and therefore should have been given in English. What most of the cast produced did quite as much violence to the original relationship of words and music as any English translation could possibly have done.'[338]

Overall, the 'spirited performance of the orchestra under the baton of Carlo Felice Cillario' was of the highest order. It was noted that the male chorus had improved 'out of sight' since the 1977 season.[339] Carmody found that Cillario presented a more 'relaxed' approach to the score than that of Georg Tintner, 'whose hard-driven performance of a few years ago was far more compelling.' According to Maria Prerauer:

The Elizabethan Orchestra, freed from the chains of the

---

[333] Ibid.

[334] Constantino, *The Sydney Morning Herald*, 15 January 1979.

[335] Cast: Anson Austin (Jaquino), Glenys Fowles and Beryl Furlan (Marzelline), Donald Shanks (Rocco), Marilyn Richardson (Leonore), John Shaw (Don Pizarro), Donald Smith (Florestan), Robert Allman (Don Fernando), Sergei Baigildin and Eric Badcock (Prisoners 1 and 2).

[336] 'E.C.', *The Australian Jewish Times* (Sydney), 1 February 1979.

[337] Constantino, *The Sydney Morning Herald*, 15 January 1979.

[338] Carmody, *The National Times*, 3 February 1979

[339] References in this paragraph are from: 'E.S.', *The Australian Jewish Times* (Sydney), 1 February 1979.

poky pit in the smaller Opera Theatre, was completely transfigured, playing as it rarely has before. Conductor Carlo Felice Cillario, proving once more that he is as much a master of the German as of the Italian repertoire, led them as though inspired. Under him, the music, full of fire and fervour, also pointed to the stars.[340]

In 1979, Cillario also led a significant new staging of *La fanciulla del West*. Due in part to its scale, *Fanciulla* has never won a lasting place in the repertoire of most opera houses, but Australian audiences have always responded to the goldrush theme which belongs to their history as much as the California of the opera's setting.[341] That sense of scale arises from the quasi-Wagnerian demands made upon its three principals as well as a large cast of supporting roles, which allowed the company to showcase its ensemble. An earlier staging of *Fanciulla* had been in the repertoire of the Elizabethan Trust Opera Company when Cillario made his Australian debut in 1968, but he had not conducted it. For this new staging Robin Lovejoy was the director and Tom Lingwood the designer with the production being widely admired at its premiere in Melbourne. The cast was world-class, led by Donald Smith as Dick Johnson, John Shaw as Jack Rance and Marilyn Zschau as Minnie.[342]

One review praised the company for having 'taken a second-rate opera and turned it into a first-rate musical and theatrical experience.' Nevertheless, 'it was the Elizabethan Melbourne Orchestra under Cillario that was the star of the evening – Puccini's star – and the playing they produced was vital and ravishing.'[343] Moffatt Oxenbould

---

[340] Prerauer, '*Fidelio* emerges from the ashes,' *The Australian*, 15 January 1979.

[341] The cast includes an Australian miner, who was apparently trying his luck in California after failing at home: 'Happy' is referred to as 'Australiano d'inferno' during Act 1.

[342] Cast: Marilyn Zschau (Minnie), Donald Smith (Dick Johnson), John Shaw (Jack Rance), Graeme Ewer (Nick), Neil Warren-Smith (Ashby), Ronald Maconaghie (Sonora), Robert Gard (Trin), Neville Wilkie (Sid), Lyndon Terracini (Bello), Robin Donald (Harry), Gordon Wilcock (Joe), Robert Eddie (Happy), Gregory Yurisich (Larkens), Erik Badcock (Billy Jackrabbit), Kathleen Moore (Wowkle), Bruce Martin and Raymond Myers (Jack Wallace), Pieter van der Stolk (José Castro), Graeme Macfarlane (Un postiglione).

[343] Glickfield, *The Australian Jewish News* (Melbourne), 25 May 1979.

has written that 'Cillario was also in his element and lavished all his experience on the wonderful score.'[344] When the project was first suggested to him, in early 1978, Cillario's enthusiasm had been palpable, and he had written to Oxenbould with a typically impish request: 'Something very important. If you choose the GIRL, you must promise that we will have HORSES onstage. In my opinion in such an opera they are more important than ELEPHANTS in AIDA (or conductor in Parsifal).'[345] The production was later received with similar enthusiasm in Sydney.

This *Fanciulla* marked Marilyn Zschau's debut with the company. She had stepped in at short notice to replace Carol Neblett, who at that time was regarded as the world's leading exponent of the role of Minnie.[346] 'Miss Zschau let go with an all-stops-out performance. She has a big, finely projected voice, and took plenty of risks, most of which came off brilliantly.'[347] Donald Smith had sung Dick Johnson in the 1968 production, and on this occasion his performance had 'the same ease and appeal'. John Shaw was 'as mean as hell' as the sheriff Jack Rance. He 'gave credibility to the role, substance to its sorrowful jealousy, and even a measure of dignity in his Act 1 solo "Minnie dalla mia casa"'. The male chorus of the Australian Opera was singled out as having 'sung splendidly' and the Elizabethan Melbourne Orchestra, under Cillario, 'played most beautifully, providing a balanced and polished response to Puccini's complex and subtle score.'[348] Roger Covell praised Cillario's conducting, relishing the 'tugging harmonies and brilliant instrumentation of Puccini's inexhaustibly fascinating score, [which] puts us in good humour, for a start.'[349] Maria Prerauer wrote that Cillario 'forced every bit of colour he could from the score, … he kept up the pace

[344] Oxenbould (2005), 332.
[345] Cillario to Oxenbould, 20 January 1978. 'Carlo Felice Cillario – Artist Files 'Misc.', Opera Australia Library archives.'
[346] See Oxenbould (2005), 330.
[347] Burch, 'A 21-carat Golden West,' *The Australian* (Melbourne), 21 May 1979.
[348] Ibid.
[349] Covell, 'Golden Girl in handsome production,' *The Sydney Morning Herald*, 8 June 1979.

and urgency in the orchestra, but he couldn't make up for the lack of action or tension on stage.'[350]

Cillario's final engagement for 1979 was an English-language production of Verdi's *Falstaff*, a pinnacle of Italian opera, a work of humour and mischief, and musically not to be taken lightly. The stage director was George Ogilvie, who had previously worked with Cillario on Mozart's *Don Giovanni* and *Seraglio*. There is no record of Cillario's specific feelings in this instance about the decision to rob Verdi's score of its association with Arrigo Boito's version of Shakespeare, but the critics approved: 'mercifully sung in English, with the accent on acting rather than in the strength of the voices.[351]

Designed by Kristian Fredrikson, the production was cast with locals[352] who created a tight, cohesive ensemble. As Falstaff, Ronald Maconaghie demonstrated 'masterly acting [and] genuine understanding for every nuance of the part.' Roger Covell praised Maconaghie as 'twinkling in manner within the padded bulk of his appearance' and Ogilvie for making 'good actors out of bad, and better ones out of the best.' Robert Allman 'subtly portrayed' Ford; Donald Shanks presented a 'swaggering, rich-voiced' Pistola; Nance Grant 'usually somewhat staid, blossomed forth as a comic' in the role of Alice.[353] For Maria Prerauer, 'Cillario in the pit and Ogilvie on stage brought it all back as alive and sparkling as the day it was written. ... This is a merry tongue-in-cheek portrait of man in all his vanity, with conductor Carlo Felice Cillario brilliantly underlining the composer's unique blend of wit and magic with orchestral fun and fantasy to match.'[354]

During 1979, Cillario also approached Hemmings about his interest in investigating the music of the First Nations Peoples.

---

350 Prerauer, *The Australian*, 8 June 1979.

351 'E.S.', *The Australian Jewish Times* (Sydney), 16 August 1979.

352 Cast: Ronald Maconaghie (Falstaff), Robert Allman and John Pringle (Ford), Paul Ferris (Fenton), Graeme Ewer (Dr Caius), Gordon Wilcock (Bardolfo), Donald Shanks and Clifford Grant (Pistola), Nance Grant (Alice Ford), Rhonda Bruce (Nannetta), Heather Begg (Mistress Quickly), Rosemary Gunn (Meg Page).

353 Covell, *The Sydney Morning Herald*, 3 August 1979.

354 Prerauer, *The Australian*, 3 August 1979.

A decade earlier he had suggested to Claudio Alcorso that talent scouts be sent to First Nations Peoples' missions in order to source voices suitable for opera. Hemmings wrote to Ian Johnstone, of the Australia Council: 'Carlo Felice Cillario has the romantic idea of spending some time in June learning about Aboriginal music. Is there anybody in the Australia Council who could help him to the right place and the right people?'[355] Cillario undertook a journey of some weeks, visiting settlements, investigating the music of the First Nations Peoples, and produced a lengthy account of his findings: 'L'Aborigeni e loro bel canto'.[356]

15: Carlo Felice Cillario, dress rehearsal for *Madama Butterfly*, June 1978.

---

[355] Peter Hemmings to Ian Johnstone, 2 April 1979. Carlo Felice Cillario – Artist Files '1', Opera Australia Library archives.

[356] Which is among his unpublished papers.

1980 was another busy season for Cillario in Australia, although most of the productions he conducted were revivals, such as *Fanciulla* which was repeated in Canberra, with the role of Minnie now sung by Catherine Duval.[357] W. L. Hoffmann wrote that he

> enjoyed this performance – for its musical qualities. The singing was first class throughout and Carlo Felice Cillario obtained excellent, supportive playing for most of the time from the Elizabethan Melbourne Orchestra. ... Catherine Duval took over at short notice, and after a somewhat tentative start, which was understandable, settled down to sing with gradually increasing assurance and tonal command, her voice having just the right 'spinto' quality for this role.[358]

Cillario led *Falstaff* and *La traviata*, in Brisbane and Melbourne,[359] where he also conducted *The Abduction from the Seraglio*. The Brisbane *Falstaff* was found to be in the best Italian tradition: 'it seemed the very strings were weeping.'[360] In *Traviata*, Joan Carden (Violetta) was the star of the evening, Anson Austin (Alfredo) 'forced his tone at times,' and Robert Allman had 'his enormous power under control and gave a masterly performance. ... Orchestral accompaniment by Carlo Cillario was first class.'[361]

At the Melbourne revival of *Falstaff,* it was reported that Ronald Maconaghie in the title role 'was often hampered by lack of vocal power. But that was the only significant error in the selection of a cast who, under Carlo Felice Cillario's sensitive and vital direction, shared the honours fairly equally'.[362] Peter Burch observed that the conductor 'moulded an affectionate reading ... there were times

---

[357] Cast changes for Canberra from previous season: Catherine Duvall (Minnie), John Serge (Trin), John Fulford (Bello), Rosemary Gunn (Wowkle), Raymond Myers (Jack Wallace), Richard Jones (Un postiglione).

[358] Hoffmann, 'An odd first night, musically fine,' *The Canberra Times*, 7 March 1980.

[359] He conducted only the opening night of *La traviata*; the season was then taken over by Peter Robinson.

[360] Val Vallis, *The Australian*, 26 April 1980.

[361] Dr W. Lovelock, *Brisbane Courier Mail*, 28 April 1980.

[362] Sinclair, 'Falstaff Fairly,' *Melbourne Herald*, 31 March 1980.

when he might have driven his singers a little more wilfully, but he generally allowed the eloquent score to read its own case.'[363]

The Melbourne season once again took place in the acoustically unsatisfactory Princess Theatre, which reportedly created problems for balance between pit and stage. Cillario elicited a visceral, expressive texture from the orchestra, but at the expense of the more fine-grained voices. The Osmin of Donald Shanks was deemed the star of the show at the Melbourne revival of *Seraglio*, with Cillario providing 'devotedly precise direction'. Glenys Fowles was singled out for her 'unfailing purity of voice, remarkable agility and in "Martern aller Arten", immense authority.'[364]

Traviata won ecstatic praise, summed up in the title of a review by Peter Burch: 'A Joan better than Joan.'[365] The context bears investigation. Richard Bonynge's tenure as Music Director of the Australian Opera, with his wife as the leading Diva, brought with it a unique imprimatur. He and Sutherland generated international publicity and valuable revenue for the company. The management of the Australian Opera built a financial and artistic model that revolved around productions which showcased their talents, effectively granting them a kind of tenure.

The husband-and-wife team supplied Australian opera-going audiences, and the Australian public more widely, with operatic glamour, international fame, and cultural excellence, to the point of them becoming regarded as a kind of 'Australian operatic royal family'. It was only a matter of time until the press would scrutinise their positions as the preeminent stars of the company. Questions began to be asked. Exactly how much better was Sutherland than other, locally resident Australian sopranos? Were the (rumoured) high fees worth it? What had happened to the notion of supporting and celebrating 'our own' (bringing the suggestion that the couple were no longer in that category)? The paradox of Bonynge and Sutherland's international celebrity made them at once bewitchingly attractive but also impossibly distant to their home audience: a

[363] Burch, 'Melbourne Falstaff', *The Australian*, 31 March 1980.
[364] Sinclair, 'Abduction worth a pardon', *Melbourne Herald*, 14 May 1980.
[365] Burch, 'A Joan better than Joan', *The Australian* (Melbourne), 7 April 1980.

paradox inherent in the cult of the operatic diva (to be observed elsewhere, for example, in the relationship between Maria Callas and her Greek public), and further sharpened by the mistrust of success known in Australia as 'tall poppy syndrome'.

In 1979, Joan Sutherland had sung the role of Violetta in Melbourne. In 1980, Joan Carden appeared in the same role. Born and initially trained in Melbourne, Carden was a fine singer, who had worked at Glyndebourne and the Royal Opera in the UK but (in contrast to Sutherland) had made her career back in her native land, where she appeared in important productions with Cillario over a period of 23 years. One year on from Sutherland's performances, Carden gave a 'very different performance, probably more successful', revealing 'a stature that looks convincing as a Parisian courtesan dying of tuberculosis, but she is also a fine actress … musical and physical phrasing go hand in hand.'[366] Carden would continue to confirm her reputation as one of the leading sopranos resident in Australia, and on the occasion of this *Traviata*, Cillario 'animated Verdi's score, and revealed the composer's intentions … it was Carden and Cillario who combined to make this a memorable *Traviata*.'[367]

A new production of Puccini's *Manon Lescaut* was created for the 1980 Sydney winter season by a triumvirate of Cillario, the director John Copley and designer Kristian Fredrikson.[368] Following its premiere in Turin in 1893, the work quickly won a place in the repertoire of European houses which the subsequent success of *La bohème*, *Tosca* and *Madama Butterfly* did nothing to dislodge. Cillario was especially drawn to the piece, perhaps due to its

[366] Ibid.
[367] Cast: Joan Carden (Violetta), Heather Begg (Flora), Cynthia Johnston (Annina), Henri Wilden and Anson Austin (Alfredo), Gregory Yurisich (Giorgio Germont), Robin Donald (Gastone), Pieter van der Stolk (Barone Douphol), John Germain and Robert Eddie (Marchese d'Obigny), Joseph Grunfelder (Doctor Grenvil), Richard Jones (Giuseppe & Servant).
[368] Cast: Leona Mitchell (Manon Lescaut), John Pringle and Pieter van der Stolk (Lescaut), Ron Stevens (des Grieux), Alan Light (Geronte), Vincenzo Nesci (Innkeeper), Robert Gard (Dancing Master), Rosemary Gunn (Singer), Neville Wilkie and Erik Badcock (Sergeant), Robin Donald (Lamp-Lighter), Guido Martin (Naval Captain).

particular blend of *verismo* and Wagner. He had begun advocating for an Australian production at the start of 1978, when he drew Peter Hemmings' attention to the work which had been 'so long ignored in Australia.' Cillario advised him that 'the Girl is a good score. *Manon* is a masterpiece.'[369] His handling of the score, and his musical rapport with Leona Mitchell in the title role, was warmly praised.

David Gyger found *Manon Lescaut* to be 'an unequivocal triumph for Leona Mitchell ... far and away her most successful opening night to date with the Australian Opera ... to a lesser extent it was also a triumph for conductor Carlo Felice Cillario and the Australian Opera ensemble.' Mitchell 'exuded 'smooth-as-silk torrents of seamless Puccini sound and was thoroughly convincing dramatically.' As the Chevalier des Grieux, Ron Stevens gave a dramatic performance, though vocally not a match for Mitchell ('he may yet develop into a lyric tenor'). There was equally qualified praise for John Pringle's portrayal of Manon's brother ('good, but not memorable'), while Alan Light was deemed 'marvellously bombastic' as the elderly lover Geronte. The Copley production was 'straightforward and non-gimmicky', while Fredrikson's designs were variable, although they improved 'from act to act'.[370]

Some of Gyger's criticisms were framed in the context of the production being a thrifty commission from the company for a set which could be reused for Massenet's *Manon* at a later date. While he remained critical of the sets and even Puccini himself (for a 'highly flawed dramatic structure'), he conceded that 'Cillario had drawn everything together musically so expertly that one could forget the flaws – almost.'[371]

Roger Covell weighed the quality of Cillario's conducting, Leona Mitchell's singing, and the well-rounded chorus work, against disappointment with the staging, designs and costumes. Mitchell 'sings

---

[369] Cillario to Hemmings, 18 January 1978. 'Carlo Felice Cillario – Artist Files 'Misc', Opera Australia Library archives.' At that time, Hemmings was the General Manager of the company.

[370] Quotes within this paragraph are from: D. Gyger, *Theatre Australia*, July 1980, 29.

[371] Ibid.

well, often superbly, with that creamy flourish of tone that can endow a Puccinian climax with a crest of vocal exhilaration,' but her 'dramatic performance leaves a great deal to be desired.' Ron Stevens, 'under voiced', did not create an equal partnership with Mitchell. According to Covell, Copley 'seems to have been defeated by the jerky but interesting dramatic momentum of the work and by the absence of an encouraging balance of necessary qualities in the casting. There is competence in this staging but no revelation and very little of the flair we have come to expect from this producer.'[372] For this company, *Manon Lescaut* was a rarity that needed more careful curating: a star soprano and a committed conductor were not enough.

1981 saw Cillario largely occupied with revivals. The Andrew Sinclair production of *La bohème* was given in the Sydney summer season, with a cast of male bohemians well known to the conductor,[373] Glenys Fowles as Mimì, and Rhonda Bruce as Musetta. According to Roger Covell, 'Cillario's conducting, vigorously urgent, when necessary, but knowing exactly when to linger and expand, helped the audience to attend with fresh receptiveness to this delectable opera.'[374] Maria Prerauer went further:

> Conductor maestro Carlo Felice Cillario is perhaps the biggest of its many assets. ... From the first chords that send the curtain shooting up without benefit of overture Cillario does not miss a single opportunity to bring out all the exotic colour and passion in the work. Just the manner in which he keeps the pace brisk and the tension high throughout the night confirms once more that he is one of the finest conductors at present on the international conducting circuit.[375]

---

[372] Covell, *The Sydney Morning Herald*, 16 June 1980.

[373] Cast: Anson Austin (Rodolfo), Glenys Fowles (Mimì), Robert Allman (Marcello), Rhonda Bruce (Musetta), Raymond Myers (Schaunard), Donald Shanks (Colline), Donald Solomon (Benoit), Pieter van der Stolk (Alcindoro), John Murray (Parpignol), John Durham (Customs Sergeant), Donald Solomon (Customs Officer).

[374] Covell, *The Sydney Morning Herald*, 12 February 1981.

[375] Prerauer, *The Australian*, 12 February 1981.

Manon Lescaut travelled to Melbourne for the autumn season, this time with Lamberto Furlan as the Chevalier des Grieux, Pieter van der Stolk alternating with John Fulford as Lescaut and a new guest soprano, Gabriela Cegolea in the title role.[376] The opening night on 7 April was billed as a 'Silver Anniversary Gala Performance', but the occasion seems to have been an artistic flop.[377] After making an apology for Puccini's early opera, Ian Hunt wrote that:

> The Australian Opera Melbourne opening had the great advantage of Carlo Felice Cillario as its conductor, but the odds were too heavily weighed against him. ... John Copley's production is conventional and, for him, strangely lacking in inspiration. The three main roles did not come to life, though Furlan sang well, after a tentative start.[378]

John Sinclair went as far as to say that Copley's staging 'put the standard of operatic performance in this country back by more than a decade.' He found Gabriela Cegolea to be a 'lyric soprano in a dramatic role' and criticised most of the other cast members.'[379] Moffatt Oxenbould recalls that Cegolea was 'disappointing' in view of her reputation earned abroad, including appearances at La Scala: she 'appeared vocally reserved and only superficially involved in the drama of the opera.'[380]

Praise for Cillario's Puccini performances continued into the Sydney winter season, which opened with *Tosca*, in a new production by Copley. In the title role Marilyn Zschau led a cast featuring Lamberto Furlan as Cavaradossi, and John Shaw as Scarpia.[381] The

---

[376] Cast: [Changes from previous year are underlined.] Gabriela Cegolea (Manon Lescaut), Pieter van der Stolk and John Fulford (Lescaut), Lamberto Furlan (des Grieux), Alan Light (Geronte), Vincenzo Nesci (Innkeeper), Robert Gard (Dancing Master), Rosemary Gunn (Singer), Constantine Mavridis (Sergeant), Sergei Baigildin (Lamp-Lighter), Guido Martin (Naval Captain).

[377] Oxenbould (2005), 364.

[378] Ian Hunt, *The Australian*, 9 April 1981.

[379] Sinclair, *The Herald*, 8 April 1981.

[380] Oxenbould (2005), 364.

[381] In the supporting roles: John Wegner and Bruce Martin (Angelotti), Graeme Ewer and Neville Grave (Spoletta), John Germain and Pieter van der Stolk (Sacristan), Robert Eddie (Sciarrone), Constantine Mavridis (Gaoler). The later performances were conducted by William Reid.

opening night was another 'Silver Anniversary Gala', given to mark the 25th anniversary of the company in Sydney, as *Manon Lescaut* had marked it in Melbourne.[382] This time, however, the performance lived up to its billing. Brian Hoad noted the 'passion (sometimes voluptuous, sometimes violent) [unleashed] by Cillario in the pit.'[383] Other reviews placed particular emphasis on the conducting, calling to mind the 1964 Royal Opera performances with Callas, Gobbi and Cillario.[384] In a similarly nostalgic vein, another reviewer praised this 1981 season of *Tosca* as the best they had seen since the 1968 Adelaide Festival.[385]

The improvement of the Elizabethan Sydney Orchestra was acknowledged: 'they are getting close to the quality of playing that one takes for granted in European and US opera houses: they played exceedingly well … and one only missed the glowing warmth from the strings that the scoring calls for.' Cillario obtained 'very responsive playing which captured the luscious beauty of Puccini's score without in any way dominating the singers.' [386] Covell wrote that 'Cillario conducts with characteristic fire and suppleness.'[387] Prerauer expanded on this:

> Puccini's music, under conductor Carlo Felice Cillario's fiery baton, seethes, as it should, with unvarnished human passions. … Cillario doesn't miss an opportunity to drive the voluptuous and deceptively difficult music along with just the correct degree of urgency, skilfully weaving the sixty or so different motives together to form a complex tapestry of sound, sometimes erotic, sometimes cruel, and always just what the composer ordered.[388]

The earlier Verdi operas belonged to the repertoire of both Cillario

---

[382] Hoffmann, *The Canberra Times*, 1 November 1981.

[383] Hoad, *The Bulletin*, 30 June 1981.

[384] 'B. Canto', '"Tosca" Opens Season,' *The Australian Jewish Times* (Sydney), 25 June 1981.

[385] Hoffmann, *The Canberra Times*, 15 June 1981.

[386] Hoffmann, *The Canberra Times*, 21 June 1981.

[387] Covell, *The Sydney Morning Herald*, 15 June 1981.

[388] Prerauer, *The Australian*, 15 June 1981.

and Richard Bonynge, and indeed, their early performance history is also a significant part of Australian operatic history, with several having been performed in this country within a few years of their premieres.[389] In 1980 Bonynge had conducted a production of *I masnadieri*, directed by Peter Beauvais with designs by Alan Lees and Michael Stennett, which Cillario then conducted in Canberra, and took to Adelaide for five performances in March 1981.[390]

The lead up to these performances was fraught with tension. On Friday 13 February 1981, Donald Smith – who was to sing Carlo in the production – suddenly announced his retirement. The opera was due to open in Canberra in just three weeks. The tenor Angelo Marenzi had just arrived in Australia to commence rehearsals for a new production of Verdi's *Otello*. He was an unknown quantity to the company, known only to Cillario who had heard him in Italy. For most tenors, the role of Otello would be an all-embracing responsibility, leaving little time for other work. The role of Carlo was completely unknown to Marenzi, but he undertook to learn it and have it ready for performance in the two and a half weeks that remained.[391]

In the event, Marenzi triumphed in both roles. As Carlo, he gave a 'most vocally assured performance', the power and Italianate ring of his voice being generally admired. As Amalia – a role sung at the 1847 premiere by Jenny Lind – Aileen Fischer was also excellent, 'in no way overshadowed by Marenzi even though her voice lacks the sheer power which, ideally, these Verdi roles require.' Robert Allman and Clifford Grant also sang admirably, and much credit for the success of the production was given to Cillario, 'who kept up the pace from the beginning and never permitted the musical interest to flag for a moment. Yet, with this more vigorous approach, he also

---

[389] See: A. Gyger, *Civilising the Colonies, Pioneering Opera in Australia* (Sydney, Opera-Opera, Pellinor Pty Ltd, 1999), 107ff.

[390] Cast: Clifford Grant (Massimiliano), Angelo Marenzi (Carlo), Robert Allman (Francesco), Ailene Fischer (Amalia), Lamberto Furlan and James Bonnefin (Arminio), Constantine Mavridis (Rolla), Bruce Martin (Moser).

[391] Michael Jacobs, 'Maestro, Marenzi, miracle,' *The Advertiser* (Canberra), 24 March 1981.

never allowed the orchestral playing or chorus singing to become rough.'[392]

Marenzi scored a huge hit with the role of Carlo, and his arrival in Australia filled a serious gap: here was a tenor who could not only sing, but also fill the dramatic requirements of the heavier dramatic roles. With *I masnadieri* in Adelaide, Marenzi was recognised as 'a real man of the theatre, of generous size, rich voice, considerable authority and with that absolute self-confidence which allows one to stand still while expressing strong emotions.' Among the cast, both Robert Allman and Bruce Martin were measured against Marenzi and found to be his equals. In the pit, Cillario conducted the Elizabethan Melbourne Orchestra, the Australian Opera Chorus and 'an excellent cast of principals in a tightly dramatic performance characterised by urgency. All concerned can allow themselves to be satisfied in terms of the powerful musical result.'[393]

During 1981, Cillario announced that he was writing his memoirs which would include his experiences in Australia.[394] He was often seen with this collection of papers under his arm, and was constantly adding to and revising them. Unpublished in his lifetime, a selection of these memoirs appear in translation in Appendix 7.

Sutherland and Cillario: *Otello*

In 1981 there took place a unique event in the company's history and in Cillario's career. In the Sydney summer season, a full staging of Verdi's *Otello*[395] was mounted in the Concert Hall of the Sydney Opera House, building on the success of productions such as the 1975 *Aida* led by Cillario, and a 1980 run of Donizetti's *Lucia di Lammermoor*

---

[392] Quotes in this paragraph are from: Hoffmann, 'Italian Tenor assured and relaxed,' *The Canberra Times*, 9 March 1981.

[393] Ralph Middenway, *The Adelaide Advertiser*, 21 March 1981.

[394] [No author named], 'Australian opera in memoirs,' *The Sunday Telegraph*, 21 June 1981.

[395] Cast: Angelo Marenzi (Otello), John Shaw (Iago), Paul Ferris (Cassio), Robin Donald (Roderigo), Clifford Grant and Donald Shanks (Lodovico), Bruce Martin (Montano), Robert Eddie (Herald), Joan Sutherland (Desdemona), Heather Begg and Kathleen Moore (Emilia).

conducted by Richard Bonynge. The *Otello* production by George Ogilvie, however, met with a mixed reception: 'somehow, the final effect was less than the sum of its parts would have suggested.'[396]

During Bonynge's tenure as Music Director, he had always conducted Sutherland's performances just as he did elsewhere. Bonynge knew his limitations as well as his specialisms, and it is a mark of the respect and trust he held for Cillario that he invited him to take charge of *Otello*, which featured Sutherland as Desdemona.

In her memoir, Sutherland recalled their work together:

> Cillario has a great sense of humour and loves spending a portion of each year in Australia, having done an enormous amount for the Australian Opera musically. He continues to encourage the singers and orchestra and I've seldom seen him without a smile on his face – only when something (or someone) is incorrect during rehearsal or performance. I remember being on the receiving end of his smile during a performance of the big third-act ensemble in Otello whilst, with a turn of his head to the left, the smile changed to a glare at a couple of other singers who were meandering along, apparently oblivious of his beat and dragging the tempo. In a flash one of Carlo's hands pinched his nose, the other made the motion of pulling a lavatory chain, then his head turned towards me again, his face wreathed in that seraphic smile. At such a dramatic point of the opera it was, perhaps, naughty, but the miscreant got the message and paid attention henceforth.[397]

Sutherland enjoyed working with Cillario, recognising in him a 'singer-friendly' conductor, no less than her husband. The pleasure afforded by their collaboration was mutual, as Cillario recorded in his memoirs (see Appendix 7) which, like most of the conductors' recollections is not without characteristic flavours of the bizarre, the irreverent and the cheeky.

The invitation to conduct *Otello* with Sutherland came with

---

[396] Hoffmann, 'Sutherland out-performed by tenor,' *The Canberra Times*, 30 January 1981.

[397] Joan Sutherland (1997), 333.

the proviso that Cillario would find a suitable tenor to undertake the title role. Cillario sought advice from Gobbi, which resulted in Angelo Marenzi auditioning for the conductor in Bologna. Cillario was attuned to the difficulties of casting this role:

> He has to have a big voice because sometimes the orchestration is very strong. But he must also be a *bel canto* singer, as there are times when he must sing softly – in the wonderful sweet lyric parts. And it is no good him just coming and singing – he must also have a big personality and be a good actor.[398]

Plácido Domingo, in an interview with Michael Parkinson, said that he set himself an annual limit of 12 to 20 performances of Otello 'for self-protection'.[399] In Australia, Marenzi sang 10 performances of the role within a month, but Cillario's instincts were once again proven to be shrewd. At home once more in the Concert Hall, he had an expanded version of the Elizabethan Sydney Orchestra at his disposal, its 75 musicians visible and audible to the audience. His musical leadership was universally admired, as was much of the casting.

For Maria Prerauer, Cillario 'coaxes, cajoles and hypnotises singers and orchestra into giving a musical reading of fire and splendour.' She went on to praise all the singers, finding the casting to be without a weak link.[400] Fred Blanks wrote that Cillario:

> ignites a rare orchestral incandescence in the Elizabethan Sydney Orchestra. He is obviously on intimate terms with every musical effect, from the sudden violent outbreak of a storm which has been gathering in ominous silence to the tensions of the final tableau. ... Angelo [Marenzi], the second main pillar of this performance, blends a heroic quality of voice, which rarely has trouble in filling the hall, with bel canto seamlessness, precision and ardour in a manner not commonly encountered in Australian opera ranks.[401]

---

[398] Jill Sykes, *The Sydney Morning Herald*, 24 January 1981.
[399] Jacobs, 'Maestro, Marenzi, miracle', *The Advertiser* (Adelaide), 24 March 1981.
[400] Prerauer, *The Australian*, 30 January 1981.
[401] Blanks, *The Sydney Morning Herald*, 30 January 1981.

Adrian Read described Cillario's conducting as 'the kind of intense commitment that unfailingly catches and holds attention. ... His was a fine, exciting performance, and it overshadowed the singers in more ways than one.'[402]

Unexpectedly, Sutherland's contribution to this *Otello* was reported as a subsidiary element to its success. 'Special honours were due to conductor Carlo Felice Cillario and to Italian tenor Angelo Marenzi, whose heroic and smooth singing impressed even more than that of Joan Sutherland, who reached her finest form in the glorious final act.'[403] Adrian Read found that:

> as Desdemona, Joan Sutherland seemed ill at ease in a role which lies towards the bottom of the soprano range and is without the cool pyrotechnics at which she excels ... it is also a dramatically exposed part, and on the huge stage her weakness in this department was all the more obvious. She restricted her acting to looking vaguely pained most of the time. Visiting Italian tenor Angelo Marenzi was the strongest in the cast.[404]

Given her association with Bonynge, there was speculation over whether Sutherland felt uncomfortable working with another conductor. She had not sung the role for two decades, but the issue was more complex. In the intervening period, she had developed both her technique and her repertoire towards roles which demanded dazzling coloratura and ornamental roulades. In agreeing to sing Desdemona once more, she was relinquishing (perhaps not without some courage) the props upon which her career had subsequently been built. She was most affecting in the Act 3 set-pieces of 'Salce, Salce' and 'Ave Maria', where Verdi recalls with great tenderness the world of Bellini and the *bel canto* tradition.

Sutherland found herself upstaged by a heroic tenor: a rarity, almost a unicorn in Australia at the time. No resident successor to Donald Smith was immediately apparent. Lamberto Furlan was held to have the right 'type' of voice but was found unreliable

---

[402] Adrian Read, *The Sunday Telegraph*, 1 February 1981.
[403] 'W. S.,' *The Australian Jewish News* (Sydney), 12 February 1981.
[404] See FN 402.

and erratic. Others possessed the looks and charm of a romantic tenor lead but were vocally inadequate. A critical debate arose over whether 'our own' – ironically casting Sutherland as an outsider in this context – were 'good enough', and even whether the cost of an imported Sutherland could be justified. Subsequently Desdemona became one of Joan Carden's signature roles, and her portrayal was favourably compared with Sutherland's.

The passionately incisive direction of her conductor on this occasion also stole the limelight from Sutherland. Bonynge and Cillario shared a strong musical rapport and mutual artistic respect. They also shared a good deal of repertoire in common, notably from the *bel canto* tradition of Bellini and Donizetti. Each of them played their part in the revival of this repertoire in the opera house as well as through recordings. It could be said that what Tullio Serafin was to Callas, so Bonynge was to Sutherland, and Cillario to Montserrat Caballé.

During the years of Bonynge's directorship, Cillario conducted very little *bel canto* opera in Australia. Nor did he ever lead the company in *Il trovatore*: a work particularly associated with Bonynge. Despite having made his enthusiasm for *Carmen* known to the management, Cillario did not conduct this work in Australia, whereas Bonynge did. He built his Australian repertoire around Puccini and Verdi, while pursuing avenues closed off to him elsewhere: notably the music-dramas of Wagner, culminating in his engagement for the company's first *Ring* cycle, planned for performance during Bonynge's tenure as Music Director.

By all accounts, Bonynge nurtured a spirit of amicable cooperation with Cillario. His own conducting centred on his home repertoire and on performances with Sutherland, while Cillario was engaged on a year-by-year basis, doing a lot of 'heavy lifting' for a Music Director who was not inclined to conduct *Otello*, *Parsifal* or the *Ring*. Bonynge has written that '[Cillario] has done more, musically, for the Australian Opera than any other conductor and has given his time generously to our singers and orchestras for many years, and continues to do so.[405] Following his return to the company in 1975, Cillario gradually lost visibility in the Australian Opera's press

---

405 Richard Bonynge (1990), 75.

releases. The focus was now on Sutherland – the Diva – and her husband. Cillario was left free to focus upon what he loved best: conducting.

During 1981, Cillario undertook two significant engagements outside the Australian Opera. He was engaged by the Philharmonia Society of Sydney, to conduct Verdi's *Requiem* for their subscription series during December. The reviews made much of Cillario's experience in the theatre to praise his conducting ('tremendous verve' and 'marvellous attention to detailed effects') of a work popularly known as 'Verdi's greatest opera'. The choir 'sounded just a bit more pleased with itself at the *fortissimo* than at the *pianissimo* end of the volume spectrum.' A significantly augmented Australian Chamber Orchestra played with 'fervour' to match the choir, while Joan Carden, Lauris Elms, Anthony Benfell and Noel Mangin formed a fine quartet of soloists.[406] Many years before, Cillario had been present when Victor de Sabata conducted the work in Rome, with Gigli, Pasero, Caniglia and Stignani – a performance which had remained in his memory and served as a model for the work's realisation.[407]

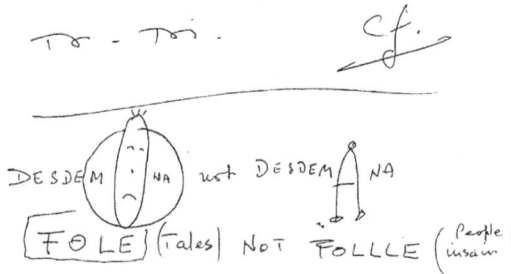

16. One of Cillario's infamous 'doodles' – corrections for Italian pronunciation.[408]

---

[406] Blanks, *The Australian Jewish Times* (Sydney), 3 December 1981.

[407] Peter Johnston, 'A "National" Treasure,' *The Melburnian*, Vol. 9 No. 9, May 1994, 33–5.

[408] The inventive graphics with which he constructed his notes to singers are intriguing. Here he asks for the pronunciation of 'Desdemona' to be made with an 'o' rather than an 'a' vowel, and highlights the difference that a single, or a double 'l' makes, altering the meaning from 'tales' to 'people insain'[sic]. At the top he writes 'toi-toi' to the recipient.

The second project was a monumental staging of *Aida*, mounted by the Canberra Opera Society (COS) for two performances, at the National Indoor Sports Stadium in Bruce, ACT. The scale of the venue and the extravagance of the production allowed for a live elephant and 400 performers, including a topless dancer. The artistic merits of the production were promoted by the participation of Cillario and several principals from the Australian Opera.

It is possible that this event was mounted as a staged protest at the dwindling presence of the national company in Canberra, with the COS making a bid to obtain increased funding in order to transform their essentially pro–am organisation. The project was directed by Bernd Benthaak. Radamès and Aida were sung by the real-life couple of Angelo Marenzi and Lorraine Nawa Jones.[409] Cillario spoke enthusiastically about the enterprise in a pre-performance interview, observing that 'different people [go] to see Aida for different reasons.... Some [go] for Verdi's music, others for the drama, others for the spectacle, including the elephant which will undoubtedly steal some of the limelight.' He praised the diversity of participants, young and old, amateur and professional, which he said would have gladdened the communitarian spirit of Benjamin Britten as expressed in works such as Saint Nicolas and Noye's Fludde. [410] There was, all the same, inevitable gossip circulating around the cost of this immense undertaking:

> Meanwhile I am unable to confirm rumours that the impov-
> erished Canberra Opera, which is employing an elephant in
> its two forthcoming performances of 'Aida' ... is planning
> to garner the waste of this colossus (let us pray that it sheds
> none during the performance) and to sell it in sacks to help
> pay the colossal fee of guest maestro Carlo Felice Cillario.[411]

Cillario had given many performances in Canberra with the Australian Opera, to enthusiastic reviews, having made his Aus-

---

[409] Cast: Lorraine Nawa Jones (Aida), Margreta Elkins (Amneris), Angelo Marenzi (Radamès), Robert Allman (Amonasro), Donald Shanks (Ramfis), Brian Dowling (Messenger), Jeanette Russell (High Priestess).

[410] Lin Enright, *The Canberra Times*, 25 November 1981.

[411] Ian Warden, *The Canberra Times*, 15 November 1981.

tralian conducting debut in the capital. On this occasion, he was conducting the Canberra Symphony Orchestra, founded in 1950, rather than one of the experienced opera orchestras of Sydney or Melbourne. Nevertheless, the reviews were glowing:

> With conductor Carlo Felice Cillario at the helm there could hardly be any doubt as to the musical quality of the overall performance; but I must say that, under his guidance, I have never heard the Canberra Symphony sound better. The strings, though not large in number, produced a fine tone, and the winds and brass were never over-dominant. And some of those difficult moments in the score where even the best orchestras have to watch themselves, went past without one being unduly aware of any problems.[412]

Cillario was very much at home, presenting the spectacle in the style of an *Aida* staged in Verona or at the Baths of Caracalla in Rome. Thousands of Canberra residents who could never normally attend an opera (4000 of them each evening) trekked from cars parked in paddocks. 'If depth of feeling was sacrificed to sheer size,' remarked one reviewer, 'there were significant gains to be had.' It was

> a community spectacle that was at once exotic and local … all made possible by a combination of vision and logistical precision from Canberra Opera's staff, and by the superhuman achievement of the man who shaped the soft, but haunting sound of the actual performances, Maestro Carlo Felice Cillario.[413]

Maria Prerauer agreed:

> The hero of the night … was the international Italian conductor Carlo Felice Cillario, well-known for his umpteen Australian Opera appearances. It was he, above all, who by some sort of obsessive hypnotic grip on his disparate forces, ranging from noted pro[fessional]s to mere weekend performers, was responsible for filling the hall with the true magic of Verdi's magnificent music.[414]

---

[412] Hoffmann, *The Canberra Times*, 12 December 1981.

[413] Ken Healey, *The Advertiser*, 17 December 1981.

[414] Prerauer, *The Australian*, 12 December 1981.

Towards the end of this year Cillario conducted Bellini's *Norma* in Melbourne, starring the noted British soprano, Rita Hunter in the title role[415] in a production directed by Christopher Renshaw. Cillario had recorded the opera commercially with Montserrat Caballé in 1973, and several pirate recordings preserve readings of the work with other leading sopranos of the day, including Elena Suliotis and Grace Bumbry. It is unfortunate that this was the conductor's only foray into the Bellini repertoire during his years in Australia. The opera was a staple of Hunter's repertoire, she had previously sung it at the Metropolitan Opera, as well as in San Francisco under Cillario's baton. Cillario had long been impressed by Hunter's voice, and had recommended her to the management in Australia, where she was also engaged to sing Brünnhilde in the 1983-4 *Ring* cycle.

Cillario also conducted a Puccini Gala concert in Melbourne at the Palais Theatre on 7 November. A planned production of *Les Huguenots* in Melbourne had been cancelled, providing a date in the theatre, and several available singers including Marilyn Zschau, Anson Austin, Paul Ferris, Lamberto Furlan, and John Shaw. The programme evolved during the season and the proceedings were dominated by Zschau, who wore a Halston dress. Moffatt Oxenbould recalled that the soprano 'looked as if she was wearing a lilac silk bath towel and revealed a great deal of flesh.'[416]

1982 brought revivals of several productions that were already part of Cillario's Australian repertoire. *La bohème* was given in Melbourne with the 1970 production being 'rejuvenated' by director Andrew Sinclair. There were several cast changes from the previous year.[417]

---

[415] Cast: Rita Hunter (Norma), Rosemary Gunn (Adalgisa), Lamberto Furlan (Pollione), Clifford Grant (Orovesco), Sergei Baigildin and Paul Ferris (Flavio), Cynthia Johnston (Clothilde).

[416] Moffatt Oxenbould, email to the author, 7 July 2023; also a cable, 7 October 1983, Oxenbould to Cillario; Carlo Felice Cillario – Artist Files 'Misc.', Opera Australia Library archives.

[417] Cast: Richard Greager (Rodolfo), Glenys Fowles and Lorraine Nawa Jones (Mimì), Robert Allman (Marcello), Jennifer McGregor and Rhonda Bruce

Carlo Felice Cillario was in top form, and his command of the orchestra was a thing of joy. The orchestra responded wonderfully throughout the opera, allowing us to savour all the felicities of Puccini's sprightly score. It really seemed like a return to the standards of old.[418]

Cillario revisited *Cav & Pag* in Melbourne, with Canio sung by Angelo Marenzi, who had established a popular presence in Australia.[419] Despite all his protestations about the *verismo* double bill, during this year Cillario accepted an engagement at the Lyric Opera of Chicago, conducting a double bill of *I pagliacci* and Poulenc's *La voix humaine*.

The John Copley production of Verdi's *Macbeth*[420] was also presented, in something more than a standard revival. The distinguished American baritone Sherrill Milnes had been engaged to sing the title role, with Rita Hunter joining him as Lady Macbeth. Reviews suggest that the production was cramped by the stage of the Princess Theatre. The singing of Donald Shanks (Banquo), Reginald Byers (Macduff), and Robin Donald (Malcolm) were found to be 'superb', with the singing 'reinforced by Cillario's attention to the detail of Verdi's magical score.'[421] Hunter was criticised for over-singing, except in the

> sleep-walking scene, where her vocal control and ability to colour, her eerie sound produced at once the finest singing

---

(Musetta), John Antoniou (Schaunard), Clifford Grant (Colline), John Germain (Benoit), Pieter van der Stolk (Alcindoro), John Murray (Parpignol), John Durham (Customs Sergeant), Guido Martin (Customs Officer).

[418] Hunt, 'As fine a bunch of Bohemians as one could ask,' *The Australian*, 28 April 1982.

[419] Cast: *Cavalleria Rusticana*: Rita Hunter (Santuzza), Rosemary Gunn (Lola), Rosina Raisbeck (Mamma Lucia), Lamberto Furlan (Turiddu), Raymond Myers (Alfio). *I Pagliacci*: Etela Piha (Nedda), Angelo Marenzi (Canio), John Shaw (Tonio), Graeme Ewer (Beppe), John Pringle and Gregory Yurisich (Silvio), Guido Martin, Anthony Clark (Two Villagers).

[420] Cast: Rita Hunter (Lady Macbeth), Sherrill Milnes (Macbeth), Donald Shanks (Banquo), Reginald Byers (Macduff), Judith Turner (Lady in Waiting), Robin Donald (Malcolm), Pieter van der Stolk (Dottore), Guido Martin (Servant to Macbeth), Geoffrey Crook, Steven Crockett, Richard Casey (Apparitions).

[421] Allan Walker, *The Sun* (Melbourne), 9 May 1982.

and the most touching theatre of the evening. Sherrill Milnes looked imposing and sang beautifully, with a clear, clean sound and a very musical line.[422]

Significant for different reasons was a revival of Puccini's *Il trittico* in Melbourne and Sydney. The production had been created in 1973 by Moffatt Oxenbould and Desmond Digby, and Cillario was conducting it here for the first time. It marked a deepening artistic collaboration between Oxenbould and Cillario that was formalised in 1984, when Oxenbould became the Artistic Director of the company. Cillario also conducted the production in 2001, in his penultimate season with the company.

Cillario was especially fond both of Puccini's trilogy of one-act operas, and Oxenbould's staging. *Il trittico* held a particular significance for the company as a trio of ensemble works offering brief but richly characterful opportunities for many principals as well as solo choristers, particularly in *Suor Angelica*.

A strong line-up of local singers,[423] was joined (in Sydney) by

---

[422] Healey, *The Canberra Times*, 6 June 1982.

[423] Full Cast: *Il tabarro*: John Shaw and Robert Allman (Michele), Etela Piha (Giorgetta), Jon Sydney and Lamberto Furlan (Luigi), Gordon Wilcock (Tinca), Alan Light (Talpa), Jennifer Bermingham (Frugola), Graeme Ewer (Song Vendor), Angela Denning, Paul Ferris (Two lovers). *Suor Angelica*: Leona Mitchell and Margaret Dixon-McIver (Suor Angelica), Lauris Elms and Rosina Raisbeck (La Zia Principessa), Heather Begg and Olga Sanderson-Smith (La Badessa), Elizabeth Fretwell (La Suora Zelatrice), Rosemary Gunn (La Maestra delle Novizie), Judith Saliba and Anne-Patricia Hemingway Kathleen Moore and Catherine Elliott (Le Cercatrici), Elizabeth Davis (Suor Osmina), Cynthia Johnston (Suor Genovieffa), Anne-Maree McDonald, Luise Napier, Helen Borthwick (Tre Novizie), Judith Turner (Suor Dolcina), Catherine Elliott (Suor Iginia*), Nicola Waite (La Suora Infermiera), Jennifer McGregor and Marie Driscoll, Bernadette Cullen (Le Converse). *For this production the director, Moffatt Oxenbould devised an ensemble of nuns, with solo profiles and musical lines, creating an 'ensemble' rather than a 'chorus'. He required an extra nun for the staging and invented 'Suor Iginia' – who he named after Puccini's own sister who, in real life became a nun. *Gianni Schicchi*: Ronald Maconaghie (Schicchi), Angela Denning and Anne-Maree McDonald and Leona Mitchell (Lauretta), Rosina Raisbeck (Zita), Paul Ferris (Rinuccio), Graeme Ewer (Gherardo), Judith Saliba (Nella), Alan Light (Simone), Robert Eddie (Marco), Jennifer Bermingham

the American soprano, Leona Mitchell in the role of Angelica and as Lauretta in *Gianni Schicchi*. These performances of the full work led critics to reconsider their attitudes to the dramatic unity of the trilogy and to the place of *Suor Angelica* in particular, which had often been considered the weak link. In Sydney, Roger Covell wrote:

> Cillario's direction of the singers and the Elizabethan Trust Orchestra is sympathetic and finely judged in *Suor Angelica*. I am inclined to think it even more effective in *Il tabarro*, the masterly piece of brutal/poetic *verismo* with which the evening begins. Certainly, the orchestra gives one of its best performances in this score.[424]

Covell singled out Robert Allman as Michele; W. L. Hoffmann found all three protagonists – Allman, Etela Piha and Lamberto Furlan – uniformly excellent in *Il tabarro*.[425] The strong casting of members of the chorus in many of the cameo roles, and the moving performance of Leona Mitchell, was much praised. Lauris Elms was lauded as the Principessa, in which she was 'regally commanding – this great lady is seen and heard too little on our opera stages.'[426] In Melbourne, Ronald Maconaghie created a 'subtle and artful' Schicchi, Rosina Raisbeck a characterful Zita; other notable accounts of smaller roles included Alan Light (Simone), Paul Ferris (Rinuccio), John Wegner (Notario), and Anne-Maree McDonald (Lauretta).'[427] In Melbourne the performances were 'stylishly conducted' by Cillario,[428] and it was acknowledged that he held the reigns in terms of the dramatic energy of the evening. His 'customary feeling for Puccini',[429] and his maintenance of excellent accord between pit and stage was praised. Cillario had now performed all the standard Puccini canon in Australia – with the notable exception of *Turandot*.

(La Ciesca), Donald Solomon (Betto di Signa), John Wegner (Amantio di Nicolao), John Germain (Maestro Spinelloccio), Joseph Grunfelder (Pinellino), John Durham (Guccio).

[424] Covell, *The Sydney Morning Herald*, 7 May 1982.
[425] Hoffmann, *The Canberra Times*, 7 June 1982.
[426] Healey, *The Canberra Times*, 6 June 1982.
[427] Ibid.
[428] Hunt, *The Australian*, 17 May 1982.
[429] Hoffmann, *The Canberra Times*, 7 June 1982.

Rysanek in *Tosca* and Pavarotti in *La bohème*

During 1983, Cillario conducted five productions for the Australian Opera, the most notable among them being the first instalment of a major and long delayed project. The company's ambition to stage Wagner's *Ring* cycle dated back at least to 1977, when General Manager Peter Hemmings proposed the idea to Richard Bonynge. The tetralogy is a test of the resources of any company, and it would be another five years before *Die Walküre* was announced as the first opera in the Cycle to be staged, with Cillario at the helm.

The conductor's schedule in the 1983 season began with a revival of *Tosca* in Sydney, where the chief attraction was Leonie Rysanek in the title role. The Austrian soprano had sung Tosca (in 1979–80) as a celebrated company member of the Vienna State Opera, as well as in Hamburg and at the Metropolitan Opera, New York. Alongside Lamberto Furlan as Cavaradossi and John Shaw as Scarpia, she scored a resounding success in Sydney, presenting 'a dramatic and, above all, musical lesson in her art.'[430]

In her portrayal of Tosca, Rysanek explored the psychological complexities of the role with a sense of true-to-life drama which embodied the spirit of *verismo*. Although her voice was not considered 'beautiful in the accepted sense of the word', she portrayed the changing faces of the diva through her voice, 'dramatically effective in its varying qualities, fiery, piercing and occasionally melting.'[431] Beyond her own performance, critics noted her capacity to 'lift the performances of the other principals,' John Shaw's Scarpia becoming 'more subtly malevolent than when he sang the role in 1981' while Lamberto Furlan (previously criticised for his variability) gave what was considered his 'best performance yet.'[432]

The role played by Cillario in igniting these highly charged performances was also evident:

> As for the conductor, it was as much Maestro Cillario's show as anybody's, and this audience recognised it. Among the present group of conductors with the Australian Op-

---

[430] 'B. Canto', *The Australian Jewish Times* (Sydney), 27 January 1983.

[431] Ibid.

[432] Hoffmann, *The Canberra Times*, 27 January 1983.

era, he towers like a colossus. The upshot was a *Tosca* of authenticity. He elicited a total commitment from the pit, with some of the playing bordering on the sumptuous – but then Cillario knows his *Tosca*.[433]

Roger Covell was also enthusiastic about the season, and cited Rysanek and Cillario as the linchpins in the production. Of the soprano he wrote

> she frankly revels in the passion, despair and fury of the part. ... The presence of John Copley, the original producer of this staging ... has obviously allowed Rysanek to work with him in fruitful partnership. There are many new details. ... The grand and thrilling moments were placed within contrasts of restrained and careful singing.' Cillario 'conducted cast and orchestra with responsive awareness of the marriage of drama and music. His musical regime was effective throughout. I thought it reached its heights in the second half of Act II and at the beginning of Act III, where much of the string playing in particular was warmly alive.[434]

The winter season in Sydney also included a revival of *La fanciulla del West*, with the original designs of Tom Lingwood and new direction by Christopher Renshaw. The American soprano Arlene Saunders sang Minnie alongside the company's long-standing Jack Rance, John Shaw, and Kenneth Collins as Dick Johnson, supported by an outstanding ensemble in the many smaller roles.[435]

In a season rich in quality, and the appearance of a number of overseas celebrity artists, the highlight proved to be the three performances of *La bohème* that featured Luciano Pavarotti as Rodolfo. The tenor was returning to Australia for the first time since

---

[433] Ibid.

[434] Covell, 'Rysanek turns on a tigress of a Tosca,' *The Sydney Morning Herald*, 21 January 1983.

[435] Cast: Arlene Saunders (Minnie), Kenneth Collins and Reginald Byers (Dick Johnson), John Shaw (Jack Rance), Graeme Ewer (Nick), Alan Light (Ashby), John Fulford (Sonora), Gregory Dempsey (Trin), Guido Martin (Sid), Anthony Warlow (Bello), Robin Donald (Harry), Gordon Wilcock (Joe), Robert Eddie (Happy), John Antoniou (Larkens), John Germain (Billy Jackrabbit), Jennifer Bermingham (Wowkle), Raymond Myers (Jack Wallace), Pieter van der Stolk (José Castro), Richard Jones (Un postiglione).

the Sutherland–Williamson season in 1965. By 1983 he was probably the world's most famous opera singer. In addition to his trio of *Bohème* performances, he had been booked to sing in a gala concert with Joan Sutherland and Richard Bonynge with the Elizabethan Sydney Orchestra, as well as recitals in Sydney and Melbourne.

As the dates for *Bohème*[436] drew near, the management became nervous. Tickets were sold out solely on the strength of Pavarotti's name. He had insisted that his protégée – Madelyn Renee – be engaged as Mimì for his performances. Shortly prior to their scheduled arrival, his manager, Herbert Breslin notified the company that the tenor was unable to perform, having developed an allergy to stage dust. [437] At this point the Sydney Opera House had been operational for just a decade, and most of the theatres in which Pavarotti regularly performed were at least a century older. He initially undertook to give a recital in place of his *Bohème* appearances (a compromise accepted by the company) before these plans were abruptly reversed. Pavarotti was 'cured': according to Moffatt Oxenbould 'there had been a temporary falling out between Rodolfo and his Mimì in their private lives – producing an allergic reaction – but all was happily resolved.'[438]

Pavarotti was considerably more rotund than on the occasion of his 1965 visit, and the author recalls a considerable hiatus during Act 1 while the tenor slowly bent over – in silence – in an attempt to pick up Mimì's key from the floor. Nevertheless, the performances were a great success, and the subsequent gala even more so. Of the seven *Bohème* performances that took place after Pavarotti's departure, all were well cast and well-reviewed, despite following on the heels of what Oxenbould dubbed the 'Pavarotti Show.'[439] They marked Marilyn Richardson's debut in the role of Mimì, in a

---

[436] 'Pavarotti Cast': Luciano Pavarotti (Rodolfo), Madelyn Renee (Mimì), Robert Allman (Marcello), Rhonda Bruce (Musetta), Raymond Myers (Schaunard), Donald Shanks (Colline), John Germain (Benoit), Pieter van der Stolk (Alcindoro), John Murray (Parpignol), John Durham (Customs Sergeant), Guido Martin (Customs Officer).

[437] Oxenbould (2005), 388.

[438] Ibid.

[439] Ibid, 389.

'restrained performance that had its touching moments', despite a perceived lack of vocal blend with the Rodolfo of Lamberto Furlan. The remainder of the cast were all praised,[440] and of the musical direction:

> Carlo Cillario and his orchestra seemed at one with this music. Though mentioned many times in this column, it is worth repeating: Cillario brings the best out of the players. His pacing and phrasing of the score is masterful. One could only wish for a comparable effort on stage. The music wins hands down, all silver macaroni – exquisitely entangled.[441]

Cillario and Pavarotti were also friends and collaborated on many projects. Pavarotti was included in Cillario's memoirs, in a piece that was adapted and published in *The Australian,* an affectionate portrait in typically irreverent style.[442]

At the end of the Sydney Season a benefit concert was hastily arranged for victims of the bushfires which had caused widespread devastation in South Australia and Victoria. Thirty singers and seven conductors, including Cillario, Richard Bonynge and Stuart Challender, took part in this fundraising initiative for victims of the disaster.[443]

The greatest challenge of the season, however, was the new production of *Die Walküre*, with which the long-awaited *Ring* cycle commenced.

---

[440] Cast: Lamberto Furlan (Rodolfo), Marilyn Richardson (Mimì), Robert All-man (Marcello), Ronda Bruce and Etela Piha (Musetta), Raymond Myers (Schaunard), Donald Shanks (Colline), John Germain (Benoit), Pieter van der Stolk (Alcindoro), John Murray (Parpignol), John Durham (Customs Sergeant), Guido Martin (Customs Officer).

[441] 'B. Canto,' *The Australian Jewish Times* (Sydney), 24 February 1983.

[442] See Appendix 7.

[443] Oxenbould (2005), 391.

Scene 3

The Forging of an Australian *Ring*

In 1970, the Australian Opera had been inaugurated with the aspiration of presenting world-class opera performances of the major repertoire in the Sydney Opera House. This was severely compromised by the final configuration of the Opera Theatre which created a severe compromise between engineering, architectural and artistic requirements. In 1975, the production of *Aida* in the Concert Hall had revealed new potential for realising works on a grand scale within the building.

By presenting *Aida* and other works in the Concert Hall, the company had sent a clear signal to the world at large that it was, from a spatial and acoustic perspective, a superior performing space. To many Australian opera goers and critics, such projects developed the expectation that a production of Wagner's *Ring* cycle would naturally find its home in the Concert Hall. What was not understood by those outside the company was that access to the Concert Hall was not guaranteed when it came to mounting opera productions. The Sydney Symphony Orchestra had first right of refusal for their season dates in what was their main home. In addition, the complex technical manoeuvres required to mount even a semi-staged opera in the Concert Hall, where no screws could be used to secure set pieces in place, made the venue a prohibitively difficult space to work in. While it was possible on occasion to secure dates to perform short runs on successive evenings (using double or even triple casting to avoid vocal fatigue), the period of occupancy required to mount a *Ring* cycle was simply not available.

Meanwhile, dissatisfaction with the limitations of the Opera Theatre threatened to overshadow the profile of the company's work. With each new production, the critics effectively placed the building on trial, and duly found it guilty. Cillario, keenly aware of these limitations, expressed his reservations both in the press and to the management. He knew at first hand the challenges presented by a pit with cramped seating, sightline issues, players exposed to unsafe levels of sound, and difficulties in hearing other instruments for the sake of good ensemble. He had made known his concerns during his earlier visits to Australia (see Ill.9 & 10), but the fact was that the final configuration of the building had been determined prior to his first visit in 1968. A change of government in 1966 had sparked a series of events that saw Utzon resign as the supervising architect and return to Denmark. During this period, the ETOC held little sway with the government, and the ABC stepped in to secure the larger performance space as a Concert Hall for the Sydney Symphony Orchestra. While this change has been much criticised, the fact is that the original plan, with the larger hall as a shared space for opera and concerts would never have been a practical option.

In terms of optimising the conditions in the Opera Theatre, Cillario, among a number of other conductors explored a variety of orchestral set-ups, but the maintenance of the design faults of the Opera Theatre ultimately rested with the Sydney Opera House Trust. The remedy lay with qualified engineers and sound technicians, who failed to agree a solution. Comments made by successive Opera House general managers made it clear that they lacked the specialised knowledge to rule on such matters and had to rely on external reports that were ultimately contradictory.[444] Plans to remove the wall between the pit and the audience came to nothing, under threat of structural damage to the building if the recommended work was undertaken. Meanwhile Cillario simply got on with the job of conducting performances in the knowledge that the Opera Theatre was not the only opera house in the world with an unsatisfactory design.

During this time performances of individual parts of the Cycle were being presented in Sydney and Melbourne,[445] in concert

---

[444] For example: [No author named], 'Size Limit on Opera Orchestra', *The Sun Herald*, 6 June 1976.

[445] See: Peter Bassett, *The RING in Australia*, online publication, September 2010. https://www.melbarecordings.com.au/sites/default/files/melba_docs/ PDF_FILES/Peter%20Bassett%20-%20The%20RING%20in%20Australia. pdf. *Das Rheingold* was given in concert in 1979 (SOH) with Mark Elder conducting. In 1981, *Die Walküre* was given in Melbourne (MSO, August) and *Götterdämmerung* was given in Sydney (SSO, October) both were conducted by Sir Charles Mackerras.

performances which served to intensify a wider perception that the Australian Opera would be judged by its ability to mount the complete Cycle in a full staging. Plans for the Australian Opera *Ring* had been under discussion since the appointment of Peter Hemmings as General Manager of the company in 1977 (with Mark Elder proposed as the conductor and David Pountney as the director).[446] As the administrator of Scottish Opera since 1965, Hemmings had been responsible for several large-scale projects, including a *Ring* cycle, and it was he who urged Richard Bonynge to programme a fully staged Australian *Ring*.[447] Bonynge had witnessed a 'golden age' of Wagner performance during his early days in London in the 1950's. At Covent Garden he heard many of the great Wagnerian singers of the day, including Kirsten Flagstad and Hans Hotter under the baton of Karl Rankl. Based upon these experiences, he felt that voices of the required calibre for Wagner were simply not available in Australia at that time. Moreover, Australia's distance from other opera centres, made flying in replacement singers at short notice an unlikely scenario, causing him to advocate double casting, to reduce the risk of performance cancellations. Double casting the *Ring* would have been, at the time inconceivable. During this period of internal conflicts and strife within the company, although the Cycle was announced, the *Ring* plans did not take concrete shape. At the time there were rumours that Bonynge and his associates had sabotaged the project, claims for which there is no evidence. Moffatt Oxenbould recalls that the conductor was 'amiable and amenable'[448] throughout planning discussions. Bonynge remained of the view that the voices required for a *Ring* were not to be found in Australia.

Following Hemmings' departure, in 1982, Bonynge had a change of heart and decided that a *Ring* could be possible, and it would be best to make a start with *Die Walküre*, the second (and best-known) opera of the Cycle. The company announced plans to commence the first Australian Opera *Ring* in 1983. Bonynge's decision was influenced by the recent influx to Australia of suitable singers,

---

[446] After a short tenure, he resigned in late 1979. Ibid.

[447] Oxenbould (2005), 302.

[448] Ibid.

including Rita Hunter (Brünnhilde)[449], Margreta Elkins (Sieglinde) and Bruce Martin as Wotan.[450] *Das Rheingold* would follow in 1984, with *Siegfried* in 1985 and *Götterdämmerung* in 1986. 1987 would see the full cycle performed, but out of order, and the complete *Ring* would finally be staged in its original order during the Australian bicentennial year of 1988. The creative team would be led by Andrew Sinclair (director), Alan Lees (set designer) and Desmond Digby (costume designer).

Not for the first time, or the last, a production of the *Ring* became an unwitting signifier for the affordances of an opera house and a lightning-rod for discontent with its limitations. In addition, this project coincided with a period of ongoing crisis and upheaval within the management of the Australian Opera. In most opera houses a new *Ring* is led by the company's music director however Wagner was not part of Bonynge's repertoire. He entrusted the music direction of the Cycle to Cillario.

The venue of the Opera Theatre called for predictable artistic compromises and attracted criticism. When Charles Mackerras conducted *Die Walküre* (in Melbourne) and *Götterdämmerung* (in Sydney) in concert form in a collaboration between the Australian Opera and the ABC in 1981, it was with an orchestra of 104 players. For *Die Walküre*, the Australian Opera 'settled for' 67 players.[451] The conductor Stuart Challender had been commissioned to undertake a reorchestration which would cover the missing instruments. In doing so, Challender was following a standard practice ('Retuschen') of middle-sized theatres in Europe which often perform Wagner and Strauss operas in this way. Nevertheless, a gestation period

---

[449] In 1978 Hunter had appeared in a production of *Nabucco* in Sydney, conducted by Bonynge. She had become enchanted by Australia and decided to relocate there.

[450] Cast: Jon Weaving and Robert Gard (Siegmund), Clifford Grant and Donald Shanks (Hunding), Bruce Martin (Wotan), Margreta Elkins (Sieglinde), Rita Hunter (Brünnhilde), Lauris Elms (Fricka). Valkyries: Etela Piha and Luise Napier (Gerhilde), Anne-Patricia Hemingway (Ortlinde), Margaret Russell (Waltraute), Lesley Stender (Schwertleite), Elizabeth Fretwell (Helmwige), Christine Beasley (Siegrune), Elizabeth Davis (Grimgerde), Patricia Price (Rossweisse).

[451] Hoad, *The Bulletin*, 18 October 1983.

of 15 years, a cost of $A102m of taxpayers' money, and the iconic stature of the Opera House, all seemed to demand more than a mere compromise for a nation which aspired to an operatic culture of international standing. Within critical and public opinion, the notion took hold that the Concert Hall would provide the affordance of a full-size Wagnerian orchestra, which would be preferable even if it resulted in a simplified staging.[452] After all, Cillario had conducted productions of *Aida*, *Otello* and *Fidelio* in the Concert Hall, where the orchestral sound was transformed, and the monumental scale of the works appropriately realised. The fact that the Concert Hall could never have been made available for such an enterprise was lost on the press and public.

This was also the era in which hi-fi and stereo sound came to the fore. With Georg Solti and the Vienna Philharmonic, Decca had begun recording the first complete *Ring* in stereo in 1959, the year construction began on the Opera House. It may have been that many Australian Wagner aficionados, somewhat naively, expected the studio-produced, high-contrast sound of the Solti *Ring* to be replicated in the Sydney Opera House when they passed through its doors to hear *Die Walküre*. Brian Hoad pointed out that 'Hi-fi freaks who have come to believe that Wagner is all about nine horns, five trumpets, five tubas and four trombones letting fly at full volume are in for a disappointment.' He went on to make a positive case for the proposed *Ring* as returning to the essential elements of Wagner's vision, with 'a strong cast of singers and a no-nonsense production which allows Maestro Cillario to explore the threads of humanity which lie beneath the bursts of pyrotechnics.'[453]

The 68-year-old conductor had never conducted the *Ring*[454]and the opportunity to do so held out great rewards, but also major responsibilities. He had a lifelong love of Wagner's music, initially kindled by discovering the score of *Die Walküre* as a child, and attempting to realise it on the piano. He witnessed the Wagner revival in post-war Italy, where the earlier operas were given in

---

[452] Ibid.

[453] Ibid.

[454] Hoffmann, *The Canberra Times*, 15 August 1982.

Italian translation, as was standard practice for the times. He had conducted three of these earlier works with success in Australia, but an entire *Ring* in a new production would be the start of his professional engagement with the Cycle. On accepting the engagement, Cillario took himself off to his farmhouse outside Bologna, and buried himself in renewed study of the tetralogy.

In accepting to conduct the *Ring* project, Cillario had to withdraw from a high-profile production of Rossini's *La Gazza Ladra*, in Cologne. The director was to be the Cologne Opera's Intendant, Michael Hampe, with whom Cillario had previously collaborated in Stockholm. While Cillario was looking forward to the Rossini project, which was part of a worldwide revival of the composer's neglected operas, the Wagner 'bug' had bitten, presenting the conductor with a dilemma, which he explained to Hampe:

> From one side the sure enjoyment of working a Rossini with you. In the other side 'The Great Magician.' He has the power to hypnotise me as he did with my father! It is a 'family disease'. ... In the first part of my life Bach and Mozart have been my only Gods. I played them spontaneously as if I knew everything about them (?!!!). BRAHMS – SCHUMANN – WAGNER: they are incercled [sic] in a big mistery [sic]. Maybe it is the last obligation of my life to try and approach them! I don't trust that you – as Intendant – will accept my reasons. So, I address this letter to THE ARTIST HAMPE; with the hope to obtein [sic] his forgiveness. He surely knows what it means for a conductor to face a Wagner opera ...! Specially for an "Italian-conductor" forced to spend most of his life with the "ABBORITO VERISMO".[455]

In inviting Cillario to conduct this *Ring*, Bonynge had wisely chosen someone who could achieve the best musical results in an imperfect performance venue, with a distinctive cast of singers, some of whose voices were on the lighter side of the Wagnerian spectrum. Bonynge, who had said that he only began to warm to

---

[455] Cillario to Michael Hampe, 24 January 1983. Copy of letter in: Carlo Felice Cillario – Artist Files '3', Opera Australia Library archives.

the composer when he heard Cillario conducting Wagner,[456] felt that Cillario's Italianate approach would work best with the vocal resources available[457], asserting the primacy of voices and text over the orchestral texture to create a lyrical, 'simpatico' *Ring*. Bonynge relied upon the Italian's ability to fine down the texture for some of the lighter voices, while being able to whip up a storm for the outpourings of a Rita Hunter.[458] There were, in any case, good historical precedents for an Italianate approach to Wagner, stretching back to the composer's esteem for *bel canto* composers and voices.

The musical rewards were considerable for opera-goers who were able to listen with open ears, setting aside the politics and the negative advance press, and Bonynge's trust in Cillario was vindicated. The staging was another matter. The production that emerged was widely held to be clumsy and provincial, falling far short of the sophisticated *Personenregie* demanded by Wagner's dramaturgy. The management stepped back while debates over the merits (and faults) of the production were rehearsed in the press.

David Gyger saw the project as:

> an acquired taste that must be nurtured over a period of years ... precisely, in fact, the sort of exposure the Australian Opera plans to give the Ring: starting with the most accessible opera, even if it happens to be Part 2 of the sequence and adding a new one each year with ongoing revivals of the parts already staged. So much for the AO's impeccable grand strategy for The Ring.[459]

Gyger asked: 'where did the actual premiere of *Die Walküre* fail

---

[456] A. Gyger (2005), 218.

[457] As indicated by Edward Greenfield in his review (below).

[458] 'It was Maestro Cillario who first suggested to her that she should sing for the Australian Opera. He had conducted her as *Aida* in 1969 in England and, in 1975, in one of her greatest roles, *Norma*, for the San Francisco Opera. Shortly afterwards Rita Hunter discovered that her admiration for Cillario was mutual: he had written to Maestro Massini who would conduct her in *Norma* at the Metropolitan, "I send you not a virgin Norma but one who has been tried and conquered all." Peter Johnston, *The Melburnian*, Vol. 9 No. 9, May 1994, 33-35.

[459] D. Gyger, 'AO Ring has debut worries,' *Opera Australia*, November 1983.

where it might have succeeded?'[460] A range of responses may be found in the leading critical voices of the day.

Maria Prerauer described the premiere as a 'good provincial repertoire performance. That is, in many ways it succeeds admirably while in others it falls somewhat short of the ideal. The Bayreuth Festival it is not, nor could it be.' Prerauer queried the decision to begin the Cycle with *Walküre*, and her other criticisms included

> some of the eccentric vocal casting and a strange mixture of production styles. Sometimes the direction, scenery and costumes were so antiquatedly naturalistic as to appear almost a send-up. At others, usually just where a little old-style realism would have helped to clarify, the complicated action became obstinately obscure, especially when sung in German.[461]

Prerauer was opposed to the work being sung in the original German, and several critics agreed, quoting comments by the composer in support of arguments to present his works in the vernacular.[462]

As to the vocal performances, John Carmody reported that Rita Hunter 'sings splendidly. I have never heard her better – powerful, expressive, and dead accurate: a born Brünnhilde.'[463] Edward Greenfield concurred: 'Rita Hunter as Brünnhilde sounds happier than she did at the [London] Coliseum, if anything sweeter of tone and by the looks as well as the sound of her, weightier as well.'[464] Greenfield was hardly alone among critics in referring to Hunter's physique in terms that have become (in the 21st century) unacceptable. Prerauer felt that Hunter

> can always say something vocally interesting about a char-

---

[460] Ibid.

[461] Prerauer, *The Australian*, 6 October 1983.

[462] The *Ring* cycle mounted at English National Opera in the 1970's conducted by Reginald Goodall, in an English translation by Andrew Porter, released on record in 1977, likely influenced these criticisms.

[463] Carmody, 'Earthbound in Valhalla: Australian Opera steps gingerly into the Ring,' *The National Times*, 14–20 October 1983.

[464] Edward Greenfield, Hand-typed review, written for publication in *The Guardian*, London. Copy of draft only in Opera Australia Press Files, 1983 Folder.

acter, it was marvellous to luxuriate in the sure warmth of her Brünnhilde.... Over and over again, in this role, she proves beyond question that Brünnhilde is the very heart of Hunter territory; she breathes life, daughterliness, fire, anger, love – above all beauty – into every phrase of this music.[465]

Margreta Elkins was also widely praised. 'Looking like the epitome of Aryan femininity,' according to John Carmody, 'she is almost an ideal Sieglinde, especially with her unforced capacity to project richly across the orchestra.'[466] Prerauer agreed that 'Elkins, translated up from mezzo status, makes a tender and touching Sieglinde.'[467] 'Lauris Elms was also vocally and dramatically formidable (and abrasively accurate) as Fricka.'[468] Reporting from slightly later in the run, Roger Covell found the cast changes to Robert Gard (Siegmund) and Donald Shanks (Hunding – 'black toned, finely projected') to be a noticeable improvement.[469]

As Wotan, Bruce Martin was recognised as the linchpin in the cast, the singer who dominated the stage and who could create cohesion in the other two works in which Wotan sings, as Carmody wrote:

> Crowning this vocal array, and bestriding the entire performance like a colossus, was the Wotan of Bruce Martin. This is a Wotan of rare magnificence. ... His command of pace, of dramatic intensity, of vocal colour and dynamics, were remarkable in the finest artistic sense. Few audiences anywhere in the world could expect to experience a finer Wotan.[470]

To which Prerauer added:

> Bruce Martin's Wotan is vocally and histrionically outstanding. He has the voluminous dramatic bass-baritone, the variety of tone colour and the physical stature to seem

---

[465] Prerauer, *The Australian*, 6 October 1983.

[466] Carmody, *The National Times*, 14-20 October 1983.

[467] Prerauer, *The Australian*, 6 October 1983.

[468] Carmody and (Prerauer), see FN 465-466.

[469] Covell, 'A stronger Hunding, a stripling Siegmund with change of cast,' *The Sydney Morning Herald*, 21 October 1983.

[470] Carmody, *The National Times*, 14–20 October 1983.

a pagan god made of flesh. He also manages to convey Wotan's fallibility and weakness, ... without ever losing his dignity.[471]

Edward Greenfield wrote of 'the splendid Wotan of Bruce Martin, true and firm, never once letting out a woolly or ugly note.'[472] David Gyger echoed these sentiments in his article 'Martin as Wotan tops Walküre'.[473] He was patient with the first steps in this enormous project and did not deny the flaws that needed to be ironed out, but he remained positive about the future – particularly in relation to the ongoing contribution of artists such as Martin. Carmody concluded that the production 'offers rewards as rich in retrospection as in the experience; for its virtues, and especially for Bruce Martin, this "Valkyrie" should not be missed.'[474]

Sharper divisions of critical opinion emerged over the reduced orchestration.[475] Roger Covell remarked on orchestral deficiencies which included 'serious gaps in the sonorities of some wind sections and gross inadequacy in the numbers of strings', leading to an 'imbalance of wind and strings'. He reminded readers that the 'Magic Fire' Music requires 'multiple harps and the careful division of exactly twice the number of violins as were available on this occasion.... Impossible, you say, within the cramped spaces of the Opera Theatre pit ... a version of the "Valkyrie" which is below provincialism in its orchestral compromises.'[476]

---

[471] Prerauer, *The Australian*, 6 October 1983.

[472] Greenfield, see FN 464.

[473] D. Gyger, 'Martin as Wotan tops Walküre,' *Opera Australia*, November 1983.

[474] Carmody, *The National Times*, 14–20 October 1983.

[475] The criticism came not only from those witnessing the performances: there was also dissatisfaction expressed from within the cast: 'Rita Hunter's radiant voice ... unfortunately unsupported by the violins in the orchestra which sounded as if they were mosquitoes humming along under the clarion ride of the horns. ... The performance was splendid as far as the singing was concerned, but the orchestral sound was so appalling that the opera company began work on enlarging and rebuilding the pit which has now (2001) achieved an acceptable sound.' Here the blame is laid squarely on the limitations of the pit. (Elms (2001), 215).

[476] Covell, 'Die Walküre needs patching,' *The Sydney Morning Herald*, 6 October 1983.

Maria Prerauer assessed it differently:

> The main assets were superb translucent playing from the pit under the quite magical baton of Carlo Felice Cillario and some fine individual performances from some, but by no means all, of the singers. Although the reduced orchestration was used, musically it lost nothing.[477]

Reviewers analysed Cillario's interpretative contribution separately from the imperfections of the resources he had at his disposal. W. L. Hoffmann found the production 'a notable start to the project'. He agreed that the pit was 'not large enough' holding only 65 players, whereas Wagner calls for closer to 100. Aurally, this impacted mostly upon the string sound, although 'Cillario obtained such excellent playing from the orchestra that this was hardly a problem. Cillario is an extremely fine conductor of the Italian repertoire, but I was pleasantly surprised at his notable realisation of Wagner's score.'[478] In considering *Die Walküre* as the first instalment of an ongoing project, undertaken by a company just over a decade old,[479] in a less than perfect theatre, Covell wrote:

> There is enough merit in the casting and much of the conducting to make it eminently worthwhile rethinking and salvaging this project before it goes too far in a direction that can bring little credit to the company's claim to be representing Wagner's music drama in a manner true to each of its vital dimensions.[480]

Covell's criticisms were particularly directed at the production, which he felt may be redeemable, and the orchestra pit, about which little more could be done. At a later performance in the run of eight, he had softened his view to some extent, writing that while there were still production weaknesses, the show had 'settled down' and

---

[477] Prerauer, *The Australian*, 6 October 1983.

[478] Hoffmann, 'Notable start to the 'Ring' cycle project', *The Canberra Times*, 14 October 1983.

[479] Referring to the Australian Opera (incorporated 1970), which had begun as the ETOC in 1957, which, in turn had grown out of the Australian Opera Company (founded 1956).

[480] Covell, *The Sydney Morning Herald*, 6 October 1983.

musically 'the conducting of Carlo Felice Cillario is now moving the work along with a relish that lifts the drama at salient moments and avoids dwelling unduly on the imbalance and faults of layering and perspective in the sound from the inadequate pit.'[481]

The Sydney press placed the project under intense scrutiny, and, like their counterparts around the world, they seemed to feel that the company's management ought to be guided by their critical voices. Overseas critics such as Edward Greenfield were more positive, impressed by the ingenuity and resourcefulness on display, and complimentary towards the musical leadership and the quality of the casting. They also held the view that the 'forging' of a *Ring* cycle is a process – an ongoing evolution, and that this was a starting point. Amid disparaging local references to 'provincial' aspects of the production, Greenfield's comments make a salutary comparison.

Greenfield introduced the projected cycle as 'now in hand at a projected cost of a million Australian dollars, the Australian Opera company at the Sydney Opera House is defying the impossible.'[482] He notes that the venue chosen was not the 'grand Concert Hall' with a capacity to seat 2700, where 'concert performances of *Das Rheingold* and *Götterdämmerung* have been given before, but the company's regular home of the Opera Theatre, seating only 1500 with room for an orchestra of no more than 70 and with hardly room to swing a cat in the wings.'[483]

In his view 'musically the limitation of scale works surprisingly well,' noting 'a slimming down of the Wagnerian upholstery' – in the arrangement of Stuart Challender.

> You have every solo on the right instrument, and only the shortage of strings brings a real change of sound. Even that had its advantages, for voices can happily ride over even the loudest tutti – as indeed one suspects they did originally at Bayreuth when Wagner's orchestra using gut strings made so much less noise than a modern band. ... The emphasis

---

[481] Covell, *The Sydney Morning Herald*, 21 October 1983.

[482] Details of the financing of the *Ring* can be found in Oxenbould (2005), 396.

[483] Greenfield, see FN 464.

on lyricism is encouraged by having an Italian conductor at the helm.[484]

By contrast the local critics tended to focus negatively upon past mistakes which were not directly relevant to the present production. 'B. Canto', for example, noted that the performance of *Die Walküre*

> produced no feelings of gratitude as far as I am concerned, not because of the performance itself, but rather a feeling of "and high time too".… The gestation of this project has been painful and not without its casualties and scandals.[485]

Cillario and Wagner

> The year went on, with an opera conducted by Cillario. He had always been a truly great conductor of Verdi and the Italian repertoire, and I was a firm admirer of his ability. But this time he was to conduct Wagner's *Walküre*! Wagner was not a great admirer of Verdi and vice versa.[486]

The above comment appears in Lauris Elms' memoirs, and is typical of the backstage talk that would take place on occasion when Cillario conducted a German opera. First and foremost, he was recognised (if not stereotyped) as an authority in the Italian operatic repertoire, so much so that his decamping from the opera pit in order to conduct performances of Verdi's *Requiem* was noted by one critic with surprise.[487] Cillario resisted such stereotypes, and his long-term relationship with Australia was based in part upon the openness of the management to offer him repertoire to conduct that he was not associated with, either in Europe or America.

The Metropolitan Opera, New York, has historically catered to audiences who arrived through a series of successive migrations to the New World. The company's conductors and music staff tended to specialise in the Italian, French or German repertoire, assuring any opera lover with (for instance) Italian ethnic roots of an

---

484 Ibid.

485 'B. Canto', 'A timid start to the Ring,' *The Australian Jewish Times* (Sydney), 13 October 1983.

486 Lauris Elms, who sang Fricka in 1983. Elms (2001), 215.

487 Blanks, *The Australian Jewish Times* (Sydney), 3 December 1981.

'authentic' experience. The notion of a particular conductor type for each of these repertoires persists to some extent to this day. Cillario embodied the 'Italian conductor' type and fulfilled this function with success and sometimes self-conscious pride during his three and a half decades in Australia. When he conducted Verdi and Puccini, he communicated a depth of personal conviction, which bore the stamp of authenticity for his audiences. He may have loved or hated *Tosca*, but the music flowed inexorably through his veins. While benefitting from this stereotyping, he was keenly aware of its limitations:

> One of the points that I was always trying to fight against is to become just a routine conductor. This is especially true in Italian opera, unfortunately. Because of my Italian name I am considered an Italian conductor, and to lead German operas is difficult for us, much more than for anybody else. An Italian conductor in the past often was just a conductor with a big experience, but not that sacred fire that you must pour forth every time you must invent something, just as I did for *Tosca* when I had Callas and Gobbi. So, I must study now.[488]

Cillario inherited his love of Wagner from his father, though he explained in 1982 that the roots of this affinity may go deeper still:

> Bologna has a wonderful Wagnerian public because Giuseppe Borgatti (1871-1950), a great Wagnerian singer, was born just near Bologna, and Giuseppe Martucci (1856-1909) was the Director of the Conservatorio, and he was mad for Wagner. … a very smart man: he translated all of the operas of Wagner, and there is a great picture in the Conservatorio which is labelled '*Riccardo Wagner, Cittadino Bolognese.*' It has been declared on a couple of occasions that *Lohengrin* perhaps was better in Italian than in German![489]

Beginning with *Tannhäuser* in 1968, Cillario's regular visits

---

[488] Cillario and Duffie, *Interview*, 1982. The reference to study relates to Cillario's preparation for the 1983 *Walküre*.
[489] Cillario and Duffie, *Interview*, 1982.

to Australia afforded him the opportunity to conduct most of the Wagner canon. Had it proceeded, this *Ring* cycle would have him seen him conduct all of Wagner's mature operas. The Cycle stalled after the first two operas, but he was well advanced with preparation for both *Siegfried* and *Götterdämmerung*; his marked-up scores contain details of projected casts and discussions about the productions which, sadly, were never realised.[490]

With typical self-contradiction, Cillario often stated that operas should be sung in the original language, although he conducted several Mozart productions and even Verdi's *Falstaff* in English. In the next breath would affirm that Wagner could be sung to good effect in Italian. He was well aware that Wagner had conducted much Italian opera in his youth, and all his life loved and admired Bellini in particular, retaining a score of *Beatrice di Tenda* which he would on occasion play and sing from. There is a point of intersection between the *bel canto* style and Wagner's vocal writing, and many conductors and coaches advocate an Italianate approach to negotiating his vocal lines.

When conducting a Wagner opera, Cillario would arrive with an Italian-language score under his arm (for example, *I maestri cantori di Norimberga*), from which he had learned all the vocal parts, in Italian, with notes about shades of meaning, etymology etc. Cillario's Wagner readings may have been more lyrical than some others, but his approach to these works carried authority, understanding, and great love.

Cillario was hardly the first 'Italian opera conductor' to suffer from being so narrowly categorised: Arturo Toscanini faced similar criticism, as the first Italian conductor to develop an international career largely in symphonic music from the German canon. He became the first conductor outside the German-speaking world to conduct at Bayreuth (followed in due course by Victor de Sabata), and in 1936 conducted a production of *Die Meistersinger* in Salzburg which retains a strong place in the opera's discography.

In 1994, Cillario was asked by a journalist if he would still like

---

[490] Scores held in the Cillario family archive, Bologna.

to conduct the *Ring*. With obvious enthusiasm he explained that he would love to 'start again' and conduct all of Wagner's music 'from the beginning', especially *Tannhäuser* and *The Flying Dutchman*, for in doing so he could 'rediscover the most profound satisfaction as expressed by Wagner himself: that while the other arts may indicate it, Music is the only art which is able to express absolute truth.'[491] Today it is often forgotten that Wagner belonged to the standard repertoire of the leading Italian houses in the early decades of the 20th century. Speaking in 1979, the soprano Maria Caniglia recalled the 'glorious tradition' of Wagner performance in Italy, which had been a central part of Cillario's musical experience.[492]

Moffatt Oxenbould, Artistic Director

17: Moffatt Oxenbould and Carlo Felice Cillario c2000.

---

[491] Johnston, *The Melburnian*, Vol. 9 No. 9, May 1994, 33–5.
[492] Ibid.

Moffatt Oxenbould had joined the staff of the Elizabethan Trust Opera Company in 1963 and just over two decades later, in 1984 he was appointed Artistic Director of the Australian Opera. His promotion marked the end of Richard Bonynge's tenure as Music Director. The decade since the opening of the Sydney Opera House had been one of enormous artistic development in the standards and profile of the company. Inevitably, it had also been marked by conflict and in-fighting within the leadership, particularly with regards to the artistic values envisaged by Bonynge and the financial realities that the company faced in realising them. The Sutherland/ Bonynge presence had become central to the company's identity– much of the strategic planning was based around that model. Sutherland was a key element in what 'opera' signified to Australians at this time, and her international acclaim was hugely attractive. There was, however, a perception in some quarters that the dual roles played by Bonynge, as Music Director of the company as well as the conductor of virtually all Sutherland's performances, created an artistically unique product, but one that was not conducive to the further evolution of the company's goals. Following his term as Music Director, Bonynge remained a sought-after guest conductor in Australia, even after the retirement of Joan Sutherland in 1990.[493]

In succeeding him, Oxenbould knew the company from the inside out. He had a clear grasp of artistic and financial imperatives and was able to tread the fine line of creating a performance programme that neither placed the company in financial jeopardy, nor allowed it to descend into provincialism. Over the next 15 years, a strong, artistically fruitful working relationship developed between Cillario and Oxenbould, based upon mutual respect and a common goal to produce operas as well as possible within the available budget.

Cillario continued to travel to Australia each year, fulfilling a significant performance schedule in both Sydney and Melbourne. In regular correspondence with Oxenbould, he advised about orchestral matters, sourced specific overseas singers, and nurtured the talents of emerging singers in the Young Artist's Programme (formed in

---

[493] Her farewell performance was in Meyerbeer's *Les Huguenots*, singing the role of Marguerite de Valois.

1984) and the chorus. He worked closely with the company's Head of Music, Sharolyn Kimmorley, to coach the resident singers in their roles and advise on musical matters. Following Oxenbould's appointment, the company shed a prevailing mood of volatile uncertainty and crisis that had characterised the first decade in the Sydney Opera House. There gradually developed a more positive sense of purposeful work and productivity.

The *Ring* Flounders

The *Ring* project continued through the change in leadership and *Die Walküre* was given again in Sydney in 1984. The staging had been reconsidered and reworked to positive effect, and the orchestra's increased command of Wagner's score under Cillario was also acknowledged. Roger Covell noted that 'Sinclair has diligently reworked his staging ... removing many of the ineptitudes ... that marred ... this production last year.'[494] He retained objections to specific aspects of the production, and to the orchestral contribution, which 'alas, is still not able to cope with the demands which the score places upon it. Though it had more spirit than last year, it faltered frequently.'[495]

The point was widely made in the press that while Lehár's *Merry Widow* was given a lavish revival in the Concert Hall during that season, *Die Walküre* was still consigned to the Opera Theatre.[496] Nevertheless, Covell conceded that 'Cillario now conducts the performance with a far surer maintenance of the flow – the Wagnerian *melos* – of its larger paragraphs.'[497] These comments were echoed in *The Catholic Weekly*: 'Cillario's conducting of the orchestra makes it have more dramatic impact, and he exposes more of the nerve centres of this marvellous, intricate score' – the reviewer found that the whole opera had been 'tightened up', and that the staging has been 'rethought in certain areas'.[498]

---

494 Covell, 'Revival of Walküre brings improved singing, staging,' *The Sydney Morning Herald*, 23 February 1984.
495 Carmody, *The National Times*, 2–8 March 1984.
496 For example, see Ibid.
497 Covell, *The Sydney Morning Herald*, 23 February 1984.
498 'RJR', 'This Wagner is a Winner,' *The Catholic Weekly*, 29 February 1984.

Among the cast,[499] two changes were welcomed: Alberto Remedios as Siegmund, 'full of ardour in vocal and interpretative terms ... his singing adhered to the true Wagnerian style,' and Marilyn Richardson as Sieglinde 'her expressive soprano went from strength to strength.' John Carmody was equally effusive about Richardson's Sieglinde – 'always with abundant, glowing vocal power' – and praised Remedios, but he felt that Rosemary Gunn as Fricka was 'not a match' for Lauris Elms.'[500] Covell wrote that

> the balance of the casting, and the intensity and vocal quality with which some key characters are realised, are immeasurably improved in this revival. ... [Remedios] brings an authentically heroic tenor to the part. ... [Richardson gave] Sieglinde's expression of both ardour and desperation a personal and vocal conviction that is thrilling.[501]

Bruce Martin meanwhile 'gained more authority in the interpretation of Wotan and displayed more vocal substance than previously.'[502]

Cillario had evidently worked hard to optimise the orchestral sound with the forces at his disposal: 'There was a touch of incandescence about their playing. Call it Italian lyricism. But when a solid phalanx of sound is required, they are betrayed by their lack of numbers' – sharply so in the 'Ride of the Valkyries.'[503]

One notable development for this revival was the use of surtitles, which had been introduced earlier in the season for Cilea's *Adriana Lecouvreur*. Roger Covell saw 'decisive value in allowing the majority of opera goers to participate in the absorbing shifts of meaning and

---

[499] Full cast: Alberto Remedios (Siegmund), Clifford Grant (Hunding), Bruce Martin (Wotan), Marilyn Richardson (Sieglinde), Rita Hunter (Brünnhilde), Rosemary Gunn (Fricka). Valkyries: Etela Piha (Gerhilde), Anne-Patricia Hemingway (Ortlinde), Margaret Russell (Waltraute), Lesley Stender (Schwertleite), Elizabeth Fretwell (Helmwige), Christine Beasley (Siegrune), Elizabeth Davies (Grimgerde), Patricia Price (Rossweisse).

[500] Carmody, *The National Times*, 2–8 March 1984.

[501] Covell, *The Sydney Morning Herald*, 23 February 1984.

[502] Horst Cybulla, *Review* – typed manuscript, dated 1 March 1984. Opera Australia Press File (1984 folder).

[503] 'B. Canto', *The Australian Jewish Times* (Sydney), 1 March 1984.

reference in Wagner's text.'[504] With the advent of surtitles, protests that certain operas should be performed in English gradually receded.

During the Winter season, *Das Rheingold* was added to the Cycle.[505] By this stage, the critics were no longer picking over details of the production; rumour was circulating that the entire project was to be discontinued. Hans Forst's review[506] summed up the judgement of critics who blamed the management for being unwilling, or unable to take the drastic steps needed to achieve a *Ring* cycle of the required quality.

In *Das Rheingold,* Bruce Martin was again singled out for praise; Covell wrote that he 'continues to be a Wotan of powerful presence and incisive voice,'[507] and Forst noted that he 'has all the vocal nobility for the top god and maintains his dignity against all the surrounding odds.' Of the remainder of the cast, Forst admired the 'world-class' Mime of Gregory Dempsey, the 'well thought out and appropriate' portrayal of Alberich by Raymond Myers, the 'lively intelligence' of Robert Gard as Loge. Rosemary Gunn presented Fricka as an 'elegant, suave hostess' which Forst took as a failing of the production. Rosina Raisbeck as Erda was likewise criticised as a piece of miscasting. [508]

Covell's reservations went further than Forst. He felt that John Wegner sang with 'a rather dry, character voice' as Fasolt; Christine Hore as Freia was an 'uningratiating soprano' who 'would have been more at home as a Walküre', while the 'tired voices of Mime and Erda throb like parodies.' He was more generous towards the Rhine

---

[504] Covell, *The Sydney Morning Herald*, 23 February 1984.

[505] Full cast: Rosamund Illing, Judith Saliba, Jolanta Nagajek (Woglinde, Well-gunde, Flosshilde), Bruce Martin (Wotan), Robert Allman (Donner), Sergei Baigildin (Froh), Robert Gard (Loge), Rosemary Gunn (Fricka), Christine Hore (Freia), Rosina Raisbeck (Erda), John Wegner (Fasolt), Clifford Grant (Fafner), Raymond Myers (Alberich), Gregory Dempsey (Mime).

[506] Hans Forst, 'Opera never did want to go another round with the Ring,' *North Shore Times*, 4 July 1984.

[507] Covell, 'Technical muddle and orchestral harshness,' *The Sydney Morning Herald*, 25 June 1984.

[508] Forst, *North Shore Times*, 4 July 1984.

maidens who sang 'capably and with some upper-level lustre', and to Robert Gard, who he felt 'has every quality necessary to make him potentially a first-class Loge, the volatile and shrewd spirit of fire.'[509] David Brown summed up the perceived failings in the cast with the barbed comment that 'Carlo Felice Cillario held the orchestra in check with great skill, so that the inadequate voices could be heard.'[510]

The orchestra attracted less harsh criticism than they had for *Die Walküre*:

> The orchestral resources are limited by the pit … particularly in the strength of the strings, but I did not find this so disturbing when the orchestral reduction has been so effectively done and when the conductor, Carlo Felice Cillario finds such a Wagnerian sweep to it, even if it does not have quite the Wagnerian sound.[511]

Forst, however, summed up the general mood, stating that while the 1983 *Walküre* had been 'half-hearted' this *Rheingold* was 'quarter hearted.' He continued: 'All deficiencies of sound are dwarfed by gigantic visual blunders' with several roles 'once again cast with staggering ineptitude.'[512] Covell criticised the 'harshness of the orchestral sound' which he saw as a

> by-product of a drastic reduction in the composer's orchestral specifications to suit the limited capacities of the orchestral pit. It is the sapping of string tone and the loss of cushioned resonance from a complete brass choir at certain moments in the score that causes the expansive, subtly coloured or emphatic passages of the work to seem bleached and threadbare.[513]

Nevertheless, he concluded that 'Cillario's conducting has energy and belief.'[514] While *Die Walküre* appeared in Sydney and Melbourne

[509] Covell, *The Sydney Morning Herald*, 25 June 1984.
[510] 'B. Canto', *The Australian Jewish Times* (Sydney), 5 July 1984.
[511] Hoffmann, *The Canberra Times*, 9 July 1984.
[512] Forst, *North Shore Times*, 4 July 1984.
[513] Covell, *The Sydney Morning Herald*, 25 June 1984.
[514] Ibid.

in 1985, *Das Rheingold* was not revived, and the planned cycle did not continue.[515]

In July, following the premiere of *Das Rheingold*, Cillario summed up his feelings about the *Ring* project in a memo he drafted to Moffatt Oxenbould:

About 'Sydney's *Ring*'

It is well known Richard Wagner's desire for having his own operas performed and his need of money.

[In] banning the King of Bavaria's project in 1870 for performing *Die Walküre* in Munich, he proved how deeply he was convinced that his 'Ring Operas' had to be performed ONLY in Bayreuth *Festspielhaus.*

May we try to imagine how he would react at the idea of using Sydney Opera Theatre for the *Ring*?!

To plan 'Der Ring' in Sydney was a noble idea supported by many arts lovers; but the performances that we did until now were very useful only for convincing everybody (the critics, the public and ourselves) that Sydney has not an adequate theatre for 'Der Ring'.

I cannot judge the technical aspects of the stage of the Opera Theatre in detail. But if I just consider the several inconveniences that we had to suffer during *Die Walküre* and especially *Das Rheingold* performances, I must think that they are scarcely acceptable for such a kind of operas.

Better I can judge the Opera Theatre orchestral pit: the worst area of such a wonderful building as the Sydney Opera House!

It is narrow, wrongly planned and built with materials producing bad sound. The worst orchestral pit that I saw in so many years of theatrical activity!!

All the players are working in difficult conditions and the little number of string players are asked to produce a sound forced in quantity (and that is prejudicial for the quality)

---

[515] For Oxenbould's summary of the *Rheingold* production issues see: Oxenbould, (2005), 415–6.

for a normal balance of the general dynamic. A very hard task for mediocre results.

Regarding 'Der Ring' I had to fight very hard for squeezing in the pit:

10 Violin I (Wagner asks for 16)

8 Violin II (Wagner asks for 16)

6 Violas (Wagner asks for 12)

6 Celli (Wagner asks for 10)

4 Double Basses (Wagner asks for 8)

When I knew that the A.O. intended to include *Die Walküre* in the repertoire I manifested my desire of conducting its FIRST ACT (I said joking!).

Then when I was offered to conduct the full *Ring,* I couldn't resist the temptation to associate myself with such an adventurous and exciting enterprise.

But at this point, looking behind us at the results obtained until today and fearing that the following two monumental operas coming in the future will create even greater problems, I am taking the painful decision of asking if [it] is not more honest and sensible to spend the subsidy that the A.O. received for 'Richard Wagner's Anniversary Celebrations' producing some other Wagner operas more suitable for Sydney's actual possibilities.

I think that would be a better way for making 'Wagner Lovers' happy and to serve at [an] artistically higher level the memory of such a great composer.[516]

Despite the ups and downs of the *Ring* project, Cillario had become, during the decade since his return to the company in 1974 a regular guest artist, and an integral part of the company's ensemble. The conductor was still represented by Gorlinsky in London, who often drove hard bargains with the company's administration, assuring that there was a parity between Cillario's Australian fees and those that he could demand elsewhere. In a nutshell, Gorlinsky 'drove a hard bargain', as the company files reveal, but at a certain

---

[516] Cillario to Oxenbould, draft letter, 20 July 1984. 'CFC – Artist Files '3', OA Library archives.'

point he made an error, demanding ten times Cillario's agreed fee. Gorlinsky subsequently brushed off the error, saying that it was 'obviously' a joke, and Oxenbould responded that it was nice to know that they were finally on joking terms. Cillario affected to be uninvolved in financial matters, and correspondence with his agent reveals that his association with the Australian Opera signified something deeper:

> I received your letter regarding TAO offer for 1986. You know that they are my First Artistic Family. A family that is having some financial problems, now. They improved the fee spontanosly [sic] and I am sure they will do it again when they can do it. My opinion is that we must accept the offer.[517]

Prior to the *Ring* production of 1984, Cillario's year had begun in Sydney with another major assignment – a revival of Verdi's *Otello* in the Concert Hall, this time with Alberto Remedios in the title role, Joan Carden making her role debut as Desdemona, and Robert Allman as Iago.[518] According to Frank Harris 'It was Carden's night', although Remedios and Allman were also very impressive. Allman created a villain about whom 'there was nothing obvious ... here was a cool, icy, coldly calculating fellow who set each step in his trap for Otello with mathematical exactness'. The 'Credo' was delivered by Allman with 'blistering force and a fiery cynicism'.[519]

Sutherland's 1981 appearances as Desdemona were still in the minds of opera goers, and a comparison was inevitable. In a changing operatic climate, Brian Hoad praised Carden's Desdemona as 'far preferable to the matronly performances of Sutherland'.[520]

---

[517] Cillario to Gorlinsky, from Melbourne, 23 April 1984. 'CFC – Artist Files '3', OA Library archives.'

[518] Full cast: Alberto Remedios (Otello), Robert Allman (Iago), Paul Ferris (Cassio), Robin Donald (Roderigo), Clifford Grant (Lodovico), Robert Eddie (Montano), Joan Carden (Desdemona), Elizabeth Fretwell (Emilia).

[519] Frank Harris, 'Joan Carden a perfect Desdemona', *Opera Australia*, March 1984.

[520] Hoad, 'Cut-price Otello didn't make a killing', *The Bulletin*, 7 February 1984.

For this production, Cillario made his entrance and launched immediately into the storm scene, 'with barely an acknowledgement of the applause that greeted his entry. It set the scene for some truly electrifying playing by the orchestra and continued throughout the night. ... I have observed before [that] when Cillario is in charge, the band takes on a new lease of life.[521]

Roger Covell concurred that

> the conducting of Carlo Felice Cillario fuelled much of the excitement given off by the first performance of the Australian Opera's summer restaging of *Otello*. ... He set the great storm chorus of Act I going, with pantherish suddenness and fiery impetus. It was a thrilling opening to an evening of considerable rewards.[522]

Frank Harris described the effect further, having witnessed that

> Cillario almost raced to the podium, wasted no time on the usual bows to the audience and with tigerish speed unleashed the first shattering chords of Verdi's raging storm scene. ... There was no personal showmanship about Cillario's entry but his lightning strike at the score was a brilliant piece of musical showmanship, thrilling in its promise of good things to come.... Cillario, conducting the Elizabethan Sydney Orchestra, was so commanding in his interpretation that he dominated the performance from start to finish. The opening storm scene was an unforgettable display of the intensity of feeling Cillario can bring to a Verdi score.[523]

Nadine Amadio wrote that:

> Carden's voice has deepened and strengthened into a golden maturity ... her Desdemona has a voice of ravishing beauty and a touching and convincing stage presence. Elegance and rare musical intelligence mark every note she sings. ...The excellent singing was accompanied by Carlo Cillario's hot-blooded yet controlled conducting. The large-

---

[521] 'B. Canto', *The Australian Jewish Times* (Sydney), 2 February 1984.

[522] Covell, *The Sydney Morning Herald*, 23 January 1984.

[523] Harris, *Opera Australia*, March 1984.

scale orchestra sounded rich, expansive, and dramatically aware in the Concert Hall venue. [524]

Finally, Hoad found that 'much pleasure is also being taken in the Elizabethan Symphony Orchestra, comfortably spread out between the stage and the audience, under the fiery baton of Carlo Felice Cillario.'[525] One wonders how the *Ring* operas would have been received had they also been presented in the Concert Hall.

18: Maestro Cillario in 18th-century costume and wig, operating the wind-machine backstage at the Court Theatre of Drottningholm, Sweden 1980s.

---

[524] Amadio, *Sunday Telegraph*, 29 January 1984.
[525] Hoad, *The Bulletin*, 7 February 1984.

Amid a busy summer season spent reviving *Die Walküre*, Cillario also found time to undertake an engagement with the Sydney Symphony Orchestra during February to conduct an all-Chopin concert with Roger Woodward as soloist. Fred Blanks praised the performance, while criticising some of the repertoire: 'much of the music itself – minor works for piano and orchestra – showed Chopin at his least inspired'. The highlight was the Piano Concerto No.2, 'beautifully executed by soloist and orchestra.'[526]

Cillario's work with the Australian Opera during 1985 was dominated by revivals. *Die Walküre*, was given again in Sydney summer, and then transferred to Melbourne for the autumn season. The Sydney cast remained essentially the same as the previous year, with the notable addition of Leonie Rysanek (Margreta Elkins later sang the role in Melbourne).[527] The cast change marked a turning-point in the fortunes of the staging – though not the Cycle as a whole – with Rysanek injecting a new level of energy and engagement into the entire production. With the *Ring* having been jettisoned (not least because of the disastrous *Rheingold*) it was as though fresh eyes were cast over the *Walküre* production, prompting a sense of what might have been.

This was captured in a review by 'B. Canto': 'The Australian Opera's aborted *Ring* was given the kiss of life in a splendid performance of *Die Walküre* to conclude the summer season.'[528] Maria Prerauer expressed similar sentiments, noting that the *Ring* had been abandoned after 'a disastrous, not to say, ludicrous, *Rheingold*. ...The present revival ... by far the best, ... shows, just what a triumph this Ring could have been if given half a chance, instead of having almost everything stacked against it from the

---

[526] Blanks, *The Australian Jewish Times* (Sydney), 21 February 1985.

[527] Alberto Remedios (Siegmund), Clifford Grant and Donald Shanks (Hunding), Bruce Martin (Wotan), Leonie Rysanek and Marilyn Richardson (Sieglinde), Rita Hunter (Brünnhilde), Rosemary Gunn (Fricka). <u>Valkyries:</u> Marjory McKay (Gerhilde), Belinda Matonti (Ortlinde), Margaret Russell (Waltraute), Lesley Stender and Jolanta Nagajek (Schwertleite), Elizabeth Fretwell (Helmwige), Kathryn Dineen (Siegrune), Jennifer Bermingham (Grimgerde), Patricia Price (Rossweisse).

[528] 'B. Canto', *The Australian Jewish News* (Melbourne), 28 February 1985.

start.' Although Leonie Rysanek was the only major cast change, 'the stage suddenly becomes sizzlingly alive ... she made the show.'[529]

Praise for Cillario was mixed with the sense of an opportunity lost.

> Even with such a reduced orchestration to fit the small pit, conductor Carlo Felice Cillario manages to draw the right spacious Wagnerian sound out of his players and singers. What a show this could have been with a full complement of musicians and streamlined sets and costumes in the converted Concert Hall![530]

Nadine Amadio seconded these sentiments 'Cillario never loses his enthusiasm for Wagner, and he drew long and spirited orchestral lines from a reduced orchestra.'[531]

Despite a history of inbuilt hostility to productions touring from Sydney, Melbourne critics and audiences received *Die Walküre* with no less enthusiasm, in what was by now the production's third revival. Brian Chalmers wrote that

> Cillario directed the 70-piece Elizabethan Melbourne Orchestra with a practiced skill ... giving emphasis and deep expression to the thoughts and feelings behind the words of Wagner's Olympian characters. ... [The production boasted] spectacular sound and visual effects adding dramatically to the impact of the staging.[532]

Tony Gould praised all the singers, particularly Margreta Elkins, who delivered 'some of the most outstanding singing and [whose] acting ... was superb. ... [Cillario] conducted the Elizabethan Melbourne Orchestra well through the fiendishly difficult score.'[533]

It is possible that the warm reception given to *Die Walküre* was partly due to the recent completion of the Victorian Arts Centre, making this the company's opening season in the new State Theatre.

[529] Prerauer, 'Rysanek resuscitates sole survivor of *Ring* cycle,' *The Australian*, 21 February 1985.
[530] Ibid.
[531] Nadine Amadio, *Sunday Telegraph*, 24 February 1985.
[532] Brian Chalmers, *Geelong Advertiser*, 20 March 1985.
[533] Tony Gould, 'Wagner, done with style,' *Melbourne Sun*, 18 March 1985.

With its construction, Melbourne now had its own home for the Victoria State Opera and the Melbourne Symphony Orchestra. They had long waited for their answer to the Sydney Opera House, and the two major arts organisations coexisted in the facility without any of the tensions that had initially characterised the Sydney model. In addition, the State Theatre boasted a wider proscenium and much more onstage space. With every passing season, it became obvious to Melbourne audiences that the Australian Opera productions had been designed for a significantly smaller stage. Attempts to adapt the stagings and mask the discrepancy in scale only served to aggravate the old rivalries between the two cities.

During this season Cillario also conducted a programme of Wagner and Richard Strauss in a Gala Concert to mark the official opening of the Arts Centre at Hamer Hall in Melbourne. The line-up of singers was appropriately first class: Leonie Rysanek, Alberto Remedios, Rita Hunter, Margreta Elkins, Jennifer Mc Gregor, and a youthful Lisa Gasteen, who had only recently joined the opera company's Young Artist's Programme.[534]

19: Music Consultant and Principal Guest Conductor of the Australian Opera, Carlo Felice Cillario 1987.

---

[534] Information in this paragraph is derived from Oxenbould (2005), 432–3.

Scene 4

Aida

The 1985 Melbourne season continued in its new home with another spectacular piece of grand opera. The *Aida* production which premiered the previous year in the Opera Theatre in Sydney, was revived in the State Theatre, directed by Christopher Renshaw, and designed by Kenneth Rowell. The impressive cast included Maria Slatinaru and Marilyn Richardson (Aida) and Fiorenza Cossotto (Amneris).[535] David Gyger reported that 'the performances, given a less inhospitable stage scape, have been quite electrifying (particularly those between Cossotto and Richardson).' Gyger found Kenneth Collins (Radamès) good but lacking the requisite vocal power. He also found that the defects of the production were 'more glaringly obvious' in the transfer from Sydney to Melbourne.[536]

John Sinclair observed that the new set fitted into the State Theatre 'with an abundance to spare'. A shortage of chorus singers apparently caused the Triumphal Scene to seem underpowered, only emphasised by 'marching the whole cast in circles.' According to Sinclair, the audience was not deceived, but some were 'vastly amused.'[537] Behind the scenes, Cillario was deeply unhappy about the staging, as he expressed to Oxenbould:

> The surprise No. 1 was to see the CHORUS spread all around the stage like a 'mayonnese' [sic] on a bread-slice … a chaos that I never saw in other theatres … [where] the chorus masters prefer to lose all their teeth instead to accept similar solutions. Knowing well that 'l'unione fa la forza.'[538]

---

[535] Full cast Melbourne: Maria Slatinaru and Marilyn Richardson (Aida), Fiorenza Cossotto (Amneris), Kenneth Collins (Radamès), Robert Allman (Amonasro), Ivo Vinco (Ramfis), Bruce Martin (The King), Robin Donald (Messenger), Bernadette Cullen (High Priestess).

[536] D. Gyger, *Opera Australia*, June 1985.

[537] Sinclair, *Melbourne Herald*, 18 April 1985.

[538] Cillario to Oxenbould, titled 'Figlio, Figlio, amoroso Giglio…', 22 April 1985. Carlo Felice Cillario – Artist Files '1', Opera Australia Library archives.

Musical values won respect despite the staging. According to Gyger, Cillario 'maintained his usual tight control in matters of ensemble', with the chorus 'giving of their best to make an impressive fist of the Triumphal Scene despite its feeble visual impact.'[539] The production transferred to the Adelaide Festival Theatre for performances from 17 to 25 May.[540] In his review, Ralph Middenway took aim at the 'Australian Opera Company … oversaddled with Mills and Boon repertoire in recent years for various private purposes,'[541] a dig at Richard Bonynge's programming. Nevertheless, he enthused about virtually every aspect of *Aida*:

> Everything depends upon consistent high-voltage perfor-mances from [all those onstage] … and from the musical director, Carlo Felice Cillario, a maestro of the old school who knows what he wants and gets it.
>
> Maria Slatinaru is Aida. With a thrilling voice, powerful enough to knock over the unwary, goes an Eastern European boots-and-all tradition that brings to life the larger-than-life Ethiopian princess. Alberto Remedios is in his element in this production, with some very dramatic and some very beautiful singing. Lauris Elms curdling the blood with her venom. … Amonasro, played by Robert Allman, takes the palm … his wonderful voice prowls in your head, as he goes about the stage, barely civilised, impossible to contain. Bruce Martin and Robert Eddie were both excellent as the King, and Donald Shanks' Ramfis 'makes Pope Paul II seem like a community liaison officer'(!). Middenway found Renshaw's direction 'creditable'.[542]

Following this success, Cillario spent the first part of the Sydney winter season rehearsing a production of *La bohème* revived by

---

[539] D. Gyger, June 1985.

[540] Full cast Adelaide: Maria Slatinaru (Aida), Lauris Elms (Amneris), Alberto Remedios (Radamès), Robert Allman (Amonasro), Donald Shanks (Ram-fis), Bruce Martin (The King), Robin Donald (Messenger).

[541] Middenway, 'Such a Grand Performance', *The Adelaide Advertiser*, 18 May 1985.

[542] Ibid.

Andrew Sinclair.[543] Perhaps his name was still tarnished by the failure of the *Ring*, but the *Bohème* production was not well received, while the music direction was:

> The AO's most experienced and best conductor, Carlo Cillario was in charge in the pit. In this Puccini *verismo* the heart-strings are crying out to be tugged at. He achieves this and more, without ever descending into bathos, conducting a vital performance, precise and splendidly paced – an aristocrat of the podium.[544]

David Gyger likewise lavished praise upon the conductor:

> I found opening night a glorious experience for the inspired conducting of Carlo Felice Cillario which produced many outbursts of the sort of thoroughly heartfelt Puccini emotionalism that had been so lamentably absent in the Victoria State Opera performance of the same work.
>
> I sat in B row of the stalls far enough to the side to have a perfect view of the maestro in profile – mouthing every word to his principals, signalling graphically when pitch seemed in danger of being lost, encouraging the musicians in the pit, his face lighting up into a broad smile when some particular moment came together particularly well.
>
> At the end of Act 1, he even conducted the audience as well as the performers, holding his left hand up, palm towards the spectators to demand silence until the last echoes of the distant lovers had died away – and then silently applauding the audience for not applauding too soon.
>
> Such is the quality of this master musician who has graced our opera pit with great regularity over the past 15 years or so, and with an enviable record of artistic achievement. We should never forget how lucky we are to be able to attract

[543] Anson Austin (Rodolfo), Amanda Thane (Mimì), John Pringle (Marcello), Christa Leahmann (Musetta), Jeffrey Black (Schaunard), Donald Shanks (Colline), John Germain (Benoit), Robert Eddie (Alcindoro), Lino Naudi (Parpignol), John Durham (Customs Sergeant), Guido Martin (Customs Officer).

[544] 'B. Canto', *The Australian Jewish Times* (Sydney), 22 August 1985.

him back year after year to our remote outpost of the operatic world. [545]

Maria Prerauer shared similar sentiments. She praised the original Tom Lingwood-designed production

> as fresh and attractive as ever, creating just the right atmosphere from start to finish. But much of this would have gone for nothing if it had not been for the inspired conducting of Carlo Felice Cillario who coaxed both the singers and the Elizabethan Orchestra to bring out the true Italianate sound in Puccini's extremely difficult score.[546]

Earlier, in the Melbourne autumn season, Cillario had also conducted a revival of *Tosca*[547] in the John Copley staging. This fixture of the company's repertoire was, during the year given in four separate runs, under four different conductors (Sydney summer, Eugene Kohn; Melbourne, Cillario; Adelaide, Stuart Challender; Sydney winter Alberto Erede). In Melbourne, Harvey Mitchell was enthusiastic about most of the cast, but particularly Marilyn Zschau, who 'dominated the production' as Tosca. He admired particularly her 'huge and dramatic voice', in full flight, noting that 'when anything less than the dramatic summit is called for, Ms. Zschau is not so successful.' He found Lamberto Furlan 'strained and brittle in the First Act', reserving plaudits for John Shaw as 'the brutal satyr Scarpia'. He 'was positively avuncular as he plotted Cavaradossi's execution and the sexual assault under cover of blackmail on Tosca' He described Cillario as 'an honourable conductor, [who] had, no doubt to cope with orchestral rostering problems.'[548]

Other reviewers were more positive, with Tony Gould writing that

> *Tosca* opened in fine style ... with conductor Carlo Felice Cillario drawing a powerful sound from the Elizabethan

[545] D. Gyger, 'Impassioned reading from maestro Cillario,' *Opera Australia*, September 1985.

[546] Prerauer, *The Australian*, 9 August 1985.

[547] Cast: Marilyn Zschau (Tosca), Lamberto Furlan (Cavaradossi), John Shaw (Scarpia), Sebastian Swan (Angelotti), Graeme Ewer (Spoletta), John Germain (Sacristan), Robert Eddie (Sciarrone), Anthony Warlow (Gaoler).

[548] Harvey Mitchell, *The Australian*, 29 April 1985.

Melbourne Orchestra.... In descending order, Marilyn Zschau sang with uncommon strength and vitality, John Shaw was excellent and Lamberto Furlan did not always match the weight of the overall performance vocally, but was still impressive.[549]

Following his intense engagement with the *Ring* and *Aida*, 1986 was a quieter year of revivals for Cillario, along with one new production. He was not involved in the Sydney summer season, but joined the company in Melbourne for three productions: *Don Pasquale*, which had premiered the previous year, *Macbeth*, and *Un ballo in maschera*. Conducting a comic, *buffo* work allowed Australian audiences to reacquaint themselves again with the lighter side of Cillario's art. He had previously conducted a single Donizetti work for the company: *L'elisir d'amore* in 1976. For *Pasquale*, he had the opportunity to work again with an excellent, mostly local cast, headed by Ronald Maconaghie in the title role. Ernesto was sung by a young American tenor, Gran Wilson, and John Pringle was Malatesta. In the role of Norina was Glenys Fowles who had begun her career with the company prior to winning a Metropolitan Opera Studio Award, and subsequently appearing at Covent Garden, Glyndebourne and New York City Opera, while regularly returning to sing in Australia.

The run was revived by the original director, Stuart Maunder, and Clive O'Connell enthused over a production that 'shows AO at best ... an almost unblemished pleasure from start to finish.' Cillario 'was in top form; not exactly skittering through this elegant work but keeping up the rapid-fire pace without blurring the edges.' He reserved special praise for Pringle as Malatesta: 'the knowing mastermind ... [who] has the enviable gift of being able to sing and act simultaneously without making the observer over-conscious of either activity – a smooth operator in both fields.' O'Connell concluded with the injunction: 'More of the same, please.'[550]

---

[549] Gould, *The Sun*, 27 April 1985.
[550] Clive O'Connell, 'Don Pasquale shows AO at best', *Opera Australia*, May 1986.

John Copley's production of *Macbeth* was revived in Melbourne with a strong team of leading villains: John Shaw as Macbeth and Rita Hunter as his wife. Macduff was played by Alberto Remedios, who had become a regular overseas guest, filling the gap of a heroic tenor among the resident ensemble, since the retirement of Donald Smith.[551]

The 1984 production of *Un ballo in maschera* had been revived at the 1986 Sydney Festival (in concert, with Bonynge conducting) and in the Sydney summer season, conducted by Vladimir Kamirski. Cillario had a strong cast for the subsequent run which he conducted in the Melbourne season, with Kenneth Collins (Gustavus III), Michael Lewis (Anckarstroem), Lauris Elms (Ulrica), and Maria Chiara (Amelia), who was renowned for her Verdi and Puccini performances.[552] Cillario had first heard talk of plans for this production during 1983, and had particularly asked to conduct it. In a letter to Moffatt Oxenbould, he outlined his history with the work:

> It is an opera that I conducted completely wrong the first time (Trieste) when I was a baby. Understanding nothing. Then I think I got my own way to interpret it enjoying immensely when I conducted Ballo in Torino (still ½ baby) and Stockholm (also touring to Germany). It was several years ago. And now I would like to have it again in my hands. Just to see if I still feel so happy. Would be enough to give me a couple of "revival performances". We can discuss that during one of Das Rheingold's intermissions ...[553]

On this occasion the performances attracted weak reviews, with

---

[551] Full cast: Rita Hunter (Lady Macbeth), John Shaw (Macbeth), Clifford Grant (Banquo), Alberto Remedios (Macduff), Elizabeth Fretwell (Lady in Waiting), Paul Ferris (Malcolm), Pieter van der Stolk (Dottore), Guido Martin (Servant to Macbeth). [This was the cast for Cillario's performances]

[552] Full cast: Kenneth Collins (Gustavus III), Maria Chiara (Amelia), Michael Lewis (Anckarstroem), Arend Baumann (Count Ribbing), John Wegner (Count Horn), John Antoniou (Cristian), Jennifer McGregor (Oscar), Lauris Elms (Mlle Arvidson), Christopher Dawes (Arnfelt), Sergei Baigildin (Servant).

[553] Cillario to Oxenbould (undated, c1983, written on Qantas 'Captains Club' letterhead). 'Carlo Felice Cillario – Artist Files '3', Opera Australia Library archive.'

complaints of an 'Unanimated Ballo.' Clive O'Connell found Collins 'a one-dimensional Gustavus', and Elms 'not at her best'. Chiara 'animated the stage for the time she was on it. ... Her soprano was powerful and almost completely satisfying.' [554] O'Connell was not complimentary to Cillario, and despite an excellent cast and an international star as Amelia, something failed to spark in this production, and Cillario was identified as the cause. It was unusual for him to be reviewed in this way, but as will be seen, *Ballo* was, in Australia, an unlucky work for him.

Eugene Onegin

In the Sydney winter season, Cillario undertook two projects, the first of which was a production of Tchaikovsky's *Eugene Onegin*.[555] This was the first time the work had been performed in Sydney since the Sutherland–Williamson season in 1965, and what was presented on this occasion was a reworking of a Victoria State Opera production, which had been directed by Anne Woolliams. Roger Covell referred to the 'truly execrable' production of the 1965 Sutherland–Williamson season, against which the new production offers 'both staging and design [which] may be counted as inspired contributions to the art of the theatre.'[556]

Joan Carden won praise as 'a beautiful Tatyana – physically, vocally and dramatically.'[557] Maria Prerauer wrote that she sang 'with a wonderful palette of vocal colours and gradations, ranging from whisper soft to huge dramatic climaxes.' [558] According to Covell, 'the gloriously sung and affectingly portrayed Tatyana of Joan Carden

[554] O'Connell, 'Unanimated Ballo', *Opera Australia*, Melbourne, April 1986.
[555] Full cast: Kerry Elizabeth Brown (Larina), Joan Carden (Tatyana), Jolanta Nagajek (Olga), Lesley Stender (Filipyevna), Richard Greager (Lensky), John Pringle (Onegin), Arend Baumann (Gremin), Graeme Ewer (M. Triquet), Joseph Grunfelder (Zaretsky), Robert Eddie (Trifon Petrovitch), Brian Messner (A Peasant Leader).
[556] Covell, 'Carden's Tatiana straight out of Tchaikovsky's imagination', *The Sydney Morning Herald*, 8 October 1986.
[557] Graham Harris, *Wentworth Courier*, 15 October 1986.
[558] Prerauer, 'Old Russia springs to life in brilliant Onegin', *The Australian*, 8 October 1986.

stands out in decisive relief', adding that 'Richard Greager began well, … [then] became over-finicky in his desire to produce special vocal effects.'[559] W.L. Hoffmann also noted that Cillario 'obtained fine playing from the orchestra … imparting an almost Italian lustre to Tchaikovsky's melodious score.'[560]

The two stars of the evening were held to be Carden and Cillario:

> Sugary though the music is, it brought out in him [Cillario] a richness and delicacy that was quite moving. The Elizabethan Trust Orchestra, under the maestro's sure touch and inspirational direction produced playing of quite superlative quality, especially from the lower strings. Carden's singing was of intelligence and refinement, a truly ravishing performance.[561]

Maria Prerauer found that the musical values complemented a sense of authenticity to the staging:

> conductor Carlo Felice Cillario also gets a similar authenticity out of the score. As so often with Tchaikovsky, the music flirts constantly with sentimentality. In less expert hands it can become quite cloyingly sickly at times. But not in Cillario's. He goes for the wide canvas, the great swelling overall line, propelled on a tide of emotion so strong that it never sounds oversweet. The passion in the music echoes the passion on stage, Tatiana's for Onegin, Olga's and Lensky's for each other.[562]

David Colville remarked that 'Cillario … extracted every ounce of the opera's romanticism.'[563] Roger Covell wrote that 'Cillario's management of lyrical trajectories at the conductor's desk is characteristically spirited. He will have to work a little longer with his orchestral forces, however, before they provide the conversational intimacy of style desirable in the prelude and elsewhere.'[564]

---

[559] Covell, *The Sydney Morning Herald*, 8 October 1986.
[560] Hoffmann, *The Canberra Times*, 27 October 1986.
[561] 'B. Canto', *The Australian Jewish Times* (Sydney), 16 October 1986.
[562] Prerauer, The *Australian*, 8 October 1986.
[563] David Colville, *The Daily Telegraph*, 8 October 1986.
[564] Covell, *The Sydney Morning Herald*, 8 October 1986.

The consensus was that this was a worthwhile production of an interesting opera, but not a great or dramatically well-constructed one. The decision to sing it in Russian was also questioned (or 'what must be an approximation of Russian')[565] in spite of the introduction of surtitles. Beyond the question of audience comprehension, these concerns extended to the preparation of the singers, and a perception that they were not being as expressive (or textually accurate) as they would be in the vernacular. Cillario, however, was enthusiastic about the decision to present a Russian *Onegin*.[566] In a 1982 interview, he recalled hearing Mussorgsky's *Boris Godunov*: 'I didn't know the Russian language when I was listening to *Boris Godunov*, and I didn't understand one word, but in my opinion, it was much more magic[al].'[567]

His knowledge of the Russian language was expanded during the year and a half that he spent in Odesa during the Second World War. While there were those who questioned the decision to entrust the score of *Onegin* to him, they would have been unaware of a momentous chapter in the conductor's past. In October 1986, an interview by Laurie Strachan uncovered the background of Cillario's relationship to Tchaikovsky's opera.[568] He had accepted a position as violin professor at the Conservatoire in Odesa and subsequently made his debut at the Odesa Opera House conducting '*Sevilsky Tsiryulnik*' (*Il barbiere di Siviglia* – it was performed in Russian),

---

[565] 'B. Canto', *The Australian Jewish News* (Sydney), 16 October 1996.

[566] In a typed list he made of his memoirs he described his linguistic skills – 'Parla – al modo suo – varie lingue'. Document (1980s) in possession of the author.

[567] This may well have been in 1942, in Odesa, when the opera was in the repertoire of the theatre. Cillario's views on sung language were based upon its 'singability', which, in turn influences the ability of the singer to sing expressively beyond the semantic content of the text. Generally, he favoured the Italian language, but typically, he threw in a few surprises: '... I think that Italian opera must be sung in Italian, because the Italian language helps the singer to sing beautifully, as do many other languages. ... Another good language for singing is Bulgarian because it's also very clear. Another is Swedish.' (Cillario and Duffie, *Interview*, 1982.).

[568] Strachan, 'Finally, Onegin under the baton of Cillario,' *The Australian*, 7 October 1986.

followed by *La traviata*. He was then asked to conduct *Onegin*. The conductor related that 'in Tsarist times … it was the tradition that *Onegin* opened the opera season in Odesa, but the communists stamped it out, ruling Tchaikovsky to be unacceptably bourgeois.' He continued:

> Talking to Russian musicians, I found that they preferred *Onegin* to *Boris Godunov*. And I think that is because the Russian people … are innocent, naïve, wonderful people. They believe in the story of love between Lensky and Olga and the wonderfully strong character Tatyana, and how Onegin discovers that everything was wrong in his life because he didn't love at the right moment.[569]

Cillario had been mid-way through the preparations for *Onegin* when the Russians advanced towards Odesa, forcing him to retreat back to Romania. Thus, he had been waiting to conduct Tchaikovsky's opera for 40 years. During his period in Odesa, Cillario evidently acquired at the very least a feel for the sound of the Russian language, as indicated by his comment 'I have heard *Onegin* in German, Italian and French, and, while it is still a good opera, it is not the same. In Russian it is a great opera.'[570]

Cillario's final assignment for 1986 was a revival of Puccini's *Manon Lescaut*. This was the third and final time that Cillario conducted the production, originally staged in 1980 by John Copley, now revived and revised by Steven Pimlott. The opening performance on 13 September was broadcast live on ABC FM Radio.

David Colville wrote that 'Saturday evening's musical honours went to celebrated Italian conductor Carlo Felice Cillario who showed what the Elizabethan Sydney Orchestra really is capable of, especially in the beautiful intermezzo between Acts Two and Three.'[571] Roger Covell agreed with the assessment of the conducting, while pointing to what he saw as defects in the opera, writing that

---

[569] Ibid.
[570] Ibid.
[571] Colville, *The Daily Telegraph*, 8 September 1986.

the 'vital ingredients' in the production are 'Cillario's conducting and Nelly Miricioiu's singing of the title role. ... They are not enough'.[572]

For each run of *Manon Lescaut*, since the production was created, the title role had been undertaken by an established overseas artist with a significant profile, beginning with Leona Mitchell in 1980 (followed by Marilyn Zschau, for the continuation of the season, which Cillario did not conduct), and Gabriela Cegolea, in 1981. For this revival, the highly regarded Romanian soprano, Nelly Miricioiu sang the title role. She was already known to Australian audiences through her appearances in 1984 as Violetta in *La traviata* and was partnered for this *Manon* by the Italian tenor, Piero Visconti, who came down with a throat infection during the rehearsals. As opening night approached, he notified his cancellation, only to learn that the understudy was also indisposed. Visconti then agreed to appear, with an announcement being made for his vocal condition.[573]

Miricioiu 'was a memorable Manon ... a sensitive actress ... finding the innocent coquetry for the first act, and suggesting Manon's boredom and worldliness in the second.'[574] However, according to Ken Healey, she 'was not helped by singing to a tenor in whom the fire of passion seemed to never to have been lighted.'[575] With Visconti effectively 'marking' his part, there could be little suspension of disbelief in this piece of *verismo* lyric theatre. Maria Prerauer suspected that Miricioiu (an 'exquisite soprano') was holding back in order to match Visconti, and found that she was hampered by the 'director's inability to fuse the passionate outpourings of the music with a cohesiveness of movement.' In the supporting roles, Michael Lewis had 'enough power and ring' for Lescaut[576] and Pieter van der Stolk stood out as Geronte. Covell was also positive about Lewis, van der Stolk and Gregory Tomlinson.[577]

---

[572] Covell, *The Sydney Morning Herald,* 9 September 1986.

[573] 'B. Canto', *The Australian Jewish Times* (Sydney), 18 September 1986.

[574] Ibid.

[575] Healey, *Opera Australia*, October 1986.

[576] Prerauer, *The Australian*, 8 September 1986.

[577] Full cast: Nelly Miricioiu (Manon Lescaut), Michael Lewis (Lescaut), Piero Visconti (Des Grieux), Pieter van der Stolk (Geronte), Gregory Tomlinson (Edmondo), Vincenzo Nesci (Innkeeper), Christopher Dawes (Dancing Master), Bernadette Cullen (Singer), Neil Kirkby (Sergeant), Jin Tea Kim (Lamp-Lighter), Stephen Bennett (Naval Captain).

Cillario's work was generally admired, with 'B. Canto' reporting that 'from the opening measures … Cillario plunged into the score with headlong vigour.… As always, he has a masterful feel for the ebb and flow of Puccini's melodies, as well as the ability to draw richly characterised playing from the orchestra.'[578] Roger Covell concluded that

> Cillario's conducting had the suppleness and conviction necessary to this urgently propelled and elaborate score. With him in command, the tenor lead in full voice and Miricioiu in unconstrained vocal flight, this *Manon Lescaut* might still come together as a drama of emotional force. The question is whether, even at its best, the performance can overcome the gracelessness of the production.[579]

20: Cillario studying a score, 1989. Photo by Andrew Tait.

[578] 'B. Canto', *The Australian Jewish Times* (Sydney), 18 September 1986.
[579] Covell, *The Sydney Morning Herald*, 9 September 1986.

La Cenerentola

The following year, Cillario took musical charge of two new productions, each of them marking new territory for the company. The first was Rossini's *La Cenerentola*, in a staging by the German director, Michael Hampe. An all-Australian cast included two singers who were about to embark on significant international careers: Bernadette Cullen, in the title role, and Jeffrey Black as Dandini. [580] This production was Hampe's Australian debut, and he would return the following year to create a classic production of *Die Meistersinger von Nürnberg* for the Australian Bicentenary. Cillario and Hampe had previously worked together on a production of *La Cenerentola* in Stockholm, where the conductor was a frequent guest during this time. [581] Hampe's invitation to Sydney was likely guided by Cillario's hand.

Cillario had never conducted a Rossini opera in Australia: not even *Il barbiere di Siviglia*, although it was a part of the company's repertoire. *La Cenerentola* was emerging at the time from relative obscurity. Vittorio Gui (a mentor to Cillario) had led a significant revival at Glyndebourne in 1952 and in 1981 Claudio Abbado had conducted a celebrated staging at La Scala, with Frederica von Stade in the title role. Cillario took immense care over the piece. He had a particular approach in mind, led by Rossini's classification of it as a *dramma giocoso* (as Mozart designated *Don Giovanni*). As he explained:

> *La Cenerentola* is not exactly a comic opera, but it is a semi-serious one with comic elements that have a great effect, as the public likes to dream and return to the world of fairy tales and the years of childhood. The tale of Cinderella, who prevails over her sisters Clorinda and Tisbe by marrying Prince Don Ramiro, enchants the spectators who admire

---

[580] Full cast: Bernadette Cullen (Cenerentola), Gary Bennett (Don Ramiro), Jeffrey Black (Dandini), Donald Shanks (Don Magnifico), John Pringle (Alidoro), Anne-Maree McDonald and Wendy Dixon (Clorinda), Suzanne Johnston (Tisbe).

[581] Armando Tornari, 'Il maestro Carlo Cillario riporta il trionfo del La Cenerentola,' *La Fiamma*, 30 July 1987.

the triumph of the humble in it. However, in comic operas, unlike tragic ones, it is very difficult to keep the audience's interest alive until the end, as Boito himself affirms in a letter to Verdi.[582]

To realise this synthesis of comic, fairy-tale and semi-serious elements, Cillario suggested that Renato Capecchi, the Italian baritone turned opera director be engaged for the preparation of the project. Invited to Australia under the auspices of The Opera Foundation, Capecchi coached the singers in collaboration with the company's principal *répétiteur* and Head of Music Staff, Sharolyn Kimmorley.[583] Cillario himself had inherited a sense of the style required from Gui and Jani Strasser at Glyndebourne. In the context of Hampe's 'stylish and witty' staging[584], an exemplary piece of modern Rossini performance came together.

Most revelatory of all was Cillario's refining of a uniquely Rossinian sound-world for the piece, close in principles of rhythm and articulation to Gui's own Rossini recordings, but communicating his own, particular and eccentric sense of fantasy. On the opening night, it was clear from the Overture that something special was unfolding, and the commercially issued video recording preserves a rare glimpse of Cillario in his element in the orchestra pit.[585] Reviewers reached for superlatives in their efforts to capture in words what Cillario was achieving with gesture and sound: according to Fred Blanks, 'surely one of the crispest, neatest and most gracefully contoured overtures ever to rise from the Opera Theatre pit.'[586] Ken Healey noted that:

> The elegant overture was begun with the soft magic that the composer intended. Throughout the performance Maestro Cillario did more than shape the instrumental music with style; he coloured and caressed the vocal lines too,

[582] Tornari, *La Fiamma*, 30 July 1987. Translation by the present author.

[583] Sharolyn Kimmorley, interview, 18 May 2023.

[584] Hoad, *The Bulletin*, 28 July 1987.

[585] This production was recorded for an 'Esso Night at the Opera' commercial video release.

[586] Blanks, *The Sydney Morning Herald*, 13 July 1987.

producing a musical unity that he, almost alone among the conductors who work regularly with the Australian Opera can achieve.[587]

For Roger Covell, 'Cillario's unmistakable tactics as a conductor could not be faulted: he wishes for a patterning lightness of orchestral and vocal delivery wherever possible, for a supple buoyancy, free of all forcing.'[588] Referring to the composer's culinary proclivities, Horst Cybulla wrote that 'Cillario at the helm of the orchestra served Rossini's score as a delicacy, and the overture was the absolute *pièce-de-résistance*.'[589] Maria Prerauer remarked that 'under the superb musical direction of Carlo Felice Cillario everything works, even the incredibly tricky vocal ensembles taken at breakneck speed.'[590] Armando Tornari concluded that:

> For this reason, the praise for the triumph of *La Cenerentola* must above all be attributed to maestro Cillario, who knows how to create a vibrant and masterful interpretation, conducting with passionate fervour, as is his custom. Critics have likened him to the man with the magic wand who makes the spectators dream, showing a particular appreciation for the execution of the overture, which they defined as the pinnacle of his creativity.[591]

The young, superbly trained cast of singers was much discussed. Tornari wrote that 'Bernadette Cullen prevailed over all in the role of Cenerentola, who showed warmth, dignity and self-confidence on stage.' Cillario himself described her as 'a star on the rise, who in her baptism by fire has already obtained a wonderful success, but she will certainly be able to achieve even better results in a couple of years.'[592] According to Brian Hoad, Cullen 'sailed through it all to

---

[587] Healey, *Opera Australia*, August 1987.

[588] Covell, *The Sydney Morning Herald*, 21 October 1987.

[589] Cybulla, 'Triumphs in Sydney – Without Sutherland,' *Orpheus* (draft), 10 September 1987. (Hand typed draft copy in Opera Australia Press File, 1987 folder)

[590] Prerauer, *The Australian*, 13 July 1987.

[591] Tornari, *La Fiamma*, 30 July 1987. Translation by the present author.

[592] Ibid.

stardom, the brilliance of her vocal art most beautifully tempered by poignancy of interpretation.'[593] For Prerauer, she emerged 'as a bright new Aus[tralian] prima donna in her own right. Indeed, her meteoric rise from chorus to lead has "Cinders" overtones of its own.'[594] Blanks saw the production as a 'stirring vote of confidence in the younger echelons of the company. Five of the seven were up and coming, or recently arrived, singers.'[595] Unusually, Healey's review remarked on the presence of the prompter, Sharolyn Kimmorley who had played a central role in the journey of musical preparation and the success of this production.[596] Amid these critical encomia, the opera also scored a palpable hit with the public.

In November, *La Cenerentola* opened the company's season in Brisbane, and Cillario, unusually, travelled north to lead the performances. Reviewers were intrigued by the storm scene, which was a highlight of the production, and had also been remarked upon in Sydney. 'Throughout all this triumph maestro Carlo Felice Cillario made more magic of the Rossini music, matching a perfectly contained Elizabethan Philharmonic Orchestra ... in complete sympathy with the fioriture that embellish the vocal lines.' This was 'a scintillating *Cenerentola* against which future productions will surely be measured.'[597]

The production's further success in Brisbane was no doubt enhanced by the return of Cullen, singing her first major role in her hometown, and Jeffrey Black as Dandini, of whom it was noted that he had evolved 'from Queensland Conservatorium to genuine stardom in four brief years.'[598] The Brisbane critic, Val Vallis wrote that the 1987 Brisbane season

> must surely be the company's pinnacle of achievement in its ventures in the field of operatic comedy. ...Cillario never deprived [*La Cenerentola*] of its humanity by stretching

[593] Hoad, *The Bulletin*, July 28, 1987.
[594] Prerauer, *The Australian*, 13 July 1987.
[595] Blanks, *The Sydney Morning Herald*, 13 July 1987.
[596] Healey, *Opera Australia*, August 1987.
[597] Patricia Kelly, *Opera Australia*, December 1987.
[598] Vallis, *The Australian*, 9 November 1987.

the combined forces of soloists, the Elizabethan Sydney Orchestra and the ... AO chorus beyond their limits. The resultant ensembles, which supply the main texture of the work, were miraculously articulate.[599]

Cherubini's *Médée*

In the winter season of 1987, Cillario went on to introduce another neglected opera to the company's repertoire, Cherubini's *Médée*. Having flopped at its premiere in 1797, the composer made extensive cuts for a staging in Vienna in 1809. During the 19th century, the opera fared best in Germany, where it was given with recitatives written by Franz Paul Lachner in the mid-1850s.[600] *Médée*, therefore exists in a plethora of versions, and in planning a new production of this rarity, Cillario was described as the 'deus ex machina' who was a decisive force in its creation. In the modern era, it took Maria Callas to revive *Médée* as a vehicle for her particular brand of histrionic intensity. Cillario had previously conducted it (like *La Cenerentola*) in Stockholm, and it was evidently at his urging that the Australian Opera mounted a new staging, directed by Ann-Margret Pettersson.

Médée makes exigent demands of its singers. The early death of the first Médée, Angélique Scio, was attributed in part to the 'excessive vocal gymnastics' demanded by the part.[601] To create the title role in Sydney, Moffatt Oxenbould turned to the South-African-born Elizabeth Connell, who had begun her career as a mezzo-soprano but was now undertaking soprano roles and winning renown worldwide. She had been singing with the company since 1974, and Oxenbould wanted to create a showpiece for her.[602] The rest of the cast was carefully chosen, with Glenn Winslade in the demanding role of Jason, and John Shaw as Créon.[603] Cillario rejected Lachner's

---

[599] Ibid.

[600] Stanley Sadie, *The New Grove Dictionary of Opera*, iii, 29. London, Macmillan Press Ltd., 1992.

[601] Ibid.

[602] Moffatt Oxenbould, interview, 11 April 2023.

[603] Full cast: Elizabeth Connell (Médée), Helen Adams (Dircé), Jolanta Nagajek (Néris), Glenn Winslade (Jason), John Shaw (Créon), Peter Talmacs (Captain of the Guard), Barbara Newton and Kathryn Dineen (Two Handmaidens).

recitatives, a sound musicological decision, but one that would leave a primarily non-French cast to grapple with French spoken dialogue. The ingenious solution adopted was an English-language narration to be spoken by the actor Ruth Cracknell.

Connell's 'electric Médée'[604] was greatly admired by most critics. David Gyger, however judged her by the light of Callas, as preserved on record, and perhaps inevitably found Connell's Médée 'less than an absolute triumph'. He objected to 'stagey posturing that undermined her dramatic credibility to a most unfortunate degree … brilliant as it was vocally … Connell's Médée was not sufficiently so [gripping as] to offset her histrionic shortfall.' When Sandra Hahn stood in for an indisposed Connell, Gyger preferred her account of the title role. Jill Sykes nevertheless credited Connell with 'that measure of humanity struggling against her murderous obsession which makes her portrayal of the character so intense.'[605] Phillip Sametz echoed these sentiments:

> Musically thrilling, full of dramatic insight, Connell's Mé-
> dée is not purely the villainess of classical mythology, but
> a woman torn between duty and revenge. … By the end
> of the performance, you're left in no doubt that you've just
> seen one of the first truly modern pieces of music theatre.[606]

W. L. Hoffmann reported fine singing from the supporting principals: Glenn Winslade (Jason), Helen Adams (Dircé), and Jolanta Nagajek (Néris) were in 'superb personal form.' John Shaw delivered 'a histrionically effective Créon but was not in particularly good singing voice.' Ruth Cracknell in the non-singing role of the Nurse was praised: 'her two brief appearances were a high point of every performance I attended during this season.'[607] Gyger thought that Cillario 'made just about as strong a case for Cherubini's decidedly patchy score as can be made, I suspect; and the Elizabethan Sydney Orchestra as well as the onstage ensemble responded with all their usual professionalism.'[608]

---

604 'B. Canto', *The Australian Jewish Times* (Sydney), 3 September 1987.
605 Sykes, *The Sun Herald*, 23 August 1987.
606 Phillip Sametz, *The Daily Telegraph*, 27 August 1987.
607 Hoffmann, *The Canberra Times*, 4 September 1987.
608 D. Gyger, *Opera Australia*, October 1987.

French works of this epoch, while containing much fine music, can be notoriously challenging to revive on the modern stage. In terms of the style of *Médée*, it was felt that the orchestra did not fully 'come to terms' with Cherubini's orchestral writing, even though Cillario did all he could with Cherubini's music, whose accents and austere measure are 'foreign to most.'[609]

Towards the end of 1987, Cillario was engaged by the Sydney Philharmonia Choirs to conduct *The Seasons* (*Die Schöpfung*) by Haydn. Both the oratorio, and the conductor's appearance on the concert platform, were relative rarities in Sydney. The Philharmonia Motet Choir, somewhat augmented, was paired with an enlarged Australian Chamber Orchestra in order to approximate to the forces Haydn would have had in mind. A strong cast of soloists featured Fiona Maconaghie, Glenn Winslade and Gregory Yurisich. David Brown found that Cillario achieved a balance 'between tragic seriousness on the one hand and the pleasures of everyday life on the other ... in an affectionate performance with the choir always responsive to the demands of the conductor.'[610]

Il Trittico

In 1987, Cillario was named Principal Guest Conductor and Music Consultant of the Australian Opera, a post which he held until 1992. He shared the role of 'music consultant' with Myer Fredman, a British conductor, who had enjoyed a long association with Glyndebourne Festival Opera, before becoming the Music Director of the State Opera of South Australia (1974-80).

In addition to *La Cenerentola* and *Médée*, Cillario conducted two revivals during the Sydney winter season. The first of them, Puccini's *Il trittico*,[611] afforded the opportunity to again work directly with

---

[609] 'B. Canto', *The Australian Jewish Times* (Sydney), 3 September 1987.

[610] 'B. Canto', *The Australian Jewish Times* (Sydney), 5 November 1987.

[611] Full cast: *Il tabarro*: Malcolm Donnelly (Michele), Christa Leahmann (Giorgetta), Lamberto Furlan (Luigi), Robin Donald (Tinca), Alan Light (Talpa), Jennifer Bermingham (Frugola), Gerald Sword (Song Vendor), Gregory Tomlinson, Helen Adams (Two lovers). *Suor Angelica*: Joan Carden (Suor Angelica), Heather Begg (La Zia Principessa), Rosemary Gunn (La Badessa), Lisa Nolan (La Suora Zelatrice), Kerry Elizabeth Brown (La Maestra

Moffatt Oxenbould on the revival of his 1973 production, which was always carefully supervised by the director himself. Cillario had last conducted the trilogy for the company in 1982, and successive revivals tended to draw out new critical preferences over the best work of the three. David Brown criticised the trilogy as a whole, even while admiring while the conductor's efforts to bring it to life. 'It was, as many times before, left to the conductor, Cillario to make much of this trilogy, and of the composer's instrumental finesses.'[612] By contrast, Hans Forst remarked that this revival allowed all three operas to 'form a unity of connected morality plays, highly critical of society and its conventional values.' In her debut as Angelica, Joan Carden's 'rare artistry, in recent years soaring from high point to high point, here reaches its zenith. Hers is a finely modulated performance, starting from submissive self-negation to the heaven-storming despair of a mother deprived of a child.' In the pit: 'Bravo Bravissimo Maestro! To the conductor Carlo Felice Cillario whose musical control is complete and inspiring.'[613] This was seconded by Roger Covell: 'Cillario respects the delicacy as well as the vivid power of the music.'[614]

David Gyger found the revival 'dramatically satisfying, musically enjoyable and even a little thought-provoking.' He remarked that *Il trittico* 'is not the ideal meat for the major *stagione* companies' lacking a platform to 'display the highly expensive talents of megastars.' The work requires 'a strong array of competent singers who are also competent actors and – most important – can blend

---

delle Novizie), Maureen Duke, Barbara Tree (Le Cercatrici), Jan Saint-John (Suor Osmina), Helen Adams (Suor Genovieffa), Barbara Newton, Helen O'Rourke, Helen Borthwick (Tre Novizie), Elizabeth Ellis (Suor Dolcina), Catherine Elliott (Suor Iginia), Nicola Ferner-Waite (La Suora Infermiera), Marjory McKay, Kathryn Dineen (Le Converse). *Gianni Schicchi*: John Shaw (Schicchi), Amanda Thane (Lauretta), Heather Begg (Zita), Gregory Tomlinson (Rinuccio), Graeme Ewer (Gherardo), Nicola Ferner-Waite (Nella), Cameron Phipps (Gherardino), Alan Light (Simone), Robert Eddie (Marco), Jennifer Bermingham (La Ciesca), Donald Solomon (Betto di Signa), Neil Kirkby (Ser Amantio di Nicolao), John Germain (Maestro Spinelloccio), Joseph Grunfelder (Pinellino), John Durham (Guccio).

612 'B. Canto', *The Australian Jewish Times* (Sydney), 6 August 1987.

613 Forst, *The Australian*, 27 July 1987.

614 Covell, *The Sydney Morning Herald*, 27 July 1987.

into an ensemble.' The work thus played to the strengths of the Australian Opera, as an ensemble company, which could cast the many secondary roles in *Il trittico, La fanciulla del West,* and *Falstaff* with artists of substance. Gyger also praised Carden as Angelica, 'soaring over the orchestra with those torrents of velvety smooth, beautiful sound that are required of most Puccini heroines, but few sopranos can deliver to perfection.' Heather Begg realised the Principessa 'to perfection: singing splendidly and demonstrating over and over again through manner and gesture what an awful person this woman is.' In *Il tabarro,* Malcolm Donnelly as Michele sang with 'splendid richness of baritone sound.' Christa Leahmann was an excellent Giorgetta, and Lamberto Furlan was in impressive form. In *Gianni Schicchi,* John Shaw and Geoffrey Chard shared the title role, and each was praised for their quite distinct portrayals. Gyger complimented the whole ensemble of the production, along with the Elizabethan Sydney Orchestra, and the presence of Cillario at the helm.[615]

21: Cillario rehearsing *Otello*, Melbourne, 1989. Photo by Andrew Tait.

[615] D. Gyger, *Opera Australia*, October 1987.

John Copley's elegant production of *La traviata* was revived and filmed for television and commercial release during the 1987 season. Leading the cast were Joan Carden as Violetta, Richard Greager as Alfredo, and Neville Wilkie as Giorgio Germont.[616] With this production it was said that Joan Carden stepped out of the larger shadow of the 'other' Joan.[617] The transformation was described by Maria Prerauer:

> Suddenly Carden, who has been steadily growing in stature as an actress, seemed to leap across an invisible barrier in a manner that is given to few opera singers. This *Traviata* was not just the performance of a fine singing actress. This was great acting full stop. The singing became a brilliant embellishment that deepened the portrayal.[618]

Roger Covell praised Carden as 'a jewel on opera's velvet.' He observed, during the course of the run, that she was

> capable of finding even more truth and feeling in the music and its action as the season proceeds. ... She is vulnerable, lovely, passionate and heartbroken; and it is all in her voice, her phrasing, her movements and gestures. ... This role has found its resident ideal in Carden.[619]

Prerauer went on to note that 'this *Traviata* would not have been half the success without the masterly musical direction of Cillario, whose affinity with the music of Verdi is now almost legendary. There is just no substitute for those wonderfully spun musical lines of sound.' Covell again concurred: 'Cillario ... controls tempos and dynamics with unfailing sympathy for the evening's heroine. The orchestra answers his demand for refinement valiantly.' David

---

[616] Full cast: Joan Carden (Violetta), Rosemary Gunn (Flora), Cynthia Johnston (Annina), Richard Greager (Alfredo), Neville Wilkie (Giorgio Germont), Christopher Dawes (Gastone), David Brennan (Barone Douphol), Robert Eddie (Marchese d'Obigny), John Wegner (Doctor Grenvil), Gerald Sword (Giuseppe), David Tapin (Servant), Neil Kirkby (Messenger).

[617] Joan Sutherland.

[618] Prerauer, 'Carden springs a big surprise – as a great actress,' *The Australian*, 30 September 1987.

[619] Covell, 'Carden: A jewel on opera's velvet,' *The Sydney Morning Herald*, 30 September 1987.

Brown felt his direction 'nearly always had the sure touch of a master at work'. A few lapses of ensemble 'did not efface some playing of incandescent beauty', particularly in the First Act Prelude.[620]

Cillario's first engagement for 1988 took place on Australia Day, 26 January, not in the Sydney Opera House, but on the outside steps of the building. If the *Ring* had come to fruition, he would now be leading the complete Cycle for the Bicentennial celebrations. Instead, he was conducting Peter Sculthorpe's *Child of Australia*, an 'Australian Anthem' with a text by Thomas Keneally, which had been commissioned to mark the 200th anniversary of the establishment of the first British colony. Sculthorpe had revised the piece after the premiere in 1987, and this was the first performance of the new version.[621] On a perfect outdoor day, Cillario conducted the Australian Youth Orchestra, the Sydney Philharmonia Choirs, and Joan Carden as the soprano soloist along with John Howard and Allan Zavod.[622] Philips issued the performance on a 'Music for Australia Day' LP (somewhat predictably illustrated by fireworks over the Sydney Harbour Bridge), and the recording captures the atmosphere of the occasion, as well as marking an all-too-rare appearance of the conductor on a major record label.[623]

---

[620] 'B. Canto' *The Australian Jewish Times* (Sydney), 7 October 1987.

[621] Blanks, *The Australian Jewish Times (Sydney)*, 6 February 1988.

[622] The performance was recorded and released on LP: 'Music for Australia Day' (Philips 834 740–1).

[623] Hoffmann, *The Canberra Times*, 26 June 1988.

Scene 5

Turandot – Sydney Festival

In February, Cillario rekindled his association with a former colleague. As artistic director of the Elizabethan Theatre Opera Company/the Australian Opera between 1969 and 1975, Stephen Hall had been instrumental in inviting Cillario to Australia in 1968 and negotiated his return to the company in 1975, when he conducted *Aida* in the Concert Hall, in a staging produced by Hall. He was then appointed Founding Director of the Sydney Festival in 1977, where he became affectionately known as 'Festival Hall' for a succession of spectacular productions and events. If Puccini's *Turandot* was a shrewd choice for the festival, so were Cillario as conductor and Rita Hunter in the title role.

Reviewing the first of two concert performances, David Gyger found Hunter 'in fine form, singing … as cold as ice through most of the opera … her posing of the riddles was fierce enough to daunt just about any contender for her hand.' As Liù, Joan Carden was 'every bit as radiant as one would have predicted … this character is one of the most alluring Puccini ever created … and she made the most of its every opportunity.' Kenneth Collins sang Calaf 'with much more warmth … than is usually present in his voice,' [624] and the rest of the cast was equally admired. David Brown remarked on the impact of Cillario's conducting:

> Breaking the sound barrier is a commonplace event these days but not when the vehicle is the Sydney Symphony Orchestra, and the pilot Carlo Felice Cillario. For the first of two concert performances of Puccini's Turandot the Italian Maestro indulged, or over-indulged himself, luxuriating in having before him 110 musicians, the Australian Opera Chorus and Children's Chorus, and the talents of some of the best singers available. Cillario, from the first moment unleashed a torrent of sound that barely let up. The audience were knocked breathless by the opening pages, some of the

---

[624] D. Gyger, *Opera Australia*, April 1988.

best in the opera, and in his interpretation the music simply goes from climax to climax, a veritable orgy of sound.[625]

Henry Pritchett added that 'chief among the heroes of the evening must be the conductor Carlo Felice Cillario, whose magical way with Puccini brought every moment of the score to life. The Sydney Symphony Orchestra clearly enjoyed working with him in what was for them, unfamiliar repertoire, and he challenged them to give their best.'[626] *Turandot* had been absent from the repertoire of the Australian Opera for some years, doubtless on grounds of scale, but the success of these concert performances encouraged the management to contemplate a full-scale production in the Opera Theatre, which took place just two years later.

La Cenerentola was revived in the Melbourne autumn season, and once more praised for a cast 'without a weak link'.[627] Hampe's staging was well received, especially the storm scene in Act 2, which showed a life-size cut-out silhouette of a horse-drawn coach careering into a blinding storm, with the passing countryside projected on to a cyclorama at the back of the stage. Perhaps ballet-going audience members were familiar with the music through John Lanchbery's use of it in his ballet score, *La fille mal gardée* (with music after Hérold, Donizetti, and Rossini, among others). Peter Burch wrote that Cillario 'delivered a tight, startling performance that propelled the music along to a most satisfactory conclusion.'[628]

John Copley's 1981 *Tosca* was also revived in Melbourne, with Marilyn Zschau, Geoffrey Chard and Lamberto Furlan.[629] Among the supporting cast was the young John Wegner singing Angelotti,

[625] David Brown, *The Australian Jewish Times* (Sydney), 26 February 1988.
[626] Henry Pritchett, *The Daily Telegraph*, 19 February 1988.
[627] Anthony Rainer, *The Australian Jewish News* (Melbourne), 3 June 1988.
[628] Burch, *The Australian*, 3 May 1988.
[629] Full cast: Marilyn Zschau (Tosca), Lamberto Furlan (Cavaradossi), Geoffrey Chard (Scarpia), John Wegner (Angelotti), Christopher Dawes (Spoletta), John Germain (Sacristan), Joseph Grunfelder (Sciarrone), Guido Martin (Gaoler).

who subsequently carved out an important career in Germany, including at Bayreuth. Burch wrote that 'Zschau's all-stops-out Tosca is a real identity. Her performance is a tribute to the occasional reality of Oscar Wilde's jest that nothing succeeds like excess. Like all the best performers, Zschau challenges herself with serious risk-taking.' Chard's portrayal of Scarpia presented a stimulating contrast to Shaw's, as a 'thoughtful and intelligent characterisation ... subtler, with a quieter – but no less strong – sense of the potential and fatal menace of the role.' Burch remarked that the seven-year-old staging had retained its freshness, and the orchestral playing on the first night was 'full of energy and colour', despite a punishing schedule of rehearsal and performance.[630]

Again under Cillario's baton, a different cast revived *Tosca* in the Sydney winter season. Maria Prerauer echoed Burch's praise for the orchestra: 'One of the evening's consistent pleasures was the playing of the Elizabethan Philharmonic Orchestra under conductor Carlo Felice Cillario ... good ensemble, fine string tone and pungent brass playing made Puccini's vivid orchestral writing one of the opening night's winning features.'[631] The US soprano Leona Mitchell was a favourite with Sydney audiences, and she was making her debut in the title role. Roger Covell praised Mitchell's performance as 'a delightful confirmation of the self-renewing character of opera and its physical circumstances ... Mitchell is a vulnerable Tosca in manner and response, but her singing is, rightly, almost an icon of courage and nobility.'[632]

While Covell expressed reservations over Lamberto Furlan as Cavaradossi, he praised Malcolm Donnelly for a 'superbly professional' assumption of Scarpia, lacking the 'air of menace' of John Shaw, but possessing its own qualities. With Cillario on hand 'to secure uncommonly good orchestral playing in general ... and to coordinate the brilliant tableaux of Puccini's score with idiomatic fluency, *Tosca* will serve very well as one of the reliable anchors of

---

[630] Burch, *The Australian*, 22 April 1988.
[631] Prerauer, 'Flaws aside, masterpiece is masterly', *The Australian*, 20 June 1988.
[632] Covell, 'Leona Mitchell's first Tosca a vivid performance', *The Sydney Morning Herald*, 20 June 1988.

AO's new season.'[633] W. L. Hoffman agreed that Cillario 'conducted with the flair and understanding he always brings to Puccini … as well as firmly shaping the performance and obtaining excellent playing from the orchestra.'[634]

Otello[635] was also revived in the Opera Theatre during the Sydney winter season. Maria Prerauer was enthusiastic about the 'no bullshit' production, first seen in 1984: 'Here [designer] Shaun Gurton's spacious setting of white Moorish arches and slim golden grills is a perfect foil for George Ogilvie's splendid direction. Ogilvie allows all the action to flow from the music-drama itself.'[636] Horst Hoffmann had been suffering from a virus prior to the premiere, but his performance was praised as 'truly magnificent, driven to despair by cunning deceit and by what he sees as betrayal. … Desdemona's killing is an act of rage and retribution.' [637]

Another US soprano, Susan Dunn, was making her Australian Opera debut, as well as her role debut as Desdemona, and the *Wentworth Courier* found that she 'acquitted herself admirably.'[638] According to R. J. Roberts: 'Susan Dunn with a comparatively brief career in opera sings the role of Desdemona beautifully, but her acting talents are still clearly in the formative stage.' Singing Iago, Robert Allman gave 'another excellent performance … as sharply delineated as ever.'[639] According to Prerauer: 'One of the chief contributors to this splendidly shaped *Otello* is … Cillario, whose grasp of the score is masterly, as is his ability to communicate what he wants to the orchestra.'[640] Roberts concurred that 'the musical direction … is in the inspired hands of a master of the art who

[633] Ibid.

[634] Hoffmann, *The Canberra Times*, 4 July 1988.

[635] Full cast: Horst Hoffmann (Otello), Robert Allman (Iago), Anson Austin (Cassio), Christopher Dawes (Roderigo), Clifford Grant (Lodovico), Stephen Bennett (Montano), Barry Patterson (Herald), Susan Dunn (Desdemona), Bernadette Cullen (Emilia).

[636] Prerauer, 'The moor the better…,' *The Australian*, 21 July 1988.

[637] [No author named], *Wentworth Courier*, 27 July 1988.

[638] Ibid.

[639] R. J. Roberts, *The Catholic Weekly*, 3 August 1988.

[640] See FN 636.

knows exactly how to let the sublime score speak for itself, who understands the style and the drama, who has the Elizabethan Philharmonic Orchestra playing in top form, and who draws the best out of his singing actors.'[641]

In another popular revival, *La bohème* was given with a cast led by Glenys Fowles and the US tenor Neil Rosenshein, in a season that won an Emmy award.[642] The scheduled conductor Rico Saccani withdrew, and Cillario took over most of the run (completed by William Reid and Omri Hadari) including a performance filmed and later released on VHS by the ABC.

In the reviews of *Otello*, discussion of previous stagings of the opera in the Concert Hall was notably absent. The orchestral pit of the Opera Theatre had recently been adapted, with the pit floor lowered by 'installing new, Tasmanian oak rostra which are stepped down from the conductor's podium towards the back of the pit.' For the first time since the opening of the Opera House, the pit was able to accommodate 'the 69 players that had originally been promised.' Cillario's reaction to the improvements is not recorded, but Sir Charles Mackerras remarked on 'a completely different sound from ever before' when he conducted a new production of *Die Meistersinger von Nürnberg* in the winter season. The remodelled pit accommodated an additional 10 string players, so that the space available for the orchestra was now 'as big as that of all but the biggest German houses.' Roger Covell's dissenting voice remained, deprecating 'pit size and orchestral deficiency.' Mackerras acquiesced to Covell's point of view: he agreed that, despite the renovation, 'the acoustics of the whole place are wrong. The amazing thing is that the orchestra sounds as good as it does.' The orchestral players remarked on the improvement, and the

---

[641] See FN 639.

[642] Full cast: Neil Rosenshein (Rodolfo), Glenys Fowles (Mimì), John Fulford (Marcello), Rosamund Illing (Musetta), David Lemke (Schaunard), John Wegner (Colline), John Germain (Benoit), Alan Light (Alcindoro), Jin Tea Kim (Parpignol), Graeme Williams (Customs Sergeant), Guido Martin (Customs Officer).

Opera House had apparently arrived at a performing space which could fulfil the conditions of its original brief, as well as meeting with the approval of both artists and audience, some 15 years after its inauguration. [643]

22: 'Andante affettuoso'.

Otello transferred to Melbourne for the 1989 autumn season.[644] Appearing again as Desdemona, Joan Carden was 'pre-eminent … she dominated the cast entirely.'[645] Horst Hoffmann reprised the title role: 'a reliable Otello … without the piercing lyricism of the Italian voice, and acting in a knockabout style.'[646] Clive O'Connell found Hoffmann's dynamic level 'more than a match for the pit at most points: a full-blooded and powerfully driving instrument that swept all before it,' though the partnership between Carden and Hoffmann 'generated very few sparks.' A stalwart in the role of Iago, Robert

---

[643] Information in this paragraph derived from: Geraldine O'Brien, 'Musos in the pits no longer,' *The Sydney Morning Herald*, 24 October 1988.

[644] Full cast: Horst Hoffmann (Otello), Robert Allman (Iago), Gerald Sword (Cassio), Christopher Dawes (Roderigo), Clifford Grant (Lodovico), Stephen Bennett (Montano), Timothy Patston (Herald), Joan Carden (Desdemona), Heather Begg (Emilia).

[645] Hince, *The Age*, 1 May 1989.

[646] Ibid.

Allman was 'dramatically convincing,' giving a performance that was 'polished and extremely well-acted … he looked and sounded much cleverer than those whose lives he destroys.' [647]

According to Kenneth Hince, 'Cillario's State Orchestra of Victoria opened with tremendous impact, as they must do in the storm chorus. In fact, they were good for most of the night with some highly delicate and, in fact, strikingly beautiful quiet playing.'[648] O'Connell agreed that the partnership between Cillario and the orchestra 'was most productive. In no mean terms the storm that opens the work ran jaggedly, setting a pitch of excitement that rarely faltered.'[649] In spite of many strong individual performances and energy in the pit, something seemed lacking from the opening night. Hince 'wished that it was a final dress rehearsal and not an opening. Perhaps it was, in some ways.'[650] The production was heard and seen across Australia as an ABC 'simulcast' on radio and television.

Cav & Pag – The Flying Bed

A new staging of Cav & Pag[651] ruffled critical feathers, though its novelties (most notoriously, a flying bed) would hardly raise an eyebrow in the 21st century. The director, John Copley had set Cavalleria rusticana in pre-war Sicily in 1938, and I pagliacci in the ruins of the same village immediately after the war. With an eye to its commercial appeal, the double bill was given nine performances in Melbourne, and no fewer than nineteen in Sydney. Cillario conducted all performances in Melbourne, and nine in Sydney (Willy Anthony Walters took over the run). Cillario was well known

---

[647] O'Connell, *Opera Australia*, June 1989.

[648] See FN 645.

[649] See FN 647.

[650] See FN 645.

[651] Full cast: _Cavalleria Rusticana_: Sandra Hahn (Santuzza), Rosemary Gunn (Lola), Heather Begg (Mamma Lucia), Bernard Lombardo (Turiddu), David Brennan (Alfio). _I Pagliacci_: Rosamund Illing (Nedda), Kenneth Collins (Canio), Robert Allman [Sydney] John Shaw [Melbourne] (Tonio), Gregory Tomlinson (Beppe), David Lemke (Silvio), Brian Messner, Guido Martin (Two Villagers). For the total of 18 performances that Cillario conducted in both seasons, the only cast change between Melbourne and Sydney was John Shaw, replacing Robert Allman as Tonio.

for both his long experience in and his ambivalence over these pre-eminent pieces of *verismo*: a flyer was published for the Melbourne run, in which the conductor protested that he 'hates violence on stage.'[652]

Singing the role of Turiddu, Bernard Lombardo had apparently been discovered in Europe by Cillario. He was a young tenor (in his late 20s) with a genuine Italianate ring, according to Andrew Bolt, and 'a secure hold on his top notes,' albeit at times overshadowed by the 'lusty singing'[653] of Sandra Hahn. Peter Burch complained about the extensive masking of the stage, once more occasioned by a staging designed for the smaller dimensions of the Sydney Opera Theatre. He felt that Hahn made less of an impact than she had done in *Andrea Chénier*, produced by Victoria State Opera in 1988. Lombardo possessed a 'beautiful tenor with something of the quality of the early Carreras,' even if his acting skills left something to be desired. Beginning a series of farewell appearances with the Australian Opera, John Shaw appeared as Tonio in *Pagliacci*; Kenneth Collins was 'in wonderful voice' as Canio (his debut in the role), while David Lemke made an 'impressive' Silvio.

Copley's staging *of Cav & Pag* divided opinion much more sharply on its transfer to Sydney. John Carmody extended his criticism to the musical direction: 'John Copley should *never* be invited back to [Australia] … It was quite the worst conducting that I have heard from Cillario, and the singing matched it.'[654] Fred Blanks was more positive about the production but objected to the 'spinning bed', as well as Copley's invention of stage action that occurred during the orchestral set pieces. The cast and conductor won his unqualified praise: Cillario 'directed with a marvellous feeling for melodic lyricism on the one hand, tension on the other.' Blanks concluded that 'it is fair to say that in this double bill The Australian Opera can stand favourable comparison with any company of equal, and some companies of better resources. Anywhere.'[655]

[652] Bronwyn Halls, *The Melbourne Times*, 19 April 1989.
[653] Andrew Bolt, *The* (Melbourne) *Herald*, 14 April 1989.
[654] Carmody, 'Tasteless and self-indulgent productions,' *The Sun Herald*, 16 July 1989.
[655] Blanks, *The Sydney Morning Herald*, 15 July 1989.

Maria Prerauer amplified reservations over the staging in her review, titled 'Sparks, mattresses fly over infidelities.' She objected to the mime scenes superimposed on the Prelude to *Cavalleria* portraying the 'betrayed and pregnant Santuzza sobbing loudly on her bed, and with passionately mimed meetings between her ex-lover Turiddu and village beauty Lola taking place all around her.' She noted that the action 'finishes with Santuzza, who seems to have popped an overdose, on a blackened stage flying through the air on a mattress.' Prerauer was however generally positive about the casting: Bernard Lombardo was 'a slightly wooden but suitably unsympathetic Turiddu ... and he sang most acceptably.' In *I pagliacci*, Robert Allman was 'magnificent' as 'the evil Tonio' and Kenneth Collins was 'in superbly ringing voice ... most convincing as Canio.' Of Rosamund Illing (Nedda), Prerauer wrote that 'her lyric soprano is just the right timbre, her small stature ... is quite perfect for this part.' Like Carmody, she was unusually critical of Cillario's conducting: '*Cavalleria* seemed musically rather limp and the orchestral playing rather uninspired, but things perked up with *Pagliacci* which had much more spark.'[656]

Ken Healey also felt that Cillario 'did little more than accompany, when we know that he has far more authority at his baton tip than that. ... The orchestral string sound was true, but underpowered for these scores; the tone of much of the solo wind playing was inferior to the Elizabethan Philharmonic's recent standard.' Healey wrote that Copley's direction failed to trust the music and summed up: 'Just get rid of that *Cav* bed!' Even those who had not seen the production had heard of the infamous bed. Healey noted the difference in reception between Melbourne and Sydney where 'opera's terrible twosome' had polarised the critics and audiences to the extent that 'it was hard to believe that some of the critics ... had been in the same building, let alone attending the same performance.' He was more positive about the singing, especially the duo of Illing and Collins: 'I have never heard a better Nedda ... and only one Canio that is superior to Collins.'[657] He found that Allman as Tonio was 'as commanding as

---

[656] Prerauer, *The Australian*, 17 July 1989.
[657] Referring to Donald Smith.

ever', and Lemke (as Silvio) had never sounded better, while Hahn made 'an acceptable Santuzza, though one with room for both vocal and dramatic improvement.'[658]

One wonders what Cillario made of it all. The *Cav & Pag* double-bill was the fifth new production that he had created with Copley in Australia, and the conductor had also led many revivals of his other productions in the repertoire. There was no clear consensus as to whether the director's approach was avant-garde, a mistake, or both. Descriptions of Cillario's contribution imply that he failed in some way to connect with the action on stage, though the cast was evidently chosen and prepared with some care. Having gone to the trouble of distancing himself from the *verismo* aesthetic with his leaflet in Melbourne, Cillario took a more nuanced stance in an interview given in Sydney: 'It's not like I don't like Mascagni or Puccini, … but you must permit me to like Haydn, Monteverdi, and Handel even more. They wrote music for the glory of God and the elevation of the spirit. I hate violence.'[659]

Werther

In the 1989 Sydney winter season, another new production was prepared by Cillario, in collaboration with the director Elijah Moshinsky. The two men had never worked together, but they went on to create productions of *Rigoletto* and *La traviata* which became staples of the company's repertoire. Massenet's *Werther* is a relative rarity, particularly in Australia, and the production was a great success. The cast was led by the rising Australian mezzo-soprano Bernadette Cullen as Charlotte, and the American Neil Rosenshein, returning to Australia in the title role.

Cillario had conducted *Werther* in Trieste, at Glyndebourne (1966), Mexico City, in Bari and at the ancient Greek amphitheatre in Lecce. His affinity with the score was clearly evident, and his interpretation underlined certain synergies between Massenet's style and *verismo*. Both in the pit and on stage, he shaped lines with subtle

---

[658] Healey, *Opera Australia*, August 1989.

[659] Ava Hubble, 'Cillario conducts his own interview', *Opera Australia*, January 1990. (Interview took place in 1989).

rubati and text-sensitive inflection, and the overall effect was stylish, fluid, and atmospheric. One critic wrote that Cillario's reading reminded him in passing that Massenet 'was not uninfluenced by Wagner': an instructive comparison, considering that Massenet took his subject from a classic of German literature and an archetypal expression of turbulent Romanticism. The same reviewer noted that Cillario 'was sensitive to linger where appropriate, willing to give the music its full measure of romantic yearning and louring fatalism.'[660]

While *Werther* is seldom staged in Germany, it holds a place in the niche repertoire of many international houses, particularly as a vehicle for a star mezzo-soprano and tenor, a director who is devoted to the spirit of the opera, and a conductor who is immersed in Massenet's world. These three elements (and more) fortuitously converged in this production. Nevertheless, John Carmody was 'bewildered by the current vogue for this opera.' He unfavourably compared the 'cool detachment' of Goethe in treating Werther's suicide with the 'sentimentally protracted death' wrought by 'Massenet and his syndicate of librettists.'[661] Maria Prerauer wrote that 'of all Massenet's operas, only *Manon* has any claim to remain in the standard repertoire,' but on the positive side, 'if you must have *Werther*, the Australian Opera has found the way to do it.'[662]

Roger Covell waxed almost lyrical over 'the many pleasures of Massenet's masterly score ... a melodiously supple musical drama,' and 'an important addition to the Australian Opera repertory.' Covell praised Rosenshein as 'a younger singer on the way up ... heard at his freshest and most eloquent.' He found 'not a hint of imperfection' in Cullen's performance as Charlotte: 'Her acting grew admirably in its intensity as her feeling progressively dominated her discipline, while her richly expressive mezzo was gloriously even throughout its range.' This was, he remarked, 'singing of rare excellence.'[663]

Despite Carmody's criticisms of the work, he was impressed

[660] 'B. Canto', *The Australian Jewish Times* (Sydney), 16 June 1989.
[661] Carmody – typed manuscript in Opera Australia press files, 21 June 1989.
[662] Prerauer, *The Australian*, 12 June 1989.
[663] Covell, 'Top performance in masterly score,' *The Sydney Morning Herald*, 12 June 1989.

by all the singing, from the children's chorus to Donald Shanks as Charlotte's 'sanguine Magistrate' father. David Brennan 'sang with a fine baritonal rotundity to match his smug and cruel prosperity,' Peta Blyth 'had a delicious freshness and pert vocal charm … musically however the night belonged to Werther (Neil Rosenshein) and Charlotte (Bernadette Cullen).'[664]

Prerauer admired the leadership of Cillario, who drew 'all the drama there is, and some there isn't, out of the musical score which, at best, is no more than pleasant after-dinner entertainment.' She nonetheless admired 'the imaginative production of Australian-born director, Elijah Moshinsky and the magnificent singing of the leads.'[665] Covell wrote that

> Cillario's conducting made it clear that he valued the privilege of conducting this delectable music, so aptly and skilfully instrumented and so fluently and naturally put at the service of its French text. Some obbligato string solos were less than thoroughly distinguished at the opening-night performance, but the musical performance of the orchestra and singers was warmly sympathetic, trenchantly emphatic on occasion and mostly idiomatic.

For Carmody: 'Cillario's conducting had an excess of "sang froid" and, though there was some eloquent clarinet and saxophone playing … the strings were a little too rough and lackadaisical.' He did, however, admire the 'filmic fluidity' of Moshinsky's staging.[666]

The success of this *Werther* occasioned several revivals. The production marked a career leap for Cullen, who had emerged as a rising star during the 1987 production of *La Cenerentola*. It showed another side of Rosenshein, previously confined to Italian roles in his Australian Opera performances, and it marked a welcome return to home shores for Moshinsky. And, as so often with new projects entrusted to Cillario, it reminded Australian audiences

---

[664] Cast: Bernadette Cullen (Charlotte), Peta Blyth (Sophie), Neil Rosenshein (Werther), David Brennan (Albert), Donald Shanks (Le Bailli), Sergei Baigildin (Schmidt), John Germain (Johann), David Hibbard (Brühlmann), Joanna Cole (Kätchen).

[665] Prerauer, *The Australian*, 12 June 1989.

[666] See FN 661.

of the conductor's unrivalled breadth of musical sympathy and experience. The production transferred to Melbourne in autumn of 1990, where it was led by Cillario, with some later performances conducted by Myer Fredman.

Tristan und Isolde

In 1990, by now 75, Cillario added *Tristan und Isolde* to his repertoire. The director Neil Armfield had created the production in partnership with Stuart Challender. Having arranged and reduced the orchestral score of the *Ring* for the ill-fated Australian Opera staging, Challender had taken on more significant conducting engagements with the company. In 1987 he was appointed Chief Conductor of the Sydney Symphony Orchestra, and this *Tristan* was designed as a staging for the Concert Hall of the Opera House, with Challender conducting his own orchestra. The production won acclaim at its premiere in Sydney in February, and then travelled with equal success to the Adelaide Festival. A run of performances in Melbourne was scheduled for April–May.

In Sydney, Marilyn Richardson made a triumphant debut as Isolde. Her Tristan was the American *Heldentenor*, William Johns, replacing the indisposed Horst Hoffmann. A closely guarded secret at the time was Challender's illness: he had contracted the AIDS virus, for which there was no known cure or therapy at that time. Moffatt Oxenbould agreed to retain Challender, who would keep Oxenbould informed of his state of health, so that arrangements to replace him, if necessary, could be made in good time. This agreement enabled Challender to continue working until 1992, when he became too ill to complete a run of *Der Rosenkavalier*. Meanwhile Cillario had generously agreed to cover discreetly for Challender, which led to him conducting firstly *Tristan* in Melbourne,[667] and then *Die Meistersinger* in the same city in 1994. In fact, Challender's Sydney Symphony Orchestra schedule already

---

[667] Full Melbourne cast: Richard Versalle (Tristan), Bruce Martin (King Marke), Marilyn Richardson (Isolde), Malcolm Donnelly (Kurwenal), Christopher Dawes (Melot), Rosemary Gunn (Brangäne), Patrick Togher (Sailor & Shepherd), John Fernon (Steersman).

prevented him from conducting the run of *Tristan* in Melbourne, and Cillario was a natural choice to step in, having been immersed in the score for decades.[668]

The production was a watershed moment for the company, with the Sydney performances giving rise to comparisons with the Cillario-led *Aida* (1975) in the Concert Hall. Richardson starred in both productions, and David Gyger had noted that she sounded 'as stunningly seductive as ever, and sang with all her customary seamless beauty.'[669] The major cast change for the Melbourne season, singing Tristan, was Richard Versalle, a noted *Heldentenor* with recent experience at Bayreuth.

Lohengrin

Cillario embarked on a further Wagnerian adventure during 1990, adding *Lohengrin* to his repertoire. In 1985, the Victoria State Opera (in Melbourne) had presented a staging by the German director August Everding; the Australian Opera took it on two years later, directed by Elke Neidhardt in Sydney. This revival was notable as one of the first Wagnerian outings of the Australian soprano Lisa Gasteen, who sang with 'engaging girliness' in the role of Elsa. Alongside her, now recovered from his Tristan-related indisposition, Horst Hoffmann sang the title role, 'superb in looks, dignity and voice, as to the Wagnerian manner born.'[670] The rest of the roles were also strongly cast,[671] and Cillario was praised for 'beautiful and almost always wholly accurate sounds from the AOBO[672] and large chorus.'

Ken Healey surmised that if all the Australian Opera revivals matched the standard of *Lohengrin*, the company would be at the forefront of world opera.' He noted that Hoffmann was not a 'true'

---

[668] Moffatt Oxenbould, interview, 11 April 2023.
[669] D. Gyger, *Opera Australia*, March 1990. (Writing of the Sydney opening).
[670] Peter Morrison, *The Australian Jewish News* (Sydney), 12 October 1990.
[671] Full cast: Donald Shanks (King Heinrich), Horst Hoffmann (Lohengrin), Lisa Gasteen (Elsa), Robert Allman (Friedrich von Telramund), Lone Koppel (Ortrud), Patrick Donnelly (The King's Herald), Jeffrey Ward, Patrick Togher, Kerry Henderson, Greg Scott (Four Noblemen of Brabant), Emma Slaytor, Leonie Cambage, Sara Dakin, Christine Logan (Four Pages).
[672] The Australian Opera and Ballet Orchestra.

Heldentenor, but that he sang with a particularly beautiful 'silver' tone. Making her debut as Elsa, Gasteen 'sounded more at home than she does in the Italian repertoire' and 'acts in an unaffected manner that brings a good deal of lustre to Elke Neidhardt's production.' Cillario won praise for 'highly musical conducting, which managed to support his singers without ever overwhelming them, but at the same time did not give the impression that the orchestra was under-strength or inhibited.' Orchestrally, Healey felt that the strings 'were full toned but without stridency in a reading that shows us how to play Wagner when the Sydney Symphony Orchestra is not available as it was for *Tristan.*' Robert Allman and Lone Koppel, made 'as lively a pair of villains as I have seen operating in tandem on the opera stage … what this pair lacks in purity of vocal tone, they more than make up for in dramatic intensity.'[673] The revival was favourably compared with the 1987 run, with this cast 'perhaps even better.'[674]

Staged *Turandot*

The success of the Sydney Festival's 1988 *Turandot* concert performances had highlighted the absence of Puccini's last opera from the then current repertoire of the Australian Opera. *Turandot*[675] had not been staged by the company since 1971, perhaps it awaited a creative solution in terms of its presentation in the Opera Theatre that would do justice to what many consider Puccini's masterpiece. The awaited solution came from the artistic director of the Sydney Dance Company, Graeme Murphy, who devised a production first presented in the winter season of 1990, with spectacular designs by Kristian Fredrikson. This was a complex, fantastical staging which took place in a busy season, competing for attention with a new production of *La bohème* directed by Baz Luhrmann, which had opened just two weeks earlier. Murphy, unsurprisingly, made dance an integral part of his staging, thus preventing the piece from

---

[673] Healey, *Opera Australia*, November 1990.

[674] Morrison, *The Australian Jewish News* (Sydney), 12 October 1990.

[675] Full cast: Galina Savova (Turandot), Kenneth Collins (Calaf), Amanda Thane (Liù), Jonathon Welch (Emperor Altoum), Donald Shanks (Timur), David Brennan, Christopher Dawes, Graeme Ewer (Ping, Pang, Pong), Greg Scott (Mandarin), Jin Tea Kim (Prince of Persia).

sinking into static colourful pageantry, as often happens.

The Bulgarian soprano Galina Savova made a considerable impact in the title role: 'an extremely fine Turandot, her voice encompassing with power and a suitable glitter the testing high tessitura [of the role].' Alongside her Kenneth Collins was 'congenial' as Calaf, and Amanda Thane scored a hit as Liù, 'touchingly sympathetic ... the best interpretation of a role she has yet given.' The powerful singing of the chorus contributed significantly to the success of the performances as did 'the fine playing of the orchestra under the assured and experienced direction of Carlo Felice Cillario.' [676] This assessment was echoed by David Brown, who wrote that 'Cillario conducted with great passion and a natural feel for Puccini's wonderful, tempestuous drama, seconded by a full-throated chorus, which bayed for blood, or was sympathetic, as the score demanded.'[677]

During the rehearsals, Cillario was interviewed by David Garrett for a promotional broadsheet published by the Australian Opera.[678] He recalled conducting *Turandot* over the decades; giving the opera's first performance in Mexico City at an entertainment centre that held 10,000 people. Cillario recalled the Calaf of Giuseppe di Stefano, but just as vividly remembered the tiny role of the emperor Altoum, sung by an unknown 19-year-old tenor called Plácido Domingo. Referring to the 1988 Sydney Festival performances, Cillario admitted that the sheer scale afforded by the Concert Hall would not be possible to match in the Opera Theatre, but he was excited about working with Murphy and seeing the physicality of the production. Turning to Savova, Cillario considered her voice to be possibly 'even too beautiful' for Turandot: 'It must sometimes be like a dagger, a cold voice, and she is a beautiful lady [with a] beautiful voice.'[679]

David Gyger enthused that 'the new AO *Turandot* is an all-round success arising very much jointly from the talents of designer and director, which are reinforced at every turn by the musical miracle

---

[676] Hoffmann, *The Canberra Times*, 18 August 1990.

[677] Brown, *The Australian Jewish News* (Sydney), 24 August 1990.

[678] David Garrett, 'Carlo ... You have been so noisy!' *The Australian Opera Broadsheet*, Issue Three, August 1990.

[679] Ibid.

that emanates from pit and stage under the veteran baton of Carlo Felice Cillario.' Savova was 'every inch a Turandot, possessing ... considerable physical presence ... but the even rarer vocal power and quality to satisfy the ear in the fiendishly demanding riddle scene.' Collins was 'in fine form ... singing strongly and ... as beautifully as I have ever heard him.' Amanda Thane's Liù was 'the obvious crowd-pleaser of the premiere.' Gyger noted that the riches of the production, and its augmented chorus were indeed cramped in the Opera Theatre, but a transfer to the State Theatre in Melbourne 'is certain to achieve that last degree of satisfying stature.'[680]

The production duly reached Melbourne for the autumn season of 1991 and was later commercially released. The US soprano Ealynn Voss replaced Savova in the title role[681] and was well received, but Amanda Thane once more attracted the most fervent acclaim for her portrayal of Liù.[682] In Melbourne, critics found that the orchestra overpowered the stage from time to time, the opposite of the effect in Sydney. Damning with faint praise, Clive O'Connell remarked that 'the experiment of inviting an outsider to direct an opera has worked.'[683]

A glance over the previous decade reveals a shift in public perception towards Cillario. From 1980, he led one or two new productions each year, typically major projects, with important directors, often in specialist repertoire. He also conducted revivals of Italian grand opera such as *Aida*, *Otello*, *Il trittico*, *La fanciulla del West* and *Turandot*. These large-scale ensemble works require a commensurate personality to galvanise them from the pit. Such repertoire was bread and butter for Cillario. The conductor also demonstrated a mastery of 'niche' repertoire that his public may not have automatically associated with him: Tchaikovsky, Cherubini, Massenet, and most impressively, his late debut conducting *Tristan und Isolde*.

Cillario's significance and status within the company continued

---

[680] D. Gyger, *Opera Australia*, October 1990.

[681] Melbourne cast changes: Ealynn Voss (Turandot), Jonathon Welch (Pang), Graeme MacFarlane (Emperor Altoum).

[682] O'Connell, *Opera Australia*, May 1991.

[683] Ibid.

to evolve with time. From now on, he would focus upon two or three productions per year, taking a step back from his previous frantic pace. Important collaborations still lay ahead, with younger directors who often brought a visual imagination to Australian audiences that invited (but did not always receive) a comparably open-minded response. In such cases, Cillario was recognised as a venerable figure of authority who gave the productions he led a hallmark of experience and quality. He had become something of an institution in Australia, an embodiment of the culture of Italian opera who could nonetheless spring the occasional surprise with his cultural sympathies.

As his schedule in Australia scaled down, Cillario began to devote time to composition: an activity which he had seriously pursued in his youth before his conducting career took him in other directions. Now, it was a pleasure, a diversion: 'What I write are just tiny caricatures, or musical jokes.'[684] Much of his new work was pastiche, based upon the styles of the composers he most admired, created with the assistance of a piece of Apple software, 'Onestep'. A firm in Brookvale, on Sydney's Northern Peninsula, had supplied the program to Cillario, and it fascinated him. He described the process of creating music with it: 'It's like a friend, like a baby – you can ask it a lot of things. ... The best aspect, from a human point of view, is that working with it is often just like discussing things with a friend. ... All the problems a friend can advise on, I can ask the computer.'[685] In another interview from the same year, journalist Jenny Brown reported that 'his compositions include variations for out-of-tune violin and another piece featuring violin, tape recorder and metronome', to which Cillario added: 'It is very interesting but that is for mental exercise, is not good music.'[686] The two compositions reproduced in Appendix 6 were notated using this technology.

Satisfaction with the expanded Opera Theatre pit proved to

[684] Cillario and Duffie, *Interview*, 1982.
[685] Alan Wood, 'Composer's computer is now his muse in a keyboard,' *The Manly Daily*, 26 October 1990.
[686] Jenny Brown, 'Cillario's score,' *The Mirror*, 31 August 1991.

be temporary. By 1991, perhaps occasioned by performing both *Turandot* and *Lohengrin* in the previous Sydney winter season, the orchestra were renewing their complaints that '70 players [were] crammed into a space designed for 50', with attendant dangers of hearing-loss and fire-safety concerns. A test had been carried out during *Turandot*, and one member of the brass section was found to be exposed to nearly three times the allowable daily decibel count. There is no doubt that the pit was overcrowded, and the stage overhang caused problems of ensemble between orchestral sections, unable to hear each other. Richard Bonynge went on record as saying that the orchestra was 'up with the best pit orchestras in the world, but the pit was the worst in the world.' A discussion was initiated about the practicality of removing the first metre of the stage overhang. [687]

There remained no straightforward solution to this intractable problem, which continually vexed the management, the orchestra and their conductors. The lack of space particularly impacted Cillario's work since he was most often assigned large-scale operas. He was working within tiny margins in order to achieve a practical, musical and artistically convincing balance of instruments and voices. Most listeners remained oblivious to the challenges he faced, and to the skill he displayed in overcoming them to present operatic performances to the highest possible standard.

New *Rigoletto*

After their successful partnership in Massenet's *Werther* in 1989, Cillario and Elijah Moshinsky were reunited to prepare a new staging of Verdi's *Rigoletto*[688] for the Sydney winter season of 1991. In a landmark staging of 1982 for English National Opera, Jonathan Miller had set the opera in Little Italy, Manhattan during the 1950's.

---

[687] Information in this paragraph is derived from: Peter Cochrane, *The Sydney Morning Herald*, 5 October 1991.

[688] Full cast: Franco Farina (Duke of Mantua), Michael Lewis (Rigoletto), Gillian Sullivan (Gilda), Arend Baumann (Sparafucile), Kirsti Harms (Maddalena), Kerry Elizabeth Brown (Giovanna), Bruce Martin (Monterone), Kerry Henderson (Marullo), David Collins-White (Borsa), Steven Gallop (Count Ceprano), Clare Gormley (Countess Ceprano), Joseph Grunfelder (Usher), Genevieve Killalea (Page). This is the cast that appeared in the performances conducted by Cillario.

Moshinsky explained why he had updated the action to 1950s Rome, the world of Rossellini's *Roma città aperta* (1945) and Fellini's *La dolce vita* (1960). He believed it was 'the nastiest, meanest, most horrible story ... those black-and-white thrillers of the '50s featured the same kind of decadence as in Verdi's opera. And as a creative team, we were attracted to the lighting, the shadows, the grittiness.'[689] Moshinsky's staging became an enduring success, and a staple of the company's repertoire.

David Gyger admired the stage action during the prelude, which showed Rigoletto getting made up for the ensuing drama (he had been much harsher on the invented action for the Copley-directed *Cavalleria rusticana*). He also sang the praises of

> that living treasure of an opera conductor, particularly Italian opera, Carlo Felice Cillario, [who] was at his usual impeccable best in delving into the score and revealing its musical treasures to maximum advantage; and his team of onstage performers as well as the musicians of the Australian Opera and Ballet Orchestra in the pit [who] were giving their all.

Franco Farina as the Duke 'could do almost no wrong ... his singing was superb,' and Gyger was equally impressed by Arend Baumann as Sparafucile: 'a thoroughly malevolent presence from the moment [he] popped out from behind a clothes rack.' He was more critical of Michael Lewis (Rigoletto), whose sound he 'found wanting in the character's big emotional moments,' and remarked that Gillian Sullivan 'could well develop into a thoroughly satisfying Gilda, but she has not quite arrived yet.' He predicted that 'with a bit of a rethink about the odd detail, and a measure more vocal guts at its heart, this new *Rigoletto* will yet be another all-round artistic feather in the cap of the Australian Opera.'[690]

In the Sydney winter season, Cillario conducted a revival of Verdi's *Otello* in the Opera Theatre. Horst Hoffmann appeared again

---

[689] Cochrane, 'Rigoletto fast-forwards to La Dolce Vita,' *The Sydney Morning Herald*, 7 June 1991.

[690] D. Gyger, *Opera Australia*, July 1991.

in the title role, with Marilyn Richardson making her role debut as Desdemona, and a return visit from expatriate Jonathan Summers to portray Iago.[691] David Gyger noted the presence of three top-rate soloists, Cillario in the pit and elements of George Ogilvie's production that had undergone 'some improvements' since its previous revival two years earlier. Gyger drew attention to how Cillario,

> in the thoroughly self-effacing way that has become his want in recent times, chose to enter the pit almost surreptitiously at the beginning of each act and creep up on the audience in absolute stealth, launching into the score before anyone even knew he was there. This ploy worked well at the beginning of *Otello*, ... before the curtain rises to the turbulence of a storm scene....

For the other acts, however, he found that such discretion 'did a significant disservice to the performance overall.' Gyger singled out Summers as Iago: 'the best sung we have had during my 35 years of opera-going in this country – and at the same time an insidious histrionic presence that increasingly made one's skin crawl as the evening wore on.'[692]

23: *'Allegro con fuoco'*.

While *Otello* completed Cillario's year with the Australian Opera,

---

[691] Full cast: Horst Hoffmann (Otello), Jonathan Summers (Iago), Gregory Tomlinson (Cassio), Jonathon Welch (Roderigo), Arend Baumann (Lodovico), Steven Gallop (Montano), John Fernon (Herald), Marilyn Richardson (Desdemona), Heather Begg (Emilia).

[692] D. Gyger, *Opera Australia*, September 1991.

he had other engagements to fulfil in Sydney. On 7 September, he conducted the Sydney Symphony Orchestra in their Annual (45th) Gala Concert, titled 'Viva Italia'. The scope of repertoire ran from Andrea Gabrieli (*Aria della battaglia*), Vivaldi (the Concerto in D for four violins) and a Boccherini symphony ('La casa del diavolo' Op.12 No.4) through to Respighi's *Pines of Rome* and excerpts from Verdi's *La forza del destino*.[693]

This was Cillario's second engagement with the Sydney Symphony Orchestra for the year. On 12 March, he had led a programme in the Bankstown Town Hall (west of Sydney), and then toured it to Penrith and Sutherland. The Bankstown concert required a last-minute rearrangement, as not all the orchestra would fit on the stage. The programme was also Italian themed, opening with Respighi's *The Birds* and closing with Mendelssohn's Fourth Symphony. The soloist in Mozart's Violin Concerto No.3 was the 20-year-old Adele Anthony, from South Australia, who was studying at the Juilliard School in New York. Reviewer Fred Blanks evoked the conductor's lively podium manner:

> Never still for an instant, he gives the impression of experiencing a profound personal responsibility for every note. He is intently alert and musically alive and shows his displeasure clearly when the response fails to satisfy him. But his energy and knowledge rub off very distinctly on the orchestra.[694]

Cillario was always enthusiastic about educating younger musicians and took great pleasure in working with emerging soloists. From the late 1970s, he worked intermittently at the NSW State Conservatorium of Music,[695] a short walk from the Sydney Opera House, where he conducted the Conservatorium Symphony Orchestra in concerts on several occasions and was held in great affection. In 1978, he gave a concert that included Schumann's Cello Concerto, with Susan Blake as soloist. In 1987 he conducted Shosta-

---

[693] Email correspondence with Alistair McKean, Head of Library Services, Sydney Symphony Orchestra, 12 April 2023.

[694] Blanks, *The Australian*, 15 March 1991.

[695] Now the Sydney Conservatorium of Music, the University of Sydney.

kovich's Fifth Symphony, which he had first conducted in Bucharest in 1944, at the start of his career.[696] He gave conducting classes, and took part in a programme of three annual 'intensive rehearsal periods', devised 'to allow visits by high-profile conductors.'[697]

For one of those projects, in 1991, Cillario led the Conservatorium Symphony Orchestra in the Overture to Verdi's *La forza del destino*, Mozart's Sinfonia Concertante K.364, with staff members Chris Kimber and Alex Todisescu as the soloists, and Franck's Symphony in D minor. In his review, David Brown applauded the initiative to bring in high-profile conductors to coach the Conservatorium orchestra, with Cillario as 'a conductor with a no-nonsense style who is able to provide inspiration as well as perspiration.' He praised the Franck as a 'warmly affectional reading', while the whole programme 'carried conviction and a high degree of musicality.'[698]

Back in 1988, Cillario had been a guest tutor at the 39th Annual National Music Camp at The King's School, Parramatta. He enjoyed the experience immensely and told the journalist Michael Shmith: 'I don't believe there is another country with such a musical force. I tell [the students] not to lose this ... try to be youthful for the rest of your life.'[699] Cillario was an ideal summer-school tutor: a perennially youthful figure despite his age, charismatic and eccentric, whose habit of speaking several languages in a single sentence unselfconsciously exuded the aura of the maestro.

---

[696] Broadsheet from Cillario family archive, Bologna. 'Carlo Felice Cillario'.

[697] Peter McCallum and Julie Simonds, *The Centenary of the Con: A History of the Sydney Conservatorium of Music 1915–2015* (Allen & Unwin, Sydney, 2015), 208.

[698] Brown, *The Australian Jewish Times* (Sydney), 12 September 1991.

[699] Shmith, 'Some even hate their cause of fame', *The Age*, 9 May 1988.

24: Cillario conducting the Sydney Symphony Orchestra in the
Sydney Town Hall, April 1992.

Cillario led four mainstage productions for the Australian Opera
in 1992, and an 'Opera in the Park' performance of *La traviata*
in Adelaide's Elder Park, as part of the festival. He also gave
several concerts with the Sydney Symphony Orchestra, including
the launch of their main season.[700] A photo-set of the concert at
Sydney Town Hall was published by the *Sydney Morning Herald*,
vividly capturing his inimitable theatrical style, which mesmerised
audiences while driving and releasing the drama of any score he
touched.

In May, Cillario was in Melbourne giving a concert with
the student musicians of the Victorian College of the Arts. The
demanding programme featured Haydn (Symphony No 99), Kodály
(the suite from Háry János), Wagner (Siegfried's Rhine Journey) and
a selection of Verdi and Puccini arias sung by Nicole Youl, a recent
VCA graduate, who went on to join Opera Australia and sing major
roles with Cillario. This was something of a gala event, given in the
'recently restored splendour' of the South Melbourne Town Hall and
broadcast live by the ABC on radio and TV: 'The amazing energy of
Maestro Cillario … made the evening a remarkable event.'[701]

---

[700] Their Chief Conductor at this time was Edo de Waart.
[701] Colin Taylor, *The Australian Jewish News* (Melbourne), 1 May 1992.

The Challender Memorial Concert

Stuart Challender had died in December 1991, of complications arising from the AIDS virus, and Cillario was asked to conduct his memorial concert with the Sydney Symphony in May 1992. Challender had been appointed Chief Conductor of the orchestra in 1987, succeeding Zdeněk Mácal, and conquering something of an Australian arts taboo, as the first resident Australian to take up so prestigious a post.[702] Challender was also the first public figure in the Sydney arts community to go on record as having contracted the AIDS virus, in an interview which was broadcast Australia-wide.

The memorial concert was designed to represent Challender's affiliations with the Sydney Symphony Orchestra and the Australian Opera, his musical affinities and passions. While the occasion was a memorial for Challender, it also had a wider resonance: the AIDS virus – seemingly unstoppable at the time – had claimed the lives of many people working in the Australian arts community, particularly in Sydney.

The concert opened with the Prelude to *Die Meistersinger von Nürnberg*, recalling Challender's deep love of Wagner, and the work that he had hoped to conduct in Melbourne in 1994. The third-act trio from *Der Rosenkavalier* (sung by Joan Carden, Joanna Cole and Kirsti Harms) represented the last opera that Challender had conducted, just weeks before his death. The second half of the concert was dedicated to Beethoven's Ninth Symphony. Cillario led a singular reading: some found the first two movements overly expansive, and the last two excessively 'urgent and aggressive', though the whole was not wanting in drama or personal insight.[703] What was not in question was Cillario's command of the orchestra, and his ability to grapple with the underlying aesthetic principles that inform the work. The concert paid a moving tribute to Challender's memory, while also revealing Cillario's affinity with a pinnacle of the symphonic repertoire.

----

[702] Sir Charles Mackerras held the same post between 1982 and 1985, and was the first Australian Chief Conductor appointed, but he had been based in London since 1947.

[703] Brown, *The Australian Jewish News* (Sydney), 15 May 1992.

During 1992, Elijah Moshinsky's much-admired staging of *Rigoletto* received its Melbourne premiere. The leading principal singers were new to the production,[704] and the cast received mixed reviews. Some coordination issues between the pit and Barry Anderson's Rigoletto were commented upon, although it was otherwise noted that Cillario kept a tight rein on the flow of the opera. Clive O'Connell remarked that Melbourne audiences had already experienced the Victoria State Opera's 'fascist' setting twice, now followed by Moshinsky's 'Fellini-inspired' production. He asked if it were not time to revive 'the old, tiresomely authentic John Copley version.'[705]

Copley's 11-year-old staging of *Tosca* was revived in Melbourne.[706] Marilyn Richardson was a 'non-fiery' Tosca according to O'Connell, producing 'mature singing which focused upon communicating warmth and depth of emotion rather than passion and volatility.' Kenneth Collins presented a 'vocally more invigorated' Cavaradossi, his third-act aria 'judged with intelligent dynamic restraint … [and] a luminous warmth that made the character's fate … all the more shocking.' Although Robert Allman's Scarpia lacked 'that overpowering menace that Shaw brought to the role [he] … sang with authority and distinction.' In the pit, Cillario directed 'with energy and a brisk approach to tempi that did a good deal to animate the work's effectiveness.'[707]

Cillario could be blunt and even rude to singers and orchestral musicians, which he tended to explain away either as honesty or

[704] Full cast: Gregory Tomlinson (Duke of Mantua), Barry Anderson (Rigoletto), Nicola Ferner-Waite (Gilda), Arend Baumann (Sparafucile), Roxane Hislop (Maddalena), Kerry Elizabeth Brown (Giovanna), Bruce Martin (Monterone), Kerry Henderson (Marullo), David Collins-White (Borsa), Steven Gallop (Count Ceprano), Lucy Macfarlane (Countess Ceprano), Joseph Grunfelder (Usher), Genevieve Killalea (Page).

[705] O'Connell, *Opera Australia*, May 1992.

[706] Full cast: Marilyn Richardson (Tosca), Kenneth Collins (Cavaradossi), Robert Allman (Scarpia), Greg Scott (Angelotti), Patrick Togher (Spoletta), John Germain (Sacristan), Steven Gallop (Sciarrone), Andrew Dalley (Gaoler), Susan Lorette Dunn (Shepherd).

[707] O'Connell, *Opera Australia*, June 1992.

the consequence of his 'poor' English. From the 1980s onwards, however, such flashes of autocratic temperament were increasingly out of step with the times. Cillario's memoir (Appendix 7) recounts the Callas *Tosca* at Covent Garden, where he remarked on a technical fault in the soprano's production. In his account, she took the criticism bravely and responded humbly to his concerns. During the 1992 run of *Tosca* in Sydney, Cillario made a critical comment to Marilyn Richardson about her performance, and the soprano felt strongly enough about the exchange to write a letter of complaint to Moffatt Oxenbould. Not for the first time where Cillario was concerned, Oxenbould found himself obliged to pour oil on troubled waters.[708] While the world of opera has never been short of strong and demanding personalities, age did not bring equanimity to Cillario, who periodically failed to see past the musical score to those who were also recreating it with him. Such lack of sensitivity led to him making errors of judgement in matters which ultimately undermined his authority.

In the Sydney winter season, Cillario conducted a run of Verdi's *Simon Boccanegra*. Originally scheduled as a revival, it became a new production on a shoestring budget, directed by Mark Gaal, with designs by Angus Strathie.[709] Verdi composed *Boccanegra* in 1867 and then revised it with the assistance of Arrigo Boito in 1881, thus placing it into a singular, transitional category between his second- and third-period styles.[710] The chronology and relations in the piece can be difficult to unravel, but no more so than in *La forza del destino*. Edward Downes, an expert Verdian had introduced *Boccanegra* to the company's repertoire in 1975. Plot intricacies aside, it was eminently suited to the strengths of the company's vocal resources. In 1992, the revival was led by Malcom Donnelly in the title role, and (as Amelia) Susan Dunn, the US soprano who had

---

[708] Moffatt Oxenbould, *Papers of Moffatt Oxenbould and Graeme Ewer, 1890-2016*. Boxes 50 and 51. Bib ID: 469317, National Library of Australia.

[709] Oxenbould (2005) 567.

[710] As defined by Julian Budden in *The Operas of Verdi* (3 Volumes); [Vol. 1: London, Cassel & Company Ltd, 1973. Vol. 2: London, Cassel & Company Ltd, 1978. Vol. 3: Oxford, Oxford University Press, 1981.]

first appeared with the company as Desdemona in 1988. The smaller roles were strongly cast,[711] and Cillario 'gave an entirely pleasing reading of the score.'

The staging was less sympathetically received, especially for 'rudimentary acting' among the principals.[712] Ken Healey noted a lack of energy, an 'ugly and distracting' set and clashing costumes, giving the impression not so much of a timeless setting as a 'half-baked concept' led by budgetary demands: 'this is clearly an austerity production.' Gaal and Strathie had come from the world of theatre, but this *Boccanegra* attracted 'an almost universally bad press',[713] notwithstanding its musical values.

Bicentennial Rossini

After the triumph of the Hampe/Cillario *La Cenerentola*, the Australian Opera scheduled another *dramma giocoso* as its contribution to the 1992 bicentenary celebrations of Rossini. *L'Italiana in Algeri* was directed by Giulio Chazalettes, with designs by Ulisse Santicchi, in a co-production with the Victoria State Opera which had first been staged in Melbourne in 1991. Preceding *Cenerentola* by five years, *L'Italiana* requires singing of virtuoso agility, precision of ensemble and a particular sensitivity to its original context in order to bring it alive for modern-day audiences. As the work of a 21-year-old prodigy, a comic force in a world of lightness, effervescence and bizarreness, this youthful score revealed another facet of Cillario's musical personality, distinct from what had become his familiar mastery of late Verdi and Puccini. Cillario counted Rossinian experts such as Tullio Serafin and Vittorio Gui among his mentors; he prepared careful notes for the staging and began to correspond with Chazalettes.[714] Aside from the veteran Donald Shanks as Mustafà, the cast was drawn from graduates of the com-

---

[711] Full cast: Susan Dunn (Amelia), Yu Jixing (Adorno), Malcolm Donnelly (Boccanegra), Arend Baumann (Fiesco), Geoffrey Chard (Paolo), Steven Gallop (Pietro), Helen O'Rourke (Lady in Waiting), Andrew Dalley (Captain).

[712] Morrison, *The Australian Jewish Times* (Sydney), 18 September 1992.

[713] Healey, *Opera Australia*, October 1992.

[714] Correspondence held by the Cillario family archive, Bologna.

pany's Young Artist Programme during the 1980s.[715] The result was a popular and critical success.

David Gyger compared the two versions of the staging in Melbourne and Sydney. He found Richard Divall's musical direction for Victoria State Opera satisfactory, but

> it did not quite scale the heights of musical affinity with the Italian operatic idiom so naturally and effortlessly achieved by Carlo Felice Cillario for the national company after so many more years' experience. ... Aided perceptibly by the much more open acoustics of the Opera Theatre pit since its most recent round of improvements, the Australian Opera and Ballet Orchestra provided a largely delicious and delightfully effervescent reading of Rossini's marvellously pleasing, if admittedly not exactly profound, score.[716]

Later in the season, Cillario conducted the finals of the McDonalds Operatic Aria Contest, with the Sydney Symphony Orchestra. On 19 August he led them once more in 'A Tribute to Dame Joan Sutherland and Richard Bonynge', which took place in the couple's presence, and was broadcast live nationally via simulcast on radio and TV by the ABC. A group of 15 singers included Deborah Riedel, Donald Shanks, Malcolm Donnelly and Kathryn McCusker. A lack of rehearsal was at times evident, as well as an edge to Cillario's conducting which sometimes surfaced when he felt that he no longer had the upper hand in the proceedings. The underlying combativeness which fuelled the energy and excitement of his performances was undoubtedly sharpened by age, but from this time, the close attention of the management became required to smooth relations between the maestro and his orchestra and singers, to cool tempers and to quell diplomatic incidents.

---

[715] Full cast: Donald Shanks (Mustafà), Lynne Murray (Elvira), Roxane Hislop (Zulma), David Brennan (Haly), David Hobson (Lindoro), Jolanta Nagajek (Isabella), Roger Lemke (Taddeo).

[716] D. Gyger, *Opera Australia*, November 1992.

25: Maestro Cillario conducting the Sydney Symphony Orchestra, Sydney Town Hall, April 1992.

ACT 3 (1993-2003)
Scene 1 – The Final Decade

An Indian Summer of Wagner

By 1993, Cillario had conducted almost all of the Wagner canon for the Australian Opera. *Meistersinger* was still to come, and only *Siegfried* and *Götterdämmerung* never came to fruition. He had long loved and studied the Wagner repertoire but had little opportunity to perform it in the theatre until after the age of 50. Cillario had conducted Neil Armfield's *Tristan und Isolde* production in Melbourne in 1990, and in the summer of 1993, the conductor unexpectedly had the opportunity to revisit it, this time in his preferred Sydney venue for such a work – the Concert Hall of the Opera House.

During 1992, Moffatt Oxenbould had approached Cillario with a proposal that he conduct a new production of *Parsifal* in 1993, to be directed by Elke Neidhardt. Cillario replied with enthusiasm from Stockholm, reminding Oxenbould of the success of the 1976 *Parsifal* in concert. He was full of ideas for the projects' realisation:

> several scenes need a visual help from the stage's set. (Changes to the 'mighty Hall' Act 1 and Act 3!) The music is sublime but not enough. PLEASE NOT just CURTAIN DOWN!!! And what about the 'Klingsor's enchanted Castle'? And the 'magic garden' taking his [sic] place? Also, the set for the opening Scene of Act 3 must be extremely Espressiva, eh…!? Love, C.[717]

Parsifal fell by the wayside due to budgetary constraints. Instead, Cillario led a revival of *Tristan und Isolde* in Armfield's 1990 staging. Horst Hoffmann finally sang Tristan in this production (having originally been scheduled to do so in 1990) opposite Marilyn

---

[717] Oxenbould, Papers of Moffatt Oxenbould and Graeme Ewer, 1890-2016. Box 50. Bib ID: 469317, National Library of Australia. 'RE; PARSIFAL RE-GIE, SET, PRODUCTION,' dated 12 January 1992.

Richardson's Isolde.[718] The simplicity of Armfield's production was again praised, as was the musical direction which 'allowed the flow of the music to be realised in the essential simplicity of the production.' In assessing the title roles, Healey noted that while neither was a 'total Wagnerian ... they are surely the first Isolde and Tristan worthy to sing with a major company of whom it can be believed that they are passionately, uncontrollably in love with each other.' Healey continued that neither singer was 'vocally too light for the Concert Hall at the Sydney Opera House, even with the full-toned Sydney Symphony Orchestra on the flat floor in front, being driven to paroxysms of the musical equivalent of orgasmic climax by Maestro Cillario.'[719]

Of the musical direction, David Brown wrote:

> Carlo Felice Cillario obviously loves this score, although in paying very close attention to it, sometimes neglects the stage[720] ... the Sydney Symphony Orchestra was a responsive instrument in Cillario's hands, producing fine string sound and ravishing woodwind. A touch more consideration of the singers is all that is required.[721]

Healey missed

> something of Stuart Challender's muscularity, though Cillario is a lively and articulate conductor to behold. ...This is a special production, already in danger of dripping with a nostalgia bestowed on it by those who fell under its spell in 1990. ... The postponement of the promised Parsifal is

---

[718] Full cast: Horst Hoffmann (Tristan), Marilyn Richardson (Isolde), Donald Shanks (King Marke), Rosemary Gunn (Brangäne), Malcolm Donnelly (Kurwenal), Dominic Natoli (Melot), David Collins-White (Sailor, Shepherd), Andrew Dalley (Steersman).

[719] Healey, *Opera Australia*, March 1993.

[720] As he approached his 80s, he routinely wore glasses when conducting, with a tendency to have his head in the score, an unnecessary posture for one who knew much of his repertoire by heart, probably caused by slowly failing eyesight and a habit of conducting from small study scores, which had been in his possession for many years, and whose yellowing pages were becoming less legible.

[721] Brown, *The Australian Jewish News* (Sydney), 19 February 1993.

made tolerable when the production substituted for it is as heroic as this one.[722]

Following six performances in Sydney, the production transferred to Melbourne, where Cillario conducted five further performances to equal acclaim: 'the State Orchestra of Victoria under the sure direction of Carlo Felice Cillario gave just the right support to the singers by paying careful attention to the glorious texture of Wagner's score.'[723]

Later in the summer, Cillario gave a concert with the Sydney Youth Orchestra in the Concert Hall of the Opera House. Weber's Overture to *Der Freischütz*[724] preceded the Violin Concerto by Beethoven, and the 4th Symphony of Brahms. David Brown found that the youthful appearance of the orchestra belied their skill and maturity: 'many a professional band would envy them their corporate sound.'[725] There was praise and the prediction of a bright future for 17-year-old violinist Natalie Chee in the Beethoven concerto. Cillario again revealed himself as a passionate educator and inspiration for younger musicians and his conducting was 'attentive' although occasionally 'over-aggressive'[726] – a criticism which became a critical refrain about his work in his later years.

Cillario returned in August for the Sydney winter season, to conduct *Un ballo in maschera* and *Tosca*. On his arrival in Sydney, he informed the company management that he had been watching a soccer match in Bologna when an explosion went off in the stands (in all likelihood a firework). He suffered injury to his eyesight from grit and particles of plastic, and it later transpired that he had also sustained hearing loss from the explosion.[727] Ignoring

[722] Healey, *Opera Australia*, March 1993.
[723] Sidney Bloch, *The Australian Jewish News* (Melbourne), 30 April 1993.
[724] While not the rule, most of Cillario's symphonic concerts generally included a nod to opera, be it an overture or a vocal selection in place of an instrumental concerto.
[725] Brown, *The Australian Jewish News* (Sydney), 19 March 1993.
[726] Ibid.
[727] Oxenbould (2005), 581–2; and Oxenbould Interview, 17 April 2023.

the advice of physicians, he had travelled to Australia to fulfil his commitments.

Ballo was set to open the season with a cast led by Elizabeth Connell as Amelia and Kenneth Collins as Riccardo. [728] It soon became apparent in rehearsals that Cillario was not on form, though he kept up a stoic demeanour. The press reception of the opening night was not favourable. Up to this point, while the merits of productions, singers, orchestral musicians and acoustics were argued out in reviews, Cillario was rarely the direct target of a bad critique, rather he was often singled out as the force that held a production together. On this occasion David Brown reported on a 'sad decline' of Cillario's powers, 'manifested in a lack of accord between pit and stage,' while 'everyone seemed to be doing their own thing.'[729]

The 78-year-old conductor rallied during the preparations for *Tosca*. The casting was far from cohesive, with Grace Bumbry, Neil Rosenshein and Joshua Hecht in the leading roles.[730] Nevertheless, Cillario made an astonishingly swift recovery and drew together this unlikely blend of personalities. David Brown posted an apology to the conductor in his review: 'I have learned [after reviewing *Un ballo in maschera*] that he was suffering from the effects (sight and hearing) of an explosion at a football match in Italy. … I regret, nonetheless the strength of my comments of a much-respected figure.' In the *Tosca* premiere, 'he was much more in control, the rise and fall of the passion of the music firmly in his grasp.'[731]

Emerging from adversity, Cillario regained his legendary energy, and declared his intention to conduct until he was 100. The incident of 1993, however, marks a line in his career in Australia,

---

[728] Full cast: Kenneth Collins (Gustavus III), Elizabeth Connell (Amelia), Jonathan Summers (Anckarstroem), Arend Baumann (Count Ribbing), Greg Scott (Count Horn), Andrew Dalley (Cristian), Rosamund Illing (Oscar), Heather Begg (Madame Arvidson), Graeme MacFarlane (Arnfelt), Michael Terry (Servant).

[729] Brown, *The Australian Jewish News* (Sydney), 27 August 1993.

[730] Full cast: Grace Bumbry (Tosca), Neil Rosenshein (Cavaradossi), Joshua Hecht (Scarpia), Joseph Grunfelder (Angelotti), Graeme Ewer (Spoletta), John Germain (Sacristan), Steven Gallop (Sciarrone), Andrew Dalley (Gaoler), Zoe Taylor (Shepherd).

[731] Brown, *The Australian Jewish News* (Sydney), 24 September 1993.

defining what became a final decade, during which the number of performances he conducted gradually diminished, and the effects of age increasingly manifested in a certain 'eccentricity' (as Oxenbould described it)[732] resulting in an unpredictability in his work, which may not always have been intentional.

Die Meistersinger in Melbourne

During 1994, Cillario returned to two of his great musical passions, with landmark productions of Verdi and Wagner. *Die Meistersinger von Nürnberg* was revived in Melbourne in Michael Hampe's 'bicentennial staging', originally conducted in 1988 by Sir Charles Mackerras. It was originally planned that Stuart Challender would conduct the season: Cillario had acted as 'cover' for him during the uncertain health of Challender's last years. The pageant-like nature of the work was more comfortably accommodated by the State Theatre in the Victorian Arts Centre. Sidney Bloch remarked that Hampe had created a vivid picture of that period in German cultural history when the middle-class citizenry pursued the artistic life with as much vigour as their trades or crafts.

> His intelligent contribution was complemented by the immaculate musicianship of Carlo Felice Cillario in the pit … Wagner's rich musical texture was given full expression by the State Orchestra of Victoria, the strings and especially the celli producing a luscious, exuberant sound.[733]

Clive O'Connell nevertheless found the stage cramped and that 'one of the few areas where expansiveness was evident came through Cillario's leisurely conducting of the work.' The cast featured Joan Carden as Eva, Christopher Doig as Walther, John Pringle as Beckmesser and Bruce Martin as Hans Sachs.[734] O'Connell welcomed

---

[732] Oxenbould noted his becoming 'more eccentric and idiosyncratic with the passing of the years' (Oxenbould (2005), 653).

[733] Bloch, *The Australian Jewish News* (Melbourne), 6 May 1994.

[734] Full cast: Christopher Doig (Walther von Stolzing), Barry Ryan (David), Joan Carden (Eva), Rosemary Gunn (Magdalene), Bruce Martin (Hans Sachs), Arend Baumann (Pogner), John Pringle (Sixtus Beckmesser), Christopher Dawes (Vogelgesang), David Brennan (Nachtigall), John Germain (Kothner), Warwick Fyfe (Ortel), Patrick Togher (Zorn), Graeme MacFarlane (Moser), Greg Scott (Foltz), Harry Coghill (Schwarz), Sergei Baigildin (Eisslinger), Richard Alexander (Nightwatchman).

Martin's Sachs as 'one of the production's greatest assets and no praise is too fulsome for his singing and acting'. Likewise, Pringle's Beckmesser 'adds to the extraordinarily successful list of roles he has offered us over the last 27 years', while Carden's Eva 'was delivered with impressive warmth and power'. Doig's Walther was sung 'determinedly but it was an effort-laden performance'. Barry Ryan, on the other hand gave 'a light and vocally energetic David, well matched by Rosemary Gunn's Magdalene'. The *Meistern* were strongly cast – 'nearly all are distinguished principals' and the director portrayed each 'as an individual'. On the opening night the audience responded with a standing ovation.[735]

Pamela Ruskin described the production as 'the jewel in the season's crown',[736] and Peter Johnston wrote that Cillario's conducting of the opera was an 'unqualified success':

> The standing ovation … was to applaud not only the magnificent singing of Bruce Martin and the work of the cast, but to acknowledge the outstanding work of Maestro Cillario who had proved once again that his stamina, intelligence, and musicianship were exactly the right ingredients. His love of Wagner was readily apparent throughout the five-hour performance as he guided the orchestra to a most brilliant climax. *Die Meistersinger* became the musical climax (thus far) of the Australian Opera's current season, in much the same way as *Tristan und Isolde* (also conducted by Maestro Cillario) was the musical highlight of 1993.[737]

The Age (Melbourne's daily newspaper) presented its annual Performing Arts Award to Cillario in 1994, for his Wagnerian achievements as 'Best Opera Music Direction'. For a conductor just shy of 80 years old, conducting *Die Meistersinger* for the first time was no mean feat. Moffatt Oxenbould recalled these performances as a high point of the conductor's later career, and in particular the Prelude to Act 3: 'It was one of those moments where time stood still … The hair still rises on the back of my neck when I think about

---

[735] O'Connell, *Opera Australasia*, May 1994.

[736] Ruskin, *Opera Australia*, June 1994.

[737] Johnston, *The Melburnian*, Vol. 9 No. 9, May 1994, 33–5.

it.'[738] Separately, he remarked that 'Bruce Martin gave one of the best performances of his career and Cillario was inspirational.'[739] The Act 3 Prelude featured in Cillario's Gala Farewell concert nine years later.

La traviata with Moshinsky

Following the success of *Die Meistersinger*, Cillario returned to Sydney for a new production of *La traviata*,[740] working again with Elijah Moshinsky and Michael Yeargan, the team with which he had created the *Werther* production in 1990. In a year of Verdi and Wagner, Cillario explained some of the contrasts between the two composers and what they demanded of a conductor. 'For Verdi, I need a good cappuccino, but for Wagner, even a double espresso would not be enough.' (In reality, Cillario disliked coffee). 'For Wagner there is no need for anything but the music … the music itself is enough … an exciting drug … [Wagner] may spend a quarter-of-an-hour building to an emotional climax, but "he always knows exactly where to grab the emotion."'[741]

A good deal of critical ink was spilled over this *Traviata*, and in particular its portrait of Violetta – 'Did she *love* Alfredo? This director's original view, slanted towards *verismo*, posits a "maybe".' From the pit, however 'Verdi's passionate music, expertly shaped by Carlo Felice Cillario, jumps from heart to mouth with an uncompromising 'yes'.[742] All the same, the production went on to become a classic of the company's repertoire. Cillario brought authority and a sense of 'rightness' to the music making, earning the respect of critics:

> Veteran conductor Carlo Felice Cillario, I thought broke

---

[738] Cosic, 'Cillario Obituary', *The Australian*, 18 December 2007.

[739] Moffatt Oxenbould, email to the author, 20 June 2023.

[740] Cast: Deborah Riedel (Violetta), Roxane Hislop (Flora), Jennifer Bermingham (Annina), Jorge Lopez-Yanez (Alfredo), Jonathan Summers (Giorgio Germont), David Collins-White (Gastone), David Brennan (Barone Douphol), David Lemke (Marchese d'Obigny), Greg Scott (Doctor Grenvil), Jin Tea Kim (Giuseppe), David Tappin (Messenger), Xiaoming Lan (Servant).

[741] Johnston, *The Melburnian*, Vol. 9 No. 9, May 1994, 33–5.

[742] Bernadette Cruise, *The Canberra Times*, 12 October 1994.

no records, but earned no demerits either, tempi just right, all very accurate and poetic, though perhaps what I missed were greater resources at his command and a touch or two more of emotion.[743]

Ken Healey reported the new *Traviata* as

a beautifully designed production, with three excellent soloists and all the usual loving support from the Australian Opera Orchestra.' Deborah Riedel as Violetta offered 'opulent singing ... [which] suits Violetta's music perfectly. She does not hold back dramatically either, trusting her director.

Of Jorge Lopez-Yanez as Alfredo 'the ardour of the young man's love is subtle in this introverted reading, but perhaps even more telling for it.' Jonathan Summers 'long ago proved the quality of his Papa Germont. He is a baritone who can be credible as a conservative country squire whose love of his daughter forces him to have truck with a soiled creature of the high demi-monde.'[744]

Healey was less favourable to the staging, criticising its failure to 'touch the emotions' and its cutting against the grain of the piece at points such as the confrontation scene between Violetta and Giorgio Germont. Moshinsky had not won over critics with a widely publicised pre-premiere remark that *Traviata* had more than a touch of the *verismo* aesthetic. Healey concluded that 'of course maestro Cillario and his orchestra did not respond like a *verismo* band. Unless the conductor speaks, we will not know how willingly he complied with this wrong-headed approach to the work.'[745] Following one performance of *Traviata* in Sydney, the full company assembled onstage, joined by the Australian Opera CEO, Donald McDonald, and Artistic Director Moffatt Oxenbould, who presented Cillario with the company's highest honour, the 'Australian Opera Trophy' an award reserved for only a handful of figures, greatly significant to the company, including Joan Sutherland.

---

[743] Morrison, 'Simply Stunning,' *The Australian Jewish News* (Sydney), 26 August 1994.

[744] Healey, *Opera Australasia*, October 1994.

[745] Ibid.

26: The presentation of the Australian Opera Trophy, Sydney Opera House, 1994, following a performance of *La traviata*.

La traviata was revived in Melbourne the following autumn[746] where 'the exquisite sensibility of the tragic trio found its match in the playing of the State Orchestra of Victoria. Conductor Carlo Felice Cillario got from the musicians the response Verdi would have welcomed – the multiple and diverse moods and contrasts of colour.'[747] In contrast to its reception in Sydney (and perhaps consciously so) Clive O'Connell wrote that the new staging 'could not be faulted as far as production values and general appropriateness were concerned ... Moshinsky animated the subsidiary characters with some personality, creating interesting cameos for them.'

Gillian Sullivan gave a 'psychologically cogent' interpretation of Violetta, and O'Connell was impressed with Lopez-Yanez's tenor,

---

[746] Full cast: Jorge Lopez-Yanez and Yu Jixing (Alfredo Germont), Barry Anderson (Giorgio Germont), David Collins-White (Gastone), David Brennan (Baron Douphol), Neil Kirkby (Marchese d'Obigny), Greg Scott (Dr Grenvil), Graeme MacFarlane (Giuseppe), Gillian Sullivan (Violetta Valéry), Julie Edwardson (Flora), Ingrid Silveus (Annina), Angus Wood (Messenger), Xiaoming Lan (Servant).

[747] [No author named], 'Stunning Traviata,' *The Australian Jewish News* (Melbourne), 31 March 1995.

'flexible and light, at its best and exploited for its characteristics most effectively in the start of Act II.' He drew attention to the unusual staging of 'Sempre libera' sung by Sullivan 'lying on her back, head towards the audience', and the unexpected caesura after the 'si redesta' chorus that concludes the first scene of Act I (Moshinsky revised these points of staging in a later revival). O'Connell further noted that Cillario accentuated 'the sad, depressing aspects of the opera, rather than following the hectic changes in emotions that typify all scenes except possibly the last.' [748]

A revival of *Turandot* in Melbourne[749] brought a new guest artist to the title role, the American soprano Ruth Falcon, who had made many appearances at the Metropolitan Opera. Falcon was praised for her singing, but seemed ill at ease with the requirements of Graeme Murphy's staging (though no more than her predecessor in the role, Ealynn Voss), particularly with the elevated position from which she was required to sing 'In questa reggia'. It made for compelling theatre, in the author's recollection, but a potentially terrifying experience for a singer required to scale heights and make precarious descents (both vocally and physically). O'Connell felt that 'while one could admire the secure and forceful power of Ruth Falcon's high register, it was near-impossible to accept her as the remote and cold character that Turandot should be.'[750]

Not for the first time in productions of *Turandot* it was Liù who stole the show, as sung by the Armenian-born soprano, Arax Mansourian, while the other main principals received only a 'lukewarm reception.'[751] Of the musical leadership, wrote O'Connell, 'Cillario conducted without urgency, apparently content to keep the singers waiting, or curbing their desire to get on with the plot. At times it sounded as though he was waiting for soloists to reach a

---

[748] O'Connell, *Opera Australasia*, May 1995.
[749] Full cast: Ruth Falcon (Turandot), Kenneth Collins (Calaf), Arax Mansourian (Liù), Robert Gard (Emperor Altoum), Donald Shanks (Timur), John Pringle, Graeme Ewer, Christopher Dawes (Ping, Pang, Pong), Greg Scott (Mandarin), Jin Tea Kim (Prince of Persia).
[750] O'Connell, *Opera Australasia*, May 1995.
[751] Ibid.

note before he brought in the orchestral support. The result sounded deliberate, weighty, and often laboured.'[752]

In the Sydney winter season, Cillario led a further revival of Puccini's *Il trittico*[753] which he had last conducted in 1987. On this occasion, David Gyger favoured *Gianni Schicchi* ('an absolute masterpiece of black comedy'), in contrast to *Il tabarro* ('inherently a pretty feeble horror show') and *Suor Angelica* ('cloyingly sloppy'). The highlight of *Schicchi*, and the evening as a whole was 'the phenomenal John Pringle, who stepped inside the shoes of the deviously wily medieval Florentine with utter conviction and brought him to life straight off with mischievous bells on.'[754]

Kosky's *Nabucco*

Cillario had first been scheduled to conduct Verdi's *Nabucco* in 1971, before the clash over the terms of his directorship led to his departure. The work itself had not been revived by the company since 1973, and a new staging in 1995 caused a stir, especially in

---

[752] Ibid. In his final years with the company, this became a regular issue, at cadence points, when the singer, clearly wishing to move to their final note, would often have to wait some time before the conductor and orchestra joined.

[753] Full cast: *Il tabarro*: Jonathan Summers (Michele), Claire Primrose (Giorgetta), Anson Austin (Luigi), Christopher Dawes (Tinca), Arend Baumann (Talpa), Anthony Elek (Song Vendor), Jennifer Bermingham (Frugola), Anthony Elek, Kathryn McCusker (Two lovers). *Suor Angelica*: Nicola Ferner-Waite (Suor Angelica), Heather Begg (La Zia Principessa), Rosemary Gunn (La Badessa), Linda Calwell (La Suora Zelatrice), Kerry Elizabeth Brown (La Maestra delle Novizie), Marjorie McKay, Sandra Oldis (Le Cercatrici), Kathleen Connell (Suor Osmina), Kathryn McCusker (Suor Genovieffa), Penelope Pavlakis, Amelia Farrugia, Julie Edwardson (Tre Novizie), Anne Way (Suor Dolcina), Catherine Elliot (Suor Iginia), Carol-Anne Petherick (La Suora Infermiera), Christine Hore, Susan Barber (Le Converse). *Gianni Schicchi*: John Pringle (Schicchi), Kathryn McCusker (Lauretta), Heather Begg (Zita), Arend Baumann (Simone), David Collins-White (Rinuccio), David Brennan (Marco), Ingrid Silveus (La Ciesca), Graeme Ewer (Gherardo), Carol-Anne Petherick (Nella), Timothy Cannon (Gherardino), Richard Alexander (Betto di Signa), John Germain (Spinelloccio), Neil Kirkby (Amantio di Nicolao), Nicholas Davison (Pinellino), David Tappin (Guccio).

[754] D. Gyger, *Opera Australasia*, August 1995.

the hands of the Australian director Barrie Kosky. Australian opera goers were largely accustomed to conventionally costumed and designed stagings, whereas Kosky's work during the 1990s stretched the boundaries of visual and conceptual language and did not shy away from graphic realism. Cillario had worked with many leading directors, but his own inclinations tended towards a traditional style, believing that not only the music but also the drama on stage should be 'come scritto'- that the composer's and librettists' instructions were both to be respected.

Cillario was hardly alone among conductors in this regard. Charles Mackerras and Richard Bonynge held similar convictions, sceptical of German-derived *Regietheater* ('director's theatre') which took an imaginative rather than historically literal approach to (for example) the setting of a piece. Whereas Mackerras or Bonynge would have been likely to withdraw from a production if they felt strongly at odds with the directorial style, Cillario looked to the musical values to make things work. He seldom expressed open dislike for a production, but there is evidence that he would have hard conversations with directors in private if he felt that the direction was 'wrongheaded' – meaning unsupported by the instructions implicit in the score.[755]

The creative partnership of Kosky and Cillario made for a complex meeting of extraordinary minds, each fundamentally European in outlook. The *Nabucco* project presented the history of the Israelites in an opera house in the Antipodes, to be judged ultimately by local audiences. Conductor and director alike were intrepid explorers in their own worlds of ideas, they were determined to question and experiment. Kosky is a widely read musician, an excellent pianist and well able to argue his decisions, however unusual, through his understanding of the inner content of the score, which he knew intimately. Identifying as a Jewish director, Kosky outlined his views about Verdi's youthful work:

> Bringing Nabucco from the score to the stage is rather like working on a wonderfully weird archaeological puzzle.

---

[755] See: Cosic, 'No truth in operatic trickery', *The Weekend Australian*, 26–27 October 1996.

Every piece of this puzzle is strange (Israelites who speak Italian, Babylonians who march to the beat of mid-19th century martial music, and characters who appear, quite often for one line of music and then disappear), or contradictory (historical accuracy is subsumed by operatic convention, characters convert in a bar of music and the horror of the destruction of Jerusalem is sung to music of foot-stomping happiness).

Nabucco is, indeed, a collage of historical fragments, political satire and nineteenth-century melodrama. It is not a piercing psychological study of tyranny. It is not an overwhelming love story with tragic implications. Rather, it is a deliciously paradoxical piece of part-documentary, part-melodrama and part-historical variety show.

Characters and situations whirl across our stage like the storms described by biblical prophets. Pages of the prophecies of Jeremiah are blown on stage and scattered throughout the opera, the works of the prophet becoming signposts or tablets. The whirlwind on stage reveals a cemetery of forgotten shoes, a landscape of fossilised debris, rubble from the past building the future. Nabucco takes place not on some nostalgic vision of the ancient world but on the landscape of an imagined nineteenth-century theatre. Painted backdrops, glaring footlights, exaggerated poses, follow-spots and bold tableaux are all combined with a deliberately brash and somewhat hallucinogenic depiction of Babylon in an attempt to shatter the boundaries of 'historical accuracy' or the 'purity of realism.'

Babylon is bestial. Birds, insects, lions and monkeys. They fly above the action, are stuck on costumes, or form giant totems. Babylon is The Animal. Jerusalem is The Word. Verdi's music holds everything together, in a monumental structure of choral music, mad scenes and vengeance arias. It too whirls across the stage, furious, passionate and unbending. Embrace the kaleidoscope of Nabucco and let yourself be whirled through the deserts of time, place and memory.[756]

---

[756] 'Director's Note' by Barrie Kosky published in the Australian Opera programme for the Melbourne Autumn season of *Nabucco* in 1996.

Within the company, everyone was anticipating a confronting, challenging production, and perhaps fireworks between Cillario and Kosky. The production's dramaturg, Antony Ernst, created an information pack for the cast and production team[757] which reproduced a Gary Larson cartoon. A venerable conductor arrives in hell, and is ushered towards his next rehearsal by the devil. There he finds a room full of musicians, enthusiastically practicing on banjos.

Regarding this partnership, Moffatt Oxenbould has written:

> Maestro Cillario adored Barrie, and although he found some of his ideas incomprehensible or crazy, he always acknowledged that they came from the mind and imagination of an excellently qualified musician. He also had long experience with so-called radical production concepts and respected the right of the artist to express himself with sincerity and integrity, no matter how eccentric he might personally consider the results to be. ... The production was provocative, daring, disturbing and often mystifying, requiring its audience to engage and exercise their imagination. Every unexpected movement or image emerged from the score and scenically reflected the brashness and blaze of the writing of a young composer ... I had not for a moment expected the production to be embraced by all our subscribers, but had no idea just how hostile most people would be towards the show. ... Nothing I said about the desirability of looking at a great work in different ways or the musical unity of the collaboration between Carlo and Barrie had any effect. I received more letters of complaint about Nabucco than about any other production I've ever been involved in presenting.[758]

The cast for the Sydney premiere included Elizabeth Connell as Abigaille, Kenneth Collins as Ismaele, and Malcolm Donnelly as

---

[757] Opera Australia press files (1996 file).
[758] Oxenbould (2005), 609–10.

Nabucco.[759] The pros and cons of Kosky's vision were played out in the press. Reviewer David Scott-Thomas, quoting Kosky, reported that the director and designer had taken *Nabucco* to 'post-modern heights of surrealism.' In so doing, the reviewer claimed that Kosky had 'completely dismissed Verdi's intentions.' Compensation was provided, however 'by some sensational singing, notably from Elizabeth Connell … one of AO's greatest assets. Long may she reign on the stage.'[760] Scott-Thomas found that:

> The conductor Carlo Felice Cillario, who is renowned for his interpretation of Verdi, did much by way of keeping sanity in the house and received much-deserved applause. The orchestra were in fantastic form, responding to even the slightest whims from the maestro. The opening night concluded with a complicated mixture of boos and hisses, alternating with bravos for Kosky and his team.[761]

There was high praise for Cillario's work – the venerable maestro had by now had become a kind of quasi-Biblical Verdian prophet pontificating from the pit, and all who witnessed the production were aware of the care and attention that the score received in his hands. Oxenbould later wrote of being 'simply in awe of Maestro Cillario's ability to conjure up a transparency and delicacy in the string sound in Nabucco and to imbue this early Verdi score with his own life experience and deep humanity.'[762]

While finding fault with aspects of *Nabucco* itself, John Carmody was impressed by the 'complex originality and cheeky vitality' of Kosky's staging. 'Cillario encouraged a clean, crisp sound from the orchestra: one can hardly ask for more with Verdi's rather unsubtle scoring.'[763] Roger Covell's criticisms were squarely aimed at the stage direction: 'Cillario, who has seen all kinds of theatrical

---

[759] Full cast (Sydney): Malcolm Donnelly (Nabucco), Kenneth Collins (Ismaele), Donald Shanks/Bruce Martin (Zaccaria), Elizabeth Connell (Abigaille), Rosemary Gunn (Fenena), John Brunato (High Priest), Christopher Dawes (Abdallo), Carol-Anne Petherick (Anna).

[760] David Scott-Thomas, *The Weekly Southern Courier*, 5 September 1995.

[761] Ibid.

[762] Oxenbould (2005), 610–1.

[763] Carmody, 'Kosky the Prophet,' *The Sun Herald*, 20 August 1995.

extravagance before and (we hope) will be spared to witness many more such audacities in the future, conducted with a calm authority that imposed itself effortlessly on pit and stage.'[764] Deborah Jones agreed that

> Cillario worked wonders ... the sound – when one could drag one's attention to it – was delicious. ... It's possible to give fullest weight to this music's driving, energetic rhythms and martial tone, but Cillario chose to emphasise the wealth of melody and lyricism. This put stage and pit totally at odds, but I was with Cillario.

Jones dismissed the production as 'director and designer's opera gone feral ... flashy, heartless, over-designed and deaf to the voice of the composer.'[765] Younger audiences were more receptive. Reviewing for the University of Sydney paper *Honi Soit*, Teng-Han Tan noted that the production had won over younger audiences, 'a section of the opera world the Australian Opera is wooing with deadly intent.' Tan appreciated the contribution of the 80-years young vintage conductor: 'Ah, and who can forget Maestro Carlo Felice Cillario, whose conducting style is matched only by the extravagance of his personality and the range of his ability.'[766]

David Gyger evoked another Biblical figure, Solomon, in weighing up the new production:

> This Nabucco overflows with highly evocative visual imagery and makes extraordinary use of the stage facilities at its disposal: sometimes it goes over the top, but far more often I found myself asking why a particular image had been put there – and finding a rewarding answer ... It would be quite wrong to question the sincerity and deep intelligence of this extraordinarily talented young director.

Gyger judged the production as 'a Nabucco, finally, to send one home pondering about human relationships and power, politics and perhaps even religion – like any exposure to the performing

---

[764] Covell, *The Sydney Morning Herald*, 14 August 1995.

[765] Deborah Jones, *The Australian*, 15 August 1995.

[766] Teng-Han Tan, *Honi Soit*, 26 Sept 1995. [University of Sydney publication].

arts ideally ought to do, but so many don't.' Gyger appreciated the 'towering performances of Elizabeth Connell and Malcolm Donnelly' and the 'monumentally sympathetic baton' of Cillario: 'Whatever one may think of the goings-on on stage, this *Nabucco* is a musical treasure.' On seeing one of the later performances, Gyger further warmed to the staging: 'I still liked it much more than the vociferous contingent of opera goers who have been making such a fuss.' Musically

> the wider ensemble, vocal and orchestral, once again gave of its best under the masterful control of that veteran conducting treasure Carlo Felice Cillario. Whatever the intrinsic demerits of this Nabucco, one could at no stage seriously fault it in musical terms.[767]

David Malouf wrote a considered appreciation for the *Australian Book Review* ('Return to Babylon,'[768] condensed in a piece for *The Age*), reflecting on the depth of imagination and ideas brought by Kosky to the stage.

---

[767] D. Gyger, *Opera Australasia*, September 1995.

[768] Malouf, 'Return to Babylon' The *Australian Book Review*, October 1995, no. 175.

Scene 2 – *Pensionamento*

27: Maestro Cillario rehearsing *La bohème*, Redfern, NSW, 1999.

Having turned 80, productions such as *Nabucco* and the *Falstaff* which followed confirmed Cillario's status in Australia as a 'National Treasure'. He retained a unique and abiding musical vision, representing an almost bygone age in operatic history. Whether engaged in core classics like *La traviata*, or rarer and stylistically more elusive works, such as *Nabucco*, his leadership resulted in musical experiences of substance, stamped with a seal of 'authenticity.'

In spite of his largely undimmed energy, in a profession where age has traditionally been associated with wisdom and transcendence, some of the younger singers and instrumentalists in the company found it difficult to relate to Cillario, and to his methods of working. His individual sense of humour, his unpredictable and occasional volatile behaviour, as well as his embodiment of the role of the 'maestro', felt increasingly out of step with changing times. Unionisation in Australia had given orchestral players an increasing degree of control over working practices, and players' committees were increasingly able to wield influence over the hiring and firing of conductors.

Cillario's hearing and sight gradually deteriorated during the second half of the 1990s. Particular frequencies became compromised, and although he knew most of his repertoire from heart, he always conducted with a score. Now, his deteriorating eyesight led to him increasingly having his 'head in the score' – a term used (misused, in this case) to denote someone inexperienced or unfamiliar with the works they are conducting. On occasion this compromised his contact with both pit and stage. Nothing was ever said openly, Cillario was still held in high regard, but it would be surprising if he was not aware of his frailties. As a result, some ugly scenes occurred with the orchestra, where he misread situations in rehearsals, and reacted in an aggressive manner that may have worked for Toscanini, but which was not acceptable in Australia of the 1990s. Cillario was still an extraordinary musical resource, but he had served with the company for almost three decades. In operational as well as interpersonal areas, he represented a bygone era, the passing of which was not lamented by most of his colleagues.

As Artistic Director, it fell to Oxenbould to guide Cillario's career to an appropriately dignified and mutually respectful close. Milestones, such as *Die Meistersinger* in Melbourne, and the presentation of the Opera Australia Trophy became part of a gradual process of farewell, which was conducted at a *lentissimo* pace, because Cillario retained his full musical sensibilities, much of his energy, and an iron determination to fulfil the role of the 'maestro', even as his health declined. This was an indivisible part of him, and letting go was not in his nature. Surviving correspondence between conductor and Artistic Director [769] documents Oxenbould's attempts, couched respectfully but with increasing firmness, to set a path for a 'farewell', with an agreed and suitably fitting end point. Verdi's *Falstaff* had received its premiere in 1893, in the composer's 80th year, and a new production was scheduled for the Sydney winter season of 1996. By this time, Cillario had already turned 81 – there was general uncertainty about the conductor's exact age – and this *Falstaff* was to become another part of the farewell process.

Falstaff

The Melbourne-based theatre director Simon Phillips directed *Falstaff*, with Jonathan Summers in the title role. Cillario himself was a veteran of six previous productions, and his experience and presence created a vibrancy within the production team and inspired its cast.[770] The premiere in Sydney was well received, 'as fresh and exuberant visually as it is musically, under the baton of Carlo Felice Cillario.'[771]

As an outcome of the Opera Conference,[772] the staging had already been given by other companies in Perth and Brisbane. Ken Healey found the production 'decidedly uneven' in Sydney, but nevertheless 'the most accessible and enjoyable *Falstaff*' he had experienced. The highlight was the great scene between Falstaff and Ford, sung by Summers and Michael Lewis: 'I should not expect to hear better anywhere.' The women presented 'a perfectly balanced

---

[769] Oxenbould/Ewer Papers, NLA Canberra.

[770] Full cast: Jonathan Summers (Falstaff), Michael Lewis (Ford), Christopher Lincoln (Fenton), David Hamilton (Dr Caius), Christopher Dawes (Bardolfo), Arend Baumann (Pistola), Joan Carden (Alice Ford), Amelia Farrugia (Nannetta), Irene Waugh and Linda Calwell [Jennifer Bermingham was indisposed] (Mistress Quickly), Rosemary Gunn (Meg Page).

[771] Morrison, *The Australian Jewish News* (Sydney), 11 October 1996.

[772] A confederation of professional Australian opera companies, established under the independent chairmanship of Margaret Whitlam. (See Oxenbould (2005), 337).

quartet,' with Carden 'relishing the ensemble opportunities provided by Alice', Rosemary Gunn 'a clear and decisive Meg', Irene Waugh 'a robust, earthy Mistress Quickly',[773] and Amelia Farrugia 'vocally almost stealing her first scene, always an enchanting Nanetta.'[774] Maria Prerauer wrote in the same vein: 'Despite the furious, manic activity of the first act and the near stasis of the last, the singing and the playing make this a *Falstaff* to treasure. And for the perfect whole, there's always the middle act.'[775]

Cillario won unanimous praise. 'A fine cast under a master conductor,' according to Healey 'ensured an evening of delight.... The AO's present cast is uniformly strong, and Maestro Cillario is back to his best form.'[776] Covell considered that Cillario was 'completely in tune with the light-fingered speed and chiming clarity of the score,'[777] and Prerauer found that the conductor brought out 'the score's many comic subtleties, revealing the special way its words and music complement each other, culminating in the final fugue that underlines its message: "All in the world is a jest."'[778]

Outside the mainstage season, Cillario also conducted a youth performance on 25 October with a young cast of emerging singers, mostly new to their roles, all anchored by the presence of John Pringle in the title role. [779] David Gyger found standard overall 'only a trifle less impressive than it had been with the first-string cast,' an impressive tribute to the skills of the company's ensemble in a work which is unique in the Verdi canon for its 'ensemble sensibilities .... At the nerve centre, of course was Cillario, for the way he was

---

[773] Jennifer Bermingham was cast in the role of Quickly but was ill on opening night.
[774] Healey, *Opera Australasia*, November 1996.
[775] Prerauer, *The Australian*, 11 October 1996.
[776] See FN 774.
[777] Covell, *The Sydney Morning Herald*, 11 October 1996.
[778] Prerauer, *The Australian*, 11 October 1996.
[779] Full cast: John Pringle (Falstaff), David Brennan (Ford), Graeme MacFarlane (Fenton), David Lewis (Dr Caius), Jamie Allen (Bardolfo), John Brunato (Pistola), Amanda Colliver (Alice Ford), Emma Lysons (Nannetta), Linda Calwell (Mistress Quickly), Ingrid Silveus (Meg Page).

constantly able to forge operatic truth in the most exalted sense from this work's often wispy instrumental and ... vocal fabric.'[780]

Cillario and Directors – *'no tricks'*

Among the productions conducted by Cillario in Australia, especially towards the end of his career, several instances arose of a sharp contrast between the reception of the musical values and the staging. With *Cav & Pag* in 1989, John Copley provoked criticism by introducing additional story elements. It was Elijah Moshinsky's turn in 1994, directing a 'verismo' *La traviata* which he eventually toned down. Barrie Kosky's *Nabucco* (1995) was in a category of its own, shocking and brilliant, provoking scandal as well as much insightful criticism. The fickle and partial nature of much of this criticism was exemplified by the reception accorded to Simon Phillips's *Falstaff*, objections to which centred on its realistic, traditional approach.

Cillario generally kept his thoughts on these matters to himself, until, following the Sydney premiere of *Falstaff*, he gave an interview to Miriam Cosic. Praising the staging as 'logical', Cillario declared that

> unfortunately, Simon Phillips will not be so famous as the others that create stupid things ... but I promise you that you will enjoy his production because it is not boring at all. It's very difficult, very new, and very Verdian and Boitoian and Shakespearean, without destroying anybody's glory. And that is the position that clever directors must take.

This may be interpreted as praise, from a veteran of six *Falstaff* productions[781] though Cosic's own position might be inferred from her description of Cillario 'defending his métier from the outrages perpetuated by new-wave directors.'

According to Cosic, 'Cillario clearly thinks that the weight of authority has shifted too far from the music – and the conductor –

---

[780] D. Gyger, *Opera Australasia*, December 1996.
[781] Mexico City 1966 with Geraint Evans; Canberra 1969 with Ronald Maconaghie; Melbourne 1969 with Tito Gobbi; Paris 1970 with Tito Gobbi; Sydney 1979 with Ronald Maconaghie; Stockholm 1984 with Björn Asker.

in favour of a star system of directors. He says that this generation of singers is becoming robotic as a consequence, losing its spontaneity and its ability to act on stage.' He speaks unhappily of the current practice of engaging a conductor after a director, when their concept and designs are already in place. Cillario prefers a system which is currently declining, where conductor, designer and director are engaged all together, with meetings and discussions and the final decision made 'all together.'

Cillario remarked that he had been engaged for *Nabucco* once the basic concept of Kosky's staging had been settled, and he was powerless to change anything. 'I was against a lot of details,' he said,

> Some things were changed, and more [occurred] when we did *Nabucco* later in Melbourne. The boos of the Sydney opening had fortunately influenced him. He didn't renounce his ideas, but he changed them, into something that was not so shocking. Melbourne was a success. Partly, of course because he was from Melbourne and also because Melbourne wished to show it was more sophisticated than Sydney. But if we performed it in Parma ... we wouldn't reach the second act, I promise you, because they just want the truth.

Cosic notes the conductor's straightforward use of leading terms such as 'truth', 'lies' and 'shock' in this context. Cillario said that he made these observations

> with great respect for Barrie, because he is a very talented man. And [Elijah] Moshinsky is extremely talented. But often they like themselves more than the masterpiece that they must interpret ... we must decide if opera is just an entertainment or an act of culture. ... we must respect what is in the manuscript. The conductor, the singers, everyone must try to get to the truth of that music. And we cannot accept the shock of having truth in the music and lies in the singing and the acting. I fight for truth, for logic in opera, no tricks.[782]

---

[782] Information on this page is derived from: Cosic, 'No truth in operatic trickery,' *The Weekend Australian*, 26–27 October 1996.

Nabucco in Melbourne

In April 1996 the notorious *Nabucco* transferred to Kosky's hometown, Melbourne. Several significant cast changes were made from
the Sydney premiere, included the appearance of Jonathan Summers in the title role.[783] Clive O'Connell referred to the 'popularly
explosive and divisive premiere' in Sydney, and drew attention to a
cast change on opening night, when Bruce Martin sang Zaccaria:
the occasion 'was chiefly a triumph for Martin, Connell, and Summers'. Elizabeth Connell's portrayal of Abigaille 'allowed humour to
emerge, chiefly in how [she] was required to behave in front of other
characters', from which there 'lurked an entertainer, a figure informed
with crude humour.'[784] For Peter Burch, Connell's performance 'was
dramatically powerful, and her naturally huge voice sat effortlessly
within the compass of this character's testing vocal demands.' In the
title role Summers was in equally fine voice, giving a performance
of 'rich intensity and dramatic power.'[785] O'Connell wrote that Summers 'was given room to express almost ludicrous megalomania and
spite', and that Bruce Martin was a 'powerful presence.'

In terms echoed by countless opera critics, 'somebody remarked
that there was nothing to stop you closing your eyes and listening to
an aurally sterling performance of *Nabucco*.'[786]

Burch wrote of Kosky's contribution:

> What has characterised critical and audience response to
> all his stagings, is that nobody has walked away feeling
> indifferent about what they've seen. People are polarised
> into those who are exhilarated by the chutzpah of his
> imagination and those who are bewildered and/or angry at
> his preparedness to saturate productions with apparently
> incomprehensible imagery.[787]

---

[783] Full cast: Jonathan Summers (Nabucco), Anson Austin (Ismaele), Bruce Mar-
tin (Zaccaria), Elizabeth Connell (Abigaille), Rosemary Gunn (Fenena),
John Brunato (High Priest), Christopher Dawes (Abdallo), Jeannie Kelso
(Anna).

[784] O'Connell, 'Entertaining and stimulating,' *Opera Australasia*, May 1996.

[785] Burch, *The Australian*, 18 April 1996

[786] O'Connell, *Opera Australasia*, May 1996.

[787] See FN 785.

There were no boos at the premiere, 'just tremendous cheers' for a performance 'that gave life to Luigi Dallapiccola's reflection that Verdi's music and libretti "formulated a style through which the Italian people found a key to their dramatic plight and vibrated in unison with it."'[788]

Burch concluded that 'Nabucco must ultimately be counted a triumph for the company, generating a strength of feeling which even resulted in an NSW Small Claims Tribunal ruling 'that a disgruntled patron's ticket should be refunded.' [789] The language of the stage would be considered tame today, in comparison to the frequently encountered practices of *Regietheater*. Even so, once past its initial runs in Sydney and Melbourne, this *Nabucco* was never revived. The Melbourne season was recorded for commercial video release.

28: 'Carlo keeps secret score,' April 1997.

1996 marked the 40th Anniversary of the company's founding. To commemorate this milestone, at the conclusion of the Melbourne autumn season a gala concert was organised, featuring singers and

---

[788] Ibid.
[789] Ibid.

staff from the original 1956 company. Cillario led the evening's climax, the 'Wachet auf' chorus from *Die Meistersinger,* honouring three former *Meistern*: Robert Allman, Robert Gard and John Germain, who were making their farewell appearances in Melbourne. Oxenbould recalled that, with past singers and staff coming onstage to join the company, 'Maestro Cillario led the throng in a moment of deep emotion, gratitude, and wonder.'[790]

In the summer season of 1997, Cillario returned to Sydney as one of five conductors for the Esso Opera in the Park, an event which attracted tens of thousands of people to the outdoor venue of the Domain, for one of the most popular events of the Sydney Festival. In addition, Cillario led two notable Verdi revivals on the mainstage.

The first of these was *La traviata*, with Cheryl Barker appearing as Violetta, and Julian Gavin as Alfredo.[791] Elijah Moshinsky returned to personally oversee the revival of his staging, having given indications that he wished to revisit some of its more controversial elements, such as Violetta singing her Act 1 scene lying on her back, and her scene with Giorgio Germont. These were summed up by Peter Morrison's criticism of what he had regarded in the original staging as 'a wilful confusion between the worlds of Mimì and Violetta ... important aspects of the production simply did not convince.' Moshinsky had apparently modified his previously circulated views that the work was 'early *verismo*, not romantic opera at all.' Morrison nonetheless reserved his highest praise for Cillario, who conducted 'with the same degree of vigour, attack and sensitivity as characterised the singing.'[792]

---

[790] Oxenbould (2005), 624. Information in this paragraph derived from this reference.

[791] Full cast: Cheryl Barker (Violetta), Julie Edwardson (Flora), Jennifer Bermingham (Annina), Julian Gavin and Du Jigang (Alfredo), Neville Wilkie and Henry Ruhl (Giorgio Germont), David Collins-White (Gastone), Richard Alexander (Barone Douphol), John Brunato (Marchese d'Obigny), Greg Scott (Doctor Grenvil), Graeme MacFarlane (Giuseppe), Robert Beasley, (Messenger), Xiaoming Lan (Servant).

[792] Morrison, *The Australian Jewish News* (Sydney), 31 January 1997.

According to Ken Healey, this 'reshaped *Traviata*' was a 'triumph'. Cheryl Barker's Violetta was 'better seen than simply heard. ... [she] is as admirable a Violetta as she has become a Mimi.' Julian Gavin's tenor had 'an almost baritonal richness ... and the power of an emerging Wagnerian at the top ... Gavin's tone would benefit from a little more Italianate burnish.' Neville Wilkie played Giorgio Germont as 'a withdrawn man, probably puritanical as well as naturally uncomfortable in Violetta's presence. The scene was a great success. ... Once again maestro Cillario conducts both orchestra and singers with loving authority...'[793]

The revival of *Falstaff* in Melbourne was another success,[794] as described by Sidney Bloch:

> Cillario is a great exponent of the Verdi oeuvre and clearly knows his *Falstaff* inside out. He inspired the forces of the State Orchestra of Victoria from the opening bars to the final fugue; what we heard was most scintillating and vibrant playing. The singers blended in resoundingly with this orchestral support, some more notably than others ... And so, the bouquets go unquestionably to Maestro Cillario and to the members of State Orchestra of Victoria. Verdi would have been most pleased to hear them.[795]

Clive O'Connell recalled the 1969 Melbourne *Falstaff*, with Tito Gobbi, and the lack of interest shown at the time by Melbourne audiences towards Verdi's final opera. He was not enthusiastic about Stephen Phillip's staging, and Cillario was damned with faint praise.[796] This was hardly the first or the last instance of the historic rivalry between Melbourne and Sydney being played out in print.

---

[793] Information and quotes in this paragraph are from Healey, 'Sensitively re-shaped La Traviata triumphant,' *Opera-Opera*, February 1997.

[794] Full cast: Jonathan Summers (Falstaff), Douglas McNicol (Ford), Anthony Elek (Fenton), David Collins-White (Dr Caius), Christopher Dawes (Bardolfo), Arend Baumann (Pistola), Joan Carden (Alice Ford), Emma Lysons (Nannetta), Jennifer Bermingham (Mistress Quickly), Rosemary Gunn (Meg Page).

[795] Bloch, 'Thank heavens for Verdi and for Carlo Felice Cillario,' *Australian Jewish News* (Melbourne), 11 April 1997.

[796] O'Connell, *Opera-Opera*, May 1997.

Following the opening of the State Theatre in 1994, Melbourne critics took exception to the presentation of revival stagings which had been designed for the smaller stage of the Sydney Opera Theatre and thus required conspicuous masking. There was also a nagging (not entirely unfounded) suspicion that the company engaged less prestigious principals and conductors for Melbourne seasons.

29: 'Dial M for Maestro,' January 1997.

In January 1997, Peter Holder explored the complex relationship between Cillario and Moffatt Oxenbould by conducting interviews with both men. Cillario recalled his introduction to the company back in 1968, when it was 'a real family, and even though it is now much bigger, it remains a family.' He had many fond memories: 'I try to forget the past and always be in the present with a mind that is in the future ... but, of course I have some special moments ... The Australian Opera allows me to work with young voices and it is much more rewarding, it allows me to mould a performer.' Oxenbould commented that Cillario 'has made an important contribution to the growth of the company and, indeed opera in Australia. ... He's a representative of a generation of conductors including

Toscanini, conductors with a link to the great Italian music tradition of Verdi and Puccini.'[797]

In speaking with each of them separately, Holder teased out moments of friction which had arisen over the years.

> 'I knew him when he was almost a boy,' says the maestro of Oxenbould, mockingly dismissive. Oxenbould says theirs is a classic love-hate relationship, and Cillario can be 'fantastically irritating. Cillario is a setter of standards … he believes in and challenges performers. One of his great strengths is that he's never rigid or stuck in the past – in fact, sometimes he can have an irritating flexibility.'[798]

In explaining his own work, Cillario recalled seeing a film about Pablo Picasso, which revealed what he could do with just a simple line. The artist began drawing a circle, which became a bullfighting arena and then a chicken. 'He was able to show how easy it was to transform a line into many different things … It was incredible to see what he could do. In many ways, a conductor can do that with a performer.'[799]

Looking Forwards

Meanwhile, Moffatt Oxenbould continued to work quietly to bring Cillario's career with Opera Australia to a dignified close. His job was not made easier by the affection and respect in which each held the other, exemplified by their address to each other as 'mio padre' and 'mio figlio'.[800] Their exchanges[801] form a model of civilised correspondence between two men sharing great mutual respect,

---

[797] Peter Holder, 'Dial M for Maestro,' *The Daily Telegraph,* 17 January 1997.

[798] Ibid.

[799] Ibid.

[800] During the 1980's another, more conspiratorial tone developed between the two, with Oxenbould signing himself as 'Dimitri' and Cillario as 'Ivan' (the Terrible). These aliases were an extension of the humour which characterised their correspondence. On one occasion 'Dimitri' (Oxenbould) sent Cillario a draft cast list for the following year, stating that it was still confidential, and asking him to eat the letter once he has memorised its contents. (Oxenbould to Cillario, 21 October 1987).

[801] Oxenbould/Ewer Papers, NLA, Canberra.

discussing a difficult, but inevitable matter. The implied father-son hegemony probably prolonged its resolution.

The Melbourne *Falstaff* of 1997 had been proposed as a *finale ultimo*, but Cillario made a case for his final appearances to occur in 1998 with *Macbeth*, which would allow him to celebrate the 30th anniversary of his first season with the company. As soon as *Macbeth* was confirmed, Cillario announced his intention to continue conducting until 2000, when he would retire. Frustrated at not being able resolve the situation, on 3 April 1997, Oxenbould wrote officially to his 'padre-maestro':

> I believe that it is the right time in 1998 for us to bring to an end the professional association which will next year have extended over a period of 30 years, during which time you have been the most significant and important musical influence in the development of our Company.
>
> I have had to take into consideration the very strong reactions and responses of players and singers to their recent collaborations with you … to the very clear feelings of recent years among singers and players, among whom are your greatest admirers, that there is an erratic and inconsistent element now present in your work that in turn creates an uncertainty and lack of clarity amongst both singers and players.
>
> The resolution of the A[ustralian] O[pera and] B[allet] O[rchestra] late last year not to work further with you may have been impetuous and ill-considered, but was serious and sincere. … I do not want such an important and wonderful artistic association to end in protest and rancour, but rather we should use the occasion of your last performances with us to celebrate our wonderful association[802]

Oxenbould's letter was friendly, open, and honest, but somewhat distanced from the tone of their usual correspondence. Cillario replied on 9 April in comparably formal terms, with a diplomatically couched and professionally typed letter. Cillario refers to his activity 'in the most important theatres in the world' before he increasingly

---

[802] Ibid.

'focussed towards Australia.' He had been given the 'certainty', he says, that 'here I would be able to work seriously.' He quotes Oxenbould's much-repeated comment: 'As long as I am here, you will be by my side.' He had received an assurance from both Oxenbould and Richard Bonynge that 'I would be coming to Australia for the rest of my life.' Now, however: 'You intend to get rid of my collaboration. Elegantly, and with no regrets.' He notes that his recent productions that 'you have entrusted me with' have enjoyed 'both public and critical acclaim.'[803]

Cillario then addresses the recent incidents cited by Oxenbould. He places them in the context of past engagements at the Staatsoper Berlin and the Paris Opéra, where he had 'found it necessary to criticise their [the orchestra's] performance … [and] both orchestras refused to play under my direction!' He acknowledges a previous failure to grasp 'other secrets, such as not raising your voice too much in Anglo-Saxon countries, and saying "stop" instead of "shut up" (I can do this!)' He finally yields to the decision to 'dissolve what you rightly describe as "our wonderful association".' On that basis, he has begun to 'reopen my links with the music scene in Europe', which has already resulted in a proposed engagement in Bergamo.[804]

Nonetheless, Cillario expresses concern that his return to European activity would be impeded by the 'international music world' learning that his 'long collaboration with Australia' was coming to an end just as the 2000 Olympic Games was on the horizon. He asks Oxenbould to extend their cooperation 'not ad infinitum' but nearer to the Olympic year when Oxenbould had also scheduled his own departure from the company. He rejects Oxenbould's proposal of a Gala Concert in Melbourne in 1998 in his honour, and makes the counterproposal of a Verdi Requiem in Melbourne, which he offers to conduct for free.[805]

> It is my belief that this would be the best way for me to conclude our exemplary artistic cooperation with my head held high. With simplicity. Without champagne or speech-

---

[803] Ibid.

[804] Ibid.

[805] Ibid.

es. Only with an affectionate embrace to the people of this
nation, whom I love so much. More than if it were my own.
… I hope with your creative fantasy and goodwill you shall
find a solution which will meet this wish of mine. I thank
you.[806]

These exchanges shed much light on the working relationship
between the two men, which had extended over 30 years, and had
become steadily closer since 1984. Cillario considered himself to
be a part of the Opera Australia family and felt the pain of their
projected separation all the more keenly. He felt that he still had
'something to say', and he was determined to leave on his own terms.

Oxenbould's 'creative fantasy' was put to work. He found suitable
projects for Cillario in the remaining years of his own tenure: in
particular a direct collaboration between the two men, as conductor
and director, in a new production of *La bohème*. Cillario continued
to lead staged performances with Opera Australia until 2002, and
his career with the company came to a fittingly memorable close,
not with the proposed Verdi Requiem but with a Gala Concert in
2003, held in the Concert Hall of the Sydney Opera House.

In January 1998, Cillario was one of several conductors at
another Esso Opera in the Park event. He could occasionally be
sighted, in the city, or near the Opera House, often walking (he was
an inveterate walker), seemingly lost in thought, or sitting, reading
a score, quietly existing in his own world. Few onlookers would
have suspected that he was the fiery maestro who galvanised an
orchestra, chorus and cast of wilful soloists in performances at the
Opera House, occasionally shouting imprecations when things did
not proceed as planned.

I was present at the dress rehearsal for the Opera in the Park
concert. Cillario sat alone in repose at the side of the stage, dwarfed
by the enormity of the venue. By this point in his career, he took care
to preserve his energy in rehearsals, and on occasion would leave the
conducting to an assistant or prompter. It was hard to imagine that

---

[806] Ibid.

he was about to take charge of the assembled company and 'break ground' – kick off the proceedings with the stirring Overture to *La Forza del Destino*. At his call, he walked out across the stage, taking in the huge outdoor audience area that was already filling up with visitors wanting to secure the best places for the evening. On the podium, he looked a little lost and unsure, some uncertainty spread among the ranks of the orchestra. An uncanny transformation took place as he gave the upbeat for the brass to begin. Their forceful, ringing tone in response to his gestures seemed to infuse him with energy. Members of the company remarked that they could not recall hearing the *Forza* overture performed with such rhythmic drive and electric dynamism. The concert that evening was no less exciting.

The flavour of that dress rehearsal was captured by the photographer Jeff Darmanin.[807] Published in a Sydney newspaper, his photo of the maestro in full flight became well known. For many former colleagues and friends, this is the image that best encapsulates Cillario, man and musician.[808] By this time his energy might wane over the course of an evening, requiring ever more behind-the-scenes support, and tempi might become erratic, but there were still moments of magic. No other conductor on the horizon had such ownership of the Italian repertoire, and such a connection with the company and its conventions – many of which he had created.

Cillario's sole engagement in the Opera House during that season was a run of *Macbeth* (due to have been his final appearance), with Michael Lewis and Claire Primrose as the murderous royal couple.[809] Cheryl Sawyer paid tribute to Cillario's 'exacting and

---

[807] See front cover illustration.

[808] Amy Egan, *The Daily Telegraph*, 10 January 1998. The accompanying text was: 'The passion of the conductor matched the devotion of the fans as the opera came to the park yesterday ... Italian Cillario is Opera Australia's visiting Verdi specialist. And he conducted the rehearsal with an energy and passion redolent of the tragic story of 'The Force of Destiny''.

[809] Full cast: Claire Primrose (Lady Macbeth), Michael Lewis (Macbeth), Donald Shanks (Banquo), Anson Austin (Macduff), Dawn Walsh (Lady in Waiting), Jamie Allen (Malcolm), Greg Scott (Doctor), John Brunato (Servant to Macbeth), David Berry, Tim Pocock (Apparitions).

dynamic conducting of Verdi.'[810] John Copley had returned to direct the revival of his own, 21-year-old staging; Cillario had shared the performances with John Pritchard during its opening season. Having sung the title role previously with the State Opera of South Australia, Lewis was now making his role debut with Opera Australia. Ken Healey found that he sang with 'thrilling clarity, all the necessary power, and a fine musical intelligence.' As Lady Macbeth, Primrose 'unexpectedly has her greatest success where one might least expect it: in soft singing. Primrose cuts effortlessly through the fortissimo ensembles, with a slightly hard edge to the tone, or at least a brilliant, steely sound at the top.' In the sleep-walking scene

> she makes as moving a Lady Macbeth as I have ever known. … Donald Shanks is in firm control of his vast, black sound as Banquo, and Anson Austin makes a mature Macduff, earning respect. Carlo Felice Cillario shows himself as truly at home as ever in this repertoire, and the Australian Opera and Ballet Orchestra maintains the high standard it so boldly displayed at the outset of the current season.[811]

Cillario was interviewed by Peter Farmer, who had been present at the dress rehearsal of *Macbeth*:

> Watching him breathe life into the score of *Macbeth* … made me realise that our definitions of creativity were at odds … the end product of a shout to the woodwinds, leaning over the podium to almost caress the strings, a joke to someone else in the pit, empathy towards the exposed singers revealed both a true artist at work, and an instinct surely refined from working with some of the great singers of the century – Callas and Gobbi amongst them.

> Carlo Felice Cillario is 83 years old. The sheer vitality of a man almost 20 years past official retirement brings to mind W. B. Yeats also writing late in life:

> > One asks for mournful melodies,
> > Accomplished fingers to play.
> > Their eyes mid many wrinkles, their eyes,
> > Their ancient, glittering eyes are gay.

[810] Cheryl Sawyer, *The Australian Jewish News* (Sydney), 6 February 1998.
[811] Healey, *Opera-Opera*, February 1998.

Not that all is high spirits and harmony for the maestro. His occasional sharp tongue or slow beat can make a singer's life hell, and attempts to achieve Verdi's ideal "ugly voice" for the character of Lady Macbeth led to fireworks in rehearsal; singers are far from keen to reverse their technique, or risk a lashing from the critics for 'creating an effect.'

Nonetheless, it's all part of a balance sheet, and Cillario, at his best, remains a wonder, which audiences recently affirmed at the Opera in the Park in Sydney's Domain – a passionate Italian in his true element on a clear summer night.[812]

30: Rehearsing *La bohème* with Moffatt Oxenbould, 1999.

---

[812] Peter Farmer, 'Basking in a sunny old age, full of humour and vigour and music,' *Opera-Opera*, April 1998.

Youthful *La bohème*

Cillario's time with the company had not yet run its course. In 1999 Moffatt Oxenbould directed a new production of *La bohème*, in response to a particular set of circumstances within the company. Baz Luhrmann had created an artistic and a commercial sensation with his 1990 staging of the opera, and went on to supervise three revivals of it, during a period when his fame and reputation skyrocketed. *La bohème* was a staple of the company's repertoire, and a production that was readily revivable was required. The evolving landscape of Luhrmann's career made his availability for further revivals an uncertainty. Oxenbould and Luhrmann reluctantly agreed that the production would be compromised if he was unable to revive it, and decided that it would be withdrawn. Unsurprisingly, the Luhrmann *Bohème* was perceived to be a hard act to follow, and directors who were approached to create a new production were unwilling to take the risk. Around this time, the company was going through a financial crisis and a new *Bohème* was urgently needed.[813]

Oxenbould decided to step into the fray. He drew upon his knowledge of the company's history of staging *La bohème*, stretching back nearly 30 years and resolved to create a production that referenced past *Bohèmes*, by incorporating recycled costumes and props from previous productions. The principal roles were triple-cast to offer opportunities to young and emerging singers, especially former members of the Esso Young Artist Programme. The Luhrmann production had demonstrated that *La bohème* may succeed using artists with lighter voices than would typically be engaged by larger opera houses. It was an approach suited both to the scale of the Opera Theatre and to the spirit of the company, presenting a cast of visually credible young Bohemians in love.

The production satisfied several imperatives. It retained *La bohème* in the company's repertoire, it met a tight budget, and it developed young, local and talented Puccini singers of the future. To complete the artistic team, Cillario's repository of stylistic knowledge

---

[813] Oxenbould (2005), 669-70.

seemed indispensable. The three casts worked in rotation to give 31 performances, with Cillario conducting 16 of them.[814]

In 1970 the company had staged *La bohème* (conducted by Cillario) featuring a youthful cast, which attracted criticism at the time for a lack of 'true' Puccini voices. While times had changed in terms of expectations regarding 'verisimilitude versus voices', Ken Healey nevertheless complained: 'What is lacking is the sort of voices that *Bohème* cannot do without.' He praised various aspects of Oxenbould's production: 'the stage very cleverly becomes a stage in the 1890s, on which a performance of the opera is being staged.' For criticism, he singled out the chair (instead of the usual bed) on which Glenys Fowles as Mimì had died in 1970 (conducted by Cillario): 'Seeing Mimì die in a chair rather than a bed seemed to upset traditionalists of 2000 as much as it did in 1970. Nonetheless', concluded Healey, 'this production will provide much joy, particularly if Maestro Cillario continues to caress sounds and musical shapes from his orchestra as he is currently doing. He never over-played the voices, and yet the score did not sound inhibited thereby.'[815] David Gyger was still more positive in his appraisal:

> The guidance of guru Cillario, to well up with those torrents of emotionally supercharged instrumental sumptuousness that cause anyone with an operatic soul to wilt into ecstasy. ... I joined willingly in the general audience acclaim which greeted Cillario after each interval and at the end, though I continued to harbour as many reservations about the production itself as ever.[816]

Amid the *Bohème* preparations, Cillario had a stroke of good fortune. It was with sadness that the company learned of the death

---

[814] Full cast: Jamie Allen, Jae-Woo Kim, Anson Austin (Rodolfo), Anke Höppner, Nicole Youl, Lisa Russell (Mimì), Douglas McNicol, Timothy DuFore, John Pringle (Marcello), Elisa Wilson, Amelia Farrugia (Musetta), Angus Wood, Joshua Bloom, John Cummins (Schaunard), Stephen Bennett, Richard Alexander, John Brunato (Colline), John Bolton-Wood (Benoit/Alcindoro), Jin Tea Kim (Parpignol), Christopher Bath (Customs Sergeant), Tom Hamilton (Customs Officer).

[815] Healey, *Opera-Opera*, September 1999.

[816] D. Gyger, *Opera-Opera*, October 1999.

of Peter Erckens, a German conductor who had made a strong impression conducting seasons of *Béatrice et Bénédict* and *Otello* in recent years. Erckens was due to arrive in Australia to conduct the Graeme Murphy production of *Turandot*. Having conducted its premiere in 1990 Cillario volunteered to step in, and the company accepted his proposal.

Leona Mitchell sang the title role, with the American tenor Michael Sylvester as Calaf.[817] In his review, Ken Healey praised Mitchell as 'the most handsome and the least strident interpreter of the title role we have seen here ... she is commanding, but truly beautiful, and she moves around the stage with a regal dignity ... [her] physicality allowed her to fully project her regal aloofness, while moving comfortably around the challenging set.' Sylvester 'very nearly sings as one would hope princes in fairy tales might sing. The voice is ample enough and wholly unforced.'[818]

These performances were considered to be the most satisfying revival of *Turandot* since the premiere in 1990.

> Just as the production mellows and improves with age, so does the work of its distinguished conductor, Carlo Felice Cillario. This revered maestro has at times during the 1990s seemed old and frail, and perhaps on the verge of retirement. But in recent seasons, perhaps starting with his *Falstaff* in 1996, Cillario grows in wisdom and mastery, in the tradition of great old conductors. His work with singers and orchestra in this revival is worthy of one of the finest productions in the company's repertoire.[819]

---

[817] Full cast: Leona Mitchell (Turandot), Michael Sylvester (Calaf), Graeme MacFarlane (Emperor Altoum), Arend Baumann (Timur), Arax Mansourian, Elizabeth Stannard and Penny Pavlakis (Liù), John Pringle and John Antoniou, Graeme Ewer and Jin Tea Kim, Christopher Dawes and Adrian McEniery (Ping, Pang, Pong), Greg Scott and Xaioming Lan (Mandarin), Virgilio Marino (Prince of Persia).

[818] Healey, *Opera-Opera*, November 1999.

[819] Ibid.

Scene 3 – The New Millennium

The new millennium saw Cillario again return for the annual 'Opera in the Domain'. This time he was the sole conductor, leading a full performance of *La bohème* in a semi-staged version, adapted from Oxenbould's production by David Crooks, with the mainstage cast of the previous year.[820] David Gyger reported that 'The biggest plus of the 2000 outcrop of Opera in the Sydney Domain was the masterful hand of Carlo Felice Cillario wielding the night's baton.' Anke Höppner's Mimì floated out 'deliciously, producing just the sort of torrents of seamless sound Puccini … needs to do him justice.' Gyger noted the difficulty of reporting on an event that was amplified and relayed to the more distant audience members on screens, with no surtitles to assist opera novices. He concluded that it was

> left to the magical wand wielded by Carlo Felice Cillario above all to infuse this *Bohème* with the emotional life, and the ebullience it needs to reach out and grab an audience by the heartstrings. … once again, he proved what a living treasure of a musician he is. We are lucky to have seen and heard so much of him over the last 30 years and more. [821]

Moffatt Oxenbould had retired at the end of 1999. He was originally scheduled to leave the company at the close of 2000, but he felt that a period of dual leadership between his departure and the commencement of Simone Young's tenure as Music Director was not the best arrangement for effecting a handover. In an unexpected turn of events, Cillario became one of the conductors[822] for the concert given to mark Oxenbould's departure on the stage of the Opera Theatre on 8 March. Cillario lead the Prelude to *Die Meistersinger*, and joined one of several speakers to pay tribute to the outgoing Artistic Director. Tucking his baton into his jacket, he

---

[820] Cast: Anke Höppner (Mimì), Jamie Allen (Rodolfo), Douglas McNicol (Marcello), Amelia Farrugia (Musetta), John Brunato (Colline), Joshua Bloom (Shaunard), Christopher Dawes (Benoit & Alcindoro).

[821] D. Gyger, *Opera-Opera*, March 2000.

[822] The conductors were Richard Bonynge, Carlo Felice Cillario, Christopher Hogwood and Simon Kenway.

presented a personal homage, which amounted to a characteristic dance, accompanied by a disc of his violin playing, recorded 60 years earlier. It was a heartfelt expression of affection for the man who had guided the company for over 30 years.

In this bicentennial year, Cillario was invited back to the Sydney Conservatorium of Music, where he conducted a Wagner evening. Jane Parkin and Ben Makesi performed scenes from Act 3 of *Lohengrin*, with the support of the Conservatorium Choir for the Bridal Procession. The programme included the *Siegfried Idyll*, along with a true rarity unearthed by the conductor: the Overture, Introduction to Act III and Devil's Waltz, from *Der Bärenhäuter* by Siegfried Wagner, in probably its first Australian performance. The concert took place in the Eugene Goossens Hall, in Ultimo, Sydney, and was an important occasion for the Conservatorium, and a revelation for the students who took part.

31: Maestro Carlo Felice Cillario, Opera in the Domain, 2000.

Cillario also conducted two productions during 2000. In Melbourne, he led a revival of Elijah Moshinsky's production of *Don Carlo* (Italian version, 1884). This was one of the few major Verdi operas that Cillario had not conducted with the company, and the production, created during the previous year in Sydney (conducted by Simone Young) was the first time the work had been produced there in over 30 years. While the company in Sydney packed up and prepared to fly or drive down to Melbourne for the autumn season, Cillario took the train, as he preferred.

In Melbourne, it transpired that the crates containing scores and other materials had not arrived. Cillario's conductor's score was among the misplaced baggage, and he had to conduct the first rehearsal from a vocal score belonging to one of the music staff. Although he had conducted *Don Carlo* around the world, he was thrown off balance by the absence of his personal score, and he apologised on several occasions, saying 'I am forced to improvise.' Eventually the missing score materialised, and rehearsals proceeded to plan. [823] The strain of conducting this long and complex opera began to tell on Cillario. Tempi became disjointed and his typically strong sense of the work's architecture was compromised.

Cillario was well-known for certain gestures and grimaces that he would make if he was displeased with a singer during a performance. As recalled by Lauris Elms:

> Carlo was always a wonderful conductor of Italian reper-
> toire and of Verdi in particular. He drew from the orches-
> tra the singing legato that most of his colleagues in the pit
> seemed unable to achieve. However, as he grew older, he
> often expressed his opinion of a singer's performance in
> very straightforward terms. Once he shouted at a soprano
> who was singing away up on the stage above him, 'Why you

---

[823] Full cast: Leona Mitchell (Elisabetta), Bernadette Cullen (Eboli), Anson Austin (Don Carlo), Kun Xie (Count Lerma), Michael Lewis (Rodrigo), Donald Shanks (Filippo II), David Hibbard (Grand Inquisitor), Tiffany Speight (Tebaldo), Elizabeth Stannard (Voice from Heaven), Jin Tea Kim (Royal Herald), Karl Huml (A Friar), Han Lim, Warwick Fyfe, John Cummins, Karl Huml, John Brunato, Joshua Bloom (Six Flemish Deputies).

sing so 'orrible?' On another occasion, he bellowed in a rage and, holding his nose, pulled an imaginary WC chain.'[824]

As he aged, the 'WC chain' was more frequently invoked, and he was also reported as having taken his shoe off and smelled it, reacting with a grimace during a performance where things onstage were not to his liking. During one performance of *Don Carlo*, a cover had stepped in for an ailing principal, and their inaccurate singing was greeted by a full-throated scream from the pit, which took unsuspecting audience members by surprise.

The run of *Don Carlo* progressed well enough, and there were always surprises in the performances, moments when you would wish for no other conductor in the pit, but it was a dicey affair '*Don Carlo* is a long work,' noted Clive O'Connell,

> even in this truncated form. On this night, the few times when this became obvious resulted from the pit where Cillario was clearly giving more attention to the orchestra than to his singers. The first two acts yielded many uncomfortable moments where individuals and ensembles were ahead of what the orchestra was up to … and cadence points in slow passages were invariably disappointing because the singers (apart from [Leona] Mitchell) got to the final note ahead of the pit.[825]

Olympic *Tosca*

Returning to Sydney from Melbourne, Cillario conducted *Tosca*, a high-profile revival which opened the Olympic Arts Festival. The cast was a disparate, though interesting mix, led by the Tasmanian soprano Elizabeth Whitehouse, who had begun her career in Germany and had recently made an impressive Australian debut in Barrie Kosky's staging of *Der fliegende Holländer*. In the role of Scarpia was Håkan Hagegård, with whom Cillario had worked and recorded some years before in Sweden, while the role of Cavaradossi was shared between Vinson Cole and Gregory Tomlinson.[826]

---

[824] Elms (2001), 184.
[825] O'Connell, *Opera-Opera*, June 2000.
[826] Full cast: Elizabeth Whitehouse (Tosca), Vinson Cole and Gregory Tomlinson (Cavaradossi), Håkan Hagegård (Scarpia), Greg Scott (Angelotti),

John Copley had been engaged to revisit his 20-year-old production. The rehearsal period was brief and made further fraught by the presence of the company's future Music Director, Simone Young, at some of the final rehearsals.[827] During this transitional year between Oxenbould's departure and the start of Young's tenure, it was sometimes unclear who was ultimately in charge.

In discussing the dynamic between the conductor and singers in performance over the years, it was often a matter of context, and the mood of the conductor as to whether Cillario expected his forces to follow him, or vice versa. With the likes of Callas and Gobbi, Cillario often seems to have been prepared to follow their lead.[828] In the case of this *Tosca*, however, the principals were looking to Cillario for leadership and guidance, and he, in turn, seemed to be waiting for them to take the lead. It took until the final stage rehearsals for this confusion to be cleared up. Cillario was not in good health during the run, and he collapsed one evening in the midst of Act 2, falling forward over the conductor's rostrum onto his music stand. The orchestra nervously continued for some bars, unsure of how to react. In fact, Cillario had fallen asleep briefly; he woke up a couple of minutes later and the performance resumed.

Medical appointments followed in the next days, and it emerged that Cillario had not been eating regularly since he had arrived in Australia and was suffering from malnutrition. He always had a rather singular relationship to food (see Appendix 9), often making what might be considered unusual meal choices. By the millennium, he had also outlived many of his friends and acquaintances in Australia, dinner invitations had fallen away, and he was often simply forgetting to eat. He was soon invited to share meals with various company members, and his health improved accordingly.

Kelly Burke noted that the 1981 premiere of this production

Christopher Dawes (Spoletta), John Bolton-Wood (Sacristan), John Brunato (Sciarrone), Joshua Bloom (Gaoler), Kate Bartlett (Shepherd).

[827] She was contracted to become Music Director commencing the following year, 2001.

[828] See Cillario's Callas memoir (Appendix 7), where he discusses the process of beginning 'Vissi d'arte' together, with Callas facing upstage; also see both Callas' and Gobbi's comments about being short-sighted, and unable to follow Cillario's lead.

had been conducted by Cillario and that, by now he had by now conducted over 30 productions of *Tosca*, from Buenos Aires to New York, via Australia.[829] David Gyger also recalled the lineage of the production 'still under the guiding hand of its original director and conductor ... [who] will celebrate his 87th birthday on February 7 next year.' Gyger praised

> an excellent trio of singers none of whom had graced this *Tosca* before ... every pertinent detail of the score was underscored by Cillario, who not only could quite probably conduct it from memory but write out the missing parts to boot if some went walkabout on the brink of a performance ... Just as every nuance of the score was given optimum prominence in Cillario's reading, there was some splendid fine tuning in John Copley's direction 19 years after its impressive debut.[830]

Cillario also took part in a concert for the Sydney 2000 Olympic Arts Festival, held between 18 August and 30 September. His request for Oxenbould to continue to engage him until the 2000 Olympics had been met.

Maestro Cillario Exposed

In his later years, Cillario was often engaged with personal projects which had been held in abeyance while fulfilling his annual engagements in Australia and commuting between other overseas opera engagements. Among these projects were the drafting of his memoirs, and a return to composition (see Appendix 6). His composition work consisted of original works, often for unusual combinations of instruments along with operatic fantasies and transcriptions. In 1998 Cillario also circulated two original compositions for voice and piano of which he was particularly proud. The company's Director of Music Administration, Sharolyn Kimmorley, came up with the idea of an event for the patrons of Opera Australia: a semi-formal concert and interview, in which Cillario would reveal something of his life and his interests outside of the opera house.

---

[829] Kelly Burke, *The Sydney Morning Herald*, 15 September 2000.
[830] D. Gyger, *Opera-Opera*, November 2000.

32: The programme cover for 'Maestro Cillario
Exposed.' Cillario's added text is a parody of an
aria from Mozart's *La clemenza di Tito*.

I accompanied mezzo-soprano Karen Cummings in one of the songs – 'L'ultimo Incontro' (*Didone languente*), a tragic scena.[831] Other musical selections included a recorded studio performance of the 'Inflammatus et accensus' from Rossini's *Stabat mater* (with Monserrat Caballé, conducted by Cillario)[832] and a sample of Cillario's violin-playing, recorded around 1937.[833] Also advertised on the programme was 'Parmi veder le lagrime,' sung by Enrico Caruso.[834] This selection was not played.

---

[831] See Appendix 6.
[832] From the disc 'Rossini Rarities' recorded in Rome with the RCA Italiana Opera Orchestra and Chorus, RCA Stereo LSC-3015.
[833] La voce del Padrone, 78rpm discs, see Appendix 5.
[834] Which was to have been played on a 78rpm disc.

It was a moving experience to perform this composition for the first time, with its composer at the function. Almost no one present knew of Cillario's compositional activities, or his career as a violinist prior to the Second World War. Sharolyn Kimmorley asked me to conduct the interview, and prompt him for details of his life, his career, and anything else that he cared to talk about. In preparation I invited Cillario to several meals, to arrive at a broad agreement on suitable topics for discussion (fruitless preparation, as it turned out). Cillario was a not infrequent visitor to my home, and I used to play him 78rpm records, on a wind-up gramophone. We would listen to early singers, pianists, and violinists, which he would accompany with a bar-by-bar verbal critique, usually rather forthright. Even Caruso was not spared his occasional derision. It was fascinating to learn how he heard these masters of the past, and how he identified what were, in his opinion, 'good habits' or 'terrible'. These commentaries (alas unrecorded) opened a window to an almost lost way of hearing and imagining music, particularly the vocal art.

Despite his criticisms, Cillario held up Caruso as a model tenor, although he also spoke with admiration about Jussi Björling and Aureliano Pertile. I took the gramophone along to the event, with a couple of Caruso recordings, and the idea that Cillario would talk to the audience about what he was hearing. We discussed this approach, and he enthusiastically agreed. I reminded him of the plan shortly before the event. I was to ask, 'Who is your favourite tenor of all time?', to which he would answer 'Caruso'.

Cillario proved to be in a boisterous and mischievous mood. The event threatened to derail at one point, as he started to interview me. He was enjoying himself thoroughly.[835] The moment finally arrived, and I asked him to name his favourite tenor, to which he answered 'Jussi Björling.' He was smiling at me, with a kind of grimace, and I was left with no choice but to change tack and move on. A wind-up gramophone stood on the corner of the stage, silent, and from time-to-time audience members would look at it expectantly.

---

[835] Ava Hubble titled her 1990 article about Cillario: 'Cillario conducts his own interview.'

I felt that the interview to that point had been a kind of performance on his part, so I turned to Cillario the man, not the maestro (if it were in any way possible to separate those two personas). We arrived at a point where he seemed to relax, and the room grew dim at the close of a long summer day. He remarked: 'You see, I think I killed my wife'. There was a slight, but audible gasp from the audience, and he proceeded to recount deeply personal life events that some may have guessed at, but no one would have ever questioned him about. He had married at the end of the Second World War II. His wife was a pianist, known professionally as Victoria Milicescu, who later gave up her career to dedicate herself to family life. Correspondence with leading musicians of the day, held by the Cillario family suggest that she could have made a significant career. At the time of writing (2024), recordings are beginning to emerge of her appearances with orchestras, often with Cillario as conductor, dating from the 1950's and early 1960's.

As Cillario recounted it, he had begun his professional life as a 'very serious musician.' His father had been thwarted in his ambition to pursue a career in music and supported his son's aspirations. In the 1930s he bought Carlo a small country house just outside Bologna. The house was to be a retreat, where he could practice, read, compose, and become a 'complete' artist. However, as discussed earlier, an accident in 1942 (or '43) put a halt to this 'serious' career as a violinist. Cillario took up opera, which he described as a mix of the 'most serious' works (*Parsifal*, Mozart) and 'entertainment' (opera buffa and the *verismo* school). He embarked on an international conducting career, travelling the world while his family remained at home. 'I became a very naughty conductor,' he told the audience.

Cillario had an ageless temperament, and until his final decade, his exact age remained uncertain: no one in the company was sure, and it didn't really matter. He did not come to Australia until he was 53, in 1968. His wife died in 1976, and photos of the conductor taken during the following years show an extremely lean, almost emaciated figure. A photograph taken at a curtain call with

Luciano Pavarotti during the run of *La bohème* in 1983, shows the conductor almost disappearing next to the rotund tenor.[836]

Few of those present at the event realised that, for the last 24 years, Cillario had been visiting Australia as a self-reliant widower. On this occasion he unburdened himself of some significant regrets about his life, how he had lived, and the price he had paid for a stellar career on the international opera circuit. Cillario would arrive in Sydney each season, and company members were often unsure where he had been. His daughter and grandson visited only once during his years of working in Australia. It was known that his 'home' was in Bologna, but 'home' was perhaps a notional concept. During the time he spent in Bologna, he rarely stayed at the family villa in the city. He more often retreated to his cottage in the country, in the midst of his scores, his books and recordings, where he could find solitude and perhaps peace.

I walked away from the event somewhat shaken. Our public conversation had apparently unlocked some previous resistance in a man whose combination of stoicism, innate theatricality and an impenetrable sense of humour often made him difficult to understand. Cillario had revealed something of his private world, and his inner feelings, to a group of strangers. Perhaps he was approaching a time when he needed to speak. Perhaps he had revealed more than he intended. It was difficult to know.

2001-2 – The Final Operas

The question of a farewell remained open. Oxenbould's early departure had left the company with a fallow year between his departure and the formal start of the incoming Music Director, Simone Young. Young greatly admired Cillario's inimitable way of music making, having begun her career as a *répétiteur* working with him. During this period of transition, it seemed easier to keep offering Cillario engagements than to terminate an association that everyone understood would cut the elderly maestro to the core. Correspondence between Oxenbould and Cillario continued, with the negotiations taking on the flavour of a musical comedy. Cillario was fully aware

---

[836] Photograph in possession of the Cillario family, Bologna.

of this – as can be seen in Ill. 32, where he has scribbled a deliberate misquote from Sesto's aria in Mozart's *La clemenza di Tito*,[837] to underline his feelings about the farewell plans that were being engineered around him.

In 2001, Cillario arrived in Melbourne to lead *La traviata*, in a revival of the Moshinsky production which he had conducted at its premiere in 1994. He showed himself as determined as ever to take an exploratory approach to the piece and to banish any hint of routine. On this occasion, however, several members of the cast were unused to working with the maestro and to accommodating his demands.[838] Coordination of the offstage *banda* and the pit orchestra had gone awry in the final rehearsals, due to the decline in the conductor's hearing. Cillario then appeared at the general rehearsal wearing headgear that resembled a Jewish kippah. He kept his reasons to himself, but all the talk at the interval centred on speculation as to whether Cillario was Jewish, which turned discussion from the musical qualities on display. In the end, both the General and the opening night were a success, but the suggestion remained that Cillario felt he needed some stratagem as a diversion in the case that things did not go so well.

The reviews were kind: this was a completely new cast from the last revival in 1998 (although Jorge Lopez-Yanez had sung in the original 1995 Melbourne season). Jennifer McGregor as Violetta was hailed as 'the outstanding performance of the company's Melbourne visit to this point.' Lopez-Yanez had sung with more energy in 1995, 'although the timbre is still a delight to experience in these times of light tenors.' David Wakeham sang Giorgio Germont with

---

[837] Cillario's 'Parto! … Ben mio … e farò quel chi mi piace! [I'm leaving, my dearest … and I will do whatever I like!] is a parody of Mazzolà's text for *La clemenza di Tito* (after Metastasio): 'Parto, ma tu, ben mio, Meco ritorna in pace; Sarò qual piu ti piace, Quel che vorrai farò.' [I'm leaving, but you, my dearest, make peace once more with me. I will be that which you would most have me be, do whatever you wish.]

[838] Full cast: Jennifer McGregor (Violetta), Rosemary Gunn (Flora), Kerry Elizabeth Brown (Annina), Jorge Lopez-Yanez (Alfredo), David Wakeham (Giorgio Germont), Jaewoo Kim (Gastone), Roger Howell (Barone Douphol), Richard Alexander (Marchese d'Obigny), Warwick Fyfe (Doctor Grenvil), Graeme MacFarlane (Giuseppe), Han Lim (Messenger), Xiaoming Lan (Servant).

a 'somewhat monochromatic, slightly stentorian delivery.' Clive
O'Connell gave Cillario uncharacteristically generous praise:

> Cillario conducted with focus and the kind of seamless drive
> that you come across pretty rarely these days. Unfazed by
> the frequent bursts of applause and some tardy brass entries
> in the opening, he maintained the pit's concentration and
> encouraged his singers with a certain amount of rhythmic
> liberty that quite properly decreased in scope as the opera
> moved to its wrenching conclusion.[839]

Cillario returned with the company to Sydney for a revival of
Moffatt Oxenbould's staging of Il trittico.[840] One of the oldest productions to have remained in the company's repertoire, the trilogy
held deep significance for Oxenbould, and Cillario had conducted
the production several times before. Once more it presented a stiff
challenge to rehearse three operas simultaneously, and then join
them together into a unified evening in the theatre. The scale of the
task sometimes showed, and Cillario often seemed fatigued. His
particular affinity with Puccini still infused the performances, but
there was a mood of valediction about them, and a sense in which
the curtain was coming down on an era of opera in Australia.

---

[839] O'Connell, Opera-Opera, May 2001.

[840] Full cast: _Il tabarro_: Barry Anderson (Michele), Margaret Medlyn (Gior-
getta), Gregory Tomlinson (Luigi), Christopher Dawes (Tinca), Arend Bau-
mann (Talpa), Jaewoo Kim (Song Vendor), Jennifer Bermingham (Frugola),
Ali McGregor, Jaewoo Kim (Two lovers). _Suor Angelica_: Lisa Russell (Suor
Angelica), Rosemary Gunn (La Zia Principessa), Kerry Elizabeth Brown
(Badessa), Irene Waugh (La Suora Zelatrice), Sandra Oldis (La Maestra
delle Novizie), Elizabeth Stannard, Susan Barber (Cercatrici), Elizabeth
Ellis (Suor Osmina), Emma Matthews (Suor Genovieffa), Ali McGregor,
Annabelle Chaffey, Vanessa Lewis (Tre Novizie), Jeannie Kelso (Suor Dol-
cina), Joanne Goodman (Suor Iginia), Nicole Youl (La Suora Infermiera),
Jennifer Barnes, Sharon Kempton (Le Converse). _Gianni Schicchi_: John
Pringle [John Bolton-Wood sang the opening night] (Schicchi), Nicole
Youl (Lauretta), Irene Waugh (Zita), Arend Baumann (Simone), Christo-
pher Lincoln (Rinuccio), John Antoniou (Marco), Rosemarie Arthars (La
Ciesca), Graeme Ewer (Gherardo), Elizabeth Stannard (Nella), Guy Brown
(Gherardino), Richard Alexander (Betto di Signa), Warwick Fyfe (Spinel-
loccio), Han Lim (Amantio di Nicolao), Tom Hamilton (Pinellino), Geof-
frey Crook (Guccio).

The reviewers largely left aside their oft-expressed reservations about this or that individual element of the contrasting pieces. Roger Covell paid his respects on several levels:

> Opera Australia has opened its winter season with a musical-theatrical experience so encouraging and satisfying that it deserves celebration as a summary of the vital things that opera can mean. Puccini as musical dramatist is responsible for most of the positive qualities of this operatic triptych ... but there is also plenty of reason to praise the revival and reworking of Moffatt Oxenbould's gratefully remembered production, Desmond Digby's beautifully literal-minded sets and costumes, and the strongly accented, yet lightly flowing musical reading of the marvellous veteran, Carlo Felice Cillario ... acting and singing in this piece was at an outstanding level of ensemble.[841]

Other long-standing reviewers such as David Gyger, sensing a farewell approaching, also paid tribute:

> At the helm of this *Trittico*, the veteran conductor Carlo Felice Cillario reasserted yet again his absolute mastery of the Puccini idiom, dwelling a trifle too lovingly perhaps on the felicities of these scores, and thus allowing the overall performance to flirt with wearing out its welcome, but laying their souls bare and underscoring their considerable charms at every turn. Despite its flaws, this *Trittico* was a pretty good curtain-raiser for the 2001 winter season.[842]

Fred Blanks, succinctly: 'Cillario conducts impeccably.'[843] During the season, journalist Bryce Hallett secured a twilight interview with the conductor, more mellow and reflective than many of his others. Hallett began by noting that:

> He is, after all, part of the Opera Australia's cultural fabric, so much so that he may sometimes be forgotten amid the fanfares given to divas, guest conductors or the latest 'hot'

---

[841] Covell, *The Sydney Morning Herald*, 11 June 2001.
[842] D. Gyger, *Opera-Opera*, July 2001.
[843] Blanks, *North Shore Times*, 20 June 2001.

director come to chance his or her arm at the Sydney Opera House. When the maestro enters the orchestra pit tomorrow evening to conduct Puccini's *La bohème*, it will mark the start of his 34th year with Opera Australia. More than that, it will be his 60th year as a conductor; if retirement is near you won't be hearing it from Cillario's lips.

Cillario spoke with Hallett about Puccini:

> He is more difficult than Wagner and people can't believe me when I say this, they think it's too much a paradox, but Wagner creates problems for the producer, the singer, [and] less problems for the conductor. ... Puccini never conducted his operas so there are big problems for the conductor ... every passage is full of different speeds and it's very difficult. Sometimes he's even funny and doesn't permit you to have your own pleasure.

He reminisced over his decades with the company:

> It has been beautiful to see slowly, the development of the opera from an amateur organisation, and for me to have been at the beginning of Opera Australia, building a marvellous public, and marvellous singers. Opera Australia is able to export artists and is not only interested in organising performances. It is forming young artists and helping them have international careers – that is noble. There are lots of very good conductors coming here now and singers, too. ... There are important artistic centres in the world which are decaying. I was born in Argentina, and it could be a [culturally] rich country, but no.[844]

As Hallett mentions, Cillario also led *La bohème*, in the production by Moffatt Oxenbould that he had premiered in 1999. Cillario conducted a cast that was a mix of experienced artists in their prime, such as Michael Lewis and Jorge Lopez-Yanez, and younger artists who had created the original production, such as Lisa Russell and Nicole Youl.[845] Over the previous decade or two, an inevi-

---

[844] Bryce Hallett, 'House master', *Sydney Morning Herald*, 1 January 2002.

[845] Full cast: Jorge Lopez-Yanez (Rodolfo), Lisa Russell and Nicole Youl (Mimì), Michael Lewis and John Antoniou (Marcello), Ghillian Sullivan and Rose-

table generational transformation took place within the company. For many years Cillario worked with an ensemble of singers who knew him, and his principles in matters of singing and declamation. Visiting international artists generally fitted smoothly into productions under his guidance, and the resident ensemble had built up a long working familiarity with Cillario's musical direction. With the emergence of a new generation of singers, particularly graduates from the Young Artist Development Programme who went on to populate the ensemble as older artists retired, there was a gap of perhaps two generations between them and their conductor. Cillario belonged to a world, and to a way of making music, that was unfamiliar to them. On occasion he would show his frustration over a perceived lack of understanding of the traditions and wider culture of the music that was so dear to him.

The demise of singing in the vernacular, which began following World War II, brought about a situation where singers would often be presenting texts that they had learned by rote, in languages that they did not speak. This has become a worldwide phenomenon which brought about a new development in the opera house, the language coach, which, along with the rise of surtitles, signalled a decline in the ability of many younger singers to use the finer detail of language to portray emotion and dramatic intent. Text and meaning were, however, central for Cillario, who was always passionately invested in every word sung by every character in the operas he conducted, and he searched endlessly for the right vocal colour to match each line that they delivered. His responsibility, as he saw it was to bring the drama alive, make it present for the public, and he would often demand a style of pronunciation that may have seemed exaggerated in the rehearsal room, but which he knew would sound just right on a large stage, and would communicate to everyone in the audience. He was, on occasion less interested in 'correct' Italian, than colourful, expressive Italian, and he often used his own rather colourful Italian to disagree with

---

marie Arthars (Musetta), John Brunato (Schaunard), Richard Alexander (Colline), Christopher Dawes (Benoit), Bob Borowsky (Alcindoro), Jin Tea Kim (Parpignol), Chris Bath (Customs Sergeant), Tom Hamilton (Customs Officer).

the company's Italian coach, Renato Verdino-Fresia, as to the right approach. This sometimes led to the two experts arguing over their respective origins (Bologna and Rome, respectively) and some fiery exchanges ensued.

33: Cillario, note to Robert Allman (performing Marcello),
La bohème, 1981.[846]

---

[846] To Marcello: 1st alternative: 'gli ho fatto fritto' – I did it fried – or 2nd: 'gli ho fatto freddo' – [I did it]cold. Bob Allman version: 'gli ho fatto fretto' (means just nothing). Puccini's one: 'Gli ho fatto fretta' (I hurried him to come) it is the best one. Try hardly [sic] to do it. 14 February 1981. CFC.

In the final act of *La bohème*, Schaunard regards the dying Mimì and sings 'Fra mezz'ora è morta!' He is directed to sing this line sadly ('tristamente') to Colline, unheard by Mimì. In rehearsal, the singer of Schaunard delivered the line not incorrectly, but without any sense of its meaning. Cillario stopped the rehearsal and focused on the line. He tried many approaches, but the young singer seemed recalcitrant or else extremely uneasy. Finally, in desperation, the conductor shouted '*Stupido*, why you sing like that? Do you know what it mean? It mean in a half an hour she will be a caaarrrrrrrrcaaassssssssssss!' A break was called.

Cillario, always passionate about text and intent, was a living example of the value of delving into the sound of the language, as a key to unlocking the emotional and dramatic significance that lies within. His notes to singers were notorious: full of humour, sometimes purposefully exaggerated, but always to the point, and many artists would retain these notes in their scores as keepsakes.

On the opening night of *La bohème*, wrote Ken Healey, 'Maestro Cillario conducted with all the love and affection for this score that a lifetime of leading it has brought. It was noticeable that he did not come to the stage for his and the orchestra's final accolade. One can only hope this results from a temporary indisposition.'[847] Cillario did not lead another opera production in Australia.

---

[847] Healey, *Opera-Opera*, February 2002.

FINALE (2003-2007)

34: A caricature of Maestro Cillario launching into a performance of *La traviata*, by Caroline Johns, tuba player of the Australian Opera and Ballet Orchestra. A copy was presented to the conductor at the gala celebration.

A Gala Celebration for Carlo Felice Cillario

The date for the farewell concert was set at 23 March 2003, and the plans for the event were negotiated in a long trail of correspondence between the company, Oxenbould, and Cillario. Fourteen singers represented a cross-section of experienced ensemble members, along with the younger singers whom Cillario had coached and mentored. Among the seasoned artists were John Pringle, Donald Shanks and Anson Austin who had sung with the conductor in his first seasons back in the 1960s. Joan Carden who had sung many leading roles with Cillario appeared, as did Elizabeth Connell, who was in Sydney working with the Sydney Symphony Orchestra at the time. Cillario conducted the Australian Opera and Ballet Orchestra – the latest iteration of the original Trust Orchestra that he had worked for many years to build – and members of the Australian

Opera Chorus sang. The programme reflected the scope of his repertoire and particular highlights of his years with the company. It began with Gluck, via Mozart to Rossini – with a dash of Cillario.

The 'Allegro Fantasia for Flute and Ensemble from *Il barbiere di Siviglia*' was an operatic potpourri which Cillario had written in a 19th-century style pastiche. The company's principal flautist, Elizabeth Pring gave a sparkling rendition of the virtuosic solo part. The Act 3 Prelude to *Die Meistersinger* and the following 'Wahn' monologue presented an aptly valedictory portrait of the ageing Hans Sachs. Cillario's innate feeling for the Italian repertoire was represented by selections from *La bohème*, *Madama Butterfly* and *Manon Lescaut*, the Intermezzo of which showcased the orchestra, to whom Cillario had given the *verismo* style. The final Verdi selections were from *Nabucco*.

Even at Cillario's final appearance, new aspects of his musical lineage were illuminated. His *Barbiere* Fantasia prompted discussion of its unexpected sound-world: 'a bit like klezmer', observed some audience members. Few of them would have made the connection with Cillario's wartime experiences in Odesa, a temporary home for countless Jews from across eastern Europe. Klezmer could be heard on the street, in cafes and beer halls. Cillario had taken up a post teaching the violin at the conservatoire, as successor to the legendary violin teacher, Pyotr (Peisakh) Stolyarsky (1871-1944) who was the son of a klezmer, and was also himself, a klezmer.[848] In composing this work, Cillario paid a musical tribute to his time in Odesa, choosing a theme from the opera which had marked his conducting debut in the city around 1942. He created the fantasia in the popular musical lingua franca found on the streets at that time, where klezmers would freely improvise upon popular operatic melodies heard in the local opera house.

David Gyger described Cillario as 'ageless, as he proceeded to demonstrate beyond doubt at the gala celebration organised for him by Opera Australia at the Concert Hall on March 23.' Gyger noted

---

[848] Iljine, Nicolas V. and Herlihy, Patricia; *Odessa Memories* (Seattle, University of Washington Press, 2003), 110.

that his own archives recorded 180 performances given by Cillario.[849] The programme was 'an encapsulation of Cillario's catholic operatic tastes,' ending with the Overture to *Nabucco*: 'a forward-looking parting shot for a concert which provided a wealth of unmistakable evidence that there's still plenty of life in the 88-year-old maestro who has played such an important role in the development of Australian opera over the last 35 years.'[850]

As Harriet Cunningham reported,

> Stephen Hall, Richard Bonynge, Anson Austin and Moffatt Oxenbould all recalled Cillario's wicked sense of humour, but also drew attention to the maestro's passion for music, his professional and personal humility and his outstanding contribution and commitment to a young company in a far-off land.

She found the *Meistersinger* Act Three Prelude particularly moving: 'Cillario's constant sparring partner, the orchestra, enjoyed its warm chorales and expansive melodies but hung nevertheless on every beat of the energetic conductor.'[851]

In the programme booklet, Moffatt Oxenbould contributed a heartfelt appreciation of Cillario's work with the company. He summed up his friend and former colleague: 'enlightening, exasperating, enriching, entertaining, enthusiastic, earnest, exuberant, eccentric, energetic, elusive, emotional, emphatic, exhausting, enterprising, erratic, even-handed, exciting and always endearing.' He evoked

> a chameleon-like character – one minute confident and even arrogant, the next vulnerable and uptight – often tough and apparently ruthless, but also surprisingly considerate and sensitive. Sometimes he seems to be a wise old patriarch but the next moment he is like a mischievous little boy.[852]

---

[849] This likely reflects Gyger's personal performance attendance – Appendix 3 lists over 1000 performances during Cillario's Australian years.

[850] D. Gyger, *Opera-Opera*, April 2003.

[851] Harriet Cunningham, *The Sydney Morning Herald*, 25 March 2003.

[852] Oxenbould, 2003 Gala Programme, *A Gala Celebration for Carlo Felice Cillario*.

Oxenbould must have pondered those words in the wake of the Gala, during which all he had described about the conductor was displayed in vivid relief. It opened with a short speech by Adrian Collette, CEO of Opera Australia, who articulated Cillario's significance for the company, and then welcomed the maestro to the stage. Cillario appeared, and those in the know were bewildered to see a microphone in his hand. There had been strict instructions among the production crew not to give him such a device. Cillario asked Collette not to leave the stage, then came forward and proceeded to congratulate him. (It had been Collette's task to congratulate Cillario, the subject of the gala).

The concert took place following the announcement that Simone Young's contract as Music Director had not been renewed; there was consternation within the company, and an element of factional behaviour which had leaked into the press. Cillario congratulated Collette for his handling of Young's departure (for which he had been widely criticised). 'You did her a favour' said Cillario and warmed to his theme: she had been 'wearing herself thin, running from rehearsal to rehearsal.' This commentary took many in the audience aback, including Young herself.

With the opera company's CEO given an unexpected welcome by the conductor, to whom he was bidding farewell, the unpredictable tone of the concert was set, and so it proceeded, accompanied throughout by a running commentary from its guest of honour. Those who had been invited to give tributes appeared onstage, many with carefully prepared speeches which were interrupted by Cillario, microphone in hand. Turning these tributes into spontaneous interviews, he delivered some subtle (and not-so-subtle) put-downs and settled some old scores. Anyone present with insider knowledge cringed; anecdotes and long reminiscences were exhumed as the minutes ticked by and the concert went into overtime. No-one was spared. Simone Young's own tribute was interrupted several times by Cillario. He jested with Richard Bonynge, that Joan Sutherland was 'una vacca placida' – a placid cow.[853] Cillario had already received the

---

[853] The background to this apparent insult can be better understood with reference to Cillario's memoir about Sutherland, found in Appendix 7.

opera company's highest award, the Australian Opera Trophy; as proceedings eventually drew to a close, Collette presented the departing maestro (perhaps fittingly, given the afternoon's proceedings) with a box which contained the indispensable ingredient for the conductor's own signature culinary dish – 'Pasta Cillario': a jar of Vegemite.

It was all over. There had been many laughs, countless awkward moments, and perhaps some hurt feelings and bruised egos. Every one of Cillario's personality traits had been systematically illustrated, according to the recipe created by Oxenbould in his appreciation of the conductor. It was a bizarre event. Cillario worked very hard – too hard – to take charge of the proceedings, which failed to conceal the fact that he did not want to go, that he felt that he was being betrayed, and that he still had much to give. He could not go quietly, and he could not hide the hurt, much as he tried.

Those close to the conductor were aware of his plight and were equally aware that this *scena ultima* had been postponed for too long. Cillario had come to love Australia as a second home. He had family at home in Bologna, whom he visited in the *intermezzi* between conducting engagements, but he spent much more time with the company members in Sydney. Some of them knew him better in their way than his own family. Fundamentally, he was sad, and grieving for this Australian family, who he was leaving for the last time.

Twilight Years

Cillario never returned to Australia. Moffatt Oxenbould remained in contact with him. Their correspondence reveals that they each felt a void following their departure from the extraordinary, close-knit company that they had each played a leading part in building over the years – a void that was at times difficult to fill. Sharolyn Kimmorley visited Cillario in Bologna. She found him unwell and confined to care. Cillario would sit quietly at his home in the city, no longer well enough to stay alone at the country cottage which his father had bought him as an artistic sanctuary.

He visited a doctor for a health check. The family wondered

what he was thinking about as he sat silently at home. Cillario told the doctor that he intended to live until the age of 100, and on that birthday, he would be invited to Teatro Colón, Buenos Aires to conduct a gala concert to commemorate the occasion. Following the concert, he would be very glad to die. Carlo Felice Cillario died on 13 December 2007, aged 92. He remained to the end the *Maestro*.

†

Maestro
Carlo Felice Cillario

Bologna 13 dicembre 2007

La tua esistenza è stato
un inno alla gioia!
Ci hai lasciato la curiosità,
il piacere della vita
e il coraggio di viverla.

Garisenda Pompe Funebri s.r.l.
Via Emilia Ponente n° 20-2 Tel 051-385858

35: Memorial card produced by the Cillario family to mark the funeral of Carlo Felice Cillario (1915–2007).

THE LEGACY

36: Faces of Cillario – Bucharest, 1944; Sydney, 1970; Sydney, 1992.

Carlo Felice Cillario first visited Australia in 1968, where he was greeted as a leading 'Italian conductor' – with all the associations that the term carries in the world of opera. He was probably the first conductor from this heritage to commit to working regularly in Australia. Colleagues and audiences alike soon perceived a dynamic figure with the rare skill to bring pit and stage together, not merely in terms of ensemble but in search of 'a total work of art', as Wagner had postulated. He challenged, he often charmed, and he brought out the best in his singers. He did not play favourites with them, working with 'star' soloists just the way he would with established locals, or returning expatriates who had carved out careers elsewhere in the world. Experienced or emerging, Cillario's one requirement was that each vocal artist took his or her work as seriously as their conductor.

Cillario was steeped in the world of Toscanini, who had emerged as a dynamic force in the late 19th century. As the roles of composer and conductor became distinct and separate from one another,

Toscanini elevated the role of the conductor-as-interpreter to a high art. Meanwhile, during the early decades of the last century, operatic traditions, repertoires and canons became more defined. The conductor became the composer's earthly representative, with a musical legacy to uphold and perpetuate. It was a role elevated by charisma to a mystical and even quasi-religious status. Toscanini also used this status to enter the realm of public affairs, where he made oracular pronouncements. Gone were the days when the conductor had been primarily a functionary tasked with faithfully adapting to the whims of star singers in performance. In this exalted role, the conductor assumed complete authority, even over the score itself.

Cillario saw this as his solemn task, evoking Toscanini, who, he said 'reclaimed the sacredness of music and the fidelity of interpretation.'[854] He knew all of the traditions surrounding the repertoire that he conducted, but his rehearsals were often an interrogation, even a deconstruction of those traditions. In his search for 'fidelity', he placed his authority in the printed score, or 'come scritto' as he would often say, echoing Toscanini without ever admitting that those concepts (fidelity and the printed score) might not be identical. Equally, he loved to invent, to create something new and spontaneous: with 'authenticity' established, he would then enjoy the freedom of improvising upon it. In this sense, he was not a creature who was at home in the recording studio, and he is best represented by live recordings.[855]

Cillario placed himself in a line of Italian *maestri* who worked to uphold and renew a particular performance tradition, imbuing it (at least for audiences) with a kind of halo. In this spirit, he also revived and rehabilitated neglected earlier works, as part of a wider rediscovery and dissemination of Italy's musical heritage during the first part of the 20th century. Cillario introduced this artistic mission to Australian operatic culture: he once commented to Moffatt Oxenbould, that 'throughout my life I dedicated my work

---

[854] Tornari, *La Fiamma*, 19 February 1981. Original: 'Toscanini ha rivendicato la sacralità della musica e la fedeltà dell'interpretazione.'

[855] Luigi Verdi, *Biographia*, c2022.

to honour the composers and not myself.' In writing the conductor's obituary, Oxenbould stated that 'from long experience of him as an artist and man, I know this to be true.'[856]

In mingling genuine humility with attention-drawing devotion to his art, Cillario belonged to an Italian culture of performing arts where the line between opera and religion can easily become blurred. Arriving in the Australia of the mid-1960s, he encountered a quite different culture. The Elizabethan Trust Opera Company had grown out of amateur music societies that produced musicals and seasons of Gilbert and Sullivan. The leaders of these organisations became the new management of the ETOC. Their mission (if they would have seen it as such) was to produce entertainment, first and foremost. Concepts of heritage, fidelity to the composer, and the primacy of the musical score as a kind of sacred text, were foreign to them, and Cillario more than anyone else introduced these precepts to Australia's nascent operatic culture. 'This is what the composer wanted,' Cillario would say, and he spoke from a wealth of experience and wisdom that no one else in Australia was in a position to challenge or refute.

Like many complex personalities, Cillario also frequently contradicted himself. In many ways, he did not conform to the stereotype of the 'maestro'. His restless nature and enquiring mind led him to explore beyond the typical repertoire of an Italian conductor. He delved into the works of Janáček, Cherubini, and Wagner, while simultaneously conducting and denouncing the *verismo* repertoire (*Cav & Pag* and *Tosca* in particular). In so doing Cillario revealed a tortured and even perverse side to his character. The attitudes he adopted towards *verismo* over the years were contradictory to the point of creating a smokescreen to hide his true feelings.

There was something deprecating in the way he described the undisputed highlight of his career, the 1964 *Tosca* at Covent Garden. He recalled people sleeping in front of the theatre for two or three days in a freezing November winter, in order to obtain tickets. 'There was great enthusiasm during the rehearsals and the general [rehearsal] was the most exciting. The first night there was great

---

[856] Moffatt Oxenbould, 'Cillario Obituary', *The Age*, 20 December 2007.

excitement, but after the first night I started to get bored. I confess that *Tosca* is not my favourite opera by Puccini.'[857] His motivation to visit Australia in 1968 was fuelled by the invitation to conduct operas by Mozart and Wagner, repertoire which he was not being engaged to conduct elsewhere.

During his lifetime, Cillario's reputation rested largely upon his presence on the international opera circuit, beyond Australia. With the passage of time, he conducted less and less in Italy,[858] and his work in Australia assumed greater significance.[859] He dedicated three decades of his life to working with a new company, in a new opera house, in a land far from the European centres of operatic excellence. It is unclear why his father, Giuseppe set out from Bologna for America in 1907, but his son seemed to inherit this spirit of restless adventure.

The responsibilities and attendant challenges of a music director's position were not for Cillario, as he admitted both to himself and to the management of the Australian Opera, during the years leading up to the opening of the Sydney Opera House. He was eventually contracted from season to season, opera to opera, as a guest conductor, an arrangement he preferred. Nevertheless, his sense of home began to drift between Bologna, where he spent little time, and Sydney. The Chairman of the Board of the ETOC, Claudio Alcorso more than once attempted to persuade the conductor into settling in Australia with his family. Cillario, wisely, resisted.[860]

---

[857] Cillario and Duffie, *Interview,* 1982.

[858] Luigi Verdi (c2022) has described him as 'one of those *eccellenze italiane* that is better recognised abroad than at home.'

[859] Verdi noted a sense of his having become a *nemo propheta in patria* ('no man is a prophet in his own land').

[860] Claudio Alcorso, *The wind you say*, (Angus & Robertson, Sydney, 1993): 'The appearance on the scene of Carlo Cillario had a significant impact on the quality of the orchestra. Carlo is a first-class lyric conductor and a profound expert in the Verdi and Puccini repertoires. He also has a warm heart, the soul of a poet and the enthusiasm of a young man. … he liked Australia … he understood the significance of the building of the Opera House at Bennelong Point. He shared my anxiety about our ability to forge a top ensemble in time for the fateful opening season. … Carlo acted as musical director in 1969 and in 1970. I believed that the position demanded long

In retirement, he dreamed of conducting a final concert (having reached his centenary) – not at La Scala, or another major Italian house, but at the Teatro Colón, which represented another notional, spiritual home.

Beyond both authority and celebrity, the practical nature of Cillario's contribution to Australian operatic culture was widely recognised. During the years that Moffatt Oxenbould was Artistic Director, Cillario functioned as the music director of the company in all but name. He was a repository of stylistic knowledge which left a deep imprint on everyone who worked with him. In particular he developed a distinctive 'Cillario sound' with the opera orchestra[861] in Sydney over the course of years. This sound was particularly evident in the Puccini and Verdi repertoire, but it also characterised his readings of Wagner. It embodied an inner lyricism, supporting a cantabile line, and a luminous transparency in the strings, cultivated through his long experience as a violinist.

Violin Studies and Career Rise

Few details survive of Cillario's early childhood in Argentina. He was born in San Rafael, Argentina, on 7 February 1915 to Italian parents of Bolognese origin; his birthplace, San Rafael is a small town in the country's mountainous northwest region of Mendoza. By all accounts he grew up in a happy home, and showed musical promise from early on. His talent on the violin was nurtured by both parents, but especially by his father, who had once contemplated a career as an opera singer. At the age of five, he entered the Atilio

---

periods of residence in Australia, so I appealed to his poetic soul by saying that the wind of life had mysteriously brought us from the Mediterranean cradle of lyric theatre, to contribute to the unfolding of a country endowed with Mediterranean traits. I told him that Australia had emerged from its colonial conditioning and was now ready to adopt mores harmonious with its environment; that he should bring his family, his teenage son, his daughter to live here … but Carlo resisted. From his point of view, he was right: I wanted a musical director who would put the needs of the Australian Opera before anything else, but for those 'few top lyrical conductors', the centre of gravity was still in the Old World.' (115–6).

[861] Today known as the Australian Opera and Ballet Orchestra.

Vincinelli-Galvini Conservatoire in Buenos Aires, where he was recognised as a prodigy.

On the family's return to Bologna in 1923, Carlo was enrolled at the Liceo Musicale G. B. Martini, considered among the foremost music schools in Europe at the time. His most influential teachers included Angelo Consolini (1859-1934) and Sandro Materassi (1904–1989),[862] who was a close friend and duo partner of the composer Luigi Dallapiccola: a notable association given Cillario's own later connection with the composer.[863]

Having graduated from the Liceo in 1932, Cillario won first prize in a national competition, organised by the *Sindacato Fascista dei Musicista*.[864] He undertook further studies with Arrigo Serato (1877–1948) at the Accademia Chigiana in Siena and the Accademia di San Cecilia in Rome, where he obtained prizes in 1934 and 1935 respectively. He went on to build a significant career as a solo violinist,[865] performing throughout Italy,[866] and demonstrating a propensity for the life of an itinerant musician. In concerto appearances, among the conductors that he played under were Francesco Molinari-Pradelli, who had been a fellow student at the Liceo in Bologna (along with Franco Ferrara). Encouraged by Molinari-Pradelli,[867] the idea was planted in Cillario's mind to pursue the career of a conductor. Meanwhile, his career as a violinist exempted him from active service during World War II, enabling him to move independently around Europe after Italy entered the war in 1940.

---

[862] Who had been a pupil of Jenő Hubay in Budapest.

[863] Cillario conducted Dallapiccola's *Il prigioniero* at the Teatro Colón, and a significant correspondence between the two is preserved in the Cillario family archive, Bologna.

[864] Fascist Syndicate of Musicians. This information is derived from: 'Carlo Felice Cillario, Violinista', Aldina, Bologna, N.D. c1936.

[865] L. Verdi, (c2022).

[866] A number of his concerts were also broadcast. The broadsheet 'Carlo Felice Cillario, Violinista' lists concerts in Genoa, Siena, Verona, Florence, Chiavari, with positive reviews.

[867] See FN 865.

Formative Figures

In a 1981 interview,[868] Cillario listed the people who has been most influential upon his formation as a musician. As 'maestri', he paid tribute to George Enescu (1881-1955), and Nicolai ('Nicola') Chernyatinsky (1897-1961). He also named two 'modelli' (exemplars), Gino Marinuzzi (1882-1945) and Arturo Toscanini (1867-1951). Each of these figures had a distinct impact upon him, which serves to illuminate Cillario's professional development during the War years, when he made the transition from violinist to conductor. Whereas for a central European, the more obvious musical centres of Berlin, Vienna or Paris might offer more traditional pathways for a musical education, the cultural axes of Cillario's life were Buenos Aires – Bologna – Bucharest – Odesa.

Bucharest - Enescu

By the time Italy entered the War in 1940, Cillario was a young man of strongly pacifistic convictions. He was none too eager to play an active part in the conflict: 'I was given this order to come and kill Englishmen, Russians and Americans – or to be killed, and I didn't like that at all'. His father, Giuseppe, was able to 'pull a few strings', and Cillario embarked on a tour of Switzerland, on the understanding that he would join the war effort on his return. The tour 'took rather longer than the Italian army probably expected.'[869] Cillario then moved to Germany, being careful to keep ahead of the bombing, then eastwards to Romania, via Bulgaria. In Bucharest he met Georges Enescu, who offered him a place to live. Whether or not this encounter with Enescu had been planned is unclear.

As a musician of apparently universal accomplishment, gifted equally as a violinist, conductor and composer, Enescu was celebrated as a pivotal figure in contemporary Romanian culture,[870]

---

[868] Tornari, *La Fiamma*, 19 February 1981.

[869] Carmody, *The Sydney Morning Herald*, 6 October 1987.

[870] For further background about Enescu see also: Gavoty and Hauert, *Yehudi Menuhin – Georges Enescu* (Geneva, René Kister, 1955); Kotlyarov, B., *Enesco, his life and times* (New Jersey, Paganiniana Publications, Inc., 1984); Malcolm, Noel, *George Enescu, his Life and Music* (Toccata Press, Exeter, UK, 1990).

known across Europe as a teacher of gifted young musicians such as Yehudi Menuhin. Cillario may have settled in the Cantacuzino Palace (today known as the George Enescu National Museum), where the composer lived with his wife. Enescu evidently held Cillario in high regard, writing letters of recommendation for him as 'l'eminent violiniste'.[871] With these letters, Cillario applied for teaching posts at music schools in Timişoara and then Odesa, where he moved around 1942.[872]

Odesa – Stolyarsky

At this time, there were two principal musical institutions in Odesa, the Conservatoire, and the Stolyarsky Music School, named after its founder Pyotr Stolyarsky (1871-1944). Stolyarsky specialised in training prodigies on the violin, counting Nathan Milstein, David Oistrakh and Ginette Neveu among his pupils.[873] The school thrived due to the large Jewish population in Odesa, as Isaac Babel (1894–1940) recalled:

> All the people of our circle – middlemen, storekeepers, clerks in banks and steamship offices – sent their children to music lessons. Our fathers, seeing they had no prospects of their own, set up a lottery for themselves. They built this lottery on the bones of their little children. Odesa was in the grip of this craze more than any other town. And sure enough, over the last few decades our town has sent a number of child prodigies onto the stages of the world. Mischa Elman, Zimbalist, Gawriliwitsch all came from Odesa – Jascha Heifetz started out with us. When a boy turned four or five, his mother took the tiny, frail creature to Mr Zagursky [Stolyarsky]. Zagursky ran a factory that churned out child prodigies, a factory of Jewish dwarfs in lace collars and patent leather shoes. He went hunting for them in the Moldavanka slums and the reeking courtyards

---

[871] George Enescu, 'Handwritten Letters,' 25 December 1942 and 27 January 1943. Cillario family archive, Bologna.

[872] Carmody, 6 October 1987.

[873] Information in this paragraph derived from: Boris Schwarz, *Great Masters of the Violin* (Robert Hale, London 1984) 457–9. Information in this paragraph derived from this book.

of the old bazaar. Zagursky gave them the first push, then the children were sent off to Professor Auer in St. Petersburg.[874]

Stolyarsky had graduated from the local conservatoire in 1898 and founded his own school in 1911. As a member of the Opera orchestra (until 1919), he was considered in some quarters to be 'a very bad violinist'.[875] Nathan Milstein later disparaged his abilities, while David Oistrakh praised his teaching skills. His school was incorporated into the conservatoire during the early 1920s, but he re-founded it as a separate institution in 1933. During the War, Stolyarsky was removed from his teaching post at the conservatoire in a purge of Jewish staff; Cillario was the replacement. In accepting the position, he was stepping into the shoes of a teacher held in some awe: 'an odd, almost fantastic figure – but a teaching genius.'[876]

In 1942, the coastal city of Odesa was under the control of the Axis powers, which included Italy and Romania, a circumstance that allowed Cillario to reside there. Following a period of inactivity after the 1941 Occupation, the conservatoire was reopened in March 1942, with Nicolai Chernyatinsky (1897-1961) as its director. It is possible that Enescu and Chernyatinsky were on familiar terms, which may explain Cillario's sojourn in Odesa, and his replacing a teacher of Stolyarsky's eminence.

Odesa - Chernyatinsky

Accounts of life in Odessa at the time[877] describe a network of close association between its cultural institutions. At least during the period of occupation, Chernyatinsky ('Н.Н. Чернятинскому'[878]) was the glue binding the musical life of the city together through his work at the Conservatoire, the Philharmonic, and the Opera House. A native of Odesa, he had graduated from the conservatoire in 1917

---

[874] Isaac Babel, quoted in: Iljine and Herlihy, *Odessa Memories* (2003), 16.

[875] Juri Jelagin, *Taming of the Arts* (1951), quoted in Schwarz, *Masters of the Violin* (1984), 459.

[876] Ibid, 458.

[877] Iljine and Herlihy, (2003).

[878] https://rdk.yarsklib.ru/doku.php?id=чернятинский_николай_николаевич, accessed 13 June 2023

and almost immediately joined the teaching staff. He went on to become the music director of the opera house in Chisinau (capital of modern-day Moldova). Back in Odesa, he became a leading force in the musical life of the city during the Occupation, but he suffered a harsh fate after the Soviet takeover in April 1945. He was arrested by the Soviet authorities 'on suspicion of anti-Soviet activities'[879] and sentenced to ten years' imprisonment. Whatever the truth of these charges, he was imprisoned until the mid-1950s, when he was allowed to resume work in Chisinau. Having died in 1961, he was posthumously 'rehabilitated' in 1993.

It is not known if Cillario was aware of his teacher's post-war fate, or if they ever had further contact after Cernyatinsky's arrest. Biographical sketches of Cillario routinely described Chernyatinsky as his conducting teacher, but their association evidently ran deeper than that. As his employer and benefactor, Chernyatinsky almost certainly facilitated Cillario's conducting debut at the opera house in 1942 (or 43), in Rossini's *Il barbiere di Siviglia*. The exact date and circumstances are lost, but there survives a startling eyewitness account of a production of *La bohème* at the Odesa Opera House in December of 1942 that gives a flavour of the times. According to this account, the dress rehearsal

> lasted a day and the next night until morning. Chelanu [the conductor] couldn't do anything. Chernyatinsky was brought in in the middle of the night ... [and] forced to literally lead Chelanu with his hand until he taught him to reproduce the correct sounds. The artists were told that if they disrupted the premiere, they would all be shot. On the second performance, the opera under the direction of Chernyatinsky was brilliant. [880]

Cillario fared better on his debut than Chelanu and, following the *Barbiere* performances, he was offered more opera productions

---

[879] Which included organising charitable concerts 'in favour of the society of officers of the former Russian army' and the 'removal of the musical library from the opera house.'

[880] https://rdk.yarsklib.ru/doku.php?id=чернятинский_николай_николаевич, accessed 13 June 2023. [From a diary kept by V.A. Shvets.]

37: The Odesa Opera House, 1941, with fortifications in place.

to conduct. On completing his studies,[881] Cillario received an award of 'Conductor of the first order' as a 'first-rate artist, for the fusion of his already known excellent musical qualities, with that of a first-class conducting technique.'[882] The source then states that he

[881] A printed broadsheet, 'CFC Sheet 1' in French (c1946). This states that he 'frequenta en 1943 le Cours de diréction d'orchestre du Mtro. Nicola Cerniatinsky au Conservatoire de Odessa.' 'CFC Sheet 3' (c1945), states that Cillario is well known in Europe and America (meaning South America) as a violinist. It also states that he studied conducting in 1943, which supports that as the year of his conducting debut, rather than 1942. It further states that immediately following his studies, Cillario was engaged by the Théâtre de l'Opéra in Odessa, where (all extant biographical sources agree that) he made his début conducting *Il barbiere di Siviglia*. Further evidence for his main activities in Odesa being placed during 1943 exists in a document issued by the Italian Embassy in Bucharest dated 16 November 1944, which states that at the beginning of 1943 Cillario was engaged as a professor of violin in Odessa: '...dans les premiers mois de 1943 a été engage par le Conservatoire d'Odessa comme professeur de violon...'. All documents referred to are held by the Cillario family archive, Bologna.

[882] 'Chef d'orchestre de premier ordre' avec la motivation suivante: 'Artiste de premier rang, pour la fusion de ses excéllentes qualités musicales déjà connues, avec une technique de chef d'orchestre de premier ordre.' See 'CFC Sheet 3' (c1945).

was immediately engaged as a conductor with Odesa Opera.[883] To summarise Cillario's own accounts (which varied slightly over the years), over eighteen months he: moved to Odesa; began teaching violin at the conservatoire; studied conducting with Chernyatinsky; graduated in conducting; made his conducting debut at the Opera and broke his arm in a soccer match.

The incident of the broken arm was often recalled by Cillario as a turning point when he was forced to pursue a conducting career. However, this path had evidently been in his mind for some time. The accident was more likely a catalyst for his decision. In the wake of his injury, Cillario may have feared that he would never again play professionally. The exact sequence of events – studying conducting, breaking his arm, making his conducting debut – seems destined to remain uncertain.[884] In the event, Cillario found he was still able to play the violin, and 'indeed that the position had considerably improved.'[885] He travelled with his violin on most of his visits to Australia, where he later acquired a violin by A. E. Smith,[886] and often played at private gatherings and ad hoc chamber-music concerts, on

---

[883] The Odesa Opera House holds significant cultural and architectural value. An opera house was built on the site in 1809, and then rebuilt in 1897, designed by Viennese architects in the Viennese Baroque style. As a cultural landmark, it was strenuously defended by the local population against the German invasion in 1941, then against the Soviets during 1944, (when Chernyatinsky played a role in its defence) and once more in 2022 during the Russian invasion of Ukraine. For more information, see https://www.hor.net.ua/?page_id=1504&lang=en

[884] Various versions of this incident were recounted by Cillario over the years, of which the following seems a likely reconstruction: 'During the war ... I was in Odesa, and I had some friends who were flying to Italy on a military plane and there were some children there, playing with a ball, and we were waiting for the departure of my friends, and we started to co-operate with the children and suddenly one of them was jumping against me and, instinctively, like that I was defending myself and I broke the wrist ... and that was the reason that I stopped playing serious. Just one week earlier I was playing Brahms Concerto and suddenly I was in the plaster, my arm, I was not sure if I could play again.' Jenny Brown, 'Cillario's score,' The Mirror, 31 August 1991.

[885] Verdi, c2022.

[886] Arthur Edward Smith (1880–1978). Interview with Sharolyn Kimmorley, 18 May 2023.

one occasion appearing as one of the soloists in Vivaldi's Concerto for Four Violins,[887] at a Sydney Symphony Orchestra concert under his baton.

It is unclear how long Cillario remained in Odesa (he referred to a period of 18 months[888]), and how extensively he conducted at the Opera. Following *Barbiere*, Cillario recalled *La traviata* as his next assignment, and then *Eugene Onegin*. At some point during the preparations for *Onegin*, the Axis powers withdrew from the city. In the face of Soviet advance, and perhaps further prompted by the Nazi occupation of Italy on 8 September 1943, Cillario returned to the relative safety of Bucharest.

Back in the Romanian capital, Cillario probably fell upon the support of Enescu once again. He undertook several engagements with the Bucharest Philharmonic, as well as with orchestras in Timișoara and Cluj,[889] no doubt thanks to Enescu's influence and proceeded to gain further valuable experience in his new career.

38: Nikolai N. Chernyatinsky c1955.[890]

A recently discovered document sheds light on this formative but obscure period of Cillario's life, and on the precarious nature of his circumstances. It describes a search of Cillario's lodgings by military police in Bucharest, and the confiscation of music scores by Soviet composers.[891] There is a grim irony that these events

[887] See p. 206.

[888] Carmody, 'Master of charm loses his cool over Puccini,' *The Sydney Morning Herald,* 6 October 1987.

[889] See: Bibliography: 'Cillario family archive, 'CFC Sheet 2'.

[890] https://rdk.yarsklib.ru/doku.php?id=чернятинский_николай_николаевич, accessed 13 June 2023.

[891] Testimony from Italian Legation, Bucharest, 16 November 1944. Original in French [English translation by Simon Lobelson]. Cillario family archive, Bologna.

took place a year before Nicolai Chernyatinsky was imprisoned by the Soviet authorities, in part for his role in protecting the library of the Odesa Opera House.[892] The possession of music by composers of the 'wrong' nationality attracted censure and even punishment. The significance of the document justifies a full transcription:

DIRECTOR OF ITALIAN LEGATION BUCHAREST No. 1495

TO THE ROYAL MINISTRY OF FOREIGN AFFAIRS November 16, 1944.

On the 9th of November a Romanian officer and two Russian officers presented themselves at the home of Mr. Carlo Felice CILLARIO, a well-known Italian musician, resident in Rue Vasile Lascar n. 186, and raided his home, confiscating a suitcase of books and scores of Russian music that Cillario had regularly bought in Odessa. Mr. Cillario himself was taken to the Soviet Military Command in Bucharest and released after an interrogation, with the promise that the music would be returned to him.

Today a commission headed by the prosecutor Mr. Miga of the Ilfov Court and by the Russian captain Scefcink of the Allied Control Commission arrived at the home of Cillario and carried out a search. Having found music that had not been confiscated in the previous search, they declared that Cillario was guilty of violation of the ordinance relating to the return of objects of Soviet property and they invited him to appear tomorrow morning at the Prosecutor's Office of the Court of Ilfov.

The Royal Italian Legation has the honour to draw the attention of the Royal Ministry of Foreign Affairs to the following facts:

1) Mr. Cillario was evidently denounced at the same time at the Soviet Military Command in Bucharest and the Allied Control Commission. He assumed that the author of the denunciation was called Mr. Johann Schmiedigen,

[892] See FN 890.

Str. Floreasca 118, Aleea C3, Romanian of German origin, whose wife is in the process of divorcing him in order to marry Mr. Cillario. The aforementioned was opposed to the divorce and made threats against Mr. Cillario.

2) Mr. Cillario, whose artistic personality is known in all musical circles in Europe and America, in the first months of 1943 was engaged by the Odesa Conservatoire as a violin teacher, following a series of concerts given in Romania with resounding success. During the time of his stay in Odesa Mr. Cillario dedicated himself exclusively to his professional and artistic activity. It was on this occasion that he regularly bought the music and books in question. At the time of the Italian crisis of September 8, 1943, Mr. Cillario – who until then had never occupied himself with political matters – freely and immediately declared himself for the Badoglio Government against fascism.

Returning soon after to Bucharest, Mr. Cillario shared the well-known vicissitudes of all the Italians who found themselves in Romania subject to German threats and reprisals and placed himself under the protection of the Royal Legation which he continues to enjoy.

3) The objects in question were regularly purchased by Mr. Cillario.

The Royal Legation of Italy consequently has the honour to request the Royal Ministry of Foreign Affairs to kindly bring the above to the attention of the Tribunal of Ilfov in order that the above-mentioned denunciations have no sequel.

It seems likely that Cillario met his future wife through Enescu and his circle. Victoria (Viky) Genoveanu Milicescu (1923–1976) was already a promising pianist, enjoying a nascent career, who counted among her mentors Walter Gieseking and Dinu Lipatti.[893] The couple married in Bucharest in 1945. During the late 1940's

[893] Cillario recorded a disc of Lipatti's compositions in 1968, and the Cillario family archive, Bologna preserves correspondence between Milicescu and Walter Gieseking.

they appeared in concerts as the duo 'Milicescu-Cillario',[894] suggesting that the accident in Odesa did not stop Cillario from pursuing the career of a violinist, rather it prompted him to make a professional choice.

There is no record of Enescu giving Cillario any formal training, but their contact exposed Cillario to the older man's contacts and deeper cultural affinities. Whatever training he received from Chernyatinsky, Cillario seems to have been recognised as a 'natural talent', who needed only a minimum of guidance and some decisive opportunities in order to set him on his way. Extant filmed performances document his idiosyncratic technique: he was not a 'textbook' conductor, and Luigi Verdi has noted that his style, especially in later years, 'was rather atypical, but highly effective.'[895] The worlds inhabited by Enescu and Chernyatinsky, along with his early years in Buenos Aires, afforded Cillario an unconventional education but one conducive to his enthusiasms and affinities.

As well as these two teachers ('maestri'), the same 1981 interview[896] cites two role models ('modelli').[897] The first is composer and conductor Gino Marinuzzi (1882–1945), now mostly forgotten except as the conductor of a landmark 1941 recording of *La forza del destino*.[898] Cillario described him as 'one of the best Italian direttori d'orchestra – who loved music more than himself and helped singers selflessly and with dedication.'[899] The circumstances of their acquaintance remain unknown, but Cillario was emphatic about Marinuzzi's role as a musical mentor, a relationship which is captured by the 'staged' atmosphere of a photo (Ill. 39) probably taken shortly before Marinuzzi's death.

---

[894] For example, a poster from 1946, advertises a recital of repertoire by Beethoven, Debussy, and Franck, performed in the Sala dei Teatini (Ciesa di San Vincenzo), Piacenza by the duo.

[895] Luigi Verdi, (c2022).

[896] Tornari, *La Fiamma*, 19 February 1981.

[897] Ibid.

[898] With Maria Caniglia, Galliano Masini, Carlo Tagliabue, Tancredi Pasero and Ebe Stignani. With the Turin Chorus and Symphony Orchestra of the Italian Broadcasting Authority. (Naxos 8.110206-07).

[899] See FN 854.

39: Maestro Gino Marinuzzi in discussion with Carlo Felice Cillario c1945.

The second 'modello' was Arturo Toscanini, who Cillario witnessed conducting as a 16-year-old in Bologna in 1931. Cillario and some fellow students gained admission to Toscanini's rehearsals, and also witnessed the politically forthright conductor being assaulted by black shirts following his refusal to play the 'Giovinezza' at the subsequent concert.[900] Between 1931 and 1946, Toscanini exiled himself from Italy, and it is unlikely that Cillario ever saw him conduct again, though he was familiar with his recordings. Cillario's reverence for him – 'Toscanini, who reclaimed the sacredness of music and the fidelity of interpretation'[901] – held true for most of his contemporaries as conductors, whether Italian- or foreign-born.

Considered together, each of these four figures held contrasting significance for Cillario. They probably never met in person, but Toscanini represented to Cillario an exemplar of musical and personal distinction. The precise significance of Marinuzzi is harder to pin down in this regard. Meanwhile Enescu's fame preceded him scarcely less than Toscanini's, while Nikolai Chernyatinsky was a more shadowy figure, whose imprisonment in 1945 has made him largely invisible outside Russia. Cillario absorbed elements of their musical personalities within his own and acknowledged their influence on numerous occasions.

Post-war Career

Cillario returned to Italy at some point in 1945. The following year, he founded a chamber orchestra in Bologna. In 1948 he relocated to Argentina, working first in the city of San Miguel de Tucumán,[902] capital of the Tucumán province in the northwest of the country, where he founded and conducted the Orquesta Sinfonica dell'Università Nazionale di Tucumán. In 1954 he moved to Buenos Aires, where he conducted the Orquesta Sinfonica Nazionale del Estado, Buenos Aires. He had already begun to work at the Teatro Colón, in 1952, conducting operas and ballets by Dallapiccola, Pizzetti, Ravel and Stravinsky, followed by standard works from the repertoire, *Aida*, *Tosca* and *La Gioconda*.[903]

---

[900] See Toscanini memoir in Appendix 7.

[901] See FN 896.

[902] Tucumán is one of the smallest, and most densely populated provinces of Argentina, located around 1000 kilometres from Buenos Aires, and about the same distance northeast from his birthplace.

[903] Printed biography c1960. 'Carlo Felice Cillario, direttore d'orchestra' (in Italian). No author or publisher named. Was probably created for programme biographies around 1960. Cillario family archive, Bologna.

Cillario had moved with his wife to Argentina, where their two children were born, but shrewdly maintained his musical connections in Italy, regularly giving symphonic concerts in Bologna from 1953 onwards. During the late 1950s he effected a gradual return to Italy, while continuing to make appearances in Argentina. The pull towards his childhood roots was strong, and this period of his life, when he effected a return 'home' not only to the cultural melting pot of Buenos Aires, but also to more distant, provincial areas such as Tucumán – underlines his sense of heritage as an Argentinian-born, Italian conductor. These roots remained deeply significant to him.

However temporary in nature, the transatlantic emigration may also have served to place emotional and physical distance between himself and his wartime experiences as well as the harsh realities of post-war life in Europe. Cillario may also have entertained the fond hope that the unruly paradise of Argentina could become for him a domain of professional success, where rivalries were not so acute, and he would not have to compete for recognition as he would back in Europe. For a time, this ambition seemed within his reach, but it came to nothing in the face of the limitations of the musical culture there which had defeated plenty of hopefuls before him. In describing his decision to return to Italy, he quoted the advice given to him by another Italo-Argentinian conductor, Ettore Panizza: 'You must leave, or South America will destroy you. If Toscanini lived here, he would be forced to return to playing the cello.'[904]

Back in Bologna, Cillario made his debut at the Teatro Comunale in 1957 with Tchaikovsky's *The Queen of Spades*. While he returned over the next few seasons, his relationship with the house ceased after a run of *La traviata* in 1963. He continued to fulfil operatic engagements elsewhere across Italy, as well as giving concerts with the Angelicum in Milan,[905] and the Accademia di Santa Cecilia in Rome.[906]

---

[904] Carmody, *The Sydney Morning Herald*, 6 October 1987.

[905] Cillario was the Director of the Orchestra dell'Angelicum for five years, making several important recordings with them during this time, including Mozart's *Lucio Silla* (1961), *Ascanio in Alba* (1959) and *Bettulia Liberata* (the oratorio's first recording, 1960).

[906] Information in this paragraph derived from Luigi Verdi, (c2022). Verdi notes that the Archive in the Accademia di Santa Cecilia contains 12 files that

Symphonic Conducting

In Australia, Cillario's appearance on the concert podium was often greeted with a sense of surprise, so etched into the public imagination was the idea of him as an Italian opera specialist. In reality, he had a wide symphonic repertoire and accepted concerts wherever they were offered. It would be a herculean task to chronicle the concerts he gave across the world. When speaking about the differences between the two genres, however, there was a sense that Cillario found symphonic work 'safe'. After the final rehearsal for a concert, he felt largely sure of what would happen on the night. 'But in opera I like this improvisation a little bit, and in opera you never know what can happen tomorrow, or even this evening. Every time it's new, and that makes excitement. It is a wonderful profession.'[907] Cillario's spirit of adventure and desire for the unknown found its natural expression in the opera house.

Operatic Rise

Cillario quickly acquired a reputation as a 'singer friendly conductor,'[908] with an expertise and a sensibility that embraced *bel canto*, Verdi and *verismo*: essentially the gamut of the 19th century Italian opera tradition. Many leading singers were eager to work with him, and his association with the impresario Sandor Gorlinsky in London facilitated engagements in the world's major opera houses. Thus, his agreement to fly to Australia and conduct three operas in the 1968 ETOC season may have looked to an outsider like a sideways, if not backwards step in his career. But Cillario, ever the wanderer, found plenty of reasons to cross the world. He was intrigued to visit so vast and distant a country (possibly reminding him his Argentinian odyssey of twenty years earlier), he was pleased

---

document Cillario's concerts between 1934 and 1952, including appearances as a violinist.

[907] Cillario and Duffie, *Interview*, 1982.

[908] At the time of Cillario's death, the Australian bass Donald Shanks, who performed in the 1968 *Tannhäuser* season, said that 'He was a singer's conductor. I look back on him as perhaps the conductor who had the most influence on my career.' (Miriam Cosic, 'Cillario Obituary,' *The Australian*, 18 December 2007).

to be visiting with his friend, Tito Gobbi, and he was excited to be leading hitherto unknown forces in a combination of his core repertoire (*Tosca*), along with two German operas by composers he revered. What started out as a singular adventure became something more, as Cillario was charmed by the atmosphere in Australia, the friendliness and directness of its people, and the talent and collective spirit of the developing opera company.

Australia

In Australia, Cillario made an immediate and lasting impact on the operatic culture that greeted him. Those who had not travelled or worked overseas had few points of reference for the expectations of a professional singer in larger operatic centres. Now they found themselves in close cooperation with a musician who had coached and conducted many of the most illustrious singers of the day. Both Cillario and Gobbi gave unstinting and invaluable help to the aspiring singers of the company. They gave advice borne of long experience to the company management as it expanded prior to the long-awaited move to the new Sydney Opera House. They also gave inspiringly positive feedback about the standard of Australian voices, and their unpretentious delight in working with their colleagues raised the entire company's morale and sense of purpose.

Among the local singers in the 1968 season was Neil Warren-Smith, who worked with Cillario until his death in 1981. His tribute to the conductor[909] holds true for many of his local colleagues in the company.

> I've got enormous respect, great affection, limitless admiration … for lots of conductors, but for Cillario I have to add love. Singing for Carlo is pure joy. He expands me. He's florid and flamboyant in the pit, and there are times when you feel he's putting on a better show than we are on stage. No matter how brilliant we're being, the audience will probably get better value for its money just from watching him. He calls me '*faccia brutta*' which roughly, means 'ugly face' and I've never felt prouder of a title.

---

[909] Warren-Smith and Salter (1983).

Carlo was the first of the truly *Italian* conductors to come to us. He brought a shimmering quality to the music of Puccini and Verdi which gave it a whole new texture and depth. And he brought this same intensely beautiful texture to Wagner: in *Tannhäuser* he produced a sound I can only define as luscious. To know what it feels like to sing, you need a Cillario in your life.[910]

Singing the role of Padre Guardiano, Warren-Smith, recalled one rehearsal of Verdi's *Forza*: [911]

During the first act ... Carlo called to me from the pit: 'Sing for me Neilo, *facia brutta*, sing for me!' ... Cillario was *wanting* me to sing, and was willing me to sing. He gave me something at that rehearsal that I've kept, an inexplicable maybe psychic something that's gone on stage with me ever since. It's a vocal freedom, an emotional freedom, it's the feeling that you *can* sing and that it's lovely, lovely, lovely to be doing it.[912]

This was Cillario at his best, and his most inspiring. He had another, more eccentric side, which could defuse or generate tension depending on the context. Lauris Elms recalled his tendency to shout while in full flow. 'From the pit he would shout indiscriminate directions to the players in the orchestra, or to the singers on the stage. If he were enjoying himself, he would often sing loudly along with whoever had the tune.' This could unsettle singers who were not used to his ways. Elms called him out on one occasion, mid-rehearsal, when his singing accompaniment threatened to upstage her own. 'I stopped singing and strode down to the footlights. "Maestro!" I shouted over the racket, "You're making so much noise that I find it impossible to hear the orchestra." He always treated me with great respect and affection after this.'[913]

Stephen Hall recalled an audition in Melbourne where a singer offered the *Ave Maria*, and it became clear after just a few notes

---

[910] Ibid, 139–40.

[911] In 1970.

[912] Warren-Smith and Salter (1983), 139–40.

[913] Elms (2001), 184.

that they were the 'absolute nadir.' During the audition, Cillario
went missing from his seat, and was next seen 'on his knees, slowly
moving down the centre aisle, waving a white handkerchief.' If he
did not like a singer, he did not hesitate to ask, 'Why you sing so
'orrible?', but to those whom he regarded as 'serious', he was greatly
admired as 'a real singer's conductor.' [914]

Moffatt Oxenbould saw both sides of this behaviour. It arose, he
thought, from the conductor's drive to

> set high standards, and he could be tough. He was a shouter
> and the stories about him still do the rounds: the time
> he held his nose and made a gesture as though pulling a
> lavatory chain; the day he took off his shoe and smelled it.
> People laugh about it now, but it was tough being on the
> receiving end.

Oxenbould admitted that 'he could be very exasperating. … He
had undoubted charm, but he was very Latin; he could be voluble,
and he made enemies.'

While Cillario's behaviour was regarded as unusual in Australia,
local singers were spared the worst of it. As General Manager of
the Metropolitan Opera (1972–4), Shuyler Chapin recalled one
particular *Tosca* performance, with Franco Corelli singing the role
of Cavaradossi:

> The conductor Carlo Felice Cillario was engaged for Tosca,
> one of the few operas that Corelli rarely cancelled. …
> "Maestro Cillario. He doesn't like me," [Corelli] said sharp-
> ly. "We disagree about everything – tempi, politics, the
> world. I don't want to sing with him." "Well," [Chapin an-
> swered], "perhaps you won't have to. The maestro will not
> be returning next season." "Ah," he sighed nervously. "But
> we still have tonight."
>
> In the performance, following Corelli's performance of "Re-
> condita armonia," there were roars of approval and shouts
> of "Bravo Corelli!" Now, there is a long-standing tradition
> that at this point in Tosca the conductor waits for the ap-
> plause to die down before continuing. The tenor usually

---

[914] Hall, Cillario Obituary, 20 December 2007.

stays frozen in front of his easel, … allowing the audience's praise to wash over him. But on this night, Cillario didn't pause; over all the applause he continued to conduct. I saw Corelli turn and stare at the orchestra pit, his face a mask of fury. When he came to his next line: "Fa il tuo piacere!" he was almost yelling.

In the second act, … Cavaradossi confronts Scarpia by singing "Vittoria! Vittoria! L'alba vindice appar…" being the only time in the act when the tenor has a chance to spin out two long solo notes. Corelli seized the opportunity to revenge himself for the first act, he held the notes longer and louder than I'd ever heard before, thus preventing the conductor from proceeding. When he finally continued, Cillario countered by increasing his tempo …

In the tenor's Act 3 aria, here again is a moment when the audience erupts into paroxysms of pleasure. Corelli had been at his best; the cheers and clapping were overwhelming. This is also the other moment where the conductor traditionally pauses for the applause – but not on this occasion. Cillario pressed on …Corelli, an apoplectic look on his face, slowly stood up and stared into the orchestra pit, flipping his thumb between his teeth in the classic gesture of defiance and walked off the stage. … boos could be heard in the distance; the smell of the mob was in the air.

The orchestra continued to play, … Tosca rushed onto the roof where she was greeted by audience confusion, then no Cavaradossi, and a third problem: she was unable to start singing because she couldn't pick up her cue note. The orchestra's sound was overwhelmed by audience hysteria … I bolted from my seat and rushed backstage … I literally pushed Corelli back on to the stage. When Corelli actually reappeared [Dorothy Kirsten, the Tosca] grabbed him firmly by both arms and forced him to look at her. Somehow her professionalism carried the day. As soon as the audience saw them together, the ruckus died down.

Dorothy Kirsten finished the opera in grand style … As the curtain came down all hell broke loose. … When Cillario appeared … Corelli leapt at him, getting his hands firmly around the conductor's throat. I tried to separate them by forcing myself between them, but each was so intent upon killing the other that I was squashed like soft sandwich filling. ...

Meanwhile, the audience was applauding and booing in about equal measure. Kirsten went out for a bow, and they cheered her enthusiastically. ... [Corelli] was given an ovation, complete with torn-up programs as confetti. His public was entirely with him. I suggested to Cillario that this was not the night for a solo conductor bow. He agreed.

Finally at the last call of the night, Kirsten and Corelli came out together. Clasping her right hand, he raised both their arms in a gesture of solidarity and victory. When they stepped backstage, I ordered the iron curtain closed.[915]

Sharolyn Kimmorley, who worked closely with Cillario from 1975 until his retirement felt that his criticisms were not meant to hurt, but that the conductor was on occasion 'missing a filter'. He sometimes blamed his 'poor English' though his meaning and intention were usually precise. When he wished to disengage himself from a tricky or awkward situation, he would feign incomprehension.[916] Recognising his complex nature, Oxenbould characterised Cillario as 'a multifaceted gem' whose bizarre sense of humour arose from a 'serious' purpose. 'He cared very much for what he did, and he respected other people who he felt had the same care, and he was very dismissive of those who didn't appreciate their opportunities.'[917] Cillario alluded to this in a comment made in 1993: 'Some artists have an opinion that conductors are beasts, but our reaction is just a reaction to the quality and results around us. We have to be diplomatic and wear the gloves sometimes and at others we take them off and bring out the claws.'[918]

Luigi Verdi knew Cillario in another context, having studied conducting with him briefly in Bologna in 1985. In an unpublished memoir, Verdi recorded some personal impressions:

[915] Shuyler Chapin, *Sopranos, Mezzos, Tenors, Bassos, and other Friends* (Crown Publishers, Inc., New York, 1995), 161–6.

[916] Sharolyn Kimmorley, interview, 18 May 2023.

[917] Cosic, quoting Moffatt Oxenbould in 'Cillario Obituary', *The Australian*, 18 December 2007.

[918] Michael Bruning, *The Manly Daily*, 17 September 1993.

As a man he was politically agnostic, disinterested in all events that weren't strictly related to music, which he understood as a mission, the bearer of a purity and superiority that nothing could scratch from the outside: detached from everything else except perhaps from the football passion … [his] faith in his Bologna team.[919]

Following a few weeks teaching at the Bologna Conservatory in 1985, Verdi reflected (following Cillario's departure for the Metropolitan, New York), that 'he was certainly of a moody temperament and with some vein of bizarreness that he could afford, given the halo of glory that surrounded him.'[920]

Cillario lived a singular life, privately as well as professionally. He ate frugally, was largely vegetarian, and rarely drank alcohol. He was fond of carrot juice, and was known to comb orange juice through his hair to style it. He liked exercise – predominantly walking and swimming – but he claimed the best exercise was conducting. To maintain his energy, he explained 'you work a lot, you do not eat too much and especially you do an activity you like. Conducting is beautiful. It is very healthy. A player at the end [of a performance] is always blaming himself and having bad feeling about things that have been wrong.' Laughing to himself, he concluded: 'But a conductor … can relax and blame everyone else!'[921]

He would often jog to the Sydney Opera House to conduct a performance, making his way through the Botanic Gardens. On some occasions, having snapped a twig from a tree on the way, he would use it as a baton in the performance. On occasion he would make his entrance into the pit late, hurriedly run into the pit and begin conducting, still wearing his white trainers. He would live simply when in Australia, for a time he stayed in an apartment in Manly, and took the ferry across to the Opera House, delighting in the journey over Sydney Harbour. In later years, he preferred a pub,

---

[919] Verdi, c2022. Verdi has published several memoirs online (http://www.luig-iverdi.it/introduction.htm) but at the date of this publication, his Cillario memoir has not been posted.

[920] Ibid.

[921] Jacobs, 'Maestro, Marenzi, miracle,' *The Advertiser*, 24 March 1981.

the Royal Exhibition Hotel in Surry Hills, ostensibly because of its proximity to the Australian Opera's rehearsal and administrative facilities. There was no direct phone line to his room, and those who wanted to speak to him would call the bar and ask to speak to 'the Maestro' as Carlo was affectionately known to the staff of the hotel. The publican would then call out in a broad Australian twang 'Is the Maestro in?', initiating a chain of enquiry through the staff and several minutes later Cillario would come to the phone.

At times, in those final years, there was a sense about him that the world had changed, in ways to which he would remain impervious, so that, in Luigi Verdi's phrase, 'nothing could scratch from the outside.'[922] I recall once browsing the shelves of a second-hand record store in the centre of Sydney during the late 1990s. I noticed Cillario enter the shop. A short while later, he was in animated conversation with the owner, brandishing an LP. I moved closer and realised that Cillario was telling the owner that he had no money with him, but that he must have the record he was holding. His requests to take the record and bring the money the next day fell on deaf ears. As I advanced towards the counter, I saw Cillario point to the cover of the record. Frustrated, he shouted, indicating a photo 'You see her, she is Caballé, she is my friend.' He then pointed to the name of the conductor on the cover – 'You see him – that is me I AM CILLARIO!' At that point, I intervened, handed over some money, and told Cillario that he could take the record. He embraced me and left. I explained to the sullen shop owner that he was indeed Cillario, and that the 'Rossini Rarities' disc in question had been made with his friend, Montserrat Caballé. My explanation was met with studied silence.

The 'Cillario Sound'

When Cillario arrived in Australia in 1968, the opera orchestra (today the AOBO) had been formed only the previous year. On his arrival, he proceeded to put the orchestra through its paces, issuing sharp criticism during his first rehearsals for *The Magic Flute*.[923] He subsequently worked unstintingly to raise the standards, and by

---

[922] Verdi, (c2022).
[923] Hall, Cillario Obituary, 20 December 2007.

the time of the *Tosca* in Adelaide that season, his uncanny ability to instil discipline, clarity, elasticity, tight ensemble, and a flexibility to support the singer's phrasing, had worked wonders.

Cillario brought all the facets of his personality to bear on his conducting: the wild 'otherness' of Argentina, the iron will and discipline of Toscanini; the rebellious streak, somehow governed by a higher authority of his own making: he would switch between these modes as the need arose, from one phrase to another, sometimes back and forth over just a few bars. Discipline – wildness; authority – freedom; structure – extemporisation. Above all, Cillario made the orchestra sing. The 'Cillario Sound' was an identifiable phenomenon, and the orchestra 'sang', accommodating the 'give and take' of the singers he had trained. This synergy between pit and stage was a fundamental concern of Cillario's[924] and his thought processes can be observed in a 1982 interview[925] where he traced his ideas from the evidence he had found in early recordings. Cillario spoke about a recording of Eugène Ysaÿe playing a Hungarian Dance by Brahms:

> In my opinion his playing was so strange that if a pupil did it today, we couldn't accept it. Perhaps it is also the same with singing, such as the voice of Maria Galvany (c1878–1927) … she had a very strange interpretation, but I don't know, because from voices we accept much more elasticity than from instruments. Sometimes I am asking my players in the orchestra to try to imitate the singers. They're the best, especially in music of Mozart or Wagner. We must ask the singers to try to imitate the instruments and the instrumentalists to try to have the kind of flexibility the singers have sometimes. Singing is the goal of the instruments, especially in opera.[926]

The essence of Cillario's art was revealed in how he shaped a score of Puccini, where he could draw out a cantabile line to the

---

[924] Appendix 9 reproduces a notice he wrote to the AOBO (one of many such missives) where he outlined his opinion about legato playing (in the orchestra) and how it supports the voice.

[925] Cillario and Duffie, *Interview* (1982).

[926] Ibid.

brink of improvisational freedom. It is this quality of apparent spontaneity which links Cillario's music-making back to a 'grand tradition', whose history may be traced through recordings from the first decades of the last century, exemplified by the violin playing of Enescu. Cillario owed his connection to this tradition to his early teachers and mentors, who had their roots in the practices of the 19th century, when performances of art music retained their origins in improvisation.

The 'Cillario Sound' imbued the opera orchestra over the course of 35 years and through several changes of musical director. Its apex could be experienced during the years between 1984 and 1999 when Cillario, in conjunction with Moffatt Oxenbould as Artistic Director, was effectively the musical voice of the company. Neil Warren-Smith paid tribute to Cillario's impact on the company orchestra, compared to the ABC orchestras who had previously played for the opera seasons: 'For the players, too, Cillario was as vital and exciting an experience as he was for us [singers]. Over a period [1968-1981] … they've come to know him very closely, because Carlo, more than any other guest conductor, has a kind of continuity of association with the company.'[927]

Cillario fought (on his own terms) many battles on behalf of the orchestra. He opposed the rostering system, which rotated players over the course of a production. He was candid about the limitations of the pit and acoustic of the Opera Theatre, and argued the case for the Concert Hall as the most favourable venue for large-scale operatic works, while leading the best performances possible under the conditions that were available. He marked his own bowings and other instructions into the orchestral material for the operas he conducted. Given his former career as a soloist rather than a rank-and-file player, it is hardly surprising that many of his bowing suggestions were creative, challenging, and not always practical for musicians working at high pressure under demanding workloads. Many of his annotations were discreetly revised over time.

For the orchestra as for the singers, Cillario was a hard but rewarding taskmaster. His unorthodox methods were mostly

---

[927] Warren-Smith and Salter (1983), 141.

well-received, and his volatile temperament mostly tolerated with affection. At the end of a long week, when the orchestra was tired, a sudden injection of energy would catapult them through another evening in the pit. Every performance for Cillario was an event, an adventure. On occasion, his demands could spill over and create tensions, particularly as he grew older and remained unmoved by the fact that the dynamic between conductor and orchestra had shifted over the decades. This created unpleasant situations, and even disillusionment and hurt on Cillario's part, in his last years. Nevertheless, surviving core members of the orchestra still recognise the legacy of the 'Cillario Sound.' They say that, when faced with a conductor who fails to convince them in Puccini or Verdi, they 'revert to Cillario'.

To a young company in 1968, Cillario brought a sensibility reaching back into the 19th century, an appreciation of the seriousness of the operatic art, of the importance of the arts generally, and the recognition that opera – which encompasses both high art and entertainment – must be treated with the utmost seriousness and engagement. While Cillario sometimes seemed unsure as to where that dividing line was to be drawn (as shown in his shifting, love-hate relationship with *verismo*), his pronouncements about the repertoire reveal a deep thinker, a musician of the utmost seriousness.

> If we talk about opera, I prefer Puccini, Wagner, Mozart, Beethoven – ... and above all Giuseppe Verdi. I think that Verdi's music holds the absolute primacy on the stages of the world, a primacy conquered at the end of the 19th century and which it still retains, despite the change of tastes and the need to mix the repertoires. When we talk about the 'rediscovery' of Verdi, we must remember that it is not [a rediscovery]. On the contrary, it has never been forgotten. Furthermore, the controversy between the supporters of the early and late Verdi operas does not rest on significant foundations, because despite the progress made by the composer in improving his means of expression, his work always had a solid unity. In the

history of opera, Verdi remains the highest and most unassailable genius.[928]

He was keenly aware of his responsibilities, and of his lineage:

> I think we all must grow, but I don't believe in interpreting too much. Toscanini was a very strong character, and sometimes he gave no answers. A lady once told him, "You are so extraordinaire! How do you do Brahms or Verdi?" he said, "I do nothing special I just do what must be!" He was being honest because each one of us must think that his interpretation is the right one![929]

Cillario was a globetrotter, and perhaps it suited him not to have a physical home. He often spoke about Bologna and Argentina, but in the year of his final concert, and his 'addio' to Australia, he confessed:

> Never was I so happy, I think, about a country that called me as I am in Australia ... Since the first time I feel it is home. The country is so beautiful, I love the sea and the people. Somebody said that in Australia [exists] inno-cence. It's true ... It is difficult to have happiness, but it is important to try ... People say that marriage is the grave of love. But one must try.[930]

---

[928] Tornari, *La Fiamma*, 19 February 1981.
[929] Cillario and Duffie, *Interview*, 1982.
[930] Crisp, *The Financial Times*, 22–23 March 2003.

CODA

Carlo Felice Cillario died in 2007. Not long afterwards, I began to reflect on his life, his career, my memories of him, and how to go about recording details of his work in Australia that were in danger of being lost to posterity. I had little idea of how I should approach the task. I envisaged a slim volume of biographical details, photos and perhaps some of the maestro's memoirs translated into English.

In January 2023, I travelled to Bologna to visit the Cillario family. I met Cillario's grandsons, Alessandro and Dario, who were charming and supportive of my research. In the Cillario family home in Via di Casaglia, I was given access to documents that illuminated the conductor's career. Chaotically bundled correspondence and other materials from leading musical figures of the 20th century fell out of envelopes, filling many gaps in his life, and linking him with people and places that I had not previously associated him with.

Dario drove me to the little farmhouse that had been a spiritual retreat for Cillario, in Castel San Pietro Terme. It had remained shuttered up since Cillario's death. We were the first people to enter in almost 15 years. The house was a living museum, the home of an enquiring musician, full of scores and books, recordings and other material. I opened a cupboard to find all of Cillario's travelling clothes, which included the tails that he wore when conducting, batons, shoes and shirts that I recalled him wearing. The house represented a moment frozen in time.

The next afternoon, I visited the Pinacoteca of the University of Bologna, a treasure house of medieval Italian art. An enormous room houses the frescoes of the Church of Mezzaratta, created by Bolognese artists in the 14th and 15th centuries. These frescoes were among the first to be detached following World War II and transferred into a museum environment. In the process of removing the frescoes, a ground layer of *sinopia*, or preparatory drawings, was revealed. These too were removed and placed in an adjoining room, allowing visitors to reconstruct the entire creative process, from preliminary sketches through to the finished work.

Preoccupied with the memories of my visit to Cillario's rural retreat, the sight of both these beautiful frescoes, and their ghostly, almost surreal prototypes caused me to consider the many layers of Cillario's life and work. It led me to reflect upon the silence that any performer has to live with whether following a performance or at the conclusion of a career, as Cillario poignantly recorded in his memoir of Maria Callas.[931] The conducting scores in his house began to form a connection with the *sinopia* of these early fresco artists. The markings found in Cillario's scores (often using the same red colour that gives the *sinopia* their name) have a related function, as sketches and preparatory maps for the performances where he brought these works to life. Cillario's scores open up a significant new area of research, but the secret, and mystery of his art ultimately lies in the translation of the score into a spontaneous extemporisation, that no marks and no score can reproduce.

These experiences have led me to write this chronicle of Cillario's years in Australia. I have aimed to document his performances, his relationships with the artists who worked with him, and the role he played in the development of the Australian Opera. Cillario's name is indivisible from that history, and equally, what he created there has come to define him. As I proceeded with my research, Cillario's life and career prior to his first visit in 1968 became impossible to exclude. He arrived in Australia at the age of 53, having already lived more than half his life. What he had learned and accomplished prior to this time had made him the extraordinary musician that I came to know.

I was associated with Carlo from 1996 to 2003, during his final years at Opera Australia. I worked with him as a musical assistant and assistant conductor, and I played rehearsals for him. He was the most fascinating, compelling and elusive conductor I have ever worked with. I wish I could have my time with him over again, when, at the completion of this book, I finally know what I would and should have asked him. He taught me to love the operas of Puccini and to see those of Verdi in a new light. He was always 'the maestro', someone I held in the highest esteem and respect.

[931] See Appendix 7.

Carlo was also my friend, and it was a foregone conclusion that I would produce this tribute to him, to assist in keeping his memory and the residue of his art alive. This book tells the story of his years in Australia. I have chronicled all of the productions he conducted, and I have included excerpts from many contemporary reviews. I have listed the 41 operas he conducted in Australia, with premiere dates and performance tallies, totalling some 1020 opera performances with Opera Australia. I have translated the bulk of his memoirs, which I often saw him carrying under his arm, and which he revised and augmented over the years. They are published here for the first time. I have also included some of his work as a composer which, during the 1930s and 1940s he approached with diligence and purpose, and which, in later years became a *divertimento*, a diversion that also became an outlet in music for his irrepressible humour. My colleague, Brian Castles-Onion, has provided a discography for those wishing to sample Cillario's art for themselves. As someone who shared meals with Cillario, I could not resist a discussion of his culinary proclivities. Such an enterprise inevitably contains omissions and inaccuracies, which I have taken every care to minimise. I have included everything that I thought relevant, but further research would reveal even more facets of this musician. Italian music-lovers and musicians of a certain generation are often perplexed as to why Cillario's name is not better known abroad. Working as he did, spending months at a time in Australia each year, he found rewards beyond the fame which accrued to some of his contemporaries. I hope that this publication may go some way to explain the forces that influenced his life and career.

Sydney, 22 March 2024

Afterword

by Moffatt Oxenbould

I was privileged to have worked closely with Carlo Felice Cillario - from his first season with the then Elizabethan Trust Opera Company in Canberra in 1968 – until his eccentric and unforgettable Opera Australia farewell concert in the Sydney Opera House in 2002. We got to know the best and the worst of each other and to call each other "*padre*" and "*figlio*". For me, he was a teacher and a counsellor as well as an authoritative but often exasperating colleague. We shared a sense of the ridiculous but, at times, our eyes filled with tears when confronted with a moment of deep emotion. We respected and we loved each other.

I am proud to have been a resource to Stephen Mould in documenting the life, career and legacy of this remarkable musician. Over the years, I have written much about Carlo, especially since he left life's stage. In now writing a final farewell to my "*padre*", I recall a rehearsal in Melbourne in 1982. The opera was *Il tabarro,* a revival of a production of the three operas that make up Puccini's *Trittico* that I had done nine years earlier for a Melbourne premiere prior to the opening season in the Sydney Opera House. At that time, I collaborated with three very different conductors – one for each opera. *Tabarro* was then the work beset by the most problems of the three. The conductor and the principal soprano simply didn't get on and there was a major clash when we got to the stage rehearsals, resulting in the soprano being removed from the cast. Then the principal tenor became ill. Any subtleties and character interaction we might have evolved in the rehearsal studio had largely disappeared by the time we got to the first night.

It was exciting to come back to *Tabarro* nine years later, collaborating with Maestro Cillario. The cast was led by two experienced performers – Etela Piha as Giorgetta and John Shaw as Michele. Both had performed the opera before, and when we gathered to rehearse, on a bleak, grey autumn afternoon in a rather gloomy hall in Fitzroy, I don't think any of us had any idea of what was to come.

Tabarro is an extraordinary piece of musical theatre – an operatic reworking of a Zola-esque play by Didier Gold that Puccini had seen and admired in Paris in 1912. It is mature Puccini and, in less than an hour, a scene is set, an atmosphere experienced and relationships revealed that culminate in a violent murder preceded by a poignant interchange between a husband and wife whose baby has died, causing their marriage to break down. It was this awkward, but heart-breaking "conversation" that we began to discuss and rehearse. We talked about the characters, their story and their text and then started to move the scene. As the rehearsal pianist began, Maestro Cillario caressed the music, subtly insinuating it into the action. Slowly, gently, a miracle seemed to happen. It was as if Puccini was somehow with us in this drab rehearsal room! The two singers started to become the characters they were intent on discovering or perhaps thought they already knew? Was it opera? Was it a play? A movie? Was it real life? The music, Puccini's music, in the hands of a true maestro, was revealing its integrity and potency and showing us "the way forward".

Perhaps the most unusual thing was that all of us in the room seemed to be having the same response to what was happening. We were exhilarated, wondering at the mastery and craft of the composer. We couldn't wait to repeat the scene to make it even richer and more real. Puccini had shared with us his love for the fallible humanity of the characters he had brought so vividly to life in music. The singers took ownership of these two challenging roles. Carlo smiled at me! *Siamo a cavallo!*

Moffatt Oxenbould 2024

APPENDICES

Appendix 1

Navigating opera in Australia

The Elizabethan Trust Opera Company was established in 1957, as a new, state-funded company to develop opera performance in Australia. The company's growth intensified after the foundation stone of the Sydney Opera House was laid in 1959. Over the course of its expansion and development, the company changed identity with a series of name changes which may easily cause confusion.

Names of the National Company

In considering the history of the company, it is important to have an overview of the succession of name changes it has undergone, particularly in the context of its activities and influence in both Sydney and Melbourne. These are the iterations of the Company since 1954.

The **Australian Elizabethan Theatre Trust** was founded in 1954, following the coronation of Queen Elizabeth II, with the aim of ushering in a 'New Elizabethan' age for the arts. In this original form, the Trust was dedicated to spoken theatre.

The **Australian Opera Company (AOC)** was established in 1956. Its function as a touring company was embedded within its formation.

The **Elizabethan Trust Opera Company (ETOC)** was established in 1957. The ETOC was a touring company, like its predecessor (the AOC), producing seasons in Canberra (until c1983), Melbourne, Sydney, Brisbane and Adelaide, including appearances at the Adelaide Festival of Arts. Its administrative operations were based in Sydney, but the company lacked a dedicated home for its performances. Plans for the Sydney Opera House (SOH) began to take shape around 1956.

In 1970 the **ETOC** was renamed the **Australian Opera (AO)** and transferred to an independent management. This transformation took place as part of a long-term plan for its move into the Sydney Opera House. The name change coincided with Cillario's appointment as the first Music Director of the company, though he left the position before the inauguration of the SOH in 1973.

In Melbourne, a professional opera company had been established in 1962. It became known as the **Victoria Opera Company** in 1964, and then the **Victoria State Opera (VSO)** in 1976. In 1996, the **Australian Opera** and the **Victoria State Opera** were joined in a government-mandated merger,[932] following the financial collapse of the **VSO**. The new company was briefly called the 'Australian National Opera'. It took Cillario to observe that ANO ('ano') means anus in Italian, and the name was swiftly changed once again, to **Opera Australia (OA),** as the company is known to this day.

Within this text, 'the company' refers collectively to this succession of entities, which together embodies the national company.

Cillario's Titles[933]

During his long association with the company, Cillario also held several titles, which suggest the nature of his changing responsibilities, while sometimes leaving unclear the precise nature of his influence over the company's musical operations.

> 1968: Guest Conductor, Elizabethan Trust Opera Company
>
> 1969: Principal Conductor, Elizabethan Trust Opera Company
>
> 1970[–71]: Music[al][934] Director, Australian Opera

---

[932] The Melbourne company was primarily state funded, with a small federal contribution https://en.wikipedia.org/wiki/Victoria_State_Opera, accessed 25 April 2023.

[933] Moffatt Oxenbould has written about the array of titles that Cillario assumed, concluding that 'whatever the title, his has been the most constant and enduring musical authority and influence upon the Company during its first half-century of life'. (Oxenbould, *Carlo Felice Cillario and Opera Australia*, 2003).

[934] In the press, as well as in company programmes, 'Music' and 'Musical' Director were used interchangeably, just as today's stage 'director' was often referred to as a 'producer'. This is a legacy of the company's origins (and that of its first administrators) in the world of musicals and light opera, and the carrying over of terminology from those genres.

1974–87: Guest Conductor, Australian Opera

1987–91: Principal Guest Conductor and Music Consultant, the Australian Opera, jointly with Myer Fredman

1992–2001: Principal Guest Conductor, Australian Opera/ Opera Australia (from 1996)

2002–03: Guest Conductor, Opera Australia[935]

Following Cillario's departure as Music Director early in 1971, the musical/artistic leadership of the company was held by the following individuals:

1973–75: Edward Downes, Music Director, Australian Opera

1976–84: Richard Bonynge, Music Director, Australian Opera

1984–99: Moffatt Oxenbould, Artistic Director, Australian Opera/Opera Australia[936]

2001–03: Simone Young, Music Director, Opera Australia

While not a conductor, Moffatt Oxenbould belongs to a direct line of artistic leadership within the company. Richard Bonynge's tenure as Music Director ended officially in 1984; in practice, however, a leadership transition was effected during 1985–86. Between 1987 and 1999, Cillario's role as Principal Guest Conductor (as well as Music Consultant,1987–91) effectively made him, a *de facto* music director. Cillario often stated that his job was to make music, not administration, and some of the ambiguity in his job titles respected this reluctance of his to assume the administrative responsibilities that would be expected of a music director, while taking into account his input and wisdom on artistic matters, and musical leadership of the Sydney orchestra.

---

[935] Cillario stated in a 1993 interview that he had been named 'Guest Conductor for Life', which may have been an off-the-cuff remark. In his final years with the Company (2002–03) he is listed in programmes on the roster of guest conductors without any official title. See: Michael Bruning, 'Lightning Conductor – Maestro strikes a chord with AO', *Timeout, The Manly Daily*, 17 September 1993.

[936] Oxenbould had intended to continue as Artistic Director until 2000, but he resigned in 1999. The following season became a period of transition between the departure of Oxenbould and the incoming leadership of Simone Young.

Orchestral Resources

Cillario first arrived in Australia in 1968, at a critical time in the expansion of orchestral resources within the country. An orchestra had been formed in 1967, specifically to play for the opera and the ballet seasons of the ETOC, services which had previously been supplied by ABC orchestras.[937] The creation of full-time ensembles for ballet and opera was widely recognised as a significant step in the development of opera in this country.

The **Elizabethan Trust Orchestra** was formed in 1967. In 1969 two full-time ensembles were established: the **Elizabethan Sydney Orchestra,** and the **Elizabethan Melbourne Orchestra.** In 1987, the Elizabethan Sydney Orchestra was renamed the **Elizabethan Philharmonic Orchestra,** and by 1989 it became the **Australian Opera and Ballet Orchestra** (AOBO) with an independent management.[938] These orchestras are today (2023) known as the **Opera Australia Orchestra** (Sydney) and **Orchestra Victoria** (Melbourne).

Touring

The company that Cillario encountered on his first visits to Australia was a touring one, which gave seasons in Sydney, Melbourne, Canberra, Brisbane and Adelaide. A full season of operas would be shared among the various cities; sometimes a return visit to Canberra would produce two seasons of one or two operas, with the entire season's repertoire then being presented in Sydney.

The long-awaited completion of the Sydney Opera House gave the company a much firmer footing in Sydney. Tours to Canberra ceased around 1984, as did regular visits to Brisbane, where an independent, state-funded company emerged in 1981. Tours to Adelaide became less frequent, and the company subsequently

---

[937] This remains the case today in Adelaide, Perth and Brisbane. Brisbane had its own opera and ballet orchestra, known as the Queensland Theatre Orchestra. Subsequently renamed as the Queensland Philharmonic, it merged with the Queensland Symphony Orchestra in 2000.

[938] See: https://thetrust.org/orchestral, accessed 27 December 2022.

divided its activities principally between Sydney and Melbourne. The construction of arts centres in most of these cities facilitated the establishment and growth of state opera companies, which were formed to provide opera for these new, well-equipped venues.

The Sydney-based company toured to Melbourne twice a year, and the ballet seasons took place at the SOH during its absence. Full-time orchestras in both Sydney and Melbourne facilitated an alternation of opera and ballet seasons year-round. Following Cillario's return to Australia for the 1975 season, his activities were largely divided between Sydney and Melbourne. The company's activities in each city were eventually referred to by season – Sydney summer (SS), Melbourne autumn (MA), Sydney winter (SW) and Melbourne spring (MS). These designations are used within the main text.

Performances and Performers

The touring activities of the company required planning contingencies to be in place. A system of double (sometimes triple) casting was developed in order to ensure that the show would go on, irrespective of vocal fatigue, illness and other cast indispositions. During the late 1960's a core of three conductors would routinely take over from one another during runs of performances in different cities. A designated conductor for each production would be present from the first day of rehearsals, taking responsibility for the musical preparation, staging and orchestral rehearsals: they were generally known as the 'musical director' of the production. They would conduct the premiere and at least the initial performances of a run. Another conductor might then take over later performances with little, if any rehearsal. These changes of conductor were often coordinated with cast changes, in order to maintain a degree of musical cohesion.

Late cancellations (even on the day of a performance) inevitably prompted a flurry of activity. Last-minute changes of personnel often went undocumented, except perhaps in stage management reports, with the changes being announced to the audience prior to the performance. The company's early records do not always reliably state who sang or even conducted at a given performance. This is still true of Cillario's performances from 1968–70; the company's record-keeping had become more reliable by the time he returned in 1975.

From 1975 onwards, Cillario would always conduct the premieres of the operas he had prepared. From time to time, he would hand over some later performances, as agreed in advance and noted in the programmes. He was not in the habit of routinely handing 'his' performances over to other conductors, and he never cancelled a performance due to illness. He rarely took over a run of performances from another conductor – with some notable exceptions, listed in Appendix 3.

The casts conducted by Cillario are listed in footnotes to the main text. Stage directors and designers are identified for new productions. Revival directors are not credited unless their inclusion is of particular significance; when their role exceeded that of merely reviving the production in accordance with the original direction (see next section).

Hybrid Productions

From its origins as a touring company, the Australian Opera developed into a busy repertory company. Successful productions might remain in the company's repertoire for many years, even decades. Such stagings would be revived by assistant directors who retained corporate knowledge and oversight from the original production period. The chronicle of operas conducted by Cillario in Appendix 2 identifies in **bold text** new productions led by him. Revival productions are in plain Roman.

Several productions do not fit the straightforward categories of new or revival stagings. A much-revived production might require a new injection of energy, or else require some revision of the staging to accommodate the casting of a significant overseas guest artist, or multiple cast changes. Depending on the amount of intervention required, such hybrid productions may be identified as 'restudied' or, in the case of a significant change of cast and venue, might be deemed to be 'redirected'. They were generally created using the original sets, with the original costumes. For example, the *Macbeth* production of 1998, was restudied by the original director, John Copley, who returned to Sydney to rework his production of 21 years earlier, tightening up detail, and introducing Michael Lewis into the title role.

Productions were also acquired from other companies, such as *Der fliegende Holländer* (1978), which began life in Bayreuth, directed by Wieland Wagner, before being restaged in Copenhagen, and then in Sydney. The production was 'new' to Sydney, but its complex lineage is part of its gestation, making it a 'hybrid' production. Such productions are identified in bold grey in Appendix 2.

The pairing of *Cav & Pag* was often revived during the late 70s and 80s by a succession of resident directors, who were charged with resolving perceived weaknesses in the original production. This is also the case with the 1970 *La bohème* production, directed by Renzo Frusca and designed by Tom Lingwood. The design was successful and became an asset for the company for 17 years. From early on, however, it was felt that Frusca's direction needed revision, and subsequently successive directors reworked the production, on Lingwood's set. Further details about such hybrid productions can be found in the main text.

Concert performances are listed in bold red. Some concert performances retained a semblance of a dramatic presentation – costumes, some props and movement, within the limitations of the stage area. A unique case is presented by the season of 1970, interrupted by a fire in Her Majesty's Theatre, Sydney, which destroyed much of the sets and costumes of the works then in repertoire. The season continued in the Capitol Theatre with concert performances. The outdoor presentation of *La bohème* in 2000 at the 'Domain Parks' presentation used singers and some stage elements from Moffatt Oxenbould's 1999 mainstage production, adapted by David Crooks. These complex processes for adapting and reusing productions were integral to the working life of the company, allowing them to maintain a large number of productions and foster a repertoire culture.[939]

---

[939] I am grateful to Moffatt Oxenbould for his assistance in clarifying these various categories of performance.

Venues

Cillario conducted his first Australian performances in Canberra. These took place at the Canberra Theatre Centre, a 1200-seat theatre, which had opened in 1965, as the first of a series of performing arts centres that were to be built around the country. Older cities – Sydney, Melbourne, Adelaide and Brisbane – had 'Her Majesty's'. These grand old theatres, (affectionately known as the 'Maj' in each case) had been built during Queen Victoria's reign. In Adelaide, the 'Maj' was replaced in 1973 by the Festival Theatre. The company gave performances both under the umbrella of the Adelaide Festival, as well as seasons promoted independently. In 1992, Cillario conducted an outdoor performance in Elder Park, Adelaide, as part of the Festival. In Melbourne, the company gave performances in several venues until the construction of the Victorian Arts Centre:

1968 Princess Theatre

1969 Her Majesty's Theatre

1970–78 Princess Theatre

1979–81 both the Princess and the Palais Theatres

1982–84 Princess Theatre

End 1984–The State Theatre, Victorian Arts Centre[940]

In Brisbane, the building of the Southbank Arts Complex led to the creation of a professional opera company in 1981, which was developed from established amateur organisations within the city. After its completion in 1985, the Lyric Theatre at Southbank became the venue for opera performances in Brisbane.

Cillario conducted his first Sydney performances at Her Majesty's Theatre. It burned down in 1970, his first year as Music Director (1970), towards the end of the season, and the remaining performances were given in the Capitol Theatre as recorded in Appendix 3. From 1975 onwards, he conducted at the Sydney Opera House, which had opened in 1973. Significantly, his first production there was in the Concert Hall – a venue where he performed gladly, for its more favourable acoustic and capacity to accommodate large

---

[940] I am grateful to Moffatt Oxenbould for supplying this information.

orchestral forces. He went on to conduct several operas in this larger space, both in concert, and in a 'semi-staged' format, with the orchestra visible, and with productions carefully designed so that nothing would be screwed into the fabric of the wooden–clad performance space. Otherwise, his usual performance home in Sydney was the Opera Theatre (today the Joan Sutherland Theatre) of the Sydney Opera House. Cillario also conducted a concert performance for the company at the Sydney Town Hall (1978), as well as *La bohème* for Opera in the Domain (outdoors presentation) on one occasion (2000).[941]

On one occasion Cillario toured to Newcastle, north of Sydney. Like many theatres of the period, the Newcastle Civic Theatre had opened in 1929 as a live-performance venue, soon to be repurposed as a cinema. During the 1970's it reverted to the city's foremost live performance venue, a status which it retains today.

---

[941] Cillario also appeared in other years as one of several conductors in programmes of operatic excerpts.

Appendix 2
Productions conducted by Cillario in Australia, 1968–2002

All performances are with Opera Australia, or one of its earlier iterations, with a single exception – a production of *Aida* for Canberra Opera in 1981.

An English-language title for a work indicate that the opera was performed in an English singing translation.

<u>Key</u>

Bold – new production

Roman – revival

Grey bold – hybrid: restudied/redirected production

Bold and <u>underline</u> – concert performance

<u>City</u>

S = Sydney

B = Melbourne

A = Adelaide

B = Brisbane

C = Canberra

N = Newcastle

<u>Venue</u>

HM = Her Majesty's Theatre (**S**ydney/**M**elbourne/**A**delaide/ **B**risbane)

CT = Capitol Theatre (**S**ydney)

OT = Opera Theatre, **S**ydney Opera House

CH = Concert Hall, **S**ydney Opera House

TH = **S**ydney Town Hall

PrT = Princess Theatre (**M**elbourne)

PaT = Palais Theatre (**M**elbourne)

ST = State Theatre, Victorian Arts Centre (Melbourne)

TC = Canberra Theatre Centre

FT = Adelaide Festival Theatre

LT = Lyric Theatre (Brisbane)

NT = Newcastle Civic Theatre

Parks = Sydney (The Domain) or Adelaide (Elder Park)

1968

Wagner – Tannhäuser (Beinl/Rowell) (C–TC; **A**–HM; **M**–PrT; **S**–HM; **B**–HM)

Mozart – The Magic Flute (Haag/Downing) (**C**–TC; **S**–HM; **M**–PrT)

Puccini – Tosca (Haag/Walton) (**A**–HM; **M**–PrT; **S**–HM)

1969

Verdi – Falstaff (Beinl/Egg/Kresta) (**M**–HM; **C**–TC; **S**–HM)

Puccini – Madama Butterfly (Fujiwara/Tosa) (C–TC; **M**–HM; **A**–HM)

Verdi – Un ballo in maschera (Brown/Digby) (**M**–HM; **S**–HM)

1970

Puccini – La bohème (Frusca/Lingwood)[942] (**S–HM/**S–CT)[943]

Verdi – Otello (Benthaak/D. Smith) (**S–HM/**S–CT)

Verdi – La forza del destino (Frusca/Lingwood) (**S–HM/**S–CT)

1975

Verdi – Aida (Hall/Lingwood) (S–CH)

Verdi – Rigoletto (Copley/Lees/Stennett) (**S–OT**)

Donizetti – The Elixir of Love (Haag/Walton/Kahan) (S–OT)

---

[942] This production stayed in the repertoire until 1988. The Lingwood design remained fundamentally unchanged, while several different directors, notably Andrew Sinclair, David Neal (1977), and at one point Lingwood himself revived the production.

[943] The final performances of this season were given in the Capitol Theatre, in concert, as a result of the fire that destroyed the sets and costumes.

1976

Verdi – Aida (Hall/Lingwood) (**S**–CH)

Verdi – Simon Boccanegra (Capobianco/Vanarelli) (**M**–PrT)

Janáček – The Cunning Little Vixen (Miller/Vercoe/Robertson) (**M**–PrT; **S**–OT)

Puccini – Tosca (Hall/Feitscher) (**M**–PrT)

Mozart – The A bduction f rom t he S eraglio (Ogilvie/ Fredrikson) (S–OT)

Verdi – Rigoletto (Copley/Lees/Stennett) (**S**–OT)

1977

Verdi – Aida (Lingwood) (**S**–CH)

Puccini – Madama Butterfly (Copley/Bardon/Stennett) (S–OT; C–TC; M–PrT)

Puccini – Tosca (Hall/Feitscher) (**S**–OT)

Beethoven – Fidelio (Copley, rev. Neidhardt/Lees) (**M**–PrT)

Wagner – Parsifal (**S**–CH)

Verdi – Macbeth (Copley/Lazaridis) (S–OT)

Wagner – Der fliegende Holländer (Peterson/Frandsen) (**S**–OT)

1978

Verdi – Macbeth (Copley/Lazaridis) (**M**–PrT)

Wagner – Der fliegende Holländer (**S**–TH)

Wagner – Der fliegende Holländer (Peterson/Frandsen) (**M**–PrT)

Mozart – Don Giovanni (Eng.) (Ogilvie/Coleman/Fredrikson) (M–PrT; N–NT)

Puccini – Madama Butterfly (Copley/Bardon/Stennett) (**S**–OT)

Mascagni – Cavalleria rusticana (Hall/Benthaak/Digby) (**S**–OT)

Leoncavallo – I pagliacci (Hall/Benthaak/Digby) (**S**–OT)

1979

Beethoven – Fidelio (Copley/Benthaak/Lees) (**S**–CH)

Puccini – La bohème (Lingwood/Lingwood) (**M**–PaT; **B**–HM)

Puccini – Madama Butterfly (Copley/Bardon/Stennett, 1977) (**M**–PrT)

Mascagni – Cavalleria rusticana (Hall/Benthaak/Digby) (**M**–PrT)

Leoncavallo – I pagliacci (Hall/Neidhardt/Digby) (**M**–PrT)

Puccini – La fanciulla del West (Lovejoy/Lingwood) (**M**–PaT; **S**–OT)

Verdi – Falstaff (Ogilvie/Fredrikson) (**S**–OT)

1980

Puccini – La fanciulla del West (Lovejoy/Lingwood) (**C**–TC)

Verdi – Falstaff (Ogilvie/Fredrickson) (**M**–PrT; **B**–HM)

Verdi – La traviata (Copley/Bardon/Stennett) (**M**–PaT; **B**–HM)

Mozart – The Abduction from the Seraglio (Ogilvie/Fredrikson) (**M**–PrT)

Puccini – Manon Lescaut (Copley/Fredrikson) (**S**–OT)

1981

Verdi – Otello (Ogilvie/Gurton/Fredrikson) (**S**–CH; **M**–PaT)

Puccini – La bohème (Sinclair/Lingwood) (**S**–OT)

Verdi – I masnadieri (Beauvais/Lees/Stennett) (**C**–TC; **A**–HM)

Puccini – Manon Lescaut (Copley/Fredrikson) (**M**–PaT)

Puccini – Tosca (Copley/Lees/Stennett) (**S**–OT)

Bellini – Norma (Sequi/Renshaw/Mariani) (**M**–PrT)

[Verdi – Aida (Canberra Opera)]

1982

Mascagni – Cavalleria rusticana (Sinclair/Digby) (**M**–PrT)

Leoncavallo – I pagliacci (Neidhardt/Digby) (**M**–PrT)

Puccini – La bohème (Sinclair/Lingwood) (**M**–PrT)

Puccini – Il trittico (Oxenbould/Digby) (**M**–PrT; **S**–OT)

Verdi – Macbeth (Copley/Lazaridis) (**M**–PrT)

1983

Puccini – Tosca (Copley/Lees/Stennett) (**S**–OT)

Puccini – La bohème (Sinclair/Lingwood) (**S**–OT)

Wagner – Die Walküre (Sinclair/Lees/Digby) (S–OT)

Puccini – La fanciulla del West (Renshaw/Lingwood) (S–OT)

1984

Verdi – Otello (Sinclair/Gurton/Fredrikson) (S–CH)

Wagner – Die Walküre (Sinclair/Lees/Digby) (S–OT)

Wagner – Das Rheingold (Sinclair/Lees/Digby) (S–OT)

1985

Wagner – Die Walküre (Sinclair/Lees/Digby) (S–OT; M–ST)

Verdi – Aida (Renshaw/Rowell) (M–ST; A–FT)

Puccini – La bohème (Sinclair/Lingwood) (S–OT)

Puccini – Tosca (Copley/Lees/Stennett) (M–ST)

1986

Verdi – Un ballo in maschera (Cox/Gunter/Stennett) (M–ST)

Donizetti – Don Pasquale (Maunder/Kirk) (M–ST)

Verdi – Macbeth (Copley/Lazaridis) (M–ST)

Tchaikovsky – Eugene Onegin (Woolliams/Fraser) (S–OH)

Puccini – Manon Lescaut (Copley, rev. Pimlott/Fredrikson) (S–OH)

1987

Rossini – La Cenerentola (Hampe/Heinrich) (S–OT; B–LT)

Cherubini – Médée (Pettersson/Friberg) (S–OT)

Puccini – Il trittico (Oxenbould/Digby) (S–OT)

Verdi – La traviata (Copley/Bardon/Stennett) (S–OT)

1988

Puccini – Turandot (S–CH)

Rossini – La Cenerentola (Hampe/Heinrich) (M–ST)

Puccini – Tosca (Copley/Lees/Stennett) (M–ST; S–OT)

Verdi – Otello (Ogilvie/Gurton/Fredrikson) (S–OT)

Puccini – La bohème (Sinclair/Lingwood) (S–OT)

1989

Verdi – Otello (Ogilvie/Gurton/Fredrikson) (**M**–ST)

Mascagni – Cavalleria rusticana (Copley/Don/Stennett) (M–ST; S–OT)

Leoncavallo – I pagliacci (Copley/Don/Stennett) (M–ST; S–OT)

Massenet – Werther (Moshinsky/Yeargan) (S–OT)

1990

Wagner – Tristan und Isolde (Armfield/Thomson/Tate) (**M**–ST)

Massenet – Werther (Moshinsky/Yeargan) (**M**–ST)

Puccini – Turandot (Murphy/Fredrikson) (S–OT)

Wagner – Lohengrin (Everding, rev. Neidhardt/Rowell) (**S**–OT)

1991

Puccini – Turandot (Murphy/Fredrikson) (**M**–ST)

Verdi – Rigoletto (Moshinsky/Yeargan) (S–OT)

Verdi – Otello (Ogilvie/Gurton/Fredrikson) (**S**–OT)

1992

Verdi – La traviata (**A**–Parks)

Verdi – Rigoletto (Moshinsky/Yeargan) (**M**–ST)

Puccini – Tosca (Copley/Lees/Stennett) (**M**–ST)

Verdi – Simon Boccanegra (Gaal/Strathie) (S–OT)

Rossini – L'italiana in Algeri (Chazalettes/Santicchi) (S–OT)

1993

Wagner – Tristan und Isolde (Armfield/Thomson/Tate) (**S**–CH; **M**–ST)

Verdi – Un ballo in maschera (Cox/Gunter/Stennett) (**S**–OT)

Puccini – Tosca (Copley/Lees/Stennett) (**S**–OT)

1994

Wagner – Die Meistersinger von Nürnberg (Hampe/Heinrich) (**M**–ST)

Verdi – La traviata (Moshinksy/Yeargan/Hall) (S–OT)

1995

Puccini – Turandot (Murphy/Fredrikson) (**M**–ST)

Verdi – La traviata (Moshinsky/Yeargan/Hall) (**M**–ST)

Puccini – Il trittico (Oxenbould/Digby) (**S**–OT)

Verdi – Nabucco (Kosky/Corrigan) (S–OT)

1996

Verdi – Nabucco (Kosky/Corrigan) (**M**–ST)

Verdi – Falstaff[944] (Phillips/Aitken/Grant Lord) (**S**–OT)

1997

Verdi – La traviata (Moshinsky/Yeargan/Hall) (**S**–OT)

Verdi – Falstaff (Phillips/Aitken/Grant Lord) (**M**–ST)

1998

Verdi – Macbeth (Copley/Lazaridis) (**S**–OT)

1999

Puccini – La bohème (Oxenbould/Cohen/England) (S–OT)

Puccini – Turandot (Murphy/Fredrikson) (**S**–OT)

2000

Puccini – La bohème (**S**–Parks)

Verdi – Don Carlo (Moshinsky/Brown) (**M**–ST)

Puccini – Tosca (Copley/Lees/Stennett) (**S**–OT)

2001

Verdi – La traviata (Moshinsky/Yeargan/Hall) (**M**–ST)

Puccini – Il trittico (Oxenbould/Digby) (**S**–OT)

2002

Puccini – La bohème (Oxenbould/Cohen/England) (**S**–OT)

---

[944] This was an Opera Conference production which had premiered in Adelaide and Perth, prior to being staged in Sydney.

Appendix 3

Cillario's Opera Performances in Australia, 1968-2002

Cillario conducted a total of 41 operas[945] in Australia. Taking into account the incomplete records that survive, particularly prior to the opening of the Sydney Opera House, it is estimated that he conducted a total of 1020 performances for the national company. The date given for each entry indicates the first performance of a run.

Verdi (12)

La traviata:

> 1980 (B) 26.4.80 (5) [+ 1 performance conducted by Peter Robinson; total 6]
>
> 1980 (M) 2.4.80 (4)
>
> 1987 (S) 26.9.87 (8)
>
> 1992 (A) 21.3.92 (1)
>
> 1994 (S) 19.8.94 (c12) [later performances were conducted by Myer Fredman]
>
> 1995 (M) 18.3.95 (9)
>
> 1997 (S) 20.1.97 (12)
>
> 2001 (M) 30.3.01 (5)

Rigoletto:

> 1975 (S) 24.7.75 (8) [William Reid = 8; Cillario 2nd run = 8; total 16]
>
> 1976 (S) 12.6.76 (2) [Cillario = 2; Reid 2nd run = 3; total 5]
>
> 1991 (S) 8.6.91 (10) [Mark Summerbell conducted final performances]
>
> 1992 (M) 7.4.92 (7)

---

[945] Counting *Cav & Pag* and *Il trittico* each as one work.

Macbeth:

> 1977 (S) 4.8.77 (c7) [John Pritchard = 8; Cillario took over the final perf's.]
>
> 1978 (M) 10.4.78 (8)
>
> 1982 (M) 17.5.82 (4)
>
> 1986 (M) 25.4.86 (4)
>
> 1998 (S) 20.1.98 (11)

Nabucco:

> 1995 (S) 12.8.95 (14)
>
> 1996 (M) 16.4.96 (8)

I masnadieri:

1981 (C) 6.3.81 (3)

1981 (A) 19.3.81 (5)

Un ballo in maschera:

> 1969 (S) 24.5.69 (8)
>
> 1969 (M) 7.3.69 (7)
>
> 1986 (M) 14.3.86 (6)
>
> 1993 (S) 19.8.93 (9)

Simon Boccanegra:

> 1976 (M) 4.3.76 (9)
>
> 1992 (S) 7.9.92 (8)

La forza del destino:

> 1970 (S) 2.7.70 (9) [6 Maj. + 3 Cap.][946]

Don Carlo:

> 2000 (M) 14.4.00 (8)

Aida:

> 1975 (S) 30.1.75 (10)
>
> 1976 (S) 13.1.76 (11)

---

[946] Six performances took place as scheduled in Her Majesty's Theatre. Following the fire towards the end of the season, the last three performances took place in the Capitol Theatre.

1977 (S) 14.1.77 (10)

[1981, Canberra Opera (2)]

Otello:

1970 (S) 10.7.70 (9) [7 Maj. + 2 Cap.][947]

1981 (S) 28.1.81 (10)

1981 (M) 20.5.81 (6)

1984 (S) 20.1.84 (5)

1988 (S) 19.7.88 (8)

1989 (M) 27.4.89 (6)

1991 (M) 5.8.91 (9)

Falstaff:

1969 (M) 21.2.68 (8)

1969 (C) 12.2.69 (2)

1969 (S) 21.2.70 (c7) [Both Cillario and Reid conducted perf's.]

1979 (S) 1.8.79 (9)

1980 (B) 25.4.80 (4)

1980 (M) 29.3.80 (7)

1996 (S) 8.10.96 (10)

1997 (M) 3.4.97 (5)

Puccini (7)

Tosca:

1968 (A) 14.3.68 (6)

1968 (M) 4.4.68 (5) [4 scheduled + 1 matinee added]

1968 (S) 15.6.68 (7)[948] [Feist conducted the final perf.; total 8]

1976 (M) 22.4.76 (4)

---

[947] As for FN 946, seven performances took place as scheduled in Her Majesty's Theatre, and the final two performances took place in the Capitol Theatre.

[948] The scheduled date for the premiere was 11 June, however both the Tosca and the Cavaradossi fell ill hours before the performance, which was cancelled until 15 June (originally to be the second performance). As a result, it may be that Cillario only conducted six performances.

1977 (S) 28.1.77 (4)

1981 (S) 13.6.81 (10) [Reid conducted later perf's.]

1983 (S) 19.1.83 (6)

1985 (S) 25.4.85 (4)

1988 (M) 20.4.88 (8)

1988 (S) 17.6.88 (10)

1992 (M) 13.4.92 (7) [Robert Rosen conducted later perf's.]

1993 (S) 13.9.93 (9)

2000 (S) 16.9.00 (6)

La bohème:

1970 (S) 20.6.70 (10) [9 Maj. + 1 Cap.][949]

1979 (M) 12.3.79 (6)

1979 (B) 2.4.79 (4)

1981 (S) 10.2.81 (6)

1982 (M) 24.4.82 (6) [Reid conducted later perf's.]

1983 (S) 10.2.83 (7)

1985 (S) 7.8.85 (8)

1988 (S) 12.8.88 (14)

1999 (S) 20.7.99 (16) [Stephen Mould conducted later perf's.]

2000 (S) (1)

2002 (S) 2.1.02 (15)

Madama Butterfly:

1969 (M) 22.2.69 (6) [Reid conducted 1 perf.; total 7]

1969 (A) 8.4.69 (5)

1969 (C) 11.2.69 (3)

1977 (S) 29.1.77 (8)

1977 (M) 24.3.77 (10)

1977 (C) 3.3.77 (4)

1978 (S) 14.6.78 (8)

1979 (M) 14.4.79 (6)

---

[949] As for FN 946, 9 + 1 for *La bohème*.

Il trittico:

    1982 (M) 13.5.82 (6)

    1982 (S) 5.6.82 (9) [Reid & Handley conducted last perf's.]

    1987 (S) 24.7.87 (8)

    1995 (S) 10.7.95 (8)

    2001 (S) 8.6.01 (11)

La fanciulla del West:

    1979 (M) 19.5.79 (3)

    1979 (S) 6.6.79 (7)

    1980 (C) 7.3.80 (3)

    1983 (S) 7.10.83 (8)

Manon Lescaut:

    1980 (S) 9.6.80 (10) [Reid conducted last perf's.]

    1981 (M) 7.4.81 (5)

    1986 (S) 6.9.86 (8) [Myer Fredman conducted last 3 (youth) perf's.; total 11]

Turandot:

    [1988 – Sydney Festival – SOH Concert Hall] 16.2.88 (2)

    1990 (S) 14.8.90 (12) [last 3 perf's (schools) cond. by Vladimir Kamirski; total 15]

    1991 (M) 5.2.91 (10)

    1995 (M) 11.4.95 (8)

    1999 (S) 17.9.99 (16)

Rossini (2)

La Cenerentola:

    1987 (S) 10.7.87 (12)

    1987 (B) 7.11.87 (3)

    1988 (M) 30.4.88 (7)

L'italiana in Algeri:

    1992 (S) 7.10.92 (8)

Donizetti (2)

The elixir of love:

>1975 (S) 21.8.75 (c10) [Peter Robinson conducted later perf's.]

Don Pasquale:

>1986 (M) 10.4.86 (4)

Bellini (1)

Norma:

>1981 (M) 17.11.81 (5)

Mascagni/Leoncavallo (1)

Cav & Pag:

>1978 (S) 19.9.78 (9)

>1979 (M) 19.4.79 (4)

>1982 (M) 2.4.82 (7)

>1989 (M) 13.4.89 (9)

>1989 (S) 13.7.89 (11) [Willy Anthony Waters conducted last 8 perf's.; total 19]

Mozart (3)

The Magic Flute:

>1968 (M) 9.4.68 (6)

>1968 (S) 12.6.68 (5) [Feist and Reid conducted the 3 final perf's.; total 8]

>1968 (C) 27.2.68 (3)

The abduction from the Seraglio:

>1976 (S) 22.6.76 (10) [Douglas Gamley conducted the second run of perfs.]

>1980 (M) 13.5.80 (6)

Don Giovanni:

>1978 (M) 6.5.78 (8)

>1978 (N)1.6.78 (3) Newcastle Civic Theatre

Wagner (8)

Tannhäuser:

>　1968 (C) 24.2.68 (2)
>
>　1968 (A) 7.3.68 (7)
>
>　1968 (M) 5.4.68 (4)
>
>　1968 (B) 21.5.68 (6).
>
>　1968 (S2) 14.6.68 (4) [Reid and Feist conducted the last 4 perfs.; 8 total]

Der fliegende Holländer:

>　1977 (S) 31.8.77 (8) [Later perf's. conducted by George Posell]
>
>　1978 (S) 27.1.78 (1)
>
>　1978 (M) 30.3.78 (8)

Lohengrin:

>　1990 (S) 1.10.90 (8)

Das Rheingold:

>　1984 (S) 23.6.84 (10)

Die Walküre:

>　1983 (S) 4.10.83 (8)
>
>　1984 (S) 21.2.84 (4)
>
>　1985 (M) 16.3.85 (5)
>
>　1985 (S) 19.2.85 (4)

Tristan und Isolde:

>　1990 (M) 17.4.90 (6)
>
>　1993 (S) 9.2.93 (6)
>
>　1993 (M) 8.4.93 (5)

Die Meistersinger von Nürnberg:

>　1994 (M) 9.4.94 (5)

Parsifal:

>　1977 (S) 2.4.77 (1)

Beethoven (1)

Fidelio:

> 1977 (M) 22.3.77 (9)
>
> 1979 (S) 13.1.79 (8)

Others (4)

Janáček: The Cunning Little Vixen

> 1976 (M) 17.3.76 (8)
>
> 1976 (S) 16.6.76 (ca. 8) [Georg Tintner took over the later perf's. The run totalled 15 perfs.]

Cherubini: Médée

> 1987 (S) 6.2.87 (8)

Tchaikovsky: Eugene Onegin

> 1986 (S) 19.7.86 (7)

Massenet: Werther

> 1989 (S) 10.6.89 (8)
>
> 1989 (M) 19.3.90 (5)

Appendix 4

Cillario Disc–/Filmography compiled and introduced

by Brian Castles-Onion

Cillario's Views on Commercial Recordings:

[On being asked if commercial recordings are 'too perfect']:

> That's the very thing which makes commercial records so terrible. I did many, and I think that this system that uses scissors is really immoral. I remember that I was given an advance copy of one and I gave the copy to my dentist in New York! The dentist is someone who makes us suffer, so now he will suffer![950]

> I have been asked what I consider my best records, and you'll be surprised but I feel that my best records are the ones I didn't get to correct. They are the pirate records. They are taken from live performances with perhaps some mistakes, but there is a line that doesn't exist in the others.[951]

Brian Castles-Onion has been a member of the music staff of Opera Australia for over three decades and is a regular conductor with the company as well as a coach and accompanist. He is a dedicated historian, researcher, and collector of recordings and ephemera related to the world of opera. He is a public speaker and author who has produced a series of CD's (released on the Desirée label) which showcase the leading Australian opera singers of the post-war era.

---

[950] Cillario and Duffie, *Interview,* 1982.
[951] Ibid.

Carlo Felice Cillario Remembered

The Australian operatic landscape experienced a welcome infusion of the Italian tradition in the late 1960s when Maestro Carlo Felice Cillario arrived in the country. There had been a string of tours of visiting Italian companies since the middle of the 19th century, culminating in the Italian Grand Opera Seasons of 1928, 1932, 1948 and 1955. While the casts for those tours featured some celebrity names onstage, on the podium were what are commonly known as 'house' conductors. The resident conductors working in Australia were mostly of English and German heritage and their standard repertoire and musical approach to it reflected that background.

It was a boon for Australia that Cillario's career in this country lasted 35 years. He returned every year, except between 1971 and 1974, to lead a considerable number of productions annually. His commitment to the development of opera in Australia was both extensive and profound. He was likeable yet demanding. His rehearsal personality was infectious and, on occasion, annoying. He could be playfully mischievous and seemed to enjoy being the 'quirky' conductor. Every musician and singer who worked under his baton has a 'Cillario' anecdote, some of which would find him in trouble today. Fortunately, he lived in an era when his manner was accepted – and encouraged.

His approach to a musical score was a revelation to those who worked with him in Australia. He created theatre in the orchestral sound itself. Singers might have questioned his guidance in rehearsal, but they never doubted his 'old school' knowledge of a piece. His reading of a score revealed the works of Verdi and Puccini as naturally organic. This also applied to his conducting of operas by Wagner, Janáček and Mozart. He was a natural storyteller on the podium. Cillario's rare excursions into the French repertoire in Australia told a similar story. His *Werther*, performed in French (he had previously conducted a production sung in Italian in 1959) was as faithful to Massenet as his *La Cenerentola* was to Rossini. But it was his readings of the Italian repertoire that made him peerless in Australia. Numerous performances of *Tosca* (which he claimed to hate because the plot was so brutal), *La bohème*, *La fanciulla del West*, *Madama Butterfly*, *Rigoletto*, *Otello* and *La traviata* clearly displayed his hallmark traits. To this day, no other conductor working in Australia has captured the essence of *La traviata*. He never just conducted the music: he took the audience on a musical journey, telling the story through the rhythms of the sung language. He did the same with his readings of *La bohème* and *Tosca*.

I began my operatic career as a member of the music staff of Opera Australia and I was fortunate to work under his guidance. I asked to spend time with him to learn *La bohème*, *Tosca* and *Médée* and he immediately took me under his wing. His personal orchestral score of *La bohème*, several decades old and well worn, contained listings of his early casts. The first page included Renata Tebaldi and Victoria de los Ángeles alternating as Mimì and, I think, the production was in Barcelona. He related the story that, as de los Ángeles was an audience favourite, they brought doves to throw on stage at her curtain call. I asked if the birds were alive – as they would surely coo during the performance and fly around the auditorium – or dead – which would not be an appropriate display of appreciation. Carlo avoided answering …

I took him my vocal score of Cherubini's *Medea* as I was about to play rehearsals of a new production with Opera Australia. The score was in the 'accepted' Italian translation. Accepted by all except Carlo, who threw my score against the wall of the rehearsal studio as the singing translation from the original French had been created by one of his own teachers, whom he despised. His outbursts of temperament were always surprising (though we quickly grew used to them) and often unnerving. For me, as well as most of my colleagues, he was an idol, a mentor and friend.

Carlo Felice Cillario was a man of the theatre who could take an audience on a journey like few other conductors of his generation. His only requirements for that journey were an orchestra, singers, and an audience. These ingredients combined in an immersive operatic experience. In the recording studio, however, one of those ingredients was missing: the audience. His studio recordings reveal a fine musician working with renowned singers. Without a live audience, however, the spark of theatre that was distinctively 'Cillario' is often absent. The earliest long-playing records on the Angelicum label are memorable mainly for the interesting repertoire – including rare works by Rossi, Leo, Perosi and Handel, and the first recording of Mozart's *Betulia Liberata*. Also dating from this period are two important first recordings of early Mozart operas – *Ascanio in Alba* (1959) and *Lucio Silla* (1961). These works were then quite rarely performed in the major opera houses of the time (they still are!), and the maestro's musical care and theatrical drive make these recordings worthwhile. In many of these recordings, the Coro Polifonico di Torino is coached by their excellent chorus master, Giulio Bertola. In these recordings, Cillario respects the composer, is truthful to the score but little more.

The 1964 recital of arias he conducted with Montserrat Caballé on Vergara is much more than competent, but the performances of individual arias rarely ignite. His two important 'Rarities' studio records, also with Montserrat Caballé, on RCA have become 'Desert Island Discs' for admirers of *bel canto* – as well as the myriad of fans of Caballé. The first, 'Rossini Rarities', recorded in 1968 with the RCA Italiana Opera Orchestra and Chorus, was musically prepared by the great American musicologist Randolph Mickelson. Cillario supports his singer at every moment but never leads. Two years later, the 'Donizetti Rarities' introduces lesser-known scenes by the composer. On this occasion, Cillario led the London Symphony Orchestra. As before, he is Caballé's faithful musical and artistic companion in the studio.

Notwithstanding the conductor's own misgivings over the recording (see p. 410–11), his most notable recorded collaboration with Caballé was the complete *Norma* made in 1973 for RCA. The supporting cast is excellent, and the only missing ingredient is a live audience, as a comparison with several live broadcast performances of the same opera from a similar period with the same singers will reveal. Cillario makes Bellini's score erupt like a volcano at climactic moments in the theatre. The two recital discs recorded in Sweden in 1975 display his feeling for the voices of the baritone (Håkan Hagegård) and mezzo soprano (Edith Thallaug) in standard repertoire. More interesting is the 1978 film soundtrack for the sublime Anna Moffo's second studio recording of *Lucia di Lammermoor*. Cillario brings a degree of dramatic licence not usually present in the recording studio.

Outside the studio, there are many live broadcast and 'pirate' recordings available either in official catalogues or in the lists of individual collectors. Without doubt, the most 'essential' Cillario recording of all is the celebrated *Tosca* from the Royal Opera in London with La Divina herself, Maria Callas: one of the great operatic performances of the 20th century. The stars were in perfect alignment in that production in London in 1964. This recording belongs in the collection of every home music library.

A lesser-known but nevertheless interesting *Tosca* was led by Cillario at the Met in New York, with Dorothy Kirsten in the title role opposite the familiar Scarpia of Tito Gobbi. The date is 7 April 1973. As recalled elsewhere in this volume, what makes this recording essential listening is the tension between Cillario in the pit and Franco Corelli onstage in the role of Cavaradossi. During the first scene of Act 3, he receives loud and long applause for 'E lucevan le stelle', but rather than stopping and waiting for the applause to fade, potentially leading to an encore of the aria, Cillario made an orchestral crescendo which led straight into Kirsten's return. Corelli stormed off the stage in disgust, before reluctantly returning to sing the remainder of the opera but, to make Cillario's task more difficult, he sings the most unexpected, unwritten, unrehearsed and unstylish rubati. Cillario, realising that he had upset the tenor, follows Corelli's idiosyncrasies at every musical turn. The recording captures this unusual and exciting moment in the theatre.

A 1966 TV broadcast from the Paris Salle Pleyel displays both Caballé and Cillario in top form. The conductor brings a Mediterranean warmth to the Granados aria and a masterly understanding of the Donizetti and Bellini scenes. The performance from both artists has a vibrancy which is missing in their studio collaborations. The 1959 *Werther* from Trieste unites Cillario with two exceptional singers, the Italian tenor Ferruccio Tagliavini and Turkish soprano Leyla Gencer. Sung in Italian, they vividly embody the emotions of Werther and Charlotte, supported and encouraged throughout by Cillario. He was adamant that one should be true to the composer (as Corelli discovered to his chagrin in that *Tosca*) but he also allowed the artist's personality to mould the phrases.

Cillario was in his element with operatic characters who projected 'real' human feelings. His reading of *La traviata* was organic rather than scholarly, drawing its detail and its energy at every stage from the text of the score. The central scene of the opera, the dialogue between Violetta and Giorgio Germont, becomes the finest stage-play under Cillario's direction, as the tempi emerge from the rhythm of the language. With Renata Scotto, Peter Glossop and Luciano Pavarotti at the Royal Opera in London in 1965, Verdi's score is again ideally realised. Two decades later, a TV broadcast from 1986 preserves Cillario directing a well-worn Australian production featuring the excellent Violetta of the Australian soprano, Joan Carden. Cillario's care for this score is evident in every bar.

Cillario's sense of operatic comedy was part of his character. I believe that Australia has never played host to a better conducted *Falstaff*. His lightness of touch (even once replacing a twig from a tree as his baton for the dress rehearsal) supported the humour in the text. The handful of live Rossini recordings also captures that light-footed comedy. A charming *Barbiere* from Teatro Colón in 1962 features Sesto Bruscantini, Luigi Alva and Victoria de los Ángeles. Two years later, from Chicago Lyric Opera, Teresa Berganza and Sesto Bruscantini feature in *La Cenerentola* with memorable charm. Equally notable is the *Barbiere* from Vienna in 1978, with Bernd Weikl, Francisco Araiza, Agnes Baltsa and Enrico Fissore heading a prestigious cast. These ensemble works show Cillario at his best. His readings sparkle through the precision of orchestral playing and the articulate delivery of the recitative.

Though Cillario has been particularly celebrated for his readings of Puccini and Verdi, he also displayed his expertise in other idioms. His early affection for Wagner developed through a friendship with the great Basque *Heldentenor*, Isidoro Fagoaga. Experienced live, Cillario's readings of *Tannhäuser, Die Walküre, Tristan und Isolde, Die Meistersinger von Nürnberg, Lohengrin* and *Parsifal* had a revelatory force. Where they survive, audio recordings confirm his authority in this repertoire.

Credit should go to the handful of anonymous collectors who attended performances with their recording devices concealed in airway bags and microphones discreetly hidden in their jacket lapels. Without their enthusiasm, the recorded legacy of Cillario would be much poorer. The long list of pirate recordings from his Australian performances is a testament to the conductor's affinity with the Australian opera scene. He was, it is fair to say, the most important player in the artistic growth of opera in Australia: a beloved friend, mentor, and idol to several generations of performers. His recorded legacy still influences and stimulates. We learn from the past, as did Cillario himself.

Brian Castles-Onion, June 2023

Cillario Disc-/Film-ography

Cillario's legacy is divided into studio and live recordings. Each reveals his artistry in different ways. Part 1 presents his discography of studio recordings, on a variety of labels, including Angelicum Records, RCA Victor Red Seal, Caprice Records and Ars Nova. His manner in the confines of the recording studio reveals him to be a musician of the highest calibre, attentive to the score, with an ear keenly focused on the singers, leading his forces with great care. The unbridled excitement he created in his live performances is not often in evidence in the studio. The recordings in Part 2 capture him in the presence of a live audience. Here, the score bristles with excitement and his brilliance as a musical risk-taker is frequently palpable. This is the Cillario who was so admired by his colleagues and his audiences.

Note: it has not been possible to date many of Cillario's studio recordings with reliable accuracy owing to the absence of supporting documentation. The dates given rely in many cases on the traceable release dates of the albums as first issued. The list of catalogue numbers is not intended to be exhaustive; in the case of Cillario's recordings with the Angelicum Orchestra of Milan, for example, the original release on the Angelicum's own label has proved elusive in several cases.

PART 1 – STUDIO RECORDINGS

1959 – **Mozart**

Le nozze di Figaro – Overture; Symphony No. 40 In G minor; *Eine kleine Nachtmusik*; Adagio and Fugue in C minor. Angelicum Orchestra. Audio Fidelity FCS 50035.

1959 – **Handel**

Concerto Grosso in D minor, Op.6 No.10; Concerto in B flat for Harp and Strings. Clelia Gatti Aldrovandi, Angelicum Orchestra. Audio Fidelity FCS 50031.

1959 – Ascanio in Alba (Mozart)

Anna Maria Rota, Emilia Cundari, Eugenia Ratti, Ilva Ligabue, Petre Munteanu. Polifonico Chorus of Turin and Angelicum Orchestra of Milan. RCA VICS-6126 (ZVRS-3586); Musical Heritage Society MHS 1755-56-57; Disques a Charlin SLC 8-9-10.

1960s – Judicum extremum, Felicitas beatorum, Lamentatio damnatorum (Carissimi)

Laura Londi, Lydia Marimpietri, Amilcare Blaffard, Teodoro Rovetta, Paolo Washington. Polifonico Chorus, Angelicum Orchestra. Angelicum LPA 5928; Musical Heritage Society MHS 1829.

1960s – Donna che in ciel, Salve regina (Handel)

Maria Manni Jottini. Polifonico Chorus, Angelicum Orchestra. Ars Nova VST 6134; Harmonia Mundi HMA 30535

1960 – Betulia Liberata (Mozart)

Emilia Cundari, Laura Londi, Adriana Lazzarini, Petre Munteanu, Paolo Washington. Polifonico Chorus, Angelicum Orchestra. Angelicum Records LPA 5918; Harmonia Mundi HM 30605/7; RCA Victrola VICS-6112

1960 – Giuseppe figlio do Giacobbe (Rossi)

Luciana Fumagalli, Pellegrina Pereno Rossi, Anna Maria Rota, Herbert Handt, Giorgio Tadeo. Polifonico Chorus, Angelicum Orchestra. Angelicum Records LPA 5914; Musical Heritage Society-MHS 1145.

1960 – La morte di Abele (Leo)

Emilia Cundari, Fernando Ferrari, Giuliana Matteini, Piero Montarsolo, Adriana Lazzerini. Polifonico Chorus, Angelicum Orchestra. Angelicum Records LPA 5912-13.

1960 – Aci, Galatea e Polifemo (Handel – excerpts)

Mariella Adani, Gabriella Carturan, Giorgio Tadeo. Angelicum Orchestra. Angelicum Records LPA 5907.

1961 – Lucio Silla (Mozart)

Fiorenza Cossotto, Anna Maria Rota, Rena Gary Falachi, Ferrando

Ferrari, Luigi Pontiggia. Polifonico Chorus, Angelicum Orchestra. RCA Victrola VICS-6117; Ars Nova C5S/149.

1961 – Transitus animae (Perosi)

Fiorenza Cossotto, Nicoletta Panni, Anna Maria Rota, Giuseppe Campora, Valerio Meucci, Teodoro Rovetta. Polifonico Chorus, Angelicum Orchestra. Angelicum Records LPA 5926; Music Guild Records M-43.

1960s – La risurrezione di Cristo (Perosi)

Nicoletta Panni, Anna Maria Rota, Giuseppe Campora, Teodoro Rovetta, Valerio Meucci. Polifonico Chorus, Angelicum Orchestra. Angelicum LPA 5915-6; Ars Nova C2S/142.

1962 – Feste romane (Respighi)

Romanian Radio Symphony Orchestra. Electrecord ECD 60.

1962 – Boléro (Ravel)

Romanian Radio Symphony Orchestra. Electrecord ECD-72; STM-ECE 01031.

1963 – Stabat mater (Rossini)

Marcella de Osma, Fiorenza Cossotto, Gianni Iaia, Ugo Trama. Polifonico Chorus, Angelicum Orchestra. Angelicum LPA 1805; Ars Nova VST 6142; Select CC-15.044.

1963 – Il natale del Redentore (Perosi)

Mirella Freni, Jeda Valtriani, Ortensia Beggiato, Giuseppe Nait, Claudio Strudthoff. Polifonico Chorus, Angelicum Orchestra. Musical Heritage Society MHS 871-3; Ars Nova C2S/144.

1964 – Montserrat Caballé: Opera Arias

Arias from *Otello*, *Un ballo in maschera*, *Anna Bolena*, *Louise* and *Tosca*. Orquesta Sinfonica de Barcelona. Vergara-781-I; RCA Red Seal LSC-3209; SER-5598.

1964 – S. Giovanni Battista (Stradella)

Adriana Lazzarini, Giogio Tadeo, Zimra Ornatt, Elena Barcis, Alfredo Nobile. Polifonico Chorus, Angelicum Orchestra. Musical Heritage Society MHS 1178.

1965 – Nisi Dominus, Magnificat (Vivaldi)

Angela Vercelli, Emilia Cundari, Anna Maria Rota. Polifonico Chorus, Angelicum Orchestra. Angelicum Records LPA 5917.

1967 – Orfeo (Monteverdi - highlights)

Andrée Aubéry-Lucchini, Giuseppe Nait, Claudio Strudthoff, Paolo Pedani, Plinio Clabassi. Angelicum Orchestra. Angelicum STA 8998.

1968 – Romanian Dances, and Concertino in Classical Style, Op. 3 (Lipatti)

Felicja Blumental. Orchestra Filarmonica di Milano. Auditorium Records AUD 102; Everest-6166; GTA Records CLA-LP 52003.

1968 – Montserrat Caballé: Rossini Rarities

Montserrat Caballé. RCA Italiana Opera Orchestra and Chorus. RCA Victor Red Seal LSC 3015-B, SB 6771,644.514 A.

1970 – Les pêcheurs de perles (Bizet)

Alfredo Kraus, Adriana Maliponte, Sesto Bruscantini, Antonio Campo. Orquesta del Gran Teatro Liceu De Barcelona. Carillon 93012.

1970 – Montserrat Caballé: Donizetti Rarities

Arias from *Torquato Tasso, Gemma Di Vergy, Belisario, Parisina*. Montserrat Caballé. London Symphony Orchestra. RCA Red Seal SER 5591 (LSC-3164) (651 027).

1972 – Norma (Bellini)

Montserrat Caballé, Fiorenza Cossotto, Plácido Domingo, Ruggero Raimondi. London Philharmonic Orchestra, Ambrosian Chorus. RCA Red Seal SER 5658-59-60 (LSC 6202/1-3).

1975 – Håkan Hagegård, baritone

Arias by Leoncavallo, Gounod, Verdi, Werle, Tchaikovsky, Mozart and Wagner. Royal Swedish Orchestra. Caprice Records RIKS LP 62, CAP 1026.

1975 – Edith Thallaug, mezzo-soprano

Arias and songs by Tchaikovsky, de Falla, Verdi and Rossini (tracks 1-4 of album only with Cillario conducting). Royal Swedish Orchestra. Caprice Records CAP 1107.

1985 – Sylvia Lindenstrand sings Mozart

Arias from *La clemenza di Tito, Le nozze di Figaro, Don Giovanni, Ch'io mi scordi di te? Exultate, Jubilate*. Chamber Orchestra of The National Museum, Stockholm. Polar POLS 397.

PART 2 – LIVE/IN HOUSE RECORDINGS

Note: Catalogue numbers are listed where it has been possible to trace them, though (as is the case with the studio recordings) most of them have long been deleted. Many of these recordings are available online, on streaming services such as YouTube. Some ingenuity may be required to locate them, using a variety of relevant search terms, but the data supplied should yield satisfactory results for the determined listener.

1957 – Manni Jottini and Lauri-Volpi in Concert

11 February 1957. Arias by Verdi and Puccini. Orchestra del Maggio Musicale Fiorentino. Fonit Cetra LMR 5021.

1959 – Werther

20 January 1959. Teatro Verdi di Trieste. Ferruccio Tagliavini, Leyla Gencer, Giuliana Tavolaccini, Mario Borriello, Vito Susca. Opera D'Oro 1234; Walhall WLCD 0259.

1960 – La Gioconda

28 July 1960. Teatro Colón. Lucille Udovick, Flaviano Labo, Aldo Protti, Mignon Dunn, Norman Scott, Luisa Bartoletti, Tulio Gagliardo, Italo Pasini, Guerrino Boschetti, José Crea. The Opera Lovers GIOC 196001, Bongiovanni.

1962 – Tosca

Teatro Colón. Régine Crespin, Gianni Raimondi, Giuseppe Taddei, Eduardo Ferracani, Juan Zanin. Ornamenti FE 114.

1962 – **Il barbiere di Siviglia** (film)

Teatro Colón. Sesto Bruscantini, Luigi Alva, Victoria de los Ángeles, Fernando Corena, Miroslav Čangalović. Sol 90 (Barcelona); Laser Disc Chile 19307.

1962 – **L'elisir d'amore**

June 1962. Glyndebourne Festival Opera. Mirella Freni, Luigi Alva, Emily Marie, Enzo Sordello, Sesto Bruscantini. Royal Philharmonic Orchestra.

1964 – **La favorita**

16 October 1964. Chicago Lyric Opera. Sesto Bruscantini, Fiorenza Cossotto, Alfredo Kraus, Ivo Vinco, Jean Deis, Luisa de Sett. Omega Opera Archive 2715.

1964 – **Tosca**

January 1964. Royal Opera, London. Maria Callas, Renato Cioni, Tito Gobbi. EMI Classics 7243 5 62675 2 7.

1964 – **Tosca** (Act 2, film)

9 February1964. Royal Opera, London. Maria Callas, Renato Cioni, Tito Gobbi. EMI DVA 4 92851 9.

1964 – **I pescatori de perle** (Bizet)

9 December 1964. Gran Teatro del Liceu, Barcelona. Alfredo Kraus, Maria Luisa Cioni, Jose Simorra.

1964 – **La Cenerentola**

21 November 1964. Chicago Lyric Opera. Teresa Berganza, Luisa de Sett, Elizabeth Mannion, Renzo Casellato, Sesto Bruscantini, Giorgio Tadeo, Renato Cesari.

1965 – **La traviata**

5 March 1965. Royal Opera, London. Renata Scotto, Luciano Pavarotti, Peter Glossop. GOP Dischi 023/4.

1965 – **La bohème**

22 October 1965. Lyric Opera of Chicago. Mirella Freni, Franco Corelli, Sesto Bruscantini, Edith Martelli, Raffaele Arié, Renato Cesari. Legendary Recordings LR 195-2.

1965 – **Roberto Devereux**

16 December 1965. American Opera Society, Carnegie Hall, New York. Montserrat Caballé, Walter Alberti, Lili Chookasian, Juan Oncina, Mauro Lampi, Ted Lambrinos. Penzance Records PR 28.

1965 – **La bohème**

Chicago Lyric Opera. Franco Corelli, Sesto Bruscantini, Raffaele Ariè, Mirella Freni, Edith Martelli, Renato Cesari. Legendary recordings LR 195-2.

1966 – **Giovanna d'Arco**

1 March 1966. American Opera Society. Carnegie Hall, New York. Teresa Stratas, Angelo Mori, Sherrill Milnes, Don Yule. Premiere Opera CDNO 1385-2.

1966 – **Il trovatore**

13 January 1966. Gran Teatro del Liceu, Barcelona. Umberto Borso, Fedora Barbieri, Montserrat Caballé, Kostas Paskalis. Opera Depot OD 11336-2.

1966 – **Carmen**

11 October 1966. Palacio de Bellas Artes, Mexico City. Elena Cernei, Pedro Lavirgen, Norman Treigle, Gilda Cruz-Romo, Alberto Hammin, Marco A. Saldana, Graciela Saavedra, Dora de la Pena, Federico Davia.

1966 – **Montserrat Caballé at the Paris Salle Pleyel** (film)

Arias from *Goyescas* (Grandos), *Roberto Devereux* and *Anna Bolena* (Donizetti), *Il Pirata* (Bellini). Orchestre Philharmonique de l'ORTF.

1967 – **Manon**

7 May 1967. Orchestra and Chorus del Teatro de la Zarzuela, Madrid. Montserrat Caballé, Alfredo Kraus, Manuel Ausensi, Silvano Pagliuca.

1967 – **Norma**

November 1967. American Opera Society. Carnegie Hall, New York. Elena Suliotis, Nancy Tatum, Gianfranco Cecchele, Luigi Roni, Joyce Mathis, Paul Franke. Celestial Audio CA 312. Opera Depot OD 11263-2

1967 – L'elisir d'amore

28 May 1967 (?). Glyndebourne Festival Opera. London Philharmonic Orchestra and Glyndebourne Festival Chorus. Adriana Maliponte, Ugo Benelli, Carlo Badioli, Zsolt Bende, Sheila Armstrong. Omega Opera Archive 4077.

1967 – Maria Stuarda

6 December 1967. American Opera Society. Carnegie Hall, New York. Montserrat Caballé, Shirley Verrett, Eduardo Giménez, Rolf Bottcher. Celestial Audio CA 253.

1967 – Otello

January 1967. Gran Teatro del Liceu, Barcelona. Nikola Nikolov, Orietta Moscucci, Louis Quilico. House of Opera CDBB 868.

1968 – Roberto Devereux

November 1986. Gran Teatro del Liceu, Barcelona. Montserrat Caballé, Piero Cappuccilli, Bianca Berini, Bernabé Marti. The Opera Lovers ROB 196801.

1968 – Nabucco

11 October 1968. American Opera Society. Carnegie Hall, New York. Kostas Paskalis, Daniele Barioni, Luigi Roni, Elena Suliotis.

1969 – Macbeth

14 October 1969. Palacio de las Bellas Artes, Mexico City. Giampietro Mastromei, Elena Suliotis, Arnold Voketatis, David Portilla, Guillermina Higareda, Rogelio Vargas.

1969 – Manon

18 September 1969. Palacio de las Bellas Artes, Mexico City. Beverly Sills, Alain Vanzo, Roberto Bañuelas, Joshua Hecht, Guillermina Higareda, Hortensia Cervantes, Guadalupe Góngora. Omega Opera Archive 2695.

1969 – La Gioconda

30 November 1969. Theatre Royal Drury Lane, London. Elena Suliotis, Bernabé Martì, Mignon Dunn, Sherrill Milnes, Franco Ventriglia, Elizabeth Bainbridge.

1969 – **Lo frate 'nnamorato** (Pergolesi)

4 September 1969. Franco Bonisolli, Francina Girones, Alfredo Mariotti, Rosina Cavicchioli, Mario Basiola, Sally Taylor Bonisolli, Agostino Lazzari, Cecilia Fusco. Orchestra 'Alessandro Scarlatti' of RAI, Naples. Foyer Live Recording CF 2026.

1970 – **Norma**

11 January 1970. Gran Teatro del Liceu, Barcelona. Montserrat Caballé, Fiorenza Cossotto, Bruno Prevedi, Ivo Vinco, Maria Teresa Batille, José Carreras. Melodram CDM 27089.

1970 – **Il pirata**

December 1970. Gran Teatro del Liceu, Barcelona. Montserrat Caballé, Montserrat Aparici, Bernabé Marti, Vincenzo Sardinero, Carlo Del Bosco.

1970 – **Falstaff** (film)

April 1970, Palais Garnier, Paris. Opéra de Paris. Tito Gobbi, Gérard Dunan, Matteo Manuguerra, Jacques Pottier, Robert Andreozzi, Gérard Chapuis, Andrea Guiot, Christiane Eda-Pierre, Marie-Luce Bellary, Fedora Barbieri. Premiere Opera Ltd. DVD 2152.

1970 – **Les pêcheurs de perles**

Gran Teatro del Liceu, Barcelona. Adriana Maliponte, Alfredo Kraus, Sesto Bruscantini, Antonio Campó. Bongiovani GB 516-517.

1971 – **Lucia di Lammermoor** (film)

Anna Moffo, Lajos Kozma, Paolo Washington, Giulio Fioravanti, Pietro Di Vietri. RAI Chorus, Rome Symphony Orchestra. VAI DVD 4211.

1971 – **La sonnambula**

Royal Opera, London. Renata Scotto, Stuart Burrowes, Forbes Robinson, Jill Gomez, George Macpherson, David Lennox, Heather Begg. Myto 2MCD 946115.

1971 – **Maria Stuarda**

13 April 1971. Teatro alla Scala, Milano. Montserrat Caballé, Shirley Verrett, Ottavio Garaventa, Raffaele Arié, Giulio Fioravanti. Opera d'Oro 1163; Myto 2 MCD 911 37.

1971 – **La bohème**

January 1971. Gran Teatro del Liceu, Barcelona. Montserrat Caballé, Nancy Stokes, Luciano Pavarotti, Vincenzo Sardinero, Carlo Del Bosco. Lyric Distribution Inc. ALD 2842.

1971 – **Il trovatore**

26 October 1971. San Francisco Opera. Plácido Domingo, Margarita Lilowa, Leontyne Price, Raymond Wolansky, Richard Mundt. Premiere Opera Ltd. CDNO 2833-2.

1971 – **Il trovatore**

29 (?) October 1971. San Francisco Opera. [See also previous entry]. James King, Leontyne Price, Margarita Lilowa, Raymond Wolansky, Raymond Michalski. Premier Opera Ltd. CDNO 1509-2.

1971 – **Edgar**

RAI Turin. Mietta Sighele, Veriano Luchetti, Biancamaria Casoni, Renzo Scorsoni, Alfredo Collela. Unique Opera Records UORC-100; Opera d'Oro OPD 1449.

1971 – **Anna Bolena**

26 November 1971. Gran Teatro del Liceu, Barcelona. Vasso Papanto-niou, Maurizio Mazzieri, Bianca Berini, Beniamino Prior, Enid Hartle. Legend 60682/60692/60702; The Opera Lovers ANN 197101.

1972 – **Caterina Cornaro**

7 October 1972. Royal Opera, London. Montserrat Caballé, José Car-reras, Lorenzo Saccomani, Enrique Serra. Opera D'Oro OPD-1266.

1972 – **Caterina Cornaro**

28 May 1972. Teatro San Carlo di Napoli. Leyla Gencer, Giacomo Aragall, Renato Bruson, Plinio Clabassi, Fernandino Jacopucci, Eva Ruta, Claudio Terni. Myto 2 MCD 921.53.

1972 – **Montserrat Caballé in concert**

15 May 1972. Orchestre de l'Opéra de Paris, Palais Garnier. Arias from *Roberto Devereux* (Donizetti), *Adelson e Salvini* (Bellini), *La donna del lago* (Rossini), *Otello* (Verdi) and *La traviata* (Caballé fainted while singing 'Addio del passato').

1972 – La sonnambula

October or November 1972. Metropolitan Opera, New York. Renata Scotto, Nicolai Gedda, Bonaldo Giaiotti, Loretta Di Franco, Richard Best. Living Stage LS 1106.

1972 – La traviata

28 June 1972. Royal Opera, London. Montserrat Caballé, Nicolai Gedda, Victor Braun, Heather Begg, Elizabeth Bainbridge, John Dobson, Richard Van Allan, George Macpherson, Eric Garrett.

1972 – Caterina Cornaro

Live, Royal Festival Hall, London. 10 July 1972. Montserrat Caballé, José Carreras, Enric Serra, Lorenzo Saccomani, Maurizio Mazzieri, Neville Williams, Anne Edwards. London Symphony Orchestra and Chorus. Opera D'Oro OPD-1266; Foyer Live Recording 2-CF 2048.

1972 – Caterina Cornaro

Live, 28 May 1972. Teatro San Carlo, Naples. Leyla Gencer, Giacomo Aragall, Luigi Risani, Renato Bruson. MYTO 921.53.

1972 – Il trovatore (in Swedish)

Royal Swedish Opera. Rolf Björling, Margareta Hallin, Sylvia Lindenstrand, Björn Asker. Lyssna 8.

1973 – Norma

17 February 1973. Metropolitan Opera, New York. Montserrat Caballé, Fiorenza Cossotto, Carlo Cossutta, Giorgio Tozzi. Bensar BRO 123084; MetOpera.

1973 – Tosca

7 April 1973. Metropolitan Opera, New York. Dorothy Kirsten, Franco Corelli, Tito Gobbi.

1973 – La favorita

7 September 1973. San Francisco Opera House. Renato Bruson, Maria Luisa Nave, Luciano Pavarotti, Bonaldo Giaiotti, James Atherton, Ariel Bybee. Frequenz 043 507.

1973 – I Lombardi

28 December 1973. Teatro Regio di Parma. Renata Scotto, José

Carreras, Maurizio Mazzieri, Bernardino Trotta, Anna Maria Borelli, Franco Federici, Bruno Grella, Rina Pallini, Mario Carlin.

1973 – Il trovatore

17 March 1973. Metropolitan Opera, New York. Plácido Domingo, Montserrat Caballé, Fiorenza Cossotto, Robert Merrill, Ivo Vinco. Celestial Audio CA 440; MetOpera.

1973 – Il trovatore

11 April 1973. Metropolitan Opera, New York. Plácido Domingo, Montserrat Caballé, Viorica Cortez, Robert Merrill, Paul Plishka, Carlotta Ordassy, Nico Castel, Edward Ghazal, Fawayne Murphy. Celestial Audio CA 564.

1974 – Il trovatore

24 July 1974. Teatro Colón. Elinor Ross, Irina Arkhipova, Flaviano Labo, Matteo Manuguerra, Nino Meneghetti. Premiere Opera Ltd. CDNO 1107-2.

1975 – Norma

31 October 1975. San Francisco Opera House. Cristina Deutekom, Tatiana Troyanos, Roberto Merolla, Clifford Grant, Janice Felty, Gary Burgess. Gala GL 100 548.

1975 – L'elisir d'amore

10 October 1975. San Francisco Opera House. Judith Blegen, José Carreras, Paolo Montarsolo, Ingvar Wixell, Pamela South.

1976 – Ernani

23 October 1976. L'Opéra de Marseille. Ghena Dimitrova, Nunzio Todisco, Franco Bordoni, Georg Papas.

1976 – Leontyne Price in Concert

Paris, Radio France. Arias from Così fan tutte, Il trovatore, Madama Butterfly, L'enfant prodigue, La forza del destino, Tosca, Manon Lescaut.

1977 – La bohème

8 June 1977. Deutsche Oper Berlin. Pilar Lorengar, Giorgio Merighi,

Ingvar Wixell, Catherine Gayer, José van Dam, Barry McDaniel, Klaus Lang, Leopold Clam, Volker Horn.

1978 – Il barbiere di Siviglia

Wiener Staatsoper. Bernd Weikl, Francisco Araiza, Agnes Baltsa, Enrico Fissore, Tugomir Franc, Cseslawa Slania.   Legendary Recordings LR 107-3.

1979 – Norma (Excerpts from Act 3)

30 October 1979. Wiener Staatsoper. Grace Bumbry, Gianfranco Cecchele, Gianfranco Caserini.

1980 – Il trovatore

17 September 1980. Teatro Municipal de Santiago (Chile). Ermanno Mauro, Cristina Deutekom, Franco Bordoni, Marta Rose, Mario Rinaudo, Cecilia Frigerio, Gabriel Sierra, Alfonso Gonzalez.

1980 – Il trovatore

19 September 1980. Teatro Municipal de Santiago. [see previous listing, same cast].

1982 – I pagliacci

3 November 1982. Chicago Lyric Opera. Jon Vickers, Josephine Barstow, Cornell MacNeil, David Gordon, Lenus Carlson. Lyric Distribution ALD 1084.

1982 – Le Voix humaine

3 November 1982. Lyric Opera of Chicago. Josephine Barstow. [In English – this and the previous listing formed a double bill].

1982 – La Vestale

December or January 1982. Gran Teatro del Liceu. Montserrat Caballé (debut in role), Bruna Baglioni, Nunzio Todisco, Vincenzo Sardinero, Walter Monachesi, Ramón Gajas, Jesús Castillón. Premiere Disc Ltd. CDNO 4992; Legendary Recordings LR 201-3.

1983 – Il fanatico burlato (Cimarosa – film)

Dröttningholm Festival. Dröttningholm Theatre, Sweden. Björn Anker, Magnus Linden, Francis Egerton, Stefan Dahlberg, Ulla Severin, Ursula Reinhardt-Kiss. House of Opera DVDCC 523.

1983 – **Don Carlo** (4-act version)

17 December 1983. Bayerische Staatsoper, Munich. Giorgio Lamberti, Evgeny Nesterenko, Wolfgang Brendel, Karl Helm, Karl Christian Kohn, Margaret Price, Agnes Baltsa, Marianne Seibel, Friedrich Lenz, Hermann Sapell, Julie Kaufmann. Audio Encyclopedia AE 204; House of Opera CDBB 645.

1984 – **Médée** (Cherubini)

14 April 1984. The Royal Opera, Stockholm. Margareta Hallin, Tord Slättergård, Iwa Sörenson, Jerker Arvidson, Inger Blom.

1984 – **Tosca**

20 September 1984. Royal Swedish Opera, Stockholm. Laila Andersson-Palme, Rolf Björling, Erik Sædén, Lars Kullenbo, Lars Bergström, Rudolf Dassie, Anders Bergström, Bo Lundborg, Sten Wahlund. Sterling CDA1837.

1988 – **Gianni di Parigi**

September 1988. Bergamo Festival. Luciana Serra, Giuseppe Morino, Angelo Romero, Elena Zilio, Enrico Fissore, Silvana Manga. Orchestra and Chorus of RAI, Milan. Nuova Era 6752-53.

1988 – **Il fanatico burlato** (Cimarosa)

20 November 1988. Orchestra Sinfonica di Sanremo. Giancarlo Ceccarini, Antonio Marani, Mario Bolognesi, Enrico Cossutta, Daniela Uccello, Gabriella Morigi. Akademia AK 107; Agora AG 064.2.

1992 – **I pagliacci**

July 1992. Teatro Colón.Vladimir Popov, Yoko Watanabe, Piero Cappuccilli, Ricardo Cassinelli, Luis Gaeta. Live Opera 09295.

1993 – **Messa di Requiem** (Verdi)

28 October 1993. The Estonian Opera Theatre Orchestra and Chorus, Talinn. Soloists: Irena Milkeviciute, Irina Arkhipova, Ivo Kuusk, Mati Palm.

1995 – **Medea** (Cherubini)

2 June 1995. Megaron Concert Hall, Athens. Grace Bumbry, Vinson Cole, Jenny Drivala, Christophoros Stamboglis, Alexandra Papadjakou.

Irma Gonzalez – compilation

Arias and scenes from *Turandot* and *Otello* with Jon Vickers and Dora de la Pena. Palacio de Bellas Artes Orchestra. Urtext JBCC189-190.

PART 3 – AUSTRALIAN PERFORMANCES

This section lists extant recordings of live performances in Australia over the full three and a half decades of Cillario's career. From the 1960s onwards, it was common for certain opera aficionados, armed with hidden microphones in their coat lapels (or, in one instance, with a reel-to-reel tape recorder in an airline bag, holding the microphone in the aisle), to make 'pirate' or 'bootleg' recordings, not necessarily for commercial gain, and many of Cillario's performances have been preserved in this way. Some of these recordings have been released on various mediums – LP, tape, cassette, CD, digital files – but many other have remained in private collections for decades.

With a little searching, many performances can be found in online catalogues as well as on YouTube. Due to the regularity of his contracts in Australia, an enormous number of his performances were captured (in sound only) from the auditorium. Two well-known collectors used to sit in opposite loge seats in the Opera Theatre of the Sydney Opera House which afforded the privacy to record with close-up superior sound. Though Opera Australia holds an extensive archive of archival audio and audio-visual material (including conductor-view live recordings filmed from the orchestral pit), it is doubtful that they will follow in the footsteps of other companies, who have begun to make some of Cillario's performances held in their archives commercially available. In the meantime, it is well worth hearing some of these 'private' recordings to experience what made Cillario such a formidable artist to his colleagues, peers and audiences.

1968 – Tosca

20 March 1968. Her Majesty's Theatre. Adelaide Festival of the Arts. Marie Collier, Donald Smith, Tito Gobbi, Elizabethan Trust Orchestra. For full cast see FN 51. Premiere Opera Ltd. 1406-2.

1970 – **Otello**

8 August 1970. Capitol Theatre, Sydney. Umberto Borso, John Shaw, Reginald Byers, Rosemary Gordon. For full cast see FN 155.

1975 – **Aida**

6 February 1975. Concert Hall, the Sydney Opera House. Elizabeth Fretwell, Reginald Byers, Lauris Elms, Raymond Myers, Donald Shanks, Alan Light.

1975 – **Aida**

15 February 1975. Concert Hall, the Sydney Opera House. Marilyn Richardson, Donald Smith, Elisabeth Connell, John Shaw, Donald Shanks, Alan Light. Celestial Audio CA 001.

1975 – **Rigoletto**

18 August 1975. Sydney Opera House. For cast see FN 236.

1975 – **L'elisir d'amore**

Sydney Opera House, 21 August 1975. Eilene Hannan, Henri Wilden, Ronald Maconaghie, Donald Shanks, Mary Hayman. Celestial Audio CA 192.

1975 – **L'elisir d'amore**

Sydney Opera House, 7 September 1975. Eilene Hannan, Anson Austin, John Pringle, Donald Shanks.

1975 – **Rigoletto**

Sydney Opera House, 26 July & 18 August 1975 [composite recording]. Peter Glossop, Glenys Fowles, Reginald Byers, Joseph Grunfelder, Jacqueline Kensett-Smith, Lamberto Furlan, Luciano Borghi, Grant Dickson, Robert Eddie, Gaye McFarlane, Robin Lawlor, Janice Hill, John Durham.

1976 – **Aida**

13 January 1976. Concert Hall, Sydney Opera House. Helena Döse, Donald Smith, Heather Begg, John Shaw, Donald Shanks, Alan Light.

1976 – Aida

16 February 1976. Concert Hall, the Sydney Opera House. Elizabeth Fretwell, Donald Smith, Margreta Elkins, Robert Allman, Donald Shanks, Alan Light.

1977 – Aida (Excerpts)

13 January 1977. Telecast ATN 7, 28 January 1977. Concert Hall, Sydney Opera House, Marilyn Richardson, Ronald Dowd, Margreta Elkins, Robert Allman, Grant Dickson, Alan Light.

1977 – Aida

21 January 1977. Concert Hall, Sydney Opera House. Orianna Santunione, Reginald Byers, Lauris Elms, John Shaw, Grant Dickson, Alan Light.

1977 – Madama Butterfly

7 February 1977. Sydney Opera House. Leona Mitchell, Lesley Stender, Lamberto Furlan, Ronald Maconaghie, Rosemary Gunn, Gordon Wilcock, Gregory Yurisich, Joseph Grunfelder, Robert Eddie.

1977 – Madama Butterfly

10 February 1977. Sydney Opera House. Leona Mitchell, Robin Donald, John Pringle, Lesley Stender, Gordon Wilcock, Joseph Grunfelder, Gregory Yurisich, Robert Eddie, Trevor Brown, Rosemary Gunn.

1977 – Madama Butterfly

14 February 1977. Sydney Opera House. Leona Mitchell, Robin Donald, John Pringle, Jennifer Bermingham, Gordon Wilcock, Joseph Grunfelder, Pieter van der Stolk, Robert Eddie, Trevor Brown, Rosemary Gunn.

1977 – Parsifal

2 April 1977. Concert Hall, Sydney Opera House (concert performance). Ronald Dowd, John Shaw, Lone Koppel-Winther, Donald Shanks, Reid Bunger, Alan Light. For full cast see FN 276. Sydney Symphony Orchestra and Sydney Philharmonia Choirs.

1977 – Tosca

5 February 1977. Sydney Opera House. Orianna Santunione, Reginald Byers, John Shaw. For full cast see FN 263.

1977 – **Macbeth**

12 September 1977. Sydney Opera House. John Shaw, Elizabeth Connell, Clifford Grant, Reginald Byers. For full cast see FN 265.

1978 – **Madama Butterfly**

7 October 1978. Sydney Opera House. Joan Carden, Lamberto Furlan, Robert Allman, Jennifer Bermingham. For full cast list see FN 328.

1978 – **Cavalleria rusticana**

14 October 1978. Sydney Opera House. Elizabeth Fretwell, Robin Donald, Neville Wilkie, Rosina Raisbeck. For full cast see FN 306.

1979 – **Fidelio**

Sydney Opera House Concert Hall, 31 January 1979. Marilyn Richardson, Donald Smith, John Shaw, Donald Shanks. For full cast list see FN 335.

1979 – **La fanciulla del West**

16 June 1979. Sydney Opera House. Marilyn Zschau, John Shaw, Donald Smith. For full cast see FN 342.

1979 – **Falstaff**

4 August 1979. Sydney Opera House. Ronald Maconaghie, Robert Allman, Nance Grant, Heather Begg. For full cast see FN 352. Celestial Audio CA 053.

1980 – **Manon Lescaut**

5 July 1980. Sydney Opera House. Leona Mitchell, Lamberto Furlan, Pieter van der Stolk, Alan Light, Rosemary Gunn, Paul Ferris, Robert Gard.

1981 – **Aida** (Act 2 only)

National Sports Stadium, Canberra. 1981. ABC Telecast. For cast see FN 409. Orchestra and Chorus of the Canberra Opera Company.

1981 – **Otello**

31 January 1981, Concert Hall, Sydney Opera House. Angelo Marenzi,

Joan Sutherland, John Shaw, Paul Ferris, Robin Donald, Clifford Grant, Bruce Martin, Heather Begg. Celestial Audio CA 074. House of Opera CDBB 875.

1981 – La bohème

27 February 1981. Sydney Opera House. Anson Austin, Glenys Fowles, Robert Allman, Rhonda Bruce, Donald Shanks, Raymond Myers. For full cast see FN 373.

1981 – Tosca

16 June 1981. Sydney Opera House. Marilyn Zschau, Lamberto Furlan, John Shaw. For full cast see FN 381.

1981 – Messa di Requiem (Verdi)

19 November 1981. Sydney Opera House. Joan Carden, Anthony Benfell, Lauris Elms, Noel Mangin. Sydney Philharmonia Choir and Australian Chamber Orchestra.

1982 – Cavalleria rusticana

April 1982. Princess Theatre, Melbourne. Rita Hunter, Lamberto Furlan, Raymond Myers. For full cast see FN 419.

1982 – Il trittico

11 June 1982. Sydney Opera House. For cast see FN 423.

1983 – La bohème

27 January 1983. Sydney Opera House. Luciano Pavarotti, Madelyn Renee, Robert Allman, Rhonda Bruce. For full cast see FN 436.

1983 – Tosca

January 1983. Sydney Opera House. Leonie Rysanek, Lamberto Furlan, John Shaw.

1983 – La bohème

12 February 1983. Sydney Opera House. Beryl Furlan, Lamberto Furlan, Robert Allman, Etela Piha. For full cast see FN 440.

1983 – La fanciulla del West

6 October 1983. Sydney Opera House. Arlene Saunders, John Shaw, Kenneth Collins. For full cast see FN 435.

1983 – **Die Walküre**

8 October 1983. Sydney Opera House. Rita Hunter, Margreta Elkins, Lauris Elms, Jon Weaving, Bruce Martin, Clifford Grant. For full cast see FN 450.

1984 – **Otello**

28 January 1984. Concert Hall, the Sydney Opera House. Alberto Remedios, Joan Carden, Robert Allman. For full cast see FN 518.

1984 – **Die Walküre**

24 February 1984. Sydney Opera House. Rita Hunter, Marilyn Richardson, Rosemary Gunn, Alberto Remedios, Bruce Martin, Clifford Grant. For full cast list see FN 450.

1984 – **Das Rheingold**

17 July 1984. Sydney Opera House. Bruce Martin, Robert Gard, Rosina Raisbeck, Raymond Myers. For full cast see FN 505.

1985 – **Die Walküre**

19 February 1985. Sydney Opera House. Rita Hunter, Leonie Rysanek, Rosemary Gunn, Alberto Remedios, Bruce Martin, Clifford Grant. For full cast see FN 527.

1985 – **Aida**

9 May 1985. Melbourne, State Theatre. Maria Slatinaru, Alberto Remedios, Lauris Elms, John Shaw.

1986 – **Manon Lescaut**

Sydney Opera House, 13 September 1986. Nelly Miricioiu, Piero Visconti, Michael Lewis. For full cast see FN 577.

1986 – **Eugene Onegin**

Sydney Opera House, October 1986. John Pringle, Richard Greager, Joan Carden. For full cast see FN 555.

1987 – **Il tabarro**

Sydney Opera House. Malcolm Donnelly, Lamberto Furlan, Christa Leahmann. For full cast see FN 611. Celestial Audio CA 428.

1987 – Médée (Cherubini)

27 August 1987. Sydney Opera House. Elizabeth Connell, Glenn Winslade, John Shaw. For full cast see FN 603.

1987 – Médée (Cherubini)

September 1987. Sydney Opera House. Performance with Sandra Hahn substituting for Elizabeth Connell.

1987 – La traviata

14 October 1987. Sydney Opera House. Joan Carden, Richard Greager, Neville Wilkie. For full cast see FN 616. ABC/Opera Australia DVD R-105750-9.

1988 – La bohème

Sydney Opera House. Television broadcast. Neil Rosenshein, David Lemke, John Fulford, John Wegner, Glenys Fowles, Rosamund Illing. For full cast see FN 642. House of Opera DVD 170.

1987 – La Cenerentola

7 August 1987. Sydney Opera House. Bernadette Cullen, Gary Bennett, Jeffrey Black, Donald Shanks, John Pringle, Anne-Maree McDonald, Suzanne Johnston. Elizabethan Sydney Orchestra. Video Selection Australia, 12861, Kultur, B0021DVUGK, DVD.

1988 – Turandot

16 February 1988. Concert Hall, the Sydney Opera House (concert performance). Rita Hunter, Kenneth Collins, Joan Carden, Bruce Martin, John Fulford, Jonathan Welch, Graeme Ewer, Ronald Dowd, Keith Hempton. Sydney Symphony Orchestra.

1988 – Music for Australia Day

Featuring Peter Sculthorpe: Child of Australia. Joan Carden, John Howard, Allan Zavod. Australian Youth Orchestra, Sydney Philharmonia Choir. Philips 834 740-1. Recorded Live.

1989 – Werther

7 June 1989. Sydney Opera House. (Dress Rehearsal). Neil Rosenshein, Bernadette Cullen, Peta Blyth. For full cast see FN 664.

1991 – Turandot

Victoria Arts Centre, Melbourne. State Orchestra of Victoria. Television Broadcast. Ealynn Voss, Kenneth Collins, Amanda Thane, David Brennan, Jonathan Welch, Graeme Ewer, Donald Shanks, Graeme MacFarlane, Greg Scott. ABC/Opera Australia DVD 0947804004, Opus Arte OAF4004D.

1992 – Tribute to Dame Joan Sutherland and Richard Bonynge

The Australian Opera and the Sydney Symphony Orchestra. ABC simulcast. Deborah Riedel, Ghillian Sullivan, Amanda Thane, Anne-Maree McDonald, Anson Austin, Heather Begg, David Brennan, Elizabeth Campbell, Andrew Dalley, Malcolm Donnelly, Graeme Ewer, Kirsti Harms, Kathryn McCusker, Jennifer McGregor, Gary Rowley, Donald Shanks.

1993 – Tristan und Isolde

12 February 1993. Concert Hall, the Sydney Opera House. Marilyn Richardson, Horst Hoffmann, Rosemary Gunn, Malcolm Donnelly, Donald Shanks, Dominic Natoli, David Collins-White, Andrew Dalley. Sydney Symphony Orchestra.

1995 – Nabucco

11 September 1995. Sydney Opera House. Malcolm Donnelly, Elizabeth Connell, Bruce Martin, Kenneth Collins. For full cast see FN 770.

1996 – Nabucco

7 May 1996. State Theatre, Victorian Arts Centre, Melbourne. Jonathan Summers, Anson Austin, Bruce Martin, Elizabeth Connell. For full cast see FN 842. State Orchestra of Victoria. ABC/Opera Australia DVD OAF4027D, Opus Arte OAF 4027 D.

1999 – Turandot

21 September 1999. Sydney Opera House. Leona Mitchell, Michael Sylvester, Arax Mansourian. For full cast see FN 817.

2000 – Moffatt Oxenbould Gala

February 2000. Sydney Opera House.

2000 – Tosca

September 2000. Sydney Opera House. Elizabeth Whitehouse, Vinson Cole, Håkan Hagegård. For full cast see FN 826.

Appendix 5

Cillario's HMV Recordings as Violinist

DA5412

Dinicu: Hora Staccato

Sammartini: Canto amoroso

DB5409

(#)Veracini, arr. Corti: Largo

(#) J.S. Bach: Solo Partita No.3 in E, BWV1006 – Preludio

DB5410

(#) Paganini, arr. Pilati: Caprice No.24 in A minor (2 sides)

DB5364/5

Mozart: Violin Sonata in B flat, K378[952] (4 sides)*

S10472

(#) Szymanowski: Mythes, Op.30 – La fontaine d'Aréthuse

(#) Sarasate, arr. Barmas: Jota navarra

GW1703

(#) Casella: Tarantella

(#) Rossellini: La fontana malata

Carlo Felice Cillario violin

Riccardo Simoncelli piano

*__Corradina Mola__ harpsichord

Recorded and issued by La voce del padrone, c1937.

---

[952] The archive: www.internetculturale.it (Accessed 18 May 2024) has further information about this two-disc Mozart set, and a selection of the discs can be accessed online.

LINK TO RECORDINGS

https://hdl.handle.net/2123/32727

This permalink will take the reader to Carlo Felice Cillario - violin recordings for 'La voce del padrone' 1930s, containing seven selections from commercial recordings that Cillario made as a violinist during the late 1930s. Produced by the Italian wing of HMV, *La voce del padrone*, these have never been reissued. By the end of the War, Cillario had largely abandoned his career as violinist for that of conductor. The purpose of including them here is to allow a glimpse into Cillario's accomplishment as a violinist, and also to provide a connection with the musical world from which he developed.

The original discs were in the possession of Cillario's sister. She made a recording onto a cassette, using a hand-held microphone to capture the sound of the 78RPM discs. The process was 'low-fi' by today's standards, and Cillario made a number of copies of the original cassette to share with friends and interested acquaintances. Among the recipients was the present author.

I am grateful to Dr David Kim-Boyle, of the Sydney Conservatorium of Music for restoring the cassette recording to digital files, and creating the best rendition of these recordings currently available.

The above discography indicates that several recordings made and released were not among this selection recorded by Cillario's sister. The author continues to search for the missing recordings, and the original discs of those currently uploaded, and will update the site as more material comes to light. Meanwhile, this material provides a glimpse into a lost world of music making, which Cillario brought into the opera houses where he worked.

il VIOLINISTA

CARLO FELICE CILLARIO

ha inciso

" HORA STACCATO ,,

di G. DINICU

per

"La Voce del Padrone,,

Dinicu - '' Hora Staccato ,,
Sammartini - ''Canto Amoroso,, - DA 5412

C. F. CILLARIO

G. DINICU

ALTRI DISCHI INCISI :

Veracini (Corti) - Largo
J. S. Bach - Preludio in mi magg.
(violino solo)
DB 5409

Paganini (Pilati) - Capriccio N. 24
(parte I e II)
DB 5410

Mozart - Sonata in si 'bem. con clavi-
cembalo (C. Mola)
DB 5364/5

Szymanowski - '' La fontana d'Aretusa ,,
Sarasate - ''Iota navarra ,,
S 10472

AL PIANO
Riccardo Simoncelli

40: Broadsheet published by the Italian branch of HMV to publicise
the release of Cillario's recordings c1937.

41: A postcard from the composer Manuel de Falla, thanking Cillario
for his recordings of Szymanowski and Bach, late 1930s.

Appendix 6
Cillario the Composer

Known Works by Carlo Felice Cillario[953]

Canzone ed Allegro su un tema bulgariano (violin and piano, 1942)

Elegy for two voices (oboe, bassoon, and pianola)

Filter, Cadenza and Potpourri (violin)

Variazioni su un tema egizio (Variations on an Egyptian Theme, c.1998)(violin and piano, revised for solo violin, on a theme from Verdi's *Aida*)

Three songs for Three Stars (voice and piano)
'Canto di un minstrello' (Luciano Pavarotti)
'Now I know for whom I sing!' (José Carreras)
'Viva los Mariachis' (Plácido Domingo)

Fantasia sul 'Barbiere' (flute and small orchestra or piano)[954]

Three Exercises (violin, recorder, and metronome)
Alla marcia (Fanfare)
Elegaic Chorale
Introduction and slightly canonical Chorale

Fantasy and Fugue for string quartet (free transcription from Verdi's *Falstaff*)

---

[953] The manuscripts of these works are held by the Cillario family, Bologna. All are unpublished, except the last two songs, which are published here for the first time.

[954] This work appears under various titles, at Cillario's Farewell Gala in 1993, it was programmed as: 'Allegro Fantasia for Flute and Ensemble from *Il barbiere di Siviglia*.'

Barbarina e il Signor Conte (mezzo-soprano and piano,1998)

L'Ultimo incontro (Didone languente) (voice and piano, April 1998)

Fantasie on Rossini's *Barbiere*, by Carlo Felice Cillario. Version for flute and piano, opening page of manuscript.

Variazioni su un Tema Egizio – Variations on an Egyptian theme [from *Aida*] for violin. First page of manuscript composed c1998.

Barbarina e il Sig. Conte

Barbarina e il Signor Conte (mezzo-soprano and piano), 1998, page 1.

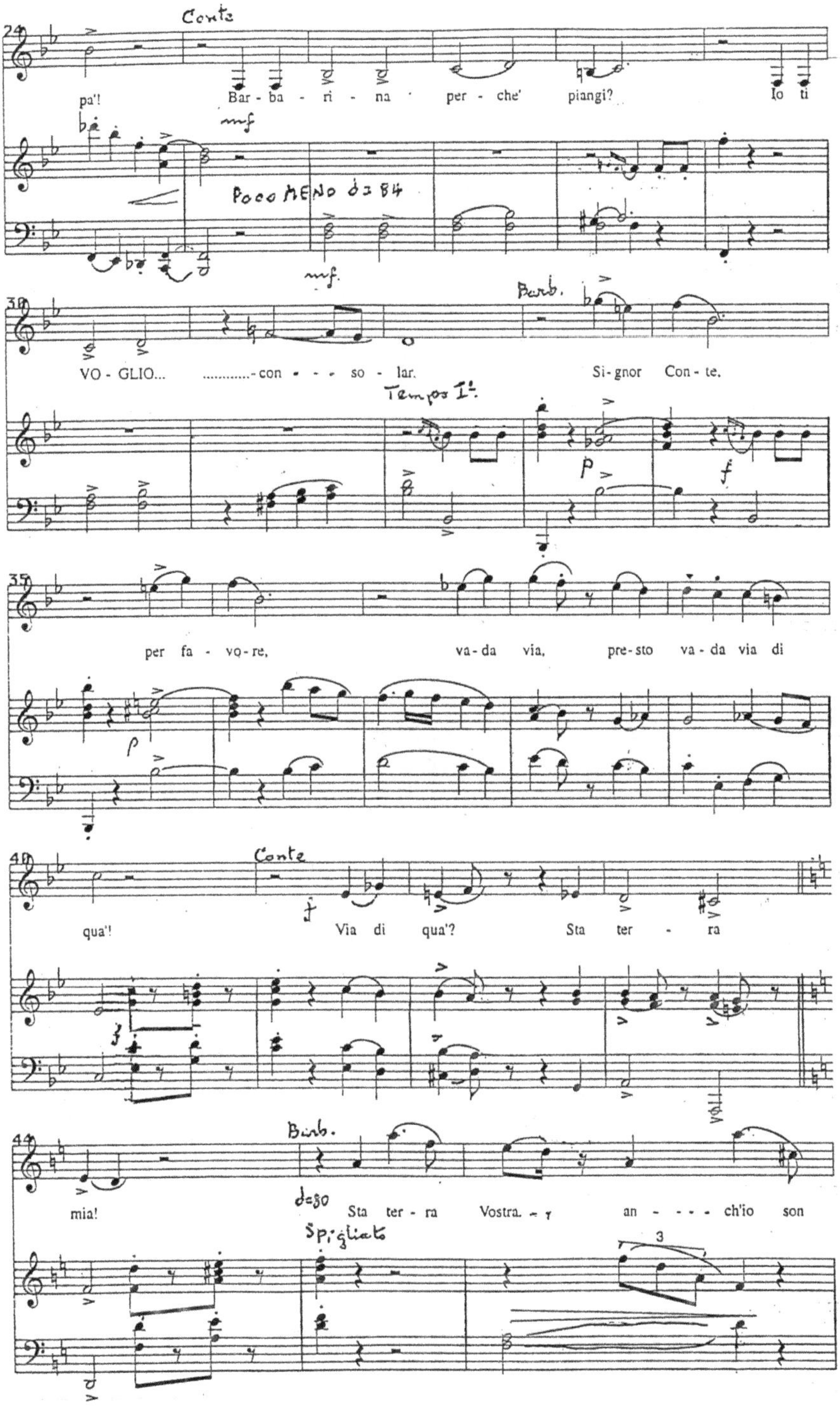

Barbarina e il Signor Conte, page 2.

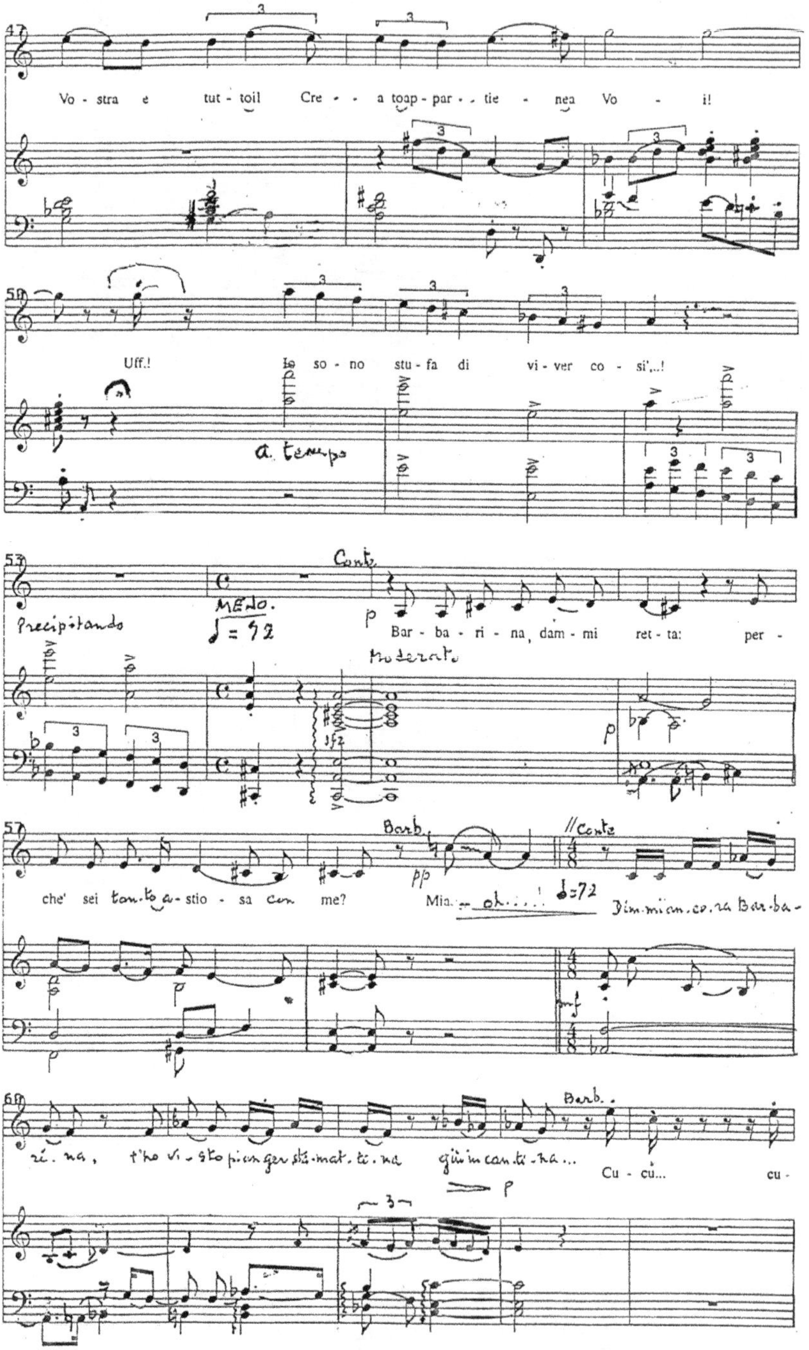

Barbarina e il Signor Conte, page 3.

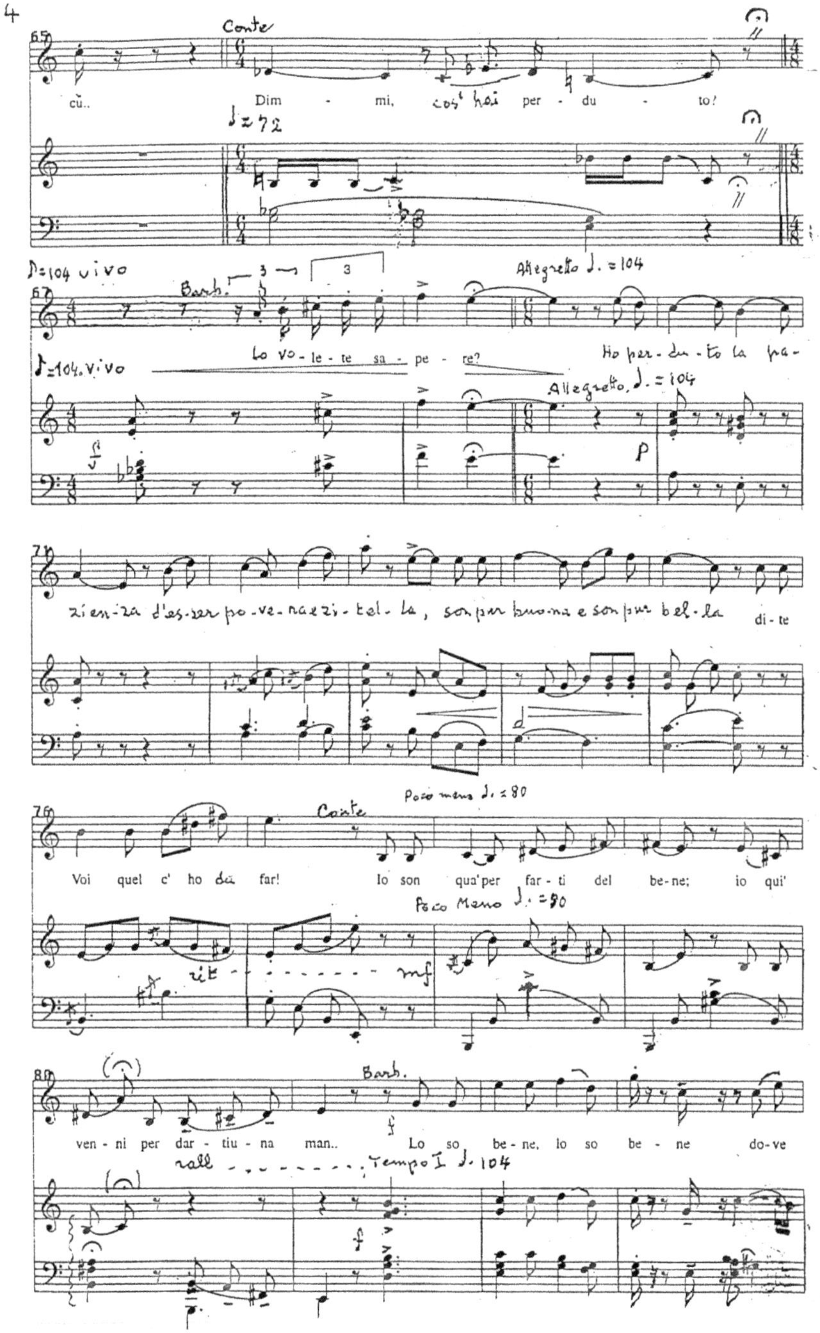

Barbarina e il Signor Conte, page 4.

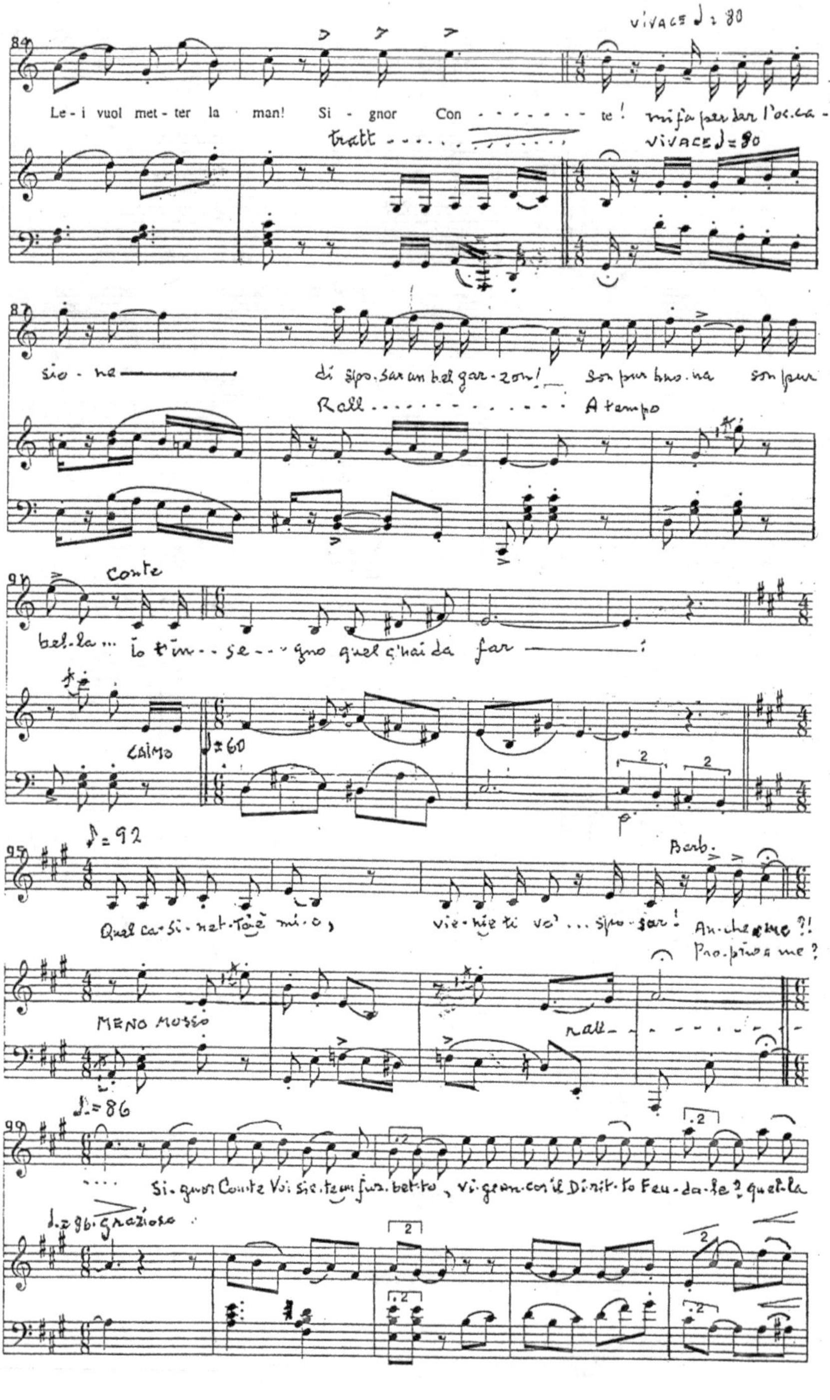

Barbarina e il Signor Conte, page 5.

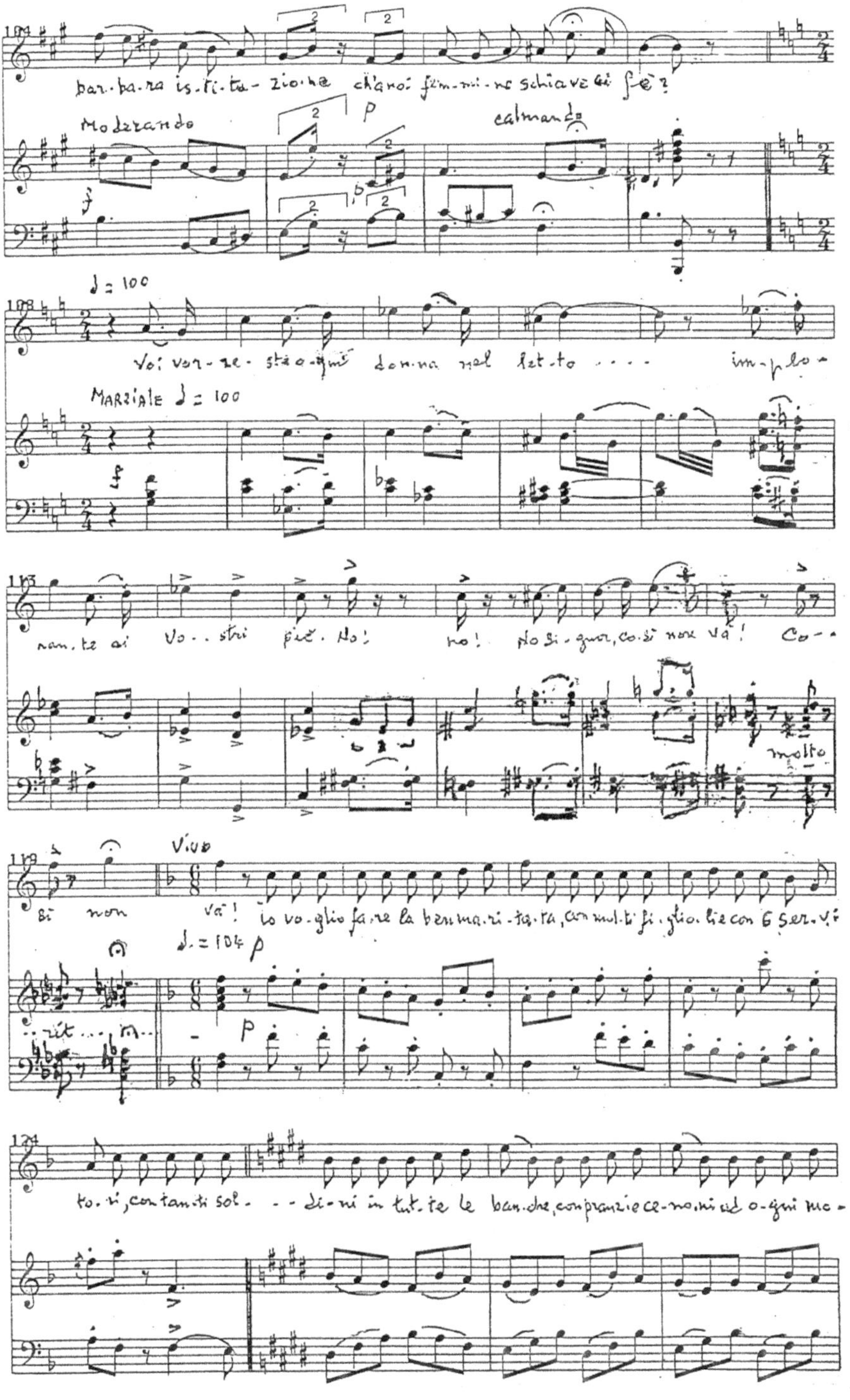

Barbarina e il Signor Conte, page 6.

Barbarina e il Signor Conte, page 7.

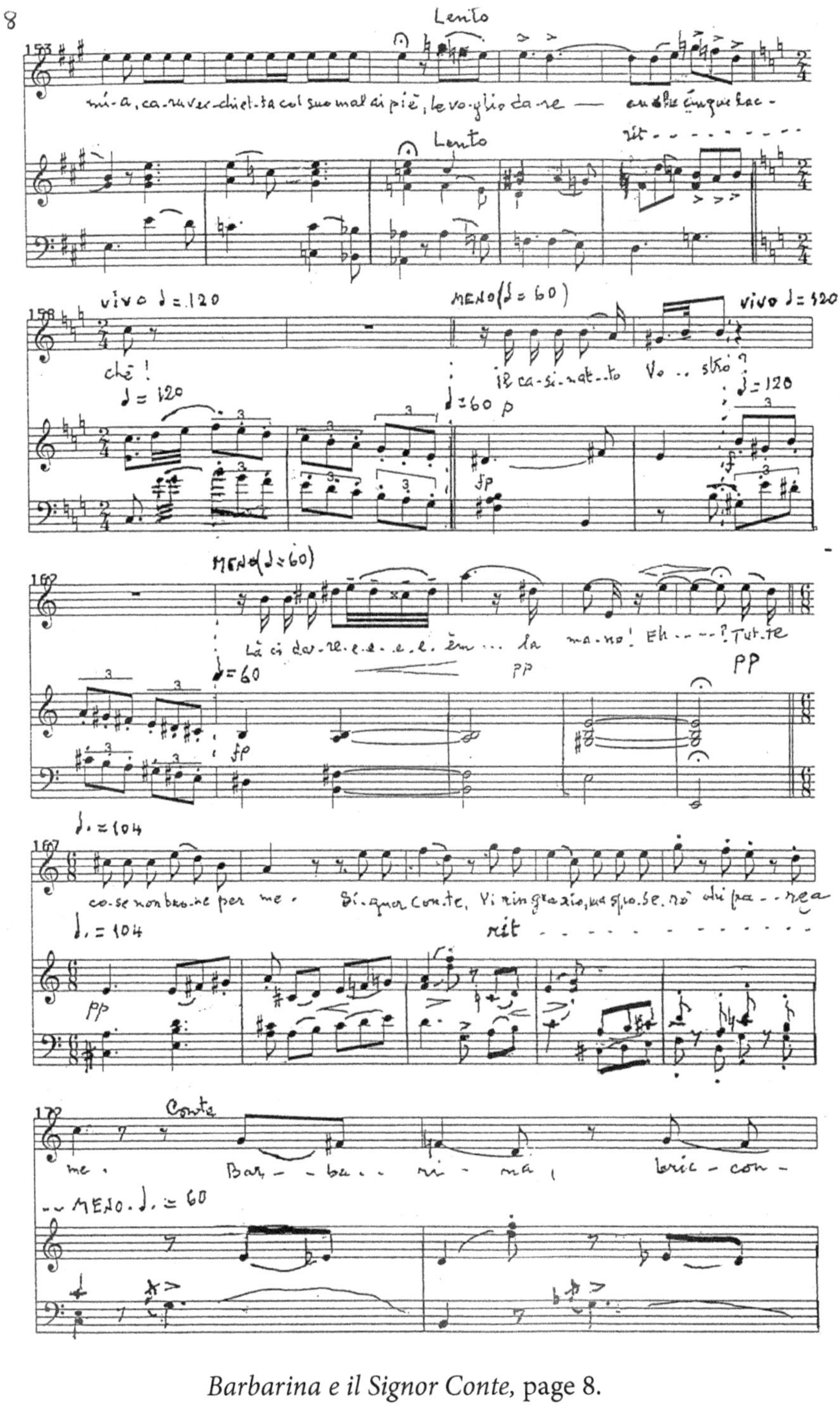

Barbarina e il Signor Conte, page 8.

Barbarina e il Signor Conte, page 9.

L'Ultimo incontro (*Didone languente*) (voice and piano, April 1998), page 1.

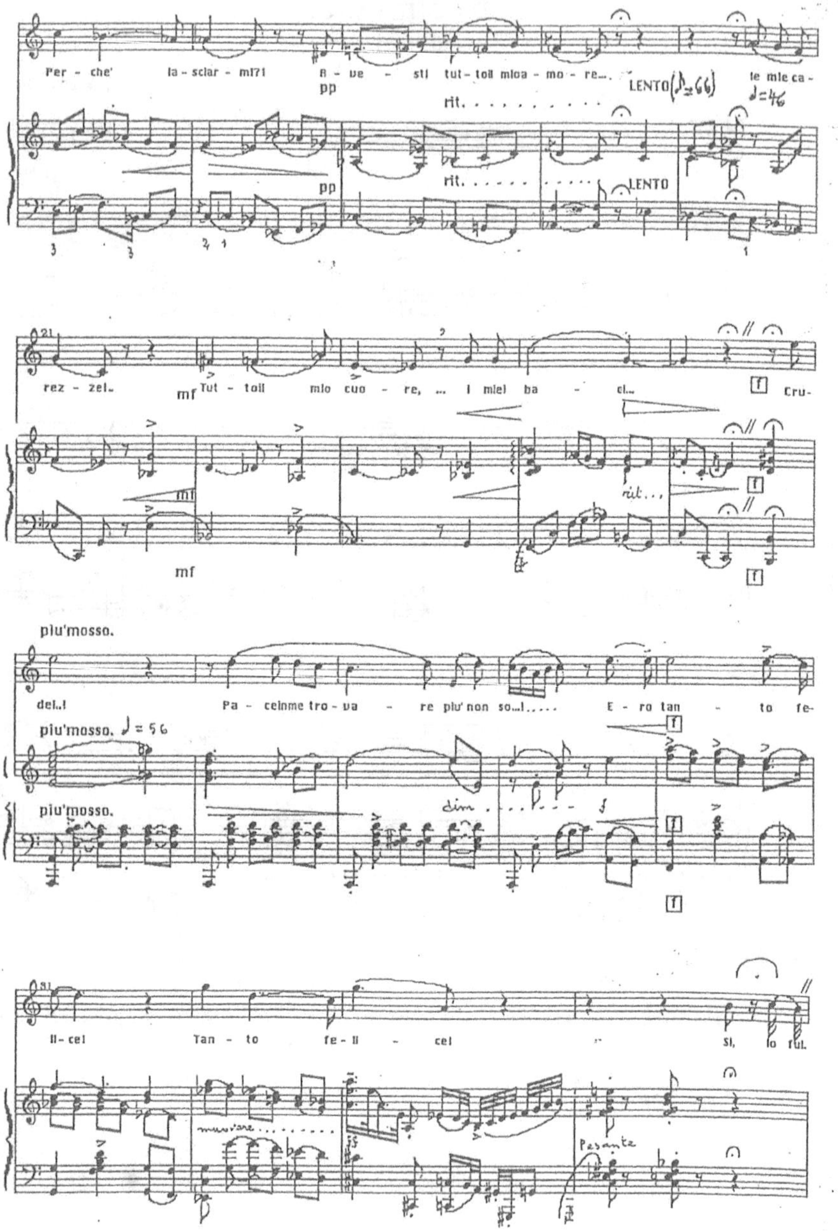

L'Ultimo incontro, page 2.

L'Ultimo incontro, page 3.

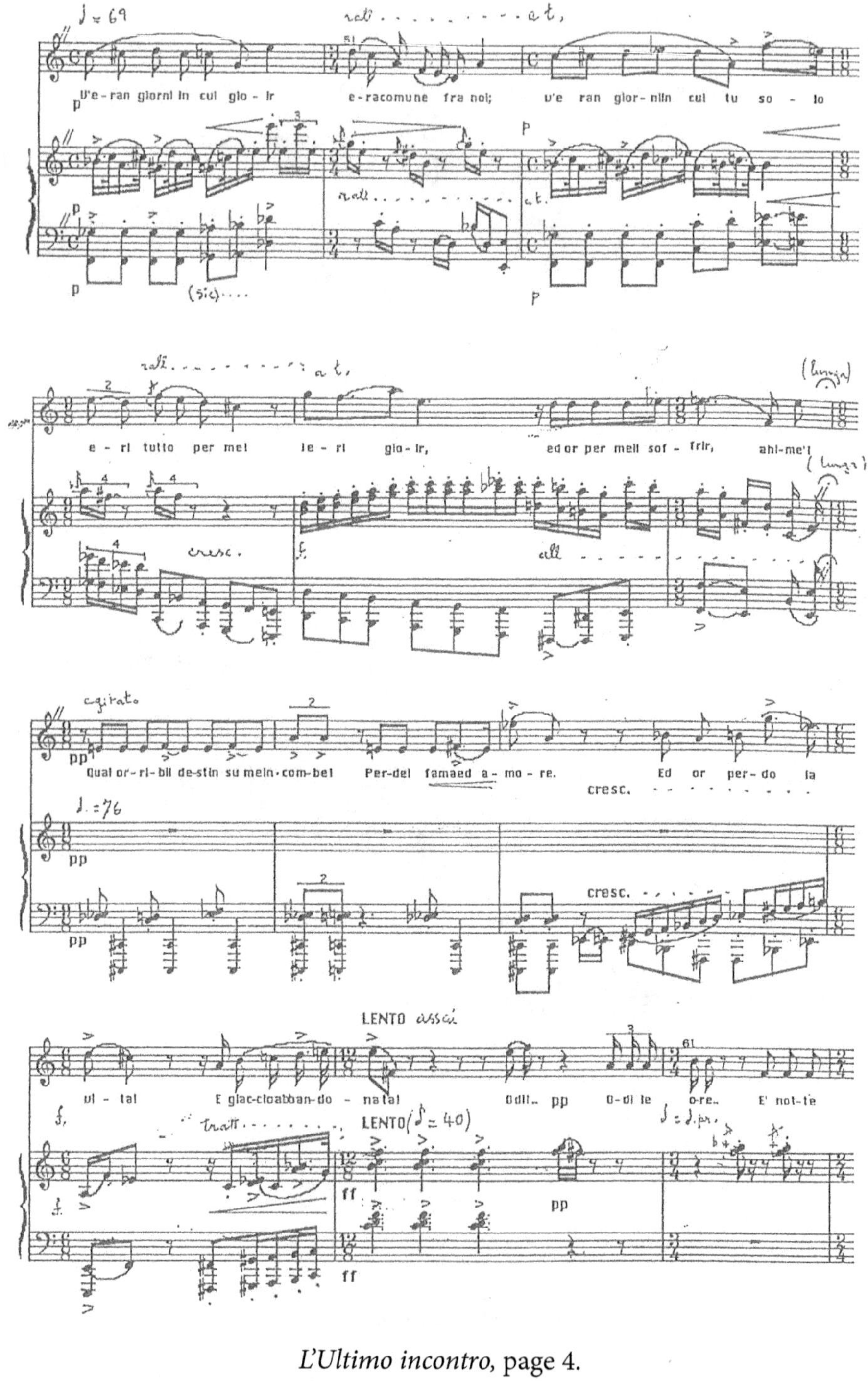

L'Ultimo incontro, page 4.

L'Ultimo incontro, page 5.

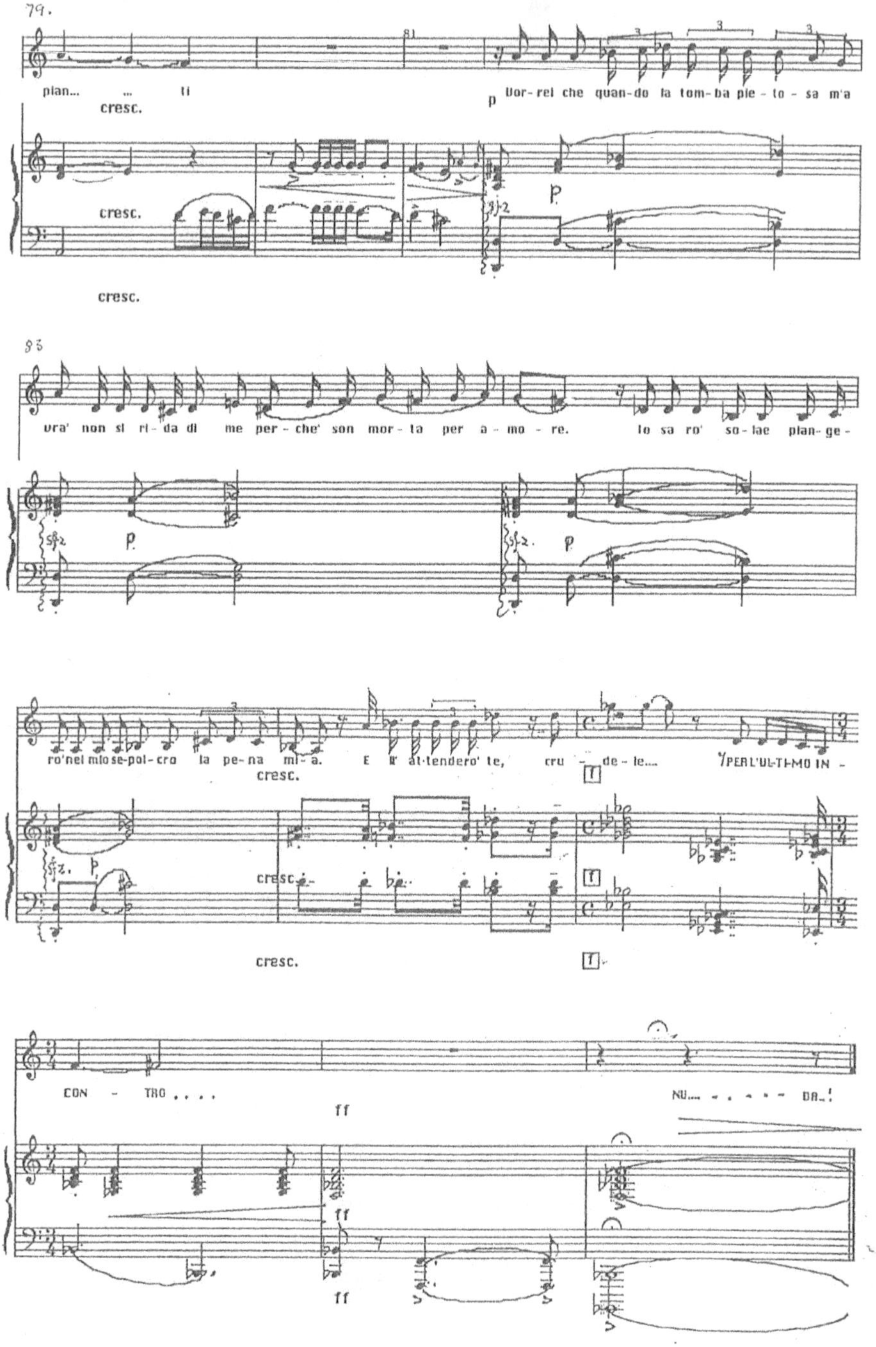

L'Ultimo incontro, page 6.

Appendix 7

Cillario's Memoirs – A Selection[955]

INTRODUCTION

Cillario began writing these memoirs during the 1970's, recalling his experiences with leading musicians, and other significant figures, that he encountered during his career. They were originally titled 'Souvenir de…'. Following his death, the conductor's grandson, Alessandro Cillario collected and compiled the memoirs under the title *"Cosi'li vidi io", racconti e memorie di Carlo Felice Cillario.*

Cillario may have originally intended to publish the memoirs singly, but as they grew in number, they came to form a collection. In 1979 he asked the Australian Opera's General Manager, Peter Hemmings to recommend him to a publisher, and Hemmings contacted Calder Publications in London, to organise a meeting which did not lead to publication. In 1985 Cillario wrote to Moffatt Oxenbould that he was in London, engaged in talks with publishers about both his memoirs and his string quartet based upon Verdi's *Falstaff*.[956] Once again, nothing came of the discussions.

Cillario supplied the following list of memoirs[957] to Hemmings:

*Arturo Toscanini

*Maria Callas

*Wilhelm Backhaus

*Tito Gobbi

*Walter Gieseking

---

[955] Cillario often referred to these *racconti*, which he carried around with him, and, at times quoted from. He would often speak of having them published. See: Lyndall Crisp, 'The Maestro at Home', *The Weekend Australian Review*, 22–23 March 2003.

[956] Cillario to Oxenbould, 4 October 1985. 'Carlo Felice Cillario – Artist Files '1', Opera Australia Library archives.'

[957] Cillario to Hemmings, hand-written note, 30 August 1979. 'Carlo Felice Cillario – Artist Files '1', Opera Australia Library archives.'

*William Kapell

**George Enescu

**David Oistrakh

*Elena Suliotis

**Karol Szymanowski

*Friedrich Gulda

**Bronislaw Huberman

*Sir John Barbirolli

Franco Corelli (this was probably the incorporated in the 'Souvenir de ... Alcuni tenori': see below)

*Montserrat Caballé

Renata Tebaldi (this may have been later merged with the Elena Suliotis memoir)

Evita Peron

**Lady Davis (New-town Wales)

Urbano, Vigile di Parma

**Don Giovanni in Israel

A single* denotes titles are included in Alessandro Cillario's selection.

A double ** denotes title of memoirs which have not been located.

The above list includes memoirs written up until 1979.

The following *racconti* were probably written after 1980. Those marked with a* appear in Alessandro Cillario's collection:

*Joan Sutherland

Benito Mussolini

*Art in the Heart

*Souvenir de …. Alcuni tenori:

    Luciano Pavarotti

    Giacomo Aragall e Josè Carreras

    Placido Domingo

    Franco Corelli

*Josef Krips

*Pablo Casals

* Bergen a prima vista

*Guitarra Adentro

*L'Australia

*Gli Aborigeni [sic] e il loro bel canto

The current selection is derived from a collection of hand-typed memoirs, copies of which were presented to this author by Cillario, as well as several other memoirs preserved in Alessandro Cillario's edited collection.

MARIA CALLAS

The first person who told me about Callas was my sister. Her friends were relatives of the Cazzaroli family, who lived in Bologna. A Veronese industrialist, Meneghini,[958] related to the Cazzaroli, had married an American opera singer of Greek origins. She was said to have an outstanding voice. A short time later, I was at La Scala, when she was singing *Norma*, her first opera from the 'Great Italian Repertoire', at a time when she was mostly performing Wagnerian operas. When the music lovers who frequent La Scala smell the birth of a new 'star', the news spreads, like on Wall Street or at Cape Canaveral: it travels by secret routes and spreads in a frenzy: 'Ten minutes of applause in the first act!' ... 'A dozen calls after the second!' Everyone is tense, waiting for the final verdict, which, as soon as it arrives, makes the blood pressure of all those present suddenly rise. 'A triumph! A real triumph, gentlemen!', ruled one. 'This will make the divas of the past pale!' 'She has two and a half octaves!' Another shouts: 'And she has three timbres of voice! And how she holds her hands!' In short: it would seem that everyone saw it and heard it.

The 'star' Callas took on an ever more consistent shape in a short time. The rivalry with Tebaldi was skilfully engineered. Meanwhile, thousands of miles away in Buenos Aires, due to one of the frequent changes of leadership in the troubled history of the Teatro Colón, the reigns ended up in the hands of one Cirilo Grassi-Diaz, strong-willed and still youthful, despite his advanced age. To his credit, he had managed the theatre during one of its most prosperous periods. At that time, a phone call to Milan or New York was enough to see a vessel loaded with Toscanini, Gino Marinuzzi, Caruso, Titta Ruffo, Claudia Muzio, Rosa Raisa, Maria Barrientos, Amelita Galli-Curci and so on, all shipped off to Buenos Aires.

Grassi-Diaz's first plan for his new management was to immediately bring to the Colón the diva who already had the international operatic world in turmoil. (Callas had appeared at the Colón several years

---

[958] Giovanni Battista Meneghini.

earlier,[959] achieving some success, but without making a sensation.) Having somehow learned that I knew her relatives, the volcanic Grassi-Diaz decided to use me as an intermediary. He asked me by telegram to convince her of the superiority of the Colón compared to the other theatres where she was singing, and above all of his great superiority – Don Cirilo Grassi-Diaz – over all the directors of all the other theatres in the world.

Through the agency of Signora Maria Cazzaroli, I was given the green light to telephone Meneghini in Milan. The Commendatore[960] was very kind, but evasive. Donna Maria, whom he called to the phone, was likewise. She made many sighs of regret: 'Ah, if I had time … I would like to, but…'. In short, a series of 'ni'[961] prompted me to communicate my doubts to Buenos Aires. Meanwhile Grassi-Diaz had pressed the Italian embassy into service. Together with a new telegram from him, I received one from the Ambassador himself. We had to proceed. I phoned Milan again, but only received more 'ni'. I telegraphed to Grassi-Diaz, saying that I considered the attempt definitively stalled. If he wished to pursue the matter for himself, he should fly to Milan, where I would arrange a meeting for him.

Two days later Grassi-Diaz landed at Malpensa, and together we went to the Meneghini apartment in Via Michelangelo Buonarroti. After the introductions, the conversation faltered. I tried to restart it somehow by entertaining Donna Maria with trivial topics that might interest her.

A couple of hours earlier I had taken part in a TV interview with Luchino Visconti. Responding to accusations of extravagance that had been levelled against his *Traviata della Scala*,[962] Visconti had retorted with impressive revenue figures. I told Meneghini the cost. And in his charming Veronese style, which he loved to use, he

---

[959] In 1949.

[960] Cillario characterises Meneghini and Callas as the 'Commendatore' and 'Donna Anna' from Mozart's *Don Giovanni*.

[961] 'No'.

[962] *La traviata* production at Teatro alla Scala, Milan, 1955.

swore: 'He talks about suuua *Traviata*, that fiol d'un can![963]... I would like to see his takings if he didn't sing his own praises!'

After a few more such pleasantries, Grassi-Diaz attacked. He said in few but weighty words that the President of the Argentine Republic had entrusted him with the task of bringing the great Callas to the Colón. Instead of answering him, Meneghini asked him which other artists he had in mind. And he naively enumerated them, 'glorious names of the past', to whom he had incurred debts of gratitude. Callas's expression, with a slight shade of haughty detachment, took on the tone of a certain amused surprise. Then Grassi listed the names that were the most popular at the time. To each of these, Donna Maria's eyebrows took on slightly different positions, between doubt and resignation. This little game was starting to boil Grassi-Diaz in his armchair.

'But I'm so expensive!', she repeated every now and then, as if in a dream.

'Don't you worry. Eso es problema mio',[964] he replied.

Eventually Callas seemed to hatch a plan, favourable for the future fate of the Teatro Colón. In her most mellifluous register, she murmured slowly: 'Why don't you take La Tebaldi? I heard she did well in America.'

And here the ingenuity of the moment was seized by the good Battista Meneghini, who, encouraged by the 'generosity' of his wife, added: 'Yes! Renata has her own works: Aida, Adriana…' – but a wordless spousal command to hold his tongue, made with two fingers in the air, arrested the Tebaldi repertoire at the letter 'A'. The ensuing silence was awkward. 'If you don't arrive at something concrete, I'm going back to Bologna,' I said, intending to stir things up.

The idea of 'concrete' seemed to disgust Donna Maria. She got up and took my hand, ushering me away to sit down with her in another corner of the large living room. 'Tell me about my dear compatriots from Buenos Aires,' she said. 'Oh…wonderful people!'

---

[963] 'Hiiiis Traviata, that son of a bitch!'
[964] 'That's my problem.'

I replied. 'Stamatàkis... Kostanìdes... Papadopulos ... everyone eager to have you there ... sentimental as they are ... far from their land, poor things....'

Meanwhile in the other corner of the room, Battista finally managed to ask Don Cirilo how much he was offering per performance. The response came straight back: 'Like at La Scala'. Donna Maria, from the opposite corner leapt at him like a tiger: 'At La Scala I'm singing practically for free!'. (Actually, I think she was getting no more than $100[965] a performance at the time). 'Tell him, you tell him Battista, how much San Francisco offers me!' she demanded. Grassi, to cut it short, offered $2000 per performance. She then struck an attitude straight out of an acting manual, from the chapter 'Disappointed-Offended-Outraged'. She murmured: 'Ah! ... but then!' 'Then how much?' Grassi urged. Meneghini calmly replied, 'Six thousand exempt from taxes.'

'I will consult the Gobierno del mio Pàis,'[966] Grassi-Diaz said abruptly as he lowered his bowler hat over his square head. 'Vàmonos,[967] Cillario!'

A few minutes later we were striding along the Via Manzoni. 'Six thousand Tax Free!!?' – hearing his outburst the passers-by turned around – 'Six thousand boos is what she will get at the Colón, if she comes and sings like she did last night!' (We had attended a rather unsuccessful *Barbiere*.) But Grassi–Diaz's scorn was not justified by the facts.

The star Maria Callas had an impressive ascent, demonstrating that in the works congenial to her – and there were many that she exhumed from oblivion – her art sometimes reached heights that could not be paid for with the currency of humans. I encountered her again a few years later.[968] Tito Gobbi and Franco Zeffirelli convinced her to accept me as the conductor for her performances

---

[965] Referring to American dollars in each case.
[966] Government of my country.
[967] 'Let's go.'
[968] They had contact by letter in 1963 in advance of the 1964 *Tosca* season.

of *Tosca* at Covent Garden, and she offered no resistance. I wrote her a note and she wrote back a nice letter[969] saying that she knew good things about my work and was delighted to work with me. She concluded: 'I'm not a tiger. I'm just a woman who tries to do things the best way possible.'

The staging rehearsals started in London, but she was still in Paris. One day Sir David Webster, manager of Covent Garden, called me into his office. I was surprised to find him unusually nervous and troubled. He said, 'She's still in Paris and she's postponed her arrival again until tomorrow. Doesn't that worry you?' 'No. I see no reason,' I replied. Later I learned why he was worried: Callas, already at the apogee of her career, had been inactive for a long time.

Was it love? Tiredness? Indisposition? Or attrition caused by having such a reputation to maintain? The fact was that when she was offered this *Tosca* in London, she refused to sign the contract. She told the impresario Gorlinsky, 'I'll do my best, I promise you. But I don't know if I'll be fit. You sign. And if I'm not okay, I'll cancel,' she said. As soon as the announcement of her return to the stage was made, the reaction was immense. And in a few hours the performances were sold out.

Eventually however, she arrived in London and immediately presented herself at the rehearsal even though she had not been scheduled to attend. (Generally, it was her habit to attend all rehearsals, even when her presence was not required.) Zeffirelli, in an interview for an English newspaper, was asked: 'Will you be able to convince Callas to follow your instructions?' He replied: 'I'm sure I will be able to transform Maria into the common *ciociara*[970] I have in mind'. So – semi-jokingly – she demanded of him at their first meeting, 'Franco I'm here. Come on, show me how you want to transform me!' And Franco, between a laugh and a hug: 'I'll make you a wet-nurse's chest this big...' (Which he really did. And she had a lot of fun with that 'windowsill,' as she used to call it.)

---

[969] See Appendix 10.

[970] A native of Ciociara, a poor district located south of Rome. It is also the title ('La ciociara') of a book by Alberto Moravia, which was made into a film, starring Sophia Loren.

We almost always rehearsed in the theatre, or sometimes at the Savoy, in her apartment. One thing that struck me above all was her commitment to giving one hundred percent in any kind of rehearsal, with or without other people present: whether in the afternoon, evening or morning. During the open General Rehearsal, a few curious things happened. Both she and Gobbi had told me that, since they were both short-sighted, I could save myself from having to worry about them – quite unusual for an opera conductor…

Finding myself free of this musical responsibility, I could fully devote my attention to the other aspects of the performance, confident that the coordination with the two of them would have been achieved without problems even if we had been divided by insulating walls. I paid so little attention to them that I was perhaps the only one present who did not notice an incident that occurred at the end of the Second Act, during the General Rehearsal: moving too close to the lit candelabra, Floria Tosca's wig caught fire. Gobbi, although already dead on the ground in the middle of the stage, leapt up to the rescue; but she, in a flash, had already nipped the conflagration in the bud. Busy with my own problems in the orchestra, I learned of this during the interval and later from the Italian newspapers, which after a few days even insinuated that the incident had been deliberately 'staged' for propaganda reasons. As if there was any need for further publicity!

A queue of several hundred people had formed around Covent Garden. They camped out for three days and two nights, shielding themselves as best they could from the damp and cold of the London winter, for one of the 40 standing room places which would be assigned at the last moment. At one of the rehearsals, it occurred to me spontaneously to congratulate Callas on her intelligence. I thought I was paying her a compliment, but she responded: 'I'm not smart. I'm just instinctive.'

At the beginning of 'Vissi d'arte', during the General Rehearsal, she placed herself in a new position, fully turned away from the conductor. I have sometimes made my own experiments in this way, and I am convinced that musical time is full of moments within the 'downbeat' and 'upbeat', and that if two or more artists are really in accord, there should be no need to give them a 'downbeat', because even without looking at each other, they should each be able to simultaneously start a speech, a musical phrase, a noise, by just instinctively picking up its signals from nature. But at that particular moment, I wasn't expecting the new position that Callas had adopted, and the strings began a moment behind the voice.

So, at the end of the act, I went directly to her dressing room. Finding the door open, I politely said to her: 'If you prefer to start facing upstage, breathe deeply, and I will understand that it is your "upbeat". She looked straight at me with two wide eyes and used them to indicate behind me. Hidden behind the door, through which I had entered without looking, were a handful of elegant women squashed like frescoes against the wall. I understood the strained atmosphere and took my leave. The next time we met she upbraided me: 'Tomorrow those loudmouths will let all of Milan know that you are making observations to me'.

The success at the General was delirious, with fanatical outbursts. But I sensed, in the air, an undertone of discontent, which I attributed to a noticeable vibrato that was felt on certain of her high notes. In such cases, I have no peace until I discuss the causes directly with the person concerned. So, on the day of a TV rehearsal, she was resting in her dressing room with her legs up on a stool, and I decided to talk to her about it. As soon as I entered, she immediately understood that I had something significant to tell her. Her lady-in-waiting was present. 'Go ahead, Mrs. Bruna is part of the family,' she said. Encouraged by this, I took a deep breath, and spoke: 'Donna Maria, you are one of the human beings closest to attaining perfection, so please explain to me why your voice wobbles in the high register'.

She leapt to her feet, and grabbed a pillow, putting it over her ears as she shouted, 'Don't tell me … don't tell me! I know, I know!' I waited for her to recover, and then added: 'If I ask you this, it is because I know that you know'. She replied calmly: 'It is a diaphragm problem. Having sung so many very high notes, I no longer have the support when I sing medium-high notes. I try to take charge, but it [the diaphragm] wins'.

I considered my mission accomplished, and a few nights later she demonstrated that she didn't hold any grudge. The performance was proceeding normally but Donna Maria began to say after the First Act that she felt her voice was not in good shape, and she thought she would have to stop. All those around her were trying to dissuade her and convince her that nothing abnormal had been heard. It sometimes happens that only the singer notices imperfections that the listener does not notice. I also approached her and told her I had heard nothing abnormal. She looked at me fixedly, with an inquiring eye, then she spoke, marking accents on each syllable: 'I believe you'. And so, we continued.

During one of the following performances, I became convinced that her explanation to me was correct. In the moment when Tosca runs to make her tragic leap into the void from the battlements of Castel Sant'Angelo, she had asked Spoletta and the other thugs who were pursuing her to realistically try to grab her. She would then take the responsibility to free herself from them. Zeffirelli had a set of narrow steps built, which leaned against the narrow and perilously high wall. Callas always climbed with mathematical precision, to reach the top just in time to sing 'O Scarpia innanzi a Dio!' But one evening her long dress, made of heavy velvet got caught between the legs of her pursuers, and although she tugged at it like mad, and I slowed down a bit to give her more time to climb the stairs, she had to sing the line when she was only halfway up the steps. She had no time to think about her diaphragm and the high B flat that night was as solid and steady as a blade.

One morning, I had asked two of my friends to record the rehearsal. When they returned to my dressing room, someone noticed the tape recorder. I soon had a visit from John Tooley, Assistant General Administrator of Covent Garden, who asked me to destroy the tape. I dissembled, offering the explanation that I was thinking of having Callas listen to some excerpts from it that afternoon. In fact, I did go to see her. She was trying on the costumes in her dressing room with Zeffirelli and the seamstresses. In the living room, some RCA employees had finished arranging a huge record player on which sat the *Tosca* recording which Callas had made with Giuseppe di Stefano and Tito Gobbi under Victor de Sabata's direction. But the turntable was silent. I got my humble tape recorder ready, placed it next to the gramophone and sat down. In the next room, Callas silenced everyone with a gesture in order to listen attentively to the music. Then she said, 'Eh! So yes, I was fit!' Michel Glotz, director of the RCA in Paris at the time, gave me a nod and I said (with a certain satisfaction): 'You must know that it was the test done this morning'.

Donna Maria suddenly felt cold, she said, and gave the sense of not wanting to continue. She dismissed the others and asked me to let her listen to the most important parts of her role. Then she said cheerfully: 'Eh ... not bad ... You're right. I've never been so fit!' I responded: 'and I have to allow the tape to be destroyed!' 'Tell them you gave it to me. They won't have the courage to ask me.' I think those six performances of Tosca in London were the last link in the long chain of her delirious successes.

She returned to Covent Garden the following season but cancelled almost all the performances. She sang only one in the presence of the Queen [of England]. She devoted her time to teaching courses, participated in a few films, went on several cruises and a few concert tours. But the light that shone on her was only a reflected light from a past that would never return. I saw her, some years later, on a boulevard near her home in Paris. But I didn't approach her. Conversation is always awkward with a person who lives on glorious memories and wears luxurious clothes, because there is no mink coat that can compare with the most worn-out theatrical costumes.

--o-o--

JOAN SUTHERLAND

This was published in The Weekend Australian *in January 1983. Another abridged version edited by Opera Australia's Italian coach Renato Verdino-Fresia was published in the programme for Cillario's Gala farewell in 2003. The version presented here incorporates elements of both versions, along with some amendments based upon the original Italian text.*

The famous baritone, Titta Ruffo had great respect for cows as singing teachers. He said he used to be able to find the right position for his voice only after he had spent many hours in the countryside, trying to imitate their mooing. But I have never believed that cows could produce a voice so agile as to reach a high E flat as Joan Sutherland. Yet she confessed it to me – and I believe everything she says – because in addition to the nickname of 'la Stupenda', I would also call her *la Simpatica* (the likeable one), *la Saggia* (the wise one), *la Semplice* (the straightforward one), *la Solida* (the sensible one) and *la Serena* (the serene one), I would also like to add: *la Sincera* (the sincere one) … taking only from the letter 's' of the dictionary.

Joan and I were returning to our dressing rooms after one of our performances of *Otello* at the Sydney Opera House when, quite unexpectedly she became talkative. 'How can you be so full of energy after you have also conducted the full General Rehearsal of *Bohème* this morning,' she said. 'How do you do it? When do you sleep?' I took the opportunity to say to her: 'Don't you ask the questions. It is I who would like to quiz you. I have been waiting for something strange to happen … I don't know … a little scandal, for example!'

She was walking ahead of me and murmured: 'I'm not good for scandals. I'm a placid old cow'. I believed not to have heard well, when she then turned around and poked me in the ribs, repeating slowly in clear Italian: 'Io sono una vacca placida'. I have never been able to find the right moment to ask her what she really meant, but it doesn't matter. *Vacca* or not, she certainly is placid. This is why it's such a pleasure to work with her. At all times, and in the face of any situation, the positive influence of her nerves of steel, her good nature and her innate sense of fun, are felt by all around. I am convinced that all of us preserve within our being the ancestry of animals from which perhaps we are descended, and they often influence our decisions and the progress of our lives. For example, I sometimes feel a horse within me – a horse who encourages me with slow laughter (using the deepest register of my voice) when he thinks I've found the right solution to some of my problems.

It must also be said that Joan was endowed by Mother Nature

with a singer's face, a face which is possible to recompose or split up like a set of kitchen cupboards, which Joan manages to rearrange into a rich array of highly effective grimaces, to express: surprise – horror – disgust – encouragement – disapproval – pleasure – complicity – reproach. These are just a few of the expressions that come naturally to her by moving her lips just a few millimetres, or by wrinkling her nose, or half-closing one eye. After a press interview with Dame Joan some time ago, an Australian newspaper published half a dozen photos of her showing several different grimaces. I cut these out and keep them in my bedroom, so that during my frequent insomniac nights I can derive comfort just by looking at them.[971]

The first time I heard her sing was in Paris. She was performing, among other things, Handel's aria 'Tornami a vagheggiar' from *Alcina*. She gave such a display of virtuosic perfection that it seemed to me beyond the possibilities of the human throat. When I saw Luciano Pavarotti the next day, he told me: 'The extraordinary thing is that Joan can sing like that even in the morning when she has just got out of bed and is boiling the water for her coffee. She warms the water and doesn't need to warm her voice!' I thought it was a natural technique but that's not true. Such perfection cost her a lot in her youth.

Later I attended her performance of *La fille du régiment* at Covent Garden, where I was impressed by her comic talent. I realised that she was as great a comedienne as Callas was in her dramatic roles. On that occasion I was surprised to meet the Glyndebourne management staff as they were leaving the theatre before the final act. 'You really don't like it?' I asked them, surprised. 'In England we don't like this kind of comedy at all,' they told me. And they strutted off. I was a little ashamed of my plebeian taste but was pleased to see that the Covent Garden audience shared my enthusiasm and declared the evening to be a real triumph.

As the time approached for the inauguration of the Sydney Opera House, Joan and I were in touch via the management of the Australian Opera. Logically, everyone wanted Sutherland to participate in the opening night. At that time, I was the Music Director: we asked her if

---

[971] These photos were published in *The Sydney Morning Herald* alongside the article.

she would sing *Aida*.[972] She said that she had heard excellent reports about me, but that she usually worked with her husband, Maestro Richard Bonynge.[973] Some of my colleagues objected to her stance, but I didn't bat an eyelid, I found her reply very reasonable. Mutual understanding is a matter of such importance in our profession, that when I find someone who works well with me, I have the strange sensation of wanting to marry them all, and establish a harem with males and females all together. I therefore understood very well that the Bonynge couple would not want to mix with strangers on such an important occasion.

Therefore, in order not to upset the apple cart for the executives of the Australian Opera, I left them free to choose whoever they wanted for the opening, and I went my own way to the Met and La Scala. I thought I had to cross Australia off my itinerary forever and I was sorry because I had liked the country from my first visit. However, neither Sutherland nor Bonynge appeared at the opening night of the Sydney Opera House, and after some time I began to be invited back each year as guest conductor.[974]

Richard Bonynge was appointed Music Director,[975] and one day he invited me to conduct *Otello* with his wife as Desdemona. From the first moment of working with Sutherland, I had the sensation of being with one of those people with whom it isn't necessary to speak in order to understand each other. During the rehearsals a few glances or some particular gestures were enough: our relations were almost always humorous and wordless.

At first, she was surprised that I was so silent. 'You never correct me!... And I'm such a disaster!' I thought that she was joking, but the next day she repeated these words, and I laughed, saying: 'You

---

[972] This is fanciful – Cillario was not Music Director at that time, he had resigned at the end of 1970.

[973] This memoir was written following the 1981 *Otello* season, the only time Sutherland appeared at the Australian Opera with a conductor other than Richard Bonynge.

[974] It was in 1975 that Cillario was invited back as Guest Conductor leading the new *Aida* production in the Concert Hall.

[975] In 1976.

must belong to some secret mafia if you are such a disaster and have such a career.'

She didn't laugh at that as I had anticipated she would; but from then on, our work continued in a more relaxed fashion. At one of the first rehearsals, it was difficult for her to coordinate the words of the second verse of the *Canzon del Salce* ('Willow Song'). Musically it is the same as the first, but with different words: 'Piangea cantando sull'erma landa, piangea la mesta' versus 'Sedea chinando sul sen la testa.'

I – without stopping the orchestra – prompted the words to her by pretending to sit down, then bow down, touching my chest and then my head (signs like these sometimes help the memory). She understood me instantly. While she was singing, she repeated the same gestures as I, and arrived at the correct moment to commence the melancholic phrase ('Salce! … Salce! … Salce! …') without however resisting the temptation to poke out her tongue at me in an attitude of triumph while she took a breath … Just like a naughty child!

Another point that needed correction was the long note (4 slow quarter-notes, then a pause) found at the beginning of the 'Ave Maria' ('Ge-su-uuuu…'). Joan mistakenly reduced it to three quarters instead of holding out five. So, at the following rehearsal, I counted them out with my left hand, 1–2–3–4–5, raising the thumb, then the index, the middle fingers and so on, towards her attentive gaze. After that time, she was always correct, and as she continued softly ('Prega per chi adoranda a te') she signed to me a few times 'bye-bye', with her fingers in the style of Laurel and Hardy; without any noticeable difference in her voice.

At the general rehearsal she seemed slightly absent. So, before the premiere, I went to her dressing room and offered her a red rose with exaggeratedly romantic gestures, saying: 'Joan: to make music together we have to love each other. So, for tonight stop thinking about Ricky and think about me.' Joan sighed, and assumed the attitude of a schoolgirl, replying with downcast eyes: 'Carlo, give me time …Next week, maybe I will be yours', to the great amusement of the seamstress and the hairdresser.

I also admire her fairness in respect of her colleagues and everything she does in her life. Richard had given me the responsibility of finding a suitable interpreter for the role of Otello. We were eager to see how tenor Angelo Marenzi would fare; he needed a couple of rehearsals in order to warm up after the long trip from Europe and the change of time zone. We left him alone and no one said anything.

By the third rehearsal he had loosened up and his voice sounded just right. I learned from the director George Ogilvie that at the end of 'Esultate', which Joan had listened to hidden in the wings, she took his hands excitedly saying: 'He is good, he is good!' That doesn't happen often. Neither Marenzi nor I interfered with the order of applause for the curtain calls. It was Sutherland who requested that Marenzi be given pride of place every night.

I would like to mention something that has been said about her because it seems to describe her most clearly: 'Apart from her glorious artistry, she is a truly wonderful person. To work with her is a joy and a delight.' And if it weren't for Richard Bonynge, who is a friend, I would feel like saying to her: 'Dame Joan: won't you be part of my artistic harem forever?'

[1981–1982]

--o-o--

MONTSERRAT CABALLÉ

During our first phone call, I apparently said, '*Signora*, don't fool me!' She is certain of this, but I deny it. She answered me: 'Maestro, I pray you …' and I responded: 'Madam, don't pray to me! Come and rehearse instead.' Sometimes we still discuss these details, because that phone call was very important to both of us. It marked the beginning of my spontaneous and affectionate friendship with the whole Caballé family, and of frequent musical collaborations with Montserrat, to whom I have always been linked by an uncommon sympathy of artistic feeling. The Gran Teatro del Liceu in Barcelona always treated me well from the beginning of my work with them, especially when it came to sopranos. I had Victoria de Los Ángeles for my first *Bohème*. Then Renata Tebaldi – also in *Bohème* – the following year. And then 'a certain Caballé', a local singer, in *Manon Lescaut*, several seasons later.

Without wishing to offend anyone, I believe that the most truthful news in theatres always comes from the humblest employees. All theatres in the world have at least one or two telephone operators, who at eight in the morning already know the news which will become official at midday. There will also be an elderly porter – respected by all – who has the gift of discovering young talent and who, according to many, would be better off sitting in the Intendant's chair. Pepe, known to all as 'Peppino', fills this role at the Liceu in Barcelona. I believe that he has always existed or that he was born along with the theatre. He is a small man, no more than 1.4 meters tall, all pepper like his name. He performs the functions of telephone operator, announcer, usher, and unloader of scenery, if there is a need. At times he runs to put on his full uniform to become an 'accommodator' or 'facilitator'. While he pollutes the air smoking terrible 'Tuscans' bigger than himself, he holds court with Ministers and other important personalities, giving his opinions on the problems of Spain and the rest of the world. His secret mission (perhaps the most important of all) has always been to tell the truth – all the truth – to conductors and directors about the real value of the artists on the stage.

Speaking of 'that certain Caballé' whom I did not yet know and who was to sing *Manon Lescaut* with me, Peppino told me: 'Maestro, go easy,' and he winked, which in his code meant high praise. So, I remained calm at the first rehearsal, even when they told me that the *Señora* would not come that day. I became a little less calm when I received the same announcement the following day, and I began to visibly tremble at the third rehearsal, when her absence was once again announced. I decided to speak to her at least by telephone, but I never managed to obtain a satisfactory explanation from whoever answered on her behalf. Her husband, the tenor Bernabé Martí who was singing the role of Des Grieux, and came regularly to the rehearsals, said to me one day: 'I think Montserrat is wrong not to come because *Manon Lescaut* is an opera that she has never sung'. Imagine then my *tranquillidad*[976] when on the third day I heard that *la Señora* was leaving to go and sing some performances in Marseille. I telephoned her with some urgency, and in response I got a promise that I could talk to her before she left.

When we finally spoke, her voice immediately struck me by its caressing sweetness: 'Maestro, please, don't worry. I have already sung *Manon* a few times' (at which point I recalled Bernabé's words). 'I'm going to Marseille today, but I promise I'll come back just to rehearse with you the day after tomorrow'. And I, fuming inside said: 'Si ... mañana!'[977] It may have been at that point that I uttered that famous '*Signora*, don't fool me' line, which we will continue to discuss.

I prepared a draft letter of resignation, to be sent to the theatre management if Caballé did not show up as agreed in two days. I waited, and she finally joined us as promised. She was smiling, rested, well-disposed and bursting with joy, just as she is when she is granted the happiness of being able to spend some time with her Catalan people. She was decked with jewels – necklaces, chains, bracelets, – which paled in comparison with the liveliness of her eyes and her smile. When she finally opened her mouth to sing, she flooded the space with all the rich range of harmonics contained in her voice. Here and there she got a few words wrong, apologising because she said she had sung *Manon* in German (and I remained silent...). She made caressing, flute-like sounds, well-balanced accents, light pinwheels. But what struck me above all was the variety of her phrasing.

Across the world there is a common thread that connects every idea and action, from its start to its point of arrival. In a speaker it can be called the thread of speech; in a building, the architectural line; in a political party, it is strategic conduct, in an athlete, competitive conduct. For musical performers, this important quality is called phrasing. There are those who break it, those who stagger it, there

---

[976] 'peace of mind' (meant ironically).

[977] 'Yes.... tomorrow'.

are those who congest it, and those who stifle it by making it asthmatic. But there are also those who craft it, in as linear and well-proportioned a fashion as a Greek temple; like a miracle (not an inch longer than necessary). There are also those singers and musicians who vary it like the dribbling runs of those football players who change their pace at any moment to confuse the opponent. Then there are also those who make you believe that it flows from them spontaneously like a natural spring, even if instead it is the result of a well-balanced calculation.

From our first meeting I tried to understand Caballé's phrasing, and I gradually discovered all these qualities. It had instinct, fresh and attractive and yet in terms of cunning it was second to none. What was less obvious – hearing her phrasing so casually – is that this spontaneity was the result of a meticulous calculation of an infinity of problems, sometimes solved during sleepless nights. She told me one day: 'If I have a performance in the evening, when I wake up in the morning, I vocalise a couple of times "Hi-Hiii" (a kind of high-pitched whistle with the voice). If the voice is there, I am at peace. Otherwise, I'll cancel immediately.' In fact, I have never heard her sing a scale or a vocalise.

The day we were to perform [Donizetti's] *Maria Stuarda* at Carnegie Hall [in 1965], I was surprised to receive a call from her at 8 o'clock in the morning. 'Maestro, I haven't slept, I've been waiting for the moment to be able to call you. The voice is there. But you have to help me by transposing the 'O nube! Che lieve per l'aria ti aggiri,'[978] half a tone up or half a tone down, as you like. But for God's sake get rid of those five flats in the key signature that disturb my voice'. Luckily it is an easy *larghetto* passage for the orchestra, so I was able to satisfy her request even though the General Rehearsal had already taken place. Evidently the sleepless hours of the night had magnified in her mind the personality of Shirley Verrett whose role as Elisabetta features prominently in the First Act. ('Don't you think she's a little too good?!' Montserrat had whispered to me,

---

[978] Maria's scene at the opening of Act 2, composed in D-flat major.

laughing, the first time we heard her sing the role.) Maybe she feared she couldn't match her in the Second Act. But at the performance they both triumphed: 'La Verrett' for the ferocity of her Elisabetta and Montserrat for the clarity of her Stuarda… 'without flats'.

We had a similar problem a few years ago, the last time we worked together at Covent Garden [in 1972]. Montserrat had resumed singing after one of her various career interruptions during that period – the birth of her daughter? Phlebitis? An operation? – I don't remember the cause, just that her nervous system was affected by something. You could also notice it when dining with her from how she ate. Years before, in trouble-free times, we were recording in Spain. As we were listening to the takes, she would greedily ask for a 'Tortilla a la española – ahy rapid que me muero – y' especial.'[979] 'Especial' meant with a double ration of all those deadly ingredients that make it up: fried potatoes – blackish sausage like a stray dog's tail – greasy onion – slices of pepper and a sea of grease. Stunned, I would watch her gulp down the dish with enthusiasm together with mugs of beer while the spinning, ethereal sounds of her voice came out of the speakers: 'Depuis le jour'[980] … 'D'amor sull'ali rosyeeee'.[981] And I couldn't believe that the same trachea was used for such different tasks - downhill and uphill.

In London, I immediately noticed that something was wrong: she ate only caviar without any enthusiasm, almost like an obligation. Before the rehearsal of *Traviata*, at Covent Garden, with only her husband Bernabé present, she burst into tears, and asked me to shift the 'Sempre libera'[982] down half a tone. I wanted to cry too, because I immediately foresaw all the trouble that the request would cause. Much higher ticket prices than usual had been charged for her return. And there was in the air – who knows why – a sense of mistrust. The reactions of the British public on certain occasions are well known. They may lose all their friends to a bomb blast yet with

---

[979] 'Spanish omelette, oh quickly, I'm dying, the special.'
[980] Louise's aria from Charpentier's *Louise*.
[981] Leonora's aria 'D'amor sull'ali rosee' from Verdi, *Il trovatore*.
[982] Violetta's Act 1 aria from Verdi's *La traviata*.

admirable coolness they manage to carry on without turning a hair. But agreeing to lower the 'Sempre libera' by half a step! What was I supposed to do? Refuse, and leave her to public opinion? Argue with the diva who raised the price of tickets in London? I placed the hood of the convict upon myself, and... I agreed to the transposition. As I anticipated, there were those who accused me of being responsible for this insult to the 'British conventions', so much so that I was never invited back to Covent Garden.

Another time I reproached her was during an incident which took place in Rome while we were making a recording for RCA. The orchestra was sitting, waiting, already tuned, and every minute that passed meant rolls of banknotes. The embarrassed sound engineers were standing around us in an effort to convince us to begin recording 'Rossini and Donizetti Rarities'.[983] In a corner of the large hall, we continued to search anxiously for the right speed for her voice for certain rapid passages. 'Let's try a little more slowly ... Ahy que me pesa! Let's see, a little faster ... Ahy que no puedo!'[984] Finally, walking towards the platform, she explained to me that such passages, when she first studied them, had lost their freshness. I watched her in silence - I had never seen her so tense. Suddenly, in the midst of her speaking, she fell in a faint, amid screams of horror from the choristers. After a few minutes of general pandemonium, she recovered and began to record as if nothing had happened, with the voice of a survivor. I needn't tell you the result... To think that a few months after that recording, she won a Grand Prix du Disque in Paris for it.

We also gave a concert in Paris at the Opéra, with skyrocketing prices and an audience that took our breath away. Her voice was in great shape. But during the intermission she had the window of her dressing room wide open, flooding it with icy air, to be able to breathe better. We returned to the stage for 'Addio del passato': she

---

[983] Two discs recorded for RCA – Rossini Rarities (1968) and Donizetti Rarities (1970). See Discography, Appendix 4.

[984] 'Oh, it's too much for me ... Oh, I really can't.'

read the letter in a voice from beyond the grave – 'Curatevi … mertate un avvenir migliore …' which ended almost in a whisper.[985] I prepared to give her the upbeat for the 'È tardi!' but I see her eyes wide open, as she falls full length and remains rigid, as if at attention, lying face up on the ground. The audience all leap to their feet in alarm, while Bernabé had already rushed from the wings and tried to lift her by grabbing her under the armpits. I took one leg, the orchestra concertmaster the other, and we carried her away, as if on an invisible stretcher, with her arms dangling down. The concert ended there, but fortunately no one thought of requesting a refund for the ticket.

Another time she made it big at Glyndebourne. She told me the following story in a London restaurant, with the air of a little girl who knows she has been naughty. She was already contracted for *Der Rosenkavalier* and *Così fan tutte* at Glyndebourne, when she received the offer for *Lucrezia Borgia* in concert performance at Carnegie Hall in New York. She lacked sufficient time to carefully – properly – prepare the three works. So, she had to make a choice and devoted herself to studying, focusing upon the pieces that seemed to her most suitable for the 'peak' of her career that had not yet occurred. Because of her awareness of herself, she felt that the time had come. She let down Glyndebourne in order to achieve a triumph in New York.

For years she had waited for that moment with patience, suffering privations and even humiliations along the way. A wealthy Barcelona family had declared their willingness to give her financial aid (these were the times when Montserrat's mother – la 'Màma' – would knit all day mending mountains of stockings to support the family). She was asked to audition to get the opinion of a famous Spanish singer, very popular at that time. The audition took place, and their opinion was negative: 'Don't throw away the money. It's not worth it'. Those who know Catalans can imagine what simmered in the heart of Montserrat.

---

[985] Violetta's letter scene from Act 3 of *La traviata*.

I learned of this incident years later. We were in the middle of giving another triumphant concert at the Liceu de Barcelona, when the proceedings were halted for Montserrat to receive membership of Spain's highest civic honour, the Order of Isabella the Catholic.[986] Admirers had travelled from far and wide, as well as many friends, international photographers and reporters. She seemed truly moved by the award. In a firm voice, albeit cracked by emotion from time to time, she expressed the hope that all Spanish artists would be able to share her great joy, and she named a few of these artists, mostly with reverence and affection. Naturally, she named first the singer who once judged her negatively. (Those who know Catalans might have expected this.) While she was doing this, she seemed to look directly at an elderly gentleman, who was almost lost among the crowd of admirers. He was the head of the wealthy family who had offered her this financial assistance years ago. The help had been given anyway, and the study abroad had occurred, despite the negative opinion of the famous singer.

Between the years 1956 to 1962, she worked in relative obscurity, singing Italian repertoire, but in German. Then she made a tour in Italy with a German company as one of the Flower Maidens in *Parsifal*. She took the opportunity to attend several auditions, with a heart full of hope, but not even Italy offered her a finger of encouragement. And now here was New York on the horizon, with a work like *Lucrezia Borgia*, that is, by her account, 'all about her'. Anyone who knows Montserrat Caballé can imagine the concentration of her will at such a decisive moment.

The artists who participated with her in that evening at Carnegie Hall later recounted to me of their amazement when, at the end of the General Rehearsal, there was a small further rehearsal for the order of applause. This Caballé directed herself. 'Now you retreat a step back ... like this. I walk slowly and there should be about two minutes of applause. Then I bow, and there will be three more. I will open my arms staring at the audience ... and the audience will start screaming. I'll take you by the hand....' And so on, all timed out with the anticipated minutes of applause. Her colleagues

---

[986] Cillario called it the 'Comedy of Isabella the Catholic.'

looked at her in astonishment, as one looks at someone who has lost her mind. Until, at the premiere, everything went exactly as predicted. Her success in New York was a sensation beyond all predictions.

Arriving shortly afterwards at Glyndebourne, the temple of punctuality, she obediently sat in the first rehearsal for *Der Rosenkavalier*, smiling and affable with everyone. Despite the meticulous musical training of each member of the company, the conductor, John Pritchard was determined to prove that he knew the work better than anyone else. When the time for the Marschallin's first line arrived, however, instead of singing, Caballé opened her mouth to announce candidly that she didn't know a note of the score. Panic. All the assembled company turn pale with shock. A glacial silence ensues, and the rehearsal is cancelled. An hour later she is received by the management who await her in a room that is set up like a war tribunal. She seems entirely unfazed, not in the least contrite, and begins by bringing her fist down on the table and ordering in full voice that no time be wasted in useless chatter. 'Give me a pianist to study at once.' Hispano–British history is filled with such clashes that brought various outcomes. In this case, England bowed to Spain. But they swore in their hearts that she would never set foot there again. She was in agreement – 'Fortunately!' she concluded. They wanted to warm up her voice two hours before each performance! ... Do her make up the way they wanted! ... Teach her where she should breathe! ... Get it into her head that 2+2 equals 4! I knew well what was being said about her.

However, it is the case that 'it' can easily be destroyed if a conductor or a director strictly observes the rule that $2 + 2 = 4$. A mathematical logic certainly exists in Caballé's art but based on a $2 + 2$ proposition that only she is able to calculate. Her main concerns resemble those of a manufacturer of model airplanes for aerobatic displays: finding the perfect balance of forces in order to caress the air without jolts. A little preparatory vibration ... and then the headlong plunge. Then a gentle glide, and when it seems that the only logical thing is to land … another proud, breath-taking ascent! Is it pure instinct? Is it mischief? One day I asked her. And she answered me: 'Carlo, I don't have the dramatic power of Callas. I don't have Joan Sutherland's technique. Not even Tebaldi's voice. Birgit Nilsson?' – she clasped her hands and raised them to the sky. Then, raising her tone, she cheerfully exploded: 'Christ! I have to have *something* if I want to make a career, right?!'

Something of that 'something', a New York critic discovered in her, as she told me herself: After our performance at Carnegie Hall of [Donizetti's] *Roberto Devereux* (exactly one year after the bombshell of *Lucrezia Borgia*), I was absent for a couple of weeks. On my return, she showed me the reviews. 'One of those scoundrels got me right!' she told me, then burst out laughing and read me the review. It was observed that she was highly skilled in the art of knowing how to sell her wares. On three occasions during the performance, she had astounded everyone with three high notes performed in such a way as to make them believe they were very different from each other and each higher than the other; each more difficult than the others. But which, upon careful examination turned out to be nothing more than 'three C naturals.' The critic continued: 'La Caballé is very skilled in knowing how to take the public by surprise, with exceptional *pianissimi* especially in moments when they are not required. She often avoids taking a breath where any other human being would….' Montserrat looked surprised that someone had discovered so many of her secrets at once. But she wasn't sorry at all; indeed, she seemed amused by it.

Then we arrived at her debut in *Norma*, which she considered the high point of her career. When we began to rehearse it, she often interrupted herself to say to me (and to herself): 'Here, I understand that it should be like this,' and she sang the passage, 'but these notes weigh me down. And I can only do them this other way.' She took long breaths and set off like a skier who has found the right wax, and knows where to place their heel in order to complete the trickiest turn. And then she enquired: 'Maestro: do you think it will be acceptable?' 'Why not?' I replied. In art, every licence becomes logical (and therefore acceptable) if it is conducted with knowledge of one's means and above all with conviction. Only inflexibility is unacceptable to a great artist. Caballé's debut in *Norma* was dedicated by her to the public of her native Barcelona, a gesture reminiscent of the bullfighter offering 'orejas y rabo'[987] to his paramour. And the Barcelona public was whipped into a frenzy by this gesture alone. But just before the General Rehearsal, in a moment when we were alone, she whispered to me: 'Now let's see how I get on. And if I don't make it… Let's do *La bohème*! I'm at home here and they would let me.'

An interviewer for an English newspaper asked, with a tone of disbelief: 'But do you really think you can get by in *Norma*?' (British interviewers are notorious for their flippant questions). Caballé replied: 'I believe that after Callas there are only "wrong" Normas, and I will be one more wrong Norma,' she said, laughing the question off. And when I asked her how she managed to parry these verbal blows so skilfully, she replied: 'Once, I was more naïve, but now I'm always ready to meet my enemies.' Her success was astonishing, the audience went crazy, and the ovations continued for dozens of minutes.

That evening Pepito almost ate the 'Tuscan' that he was smoking. All the owners of the private boxes in the Liceu stayed until the end (which rarely happens). Afterwards, the backstage corridors became clogged by a stream of people who wanted to reach the stage at all costs, to see us up close, to touch us…. She and I seemed to be the only two people who had kept our heads. In a moment of quiet, she whispered to me (and winked as she did so): 'Maestro! Now I can tell you: in two years, I will be Norma. I promise you.' To which I whispered back to her: 'Why two years? Try six months.'

The following morning, I received a call from a stranger. He introduced himself as the owner of a modest house, but of an excellent tape recorder, and he invited me for 'arroz a la Valenciana'[988] and the opportunity to listen back to our *Norma* from the night before. I

---

[987] The ears and the tail.
[988] Valencian rice.

gladly accepted. At the end of the First Act, surprised and moved, I asked permission to make a phone call: 'Monte! They were right. I'm listening to *Norma* and it's really beautiful!' And she: 'Carlo! I'm listening to it too and I'm surprised and happy! But I'm just at the end of the First Act and I've already counted six chest notes! In six months, I will do fewer. I promise you.'

After the final performance she threw a party at her house, and I was honoured to be present. She had invited only those whom she considered her closest friends: Don Antonio Pamias, her first impresario; Louie Andreu, faithful friend; the seamstress of the Liceu; the hairdresser; Pepito (for once without 'Tuscan'), and a lady who was presented with particular respect. It was she who, when Montserrat was nothing more than a poor girl studying singing, sent *la Màma* mountains of stockings to be mended. And there was – of course – in full force as always – the Caballé family. All composed, in a circle, gazing at their Montserrat, who sat with her child on her lap like a Madonna and Child. We hardly spoke, we were all wrung out. We looked at each other and exchanged smiles, chewing a *Jamòn cerrano* cut into large pieces with peasant bread that would resurrect the dead. To drink, there was wine sent from the Aragonese vineyard belonging to Bernabé, the colour of a blood transfusion. Bernabé looked after everyone, he who, without ever making it obvious, had played so central a part in the success of Montserrat. For his innate common sense, for his open and frank character, for his advice that she always asked him before making any important decision.

I remember making a record together with him in Spain, while Montserrat sat in the control room. When, after hours of recording, it seemed to everyone that we had 'Di quella pira' in the can, her persuasive voice would come over the loudspeaker: 'Bernabé mi amor; hazlo una vez màs, por amor mio....'[989] And he, da capo: 'With your saaaangue...'. Over the next ten minutes he pulled out another seven high C's. Later, he stopped singing in public when they found a lung defect. I asked him one day in London how he felt in the

---

[989] 'Bernabé, do it once more please, my love.'

guise of 'Mr. Caballé', a qualification that is generally used for the husbands of famous female artists. He replied: 'Carlos, my destiny was to graze sheep on my hillsides. Now I find myself here, with all these gold buttons (in fact he was wearing an elegant blue jacket with six gold buttons) ... do you really want me to kick up a fuss?'

Nevertheless, his health picked up once he began taking care of the land they bought in Catalonia. Montserrat has had no time to enjoy it yet, but he has. A few days before the *Norma* debut, we were sitting in her living room with a group of international journalists who had come to interview us. While we discussed aesthetic problems, stylistic purity, Bellinian melody, Maria Malibran and Giuditta Pasta, Bernabé made an entrance, having come from their farm. On his expensive carpets he set down two boxes with holes in, full of hens, who proceeded to cluck away, demonstrating their loud voices, and drowning out our elevated conversation.

It was during that post-premiere party for *Norma*, while nibbling on a slice of *Jamòn cerrano*, that I brought up the story of our first phone call. 'You came three days late for the first rehearsal,' I recalled to her. 'But I have to admit that you did come back from Marseille and kept your promise.' I began to notice some funny faces among the Caballé group. I didn't understand until Montserrat turned to the others: 'What are we going to do? Shall we tell him?' She giggled softly. 'Eh ... shall we tell him?'. 'Yes, let's tell him...' said Màma. 'Now we can tell you,' she sighed as she stared into my eyes. 'I never went to Marseille', she laughed. 'I stayed indoors studying *Manon Lescaut* because I didn't know it. I'd never sung it before!' And I was stunned into silence as I looked at good Bernabé, the only person present who shook his head, instead of laughing.

--o-o--

ELENA SULIOTIS (and RENATA TEBALDI)

It can truly be said that the world of opera is beautiful because it is varied. I went on a concert tour in Germany with Renata Tebaldi at the time when the rivalry between her and Maria Callas was at its height. Our concerts took place in the very same cities where Callas had sung only a couple of months earlier, with sold-out houses for both. But I learned from the organisers that while it took at least two days to sell all the tickets for Tebaldi, for Callas they were snapped up in just a couple of hours. As justification, they added: 'It is logical, Callas has much bigger scandals in her private life'. But everyone recognised that from an artistic point of view Tebaldi was superior. Having heard from Renata herself that she loved giving these concerts, I thought she would make use of her first-class instrument to present music of exceptional interest. Vain hope: the most substantial item was the 'Willow Song' and Ave Maria from *Otello*. For the rest of the programme, she sang brief operatic selections such as 'Vissi d'arte' and 'O mio babbino caro', interspersed with long stretches of orchestral interludes for which I took responsibility.

Callas had been boxed in by the constraining space on the concert platform – trapped inside a few square meters – without the possibility to unleash the full force of her power as an actress. She suffered in direct comparison with her rival. Some of the audience even ridiculed her for attempting to dramatise the scene from *Il Pirata* of Bellini. By contrast, Tebaldi had the advantage of her voice and celestial charm, and she was greeted with rapture. At the close of the concert, compact bouquets of flowers would rain down on the stage, catapulted by muscular *fräuleins* from close range, constituting a danger to our safety.

One evening, having arrived at the theatre at the time when Tebaldi usually warmed up her voice, I saw on the faces of the organizers that particular pallor which usually heralds serious problems. 'The young lady doesn't want to see anyone, and we don't know if she will sing', they reported. Her voice emerged from the dressing room endlessly repeating slowly and with great care, only two notes. After a while I went in and saw her:

'Maestro! Tonight, I can't dampen the A flat!'

... 'Then don't dampen it.'

'But I've always toned it down.'

... 'Well, not tonight.'

She sang nervously all evening up to that famous A flat in 'Vissi d'arte' and from then on she seemed liberated from a nightmare, triumphing as usual. I recalled this moment in another difficult moment of my life, when I was working with another diva, Elena Suliotis.

Of all the oddities that occur even in the best theatres, at Covent Garden in London I had the dress rehearsal of *Macbeth* on a Friday morning, and the first night four days later, on Tuesday evening. Suliotis [performing Lady Macbeth] had asked me to run through her arias with her before the performance, so I arrived quite early. At Covent Garden the maestro's dressing room is located high up, in a sort of turret, from where one may look down on the comings and goings of the fruit and vegetable market, which surrounds the theatre like the moats around old castles. The voices of the singers in their own dressing rooms thus reach the conductor's room from anywhere in the theatre. There I was, when suddenly a voice rent the air.

At first, I was not sure if the voice was coming from one of the dressing rooms or from the pub over the road. It was a full and strange voice, rather thick and cavernous, which seemed to contain crushed stones, bits of shell and a good deal of tar. In rising to the top, it broke into a fabulous 'false' note; one of the longest, bravest, most insistent false notes I've ever heard in my life. Then there was silence, broken after a while ('broken' is the right expression) by another vocalised expression, now half a tone higher, which reached the exact same out-of-tune conclusion. Perhaps this one was even longer, more squeezed and insistent than her preceding sister.

As this series of vocalisations continued – gradually a little more acute and always similar in their abstract deformity – I made my way, with understandable horror, to the door of the prima donna's dressing room, to be certain that it was indeed the voice of Elena Suliotis which was producing such strange effects. At the first opportune moment, I gathered my courage and knocked. 'Come in,' replied a full, grave, solemn voice. 'How is it going?' I asked, 'Very good' (?!!) she replied. 'Shall we run through some passages?' I suggested. 'All right.'

That evening Suliotis gave one of her most characteristic performances, displaying incredible qualities in her voice and her heart. Yet this wonderful girl used them in an unconventional way and with apparent indifference. Her performance polarised the audience: fantastic enthusiasm came from one section of the public, and enduring scepticism from many others. Following the performance, we found ourselves together in a Greek restaurant. Its deafening noise seemed finally to put her at ease. I told her how alarmed I was when I had heard her 'move her voice'; I could have said to 'smash it to bits', because it was just as if a violinist had chosen to warm up their Stradivarius before a concert by using it to squash flies against a wall. 'Everything is normal,' she said. 'During the three days off I went to the beach, and after that I have to do this'.

What a contrast to Renata Tebaldi! In between the exhausting rehearsals and concerts on our German tour, she took refuge in her hotel room, lowering the shutters on the windows for fear that a breath of air or a faint ray of light might damage her voice. It would seem that even the 'angels' – as Toscanini called divas – must take care of themselves.

But Elena Suliotis had no time for such appellations. She, like the angels, certainly came from above – but more in the manner of a meteorite hitting Greek soil with a resounding roar, bouncing up again and landing in the middle of the Argentine pampas. It was here that she spent her youth driving trucks and operating bulldozers on her father's land. She terrified herds of wild animals with thunderous curses, until the beasts noticed and winked at her.

Later, she left her worker's clothes behind and put on silky robes. She passed the care of the wild herds to others and bent her voice to the discipline of the printed and orderly 'bel canto'. Reassurances were given to her that 'We won't make up your eyes. And your face will appear on the covers of thousands and thousands of record albums. And if we make good money from you, maybe one day you'll even be on the cover of *The Times*'. And she – a little ambitious, a little indolent – accepted to play the game and let it unfold. But with no great enthusiasm.

For the gala concert at Carnegie Hall where we performed *Norma* in concert [in 1967], Suliotis spent all of her fee on an evening gown created especially for her by New York's most famous Greek tailor. The dress was a dream. Of a beautiful *framboise* colour, edged with a striking black Greek design along the fringes of dress and accompanying shawl. But when she made her entrance as Norma she seemed to walk on her stomach, with her feet spread out, as if she had just preceded the arrival of Pancho Villa.[990] At that gala event, which was to signify her definitive 'arrival', the promoters had charged astronomical sums for tickets. Intending to give the public their money's worth, these promoters had the idea to invite various operatic stars who were dear to the hearts of the New York public; among them Zinka Milanov, the tenor Giovanni Martinelli and even Maria Callas.

The First Act passed without incident. Then Callas arrived, direct from Paris, with a bottle of champagne and a retinue of excited photographers who captured her in all her poses. She went straight to Suliotis' dressing room where we were trying to focus our energies in view of the challenges yet to come. The 'star of the evening' had curled herself up in a corner of the sofa, like a child being punished. Returning to the stage at the end of the intermission, we were greeted with a roar of enthusiasm – or so we imagined. Instead, we found ourselves standing on stage while the entire audience had turned towards the seat, highlighted by spotlights, where Callas theatrically bequeathed kisses and smiles on the public, 'old glories'.[991] It took some time and effort on our part to turn the public's attention back to the musical glories of Bellini.

Despite playing the role of the opera star, Suliotis seemed incapable of climbing the greasy pole for the sake of her career. She would say: 'I am rich. If I lose my voice, I'll get married.' She was hated by many who were unable to forgive her for coming from a wealthy family. They judged her aloof and unfriendly, mistaking her natural reserve for haughtiness. Publicity-hungry impresarios are always looking for labels and slogans, working along the usual

---

[990] A Mexican revolutionary and one-time Governor of Chihuahua.
[991] Retired world-famous singers of the past, including Martinelli, Milanov and Callas.

lines of 'squeeze until there's nothing left, then throw it away'. They certainly did her no favours by making up the myth of 'the new Callas' based on her Greek origins and on the particular sound of some notes that – even if Callas had wished to use them – it would have been better not to share with the public. Meanwhile Suliotis always carried herself with amused indifference above praise and insults.

Her premieres didn't excite her. And as for criticism, it was like throwing a punch at a boxing-ball. Maybe a little sand stirred inside her, but you could hardly tell. I tried repeatedly, but only once was I able to make her lose her composure. It was when I told her that, with her qualities, she could have made much more of herself if she had just used a crumb of Caballé's shrewdness (for which, incidentally, she always showed great admiration). She yelled back: 'You've already broken my balls with your bullshit,' and from the sound of her voice I thought at that moment that she might actually be right.

We worked together on various occasions, and I was able to witness her special qualities at close quarters: a straightforward approach to human problems and an extreme respect for every form of life. When we had a free afternoon in Genoa, she often asked me to come with her to Portofino. Driving – both there and back – she would start humming Greek songs in a low and sweet voice. No one could do it quite like her, because she would impart in those songs, sometimes profoundly melancholy or strictly rhythmical, a nuance of boundless expression that seemed to come from the steppes of Asia and the Argentine pampas. In Portofino we would sit in companiable silence with an orange soda, looking at the sea. One afternoon, walking across the small inlet where the boats dock, she moved ahead of me, suddenly quickening her pace and heading towards a group of people who were looking down into the water.

Her voice thundered out, vibrant and spontaneous, a phenomenon of nature, raw and untamed: 'Who did it?' she demanded. The group crumpled under the vocal assault, but no one answered. 'I asked, who did this?!' she repeated. A man dressed in blue overalls –

evidently a worker – murmured: 'Me'. 'Now save him!' she ordered. And the natural acoustics of the small cove amplified the command, vibrating in all its vegetation and reverberating in the rocky walls. The group spread out, trembling at her arrival. With the aid of a few onlookers, the wretched man frantically dedicated himself to a rescue operation. He jumped into a boat, took a bucket and a rope, and with the help of a piece of wood he managed to get a poor, large toad into the bucket which until then, to the delight of the curious spectators, had not managed to do anything other than swallow large gulps of salt water, probably resigned to meet his maker. All of a sudden, thanks to this fairy with a voice of thunder, the toad, as if transformed by magic into Prince Charming, enjoyed the frantic attentions of everyone.

A little reverent and a little fearful, the group shrank away and dispersed, leaving the two of us alone, in the middle of the deserted bay of Portofino, with a toad that continued to make strange noises and vomit salt water. With gentle motherly care she hastened his recovery by tenderly rubbing his stomach. I had engaged in a similar operation myself. One day, sailing off the coast of Milano Marittima, I managed to bring back to shore and save a bat which – who knows how – had become lost on the high seas and was flying blindly in the sun of a summer noon. So, I gladly gave my energies to finding a suitable new home for the toad. When he seemed to us sufficiently recovered and able to get by on his own, we succeeded in slipping him, with great care, through a net, into a meadow overlooking the wall which surrounds the bay. We took this grave responsibility upon ourselves, having no further information about where he belonged. Did he find his family? Will he form another family? We had done our best, and left with a clear conscience.

Luckily, we didn't have immediate commitments that afternoon, otherwise what would we have done if we had to go back to the theatre early? Could we have returned with a toad on a leash? Perhaps we would have abandoned the rehearsal because we certainly would not have abandoned him in the company of those savages. I care deeply for all the problems of this world, including the artistic ones, but they pale in significance compared to the life of a living thing, man or beast, however small or large. I am convinced that if Destiny had given me, in a past life, the possibility of an intimate dinner with 'Nefertiti the Beautiful', and I had read in her bewitching eyes a promise of amorous pursuits; and if in the meantime she had done what elegant ladies do at the table on summer evenings (that is to say, absent-mindedly place their ringed hands on poor insects attracted by the light and by our crumbs) well, I'm sure I would have given 'Nefertiti la Bella' a hard slap.

Elena: with your voice you certainly sold the thousands and thousands of records that the promoters and record companies dangled in front of you. Perhaps they exploited you. I don't know if you will continue to sing and cause an uproar, as happened in Mexico City where your supporters and your enemies began to pick a fight during your performance. In my eyes, your greatest act was the thunder that you let off in Portofino. I wish all the hunters on earth could hear the thunder that roared on that afternoon. I would hammer it into their brains when they exult in the blood they have spilled. And I wish that the beautiful ladies could hear it too, when they absent-mindedly squash midges on white tablecloths.

--o-o--

SOUVENIR DE ... ALCUNI TENORI:

The following introduction and the Pavarotti memoir exist in two versions – Cillario's own manuscript, and a published newspaper article 'Love, Women and Big Luciano', which appeared in The Weekend Australian Magazine, *11-12 December 1982. This is a conflation of the two versions.*

Could the insults so often aimed at tenors possibly be fuelled by envy? I am sure this is the case because tenors themselves are able to find easy consolation in their expensive cars and in dressing their wives in mink and jewels from top to toe. They deserve some respect, for filling theatres and swelling box-office returns, if for nothing else. And here's the reason: theirs is the most unnatural of all voices, the most unpredictable in performance, and the most difficult to dominate. It is a hybrid of voices: a contralto bud grafted onto a baritone rootstock. And (to admit a note of malice), somehow related to a castrato or even a hunchback. In spite of all this, it is considered the most attractive voice of all – and the most exciting.

A soprano's perfect top note is… still just a top note. A tenor's high note, even from an average singer, can be compared to the gymnast in a circus troupe of acrobats, ascending the pyramid and arriving triumphantly on unknown shoulders. This advantage of theirs leads some of them to engage only cursorily with musical notation: but let us not forget Enrico Caruso, who has gone down in history as one of the greatest tenors of all time, precisely because of his freedom in music-making and his incomparable phrasing.

I have an English friend who is a fanatic (as only certain English people know how to be) for Handel, who has dedicated part of his life and fortune to collecting all kinds of Handel recordings. He had me listen to the most rare and precious items in his collection. 'I consider this the most perfect interpretation of Handel,' he said, and showed me a recording of 'Ombra mai fu', from *Serse*, sung by Caruso. I thought he was joking, or that he had said it out of extreme courtesy to my race. But, listening to the disc, I had to agree. Caruso – perhaps unconsciously – had distilled all the expressive emotionality of his heart within a stylistically valid framework. This is a goal that even artists of the calibre of Toscanini, Huberman or Furtwängler – citing only the major ones – spent their lives in pursuing. Perhaps only Pablo Casals, born like Caruso in the Mediterranean basin, was able to access such artistic mysteries and illuminating insights, with his interpretations of Bach.

It is well known that Caruso did not reach the 'high C'.[992] So is that famous 'high C' so important? In the world of opera it certainly is. To make a great career, some would sell their soul to the devil for it. In the past there were certain apocryphal accounts which fuelled the myth of the 'high C', bestowing upon it the power to shatter chandeliers and turn the pages of music on faraway music stands.

---

[992] This has been challenged – while he had trouble at certain times in his career producing the note, he apparently sang it in public performances on numerous occasions.

Even today this fantasy retains a certain appeal for some opera lovers. But today we are more objective, thanks to a recent generation of opera conductors who continue the work of reinstating the old traditions begun by Toscanini and others of his time, steering the operatic spectacle onto a path of more correct foundations.

Let us recall the tale of Luciano Pavarotti (present standard-bearer of the 'high C' possessors), of how his great success grew suddenly from the moment when in New York – instead of the occasional 'C' here and there, as required in other operas – he rattled off nine 'high C's' in the space of a minute in Donizetti's *La fille du régiment*. We can reduce the tenor with the 'Do in petto'[993] to the following formula: One 'C' here and there equals a run-of-the-mill Fiat plus an apartment in Milan's outer suburbs. For nine 'high C's' a minute – bonus dollars, a custom-made Maserati and a beach villa.

But the tenors of the 'high C' differ from their colleagues also in the number of murmured prayers and signs of the Cross they make when they enter or exit the stage, often bearing amulets and small pictures of saints ('holy card collectors') in hope of divine protection. This is the price they pay for their 'high C's'. In Pavarotti's words 'Every time I must go on stage I feel as if I have taken castor oil' – and he is the greatest, in spite of the dark overtones of his high register.

LUCIANO PAVAROTTI

Now, some of his friends have valid reasons for calling him Lucianone (big Luciano). But in 1965, when we went to London for *La traviata* at Covent Garden, he was an elegant Alfredo, slender as an asparagus. And like asparagus he bore the fresh and healthy fragrance of sunny fields, and the forbearance of those who know nature's secrets well. He came from his home in Modena to sing for me. We spoke a little about the odd 'rattle' that sometimes broke the flow of his singing. I called them 'little brays' and he laughed: 'Well, anyway, better to be a donkey than a capon!'

---

[993] The 'high C' sung from the chest, most famously at the premiere of Rossini's *Guillaume Tell* in 1829.

My maid was listening behind the door while he was singing, and like all Italian girls she had a good knowledge of voices. After accompanying him to the front door, she turned to me: 'Don't say you didn't like him?' And then, with a sigh, 'He is such a nice lad.' The girls in London also liked him. Pavarotti smiles at his public and gets smiles back. He gives comfort and trust and asks, in turn for comfort and reassurance. He can convince 20,000 people that he is addressing each one of them individually. Like the Halloween masks that children make in America, by hollowing out a pumpkin and placing a candle inside, Pavarotti also seems to have inside himself a little candle, perpetually lighting up his smile. Whenever I see him, a poem by Giosuè Carducci[994] always enters my mind – why, I don't know:

> 'T'amo o pio bove
>
> E mite un sentiment
>
> Di pace e di vigor
>
> Al cor, infondi…'[995]

The London *Traviata* was a good success even if some of the critics did not realise that this young man with a gentle rustic appearance would one day emulate the most famous of the Medici's, becoming – no less – 'Luciano the Magnificent' as many in England now call him. He was sad about the chilly reception from the English critics. Lord Harewood, the Queen's cousin, cheered him up in my presence by saying: 'Let them say what they like! You will be one of the greatest tenors in the world.'

I have always admired his qualities: his solidity, his good temper and his common sense. But one evening when he wasn't singing and I wasn't conducting, I admired him for another aspect of his nature which is rare in our profession. We were at the Arena di Verona, Luciano was singing in *La bohème,* and I was conducting The Nutcracker.[996] One evening *La Gioconda* was performed, with Carlo Bergonzi as the tenor lead. We were together in the small area

---

[994] Carducci (1835-1907) was a leading Italian poet, writer and literary critic.

[995] 'I love you, pious cow, with mild sentiments of peace and vigour you enfold my heart.'

[996] Tchaikovsky's ballet.

reserved for the Intendant and his guests, where we had to stand, packed in like sardines. Lucianone was standing behind me, and at the end of each act he shouted 'Bravo Carlettooh' at the top of his lungs, like the most fanatical *loggionista*, which prompted people in the parterre to turn around and made my ears buzz.

A few evenings later I went to hear Luciano in *La bohème*. In front of me – with everyone crowded together, standing as usual – was 'Carletto' Bergonzi. When Luciano sang, Bergonzi turned around, touched my arm, and murmured: 'Oh God, how beautifully he sings!' It seemed as though he was hearing singing for the first time. So, I ask – who will be rude about tenors? For singers, the problem of what they will do at the end of their career often arises. Some become owners of petrol-station chains, some open restaurants, or manage a hotel of their own. Others go to the casino and gamble away all their money and finish their lives in an artists' asylum.

It is my opinion that Luciano Pavarotti has the qualities to excel in any profession. Whether it be as a doctor or a stockbroker, I feel that I could trust him. If he were a priest, I could believe him (and perhaps even if he were a politician). I could even see him mastering the profession that I consider the most difficult of all: that of a waiter. One of those marvellous 'family restaurant' waiters who is able to remember everybody's orders and special requests, while at the same time carrying piles of dishes on his arms and gliding between crowded tables, distributing a kind word, a smile, some advice, suggestions, and recommendations.

I must say that I find Pavarotti's perspiration a mystery! In the US I saw lines of women of all ages waiting for their turn to touch him, even to kiss him, regardless of the flood of perspiration bathing his body after a performance. Perhaps they don't see the perspiration, or else they consider it purifying, like holy water. They stay in line patiently just exchange a few words with him. And a kiss. Yes, because Lucianone kisses each one of them, especially those under 40. Calmly and conscientiously. Sweet lover's kisses with others waiting their turn, under the supervision of his wife, the level-headed and understanding Signora Adua.

She declares that between Luciano and women there exists some kind of primal rapport, and in these moments, she is probably thinking that the career of her man is more important than a few kisses lost (I mean a few kisses stolen from her). She says: 'Luciano needs women close to him. He observes them, studies them, he needs to be surrounded by them. It has been like this since he was a child.' Because of such good common sense on her part, and Luciano's open nature, the Pavarotti marriage has not suffered the quakes that so often shake other unions in the world of 'stars'. When the family are all together, they form a group that could well appear in the *Family Weekly* magazine. Papa Luciano and Mamma Adua in the centre, seated on the sofa, and around them, in silent adoration, their three girls.

I think that Adua is right: Luciano observes women, studies women, and tastes women. Before travelling to Australia for the first time I asked him – since he had already been there – what he thought of the country. We were in his dressing room at La Scala. He was dressed as a monk for the last act of *La favorita*, so I expected a serious answer. But only one sentence passed his lips, murmured with his eyes pointing to the sky: 'Dio, quanta gnoca.'[997]

As I write I feel God in my presence, shaking his head in disapproval. I distinctly hear him say: 'Carlo, please don't translate that into English.' Evidently God understands Emiliano dialect.

GIACOMO ARAGALL AND JOSÉ CARRERAS

To be honest, the encounter which took place between Giacomo Aragall and José Carreras in London, before my very eyes, was much less noble than the previous memoir. The two tenors were not to blame. Aragall, although he likes to introduce himself as Giacomo, is just as Catalan as Carreras, hailing from that glorious and inexhaustible incubator of singers which is the city of Barcelona. A few hundred metres from the Gran Teatro del Liceu, there is a wonderful market, 'El mercato de San José', which I have nicknamed 'El mercato que canta'. At any time of day, until closing time, it resounds with the most beautiful and natural voices in the world.

---

[997] A cleaned-up translation: 'So many lovely women.'

The fishmongers banter with the greengrocers or the cheesemakers, the chicken vendors scold their children. It is a rich tapestry of calls and responses, a curtain of sound that hangs over everyone like an umbrella, produced by the healthiest and most resonant throats, never hoarse or weakened despite humidity, cold, and continuous use. Italy perhaps gives us singers with a more rigorous education. But in the number of throats touched by the finger of God, Spain undoubtedly takes the first place.

Giacomo Aragall's larynx is also very healthy and resonant, incorporated within an athletic physique. Yet there is a vulnerable spot, a kind of 'Achilles heel' situated in his brain. It is enough for one to stare at Aragall fixedly, squint a little and emit a diffident 'Ehm...' for him to put his hand over his throat, and complain 'Ah yes, I'm ill!' Then he hurries off to cancel the performance. He is an excellent musician with exceptional talents, and any theatre director may rest easy if they engage him: as long as his enemies do not come near him.

In London [in 1972] we were due to perform Donizetti's *Caterina Cornaro* in concert at the Royal Festival Hall. He was singing beautifully, but he made the mistake of being absent for two days to go to Parma and complete a recording. He missed one day of rehearsals, which was enough to mobilise another group of opera fans who were waiting for just such an occasion to launch the new tenor: José Carreras. This tenor was also blessed by Mother Nature, fresh out of his studies, smiling, and in possession of bombproof nerves. He just happened to be there in London and – in my opinion – he must already have studied *Caterina Cornaro* for performances that he was to give later, in another city.

Aragall reappeared at the appointed rehearsal. He had barely sung a note when someone stared at him, gave him the fateful 'Ehm!' and rapidly persuaded him to conclude that he was ill. I can imagine how he must have felt knowing that another Barcelonan would replace him. I don't know if other professions are similarly affected, but in ours there are remarkable reactions when we learn that one of our fellow citizens is ready to take our place. Not a few moribund artists have suddenly found themselves cured, filled again with life-force.

But in the case of Aragall–Carreras, the change of cast had already been confirmed.

With Carreras stepping in, the press were invited to attend a private rehearsal at which this 'new Mozart' would prove his skill by sight-reading the entire opera from cover to cover. Carreras undertook the task in front of all the assembled company, displaying great musicality and also shrewdness, because he did not fail – here and there – to make a few small mistakes while furtively glancing at me as if to say: Do not worry, tomorrow everything will be fine. In fact, at the performance everything was perfect, and Aragall applauded us from the front row. Luckily, they are such fine singers, and Aragall has so few enemies, that both of them are making great careers. The Catalan saints rejoice from their altars and wink slyly with their long, Romanesque eyes.

PLÁCIDO DOMINGO

It was the 1960 Temporada Liric Internacional in Mexico City. Among the five operas on the bill – all sung by Pippo Di Stefano – were *Tosca* and *Turandot*. For the role of Spoletta in *Tosca*, they had chosen a young local lad: tall, lanky and 19 years of age. 'He will be inexperienced,' I thought. And yet he did very well. He made of this small role a new character, a bloodhound, alternating between indolent and itchy. He was musical and well-coordinated in every respect. In *Turandot*, this same 19-year-old was entrusted with the role of Altoum, the celestial, decrepit old Emperor. 'He is too young,' I thought. But I had to eat my words once more, and admit that he knew exactly how to imitate the weak and strained voice of an ancient old man, as Puccini envisaged.

A few years later, I encountered him again in Mexico City. He was happy to be back at his parents' home (both were well-known zarzuela singers) after two years of working in Israel. He now felt ready for leading roles, and sang *The Tales of Hoffman* as best he could. One critic wrote that a tenor such as this should leave the singing to his family, because he was not suited even for the zarzuela. I knew the critic personally and told him that he would soon be proven wrong – that tenor will soon be singing at the Met. In fact, six months later, that is exactly what happened. And today we all know what he has achieved.

Unfortunately, when we recorded *Norma* for RCA in London I didn't see him enough. Plácido arrived just before the start of the recording, so late that we didn't even have time to greet one another. He felt tired because he had sung the night before in New York and he asked me to leave Pollione's 'high C', (which all Pollione's dislike) for the last session, two days later. I don't believe he was interested in having *Norma* in his repertoire. In the large studio on the outskirts of London, the distance between the soloists and the conductor is enormous. Plácido placed the score against his nose, so I couldn't see him. Two days later we received bad news: the Met was threatening legal action against RCA if Domingo did not make it back to New York on the afternoon plane. We still had a lot left to record.

We tried to get the job done as quickly as possible, but in the middle of our work, a group of uniformed English policemen entered the studio, interrupting the recording, seized Plácido, and led him to one of their cars. Speeding off for a few hundred metres, they took him to a waiting helicopter, surrounded by onlookers who imagined they were witnessing the capture of some dangerous IRA terrorist. I was among them. And as the helicopter sputtered away, I shouted at him: 'What about the "High C"?' 'We'll record it in New York … si Dios lo quiere!'[998] he shouted back at me from the still open door, throwing his arms to the sky. The helicopter was soon barely visible in the distance.

That is how the *Norma* recording progressed: our Pollione, the Roman pro-consul, was hustled off to Scotland Yard and kidnapped. Norma fell sick! Adalgisa was tired! And everyone glowered at the good Ruggero Raimondi because he candidly declared that he felt good and had no problems. Frankly, I thought little of that recording; maybe it was the worst thing I've done. So much so that when I received my copy, I immediately gave it to my dentist. I still can't believe it was awarded a Grand Prix du Disque!

---

[998] '… if God is willing!'

FRANCO CORELLI

Piece by piece, Franco is a fine specimen. Impeccable. <u>Voice</u>: masculine, confident and tense. Handsome. Velvety. <u>Physique</u>: like a gladiator. Head: Greco–Roman, beautiful both in front and in profile. <u>Legs</u> which send directors and audiences into paroxysms when he plays characters in a cloak. (And for the tenor there are many, from Julius Caesar to Pollione, from Samson to Radamès.) <u>Diction</u>: clear and flawless, with the syllables supporting the line of the music like sturdy pillars. I remember when we were rehearsing *Carmen*, I was surprised at his bad pronunciation. He sang: 'La fler che tu mavè getè.'[999] I told him: 'Franco: don't you think your French sounds rather "made in Italy"?' 'I know that' he replied, 'but do you really want me to change the position of my voice to produce perfect French?!' (An instance of deliberate and well-studied cunning).

Nevertheless, despite so many advantages bestowed upon him by Mother Nature – voice, physique, personality – it would seem that Corelli belongs to the category of those 'born to suffer'. His voice drags him out of his everyday life for three or four days before each performance. And since he generally has a performance every three or four days, he ends up never using it other than in public performances.

I have a friend who was present at a scene that took place in Franco Corelli's apartment in New York, and he related it to me in such detail that I felt as though I had witnessed it myself. While his wife was preparing dinner, she dropped a massive Patek Philippe gold bracelet down the garbage disposal. Franco rushed to her desperate screams and his lips articulated the most acerbic and reproachful profanities, accompanied by rolling of the eyes and suitable dramatic gestures. But he did all of this without making a whisper… because the following day he had a performance at the Met.

I recall an incident at the Met itself where we were to perform *Tosca*.[1000] I had envisaged that we would confer about how to conclude

---

[999] Don Jose's aria from Carmen – the first line rewritten to show that Corelli would open the final 'e's' as is usual when singing Italian, but not French.

[1000] This is Cillario's own account of the scandalous performance at the Met.

his 'Addio alla vita' from Act 3. Puccini – of course – calculated things well, allowing time for the tenor's fan-club to shout their 'Bravo... sei grande...', repeated many times while the orchestra continues for about half a minute with low, slow, and *pianissimo* harmonies that smoothly transition into Flora's anxious arrival with the letter of safe conduct, her frantic embrace and the news of her unexpected freedom. But some tenors think that half a minute of applause is not enough. And so, with the complicity of some conductors who are unwilling to follow the precise indications of the composer, a bad tradition was created so that the conductor folds his arms, and the music stops. The orchestra players resume reading the magazines they often keep close at hand under their music stands, Floria Tosca waits in the wings while the gallery continues its shouting, and the tenor can assume a contrite air as if to say: 'I would like to do an "encore", but they won't let me ... To you who praise me I would embrace you one by one ... and maybe I would also give you a little present for your children... but I just can't... But if you continue to applaud me, I will raise my head towards you ... slowly ... like this ... then I will put my hand on my heart ... I will say goodbye ... and I will also send you some kisses....'

At the Met, either to prevent his voice from wearing out, or because he was indisposed, Corelli hadn't attended rehearsals, not even those with the orchestra. He only came to the General Rehearsal and, whether he was distracted or worried about problems of his own, he didn't notice that when I reached the fateful point, following this aria, I didn't stop. Nor did I stop in the performance, but then he noticed it – and how. When he realised the music had continued, he leapt down to the edge of the footlights and placing his foot on the prompter's box, he let out a tremendous 'Noooo ... Noooooo ...' at me: out loud this time, with no regard for his larynx. I ignored him, as of course I had to. Then he began to gallop up and down the battlements of Castel Sant'Angelo, until by chance he ran into the soprano who didn't know where to find him. And when she managed to get the safe-conduct document into his hands, he

---

Shuyler Chapin's account can be found on p. 250-1.

ripped it in four pieces and came downstage to throw the pieces into the pit. Then he was up again dashing along the ramparts without paying any attention to the difficulties that Floria Tosca was recounting, of the night before with Baron Scarpia which occurred precisely because of him.

Musically, the performance felt like a rodeo for the soprano, the orchestra, and me – taking care not to be thrown off by the enraged bullock. Meanwhile, the stage director looked on from the wings, tearing out his hair. Finally, the firing squad arrived to mete out justice. The audience didn't seem to notice the little, unscripted dramas that were additional to the main *melodramma*. Maybe they thought they were witnessing the eccentricities of a radical 'new' production, which are becoming ever more common. Eventually, though, Corelli was well received and seemed to make peace with me and with life. Many years have passed since Toscanini and other honest 'men of the theatre' decreed – at the price of hard-earned battles – that the show does not have to suffer 'optional hiatuses' or forced 'backtracking'. But in opera, much more than in other art forms, the winds of passion blow. And they often cover the paved streets of good intentions with sand. Up on stage, 'lucevan le stelle', but down here we have too many stars who are addicted to the lure of 'encores'.

--oo-oo--

TITO GOBBI

All those who knew him will agree that Tito Gobbi was a 'fine example of a man'. In appearance he recalled those captains of fortune, bold and courageous, who by their mere presence had the power to inflame and inspire crowds of followers. I am surprised that no composer has written an opera which would cast him in the role of Giuseppe Garibaldi. He had the appearance of a beneficent curmudgeon, which in a nutshell, he was. I have often heard him raise his voice very severely, to reprimand laziness in the young singers from whom he demanded the same sacrifices that were his lot at the start of his career. However, he was also ready to give them a pat on the shoulder and an encouraging half-smile when it was justified. He became tense when imposing his will, like all those who know exactly what they want, but are always willing to listen to new opinions and to change their mind if they found them to be correct.

Personally, I think Tito's problems began with his birthplace, Bassano del Grappa, in the Province of Vicenza. Throughout the Veneto region I have many friends, and relatives too – in Venice, Vicenza, Padua, Treviso and Verona. They are lovely, modest people and warm companions, generous conversationalists, whose long chats captivate the listener more by their intonation than by their content. Whatever their origins, these people share a common gentleness. Even when they shout, their voice never rises above a *mezza voce*. When they leave, they quietly slip away, as stealthily as they arrived, leaving no footprints or other trace: you are left with the suspicion that they may have been wraiths. Even if they move abroad for decades, the Venetian remains a Venetian, maintaining at all times a sad-cat face.

I don't know anyone else from Bassano del Grappa, but if Tito is representative of them, Bassano should be moved south a few hundred kilometres and placed in the middle of Friuli. In my opinion, Tito unites all of the characteristics of these people. If there is an earthquake, they remain stay put, holding up their house up if necessary. In times of scarcity, they tighten their belt and carry on. If there is a dance, everyone dances together. If there is digging to be done, they dig together, all the way down to the seam, and if they don't find what they seek, they start again. They keep both feet firmly on the ground even while the earth trembles, and their minds are full of fantasy. In one moment, they may be smiling, the next severe, frowning, semi-serious, gallant or majestic. They display a whole kaleidoscope of rapidly changing expressions that I find in the music of another Austro–Italian who travelled the world: Wolfgang Amadeus Mozart. His complex character took me some time to grasp for myself.

Tito and I had our first business contact in Australia.[1001] He liked

---

[1001] In 1968, however they had worked together before, notably in the 1964 *Tosca* with Callas.

the country as soon as he stepped off the plane. The organisation of the Elizabethan Opera Trust was, at that time in the hands of three enthusiastic gentlemen who had succeeded in giving it the character of an artistic family. We all felt ourselves to be part of a team that discussed and resolved problems together. It was a real joy to be able to work in this way, a joy that also permeated our personal lives. It was the only example in the world at that time of an amateur organization dedicated to scrupulously professional purposes, and we found carefree friends thanks to whom we all felt like children again.

Marie Collier also arrived there in Australia, unusually cheerful and serene. After the rehearsals were over for the day, the three of us often went to an ice-cream vendor who had emigrated from Forlì, to eat a cone that was bought for us by 'Oncle Tito'. As we stood in the street with our ice-creams, Tito would protest loudly that his ice-cream had all melted in the bottom of the cone, to the great amusement of the passing children, who waited around and often received a cone as well. One evening we played a frenetic game of soccer (two-a-side) in Marie Collier's luxurious apartment at the Southern Cross Hotel in Melbourne, using a ball of newspaper rolled up with a shoelace. Marie revealed a hitherto unsuspected talent, giving the ball a wallop as well as our ankles. I also recall a tennis match I played with Tito. We hadn't touched a racket since childhood, so we played without putting the net in place (Tito's suggestion to make less work for us). The ball travelled from one side to the other, far too close to the ground, without either of us wanting to admit defeat. It looked more like a polo match between two tired statues than tennis.

The following year, Tito and I returned to Australia for *Falstaff*. His flight arrived a day late and he came directly to the *Sitzprobe*, potentially taking a big risk. In the event, everything went smoothly between us, as if we had performed the opera together many times. And at the end of the rehearsal, raising the right corner of his mouth in his characteristic smile, he said to me: 'It is evident that we ate the same polenta.' However, one evening something took place that hinted at a cruel side to his personality. It was often difficult to get rid of the crowds of fans who stood around the theatre, demanding autographs and requesting demonstrations of how to put on stage makeup or attach a fake nose. Tito was always patient, albeit tired from rehearsals; he would open up his make-up case in the middle of the street and put on Falstaff's nose with the same meticulousness as he would in the dressing room at the Met. On this particular evening, the crowds slowly receded, until only Tito's closest friends remained with us: Friulian emigrants, lovers of opera, and he was pleased to have them around for a few relaxing *ciàcole*.[1002] The group followed us into our hotel.

There were about 15 of us assembled in the hotel lounge, and Tito came up with the idea of ordering champagne. 'French or Australian?' he enquired. 'There's an Australian one that's not bad,' someone suggested, so he said 'Let's try it! Bring the Australian!' Then he resumed the conversation to which, as it progressed, I became increasingly inattentive as I followed the comings and goings of an elderly waiter, who – unknowingly – was tightening a noose around his own neck. He brought us five bottles of champagne and, so as not to disturb the talk, he set about uncorking them all, silently, and with great care. When he was finished, he finally did what he should have done earlier. He attracted our attention and poured a little champagne into a goblet for Tito to taste. He savoured it, clicked his tongue, made a face and broke the expectant silence with … 'I don't like it.'

The old waiter must have been slightly deaf, or slow, because he giggled and with more bowing and scraping poured out glasses for two more of the company. They also said: 'It's not good – it's certainly not the best.' Then Gobbi decided: 'Bring some French. I don't want this.' The waiter stopped smiling as he began to realise many things. He explained that by now he had opened five bottles … and he murmured evermore softly that Tito would have to pay for them. 'And drink them too,' Tito hissed back at him, with a smile full of anger: 'I wasn't wrong! You were wrong ... I don't want these.' In similar situations I am more conciliatory, and I swear I would have encouraged those present to empty those five damned bottles even if they were full of pee.

As this unfolded, I imagined the stunned waiter in the guise

[1002] Venetian word for chat, gossip.

of an emigrant with a bundle on his shoulder, the grandfather of dozens of grandchildren piled up in a sordid hovel, with his old wife interrupting the darning of mountains of socks and brushing his jacket so that 'grandfather can go to work.' And now there he was, in front of us, pulling at his fingers nervously and attempting to smile. When the bar closed, he would probably run home to hang himself from the beam of a deserted attic. With five bottles of Australian champagne under his feet dangling in the air... ('Ahhh! that Gobbi deserved Floria Tosca's stabs at the end of the Third Act!'). Despite (or because of) the French champagne, the evening was not the most convivial. Tito probably sensed a certain hostility from me, because when we were alone, he said: 'When you make a mistake, is it right that you pay – or not?' Then he added in a low voice: 'Anyway, even the Australian bottles are added to my account.' Tito, Tito, Tito...

Every two years a very popular event takes place in Melbourne: the 'King of Moomba' Parade. Everyone pours into the streets to watch the parade and pay homage to the King of the Festival who slowly passes among his people in a luxurious open-topped car, smiles at them, and bestows on them his them good wishes. John Young, Manager of the Elizabeth Opera Trust, managed to get Tito elected 'King of Moomba'. The reaction of the citizens of Melbourne was extremely hostile, even violent. In Melbourne opera afficionados may number in the thousands, but imagine how many more pop music fans, Australian rules football or boxing fans there are. Threats of reprisals and even of shootings were made, and became more and more frequent. And – just to show that they were serious – during the night someone shot at a huge 'balloon' that had been inflated and placed on the building of a city newspaper office.

After a couple of days, it was replaced, but even the replacement was blown up with a well-aimed shot. Tito also received many anonymous and threatening letters. 'We want an Australian King of Moomba!' 'Go back to *Surriento* or you too will end up like the balloons!' The situation had become so grave that the Italian Ambassador intervened. Although he was delighted that such a singular honour had been bestowed upon an Italian artist, he advised prudence, even suggesting that Gobbi resign from his office. But

Tito showed courage and determination, saying that a public figure such as he considered himself to be, could not make decisions which were dependent upon on the mood of the masses. He said that he had accepted his assignment and was honoured to represent Italy in a popular Australian festival. He would not consider resigning from his duties.

On the appointed day, he was enthroned in a red Alfa Romeo Spider that was almost covered by his golden royal mantle, his crown was slightly askew on his head, as he passed majestically between two flanks of applauding crowds. More than a million people lined the route that crossed the length and breadth of the city. I followed him – at a crawl – hiding among the confusion of the paparazzi, fearful that some fool would cause him the same fate as John Kennedy. But nothing went amiss. The following morning, he was flying back to Rome, and I was certain that the airport would be overrun by crowds to see off their sovereign. But the masses, particularly in Australia, forget so easily, and it was just us musicians who came to see him off. The 'king for a day' returned quietly to the world of opera.

Tito and I worked together on one further *Falstaff* production. He had filed a lawsuit against the Paris Opéra, and instead of just accepting the money as compensation, he proposed that he would sing the title role and direct the staging of *Falstaff* thereby earning the settlement fee. I had conducted a successful *Don Carlo* in Paris a year earlier and the orchestra of the Opéra had included me on a list of three conductors that they liked. I was invited to conduct this new *Falstaff* [in 1970], a work which had previously belonged to the repertoire of the *Opéra Comique*, and was to be staged at the *Opéra* for the first time. This was in the era prior to Liebermann,[1003] during a time when the theatre lacked an artistic director. Gobbi was in the United States, and I was charged with the responsibility for choosing the singers to form two casts, agreeing the number of rehearsals required, and a thousand other details.

[1003] Rolf Liebermann (1910-1999) was the artistic director of the Paris Opera from 1973-1980.

42: 'King had a right royal time.' Tito Gobbi in the Moomba
Parade, crowned 'King of Moomba.' March 1969.

The first orchestral reading began in the most promising fashion:
'*Enchanté* to play again *avec vous…*'; '*Enchanté* to conduct you since
you are such an excellent ensemble.' At the following rehearsal
I was surprised to find new faces in front of me. I knew that the
cursed system of rostering ('tournements') was widespread and
supported by the members of the various orchestras. In my opinion
it is tantamount to swapping a few violinists every day for a concert

pianist, or to Gianni Agnelli's workers.[1004] I called meetings and held discussions with those in charge and finally they promised me that I would have the same players for the pre-General and General rehearsals as well as for the first night. At the opening, there was great expectation, and the audience was peppered with government ministers and crowds of celebrities. I entered the pit, acknowledged the ovation and turned to the orchestra. At that moment I saw a new third horn sitting in the orchestra. Suddenly my legs took me off, out of the pit and back to my dressing room. There followed animated discussions for more than 25 minutes with the leaders of the orchestra who had followed in the wake of my departure.

The public was ignorant of the cause of the delay, as was a furious Tito, who was already on stage inside his enormous foam rubber armour kicking the furniture around. I later learned that he cursed and called me names that are better not to recall here; best to say that he vowed never to work with me again. After the show we had dinner together and despite the success he was ill-tempered and wouldn't even look at me, until Tilde,[1005] with her common sense, exclaimed: 'Tito, enough with this nonsense. Carlo did the right thing, and you would have done the same.' Slowly, the half-smile in the corner of Gobbi's mouth reappeared, and we have worked together many more times since then.

We were both working at the Met when he asked me if I knew a dentist in New York. I was happy to recommend to him Gustave Dürrer, who was famous for his skill. He was Swiss, and a professor at Columbia University, with offices at the Rockefeller Plaza Centre, where patients enjoyed piped music, looked after by beautiful nurses in white uniforms who looked like little angels. There was one to open the door, one to make appointments, another to answer the phone, and so on. Tito didn't need much coaxing. The tip of one of his 32 healthy teeth was slightly chipped and he just wanted to have it rounded. He decided to see Dr Dürrer, who is generally so busy that if an ordinary person asks for an appointment in the month of

[1004] Gianni Agnelli (1921-2003) was an Italian industrialist and the main shareholder in Fiat.
[1005] Tito Gobbi's wife.

November, he is forced to wait until March or April. Dürrer is a man of exquisite taste, and a lover of the arts (including opera). He was very grateful to me because I was able to satisfy one of his dreams: one night at the Met I managed to have him seated on a light tower onstage and from that unusual angle he enjoyed the show in reverse, from behind the scenes. He was also a great admirer of Tito Gobbi, so he immediately found space in his diary.

On the day, Tito made his entrance with the gravitas of Doge Simone Boccanegra, refusing mouthwash and stating that he would treat himself. All he asked of Dürrer was to lend him the drill and he'd do the rest. All the little angels looked on with astonishment as a tug-of-war took place between Tito, who refused to open his mouth and Dr Dürrer, who, while retaining a tense smile, was almost amused. Finally, Tito had to give in, but he abandoned the session after a few minutes leaving unceremoniously, and visibly dissatisfied.

There are many revealing anecdotes that I could recount about him. As an animal lover, I especially like to remember the time when we were in New York and decided one evening to go to a nearby restaurant, just a short walk from our hotel. As we made our way, we began to discuss music and the events of the day. At one point Tito left Tilde and me, and approached the edge of the sidewalk. A lady was tying up her dog in order to go into a shop. The dog, not happy to be left in solitude, whined pitifully. Tito stood next to him and said to the lady: 'Go, I'll keep him company.' He said nothing to the dog. He didn't stroke it. He didn't even look at it. He just stayed beside him, pulling up his collar because the evening was damp and cool. We were all silent for about ten minutes: Tito, Tilde, the dog, and me. Finally, the lady returned, and we all went off to the restaurant, with the air of having fulfilled a duty and nothing more. The dog did not look at Tito but barked gratefully.

--o-o--

ARTURO TOSCANINI –

The good Grandfather who took the 'smack'[1006]

These events took place in Bologna in May 1931.

The students in my composition class at the Bologna Conservatory all had the privilege of attending rehearsals held at the Teatro Comunale during each symphony season. In 1931, Arturo Toscanini was coming to direct a commemorative concert for Martucci,[1007] but it was with great disappointment that we learned that the maestro would not admit anyone to his rehearsals. However, some days later, I saw the Director, Maestro Cesare Nordio[1008] in the corridor of the conservatoire, approaching me, and waving a blue letter. With a bemused smile he said to me: 'Did you know that your mother was successful?' And I, who knew nothing of the situation, asked: 'How? What did she do?' 'Don't you know that she wrote to Maestro Toscanini asking him to let you all attend his rehearsals? This morning, he himself gave me her letter, instructing me: tell those boys to hide, so that they are not seen. But let them come.'

The following morning our small group sat on the floor of one of the highest boxes, to attend – silently – the rehearsals for the commemoration concert of Giuseppe Martucci. The soloist for the piano concerto was Ferrari Ariani, an Italian musician living in the United States, to whom Maestro Toscanini had also entrusted the task of conducting the first orchestra rehearsals. On the day of his arrival in Bologna, Toscanini attended the evening rehearsal, sitting

---

[1006] The account in Harvey Sachs, *Toscanini, Musician of Conscience* (2017), 505-9 is recommended as a comparison.

[1007] Giuseppe Martucci (1856–1909) was an Italian composer who was influential in introducing Wagner's operas in Italy. Toscanini championed Martucci's compositions during his later career, and may have been influenced in his thinking by the composer's often-stated conviction that absolute (instrumental) music was the highest goal of composition.

[1008] Cesare Nordio (1891–1977) was an Italian composer and director of the Bologna and Bolzano Conservatoires.

in a box from which, at times, he stopped Ariani and the orchestra with a shout, in order to make observations and corrections. He specified the exact bar and which instrument to correct, giving precise indications without the aid of a score, revealing a prodigious memory. With our noses to the edge of the stage, we all remained invisibly engrossed in the proceedings.

The following morning, Toscanini himself began to rehearse. He seemed in a good temper. The musicians formed an orchestra, which he acknowledged was 'almost' worthy of his needs. He had loved Giuseppe Martucci as a friend and as a musician, and he venerated his friend's memory for what Martucci had done in Italy for music in general, and for Wagner in particular. The Maestro began the rehearsal in good cheer and went on to break a lot of batons. Anticipating this outcome, he brought a bundle to each rehearsal. They were not the batons of a professional, just sticks taken from country hedges. As soon as something didn't align with his will, he smashed the one he was using with an angry gesture and threw the broken pieces into the auditorium. In those moments we ceased breathing, as did the orchestra. During the stormy silence that followed, the leader of the orchestra – Enrico Campajola, had the task of picking up another baton from the foot of the podium and handing it to the Maestro. An electrical tension was in the air!

During the first rehearsal, an elderly violinist who had been Toscanini's friend when they were students together, resigned. He had white hair like the maestro and had asked for the honour of ending his career by playing once more under Toscanini's baton. He had spent his life as a conscientious and respected professional, and in order to accede to his request, the management had placed him on the last desk of the second violins, hoping that the maestro would not notice him. On learning of this during the rehearsal, Toscanini protested silently, by breaking a 'wand' every now and then and staring at the man for a long time with his tired eyes; glaring like a hunting dog in the direction of the poor fellow, who, in the first break, hastened to resign. On that day, everyone present learned that at a certain age it is more prudent to conduct an orchestra than to play an instrument.

As the rehearsals progressed, the mood become more and more congenial. Just when everyone had started to relax, Toscanini suddenly interrupted the orchestra. 'Who is the first horn?' Breathless silence. 'Let the Primo Corno rise', he ordered. The 'primo corno' was Pietro Righini, a young, thin man who, at that moment became as pale as a sheet. He stood up hesitantly. 'Bravo! Bravo indeed!' said Toscanini. 'No one has ever performed this "solo" in the symphony as you have done now. Bravo!' Toscanini took particular care and affection in shaping the *Novelletta–Notturno* and *Tarantella* – particularly the *Novelletta*. His voice, already rather hoarse, became softer and more mysterious when he described the old woman who tells the children an old tale by the fire. Hidden in our box we too felt close to that fire. Toscanini had become our 'good grandfather', who had the skills and found the right words to convince us and make us dream. Everything continued to proceed well. The theatre had been sold out for months, and all the *crema* of musical and worldly Europe would be present in Bologna for the concert. But suddenly the Devil showed his tail.

On the day of the concert, the Bologna-San Luca cableway would be inaugurated in the presence of some Fascist ministers. One of them, Leandro Arpinati,[1009] was an ex-railway man who certainly didn't care about nocturnes or novelettes, but he would have to attend the concert. Therefore, Maestro Toscanini was asked to conduct the 'Marcia Reale' and the 'Giovinezza'. He refused: 'It is a festival dedicated to commemorating the memory of Giuseppe Martucci. Other music has nothing to do with it'. There was an effort to find a compromise: to have the concert master, Enrico Campajola conduct the anthems before Toscanini took the podium. But the maestro was adamant. The day was spent in useless negotiations.

Before the concert, I was standing at the artists' entrance with Mario Medici, who later became Director of the Istituto di Studi Verdiani in Parma. We entertained the hope that the doorman would be distracted for a moment, allowing us to slip into some dark corner of the hall. We were surprised to see the comings and goings

[1009] 1892-1945, was an anarchist turned follower of Mussolini.

of a group of 'black shirts' who were clearly agitated and speaking amongst themselves. We were even more surprised by the fact that Toscanini – the most punctual man in the world, both in art and in life – was not yet in the theatre, even though it was almost time to begin the concert. Then we learned what was happening: a person close to the authorities had informed Toscanini by telephone that due to his stance against the 'Giovinezza', a political demonstration against him was brewing. He was advised not to come to the Comunale. There was a heated discussion at the hotel between Donna Carla,[1010] who would have preferred to accept the suggestion, and the maestro who, stamping his feet furiously, insisted on going. And of course, he prevailed.

About ten minutes after the scheduled starting time, the huge RCA Rolls Royce pulled up in front of us, silent as a gondola, with the maestro and his family inside. An imposing chauffeur in a blue and white uniform got out of the limousine and as he was opening a door to allow Toscanini to alight, some little men dressed in black[1011] appeared beside us, through the artists' entrance, forming a wall around the open door of the car. 'Will you conduct the "Giovinezza"?' one of them shouted. 'No.' was the maestro's reply: sharp, dry, like the crack of a whip. We could see only Toscanini's head, bent in the act of alighting from the car. Above him, fists were raised menacingly. I didn't see the famous smack, but I heard women's screams from inside the car. The chauffeur pushed the protesters away. They fell back, staggering off and quickly dispersing. The driver locked the car, got back into his seat and sped away. This all happened within about 20 seconds, a blink of an eye that was to have long-lasting consequences for musical and non-musical Italy. Medici and I were completely beside ourselves with shock. Our idol had been attacked before our eyes. Politics had interfered and struck the arts a resounding blow. An evening that was to be dedicated to joy had been silenced.

Meanwhile, it had been announced inside the theatre that the

[1010] Toscanini's wife.
[1011] In another version of the memoir, Cillario describes them as 'cockroaches' (*scarafaggi*).

concert would not take place. Groups of elegant and incredulous spectators began to pour into the square, asking each other, in a mixture of languages, what had happened. One of the Fascists improvised an oration: standing on a curb-stone he harangued the crowd, describing Toscanini with the most insulting epithets. The maestro was in his apartment at the Hotel Brun packing his bags. Mussolini, already informed of these events, immediately grasped that his zealous subordinates had overstepped their duty, creating a further reason for the international discredit of fascism. After a few minutes a waiter knocked on the maestro's door announcing that the 'Honourable Arpinati' wanted to speak to him and sort out the incident. The answer was clear: 'Tell His Excellency not to break my c...', and from that moment relations between Toscanini and Fascism, between Toscanini and Italy were severed. A few months later, he was invited by Bronislaw Huberman to Tel Aviv to conduct the inaugural concert of the Palestine Symphony Orchestra.[1012] At the end of the first rehearsal he declared: 'Finally I feel at home!' Then he moved to the United States and did not return to Italy until after the war.

Immediately after this outrage, the guerrillas resumed their activity. The Fascists knew that the conservatoire was a Tuscan refuge, and they came to paper the walls with the front pages of newspapers carrying headlines full of outrageous slurs directed at Toscanini. As soon as the Fascists had left, we students ensured that they were torn down or defaced. There weren't many skirmishes at first, because at any sign of trouble, such as a group of Fascists appearing in Piazza Rossini, we would scamper like rabbits up the stairs and barricade ourselves inside the classrooms. ('Art is fine, but if they break my fingers who plays the violin anymore?') Then we hit upon a Machiavellian solution that allowed us to keep faith with our ideals while minimising personal risk.

[1012] The Palestine Symphony Orchestra was later renamed the Israel Philharmonic, the name by which it is still known today. Cillario has miscalculated the time elapsed from the aborted Bologna concert in 1931, to the Tel Aviv inaugural concert, which took place on 26 December 1936 – a few years, rather than a few months later. The Palestine orchestra was founded by Bronislaw Huberman.

There were a couple of brothers who came from the Romagna countryside: the Sibani brothers. One studied the trombone and the other the double bass. I don't think they had high intellectual aspirations, but they cared about Toscanini – and perhaps also about the musical art – up to a certain point. They had solid shoulders and big muscles, and an odd spirit. Using our skilful words of persuasion, along with helpings of pasta at times when they were suffering from hunger, we convinced them to take a stand against the overbearing Fascist aggression. They declared themselves proud to be chosen and eager to demonstrate the power of their biceps in our presence. And so, often, at the end of the lessons, we witnessed – from a prudent distance – the skirmishes that they waged with the Fascists. They were our pride, our freedom badges, and they fought bravely. Every day they returned home covered in scratches and with their shirts in tatters, which caused them to be continuously beaten by their mother. They soon gave up their 'heroic resistance' and a rumour spread that in order to have no more problems with the Fascists they had joined the Party. How did they end up? Since then, there have been many skirmishes in Italy – Fascists – Communists – perhaps they went to meet their maker before their time?

In Italy, a series of rumours arose about Arturo Toscanini during those turbulent war years. The cruellest and most unlikely was the one that accused him of donating money to America to bomb the enemy with more ferocity than he had done himself. Others maintained that he had kicked a journalist out of his dressing room in New York who was trying to extract some statements against Italy from him. But denials can never completely obliterate malicious claims. The fact is that Italy was none too moved when the maestro died. Perhaps this was because, with the wartime deaths of so many – adults and children, good and bad – everyone had become desensitised to death. When the news of Toscanini's passing reached Milan from America, La Scala suspended the rehearsals that were in progress as a sign of mourning. Several players from the orchestra and some members of the chorus were able to resume their usual games of chess or *scopone*.[1013]

[1013] An Italian card game of Neapolitan origin.

As for His Excellency Arpinati, an independent and proud spirit, there came a time when he disagreed with the Duce. And he ended up in detention. Released as soon as the war ended, he was standing one evening in the countryside, his hands in his pockets, watching a column of trucks loaded with partisans pass by, just to see if there were any faces he knew among them. When one of the trucks stopped, one of the partisans recognised him. I don't know what crime they accused him of, but they shot him in the chest, leaving him in the middle of the damp countryside, with his hands still in his pockets.

In the crystal ball of the future, everything is confused and obscured by fog. In the crystal ball of the past, we leave behind ditches full of idols torn down and beaten, twisted iron, broken and forgotten dogmas, rotting corpses. Amid so much horror, there is also the memory of 'Grandfather Toscanini', narrating Martucci's *Novelletta* for good children, by the hearth. But his presence keeps slipping farther and farther away, smaller and older. His voice becomes more and more faint, more tired, almost inaudible – just like the 'Marcia Reale' and the 'Giovinezza'...

--o-o--

PABLO CASALS

I first met Enrique Casals, his violinist brother, who was the concertmaster when I played a concerto with the Barcelona Symphony Orchestra. At the end of the first rehearsal, he approached me cautiously, with a courtesy that could be mistaken for humility, and complimented me. I had recently listened to the records of Pablo Casals playing Bach's Cello Suites. It was one of those rare experiences that have remained forever sublime in my experience of music. Casals completely dissolves the conventions of notation, blends them, makes them invisible, so that the music transfigures itself and emerges as something else. There are no more bar-lines or time-signatures: 6/8 and 4/4, the beat and the upbeat, the sharps and the flats, they all disappear. Bach's music dissolves all nationality, all texture and even gender – assuming that music has one. I will try to express it poetically: it became like an ocean wave, a sky full of pearly clouds over the desert, a flicker of flame, a flowing stream. I'm sorry if that's inadequate....

During my life I have experienced similar moments of freedom only a handful of times: from the Polish Jew Bronislaw Huberman in Beethoven's Violin Concerto; in the Venetian Antonio Guarnieri's conducting of *Tristan und Isolde*;[1014] and the recording of Enrico Caruso – Neapolitan by birth – singing Handel. But at that moment in Barcelona, I was very young, and I couldn't say anything other than 'Your brother, he's good!' and Enrique Casals seemed almost surprised by that idea. He said, 'Do you like his playing?' But he said it with such an air of shyness that he could have been asking my opinion of his brother's first school essay. I thought he was not being serious, so much so that if I had been Roman and more familiar with him, I would have gladly given him a slap on the stomach saying: 'Aoh! C'è sei o c'è fai?' But later I discovered that simplicity and modesty were genuine characteristics of the Casals family, including the great Pablo.

Once, I was driving from Rome, heading north along the Via Cassia. I wasn't intending to pass through the city of Siena, but in spite of following the road signs, I found myself in the city. At a given moment, the arrows led me to unexpectedly enter the Piazza del Palio. This seemed to me to be almost a blasphemy: the sheet metal of my car in that sacred place of steed hooves. The stench of my exhaust instead of the frantic, galloping breath of the horses launched into the final gallop. The Piazza del Campo di Siena, stained by Fiat, Ford, and Chevrolet. But since I was there, I decided to park, and I walked up to the Palazzo Chigi–Saracini, to speak to Count Chigi whom I hadn't seen for years. I enquired after him on the first floor and I was told: 'Count Guido has left just now. Maybe you can join him if you go through the downstairs door into the courtyard.' Years before, when I had studied at the Accademia Chigiana, that door did not exist. So, when I opened it, I didn't know where it would take me.

[1014] Guarnieri conducted Wagner's *Tristan und Isolde* for the first time at La Fenice, Venice in the 1908/9 season. It is not known when and where Cillario may have heard him conduct the opera.

I pushed the door with some force and suddenly found myself on a wooden stage less than half a metre from Pablo Casals's cello. He had just begun playing the Sonata in E minor by Brahms. I stood, frozen. The low notes of the cello made the wooden stage vibrate, and my feet tingled as if I were standing on one of those machines designed to improve the blood circulation of old people. All around the stage in a semicircle were seated students from the cello course of the Academy who were experiencing a lesson from Casals. I later learned that he did not give lessons in the usual sense. He simply sat down and played a major work from the repertoire, as if he didn't dare to give advice. He was so immersed in his playing that he hadn't even noticed that I was so close. His eyes were closed, as always when he played, and he would only emerge from his reverie after the close of the sonata.

I have often thought that those who make a profession of music and go to great efforts to analyse it, especially if they have absolute pitch, can rarely enjoy it with the same abandon which is granted to a listener who is without technical knowledge. Listening to music for us musicians is a struggle, and not infrequently unpleasant. We love to read it or perform it ourselves for the enjoyment (or annoyance) of others. If I feel the need to relax, however, I prefer to kick a ball against a wall. I would not usually go to a concert, unless it was to listen to one of the artists I have mentioned. Only they can make me forget the rules of music and what key the piece is in. They allow me to dream their dream.

Listening to Casals I closed my eyes, and let him take me on an interior journey, to the Calchaquí valleys in northern Argentina. Above the town of Tafí del Valle is a holiday resort, more than 2000 metres above sea level and the plain below. To get there, you travel through beautiful mountains along a dangerous road, winding around sharp curves, over deep ravines with the river below, separated from us by only a simple wooden post placed on the edge of the precipice by some kind soul. The coach made this long journey and finally arrived at Tafí for lunch. The passengers ate heartily, happy to be amid the beauty of the scenery and the sparkling air. And in proportion they also drank. The driver too.

The rickety coach set off again as soon as lunch was over, and there was a little regret in everyone's hearts because it was cool up in Tafí, whereas the heat became more intense with each of the countless bends down towards the plain, until it became unbearable. During the journey, people gradually fell asleep. So did the driver.

Known as 'Chazampy,' he was reputed to be an excellent driver who had never plunged into the ravine. On this occasion, he proved very good, maintained an even pace and took turns in the safest way. He didn't speed too much, but he did have a habit of falling asleep. Not for the entire journey, of course. He only nodded off during the short, straight stretches between one bend and the next. He knew the road so well that it was enough for him to come to his senses and open half an eye (or sometimes a whole one, depending on the danger) just at the right moment to brake as much as necessary. After my initial shock, I came to understand that I could trust his reflexes. My close study of his driving technique absorbed me completely, and did not allow me to admire the spectacle of the peaks, the green plains, the ravines, or the dense forests as we descended.

Back to Casals, playing Brahms. I was fascinated to observe his closed eyes. Even his lowered lids exuded a transcendent expression of peace and security, of consciousness, concentration, and familiarity with places in higher spheres. I was standing so close to him – almost above him – that I could perceive the play of a network of tiny wrinkles, each of which corresponded perfectly to the most intimate sense of musical expression. But that didn't stop me from enjoying the impervious peaks of the Brahms Sonata, its green esplanades, its ravines and uphill forest – far from it! After what seemed a lifetime, this beautiful journey came to an end.

Casals opened his eyes, stood up, holding his bow with two fingers, opened his arms, smiled, and said out loud to everyone: 'La leçon est finie!' Simply, like a good country parish priest who says: 'Ite missa est. Go in peace.' The retreat from the hall was hasty because it was already past midday, and everyone hurried to get the best places in the students' cafeteria. As they dispersed, the pupils seemed quite indifferent to the gift that Casals had bestowed upon them. For a whole month this occurred almost every morning, just like daily Mass. One of the students walked away whistling the theme from 'The Bridge over the River Kwai'.[1015] Casals lingered a bit, stroking his cello, rubbing its strings, carefully loosening the bow as if he had become confused at being back amongst people. And rather than the grand master of the cello, he had about him an air of nothing more than an elderly student who had presented his essay. But what wisdom!

--o-o--

WILLIAM KAPELL

The poor boy! He had, like so many pianists, American or Russian, embarked on a stellar career, armed with a dizzying technique. For many, that's enough. But a critique from Olin Downes in the New York Times, made him stop and think. 'He possesses the necessary velocity', wrote the powerful critic. Suddenly Kapell understood that he was more of a 'counting machine' than a soulful musician. He began to realise that the breakneck speed required by American and international concert promoters has little to do with art. Furthermore, performers who are merely fast and correct (as required by today's current taste, based on that deceptive element which is the recording) no longer merit the epithet of 'artist'.

So, Kapell dived into the unknown, listening to mountains of old recordings by performers famous for their disregard of technical perfection such as Alfred Cortot, Edwin Fischer and Bronislaw Huberman. In the midst of his artistic crisis [1953], he came to San Miguel de Tucumán.[1016] A couple of years earlier he had played a recital there, consisting of the most pyrotechnic piano acrobatics, which won him immense success. This time he returned humble, worried, and anxious, with a programme entirely dedicated to Mozart. When he played, his demeanour was reminiscent of a thoroughbred racing horse who had been forced to give up racing in order to pull a carriage in the heart of a metropolis. Firm hamstrings

---

[1015] From the 1957 film.
[1016] Where Cillario was based during the late 1940's and early 1950's.

and gleaming muscles aren't always enough: playing Mozart is a more finely calibrated task. It takes a lot of sensitivity, philosophical enquiry, experience, and contact with the worn cobblestones of old Europe: more reincarnations, more inward smile. America has produced imitation whiskey, but bourbon is something else altogether. Cask-aged scotch is better.

After his concert we had dinner together. At one point, he interrupted our conversation: 'How did you like my Mozart?' An awkward silence ensued. We in Tucumán treated Mozart as one of the family. With much simplicity. We felt a little bit like priests, like servants of our own Mozarteum which we had founded without a penny.[1017] Whoever played or sang there had to put away the music stands themselves, close up the piano or the harpsichord, and turn off the lights behind them. We stood in judgement of those who came from skyscrapers and the sound of many dollars, trapped in the whirlwind of a dizzying international career.

I took a deep breath. (You can tell Americans hard truths. Either they don't believe you, and then nothing happens, or they take you seriously, and then all the better). 'Here is my honest opinion: yours is a Mozart who knows about Palmolive, who travels by plane, who is too straightforward. Mozart is two-faced, four-faced, all-facing. You Americans do not have this defect yet. America's most savvy gangster is a lamb compared to this lovable marauder.' Kapell gathered himself up to consider my words, then he stood up and said, 'Let's go to the theatre'.

When we arrived, the theatre was closed. We found the old caretaker, who at first resisted, but finally let us in. Kapell and I spoke a little, around the piano, in the empty hall. Then he played until the small hours, without further words. I sat while he played. The spirit of Mozart dwelt among us. And he enjoyed seeing how easy it was for Mozart to intrigue human beings. With simple things. With the right speed. He had intrigued humans even during his lifetime. And the mystery of why they didn't understand him and let him die will always remain.

[1017] Cillario refers to the teaching courses in the 'Mozart style' that he had developed at the local University.

The next day Kapell left for the United States. There were many of us at the airport, we loved him. The Aereolineas aircraft had a two-hour delay, and we were happy about that, giving us more time to talk. But he was nervous. He openly cursed Perón, Argentina, and his delayed planes. A few months later he died in a plane crash in the United States. I wonder if anyone still remembers it?[1018]

--o-o--

CORDE E PEDALI – DUE DIVERSI SISTEMI DI INSEGNAMENTO[1019]

I - WALTER GIESEKING

1949 was a year of great significance for the musical life of Tucumán. Walter Gieseking was coming, not only for a series of concerts with the new University Symphony Orchestra I had formed, but also to give a course in interpretation that was to last for more than a month. Young pianists had flocked to this course from every corner of America, including the United States. The University had managed to convince Gieseking to visit by giving the false assurance that he could find rare specimens for his butterfly collection in their province of northern Argentina. On the day of his arrival, we all greeted him at the airport. He gave a few slaps on the shoulders to those he knew, before disappearing in a long procession of cars. He put his nose against the window, carefully observing each tree with his sly little eyes; and in so doing he began to feel a little panic. Everyone knows well that at that time of year, there is not even a shadow of a butterfly in the province of Tucumán.

On arriving at the Savoy Hotel, a few people timidly tried to break the news to him, but he ran off to change, and returned after a few minutes equipped with a net, jars filled with chloroform, a wide-brimmed hat and a jacket marked with old sweat stains. He stood

---

[1018] Kapell played his last recital in Australia, in Geelong, Victoria on 22 October 1953. The plane on which he returned to the United States crashed, killing all those on board. On the programme of what proved to be his final recital, he played Chopin's 'Funeral March' Sonata.

[1019] 'Strings and pedals, two different teaching systems.'

in front of the first tree he found. The Savoy Hotel in the city of San Miguel de Tucumán is located in an area that becomes magical at this time of the year. The Avenue Sarmento is lined with *lapachos,* loaded with pink and yellow flowers.[1020] Where it crosses with the Calle Salta, all flowering in blue, it creates a wonderful carpet of tropical colours made by the flowers falling from the trees. And on the horizon, the view of the Calchaquies Valleys that divide Chile, washes the backdrop with shades of pale blue.

But Gieseking paid the panorama neither a glance nor a thought. He stood motionless and silent, observing a spot on the tree that seemed to us all to be rather insignificant. Time passed. Those present, standing in a circle around him, became increasingly nervous: There are whispers of 'When he realises that there are no butterflies, he will surely leave us, and then, goodbye piano course!' Finally, a *bagaién* emerged from a crack in the tree, some kind of giant moth. Gieseking dexterously wielded his net, and soon trapped the poor thing inside the bottle for a painless death. At this point our prominent guest relaxed and laughed uproariously. 'You understand nothing! There are butterflies! Here's a butterfly! Look!!' And triumphantly he held aloft the yellow bottle with the poor giant moth that saved the Tucumán Piano Course. More slaps on the shoulders and general relief: the guest stayed put.

The course, dedicated to the interpretation of Debussy, was strange. Gieseking spoke very little. He listened very attentively to the young pianists, but instead of correcting them verbally, he would take his seat in their place, and play the piece right through. Then he stood up, swelled to his full size and, with a gesture that the Germans also must have mimicked from the Neapolitans, he buried his head between his shoulders and half-opened his forearms, with the palms of his hands turned upwards, as if to say: 'It can only go like this! It's that simple!'

To allow everyone present to understand his secrets when operating the pedals, I had invented a device which, when placed correctly, lit up a red light-bulb when he pressed the right pedal; and a green one when he used his left foot. The pupils marked everything

---

[1020] Known as the 'pink trumpet tree.'

in their scores. But in art, the most important secrets seem to arise from the artists' fervent imagination and their instinctive ability to dream. Antonio Stradivari is said to have improvised his varnishes and the thickness of his instruments according to the quality and degree of seasoning of the woods he found, and the masterpieces of the great Renaissance painters reveal many 'afterthoughts' if they are observed with X-rays. Thus, it was discovered that Gieseking used a different pedalling each time he played a piece.

Another surprise came when, at the end of each session, he was supposed to answer the questions that were handed to him at the end of the previous meeting. Some were really too naïve for him to engage with, others not. For example, I remember: 'What is the difference between a Beethoven *forte* and a Debussy *forte*?' We all imagined that an opportunity had arisen for an exhaustive outpouring of wise advice, on a subject that lent itself to a thousand nuances and revelations. But Gieseking thought otherwise. He repeated his Neapolitan-German gesture, with his head between his shoulders, while he waved the question slip: 'What do you want me to tell you?!' Then he sat down at the piano and played the first movement of Beethoven's *Appassionata* Sonata, followed by the Debussy 'Clair de lune'. And while we initiated discussions about green and red lights and keys stroked with fingertips or hammered fingers, he went to stand in front of a tree in the garden. And he shrugged his shoulders violently, laughing behind our backs at the ignorant creatures who didn't even know how to recognise butterflies.

II - FRIEDRICH GULDA

The occasion was the 'Temporada Lirica Internacional' in Mexico City, and we were using the reception hall on the top floor of the Alffer Hotel for piano rehearsals. I arrived before everyone else and peered through the darkness to find a figure walking around the piano. I turned on the lights and was met with a look of antipathy whether for the electric glow, or for my presence. The figure demanded to know what I was doing there. I knew that Friedrich Gulda (for it was he) had a concert in Mexico City around that time.

I explained to him that I had arrived to lead a piano rehearsal of *Così fan tutte*. His face lit up, and he asked: 'Would you let me play for your rehearsal?' (How could you say no?!!) The rehearsal was supposed to be dedicated to the recitatives, but given his strange request, I decide to rehearse the musical numbers to give him more satisfaction. When the artists arrived, I introduced him, half-jokingly as the pianist. But he was quite serious.

Those of us present on this extraordinary occasion found that Gulda gets excited when he's in dialogue with Mozart. He occasionally inserts, by memory, fragments of *Don Giovanni* and the *Die Zauberflöte*, or of sonatas and concertos. He improvises as if inspired like a god. We all participated in his enthusiasm, even if our rehearsing could be considered a failure. And meanwhile the telephone at the back of the long room rings and rings continuously. Eventually I go to answer it. A gentleman's voice shouts: 'Se puede saber andonde se metió Friedrich Gulda? Hace mas de media hora que la sinfonica y su director lo estan esperando para ensayar el Emperador!'[1021] I didn't have the courage to inform him that, at that precise moment, Gulda didn't seem to feel much respect for His Majesty the Emperor, and preferred flirting with two frivolous little sisters from Ferrara. I reported the call to Gulda somewhat apprehensively, but he was in no hurry. He carried on playing for a while then closed the keyboard and took his leave, grumbling.

On the Sunday I felt obliged to attend his concert, even if I was more attracted by a gloriously sunny Mexican morning than by the prospect of a 'long-deceased Emperor' packed away into a black coffin called a piano. It was, however, an extraordinary and unforgettable concert. I had recently attended a séance in Mexico. I'm not saying that I was completely convinced of the presence of otherworldly entities among us, but they had certainly forced me to take a long overdue look at myself and open my eyes to some problems which until then I had found it convenient to ignore. It

---

[1021] 'Do you know where Friedrich Gulda went? The orchestra and the conductor have been waiting for him for more than half an hour to rehearse the Emperor!'

was hard to explain, but some strange process had occurred within me. In search of further explanation, I read treatises on the origins of man, on the possibility of his derivation from worlds preceding animals (or of metempsychosis), of detachment from God and of the ways to make a return to Him at the end of our earthly journey, as well as other volumes on reincarnation and the like.

On that Sunday morning, Beethoven's 'Emperor' Concerto - which I had always found solidly earthbound – took on another dimension. I heard within it perfumed flowers, precious minerals, a connection to the sounds of distant planets. Beethoven himself seemed disembodied to me, like certain portraits by 17th-century painters. He was no more a man made of flesh, no longer weighed down by problems with his cruel nephew or unpaid bills. He had carrots for fingers, a scarlet radish for a nose, and shells for eyes.

My imagination was liberated by travelling through space and time in this way, and I was enjoying the forceful Rondo finale when, during a *tutti* from the orchestra, Gulda darted from the piano and ran into the wings, shouting like a madman. From a distance, he issued terse and imperious orders: 'Vengan! Quick! Se cayò la pedalera!'[1022] While the orchestra continued to play, he dashed back on, and pushed two sleepy Mexican attendants under the piano. Then he took his seat at the keyboard just in time to play the next 'solo'. The two poor fellows, face up under the instrument like car mechanics, had no idea where to put their hands. They attempted to hold on to the pedal board which had come unscrewed, a futile manoeuvre because the pedals no longer worked. The piano really looked like a crazed spaceship, with those poor fellows floating around, without the force of gravity in a splash of arpeggios in E flat major, the lunar key.

The performance was a success all the same. To begin a series of encores, Gulda played a Prelude and Fugue by Bach, in a dry and 'harpsichord-like' performance. Then Scarlatti. He kept his legs wide apart, with his feet up against the rear legs of the piano stool [to emphasise that he was not using the pedals]. The expression of his nose – always a little noble – demonstrated his disdainful

---

[1022] 'The pedal board has fallen off!'

detachment. And yet how eloquently his feet spoke at that moment! They seemed to be holding a master class on the use of pedals. Logically, there is no need to use them when playing music written for the harpsichord; but they also handed down a stern judgment on the efficiency of an organisation that entrusted him, Friedrich Gulda, with a piano under these conditions! His feet were expressing certain words that are better not to repeat.

--o-o--

WILHELM BACKHAUS

I had the good fortune in that year [c1951] to conduct a cycle of Beethoven concertos given by Wilhelm Backhaus in Argentina. We were to start with a concert in Buenos Aires, and I went to his hotel apartment where an excellent grand piano had been provided. It took him a long time to adjust the piano seat to the correct height and distance. He did this methodically, without haste, without wincing, and smiling like a good nurse who arranges a new-born's legs in diapers. I stood expectantly, admiring his sure, supple, and well-coordinated movements. Finally, everything was in order. He flicked the sleeves of his shirt and looked at me with his immense blue eyes, as he would do again, on the evening of the concert when I commenced the concerto.

At this point, I imagined that he wished to hear the orchestral introduction, so I took my seat next to him and began to hum the Concerto No. 3 in C minor: 'Do- mi- sol- fa-mi- re'. Whereupon my humming was broken off by a mellow, well-supported chord of G major, followed by much roaring and groaning! 'Eeeeh?!... Aaaah?!... G-Dur! G-Duuur!... Nein c-Moll! ... G-Dur!'. He stood up, kicking the seat. 'Number 4. I perform number 4! No c-Moll!' ... Then he concentrated for a moment, and burst out again, even more enraged: 'Aaaach ... Schwein! Grosse Schwein ...! They protect little Weiss ...! Ja! Ja!' (He is still kicking the seat). 'I talk. You wait.' And he grabbed the phone.

What he said to the impresario on that phone call was something straight out of Wotan's monologue when he was forced out of Walhalla. The name 'klein Weiss' was often invoked; a promising young pianist – also represented by this impresario – who just a few days earlier had performed Beethoven's Concerto No. 4 in Buenos Aires. And Backhaus suspected that an attempt was being made to prevent him – 'Wilhelm der Grosse' – from destroying the impression made by the young man with a demonstration of superiority. The first phone call was soon followed by others, while the impresario's office worked to find another free date; meanwhile 'Wilhelm der Grosse', between one telephone call and another, paced like a lion from one corner of the room to the other. At that moment I am sure that because of his deep love for the G-Dur, and the extraordinary situation, he was deeply hating the c-Moll, No. 3. Even in art, love may blind us.

At length, Backhaus calmed down when he was informed that a free date had been found; when we returned from the tour to other Argentine cities, we would also perform No. 4 in G-Dur in Buenos Aires. But these revelations had ruined his mood for the day, so he begged me to come back the next day so we could discuss the c-Moll together. I had considered the various interpretative doubts that had remained with me even after conducting Beethoven's concertos with other great interpreters such as Solomon and Walter Gieseking. I had hoped that my uncertainties would be conclusively resolved by Backhaus, at that time considered to be the custodian of the most authentic Beethovenian tradition. These doubts concerned in particular some orchestral passages in relation to the piano solo text, and I raised them with him the following day. He ruminated a little, thinking about the problems that I presented to him and then he asked me: 'What do you think?' I told him, and he concentrated again, in silence, as if these were questions he had never encountered. Then he said, 'You can stay.'

I had expected to find myself dealing with an artist who, having reached a summit of wisdom and fame, would make music as if riding in a presidential convoy. Instead, his desire to continually renew himself was one of the most surprising aspects of our performances together. As we performed the same concertos several times, the harmony between us deepened: especially in the finale of the Third Concerto, where he allowed himself certain rhythmic liberties that I would never have anticipated. He even tended towards a declamatory style of improvisation, resembling the *rubato* of a Latino singer. I told him so during one of our last flights, and I was gratified to note his pleasure at my observation. It was clear that, by this point, he had found a new purpose in life by cultivating a spirit of interpretative freedom. Not in just giving a few more concerts: he had no interest in the financial gain that his activity brought him, but rather in experimenting to see whether music could still draw from him something that he had not yet achieved. Perhaps this was why he still felt himself in competition with younger artists such as 'klein Weiss' (excellent pianist) in one of his 'war horses', No. 4 in G-Dur (indeed his favourite concerto). Backhaus spoke little, preferring to smile or become withdrawn.

Arriving in a new city – Mendoza I think – the hotel porter, not knowing how to write his surname correctly, politely asked him to spell it out to him letter by letter. Backhaus affected not to understand. He inclined his head, looked at me, and stamped his foot hard on the ground without opening his mouth, as if so say, 'Look at this imbecile who doesn't know my name!' Then he barked (in Italian): '"B" for beast – "A" for donkey – "C" for dog' … 'Kappa-Hotel-Arezzo-Udine and Siena', I completed, to end the situation peacefully. Backhaus was haughty with men, but he made up for it by bringing humility to the keyboard.

Our tour took us to all the major Argentinian cities. During each flight, he invariably asked me: 'Do you know anyone who owns a piano and would allow me to go and practise?' He wasn't far from the end of his long career. And he surprised us all with his new interest in performing a lot of Chopin: études, polonaises, and mazurkas, a genre we didn't think interested him. Instead, he included these pieces in his solo recitals, particularly as encores. Perhaps his interpretative style in Chopin was open to debate, but not his technique, which was flawless. His hands had the texture and the aroma of freshly baked bread…

--o-o--

ART IN THE HEART,

or, in Memory of "Papà Pinotto"

When my father was young, he didn't have much money in his pockets, but many beautiful things were inside his heart. He had memorised many poems and he often recited them to his friends. Carducci, Pascoli, D'Annunzio, Heine, even passages of Dante's *Divina Commedia*. Such things are generally the privilege of drunkards in Italy, but he did not drink at all. Emigrating, he ended up in the Argentine pampas where he went to work on horseback, singing opera fragments at the top of his lungs. He sang to the animals in the bush, or to anybody who would listen. (In those days television did not yet exist, and people enjoyed being together and making friends). 'Salute demeure chaste et pure' ... 'A throne near the sun ... a throne near the sun...'

'Go to the city! You must study!' everyone advised my father. So, he left the pampas and the horse behind and made his way to the Big City to work in a tiny, cramped office. Thus, he was able to take singing lessons ('Open-close-smile. Lean-up. Strengthen-down ...'), and in just a couple of years his teachers managed to destroy his voice. He was rendered completely aphonous. This was the great tragedy of his life! He renounced his dream of becoming Siegfried or Radamès and devoted himself to other professions, always in neon-lit offices.

My father spent his spare time in museums and art galleries. But he favoured music above all the arts, and especially opera, and most of all the works of Richard Wagner, the composer who – with music sometimes heroic, or sensual, rebellious, and desperate – inflamed the imaginations of the young people of his day who were searching for answers to complicated problems. My father learned Wagner's music-dramas off by heart, both in German and in Italian – 'Celeste amor, desìo febbril', 'Sehnender Liebe, sehrende Not' – he also sang the themes entrusted to the trumpets and trombones and he played 'pum-ratapum' instead of the timpani (in those days there weren't as many records as now and you had to feel the music inside your heart, not just in your ears). When I began to play the piano he put the score of *Die Walküre* in front of me. I was eight or nine years old, and I only knew about music: nothing about Schopenhauer, Freud, Nietzsche. As for love, I only felt that for my parents and for the neighbour's cats.

Of all that Sieglinde and Siegfried said to each other as they sang, I only understood that she was inciting him to pull a sword from a tree that she had in the house; then together, in sweet voices, they planned to have a baby. I remembered hearing that kind of talk from my parents before my little sister was born. But I didn't understand why, in *Die Walküre*, there was a big man who raised his voice and stood in their way; at that time 'porn' films had not yet been invented for the education of youth, and we were forbidden to know many things.

It was the music that struck me above all. This was a music that at times rose loudly and desperately, only to fall away again, murmuring many strange things. I think it still expresses this to everyone, young and old. Come and listen to it, and please tell me if I'm right. I, who have never tried drugs, can only say that it has the effect of several coffees taken together.

I mentioned the strong feelings that Wagner's music provoked in my father, but I also remember an anecdote about my mother. She didn't care so much about music. But – since female liberation wasn't very developed in those days – she generally followed my father's tastes and desires. So, one evening when *Die Walküre* was playing at the opera house, my father persuaded her to attend the performance with him. The only problem was leaving me, as I was just a few months old in those days, at home. My mother rigged up a barricade of tall furniture around my crib, and after checking all the gas taps several times, she went off to the opera with my father.

At the theatre, everything went well up until the last scene, when Wotan intoned the sublime 'Leb wohl, du kühnes, herrliches Kind!', and began to draw a line of fire around the body of Brünnhilde, leaving her asleep in an open space between high mountain peaks, to punish her for disobedience. At the sight of the smoke, and little flames made of harmless strips of red paper with fans underneath to move them, my mother saw and heard nothing more! Heedless of the disturbance she was causing, she got up and dashed home, dragging my father with her, to reassure herself that nothing similar had occurred in my room. When this incident was retold to me some years later, I was unable to suppress a certain pride in the thought that Richard Wagner, for all his wisdom, his creative and dramatic power, and all his trombones and tubas, failed to surpass the power of attraction I exercised on that occasion over my mother and father.

And without any effort on my part!

--o-o--

SIR JOHN BARBIROLLI

It was Sir John who introduced me to England. Even before I knew him, I had attended one of his concerts in London with the Hallé Orchestra from Manchester, of which he was the Chief Conductor. After the section leaders had carefully tuned, the orchestra sat quietly, coolly composed. Sir John appeared on the platform, his short legs leaping in great strides, as if he were steering a gondola. He then waved his baton in the air, which caused a rush of fire to flood the lungs of the audience, who welcomed him with enthusiastic demonstrations that would convince you that Beethoven's Ninth had just concluded! Even before bowing, Barbirolli had given the upbeat, with his face to the audience and his back to the orchestra, who struck up 'God save the Queen', and he urged everyone to sing along – me included – with a profusion of dynamic and inviting gestures.

The Anglo–Saxons, along with their German cousins, have the best possible music for a National Anthem. But they themselves are not too convinced of this! In peaceful times they don't always take advantage of it. Sometimes they perform their Anthem as if they were bored, and they often disfigure it in their rendition. They will perform it in full only if the Queen is present. For less regal figures they play just a few bars, and in these times of short measures I fear that one day they will be reduced to performing only the drum roll, just to lift the buttocks of the audience members from their seats.

Sir John, however, with the Queen present or not, conducted the entire 'God save the Queen'. And how! In an emphatic and Latin-style of execution, vibrant, and bringing great satisfaction to the players of the *gran cassa* and *piatti*! If all of England took that style of execution as a model, I am convinced that it would take them less time to win wars…

I had the pleasure of meeting Sir John personally in Bucharest. It was the inaugural Enescu Festival and Competition of 1958, dedicated to the memory of the composer, who had died three years earlier. The jury members for the competition included Yehudi Menuhin, David Oistrakh and Claudio Arrau, along with French, Swiss and Americans, and a large contingent of Romanian musicians. I was there on the jury, and Sir John was there too, at least on paper. In fact, his attention was focused more on rehearsing for his concerts with the Bucharest Philharmonic than on the playing of the young contestants. He rarely appeared, and when he did, he stood in the doorway, stirring the air with broad gestures of satisfaction for whoever was playing and then he would disappear as quickly as he had arrived!

After the first round, an interesting duel took shape between a Romanian violinist and a Russian pupil of David Oistrakh. Both were excellent, albeit diametrically opposed in their ways of playing. There was the Russian 'tightrope walker', and the Romanian who was a good interpreter of Bach, and my preferred candidate. At this point, a sort of 'cold war' arose within the jury – who were undecided as a collective, but had clearly defined preferences – between the group of Romanians and David Oistrakh. He spoke no Romanian and was unable to understand what the others were plotting, so he kept a dignified distance in the background.

However, I understand Romanian, and I also know Romanians well! They are one of the most sympathetic and handsome people, sharing many traits with Italians; their country welcomes us and offers us an oasis, surrounded as they are by Russians, Hungarians, Bulgarians, and Yugoslavs. The Indo–Germanics created their history, tormented as it is by attacks and invasions of fiery Turks and Lipovans, arrogant Tartars and persuasive Greeks; Goths, Huns, and Visigoths; Avars, Sarmatians, Gepids, Magyars, Peccenighi, Ottomans, Gypsies and Caucasians. They were all attracted, in different eras, by the richness of that land with its fertile soil and subsoil rich in minerals. While many of them have left their marks, the most lasting imprint was that left by the Emperor Trajan with his Roman and Neapolitan legionaries, who arrived as valiant fighters and then became peaceful colonisers.

The result was a strong but peace-loving and flexible population, which inherited more from the Neapolitan colonists than from the Roman legionaries: the principle of 'Flectar non Frangar' and an open heart; also, the liveliness of the Mediterraneans, combined with the fatalism, the patience and wisdom of Asian races. All of these qualities I saw placed on the carpet, on the table and under the table, when the Romanian members of the jury began to make use of their complex heritage, in order to ensure that their preferred candidate would triumph.

I understood their reasons. Nowadays those who excel in virtuosity have more chances of making a great career than those who excel in the interpretation of the classics. There was also national pride at stake, as well as the outcome of a battle in which, at the end, it was unclear if Romania had won or lost! They were against the Russians – their not-too-hated enemies – at first; and then with the Russians – their not-too-beloved allies – then.... But their stance against the gifted interpreter of Bach didn't seem right to me. The President of the Jury was George Georgescu, a famous conductor of international renown and no less celebrated as a person of wit and a charming man of the world [he had organised the festival].

In order to make Georgescu understand that their manoeuvre hadn't escaped me, I pointed the index finger of my right hand at him and moved it up and down, starting a wordless dialogue with him. He winked back at me. I wrinkled my nose and moved my head left and right a few times. He frowned, pursed his lips, and tapped his forefinger on the tip of his nose, which means in Romanian, 'Taci din gura' ('Keep your mouth shut'). I nodded my head and then Georgescu remarked: 'Even Barbirolli agrees!', surprising the jury with this sudden outburst. Naturally Barbirolli was not present, and I said: 'Barbirolli doesn't count. He's never here so we can't hold him responsible.' And Georgescu, opening his arms: 'Vorbest de el cum de un prost! Barbirolli este un Siiiir, Domnule', ('You speak about him as though he is an idiot! Barbirolli is a "Siiiiir", dear Sir.') The joke made those present laugh a lot because it was delivered with a mixture of envy and burlesque good humour.

While they continued with their deliberations, Sir John appeared at the door. We asked him to come in and have his say. He shared with us some unusual insights: 'Competitions are useless! The important thing is to love music and have the courage to play an instrument. My porter's son blows into a trumpet, and I'd give him a prize, because it's better than him killing people or working on the black market! These people are all good because they all love music and have courage. I propose a prize for all of them ... they are all excellent!' He had already turned his back to us, and was walking away to return to his rehearsal, making swirling gestures in the air...

His proposal was generally accepted by all. Not everyone was awarded a prize, but the First Prize was divided between the Romanian and the Russian violinists. As far as I know, neither of them made a 'great career'. A few days later, while I was rehearsing Respighi's *Feste romane* with the Bucharest Philharmonic, Sir John entered the room and said to me discreetly: 'I'll organise an invitation for you to conduct my orchestra.' Such promises are often made, I thought. However, a few months later I received a formal invitation, and at that moment I thought: 'Ah yes! Barbirolli really is a "Sir!"'

--o-o--

TWO POLITICIANS: EVA PERON AND BENITO MUSSOLINI

Politics is one of the most damaging threats to the beauty – internal and external – of mankind. It corrodes the hearts and darkens the faces of those who practise it. When they are bitten, politicians react badly. They bite back, they laugh at the wrong moments, and when they take on a contrite look (which they often need) there is an acrid smell of falsehood around them. Women are not exempt from these defects.

EVA PERÓN

I once had the opportunity to observe Eva Perón at close quarters when she was speaking to a group of workers. I saw her face tense with hatred. Her skin was wrinkled and yellowed, her feline eyes were restless, and her lips were pursed in a cruel smile. I tried to imagine what truths people could expect from someone whose spirit was twisted in such a way. She would have been much more attractive if she had continued her career as a film-star, instead of climbing to political glory! The poor woman did not live for long after the day I saw her. And it was precisely her death that makes me consider her now as a benefactor – even if only for a few hours – of good musical taste. The moment her light went out, people gathered silently in the darkness, weeping heartfelt tears.

Her death released a great wave of sentiment, in the kind of poor taste that readily surfaces in the souls of South Americans. There was talk of embalming her body: it was said that she had asked the Vatican for her beatification. It was officially decreed that all performances of popular music would be suspended in Argentina for three days following her death, leaving only classical and religious music. There would be no tangos, milongas or carnavalitos, no fox-trots or boogie-woogies – all that insipid music that is gradually overwhelming our everyday lives. We are subject to it in elevators, department stores, dentists' waiting rooms.... In its place, from dawn until the daily shut-down of radio stations and the closure of public places, there would only be masses, oratorios, quartets, symphonies – by Bach, Beethoven and Brahms; Mendelssohn, Bruckner and Stradella.

Some years ago, a malicious rumour circulated in Italy regarding a high-ranking RAI official, known for his musical ignorance. Having become terribly bored while listening to the intricate 'Mozart Variations' by Max Reger, he apparently issued an edict to the Italian radio, suspending broadcasts of 'variations' of every type, of any era and of any composer! I wondered if the Argentinian leaders made a similar miscalculation when they issued their orders. Without doubt, something happened: the sound of Argentina changed overnight!

One morning, towards midday, I was walking home through the deserted streets of Tucumán, past low-set houses. When sunset comes, the pavements are populated by entire families who carry chairs, sofas, tables, radios, and televisions into the street. They eat sausages and guzzle mate, wine, beer and Coca-Cola to quench their accumulated hunger and thirst from the day. They play cards, dominoes or chess while the boys kick balls into the better-lit areas and roam up and down on bicycles and scooters among the family members who meanwhile chat loudly with the neighbours. Everyone looks forward to the cooler weather which will eventually descend from the nearby mountains. The streets transform into a lively communal living room, following days of heavy heat that recall the last days of Pompeii during the fall of fiery ash from Vesuvius!

Around midday, the scene shifts. The sun is high above the heads of the rare passers-by, who hurry – but not too quickly! – to reach their homes, take off their clothes , take a cold shower and doze off in a cool corner. The streets were deserted. I saw only my shadow, which I regularly stepped on, it having been reduced to a round stain under my feet. Suddenly, from a distance, but slowly approaching, I heard the sound of an organ playing J.S. Bach's famous Toccata and Fugue in D minor. A vision of white marble cathedrals, filled with masses of heads invaded my thoughts, of blond congregations processing under snowy skies and the dark shadows of foggy forests, dripping like the notes of a Bach fugue:

I asked myself, 'What is this music doing here? And at this time of day?' The sound of the organ, so loud as if to fill every corner of a cathedral, came from a van – one of those vehicles topped with a loudspeaker and used by political parties to spread propaganda. Or even by businesses announcing their imminent liquidation. Even driving at a very slow pace, the van soon reached me. When it stopped, the music retreated to the level of soft background music. A grave and cavernous voice (one of those fascinating male voices that tango singers use to narrate their sentimental misadventures and their dreams devoid of a future) spoke slowly, ignoring the Bach in the background: 'Seiioras y Senores: auti en momentos de duelo, nunca te renas Alpargatas Pampero'.[1023] And then, Bach's Fugue swelled into life once more, flooding the surrounding houses and streets.

Reflecting on it now, this may seem just a light-hearted little story. But when it took place - perhaps partly because of the sun shining directly on my head, and the enveloping heat that made my bones and brain smoke – I entered a sort of delirium. 'Deep within this world of ours, in which we feel so dissatisfied,' I said to myself, 'lies an impediment to a state of perfection that we don't even dare to dream of! See how the death of a fragile blonde woman is enough to transform San Miguel de Tucumán, this remote corner of the universe, into a sort of Promised Land where every form of vulgarity in art has disappeared, leaving only propaganda and the sound of Bach's fugues ... but yes ...! Let's make her a Saint, I thought.' The illusion, however lasted only three days. Then everyone went back to selling Alpergatas Marca Pampero again, thanks to the tangos and the milongas ... and the ever-increasing prices...

[1023] 'Ladies and Gentlemen, we beseech you at this time of mourning, never forget Alpargaita Pampero' (a brand of shoes).

BENITO MUSSOLINI

In 1936, the bicentenary of the birth of Antonio Stradivari, all of his surviving instruments were gathered together in Cremona, sent from all parts of the world, along with those of other leading luthiers of his era: the Amati family, the Guadagni, the Bergonzi, and of course, the prodigious lineage of the Guarneri. This was a unique event – unrepeatable – because even if something similar were to be organised in 2036, we cannot know what effect the ravages of time will have wrought on the instruments, or how many of them will even exist! The instruments were loaned from the most famous collections in the world, gathering like a flotilla of oddly shaped objects, like small boats (violins, violas, 'cellos, and basses) to be conveyed to their port of origin, where – by some strange fate – they were reunited.

To organise this event involved an enormous insurance cover, as well as the presence of armed police. As they arrived in Cremona, each instrument was placed in purpose-made display cases, for the delight and astonishment of the many connoisseurs who had gathered from all over the world to admire the beauty of the forms and the patina of the varnishes. A number of prominent Italian musicians, along with Adolf Busch and the members of his Quartet (because they all owned Cremonese instruments) agreed to form an orchestra to bring these famous, precious objects to life.

To list the musicians in alphabetical order, the concert master was Michelangelo Abbado, along with Abussi, Brengola, Carpi, Cillario and so on, down to Arrigo Pelliccia and Arrigo Serato, who closed the ranks of the second violins. We were all professional soloists (who played all the notes!) and we each had one of these world-famous instruments entrusted to us for the occasion (with the police ever present), and we were all eager to assert our own artistic personality over that of our colleagues. So strong was our passion for this task that Antonio Guarnieri[1024] who conducted

---

[1024] Antonio Guarnieri (1880-1952) was an Italian conductor and cellist. He took up conducting in 1904 and succeeded Toscanini at La Scala, Milan in 1929. See also FN 1014.

us, was determined to throw water over our excessive ardour: he remarked at one rehearsal that he felt nostalgic for his time in front of amateur orchestras! In the end, by exercising his ability to subjugate anyone to his musical will, he achieved the results that he sought. We gave two concerts in Cremona under the patronage of the Princess of Piedmont, Maria José,[1025] and those present said that they had never heard such a sound, nor had they imagined that it could exist.

Two years later, in 1938, we gathered once more, in order to commemorate another great Italian: Nicolò Paganini. But the atmosphere was different. Genoa is certainly an important city, beautiful and vibrant, but it lacks the exquisite provincial quality of Cremona. Paganini was undoubtedly one of the most interesting musicians of all time, perhaps the unsurpassed precursor of the current acrobats of that diabolical instrument that is the violin. He was inspired, imaginative and brilliant as both a composer and a performer, though he never cultivated the arcane charm of an Antonio Stradivari. Although illiterate, Paganini understood mysteries that not even science can reveal. He was a craftsman capable, using simple pieces of wood, of obtaining sonic balances that no one else has achieved.

At the time of the Paganini commemoration, the world was in a turmoil; storm clouds were brewing over Europe, threatening to spread far and wide. Violence was on the rise everywhere. The Munich conference, attended by Neville Chamberlain with his umbrella, raised ironic smiles while the world helplessly looked on. Il Duce banged his fists even harder on the windowsill of the balcony of the Palazzo Venezia.[1026] In spite of this, our musical venture was another success, but hardly comparable to the previous, Stradivarian one. Everyone around us was distracted by an overwhelming anguish in their hearts.

After the concert in Genoa, we were invited (if that is the word)

[1025] Marie-José of Belgium (1906-2001) the last Queen of Italy. Her tenure of only 34 days, gave her the nickname of 'the May Queen'.

[1026] The palazzo housed the personal office of Mussolini and was the headquarters of the Fascist government.

to repeat it at Villa Torlonia,[1027] in a private setting for Il Duce. The audience consisted of his children, their ski instructor Eraldo Monzeglio (a former Bologna footballer), and some political figures. During the concert I occasionally glanced at Il Duce, and became convinced that he was bluffing even when he was listening to music! He widened his dark eyes and shot murderous glances at the row of double basses when they were doing nothing worthy of note. Then he suddenly pointed at us violinists with feigned interest, while we were performing an insignificant harmony.

This behaviour would not have been surprising were it not for the rumours in circulation that he loved music. I had received a postcard from a friend which contained a photo of Il Duce holding a violin! He faced the camera grimly, as if to say: 'Be careful, if you piss me off, I'll break my bow on your skull!' As for his musical taste, I learned from Arrigo Serato (who considered himself his teacher) that Il Duce's favourite piece of music was the Intermezzo from Mascagni's *L'amico Fritz*. I rest my case.... A delegation of Italian instrumentalists had apparently asked for his assistance to get foreign-made strings imported into Italy despite the economic restrictions, and he replied: 'Paganini was the greatest violinist in the world and always played with gut strings made in Naples!' – which would be tantamount to fitting out an army with 19th-century rifles and sending them off to fight against an enemy who has atomic weapons!

Following our performance at Villa Torlonia, Il Duce took to the podium alongside Maestro Guarnieri. He addressed four well-spoken words to us: 'You are good. Congratulations.' Then he stepped down from the stage, and began talking with Guarnieri. Il Duce spoke first; Guarnieri, still elevated on the podium, replied with words inaudible to us, though we could see him make lazy histrionic gestures like an old Venetian cat. Mussolini retorted; his words were accompanied by sharp, decisive gestures. Guarnieri's body simply swayed, and he shook his big head. Finally, Il Duce threw his arms in the air and marched away with angry steps.

[1027] The villa became the state residence of Mussolini in Rome during the 1920s.

We waited silently for the order to 'break ranks', and then retreated into an adjacent room to speculate about what the two leaders had said to each other. A minor politician burst out: 'Don't you understand? He asked the Maestro to repeat the concert in Rome under his patronage, and then take it on tour through Italy and Germany!'

Guarnieri then joined our group and explained what had taken place: 'I was happy to say no. I told him: "Duce! Before we do that, let us end this storm which is swirling over Europe." Il Duce said: "No. Immediately! I want it to happen immediately!" And I replied that "immediately" I intend to go to Riccione and get some sun on my balls. I suggested that we meet in Riccione and talk about it then – but he stormed off and left me there!' Guarnieri kept swinging his head.

> The storm did not pass.
> Other music sounded.
> Paganini has no encore.
> And Il Duce is no more.

(To the Creator! Feet up and heads down!)

I write this with disgust because I hate violence with all my heart: in every form – even when we invoke patriotism to justify it. But – and it may be macabre – I was left with the desire to know whether at the moment of his truth, in front of his executioners, Mussolini looked them in the eye, or not.... Who knows? Sometimes politicians are so stubborn! They remain actors right to the end.

--o-o--

URBANO, VIGILE DI PARMA

The place I have just entered looks like a wartime bomb shelter. But no: I find myself in the headquarters of the famous 'Hideaway of Verdians' in Parma. It is located in a long brick and stone basement, under a famous restaurant. From the gloom there slowly emerges a bust of the Master, wearing an expression somewhere between a smile and scowl. One of the walls is covered with Verdi memorabilia, another is laden with hams and bottles of local wine. Seated along the wall as you enter, are the citizens who have been elected as lifelong custodians of the composer's works. They are chosen from among the most enthusiastic supporters of Giuseppe Verdi's operas, and each of them has been assigned the name of one of his works as a *nom de plume*.

The members are all men, meaning that some are obliged to introduce themselves in a curious way: 'I am *Luisa Miller* ... a pleasure to meet you.' 'My name is *La traviata* ... most honoured', and so on. There is even a 'Signor Messa da Requiem' among them looking in the prime of life! I have been invited here to receive the 'symbolic baton' which is presented to those conductors who manage to open the opera season of the Teatro Regio di Parma without creating an apocalyptic scandal.

I feel that I deserve it, not least because I have refused two previous invitations, sensing that some of my fellow artists who would be singing with me were doomed to certain destruction (as occurred in both cases; the curtain fell hastily before the performance had even finished!) It is well known that Parma has the most demanding audience in the world when it comes to the appreciation of Verdi voices and traditions.

The *loggionisti* of the Teatro Regio certainly don't go to the opera to show off fashionable clothes. They often arrive pedalling a bicycle through the snow. But when they are sitting on their seats in the dress circle, they feel invested with high powers and great responsibility, and they don the imaginary robes of judges of popular opinion. The finely-tuned alertness of their reflexes is not open to question. Before anyone else detects the slightest vocal imperfection, the Parma *loggionisti* have unhesitatingly issued their judgment! I believe they have developed the ability to intuit the quality of each phrase even from how a singer takes a breath or places their feet!

Some of their witty remarks have become famous and almost all reports are accurate: sharp, withering quips and cruel barbs hurled at the top of their lungs from one corner of the theatre balcony to the other. There are stories such as that of the porter at the train station, who refused to carry the luggage belonging to the baritone who had been booed the night before. Even more unfortunate, the acclaimed Divo (this too can happen!) who gave into insistent demands for an encore, only to be met with derisive whistles afterwards. Toscanini contributed significantly to developing the high musical standards of his fellow citizens, when he declared that the correct speed to perform 'Va pensiero' is the one heard on the weekends, when it is sung in the taverns outside Parma.

The opening night of the 1972 season went off without a hitch. Renata Scotto and José Carreras showed off their technical prowess, and the other singers were kindly received due to their youth, or being fellow citizens of Parma. If anything, on this occasion the public showed unusual and, in my opinion, excessive generosity. The Regio Orchestra had agreed – unusually – to meet half an hour before the theatre opened to the public, for a short warm-up session in order to ensure the best ensemble for the evening. I was driving from Bologna when, alone on the outskirts of Parma, I lost my way. In the foggy darkness passers-by were few and far between, and their advice was confusing: 'Go down there, then turn left ... eh, no...' 'It's better that you go back ...' 'Well, frankly I can't say.'

I continued to drive around in circles, becoming more and more anxious as the time passed. Having obtained extra rehearsal time from the orchestra, my absence would be treated as a serious matter, for the orchestra, the theatre, for Verdi and myself! Following several handbrake turns which caused the engine palpable strain, I finally emerged onto the Piazza della Pilotta and immediately noticed that there was no authorised parking available. Summoning the spirit of Verdi, I authorised myself to park my car in a dark corner of a *loggia*. I grabbed my score and baton, and made a quick mental calculation that as soon as the warm-up was over, I would have time to return to the car and re-park it next to the theatre. Darting down the street, I made out the dark silhouette of a policeman approaching in the dim light, with measured steps.

The sight of a *poliziotto* has the power to make me fear the worst: on this occasion it took me back to an incident that occurred some years earlier, when I almost found myself thrown into a pen for stray dogs and crazy people in Melbourne. I had finished an evening rehearsal of *The Magic Flute* [in 1968], and I was crossing the road to return to my hotel when a van with wire-mesh sides pulled up next to me. Two policemen alighted and demanded to know where I had been and what I was doing. In my post-rehearsal euphoria, I unwisely decided to joke with them, replying: 'First of all, it is clear that I am walking. And if you want to know where I have been, I have just come from a meeting with the Queen of the Night, who has a daughter who is kept prisoner by a black man. A bird-man manages to find her, thanks to a whistle that makes a strange sound….' The two policemen looked at each other and, without another word, attempted to force me into their mobile cage! On that occasion I learned that despite their friendly demeanour, the Australian police are not very well versed in Mozart's opera libretti. And they enforce their laws with great energy and few words!

Back to Parma, where I was overcome with dread as the policeman approached. What would happen to the rehearsal that I was due to conduct? When the policeman spoke to me, his words were friendly, and his baritone voice was velvety. Nevertheless, he expressed the terrible reality of my situation: 'Oh no, dear sir, you really can't leave your car here.' I stammered: 'Look, give me the fine… take the car away…burn it… but I have to be at the Regio in three minutes! Seventy-five people are awaiting me and perhaps, if I run down that little street I'll just get there.' A pause followed – a long pause – too long for my growing anxiety. Finally, he enquired: 'What are you going to do at the Regio?' I was careful not to play the clown again and tell him about the Crusades, so I shouted: '*I Lombardi*! Verdi's *I Lombardi*. I have to conduct *I Lombardi* at the Regio this evening, do you understand?' Already starting to run down the street, I added: 'I don't care about the car. Destroy it, do whatever you want with it.'

The policeman let out a long, encouraging sigh: 'Eh, you don't need to turn it into a *melodramma*! I'll write you a permit, so you can drive on the wrong side of the road for 10 minutes.' I was confused: 'Wrong side?! Forwards?!! … Should I sound the horn?

... Oh no!!' Getting into the car, I again pushed the engine into overdrive. I didn't have time to hug the policeman. I never saw him again. Afterwards, I was left wondering whether the authorisation he gave me on a yellow piece of paper with his signature was legal, or whether he risked being put in the gaol for crazy policemen. Perhaps he did it out of a shared passion for Verdi. From the slip of paper that I have kept, I was unable to decipher his name. So I made one up: 'Urbano, Vigile di Parma' (Urban Sergeant from Parma). And I would like to recall him here, with much gratitude.

--oo-oo--

GUITARRA ADENTRO[1028]

Ilanded at Rome's Fiumicino airport on a flight from Cairo. The cold, early morning, was accompanied by a bitter wind which slid between collars and caps and nipped at the necks of the arriving passengers. We were all obliged to stand in front of an outdoor counter, waiting for our suitcases. Even the porters seemed annoyed by the conditions, and put even more ardour than usual into throwing down luggage with their typical bad temper. As we waited, we took in a cacophony of curses and shouts; the thuds, crashes and sinister creaks of suitcases at the limit of their resistance, thrown about by muscled arms and calloused hands. Everyone was in a hurry, and the insistent, icy gusts of wind were such that – in spite of the danger to our luggage – the porters worked as fast as possible. Suddenly there was silence. Looking around, I caught my breath in astonishment.

In the midst of the luggage, I saw an object, like one of those plaster Madonnas that are carried on the shoulders of the faithful at village festivals. Beautifully carved from golden wood, slender but majestic, noble and haughty she stood ... a harp! A concert harp. Completely bare, deprived of a case or cover; not even the shadow of a handkerchief resting on the transparency of her multi-coloured strings.

[1028] Inside the guitar.

In that moment I imagined that the appearance of Joan of Arc, amid the blood and sweat of battle, must have produced a similar magical and paralytic effect upon the armour-clad soldiers. I tried to think of Joan naked, beautiful, or perhaps ugly. And, leaving aside any base or impure instincts, I had to admit that her magnetic effect upon the armies would have spurred them to greater and more decisive deeds.

The porter who was carrying the harp held the pedal-board firmly against his chest. He betrayed no surprise at carrying such an unusual cargo in his arms, in fact he carried out his duty with the greatest seriousness. He was strongly built like his colleagues, but in that moment he appeared transfigured. As he advanced with the harp, a circle full of respect formed around him and his cargo, as though a drop of holy oil had been imparted to a congregation.

The harp was gently set down on the counter, in front of a distinguished gentleman who sat quietly to my side, almost abstracted from the events taking place around him. Studying his profile, I recognised a singular character: Nicanor Zabaleta,[1029] who during the course of his career had been a remarkable figure in the music world. At a time when Rubinstein, Gieseking, and Małcużyński, the most popular international soloists would tour South America, giving perhaps thirty concerts, Zabaleta would arrive with his harp and play two hundred. He had discovered that, due to the Spanish conquest, the harp is just as popular as the guitar in the rural areas of South America.

Zabaleta played an unsophisticated instrument, made with any local wood available and used outdoors to accompany dancing. On these occasions the instrument was placed directly on the bare earth, or even in the middle of the mud. Zabaleta would load his instrument onto a pickup truck and take his classical and modern programmes on a zig-zag itinerary through small, semi-remote villages on the edge of the Argentine pampas or tropical forests. His concerts were invariably sold out, with entire villages attending. But arriving at Rome airport with a naked harp … 'Nicanor!? Que

---

[1029] 1907-1993, Spanish harpist.

pasò?' 'I've come from Greece,' he answered softly. 'Yes ... but ... the harp?' 'Ah...'– he seemed to wake up from a dream, and with a sweet smile he explained: 'For many years I packed her up in a protective box. And she often arrived smashed to bits. For two years I have been experimenting, travelling with her like this. And so far, she has been fine.'

While he was speaking to me, Zabaleta had placed the harp on a pair of wheels and was walking away, like a lady with a shopping trolley. I watched him go and in my mind's eye the scene became transfigured, emptied and compressed like a surreal canvas by De Chirico or Dalì. I saw the harp in the guise of a tyrannical mistress and Nicanor Zabaleta as her slave. He became the servant sent to earth in order to deliver the message that she had the task of transmitting to men. Pablo Casals must have felt something similar when he spoke to a colleague who was surprised that the greatest living cellist did not use a Stradivari: 'The Stradivarius has too much personality. And I have to find mine,' he replied. (Who knows how many hours of stubborn fights took place between the great Casals and some Stradivari cellos before the cellist renounced them).

Zabaleta and his 'mistress' went off to their Parisian or Patagonian audiences, leaving me with a host of unanswered questions. Are musical instruments really inanimate objects, as believed by many, or are they sentient beings belonging to another world, carrying precise and well-defined messages in their bodies? Are they distant relatives of the common block of wood, destined to become a table-leg – even the kind which, transformed into Pinocchio, dared to pull Geppetto's nose? I have tried to talk about this subject with some luthiers, but it is clear that they hide behind a collective secrecy. They play dumb, and they all respond the same: first they give a little laugh and then say 'Eh! Yes! ... the soul? ... Mah.'

There are many kinds of instruments, and each has a temper of its own. There are the good-natured ones, among which we can include the piano. Aware of his strength, he is generally good-natured. Open his mouth and he will smile at you with a long row of very black and very white teeth (or yellowed or bitten – depending on age). If you raise the upper side of the chest that covers his body the inside belly is revealed, the strings taut and criss-crossed like a well-ordered vascular system, surrounded by gold.

The flute holds few hidden secrets. Put an eye to one of its ends and it is like looking down a tube of surprising simplicity, revealing its pastoral origins as a plaything of nymphs and fauns. The horn, on horseback, summons people and packs of dogs, who chase after poor frightened animals. In his natural state, he is easily held in the arm, while the tube, curved in concentric circles, looks like a labyrinth. But if he allows himself to be stretched out, by grabbing him by the bell at one end and the mouthpiece at the other, he will uncoil like a snake, until he reaches a full 16 feet in length. He would look like a long telescope without lenses.

Next, look inside the soul of a violin, a viola, a 'cello, or a double bass. The violin is the most manageable but also the most capricious member of the family, whether it is coloured a yellowish blond that seems to be suffering from jaundice, or a tomato red, or else one with a dark complexion. Through the 'f – those two looping holes next to the bridge – you may glimpse its interior. There may be a label with the identity of its maker (often false): '*TIZIUS CAIUS facebat Anno Domine...*'. If you want to examine it thoroughly, loosen the strings that press upon it until it becomes mute, and gently remove the bridge. The instrument will be like a person under narcosis, with its strings dangling uselessly down like the hair of corpses. It won't react anymore. No more trills, no more tantrums … reduced to silence!

At that moment, taking advantage of its sleep, you can pull towards you a kind of navel – an endpin that is in its tail. This rests against the violinist's neck while they play. When you remove it, a little hole the size of a pea will remain, through which you can finally look inside the instrument along its full length. There isn't much to see, but the interior appears eerie. The light only penetrates the two 'f holes, so you will have to manoeuvre the instrument in order to illuminate the farthest corners. The colour has nothing in common with the shiny, varnished exterior; it is grey and generally dusty, with an hallucinatory quality shared by empty theatre stages or the holds of ships waiting for cargo.

A little to the right, you will see a vertical post between the back and the soundboard. It looks like a pillar placed there at random, isolated from everything else and it's called the 'anima'.[1030] It is extremely important! Without that soul, the pressure of the taut strings would destroy the instrument in an instant, reducing it to a pile of splinters. Moving it just a millimetre, to the right or the left, changes the sound quality enormously. To the left, as you look up, is a softwood keel known as the bass-bar – long, white and thin – which is glued to the top-plate (the 'belly') of the instrument. It stretches under the lowest string (the '4th') of the violin to offer support, like a mother who breastfeeds her strongest child more. Along the inside and the fascia, there are many pieces of wood in the shape of a stamp. They recall the look of warriors from far-off times, when scores were settled with swords, pikes, and halberds, and they returned from wars covered in bandages. The interior of the instrument has been like this since its birth. Then gradually, suffering fractures at the hands of time, the 'bandages' of age increase, above and below. As they multiply, the value of the instrument decreases. There is nothing more to the interior of the violin, and perhaps described thus it seems insignificant. However, if you have the chance to undertake this journey, I advise you not to miss the opportunity.

By allowing strangers to fix their gaze through that little pea-sized hole, I have made new friends. Some of them described an abandoned ballroom, others a circle of Dante's *Inferno*, or the interior of the Teatro Bibiena di Mantova – another hallucinatory vision.[1031] Yet, it is simply a space destined to create impalpable sounds, a box that has not changed its shape for more than 300 years. It was created with minute precision to generate sound that emerges freely and is projected into space as soon as it is born. The sound encircles the post, intoxicating it with vibrations, allowing that 'anima' to support the whole edifice.

I have characterised the violin as the most capricious being

[1030] The soundpost.

[1031] The 'Teatro Bibiena' or the 'Scientific Theatre of Bibiena' in Mantua was created by Antoni Galli da Bibiena between 1767–1769.

of the family, to which I should add the most delicate, prone to deterioration of the lungs and weakening of the voice. It is also the most sensitive and impressionable. It has been proven many times that if the owner of a fine old instrument is foolish enough to lend it to another performer, it will return with a different sound – with that of whoever used it last. It will take several days to tame it again, and convince it to accept you. But the title of this memoir has wider significance…

We once travelled from San Miguel de Tucumán to Tafí del Valle for the weekend. It is about 40km as the crow, or the aeroplane flies, if one wanted to take the fastest route, but you would run the risk of crash-landing, into a valley full of animals. Travelling by road during the rainy season, however, brings the danger of getting stuck halfway. In fact, this is what happened to us, one evening with a beautiful full moon, so bright that we could see one another almost as if in daylight. No one thought of turning back, because the road was blocked by a long, serpentine line of cars, all waiting for the morning.

In a nearby clearing, everyone joined forces to make a fire, shared their provisions and improvised an 'asado'. Someone began to softly strum a guitar, and soon they were joined in song. It was that evening when I first heard the words of an old nortena[1032] song that is still remembered and sung in those valleys: 'Llevarte quisiera guitarra adentro hasta al tempo de la madera'.[1033] The singer expresses to his beloved the desire to take her on a journey towards the inside of the guitar, until the 'tempo de la madera', back through the centuries when that thin piece of wood ('anima') in the sun and the winds, was still part of a living, intact, vibrant, happy nature…

I believe that no one has ever said something so beautiful about being loved, because going back in time would take place in a kind of sonic 'Milky Way'. Sound is the greatest mystery of the universe, perhaps even more than light, and undoubtedly more than the word.

[1032] Folk music of northern Mexico, with Spanish lyrics and accompanied on an accordion or 12-string guitar.

[1033] 'I would love to carry you, dear guitar, within me, back until the time of the wood.'

Because the word acts on reason, whereas sound carries the word to the senses. 'Happy voyage, happy couples who manage to put your dreams inside the guitar. Try to stay there as long as possible ...'

43: Carlo Felice Cillario, rehearsing in the Opera Theatre orchestra pit, Sydney, c1999.

Appendix 8

Cillario the cook

44: 'Tuxedo or Apron, he's a Maestro,' Cillario in the kitchen, 1979.

Cillario's culinary proclivities were singular, and often the source of comment. His diet was unusual – he was a self-proclaimed 'pescatarian', and he seemed to survive on little sustenance. He regulated his diet for health, as much as any ethical concerns. He loved carrot juice, and once said that on being offered some on his first trip to Australia, he decided that any country where carrot juice could be readily obtained was a place to revisit often.

In an interview in 1979, Barbara Hooks questioned Cillario about his culinary preferences, and he shared two of his favourite recipes:

UOVA CON AGLIO[1034]

For each person take three eggs and three 'or more' cloves of garlic.

Chop the garlic coarsely. Heat some safflower oil in a heavy frying pan and sauté the garlic without allowing it to brown.

Break in the eggs, add some salt and scramble the mixture.

[Cillario discovered this recipe while living in Romania during World War II.]

SALATE DE VINETE ('Poor man's caviar')

(serves 4)

2 kg eggplants

Olive oil

A few drops of vinegar

Finely chopped onion

Slices of radishes

4 hardboiled eggs quartered.

Barbecue or grill whole eggplants until charred. Remove the skin under cold running water and mash the pulp in a wooden bowl. Add a few drops of vinegar to prevent browning.

Add the oil 'like for mayonnaise, by instinct' – the mixture should be quite thick.

Chill two to three hours then garnish with the onion, radish slices

---

[1034] These recipes were published in a newspaper article 'Tuxedo or Apron, he's a Maestro', Cillario is interviewed by Barbara Hooks, *The Age*, 5 June 1979.

and quartered eggs. Serve with toast and smoked ham, or bacon.

Poor man's caviar is traditionally accompanied by Tzvika, a spirit made with plums. Vermouth or a light vodka could be substituted.

PASTA CILLARIO

Cillario often ate a simple pasta meal accompanied only by olive oil, perhaps with some cheese added. However, over the years he developed his own recipe – 'Pasta Cillario' which was notable for the addition of Vegemite to the basic dish. He cooked it regularly, and friends did their best to avoid eating it. Due to this predilection, at the conclusion of his final, Gala Celebration Concert in 2003, the company presented the maestro with 'a red cedar deed box, with a sterling silver gumnut motif, containing a jar of vegemite.'[1035]

[1035] Angus Grigg, *The Australian Financial Review*, 25 March 2003.

Appendix 9
Cillario on legato, 2001

TO AOBO STRINGS (To whom it may concern)

<u>My opinion about LEGATO ;</u>

I notice with pleasure that TRITTICO is receiving a good success
from the pubblic. I am convinced that it depends in great proporćion
from AOBO playing better than never. <u>CONGRATULATIONS TO ALL OF YOU !</u>

But without the possibility to talk with you I send this notice that
repetes what I was already asking to the strings during the rehearsals:
PLEASE NEVER PLAY A LEGATO PHRASE ADDING ⟶ - -- ---- ON EACH NOTE.
I know that is used in other Orchestras and even by some "international
virtuoso"beleiving that they enrich the expression of the phrasing.
The intention is good , but in my opinion the result is negative!
The instruments have the task of imitating the BEL CANTO of the best
singers; and never a good soprano will sing

After so many years working with you,
I feel affectionatly towards you ; and if
I did not speak of this details I would
feel guilty.

correct: ca———— sta pi—.va,

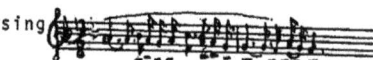

I advise you to play a few bars as the Violins lines of TABARRO n.48
until after 49 in the 2 different manners:

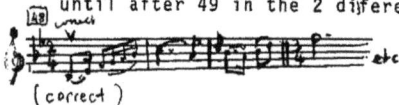

(correct)

etc.

etc.

and then tell me wich one is more closed] to BEL CANTO...
Thanks for your attention and much love.

Sydney 01

Yours C.F. Cillario

Carlo Felice Cillario, note to the Australian Opera and Ballet
Orchestra, written during the 2001 season of Puccini's *Il trittico*.

Appendix 10

Maria Callas: letter to Cillario, 6 December 1963

Caro Maestro -

Ho ricevuto la sua lettera e le rispondo subito.

Ho sentito molto belle cose su di lei. Spero e mi auguro che avremo un perfetto affiattamento. Lei e giovane ed io matura ma la musica e un unico linguaggio uni-versale. Chi la sente subito anche se giovane o chi non la sente mai anche se e vecchio.

Quindi sono sicura che tutto andrà bene - Basta che non si terrorizzi di me perché se dicono tante sul mio conto - In realtà sono assai facile - Basta fare della musica

45-6. Maria Callas - letter to Carlo Felice Cillario.

Caro Maestro,

I received your letter and I reply immediately.

I've heard many nice things about you. I hope that we will have a perfect accord. You are young and I am mature, but music is a single universal language, although there are those who feel it immediately when they are young, or those who never feel it even when they are old.

So, I'm sure everything will be fine – Just don't be terrified of me because they say a lot about me. Actually, I'm very straightforward – we just need to make some good music – right?

In any case, we will see each other on 8th January. I wish you all the best for your work and for the upcoming holidays –

Sincerely, Maria Callas.[1036]

[1036] I am grateful to Mr Alan Hicks for his advice regarding this translation.

Bibliography

Books

Claudio Alcorso, *The Wind You Say* (Collins Angus and Robertson Publishers, Pty. Ltd., Ryde, NSW, 1993).

David Bret, *Maria Callas – The Tigress and the Lamb* (Robson Books Ltd., London, 1997).

Richard Bonynge, *Joan Sutherland and Richard Bonynge with the Australian Opera* (Craftsman Press, Roseville, NSW, 1990).

Stephenie Cahalan, *Colour and Movement – the life of Claudio Alcorso* (Tasmania Forty South Publishing Pty. Ltd., Hobart, 2019).

John Cargher, *Opera and ballet in Australia* (Cassell Australia, Stanmore, NSW, 1977).

Shuyler Chapin, *Sopranos, Mezzos, Tenors, Bassos, and other Friends* (Crown Publishers, Inc., New York, 1995).

Roger Covell, *Australia's Music, Themes of a new Society* (Sun Books, Melbourne, 1967).

Lauris Elms, *The Singing Elms: The Autobiography of Lauris Elms* (Bowerbird Press, Terrey Hills, NSW, 2001).

Alison Gyger, *Civilising the Colonies, Pioneering Opera in Australia* (Opera–Opera (Pellinor) Pty. Ltd., Sydney, 1999).

Alison Gyger, *Opera for the Antipodes* (Currency Press, Pty. Ltd., Sydney, 1990).

Alison Gyger, *Australia's Operatic Phoenix, From World War II to War and Peace* (Pellinor Pty. Ltd., Sydney, 2005).

Ava Hubble, *The Strange Case of Eugene Goossens, and other tales from the Opera House* (Collins Publishers, Australia, Sydney, 1988).

Rita Nellie Hunter, *Wait Till The Sun Shines, Nellie* (Hamish Milne Ltd., London, 1986).

Nicolas V. Iljine and Patricia Herlihy, *Odessa Memories* (University of Washington Press, Seattle, 2003).

Viktor Jusefovich, *David Oistrakh, Conversations with Igor Oistrakh* (Cassell and Co. Ltd., London, 1977).

Harold Love, *The Golden Age of Australian Opera, W. S. Lyster and his Companies 1861–1880* (Currency Press Pty. Ltd., Woollahra, 1981).

Peter McCallum and Julie Simonds, *The Centenary of the Con: A History of the Sydney Conservatorium of Music 1915–2015* (Allen & Unwin, Sydney, 2015).

Helena Matheopoulos, *Diva* (Gollancz, London, 1991).

Wenzel de Neergard, *The Australian Opera: The first twenty years* (The N.S.W. Friends of the Australia Opera Ltd., Brickfield Hill NSW, 1977).

Moffatt Oxenbould, *Timing is Everything: A life backstage at the opera* (ABC Books, Sydney, 2005).

Harvey Sachs, *Toscanini, Musician of Conscience* (Liveright Publishing Corporation, New York, 2017).

Boris Schwarz, *Great Masters of the Violin* (Robert Hale, London, 1984).

Joan Sutherland, *A Prima Donna's Progress, The Autobiography of Joan Sutherland* (Orion Books, Ltd., London, 1997).

Neil Warren-Smith and Frank Salter, *25 Years of Australian Opera* (Oxford University Press, Melbourne, 1983).

John Yeomans, *The Other Taj Mahal, What Happened to the Sydney Opera House* (Longmans, Green & Co Ltd, London & Harlow, 1968).

Programme essays / monographs / journal articles

Moffatt Oxenbould, *Carlo Felice Cillario and Opera Australia*, essay in 'A Gala Celebration for Carlo Felice Cillario' commemorative programme. Opera Australia, Concert Hall, Sydney Opera House, 23 March 2003.

Oksana Salata, *Activity of the Odessa Opera and Ballet Theatre in August 1941-1942* (East European Historical Bulletin, 12, 137-148).

Luigi Verdi, *Cillario Biographia*, unpublished manuscript, c2022.

[No author named], 'Carlo Felice Cillario, Violinista', Aldina, Bologna, N.D. Copy held in the 'Civico Museo Bibliografico Musical, Bologna'. Inventory No. 15918, found at 20.F.1185. Published c1936. 14 pages, stapled in paper covers.

Interviews (listed chronologically)

David Malouf, 'Cillario the aristocrat', *The National Times*, 12–17 July 1976.

Nadine Amadio, 'Parsifal: at last we can see Wagner's dynamic 'farewell',' *The Financial Review*, 25 February 1977.

Stephen Downes, 'Cillario: noble maestro of the opera world', *The Age*, 18 April 1977.

Maria Prerauer, 'Hooked, Happy, High', *The Australian*, 28 January 1977.

Nadine Amadio, 'Sydney in for a Dutch treat of Wagner – Italian style', *The Financial Review*, 26 August 1977.

Nadine Amadio, 'Conductors and the sound of music', *Hi-Fi and Music*, November 1978.

Romola Constantino, 'Cillario against the wind', *The Sydney Morning Herald*, 13 January 1979.

A. Tornari, 'Carlo Felice Cillario: un direttore d'orchestra che si diverte con la sua professione,' *La Fiamma*, 19 February 1981.

Michael Jacobs, 'Maestro, Marenzi, miracle', *The Advertiser*, 24 March 1981.

Carlo Felice Cillario and Bruce Duffie, *Conductor Carlo Felice Cillario: A conversation with Bruce Duffie*. A conversation recorded in Chicago, November 8, 1982, and portions broadcast on WNIB in 1986, 1990, 1995 and 2000. The conversation was transcribed in 2015 and is available at: http://www.bruceduffie.com/cillario.html.

Carlo Felice Cillario, 'Love, Women and Big Luciano', *The Weekend Australian Magazine*, 11–12 December 1982.

Peta Landman, 'Cillario's Scenario', *Xpress*, November 1985.

A. Tornari, 'Il maestro Carlo Cillario riporta il trionfo de La Cenerentola,' *La Fiamma*, Sydney 30 July 1987.

John Carmody, 'Master of charm loses his cool over Puccini,' *The Sydney Morning Herald*, 6 October 1987.

Judy Robinson, 'The ever-welcome visitor,' *Opera Australia*, December 1987.

Michael Shmith, 'Some even hate their cause of fame,' *The Age*, 9 May 1988.

Ava Hubble, 'Cillario conducts his own Interview,' *Opera Australia*, January 1990.

David Garrett, 'Carlo...You have been so noisy!' *The Australian Opera Broadsheet*, Issue Three, August 1990.

Alan Wood, 'Composer's computer is now his muse in a keyboard,' *The Manly Daily*, 26 October 1990.

Jenny Brown, 'Cillario's score,' *The Mirror*, 31 August 1991.

Robert J. Stove, 'The Modest Maestro Carlo Felice Cillario,' *The Canberra Times*, 18 October 1992.

Michael Bruning, 'Lightning Conductor – Maestro strikes chord with AO' *Timeout, The Manly Daily*, 17 September 1993.

Peter A. Johnston, 'A 'National' Treasure,' *The Melburnian*, Vol. 9 No. 9, May 1994, 33–5.

Miriam Cosic, 'No truth in operatic trickery,' *The Weekend Australian*, 26–27 October 1996.

Peter Holder, 'Dial M for Maestro,' *The Daily Telegraph*, 17 January 1997.

Bob Crimeen, 'Carlo keeps secret score,' *The Sunday Herald*, Sun 6 April 1997.

Peter Farmer, 'Basking in a sunny old age full of humour, vigour, and music,' *Opera-Opera*, April 1998.

Bryce Hallett, 'House master', *The Sydney Morning Herald*, 1 January 2002.

Kylie Keogh, 'Keeping in tune,' *The Sun Herald*, March 2003.

Lyndall Crisp, 'The Maestro at home', *The Financial Times*, 22–23 March 2003.

Harriet Cunningham, 'Swan song for veteran opera maestro', *The Sydney Morning Herald*, 25 March 2003.

Obituaries

Elizabeth Forbes, 'Obituary of Carlo Cillario Conductor of the Zeffirelli production of Tosca who later led Opera Australia', *The Independent*, 24 December 2007.

Stephen Hall, 'Opera conductor a humble wizard in Oz', *The Australian*, 20 December 2007. [Referenced as: Hall, Cillario Obituary, 20 December 2007.]

Moffatt Oxenbould, 'Maestro nurtured Australian opera', *The Sydney Morning Herald*, 19 December 2007. [Referenced as: Oxenbould, Cillario Obituary, 19 December 2007.]

Moffatt Oxenbould, 'Early guiding light shone brightly for Opera Australia', *The Age*, 20 December 2007. [Referenced as: Oxenbould, Cillario Obituary, 20 December 2007.]

[No author named], 'Obituary: Carlo Felice Cillario', *Opera* (London), 59(3) March 2008, 281.

Archival / Unpublished Material

Material held by Opera Australia Music Library Archive

Programmes for seasons dating between 1968–2002.

Opera Australia company press files, 1968–98.

Opera Australia Artist files: 4 folders labelled 'Carlo Felice Cillario' containing documentation between 1968 -1988. Cited as 'Carlo Felice Cillario – Artist Files 'x', Opera Australia Library archives.' [There are 4 folders – '1', '2', '3' and 'misc.'].

Opera Australia library archive. File containing publicity photos of Carlo Felice Cillario, between c1961 to 2002.

Cillario memoirs and related materials

Hand-typed copies of 17 memoirs, photocopies presented to this author by Carlo Felice Cillario c2000. (in Italian).

'Cosi' li vidi io' edited version of the above, by Alessandro Cillario, 2020. (in Italian).

Miscellaneous papers (photocopies) of notes, doodles and typed documents, given to the author by Cillario c1999–2002.

Copies of manuscripts of musical compositions (photocopies) given to the author by Cillario c1999–2001. (See Appendix 6.)

Cillario family archive, Bologna

Printed Broadsheets and Biographies

'CFC Sheet 1'. [No author or publisher named] 'Carlo Felice Cillario', Printed broadsheet in French, with image of Cillario conducting in the Atheneum, Bucharest, (4 pages) c1946. Gives the outcome of his conducting 'cours' in Odessa, and reviews of conducted performances in Odessa, Timisoara, Bologna, and Bucharest. No publication details, states: 'Printed in Italy' (in English). Gives Cillario's address as: Piazza Calderini, 2, Bologna. Cillario family archive, Bologna.

'CFC Sheet 2'. [No author or publisher named] 'Complessi diretti dal 1942' and 'Attiva lirica'. Printed sheet, no publisher or further information given. 21 orchestras are listed, in Ukraine, Romania, Italy, Argentina, Spain. Seven theatres in Odessa, Argentina, Italy and Spain are also listed. Probably a publicity brochure, created after 1956. Cillario family archive, Bologna.

'CFC Sheet 3'. [No author or publisher named] 'Carlo Felice Cillario, Direttore d'Orchestra'. Printed sheet, companion publication to previous entry. A biography of six paragraphs, probably meant for use in programmes. Created after 1956. In Italian. Cillario family archive, Bologna.

Selected correspondence and other documents consulted

<u>Testimony</u> from the Italian Legation, Bucharest – 16 November 1944.

Sir John Barbirolli to Cillario – 28 November 1958 (in English).

Sir John Barbirolli to Cillario – 27 December 1962 (in English).

Sir John Barbirolli to Cillario – 1 July 1966 (in Italian).

Montserrat Caballé to Cillario – 30 September 1969.

Montserrat Caballé to Cillario – 12 December 1970.

'Callas to CFC' Maria Callas: letter to Carlo Felice Cillario dated 6 December 1963. 2 handwritten pages in original envelope. Courtesy of the Maria Callas Foundation (Fonds de Dotation Maria Callas).

Luigi Dallapiccola to Cillario – 14 March 1946.

Luigi Dallapiccola to Cillario – undated letter (c1953 regarding *Il prigioniero* and discussing Scherchen's recording; two closely typed pages).

Luigi Dallapiccola to Cillario – 4 June 1954.

Cillario to Luigi Dallapiccola – 13 June 1954.

Cillario to Luigi Dallapiccola – 5 August 1954.

Luigi Dallapiccola to Cillario – 10 August 1954.

Luigi Dallapiccola to Cillario – 11 August 1954.

Luigi Dallapiccola to Cillario – relating to *Il prigioniero*, dated 7 September 1954.

Luigi Dallapiccola to Cillario – 18 October 1954.

'Enescu for Cillario' Two letters of recommendation, in favour of Carlo Felice Cillario, dated 25 December 1942, and 27 January 1943 handwritten by Georges Enescu (in original envelope, in French).

Manuel de Falla to Cillario, postcard with photograph of the composer, late 1930's. Expressing thanks and admiration regarding Cillario's HMV recordings.

Gianandrea Gavazzeni to Cillario – 18 January 1963.

Gianandrea Gavazzeni to Cillario – 23 March 1963.

Gianandrea Gavazzeni to Cillario – 4 August 1978.

Gianandrea Gavazzeni to Cillario – 28 April 1984.

Walter Gieseking to Victoria Genoveanu Milicescu – .. January 1948 (letter is damaged).

Sandro Gorlinsky to Cillario (in Rome) – 9 September 1963 (information about the forthcoming *Tosca* in London with Callas).

Vittorio Gui to Cillario – 3 March 1960.

Vittorio Gui to Cillario – 18 May 1960.

Vittorio Gui to Cillario – 23 August 1961.

Vittorio Gui to Cillario – 31 August 1961.

Vittorio Gui to Cillario – 12 September 1961.

Vittorio Gui to Cillario – 17 November 1961.

Vittorio Gui to Cillario – 17 September 1962.

Vittorio Gui to Cillario – 7 October 1962 (2 typed pages).

Vittorio Gui to Cillario – 12 December 1962.

Vittorio Gui to Cillario – 22 September 1963.

Vittorio Gui to Cillario – 15 February 1964.

Vittorio Gui to Cillario – undated, 2 typed pages in blue ink.

Giacomo Lauri-Volpi – 31 January 1957.

Giacomo Lauri-Volpi – 4 March 1967.

Dinu Lipatti to Milicescu/Cillario –15 November 1947 (2 pages typed, in French).

Riccardo Malipiero to Cillario – 16 February 1954.

G. Francesco Malipiero to Cillario – 26 June 1954.

G. Francesco Malipiero to Cillario – 5 November 1954.

G. Francesco Malipiero to Cillario – 17 February 1955.

G. Francesco Malipiero to Cillario – 31 November 1956.

G. Francesco Malipiero to Cillario – 22 March 1958.

Ildebrando Pizzetti to Cillario – 6 June 1955

Ildebrando Pizzetti to Cillario – December 1956.

Moffatt Oxenbould and Graeme Ewer Papers

Oxenbould, Moffatt; Papers of Moffatt Oxenbould and Graeme Ewer, 1890-2016. Bib ID: 469317. Unit ID: MS Acc09.020, MS Acc09.101, MS Acc09.136.MS Acc09.200, MS Acc16.144.

National Library of Australia. Documents related to Carlo Felice Cillario are stored in Boxes 50 and 51.

Papers of Claudio Alcorso, relating to Carlo Felice Cillario

Tasmanian Archives and Heritage Office, Hobart. Item NS3001/1/14: 'Correspondence Claudio Alcorso and Carlo Cillario, a conductor and at one time Musical Director of The Australian Opera.' Contains correspondence between Alcorso and Cillario along with other documentation.

Online resources

https://trove.nla.gov.au/

www.ausstage.edu.au

https://www.hor.net.ua/?page_id=1504&lang=en

https://rdk.yarsklib.ru/doku.php?id=чернятинский_николай_николаевич

Live interviews

Moffatt Oxenbould, interviews, Mosman NSW, 11 April 2023 and 17 April 2023.

Sharolyn Kimmorley, interview, Randwick NSW, 18 May 2023.

Index